MW0065O947

VERISSIMUS

Also by Donald J. Robertson

How to Think Like a Roman Emperor
Stoicism and the Art of Happiness

VERISSIMUS

The Stoic Philosophy
of Marcus Aurelius

DONALD J. ROBERTSON

Illustrated by Zé Nuno Fraga

ST. MARTIN'S PRESS
NEW YORK

First published in the United States by St. Martin's Press,
an imprint of St. Martin's Publishing Group

VERISSIMUS. Copyright © 2022 by Donald J. Robertson. All rights reserved.
Printed in China. For information, address St. Martin's Publishing Group,
120 Broadway, New York, NY 10271.

www.stmartins.com

Illustrated by Zé Nuno Fraga

Library of Congress Cataloging-in-Publication Data is available upon request.

ISBN 978-1-250-27095-5 (hardcover)
ISBN 978-1-250-28265-1 (ebook)

Our books may be purchased in bulk for promotional, educational,
or business use. Please contact your local bookseller or the
Macmillan Corporate and Premium Sales Department at 1-800-221-7945,
extension 5442, or by email at MacmillanSpecialMarkets@macmillan.com.

First Edition: 2022

10 9 8 7 6 5 4 3 2 1

For Poppy, for philosophy and imagination

PREFACE

I'd like to welcome you to the world of Marcus Aurelius, second-century Roman emperor and Stoic philosopher.

The book you are now holding in your hands is the product of nearly twenty-five years of research. While writing my preceding book, *How to Think Like a Roman Emperor,* I was contacted by a young Portuguese illustrator named Zé Nuno Fraga. Zé showed me some amazing work he'd been doing on a play by Aristophanes. We began experimenting with ideas for illustrations about the life and thought of Marcus Aurelius, and eventually found ourselves at work on a graphic novel for St. Martin's Press, which acquired the title *Verissimus.*

A lot of patience was needed to verify the accuracy of the philosophical and historical content of this book, including spending time at the magnificent archaeological park in Carnuntum, and interviewing scholars for our research. I also have to thank our "focus group" of philosophy, comic book, and Roman history enthusiasts for their invaluable feedback on the initial drafts. You're about to read a truly epic story told in a sweeping cinematic style. As well as Marcus Aurelius the philosopher and statesman, you'll see him in action as *imperator* or commander in chief of the Roman legions. However, there's no way we could have hoped to cover the whole of Marcus's life and the whole of Stoic philosophy. We had to be selective and focus on specific ideas and events.

This book isn't intended as an introduction to Stoic philosophy. *How to Think Like a Roman Emperor* and *Stoicism and the Art of Happiness* serve that purpose well enough, I hope. Instead, we chose to do something completely new by presenting Marcus's philosophical precepts and psychological techniques in a more concrete way, placing them within the context of real events from his life. We show how Stoicism influenced some of his decisions as Roman emperor and helped him to cope with the many challenges he faced, in particular the problem of anger and revenge. You'll find an appendix at the end of this book outlining the main psychological techniques used by Marcus, and indeed by many modern Stoics, for managing anger.

I know some readers are probably unaware of how much historical information we actually possess about the life of Marcus Aurelius. The Roman histories of Cassius Dio, Herodian, and the *Historia Augusta* are our main sources. We also have fragments of evidence in many other ancient texts, even quotes from Marcus's rescripts in Roman legislative records, and archaeological evidence from monuments, coins, etc. However, it would, of course, be impossible to retell the story of Marcus Aurelius's life verbatim. There are gaps, ambiguities, and contradictions in the surviving record, as you'd expect.

Our goal was to remain as faithful as possible to the historical evidence while also engaging the reader in an exciting story and teaching them some valuable things about Stoicism along the way. Where there's information in our sources that seemed dubious or contradictory, we employed the device of presenting it in differently shaped panels, denoting the character's imagination, or as gossip, to place its reliability more obviously in question. See also the notes at the end of this book for some examples of decisions that were made regarding historical controversies. However, we don't expect you to read this book as a conventional biography or a philosophy textbook . . . No, this is a "ripping yarn" about a great man's philosophical, psychological, and spiritual journey.

My main goal in writing *Verissimus* was to help you . . . I want Marcus's story to bring his philosophy to life for those finding out about it for the first time. I also want to give those familiar with Stoicism a new perspective on some of its main teachings and practices. I hope it inspires you to learn more about Marcus's life and the philosophy of Stoicism, perhaps by reading *The Meditations,* if you haven't already done so. Fate permitting, some of you will find that the remarkable story of Marcus's personal challenges resonates very deeply with you. May it even help liberate you from the grip of anger and the other toxic passions against which Stoics waged their inner war.

Donald J. Robertson
Athens, Greece

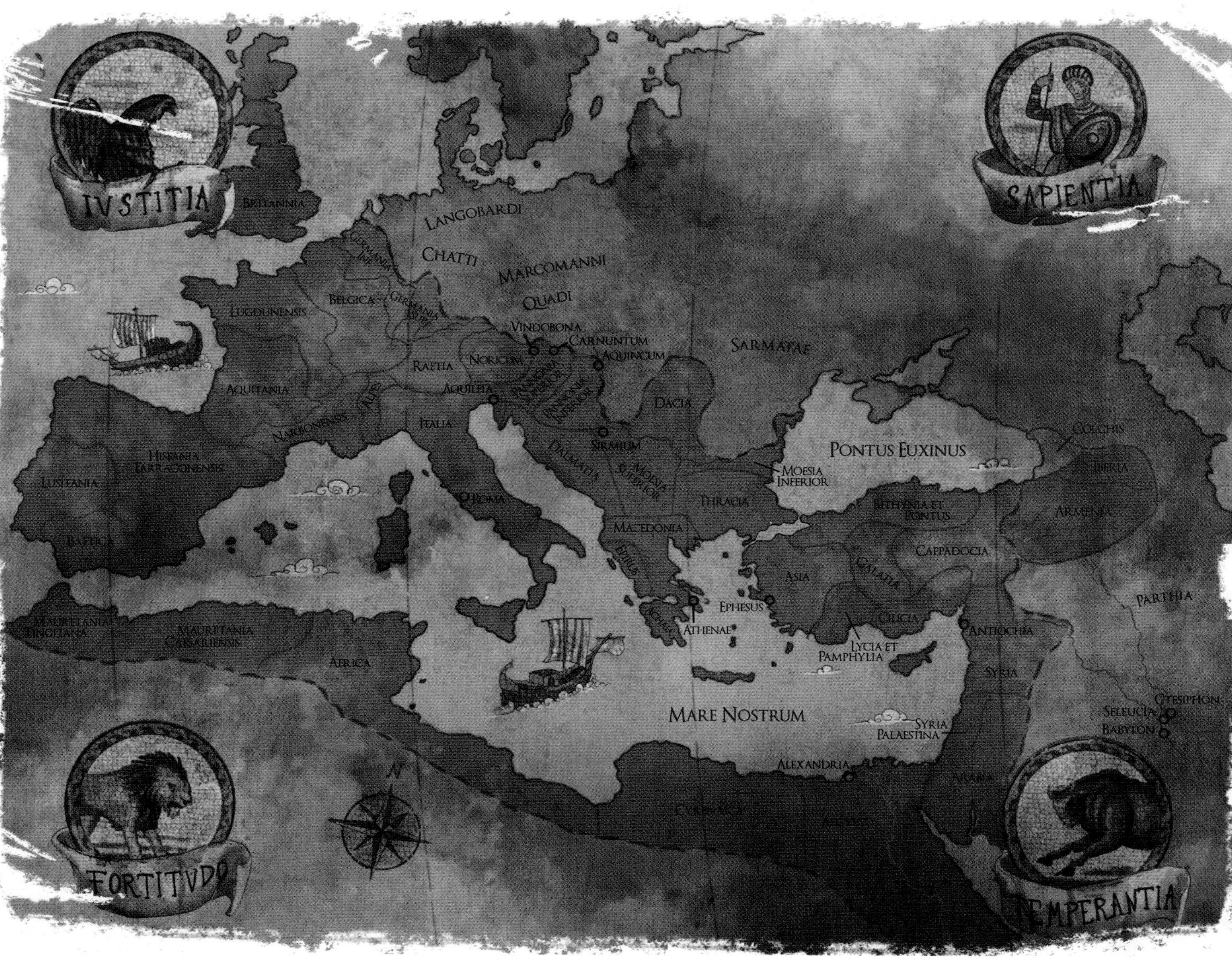
IVSTITIA
SAPIENTIA
FORTITVDO
TEMPERANTIA
BRITANNIA
LANGOBARDI
CHATTI
MARCOMANNI
QUADI
GERMANIA INF.
GERMANIA SUP.
BELGICA
LUGDUNENSIS
AQUITANIA
NARBONENSIS
ALPES
RAETIA
NORICUM
VINDOBONA
CARNUNTUM
AQUINCUM
PANNONIA SUPERIOR
PANNONIA INFERIOR
AQUILEIA
ITALIA
ROMA
SIRMIUM
DALMATIA
DACIA
SARMATAE
MOESIA SUPERIOR
MOESIA INFERIOR
THRACIA
MACEDONIA
EPIRUS
ACHAIA
ATHENAE
EPHESUS
PONTUS EUXINUS
COLCHIS
IBERIA
ARMENIA
BITHYNIA ET PONTUS
CAPPADOCIA
GALATIA
ASIA
CILICIA
LYCIA ET PAMPHYLIA
ANTIOCHIA
SYRIA
PARTHIA
CTESIPHON
SELEUCIA
BABYLON
SYRIA PALAESTINA
ALEXANDRIA
MARE NOSTRUM
HISPANIA TARRACONENSIS
LUSITANIA
BAETICA
MAURETANIA TINGITANA
MAURETANIA CAESARIENSIS
AFRICA
CYRENAICA
N

A Guide to Marcus's Empire

Marcus was born in Rome and spent most of his youth there or visiting nearby Italian towns and cities.

During the Parthian War, Marcus's brother, Lucius Verus, based himself in the capital of the Roman province of Syria, the city of Antioch, near modern-day Antakya.

Carnuntum, the capital city of the Roman province of Pannonia Superior, was situated on the River Danube, near modern-day Vienna in Austria. It was the site of a major legionary fortress in the Marcomannic Wars, where Marcus stationed himself and wrote part of *The Meditations*.

Alexandria, the capital of the Roman province of Egypt, provided the base for Avidius Cassius's campaign against the herdsmen.

During the Roman civil war, the province of Cappadocia in northeastern Anatolia, now part of modern-day Turkey, became the last bastion of loyalist support for Marcus's rule.

Marcus died at Vindobona, in the Roman province of Pannonia–modern-day Vienna, Austria.

CONTENTS

THE
DEAD
EMPEROR

*Very soon you will be ashes or a
skeleton, and then merely a name,
or not even a name.*

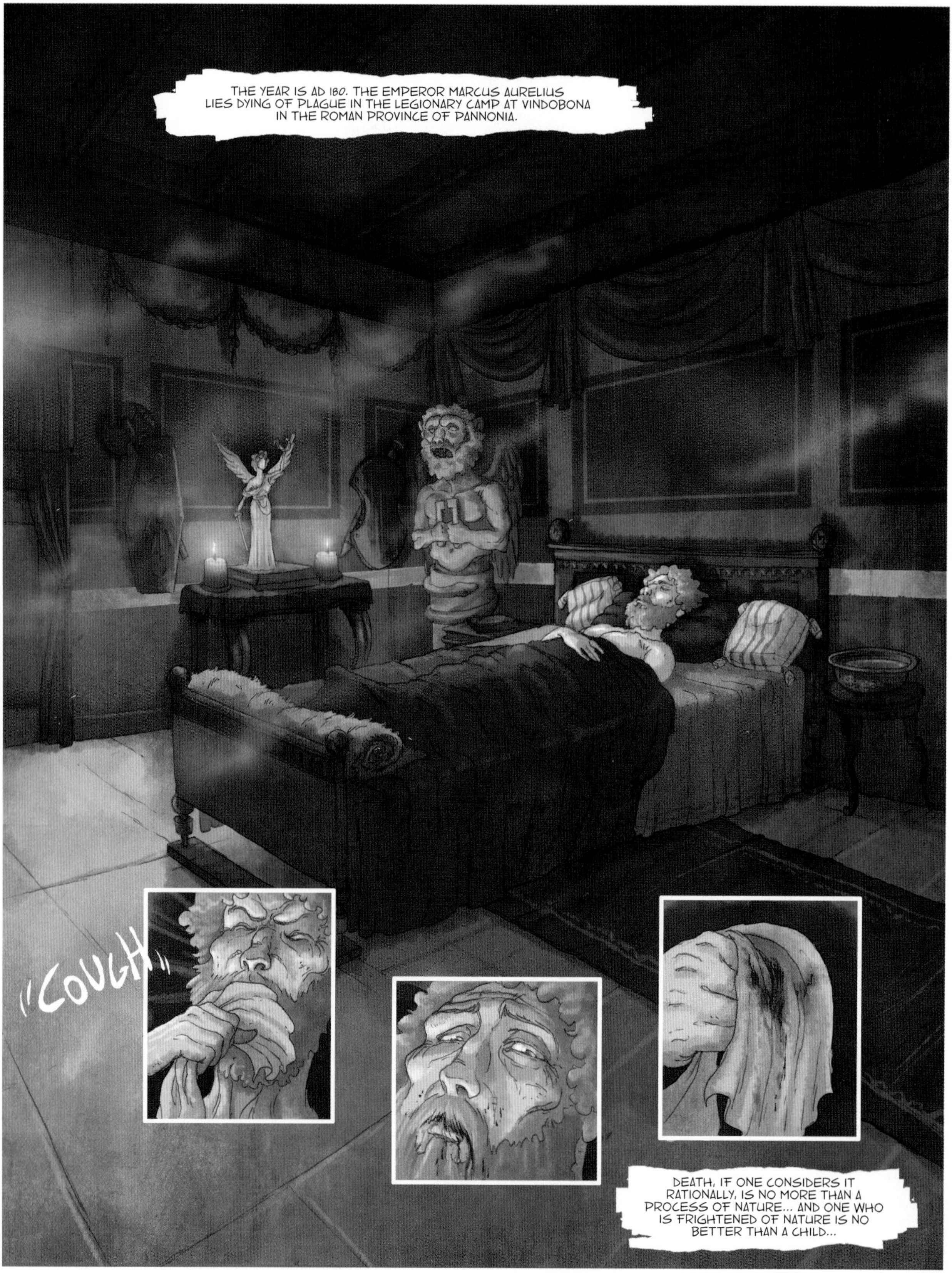
THE YEAR IS AD 180. THE EMPEROR MARCUS AURELIUS LIES DYING OF PLAGUE IN THE LEGIONARY CAMP AT VINDOBONA IN THE ROMAN PROVINCE OF PANNONIA.
"COUGH"
DEATH, IF ONE CONSIDERS IT RATIONALLY, IS NO MORE THAN A PROCESS OF NATURE... AND ONE WHO IS FRIGHTENED OF NATURE IS NO BETTER THAN A CHILD...

HOW MUCH LONGER NOW, GALEN?
THOSE WHO CAN BE SAVED FROM THE GREAT PLAGUE BREAK OUT IN DARK PUSTULES ALL OVER THEIR BODY BY THE NINTH DAY. COUGHING DUE TO ULCERS IN THE WINDPIPE IS A COMMON SYMPTOM, AS ARE FEVER AND DIARRHEA. THOSE WHOSE STOOLS ARE BLACK DUE TO INTERNAL BLEEDING RARELY SURVIVE.
THE COUGHING IS GETTING WORSE, LORD CAESAR... I COULD EASE YOUR PAIN BY INCREASING THE DOSE OF POPPY JUICE...
I DON'T WANT THE DRUG CLOUDING MY MIND.
YOU PHYSICIANS MERELY PRESCRIBE REMEDIES FOR THE BODY, YET EACH MISFORTUNE PRESCRIBED BY NATURE, EVEN SICKNESS AND DEATH, COULD BE A MORAL REMEDY IF WE ONLY KNEW HOW TO TURN IT INTO ONE.
PERHAPS THERE'S STILL SOME CHANCE... WE COULD TRY PURGING AND BLEEDING YOU AGAIN...
NO! DEATH COMES TO US ALL EVENTUALLY... HOW MANY EXPERTS IN THE ART OF MEDICINE NOW LIE BENEATH THE GROUND THEMSELVES?
"COUGH"
JUST AS DOCTORS KEEP THEIR KNIVES AT HAND TO DEAL WITH URGENT CASES...
...I HAVE KEPT THE DOCTRINES OF PHILOSOPHY IN MIND, READY TO MEET MY FATE WITH GOOD CHEER.

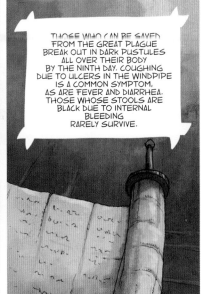

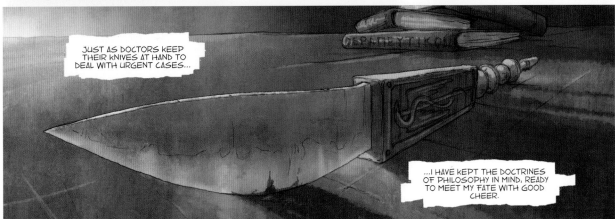

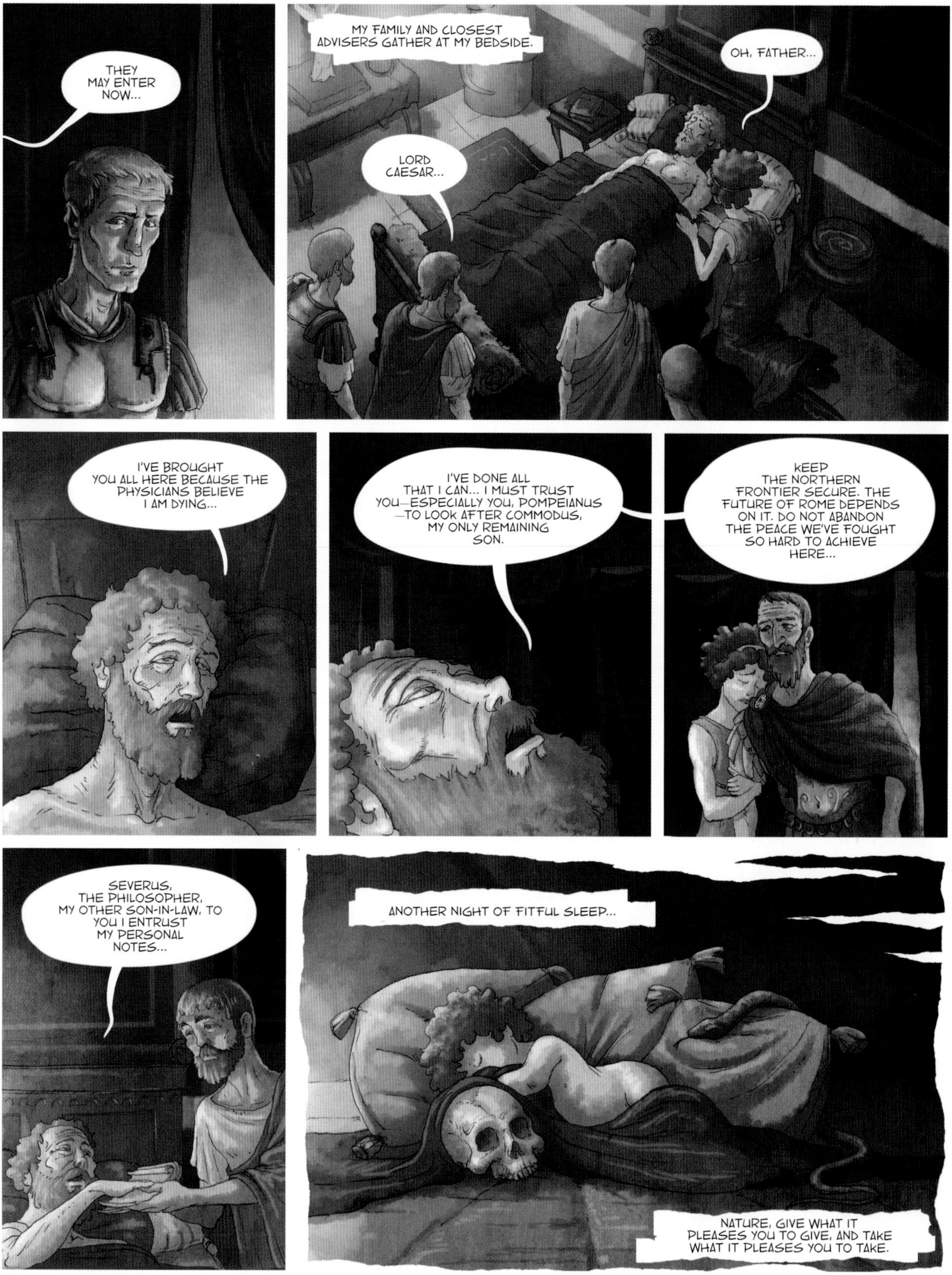
THEY MAY ENTER NOW...
MY FAMILY AND CLOSEST ADVISERS GATHER AT MY BEDSIDE.
OH, FATHER...
LORD CAESAR...
I'VE BROUGHT YOU ALL HERE BECAUSE THE PHYSICIANS BELIEVE I AM DYING...
I'VE DONE ALL THAT I CAN... I MUST TRUST YOU—ESPECIALLY YOU, POMPEIANUS —TO LOOK AFTER COMMODUS, MY ONLY REMAINING SON.
KEEP THE NORTHERN FRONTIER SECURE. THE FUTURE OF ROME DEPENDS ON IT. DO NOT ABANDON THE PEACE WE'VE FOUGHT SO HARD TO ACHIEVE HERE...
SEVERUS, THE PHILOSOPHER, MY OTHER SON-IN-LAW, TO YOU I ENTRUST MY PERSONAL NOTES...
ANOTHER NIGHT OF FITFUL SLEEP...
NATURE, GIVE WHAT IT PLEASES YOU TO GIVE, AND TAKE WHAT IT PLEASES YOU TO TAKE.

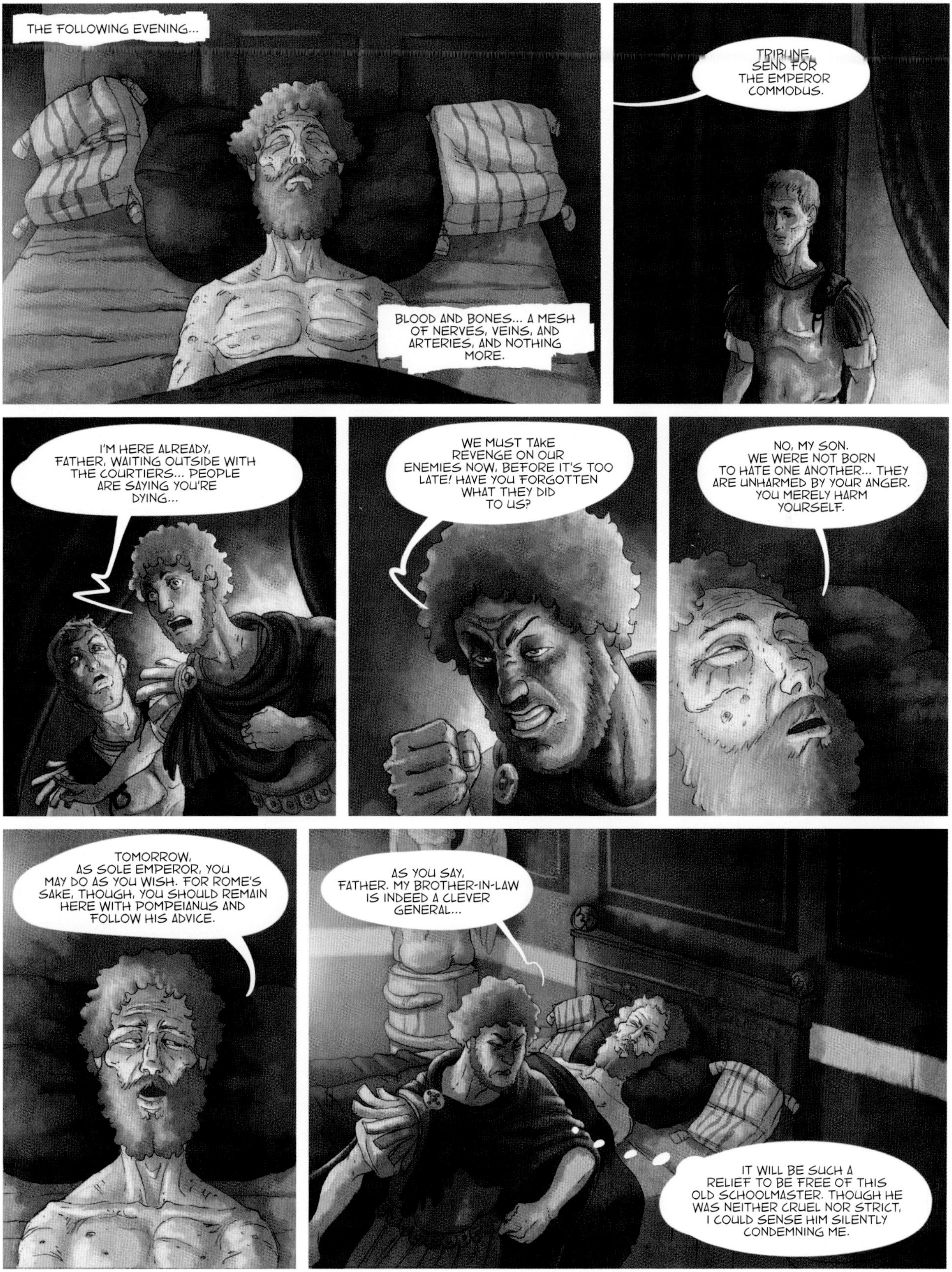
THE FOLLOWING EVENING...
BLOOD AND BONES... A MESH OF NERVES, VEINS, AND ARTERIES, AND NOTHING MORE.
TRIBUNE, SEND FOR THE EMPEROR COMMODUS.
I'M HERE ALREADY, FATHER, WAITING OUTSIDE WITH THE COURTIERS... PEOPLE ARE SAYING YOU'RE DYING...
WE MUST TAKE REVENGE ON OUR ENEMIES NOW, BEFORE IT'S TOO LATE! HAVE YOU FORGOTTEN WHAT THEY DID TO US?
NO, MY SON. WE WERE NOT BORN TO HATE ONE ANOTHER... THEY ARE UNHARMED BY YOUR ANGER. YOU MERELY HARM YOURSELF.
TOMORROW, AS SOLE EMPEROR, YOU MAY DO AS YOU WISH. FOR ROME'S SAKE, THOUGH, YOU SHOULD REMAIN HERE WITH POMPEIANUS AND FOLLOW HIS ADVICE.
AS YOU SAY, FATHER. MY BROTHER-IN-LAW IS INDEED A CLEVER GENERAL...
IT WILL BE SUCH A RELIEF TO BE FREE OF THIS OLD SCHOOLMASTER. THOUGH HE WAS NEITHER CRUEL NOR STRICT, I COULD SENSE HIM SILENTLY CONDEMNING ME.

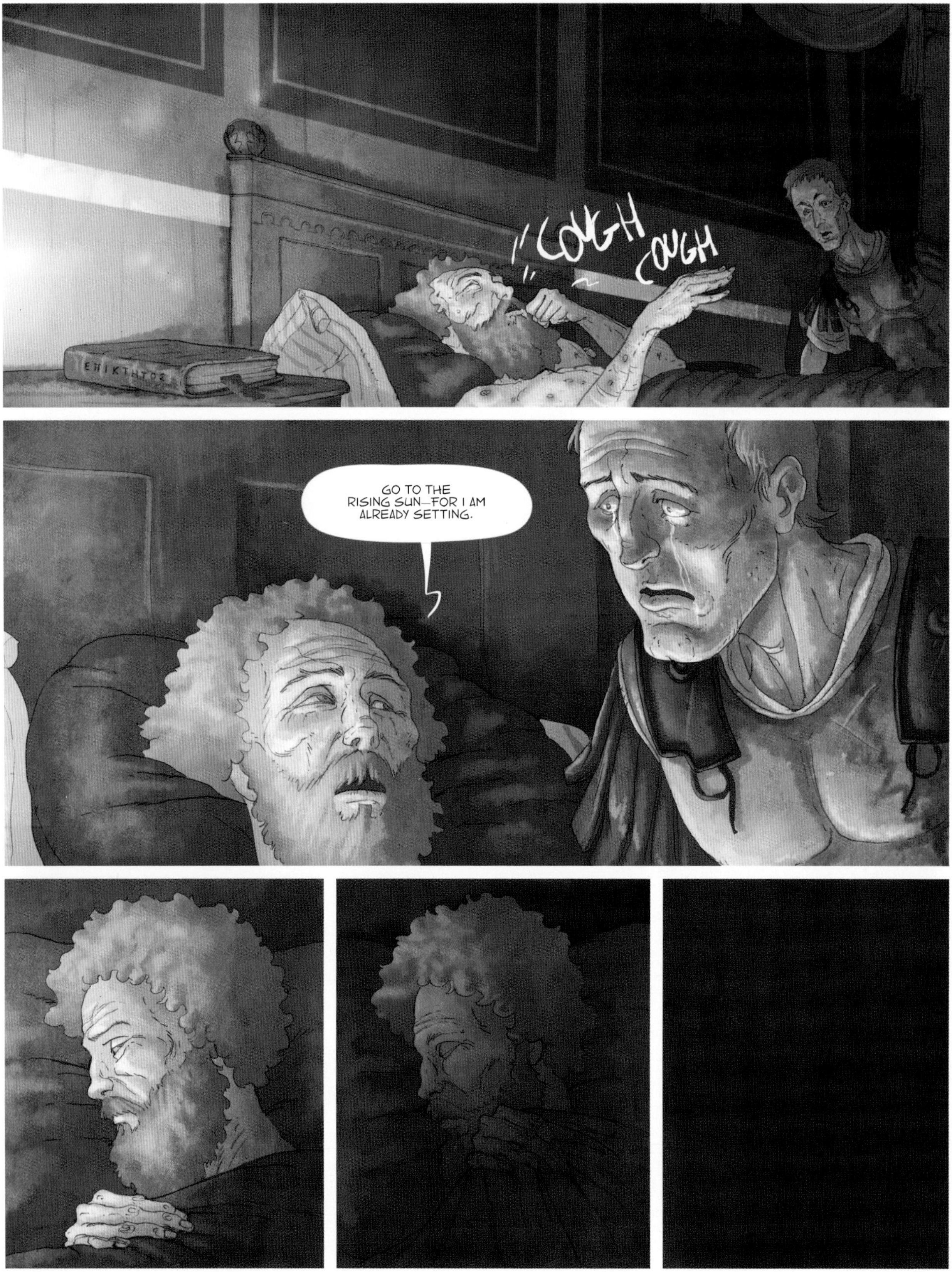
COUGH COUGH
GO TO THE RISING SUN—FOR I AM ALREADY SETTING.

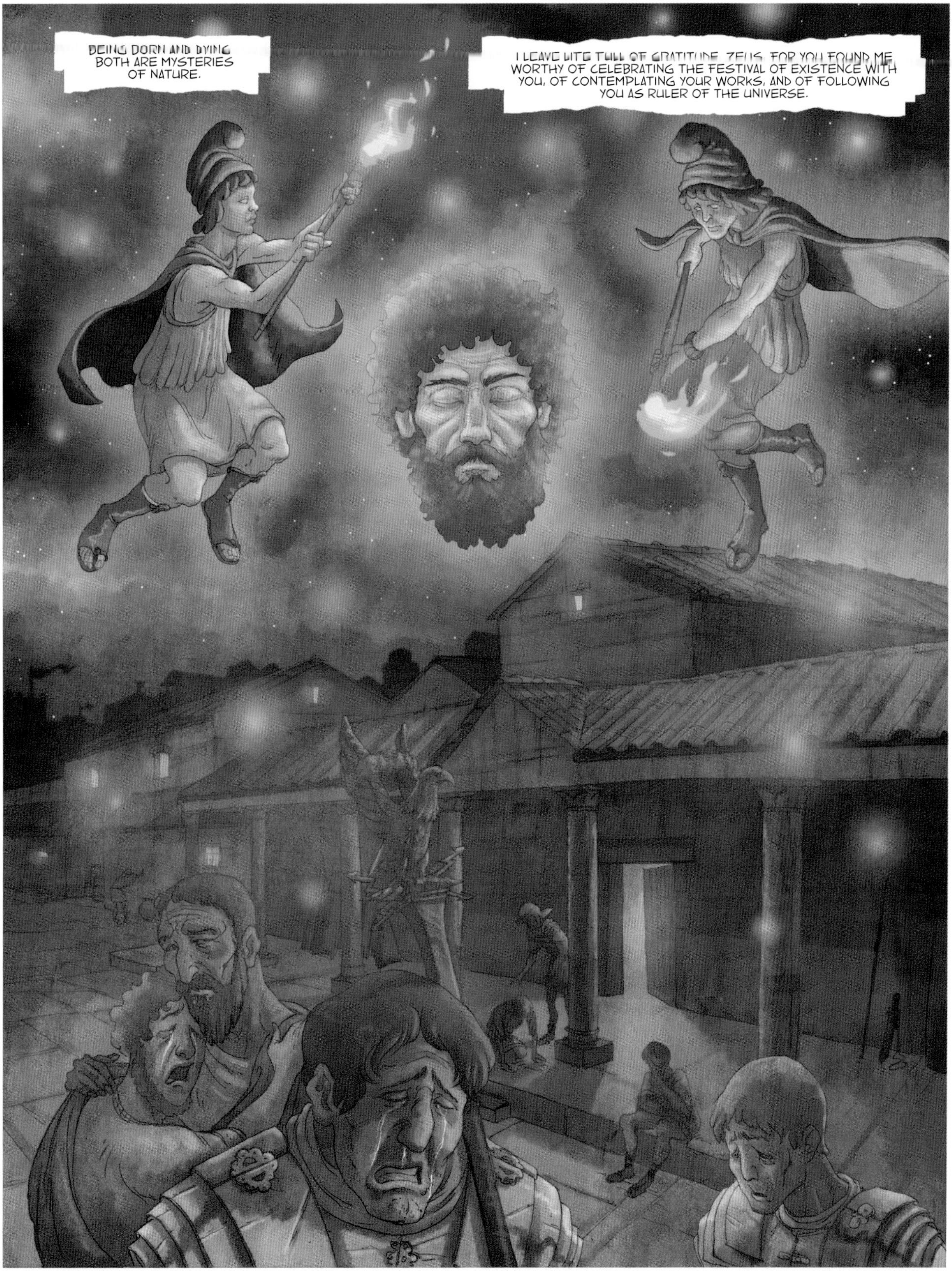
BEING BORN AND DYING
BOTH ARE MYSTERIES
OF NATURE.
I LEAVE LIFE FULL OF GRATITUDE, ZEUS, FOR YOU FOUND ME
WORTHY OF CELEBRATING THE FESTIVAL OF EXISTENCE WITH
YOU, OF CONTEMPLATING YOUR WORKS, AND OF FOLLOWING
YOU AS RULER OF THE UNIVERSE.

THE
MOST TRUTHFUL
CHILD

Expect nothing, fear nothing, be satisfied to act in accord with nature, with heroic truth in every word you utter, and you will live fulfilled. For no man will be able to prevent this.

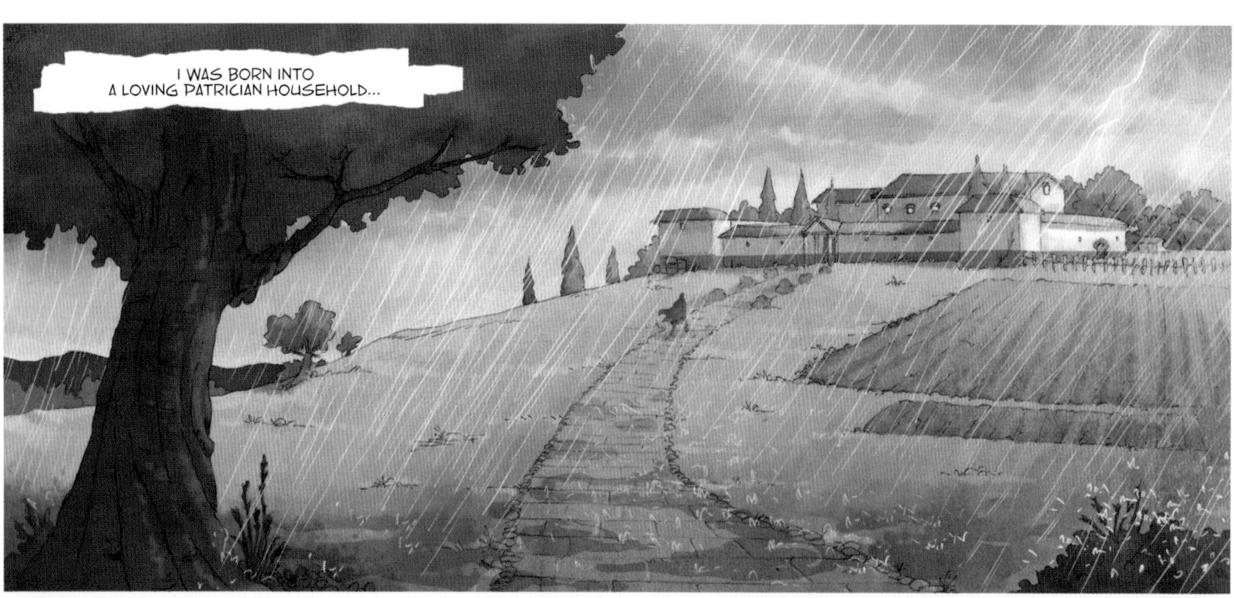
I WAS BORN INTO A LOVING PATRICIAN HOUSEHOLD...

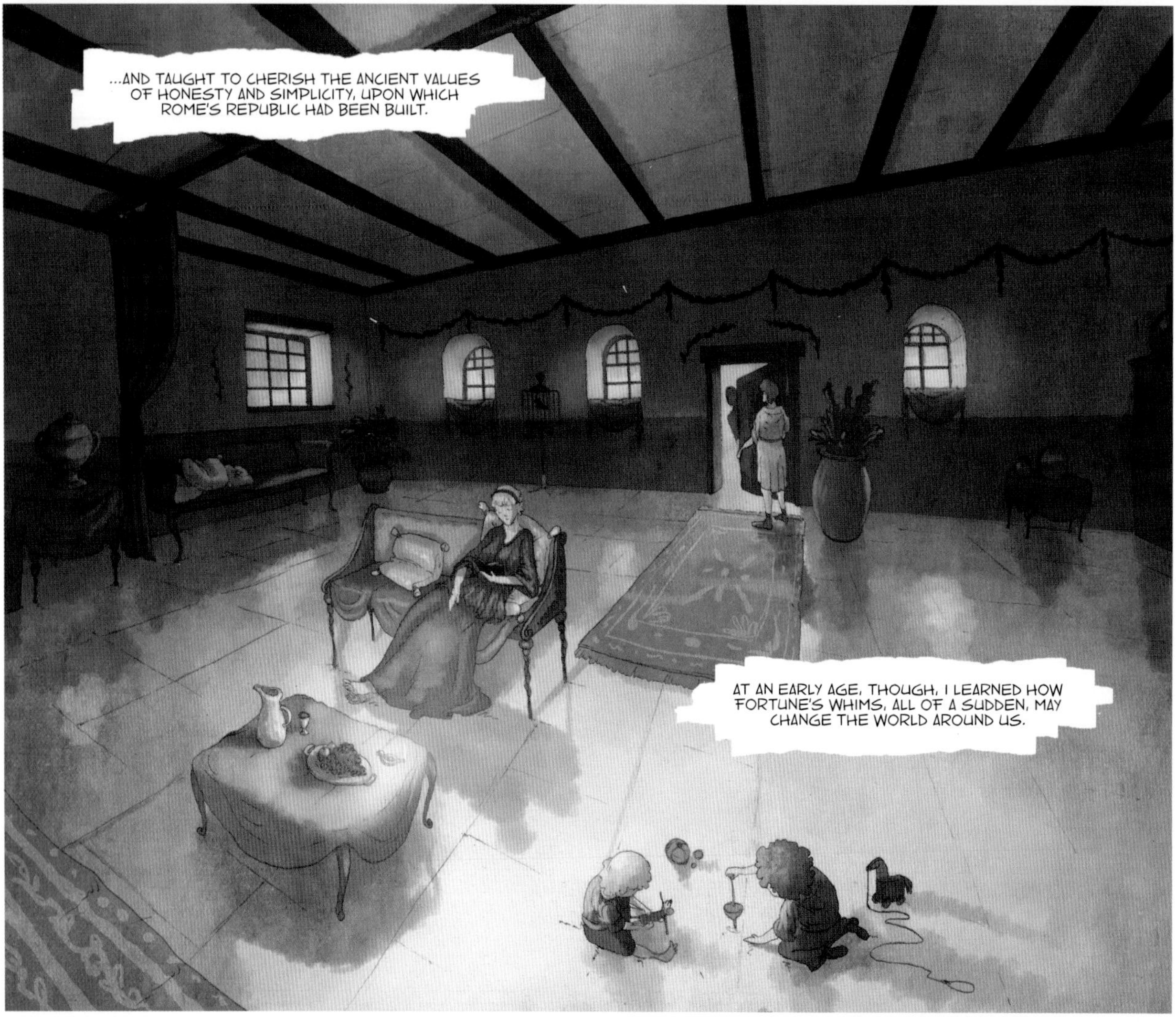
...AND TAUGHT TO CHERISH THE ANCIENT VALUES OF HONESTY AND SIMPLICITY, UPON WHICH ROME'S REPUBLIC HAD BEEN BUILT.
AT AN EARLY AGE, THOUGH, I LEARNED HOW FORTUNE'S WHIMS, ALL OF A SUDDEN, MAY CHANGE THE WORLD AROUND US.

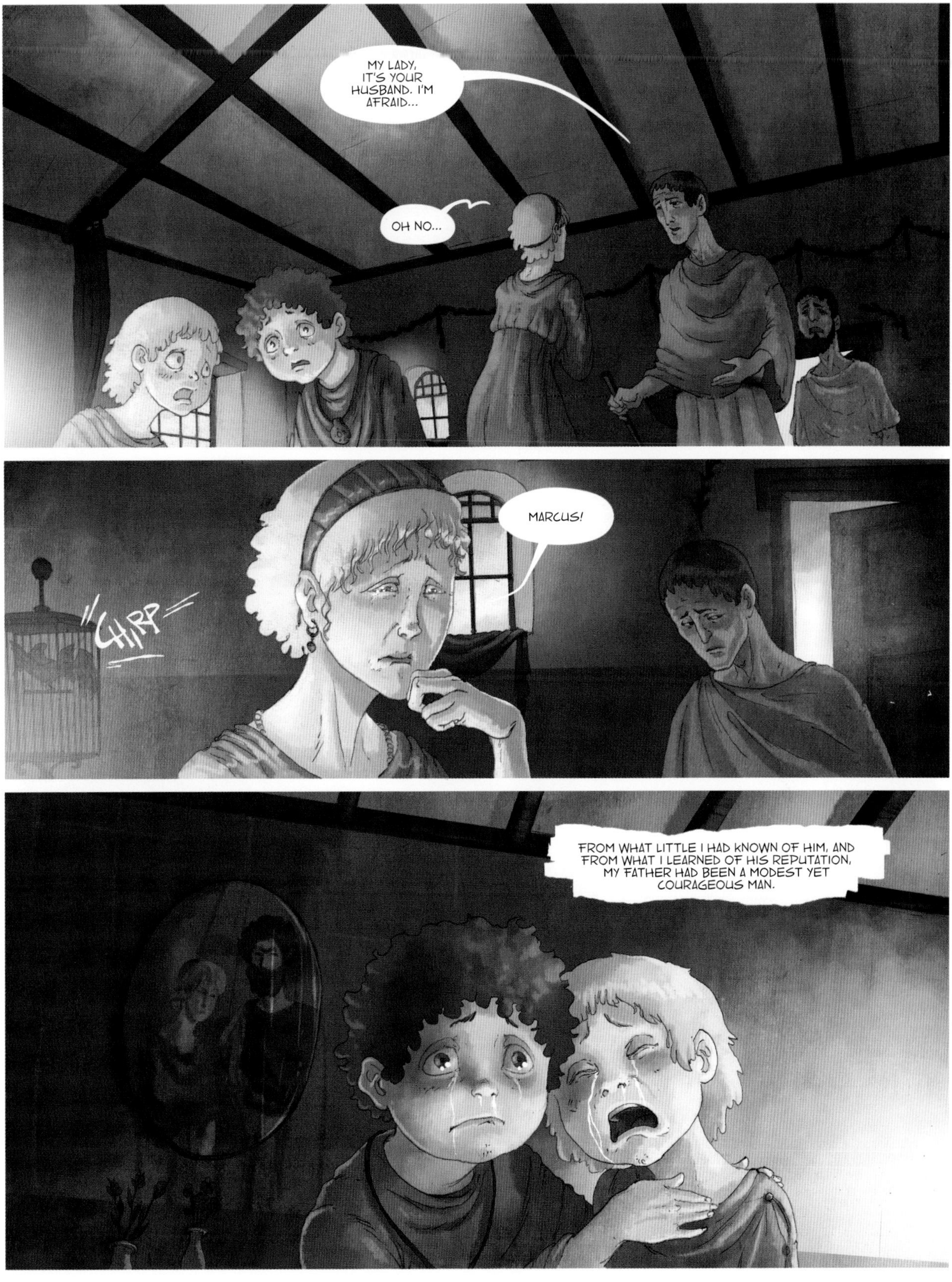
MY LADY, IT'S YOUR HUSBAND. I'M AFRAID...
OH NO...
MARCUS!
CHIRP
FROM WHAT LITTLE I HAD KNOWN OF HIM, AND FROM WHAT I LEARNED OF HIS REPUTATION, MY FATHER HAD BEEN A MODEST YET COURAGEOUS MAN.

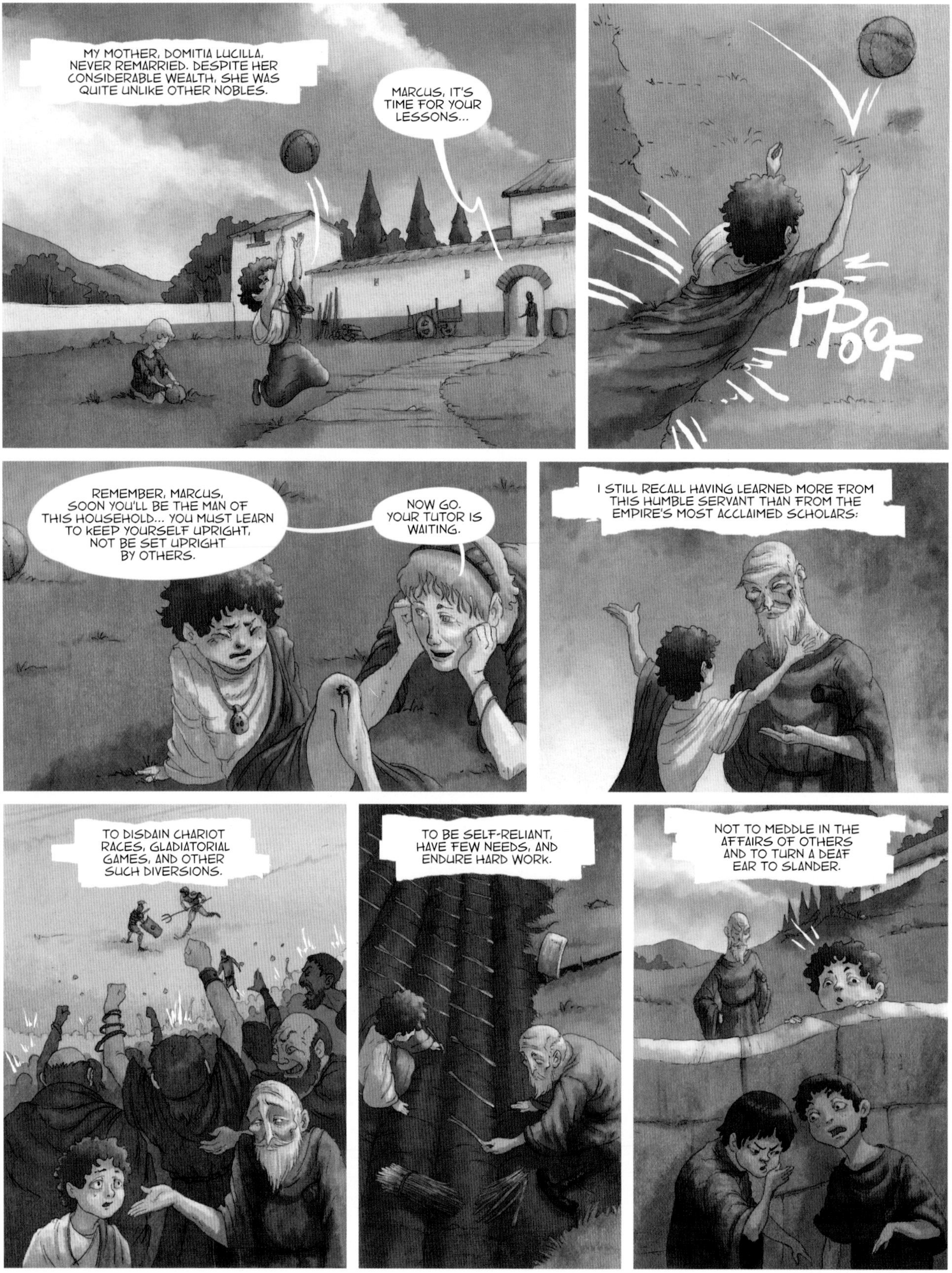
MY MOTHER, DOMITIA LUCILLA, NEVER REMARRIED. DESPITE HER CONSIDERABLE WEALTH, SHE WAS QUITE UNLIKE OTHER NOBLES.
MARCUS, IT'S TIME FOR YOUR LESSONS...
PPOOF
REMEMBER, MARCUS, SOON YOU'LL BE THE MAN OF THIS HOUSEHOLD... YOU MUST LEARN TO KEEP YOURSELF UPRIGHT, NOT BE SET UPRIGHT BY OTHERS.
NOW GO. YOUR TUTOR IS WAITING.
I STILL RECALL HAVING LEARNED MORE FROM THIS HUMBLE SERVANT THAN FROM THE EMPIRE'S MOST ACCLAIMED SCHOLARS:
TO DISDAIN CHARIOT RACES, GLADIATORIAL GAMES, AND OTHER SUCH DIVERSIONS.
TO BE SELF-RELIANT, HAVE FEW NEEDS, AND ENDURE HARD WORK.
NOT TO MEDDLE IN THE AFFAIRS OF OTHERS AND TO TURN A DEAF EAR TO SLANDER.

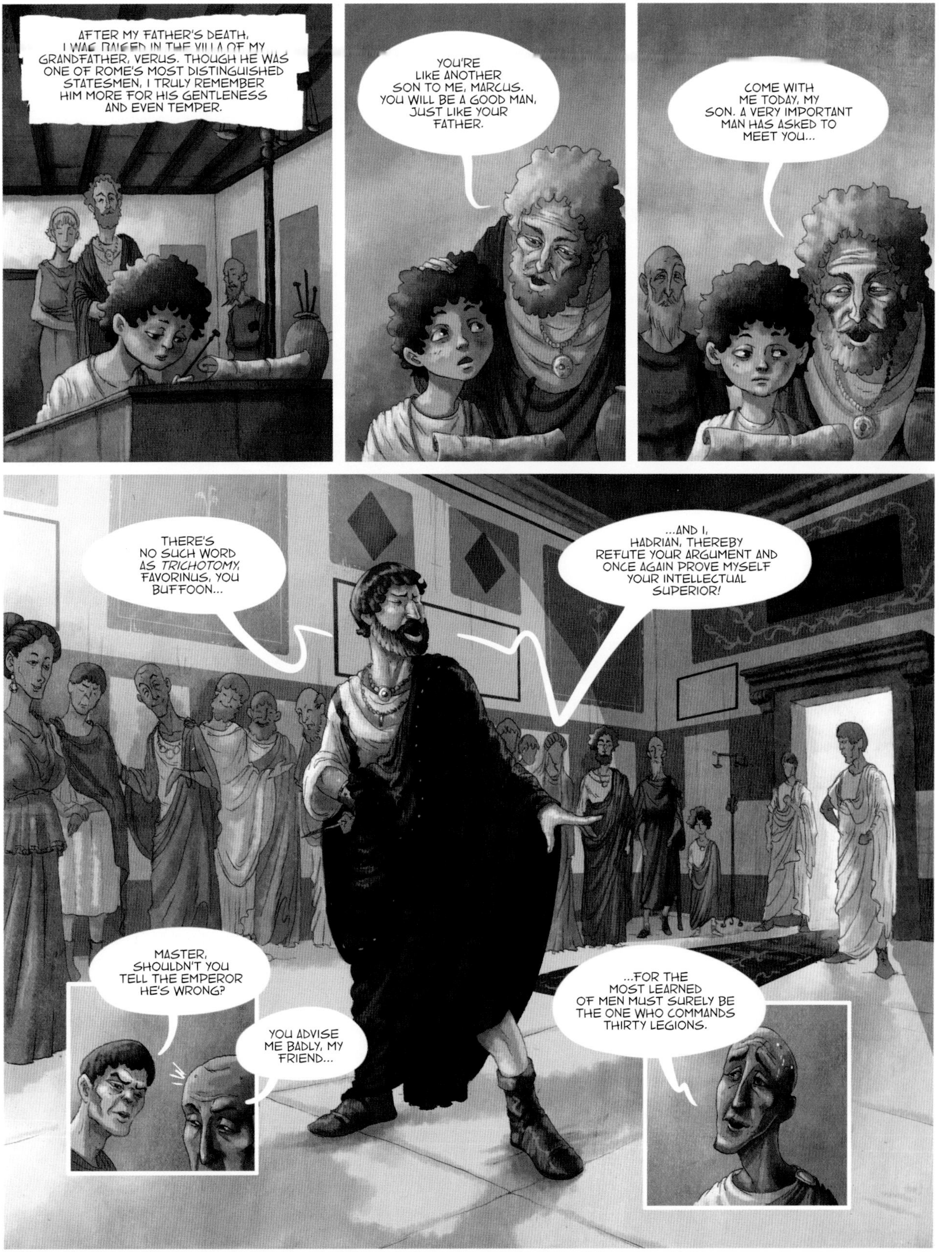
AFTER MY FATHER'S DEATH, I WAS RAISED IN THE VILLA OF MY GRANDFATHER, VERUS. THOUGH HE WAS ONE OF ROME'S MOST DISTINGUISHED STATESMEN, I TRULY REMEMBER HIM MORE FOR HIS GENTLENESS AND EVEN TEMPER.
YOU'RE LIKE ANOTHER SON TO ME, MARCUS. YOU WILL BE A GOOD MAN, JUST LIKE YOUR FATHER.
COME WITH ME TODAY, MY SON. A VERY IMPORTANT MAN HAS ASKED TO MEET YOU...
THERE'S NO SUCH WORD AS *TRICHOTOMY*, FAVORINUS, YOU BUFFOON...
...AND I, HADRIAN, THEREBY REFUTE YOUR ARGUMENT AND ONCE AGAIN PROVE MYSELF YOUR INTELLECTUAL SUPERIOR!
MASTER, SHOULDN'T YOU TELL THE EMPEROR HE'S WRONG?
YOU ADVISE ME BADLY, MY FRIEND...
...FOR THE MOST LEARNED OF MEN MUST SURELY BE THE ONE WHO COMMANDS THIRTY LEGIONS.

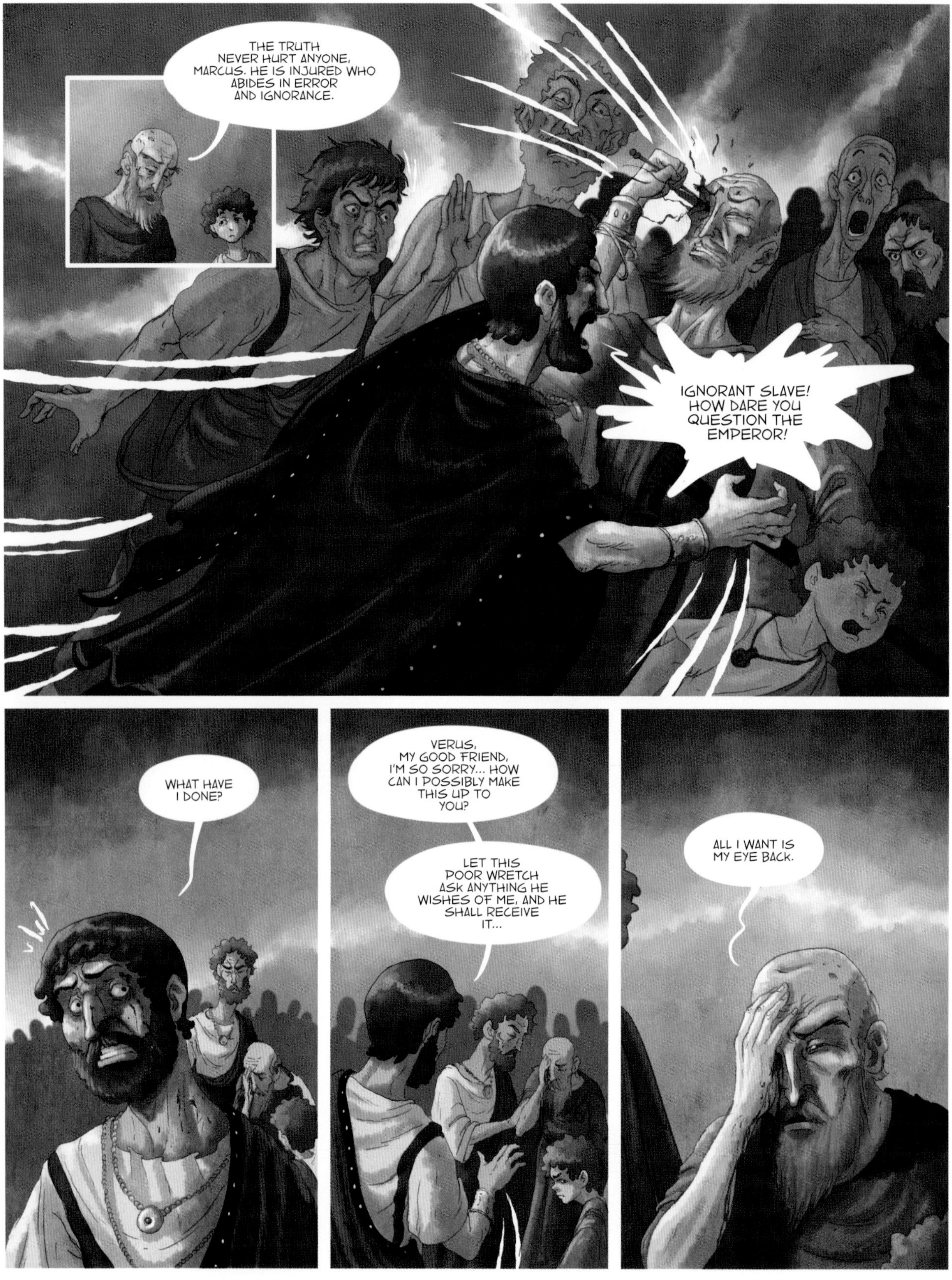
THE TRUTH NEVER HURT ANYONE, MARCUS. HE IS INJURED WHO ABIDES IN ERROR AND IGNORANCE.
IGNORANT SLAVE! HOW DARE YOU QUESTION THE EMPEROR!
WHAT HAVE I DONE?
VERUS, MY GOOD FRIEND, I'M SO SORRY... HOW CAN I POSSIBLY MAKE THIS UP TO YOU?
LET THIS POOR WRETCH ASK ANYTHING HE WISHES OF ME, AND HE SHALL RECEIVE IT...
ALL I WANT IS MY EYE BACK.

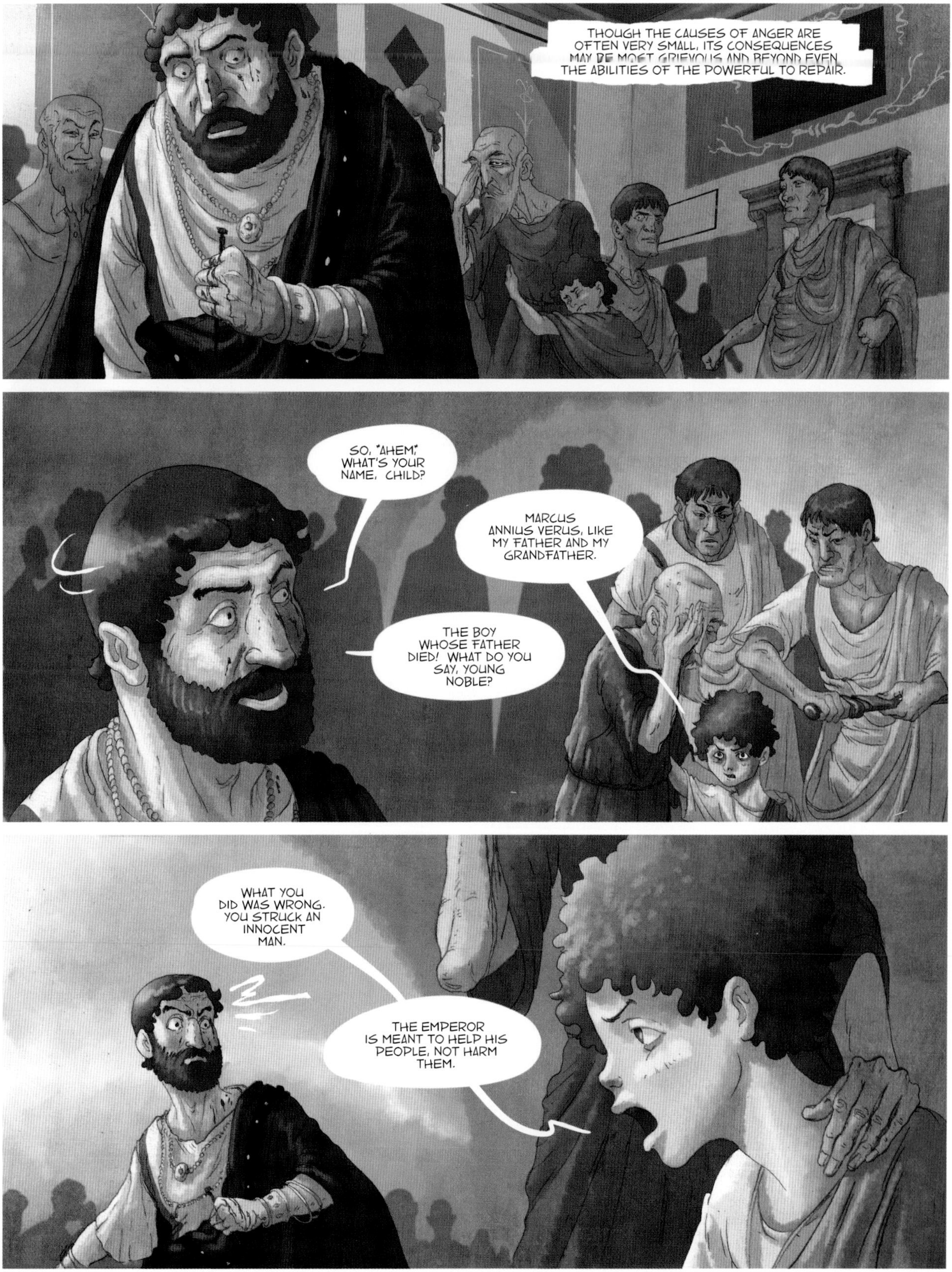
THOUGH THE CAUSES OF ANGER ARE OFTEN VERY SMALL, ITS CONSEQUENCES MAY BE MOST GRIEVOUS AND BEYOND EVEN THE ABILITIES OF THE POWERFUL TO REPAIR.
SO, "AHEM," WHAT'S YOUR NAME, CHILD?
MARCUS ANNIUS VERUS, LIKE MY FATHER AND MY GRANDFATHER.
THE BOY WHOSE FATHER DIED! WHAT DO YOU SAY, YOUNG NOBLE?
WHAT YOU DID WAS WRONG. YOU STRUCK AN INNOCENT MAN.
THE EMPEROR IS MEANT TO HELP HIS PEOPLE, NOT HARM THEM.

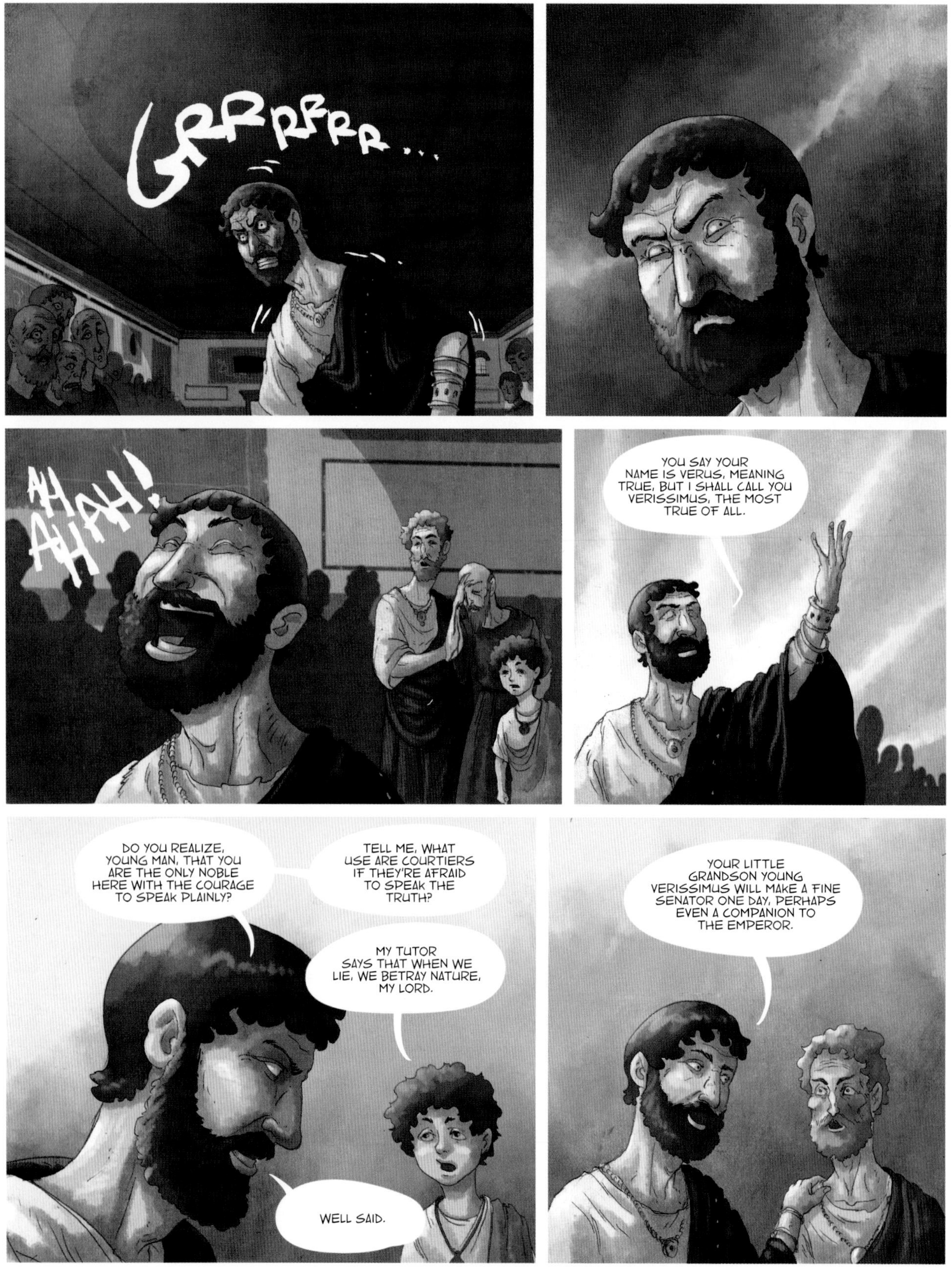
GRRRRRR...
AH AH AH!
YOU SAY YOUR NAME IS VERUS, MEANING TRUE, BUT I SHALL CALL YOU VERISSIMUS, THE MOST TRUE OF ALL.
DO YOU REALIZE, YOUNG MAN, THAT YOU ARE THE ONLY NOBLE HERE WITH THE COURAGE TO SPEAK PLAINLY?
TELL ME, WHAT USE ARE COURTIERS IF THEY'RE AFRAID TO SPEAK THE TRUTH?
MY TUTOR SAYS THAT WHEN WE LIE, WE BETRAY NATURE, MY LORD.
WELL SAID.
YOUR LITTLE GRANDSON YOUNG VERISSIMUS WILL MAKE A FINE SENATOR ONE DAY, PERHAPS EVEN A COMPANION TO THE EMPEROR.

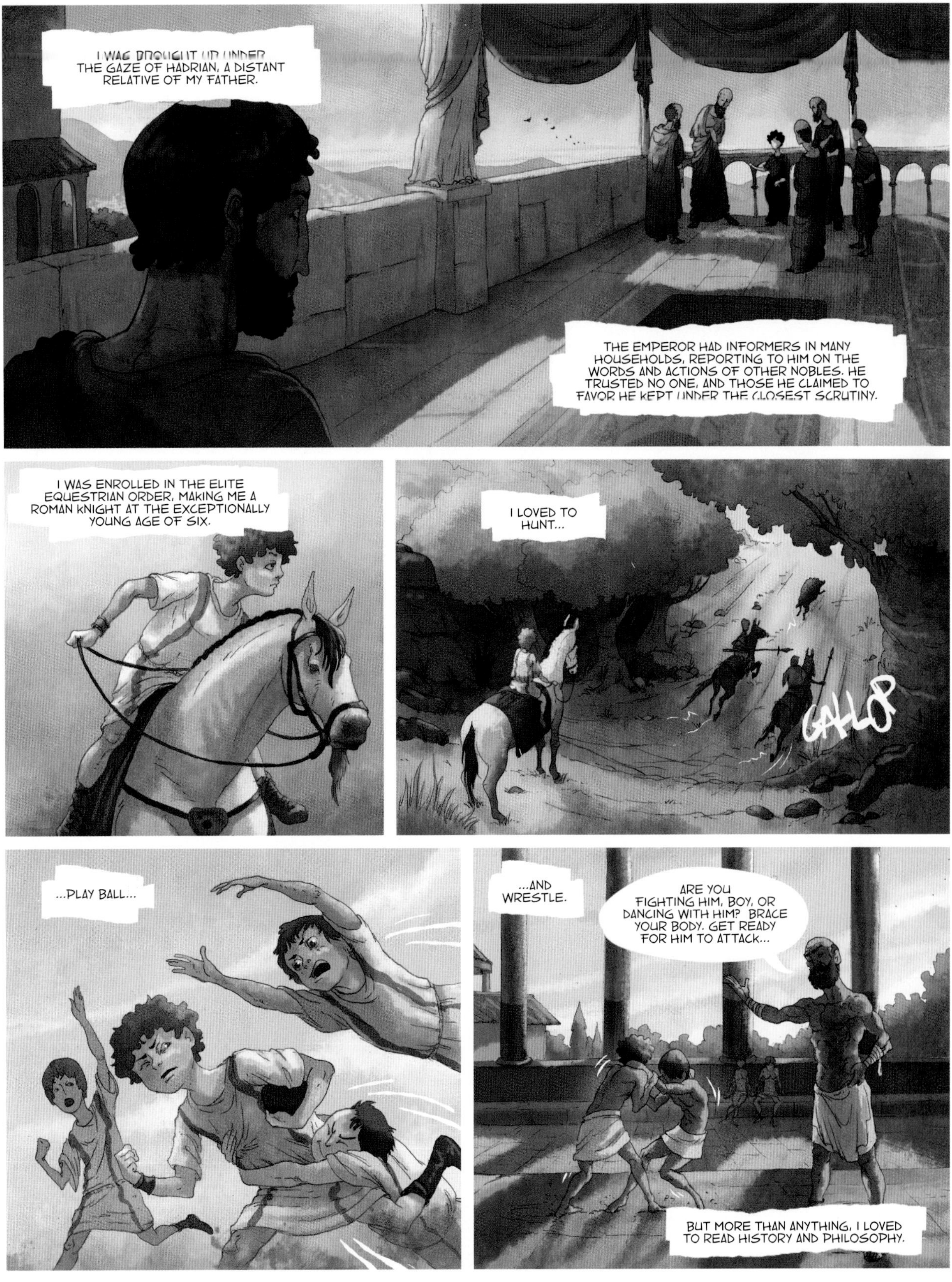
I WAS BROUGHT UP UNDER THE GAZE OF HADRIAN, A DISTANT RELATIVE OF MY FATHER.
THE EMPEROR HAD INFORMERS IN MANY HOUSEHOLDS, REPORTING TO HIM ON THE WORDS AND ACTIONS OF OTHER NOBLES. HE TRUSTED NO ONE, AND THOSE HE CLAIMED TO FAVOR HE KEPT UNDER THE CLOSEST SCRUTINY.
I WAS ENROLLED IN THE ELITE EQUESTRIAN ORDER, MAKING ME A ROMAN KNIGHT AT THE EXCEPTIONALLY YOUNG AGE OF SIX.
I LOVED TO HUNT...
GALLOP
...PLAY BALL...
...AND WRESTLE.
ARE YOU FIGHTING HIM, BOY, OR DANCING WITH HIM? BRACE YOUR BODY. GET READY FOR HIM TO ATTACK...
BUT MORE THAN ANYTHING, I LOVED TO READ HISTORY AND PHILOSOPHY.

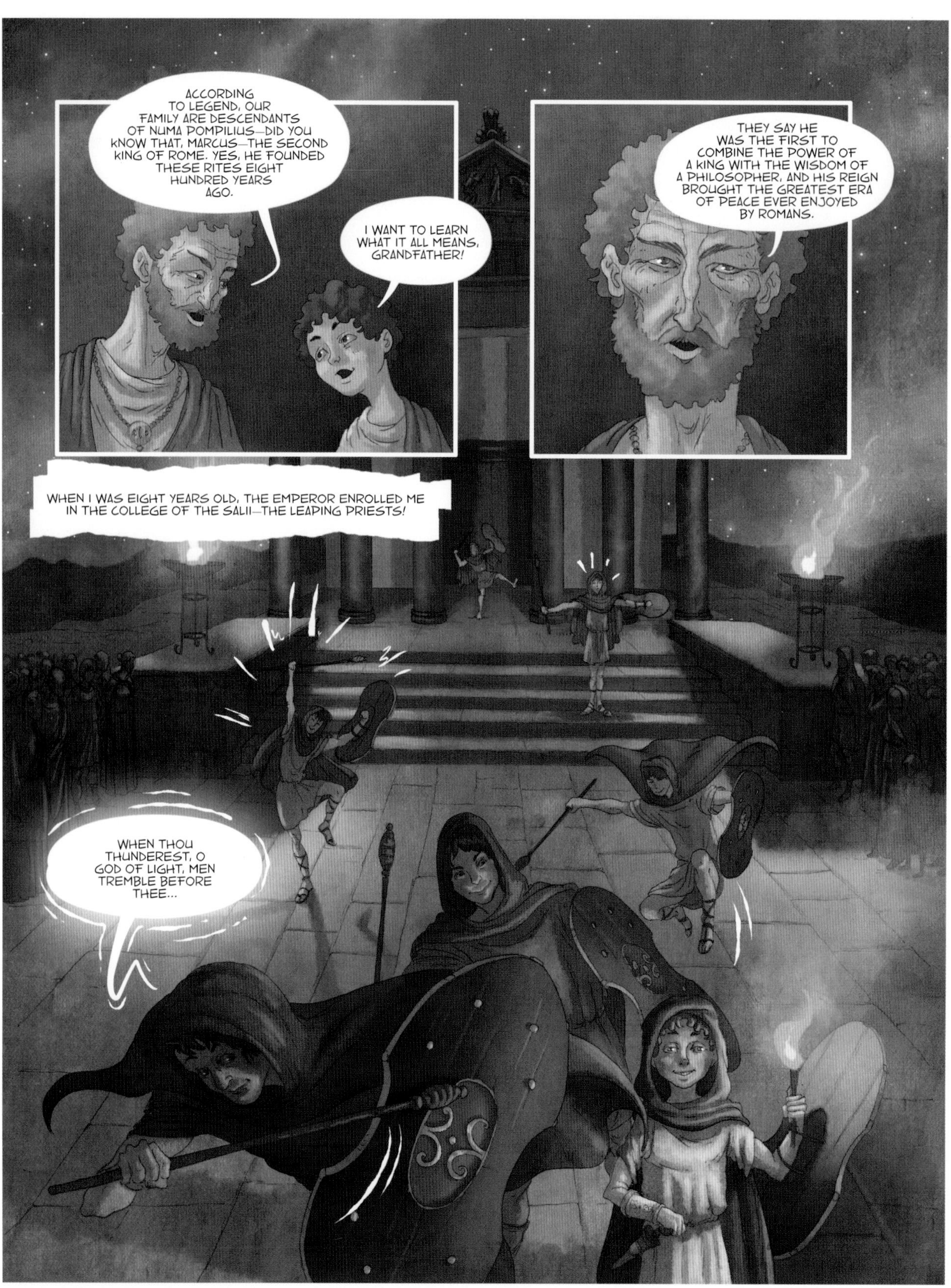
ACCORDING TO LEGEND, OUR FAMILY ARE DESCENDANTS OF NUMA POMPILIUS—DID YOU KNOW THAT, MARCUS—THE SECOND KING OF ROME. YES, HE FOUNDED THESE RITES EIGHT HUNDRED YEARS AGO.
I WANT TO LEARN WHAT IT ALL MEANS, GRANDFATHER!
THEY SAY HE WAS THE FIRST TO COMBINE THE POWER OF A KING WITH THE WISDOM OF A PHILOSOPHER, AND HIS REIGN BROUGHT THE GREATEST ERA OF PEACE EVER ENJOYED BY ROMANS.
WHEN I WAS EIGHT YEARS OLD, THE EMPEROR ENROLLED ME IN THE COLLEGE OF THE SALII—THE LEAPING PRIESTS!
WHEN THOU THUNDEREST, O GOD OF LIGHT, MEN TREMBLE BEFORE THEE...

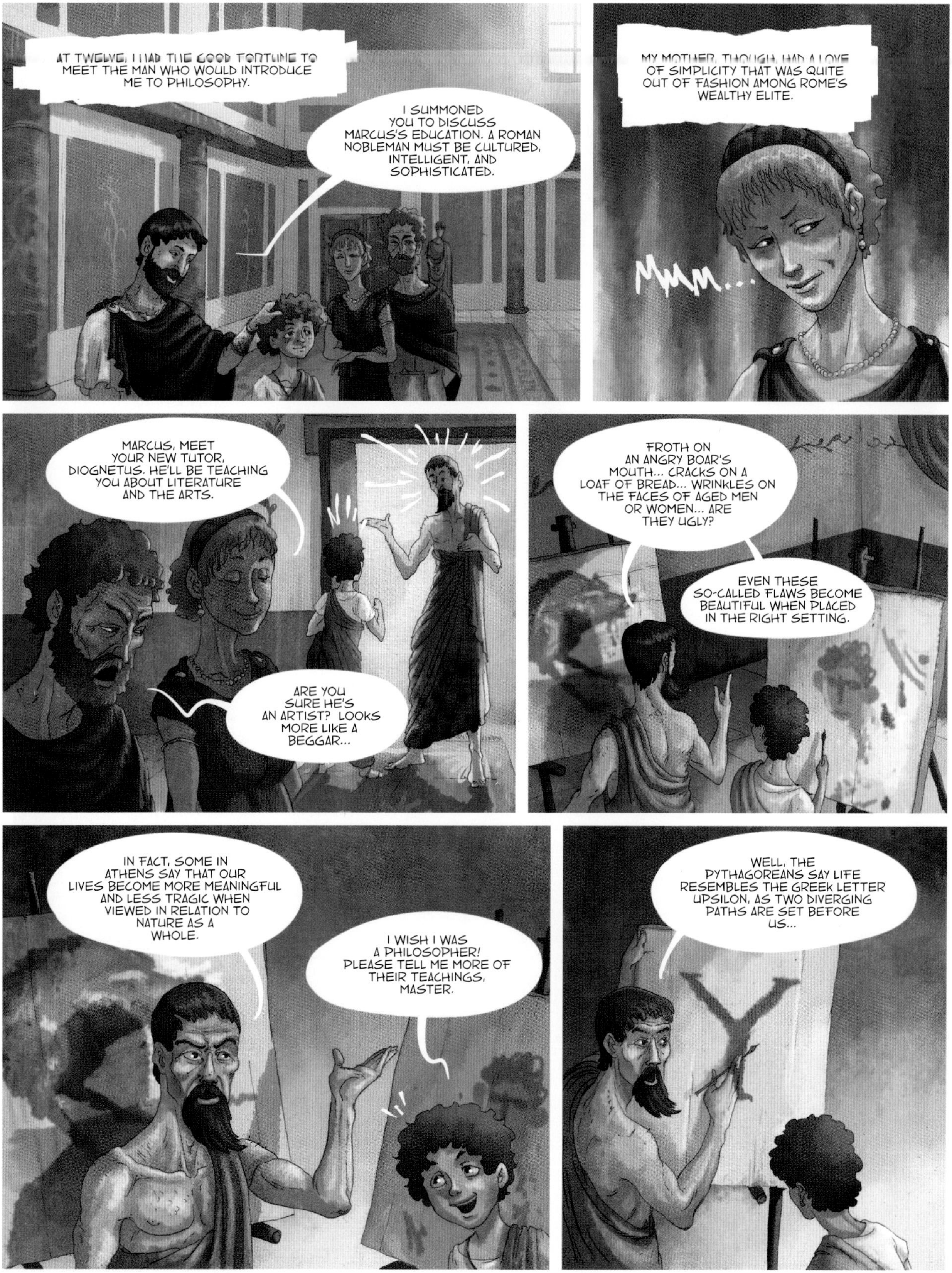
AT TWELVE, I HAD THE GOOD FORTUNE TO MEET THE MAN WHO WOULD INTRODUCE ME TO PHILOSOPHY.
I SUMMONED YOU TO DISCUSS MARCUS'S EDUCATION. A ROMAN NOBLEMAN MUST BE CULTURED, INTELLIGENT, AND SOPHISTICATED.
MY MOTHER, THOUGH, HAD A LOVE OF SIMPLICITY THAT WAS QUITE OUT OF FASHION AMONG ROME'S WEALTHY ELITE.
MMM...
MARCUS, MEET YOUR NEW TUTOR, DIOGNETUS. HE'LL BE TEACHING YOU ABOUT LITERATURE AND THE ARTS.
ARE YOU SURE HE'S AN ARTIST? LOOKS MORE LIKE A BEGGAR...
FROTH ON AN ANGRY BOAR'S MOUTH... CRACKS ON A LOAF OF BREAD... WRINKLES ON THE FACES OF AGED MEN OR WOMEN... ARE THEY UGLY?
EVEN THESE SO-CALLED FLAWS BECOME BEAUTIFUL WHEN PLACED IN THE RIGHT SETTING.
IN FACT, SOME IN ATHENS SAY THAT OUR LIVES BECOME MORE MEANINGFUL AND LESS TRAGIC WHEN VIEWED IN RELATION TO NATURE AS A WHOLE.
I WISH I WAS A PHILOSOPHER! PLEASE TELL ME MORE OF THEIR TEACHINGS, MASTER.
WELL, THE PYTHAGOREANS SAY LIFE RESEMBLES THE GREEK LETTER UPSILON, AS TWO DIVERGING PATHS ARE SET BEFORE US...

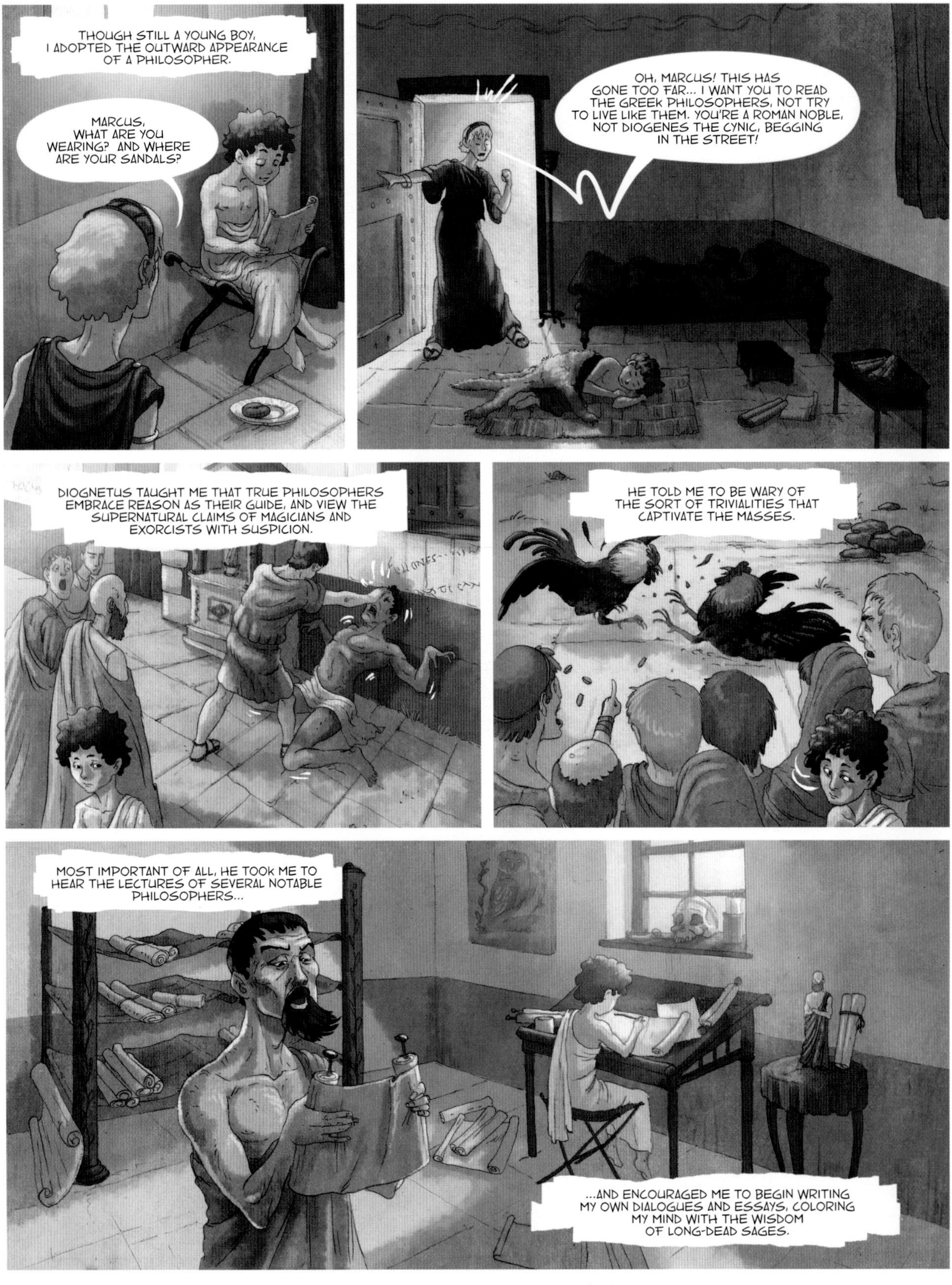
THOUGH STILL A YOUNG BOY, I ADOPTED THE OUTWARD APPEARANCE OF A PHILOSOPHER.
MARCUS, WHAT ARE YOU WEARING? AND WHERE ARE YOUR SANDALS?
OH, MARCUS! THIS HAS GONE TOO FAR... I WANT YOU TO READ THE GREEK PHILOSOPHERS, NOT TRY TO LIVE LIKE THEM. YOU'RE A ROMAN NOBLE, NOT DIOGENES THE CYNIC, BEGGING IN THE STREET!
DIOGNETUS TAUGHT ME THAT TRUE PHILOSOPHERS EMBRACE REASON AS THEIR GUIDE, AND VIEW THE SUPERNATURAL CLAIMS OF MAGICIANS AND EXORCISTS WITH SUSPICION.
HE TOLD ME TO BE WARY OF THE SORT OF TRIVIALITIES THAT CAPTIVATE THE MASSES.
MOST IMPORTANT OF ALL, HE TOOK ME TO HEAR THE LECTURES OF SEVERAL NOTABLE PHILOSOPHERS...
...AND ENCOURAGED ME TO BEGIN WRITING MY OWN DIALOGUES AND ESSAYS, COLORING MY MIND WITH THE WISDOM OF LONG-DEAD SAGES.

"IN MY MIND'S EYE, I LOVE TO SOAR AMONG THE STARS OR STAND ON MIGHTY ATLAS'S SHOULDERS, AND FROM AFAR TO LOOK DOWN UPON MEN'S WANDERINGS BELOW."
THAT'S FROM OVID, MASTER, ISN'T IT?
YES, THE PHILOSOPHY OF PYTHAGORAS, WHICH HE SAYS YOUR FOREBEAR, NUMA BROUGHT TO ROME...BUT THAT'S PROBABLY JUST A LEGEND. ANYWAY, TRY TO WRITE ABOUT THIS IDEA, PUTTING IT IN YOUR OWN WORDS.
HAVE YOU NOTICED, MARCUS, HOW LOOKING AT EVENTS FROM A DIFFERENT PERSPECTIVE CHANGES THE WAY WE FEEL ABOUT THEM?
LIKE IN A WORK OF ART...
INDEED. THOSE MEN ARGUING IN THE STREET BELOW ALMOST CAME TO BLOWS... ALARMING OTHERS WITH THEIR SHOUTS... AND YET, A PAINTING OF THEIR BRAWL WOULD NOT ALARM US.
BUT THE PAINTING ISN'T REAL...
NEITHER ARE THE THINGS THEY'RE ARGUING ABOUT.
PERHAPS ONE DAY, LOOKING BACK ON THEM, WORRIES THAT NOW DOMINATE OUR WAKING HOURS WILL SEEM NO MORE IMPORTANT TO US THAN DREAMS THAT ONCE AGITATED OUR MINDS WHILE WE WERE ASLEEP.

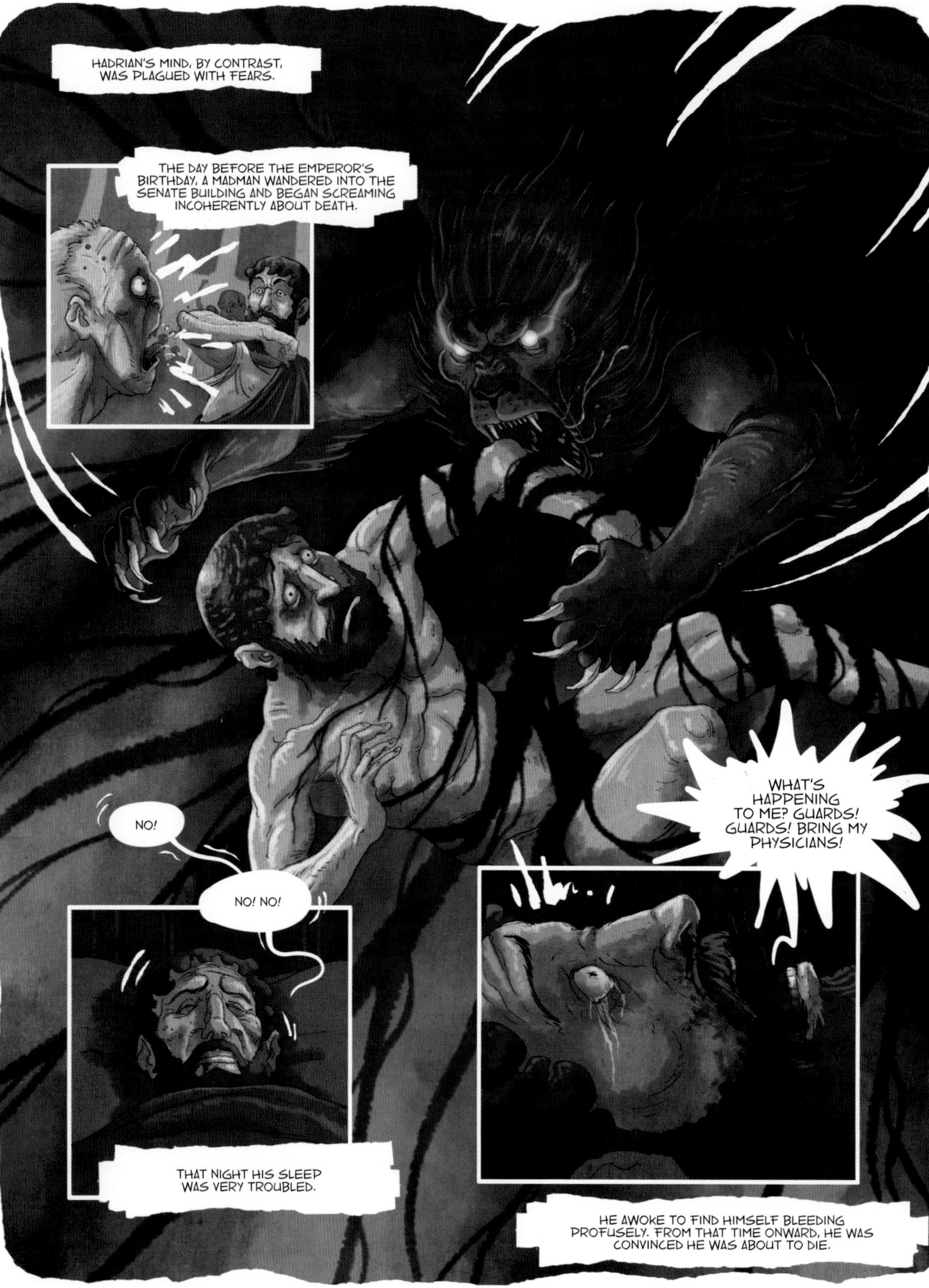
HADRIAN'S MIND, BY CONTRAST, WAS PLAGUED WITH FEARS.
THE DAY BEFORE THE EMPEROR'S BIRTHDAY, A MADMAN WANDERED INTO THE SENATE BUILDING AND BEGAN SCREAMING INCOHERENTLY ABOUT DEATH.
NO!
NO! NO!
THAT NIGHT HIS SLEEP WAS VERY TROUBLED.
WHAT'S HAPPENING TO ME? GUARDS! GUARDS! BRING MY PHYSICIANS!
HE AWOKE TO FIND HIMSELF BLEEDING PROFUSELY. FROM THAT TIME ONWARD, HE WAS CONVINCED HE WAS ABOUT TO DIE.

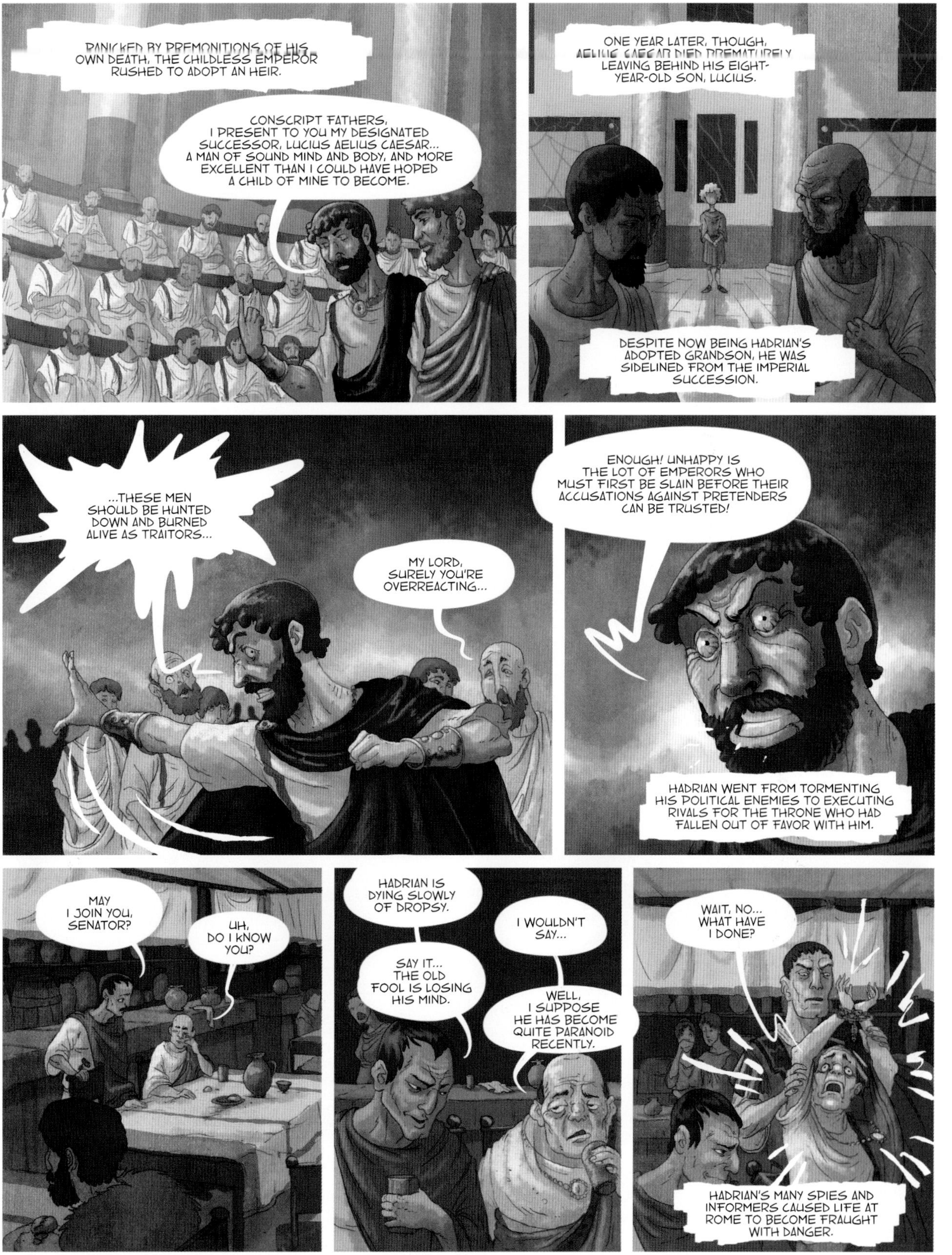
PANICKED BY PREMONITIONS OF HIS OWN DEATH, THE CHILDLESS EMPEROR RUSHED TO ADOPT AN HEIR.
CONSCRIPT FATHERS, I PRESENT TO YOU MY DESIGNATED SUCCESSOR, LUCIUS AELIUS CAESAR... A MAN OF SOUND MIND AND BODY, AND MORE EXCELLENT THAN I COULD HAVE HOPED A CHILD OF MINE TO BECOME.
ONE YEAR LATER, THOUGH, AELIUS CAESAR DIED PREMATURELY LEAVING BEHIND HIS EIGHT-YEAR-OLD SON, LUCIUS.
DESPITE NOW BEING HADRIAN'S ADOPTED GRANDSON, HE WAS SIDELINED FROM THE IMPERIAL SUCCESSION.
...THESE MEN SHOULD BE HUNTED DOWN AND BURNED ALIVE AS TRAITORS...
MY LORD, SURELY YOU'RE OVERREACTING...
ENOUGH! UNHAPPY IS THE LOT OF EMPERORS WHO MUST FIRST BE SLAIN BEFORE THEIR ACCUSATIONS AGAINST PRETENDERS CAN BE TRUSTED!
HADRIAN WENT FROM TORMENTING HIS POLITICAL ENEMIES TO EXECUTING RIVALS FOR THE THRONE WHO HAD FALLEN OUT OF FAVOR WITH HIM.
MAY I JOIN YOU, SENATOR?
UH, DO I KNOW YOU?
HADRIAN IS DYING SLOWLY OF DROPSY.
I WOULDN'T SAY...
SAY IT... THE OLD FOOL IS LOSING HIS MIND.
WELL, I SUPPOSE HE HAS BECOME QUITE PARANOID RECENTLY.
WAIT, NO... WHAT HAVE I DONE?
HADRIAN'S MANY SPIES AND INFORMERS CAUSED LIFE AT ROME TO BECOME FRAUGHT WITH DANGER.

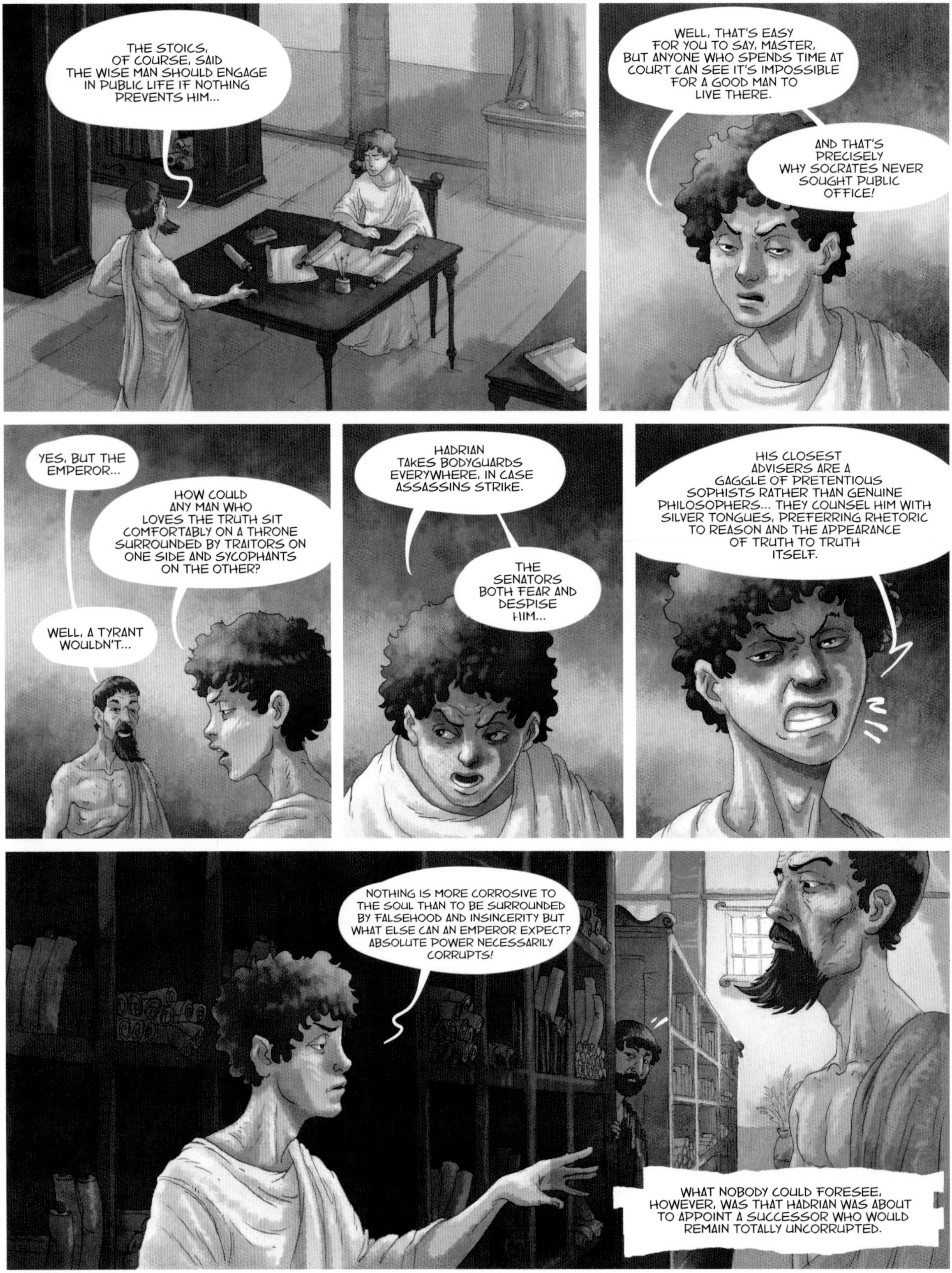
THE STOICS, OF COURSE, SAID THE WISE MAN SHOULD ENGAGE IN PUBLIC LIFE IF NOTHING PREVENTS HIM...
WELL, THAT'S EASY FOR YOU TO SAY, MASTER, BUT ANYONE WHO SPENDS TIME AT COURT CAN SEE IT'S IMPOSSIBLE FOR A GOOD MAN TO LIVE THERE.
AND THAT'S PRECISELY WHY SOCRATES NEVER SOUGHT PUBLIC OFFICE!
YES, BUT THE EMPEROR...
HOW COULD ANY MAN WHO LOVES THE TRUTH SIT COMFORTABLY ON A THRONE SURROUNDED BY TRAITORS ON ONE SIDE AND SYCOPHANTS ON THE OTHER?
WELL, A TYRANT WOULDN'T...
HADRIAN TAKES BODYGUARDS EVERYWHERE, IN CASE ASSASSINS STRIKE.
THE SENATORS BOTH FEAR AND DESPISE HIM...
HIS CLOSEST ADVISERS ARE A GAGGLE OF PRETENTIOUS SOPHISTS RATHER THAN GENUINE PHILOSOPHERS... THEY COUNSEL HIM WITH SILVER TONGUES, PREFERRING RHETORIC TO REASON AND THE APPEARANCE OF TRUTH TO TRUTH ITSELF.
NOTHING IS MORE CORROSIVE TO THE SOUL THAN TO BE SURROUNDED BY FALSEHOOD AND INSINCERITY BUT WHAT ELSE CAN AN EMPEROR EXPECT? ABSOLUTE POWER NECESSARILY CORRUPTS!
WHAT NOBODY COULD FORESEE, HOWEVER, WAS THAT HADRIAN WAS ABOUT TO APPOINT A SUCCESSOR WHO WOULD REMAIN TOTALLY UNCORRUPTED.

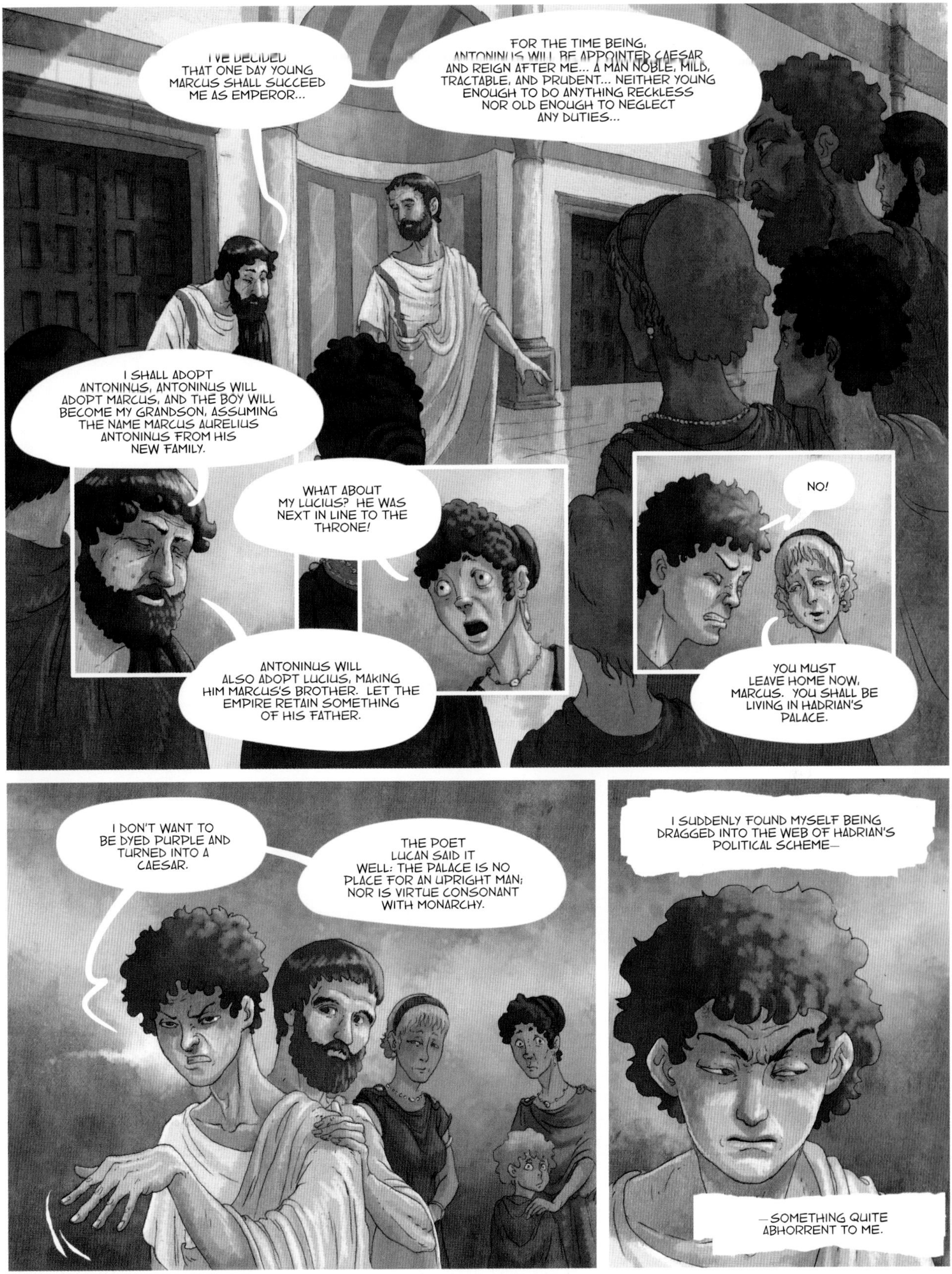

I'VE DECIDED THAT ONE DAY YOUNG MARCUS SHALL SUCCEED ME AS EMPEROR...
FOR THE TIME BEING, ANTONINUS WILL BE APPOINTED CAESAR AND REIGN AFTER ME... A MAN NOBLE, MILD, TRACTABLE, AND PRUDENT... NEITHER YOUNG ENOUGH TO DO ANYTHING RECKLESS NOR OLD ENOUGH TO NEGLECT ANY DUTIES...
I SHALL ADOPT ANTONINUS, ANTONINUS WILL ADOPT MARCUS, AND THE BOY WILL BECOME MY GRANDSON, ASSUMING THE NAME MARCUS AURELIUS ANTONINUS FROM HIS NEW FAMILY.
WHAT ABOUT MY LUCIUS? HE WAS NEXT IN LINE TO THE THRONE!
ANTONINUS WILL ALSO ADOPT LUCIUS, MAKING HIM MARCUS'S BROTHER. LET THE EMPIRE RETAIN SOMETHING OF HIS FATHER.
NO!
YOU MUST LEAVE HOME NOW, MARCUS. YOU SHALL BE LIVING IN HADRIAN'S PALACE.
I DON'T WANT TO BE DYED PURPLE AND TURNED INTO A CAESAR.
THE POET LUCAN SAID IT WELL: THE PALACE IS NO PLACE FOR AN UPRIGHT MAN; NOR IS VIRTUE CONSONANT WITH MONARCHY.
I SUDDENLY FOUND MYSELF BEING DRAGGED INTO THE WEB OF HADRIAN'S POLITICAL SCHEME—
—SOMETHING QUITE ABHORRENT TO ME.

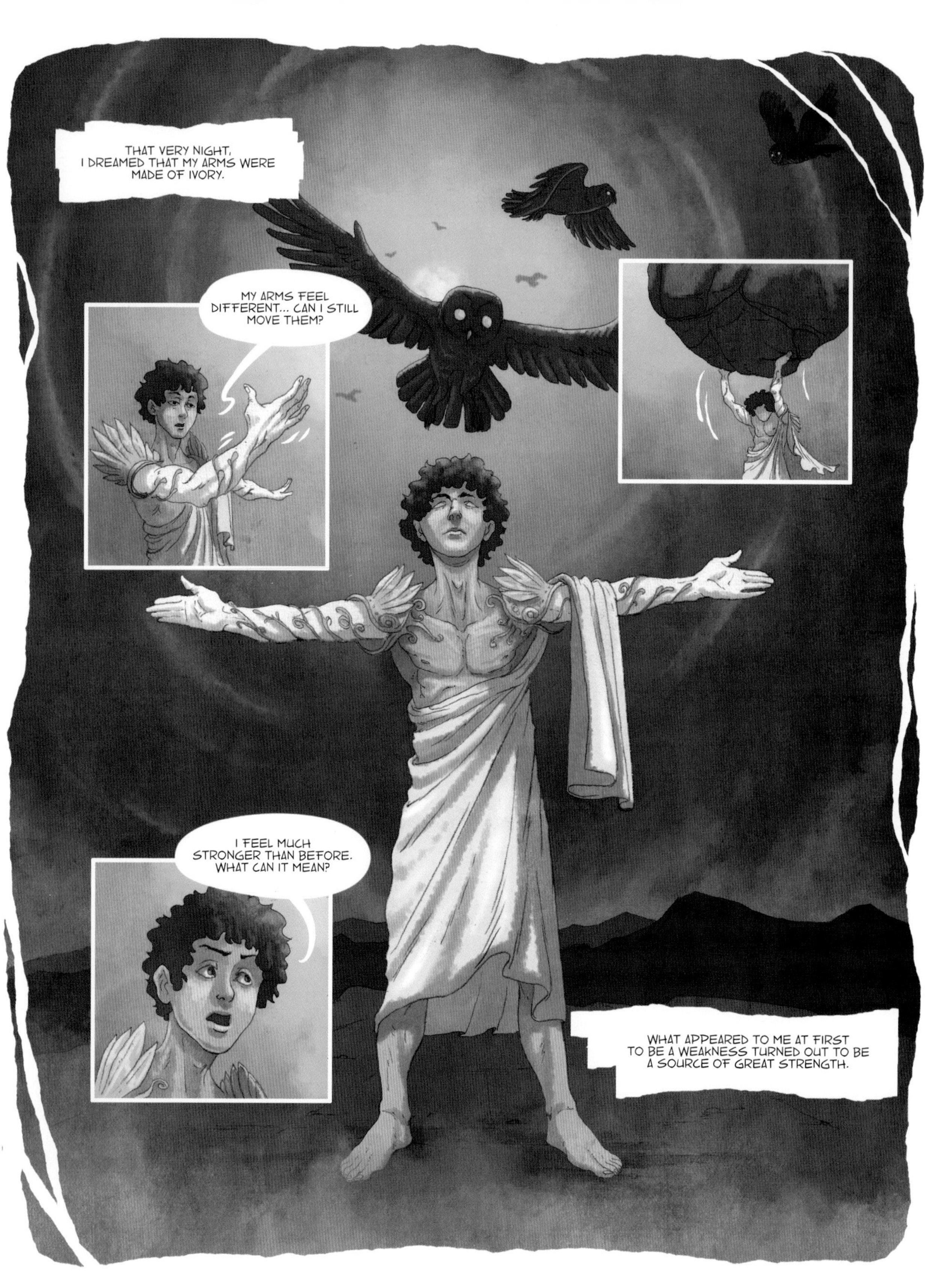
THAT VERY NIGHT, I DREAMED THAT MY ARMS WERE MADE OF IVORY.
MY ARMS FEEL DIFFERENT... CAN I STILL MOVE THEM?
I FEEL MUCH STRONGER THAN BEFORE. WHAT CAN IT MEAN?
WHAT APPEARED TO ME AT FIRST TO BE A WEAKNESS TURNED OUT TO BE A SOURCE OF GREAT STRENGTH.

THE
STOIC
MASTER

We should not hold on to the opinions of everyone, but only to those of such men as live in accord with nature.

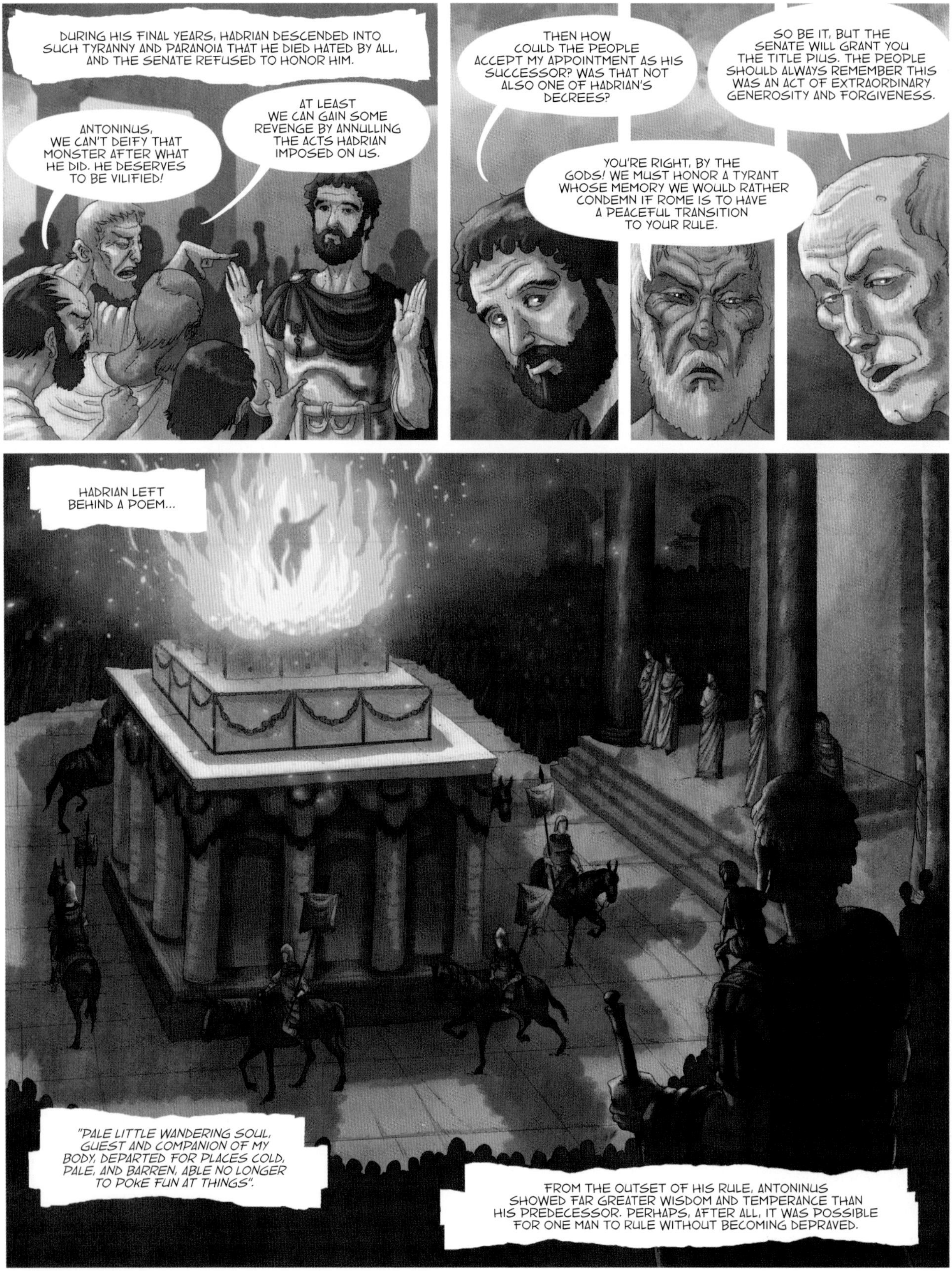
DURING HIS FINAL YEARS, HADRIAN DESCENDED INTO SUCH TYRANNY AND PARANOIA THAT HE DIED HATED BY ALL, AND THE SENATE REFUSED TO HONOR HIM.
ANTONINUS, WE CAN'T DEIFY THAT MONSTER AFTER WHAT HE DID. HE DESERVES TO BE VILIFIED!
AT LEAST WE CAN GAIN SOME REVENGE BY ANNULLING THE ACTS HADRIAN IMPOSED ON US.
THEN HOW COULD THE PEOPLE ACCEPT MY APPOINTMENT AS HIS SUCCESSOR? WAS THAT NOT ALSO ONE OF HADRIAN'S DECREES?
YOU'RE RIGHT, BY THE GODS! WE MUST HONOR A TYRANT WHOSE MEMORY WE WOULD RATHER CONDEMN IF ROME IS TO HAVE A PEACEFUL TRANSITION TO YOUR RULE.
SO BE IT, BUT THE SENATE WILL GRANT YOU THE TITLE PIUS. THE PEOPLE SHOULD ALWAYS REMEMBER THIS WAS AN ACT OF EXTRAORDINARY GENEROSITY AND FORGIVENESS.
HADRIAN LEFT BEHIND A POEM...
"PALE LITTLE WANDERING SOUL, GUEST AND COMPANION OF MY BODY, DEPARTED FOR PLACES COLD, PALE, AND BARREN, ABLE NO LONGER TO POKE FUN AT THINGS".
FROM THE OUTSET OF HIS RULE, ANTONINUS SHOWED FAR GREATER WISDOM AND TEMPERANCE THAN HIS PREDECESSOR. PERHAPS, AFTER ALL, IT WAS POSSIBLE FOR ONE MAN TO RULE WITHOUT BECOMING DEPRAVED.

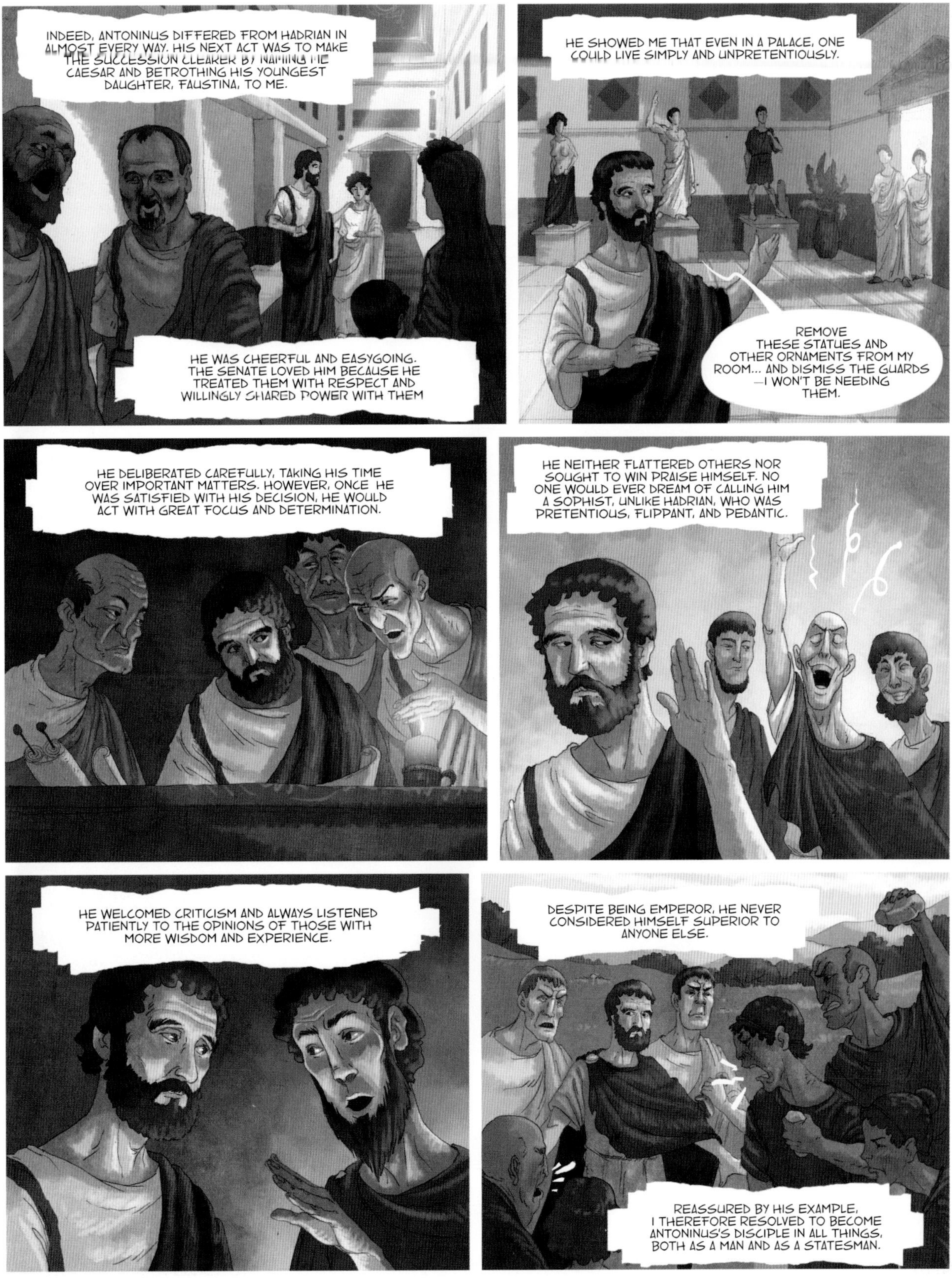
INDEED, ANTONINUS DIFFERED FROM HADRIAN IN ALMOST EVERY WAY. HIS NEXT ACT WAS TO MAKE THE SUCCESSION CLEARER BY NAMING ME CAESAR AND BETROTHING HIS YOUNGEST DAUGHTER, FAUSTINA, TO ME.
HE WAS CHEERFUL AND EASYGOING. THE SENATE LOVED HIM BECAUSE HE TREATED THEM WITH RESPECT AND WILLINGLY SHARED POWER WITH THEM
HE SHOWED ME THAT EVEN IN A PALACE, ONE COULD LIVE SIMPLY AND UNPRETENTIOUSLY.
REMOVE THESE STATUES AND OTHER ORNAMENTS FROM MY ROOM... AND DISMISS THE GUARDS —I WON'T BE NEEDING THEM.
HE DELIBERATED CAREFULLY, TAKING HIS TIME OVER IMPORTANT MATTERS. HOWEVER, ONCE HE WAS SATISFIED WITH HIS DECISION, HE WOULD ACT WITH GREAT FOCUS AND DETERMINATION.
HE NEITHER FLATTERED OTHERS NOR SOUGHT TO WIN PRAISE HIMSELF. NO ONE WOULD EVER DREAM OF CALLING HIM A SOPHIST, UNLIKE HADRIAN, WHO WAS PRETENTIOUS, FLIPPANT, AND PEDANTIC.
HE WELCOMED CRITICISM AND ALWAYS LISTENED PATIENTLY TO THE OPINIONS OF THOSE WITH MORE WISDOM AND EXPERIENCE.
DESPITE BEING EMPEROR, HE NEVER CONSIDERED HIMSELF SUPERIOR TO ANYONE ELSE.
REASSURED BY HIS EXAMPLE, I THEREFORE RESOLVED TO BECOME ANTONINUS'S DISCIPLE IN ALL THINGS, BOTH AS A MAN AND AS A STATESMAN.

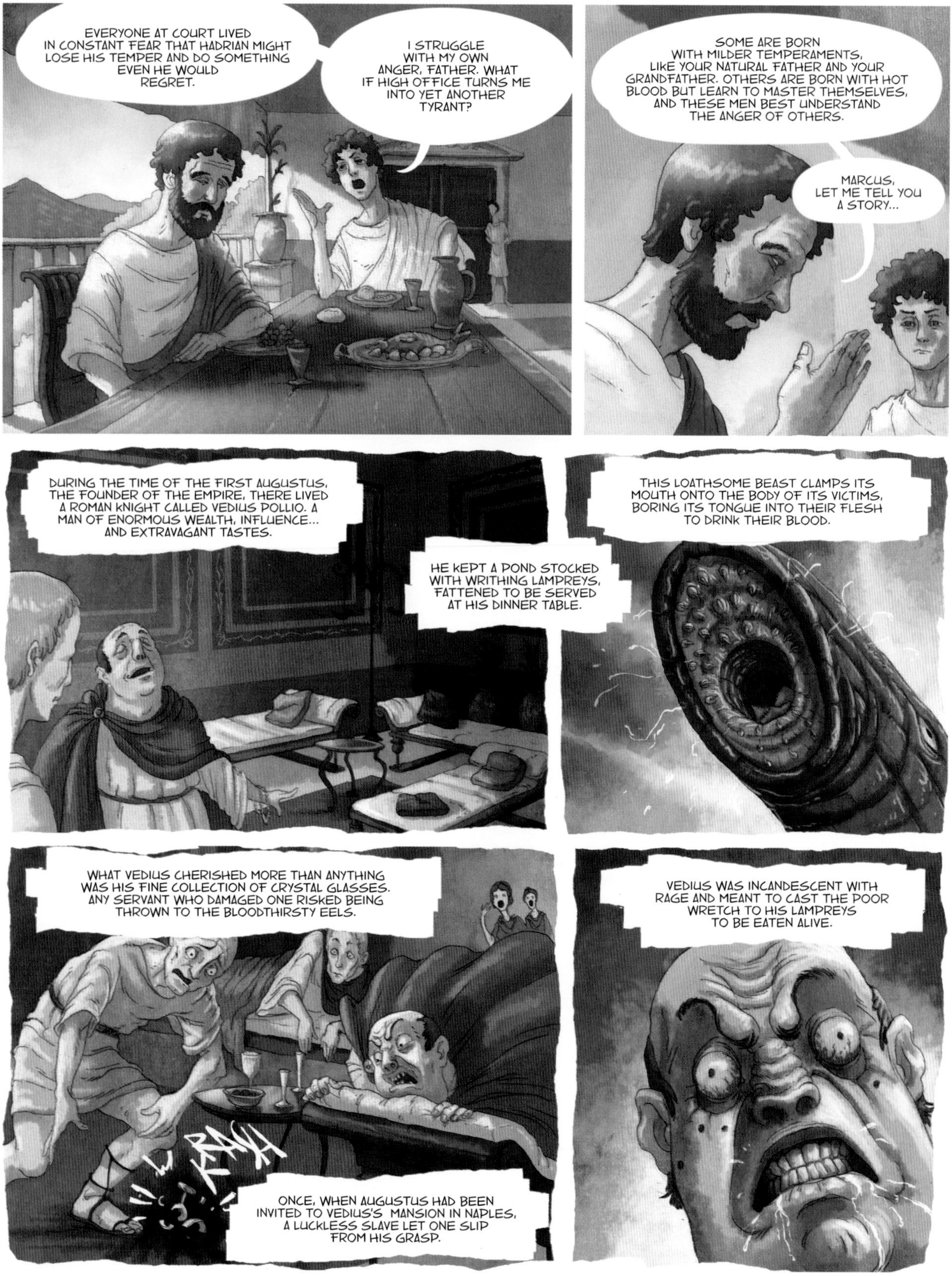
EVERYONE AT COURT LIVED IN CONSTANT FEAR THAT HADRIAN MIGHT LOSE HIS TEMPER AND DO SOMETHING EVEN HE WOULD REGRET.
I STRUGGLE WITH MY OWN ANGER, FATHER. WHAT IF HIGH OFFICE TURNS ME INTO YET ANOTHER TYRANT?
SOME ARE BORN WITH MILDER TEMPERAMENTS, LIKE YOUR NATURAL FATHER AND YOUR GRANDFATHER. OTHERS ARE BORN WITH HOT BLOOD BUT LEARN TO MASTER THEMSELVES, AND THESE MEN BEST UNDERSTAND THE ANGER OF OTHERS.
MARCUS, LET ME TELL YOU A STORY...
DURING THE TIME OF THE FIRST AUGUSTUS, THE FOUNDER OF THE EMPIRE, THERE LIVED A ROMAN KNIGHT CALLED VEDIUS POLLIO. A MAN OF ENORMOUS WEALTH, INFLUENCE... AND EXTRAVAGANT TASTES.
HE KEPT A POND STOCKED WITH WRITHING LAMPREYS, FATTENED TO BE SERVED AT HIS DINNER TABLE.
THIS LOATHSOME BEAST CLAMPS ITS MOUTH ONTO THE BODY OF ITS VICTIMS, BORING ITS TONGUE INTO THEIR FLESH TO DRINK THEIR BLOOD.
WHAT VEDIUS CHERISHED MORE THAN ANYTHING WAS HIS FINE COLLECTION OF CRYSTAL GLASSES. ANY SERVANT WHO DAMAGED ONE RISKED BEING THROWN TO THE BLOODTHIRSTY EELS.
KRASH
ONCE, WHEN AUGUSTUS HAD BEEN INVITED TO VEDIUS'S MANSION IN NAPLES, A LUCKLESS SLAVE LET ONE SLIP FROM HIS GRASP.
VEDIUS WAS INCANDESCENT WITH RAGE AND MEANT TO CAST THE POOR WRETCH TO HIS LAMPREYS TO BE EATEN ALIVE.

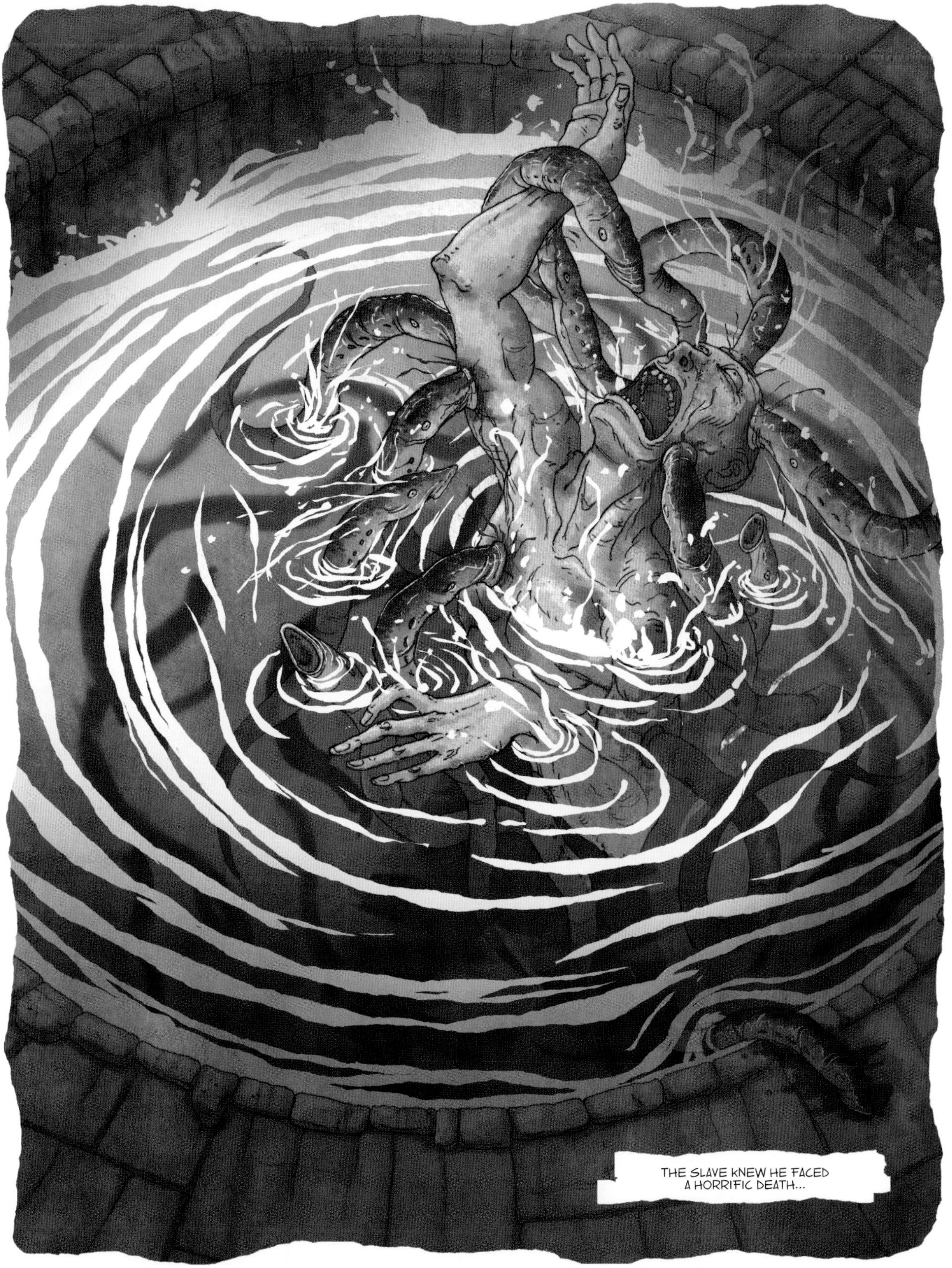
THE SLAVE KNEW HE FACED
A HORRIFIC DEATH...

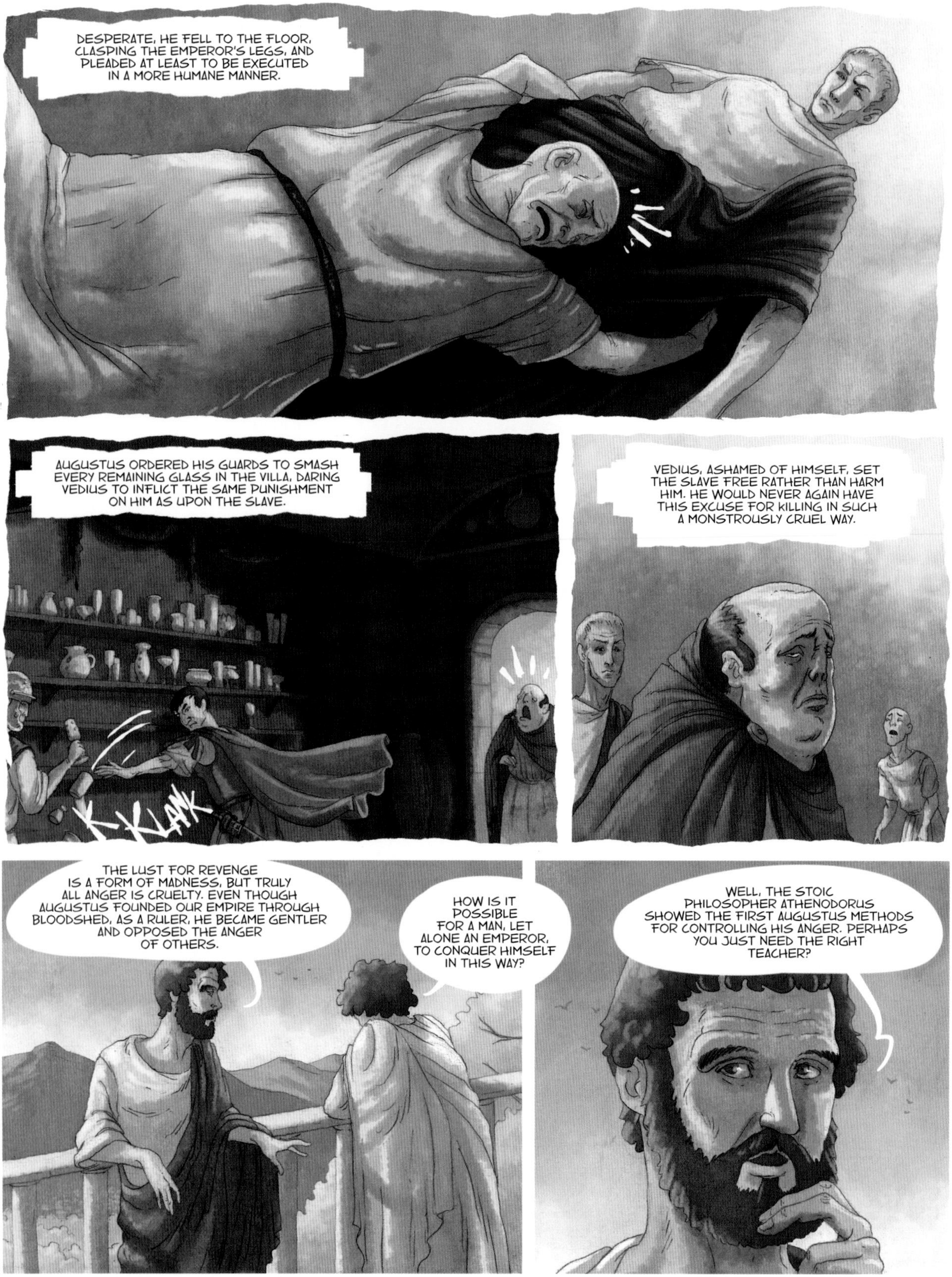

DESPERATE, HE FELL TO THE FLOOR, CLASPING THE EMPEROR'S LEGS, AND PLEADED AT LEAST TO BE EXECUTED IN A MORE HUMANE MANNER.
AUGUSTUS ORDERED HIS GUARDS TO SMASH EVERY REMAINING GLASS IN THE VILLA, DARING VEDIUS TO INFLICT THE SAME PUNISHMENT ON HIM AS UPON THE SLAVE.
K-KLANK
VEDIUS, ASHAMED OF HIMSELF, SET THE SLAVE FREE RATHER THAN HARM HIM. HE WOULD NEVER AGAIN HAVE THIS EXCUSE FOR KILLING IN SUCH A MONSTROUSLY CRUEL WAY.
THE LUST FOR REVENGE IS A FORM OF MADNESS, BUT TRULY ALL ANGER IS CRUELTY. EVEN THOUGH AUGUSTUS FOUNDED OUR EMPIRE THROUGH BLOODSHED, AS A RULER, HE BECAME GENTLER AND OPPOSED THE ANGER OF OTHERS.
HOW IS IT POSSIBLE FOR A MAN, LET ALONE AN EMPEROR, TO CONQUER HIMSELF IN THIS WAY?
WELL, THE STOIC PHILOSOPHER ATHENODORUS SHOWED THE FIRST AUGUSTUS METHODS FOR CONTROLLING HIS ANGER. PERHAPS YOU JUST NEED THE RIGHT TEACHER?

MY EDUCATION WAS TO BE SUPERVISED BY LEADING REPRESENTATIVES OF THE SECOND SOPHISTIC, ROME'S REVIVAL OF A TRADITION THAT ORIGINATED IN THE ATHENS OF SOCRATES.

THE SOPHISTS TAUGHT RHETORIC AND ORATORY, THE ART OF INFLUENCING OTHERS THROUGH VERBAL PERSUASION. HOWEVER, THEY ALSO PROFESSED TO IMPROVE THE CHARACTER OF YOUNG MEN BY IMPARTING CULTURAL SOPHISTICATION.

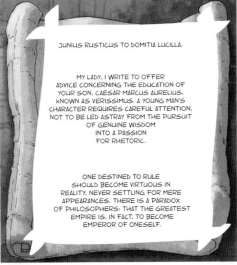

JUNIUS RUSTICUS TO DOMITIA LUCILLA,

MY LADY, I WRITE TO OFFER ADVICE CONCERNING THE EDUCATION OF YOUR SON, CAESAR MARCUS AURELIUS, KNOWN AS VERISSIMUS. A YOUNG MAN'S CHARACTER REQUIRES CAREFUL ATTENTION, NOT TO BE LED ASTRAY FROM THE PURSUIT OF GENUINE WISDOM INTO A PASSION FOR RHETORIC.

ONE DESTINED TO RULE SHOULD BECOME VIRTUOUS IN REALITY, NEVER SETTLING FOR MERE APPEARANCES. THERE IS A PARADOX OF PHILOSOPHERS: THAT THE GREATEST EMPIRE IS, IN FACT, TO BECOME EMPEROR OF ONESELF.

DIOGNETUS HAD INTRODUCED ME TO PHILOSOPHY, BUT IT WAS JUNIUS RUSTICUS WHO BECAME MY GREATEST PERSONAL MENTOR AND GUIDE.

SOME PHILOSOPHERS SPEND THEIR LIVES ENGAGED IN ABSTRACT THEORETICAL DEBATE, BUT STOICISM IS DIFFERENT. IT SHOWS US HOW TO LIVE AND, IN YOUR CASE, RULE MORE WISELY.

PHILOSOPHY ISN'T JUST ABOUT BOOKS AND LECTURES, MARCUS. TO REALLY IMPROVE, YOU HAVE TO ALLOW OTHERS TO QUESTION YOUR VERY CHARACTER.

THE STOICS CALLED THIS PROCESS "THERAPY," OR THERAPEIA IN GREEK.

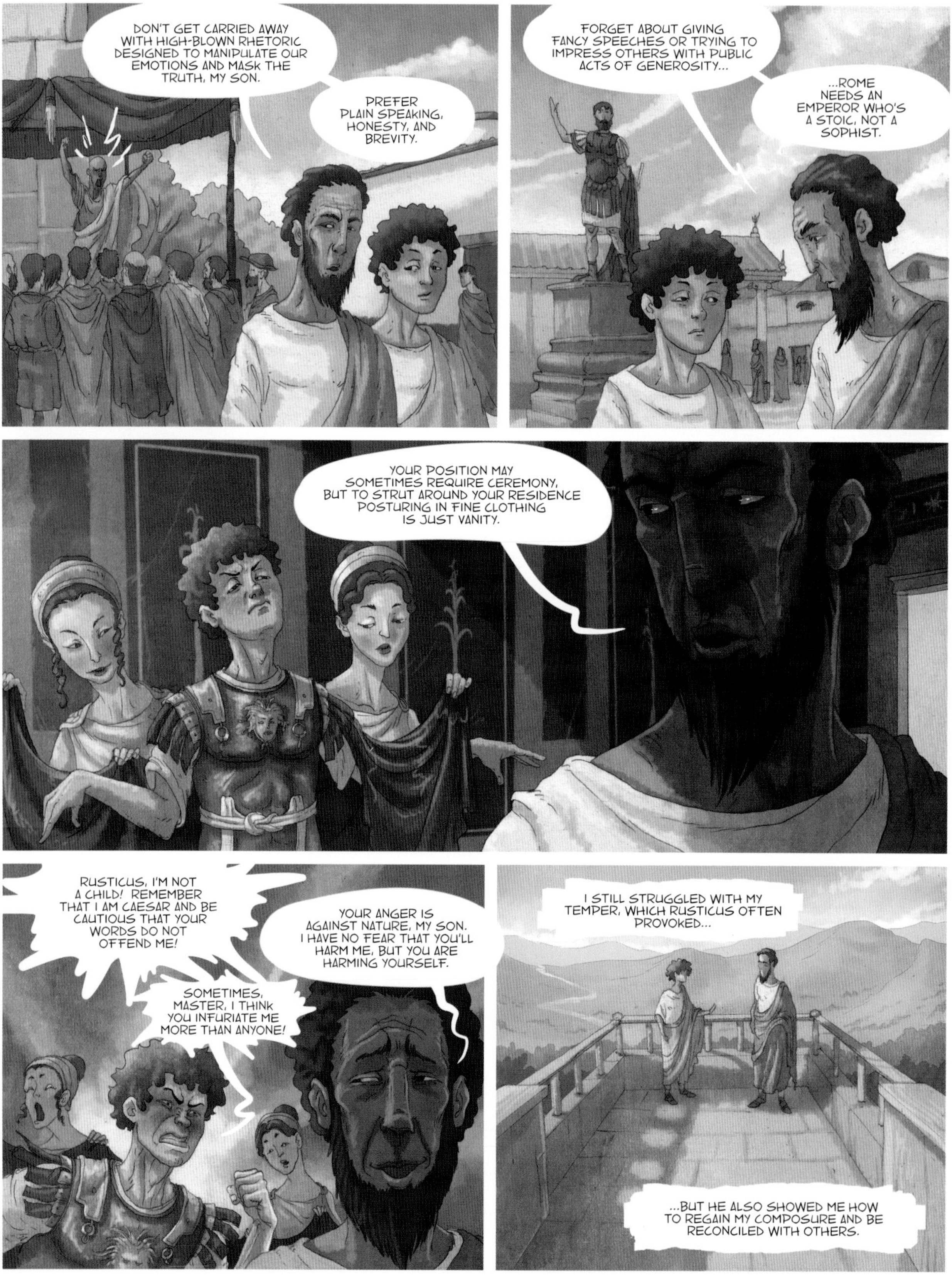
DON'T GET CARRIED AWAY WITH HIGH-BLOWN RHETORIC DESIGNED TO MANIPULATE OUR EMOTIONS AND MASK THE TRUTH, MY SON.
PREFER PLAIN SPEAKING, HONESTY, AND BREVITY.
FORGET ABOUT GIVING FANCY SPEECHES OR TRYING TO IMPRESS OTHERS WITH PUBLIC ACTS OF GENEROSITY...
...ROME NEEDS AN EMPEROR WHO'S A STOIC, NOT A SOPHIST.
YOUR POSITION MAY SOMETIMES REQUIRE CEREMONY, BUT TO STRUT AROUND YOUR RESIDENCE POSTURING IN FINE CLOTHING IS JUST VANITY.
RUSTICUS, I'M NOT A CHILD! REMEMBER THAT I AM CAESAR AND BE CAUTIOUS THAT YOUR WORDS DO NOT OFFEND ME!
YOUR ANGER IS AGAINST NATURE, MY SON. I HAVE NO FEAR THAT YOU'LL HARM ME, BUT YOU ARE HARMING YOURSELF.
SOMETIMES, MASTER, I THINK YOU INFURIATE ME MORE THAN ANYONE!
I STILL STRUGGLED WITH MY TEMPER, WHICH RUSTICUS OFTEN PROVOKED...
...BUT HE ALSO SHOWED ME HOW TO REGAIN MY COMPOSURE AND BE RECONCILED WITH OTHERS.

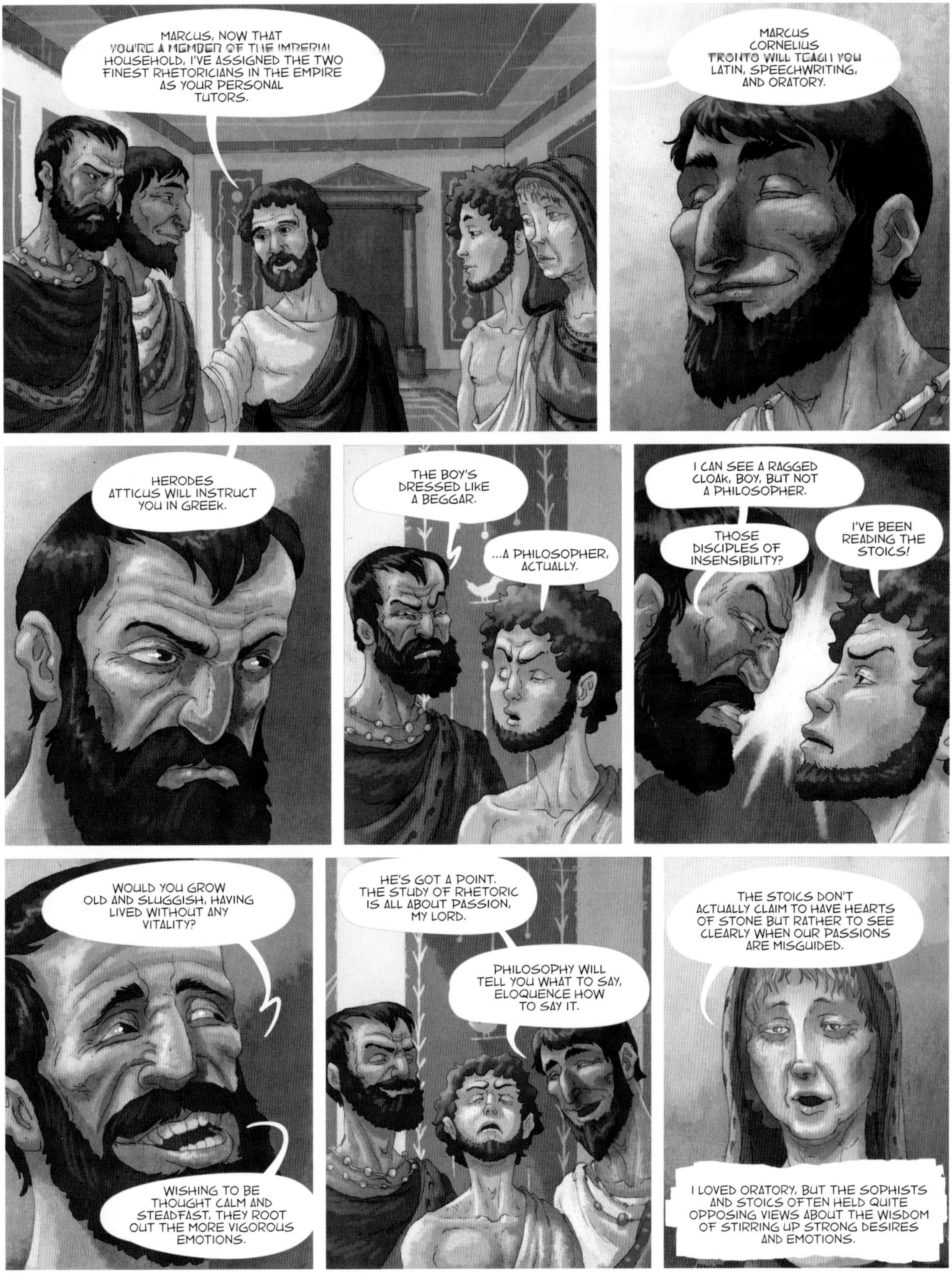
MARCUS, NOW THAT YOU'RE A MEMBER OF THE IMPERIAL HOUSEHOLD, I'VE ASSIGNED THE TWO FINEST RHETORICIANS IN THE EMPIRE AS YOUR PERSONAL TUTORS.
MARCUS CORNELIUS TRONTO WILL TEACH YOU LATIN, SPEECHWRITING, AND ORATORY.
HERODES ATTICUS WILL INSTRUCT YOU IN GREEK.
THE BOY'S DRESSED LIKE A BEGGAR.
...A PHILOSOPHER, ACTUALLY.
I CAN SEE A RAGGED CLOAK, BOY, BUT NOT A PHILOSOPHER.
THOSE DISCIPLES OF INSENSIBILITY?
I'VE BEEN READING THE STOICS!
WOULD YOU GROW OLD AND SLUGGISH, HAVING LIVED WITHOUT ANY VITALITY?
WISHING TO BE THOUGHT CALM AND STEADFAST, THEY ROOT OUT THE MORE VIGOROUS EMOTIONS.
HE'S GOT A POINT. THE STUDY OF RHETORIC IS ALL ABOUT PASSION, MY LORD.
PHILOSOPHY WILL TELL YOU WHAT TO SAY, ELOQUENCE HOW TO SAY IT.
THE STOICS DON'T ACTUALLY CLAIM TO HAVE HEARTS OF STONE BUT RATHER TO SEE CLEARLY WHEN OUR PASSIONS ARE MISGUIDED.
I LOVED ORATORY, BUT THE SOPHISTS AND STOICS OFTEN HELD QUITE OPPOSING VIEWS ABOUT THE WISDOM OF STIRRING UP STRONG DESIRES AND EMOTIONS.

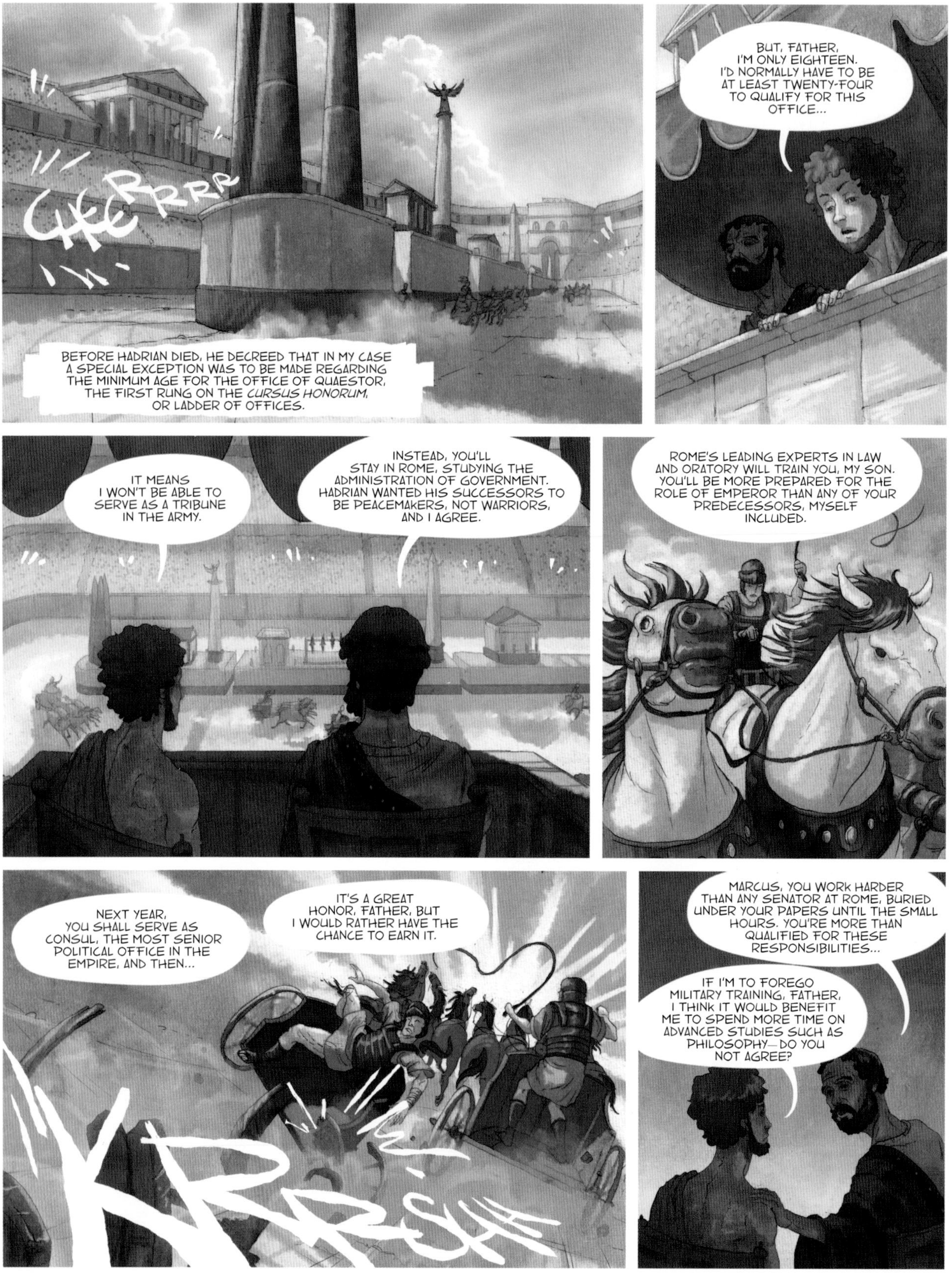
BEFORE HADRIAN DIED, HE DECREED THAT IN MY CASE A SPECIAL EXCEPTION WAS TO BE MADE REGARDING THE MINIMUM AGE FOR THE OFFICE OF QUAESTOR, THE FIRST RUNG ON THE *CURSUS HONORUM*, OR LADDER OF OFFICES.
BUT, FATHER, I'M ONLY EIGHTEEN. I'D NORMALLY HAVE TO BE AT LEAST TWENTY-FOUR TO QUALIFY FOR THIS OFFICE...
IT MEANS I WON'T BE ABLE TO SERVE AS A TRIBUNE IN THE ARMY.
INSTEAD, YOU'LL STAY IN ROME, STUDYING THE ADMINISTRATION OF GOVERNMENT. HADRIAN WANTED HIS SUCCESSORS TO BE PEACEMAKERS, NOT WARRIORS, AND I AGREE.
ROME'S LEADING EXPERTS IN LAW AND ORATORY WILL TRAIN YOU, MY SON. YOU'LL BE MORE PREPARED FOR THE ROLE OF EMPEROR THAN ANY OF YOUR PREDECESSORS, MYSELF INCLUDED.
NEXT YEAR, YOU SHALL SERVE AS CONSUL, THE MOST SENIOR POLITICAL OFFICE IN THE EMPIRE, AND THEN...
IT'S A GREAT HONOR, FATHER, BUT I WOULD RATHER HAVE THE CHANCE TO EARN IT.
MARCUS, YOU WORK HARDER THAN ANY SENATOR AT ROME, BURIED UNDER YOUR PAPERS UNTIL THE SMALL HOURS. YOU'RE MORE THAN QUALIFIED FOR THESE RESPONSIBILITIES...
IF I'M TO FOREGO MILITARY TRAINING, FATHER, I THINK IT WOULD BENEFIT ME TO SPEND MORE TIME ON ADVANCED STUDIES SUCH AS PHILOSOPHY— DO YOU NOT AGREE?

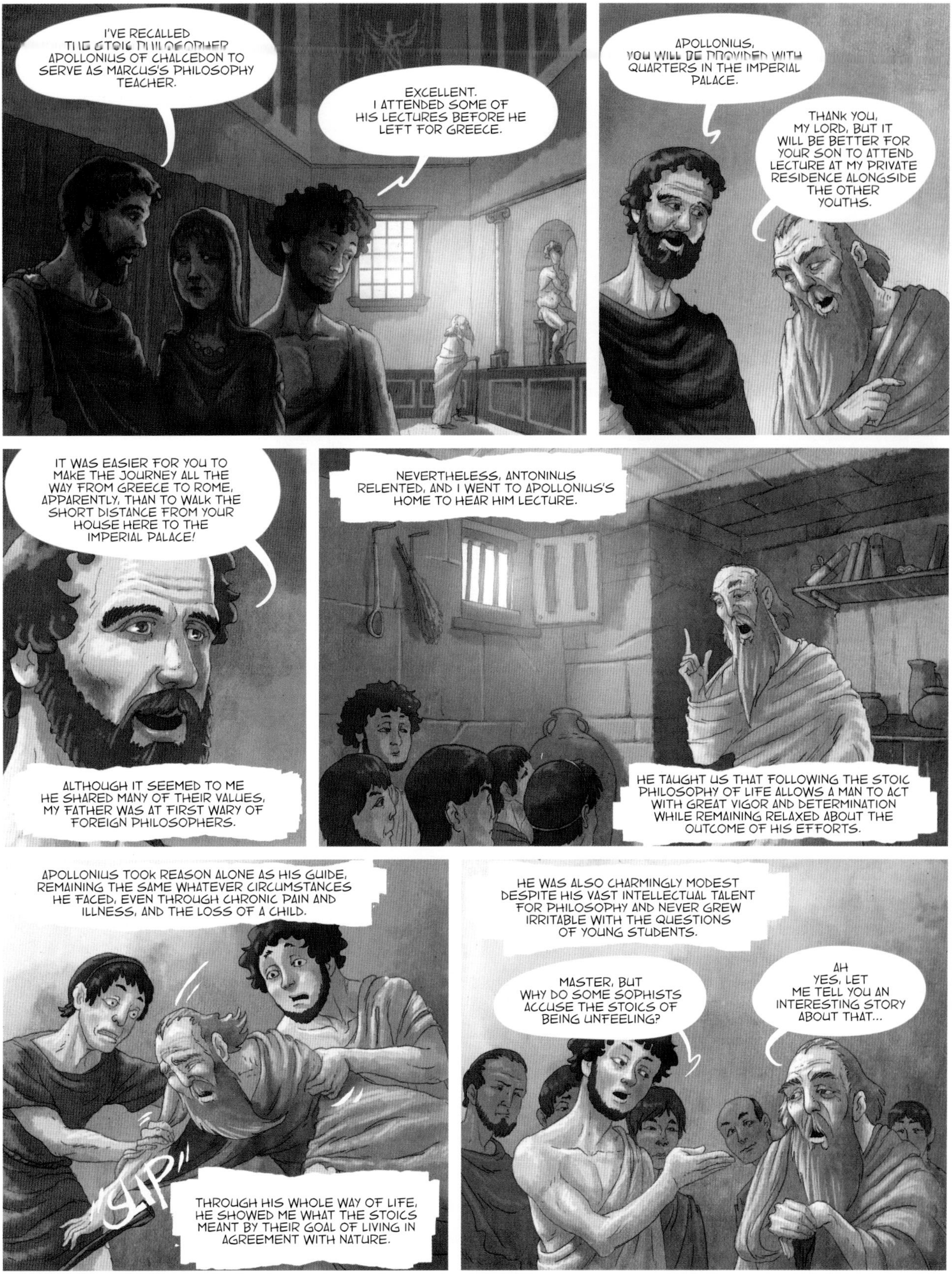
I'VE RECALLED THE STOIC PHILOSOPHER APOLLONIUS OF CHALCEDON TO SERVE AS MARCUS'S PHILOSOPHY TEACHER.
EXCELLENT. I ATTENDED SOME OF HIS LECTURES BEFORE HE LEFT FOR GREECE.
APOLLONIUS, YOU WILL BE PROVIDED WITH QUARTERS IN THE IMPERIAL PALACE.
THANK YOU, MY LORD, BUT IT WILL BE BETTER FOR YOUR SON TO ATTEND LECTURE AT MY PRIVATE RESIDENCE ALONGSIDE THE OTHER YOUTHS.
IT WAS EASIER FOR YOU TO MAKE THE JOURNEY ALL THE WAY FROM GREECE TO ROME, APPARENTLY, THAN TO WALK THE SHORT DISTANCE FROM YOUR HOUSE HERE TO THE IMPERIAL PALACE!
ALTHOUGH IT SEEMED TO ME HE SHARED MANY OF THEIR VALUES, MY FATHER WAS AT FIRST WARY OF FOREIGN PHILOSOPHERS.
NEVERTHELESS, ANTONINUS RELENTED, AND I WENT TO APOLLONIUS'S HOME TO HEAR HIM LECTURE.
HE TAUGHT US THAT FOLLOWING THE STOIC PHILOSOPHY OF LIFE ALLOWS A MAN TO ACT WITH GREAT VIGOR AND DETERMINATION WHILE REMAINING RELAXED ABOUT THE OUTCOME OF HIS EFFORTS.
APOLLONIUS TOOK REASON ALONE AS HIS GUIDE, REMAINING THE SAME WHATEVER CIRCUMSTANCES HE FACED, EVEN THROUGH CHRONIC PAIN AND ILLNESS, AND THE LOSS OF A CHILD.
SLIP
THROUGH HIS WHOLE WAY OF LIFE, HE SHOWED ME WHAT THE STOICS MEANT BY THEIR GOAL OF LIVING IN AGREEMENT WITH NATURE.
HE WAS ALSO CHARMINGLY MODEST DESPITE HIS VAST INTELLECTUAL TALENT FOR PHILOSOPHY AND NEVER GREW IRRITABLE WITH THE QUESTIONS OF YOUNG STUDENTS.
MASTER, BUT WHY DO SOME SOPHISTS ACCUSE THE STOICS OF BEING UNFEELING?
AH YES, LET ME TELL YOU AN INTERESTING STORY ABOUT THAT...

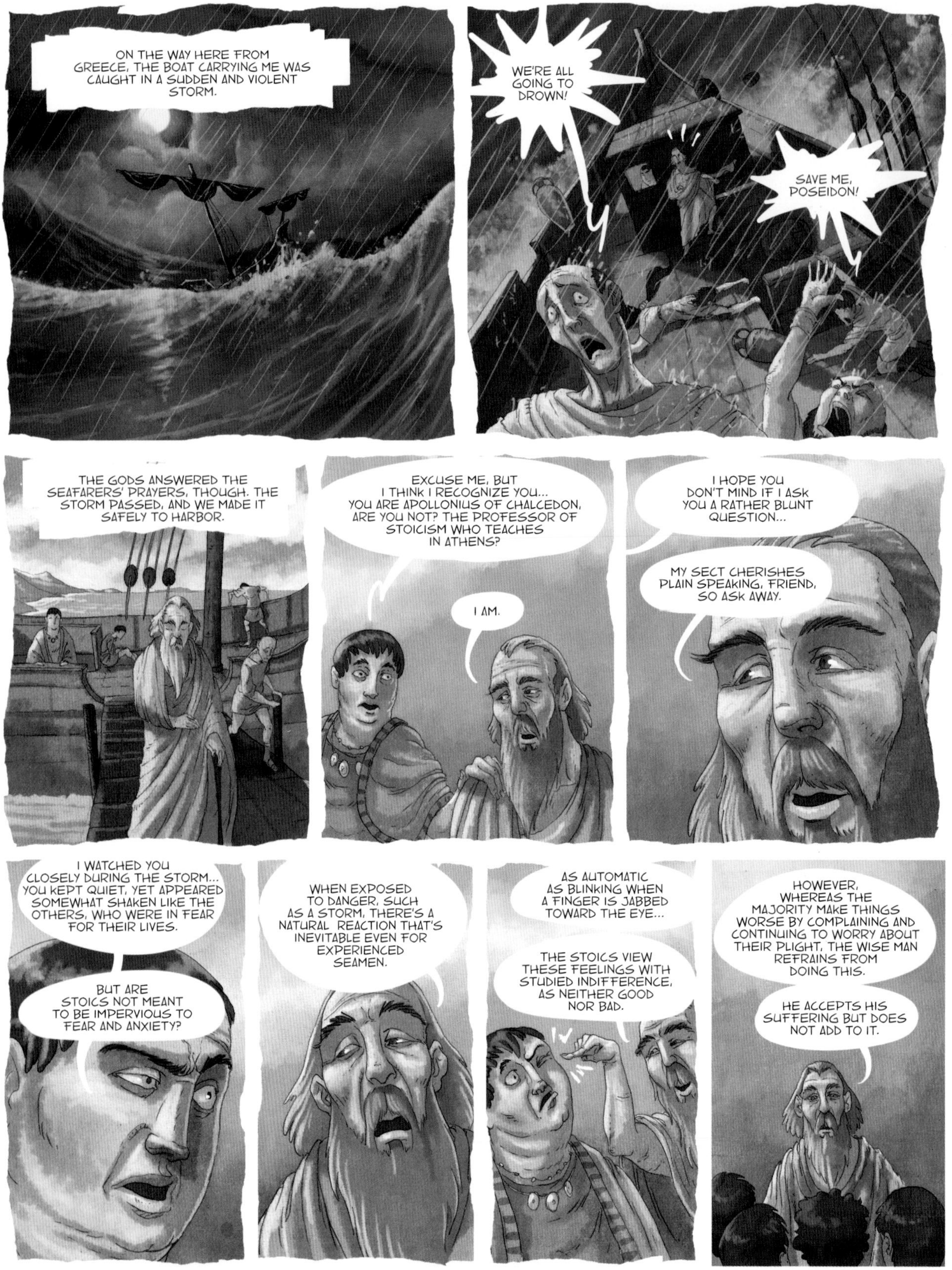
ON THE WAY HERE FROM GREECE, THE BOAT CARRYING ME WAS CAUGHT IN A SUDDEN AND VIOLENT STORM.
WE'RE ALL GOING TO DROWN!
SAVE ME, POSEIDON!
THE GODS ANSWERED THE SEAFARERS' PRAYERS, THOUGH. THE STORM PASSED, AND WE MADE IT SAFELY TO HARBOR.
EXCUSE ME, BUT I THINK I RECOGNIZE YOU... YOU ARE APOLLONIUS OF CHALCEDON, ARE YOU NOT? THE PROFESSOR OF STOICISM WHO TEACHES IN ATHENS?
I AM.
I HOPE YOU DON'T MIND IF I ASK YOU A RATHER BLUNT QUESTION...
MY SECT CHERISHES PLAIN SPEAKING, FRIEND, SO ASK AWAY.
I WATCHED YOU CLOSELY DURING THE STORM... YOU KEPT QUIET, YET APPEARED SOMEWHAT SHAKEN LIKE THE OTHERS, WHO WERE IN FEAR FOR THEIR LIVES.
BUT ARE STOICS NOT MEANT TO BE IMPERVIOUS TO FEAR AND ANXIETY?
WHEN EXPOSED TO DANGER, SUCH AS A STORM, THERE'S A NATURAL REACTION THAT'S INEVITABLE EVEN FOR EXPERIENCED SEAMEN.
AS AUTOMATIC AS BLINKING WHEN A FINGER IS JABBED TOWARD THE EYE...
THE STOICS VIEW THESE FEELINGS WITH STUDIED INDIFFERENCE, AS NEITHER GOOD NOR BAD.
HOWEVER, WHEREAS THE MAJORITY MAKE THINGS WORSE BY COMPLAINING AND CONTINUING TO WORRY ABOUT THEIR PLIGHT, THE WISE MAN REFRAINS FROM DOING THIS.
HE ACCEPTS HIS SUFFERING BUT DOES NOT ADD TO IT.

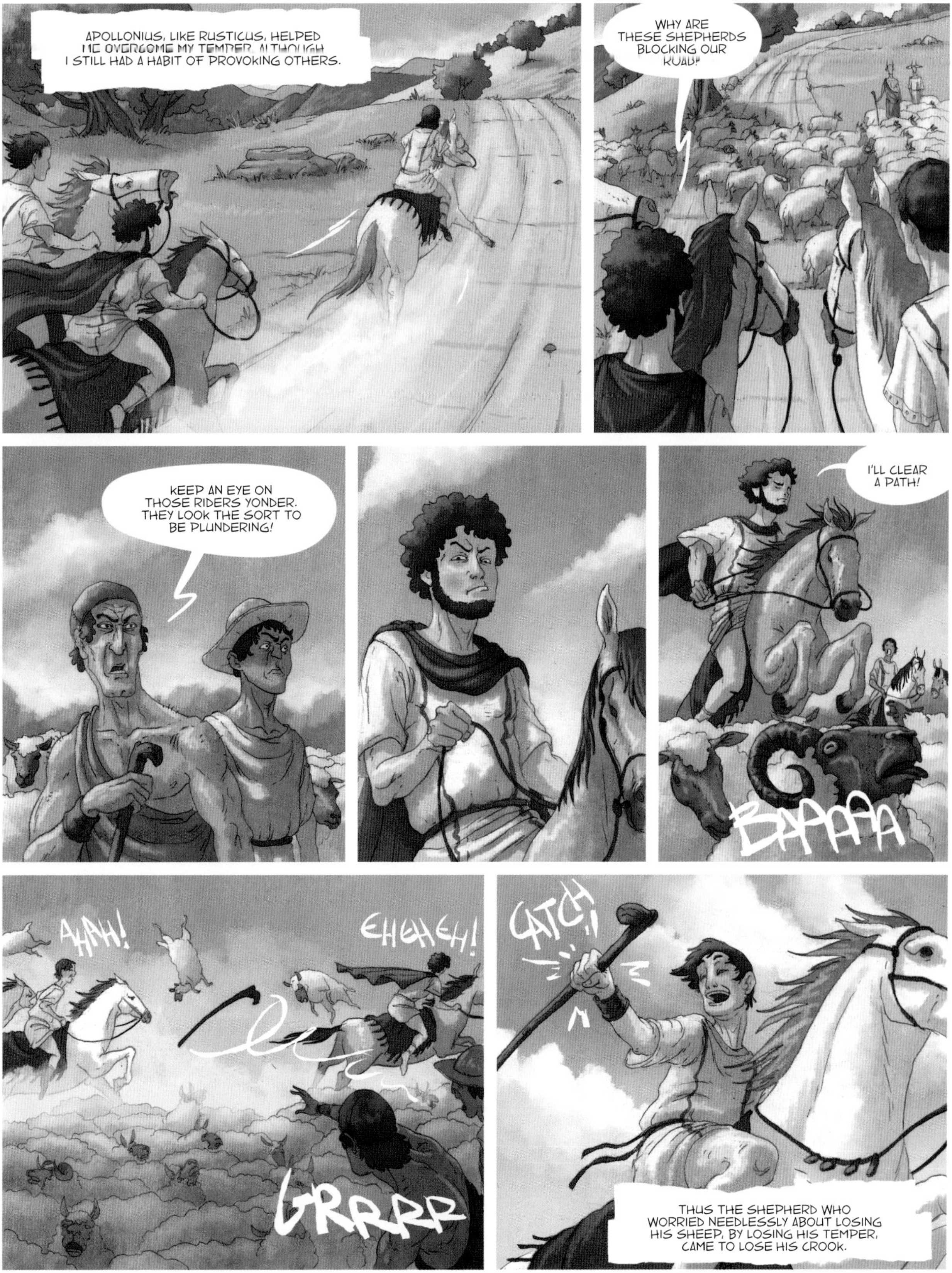
APOLLONIUS, LIKE RUSTICUS, HELPED ME OVERCOME MY TEMPER, ALTHOUGH I STILL HAD A HABIT OF PROVOKING OTHERS.
WHY ARE THESE SHEPHERDS BLOCKING OUR ROAD?
KEEP AN EYE ON THOSE RIDERS YONDER. THEY LOOK THE SORT TO BE PLUNDERING!
I'LL CLEAR A PATH!
BAAAAA
AHHH!
EHEHEH!
GRRRR
CATCH
THUS THE SHEPHERD WHO WORRIED NEEDLESSLY ABOUT LOSING HIS SHEEP, BY LOSING HIS TEMPER, CAME TO LOSE HIS CROOK.

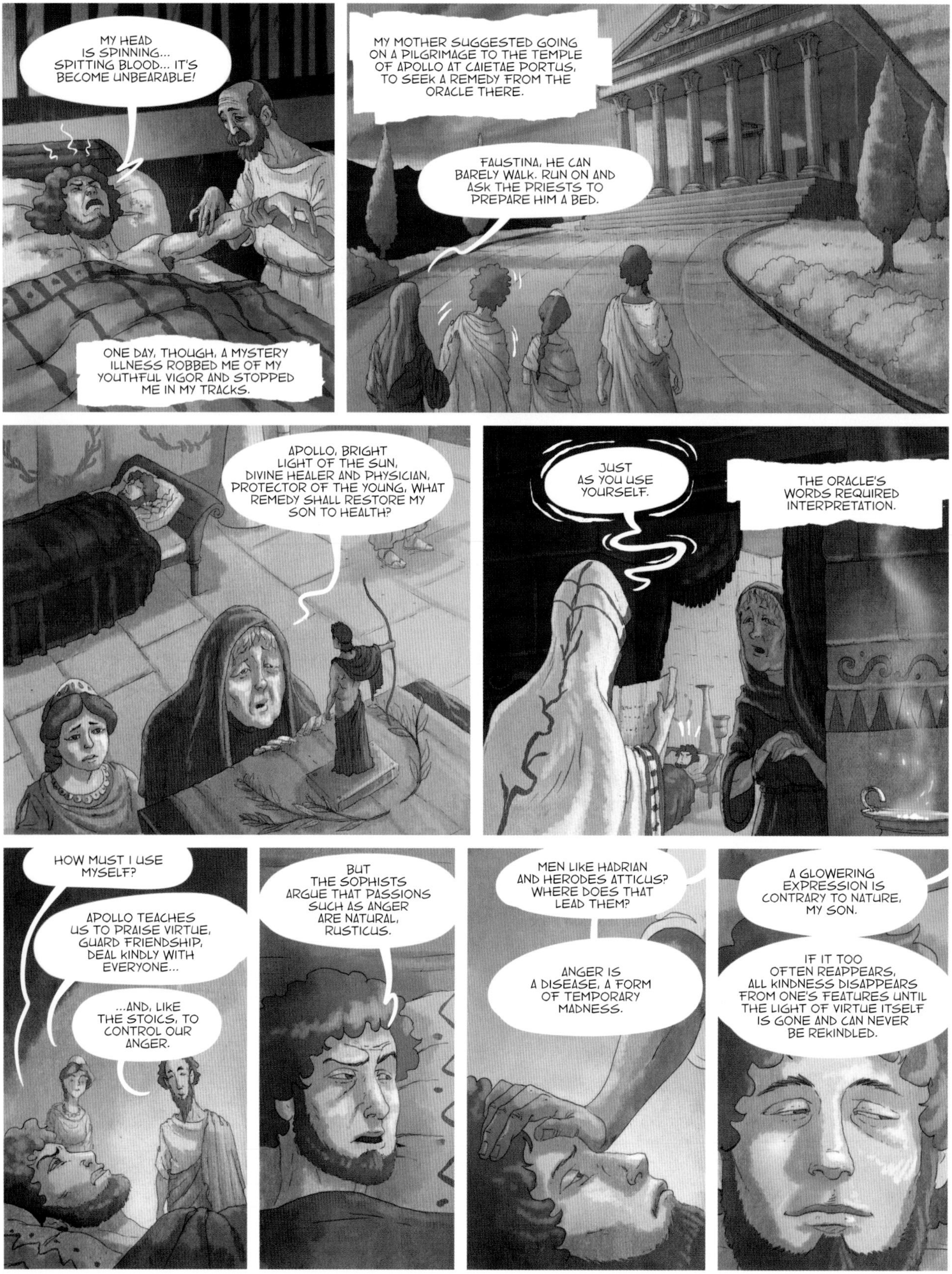
MY HEAD IS SPINNING... SPITTING BLOOD... IT'S BECOME UNBEARABLE!
ONE DAY, THOUGH, A MYSTERY ILLNESS ROBBED ME OF MY YOUTHFUL VIGOR AND STOPPED ME IN MY TRACKS.
MY MOTHER SUGGESTED GOING ON A PILGRIMAGE TO THE TEMPLE OF APOLLO AT CAIETAE PORTUS, TO SEEK A REMEDY FROM THE ORACLE THERE.
FAUSTINA, HE CAN BARELY WALK. RUN ON AND ASK THE PRIESTS TO PREPARE HIM A BED.
APOLLO, BRIGHT LIGHT OF THE SUN, DIVINE HEALER AND PHYSICIAN, PROTECTOR OF THE YOUNG, WHAT REMEDY SHALL RESTORE MY SON TO HEALTH?
JUST AS YOU USE YOURSELF.
THE ORACLE'S WORDS REQUIRED INTERPRETATION.
HOW MUST I USE MYSELF?
APOLLO TEACHES US TO PRAISE VIRTUE, GUARD FRIENDSHIP, DEAL KINDLY WITH EVERYONE...
...AND, LIKE THE STOICS, TO CONTROL OUR ANGER.
BUT THE SOPHISTS ARGUE THAT PASSIONS SUCH AS ANGER ARE NATURAL, RUSTICUS.
MEN LIKE HADRIAN AND HERODES ATTICUS? WHERE DOES THAT LEAD THEM?
ANGER IS A DISEASE, A FORM OF TEMPORARY MADNESS.
A GLOWERING EXPRESSION IS CONTRARY TO NATURE, MY SON.
IF IT TOO OFTEN REAPPEARS, ALL KINDNESS DISAPPEARS FROM ONE'S FEATURES UNTIL THE LIGHT OF VIRTUE ITSELF IS GONE AND CAN NEVER BE REKINDLED.

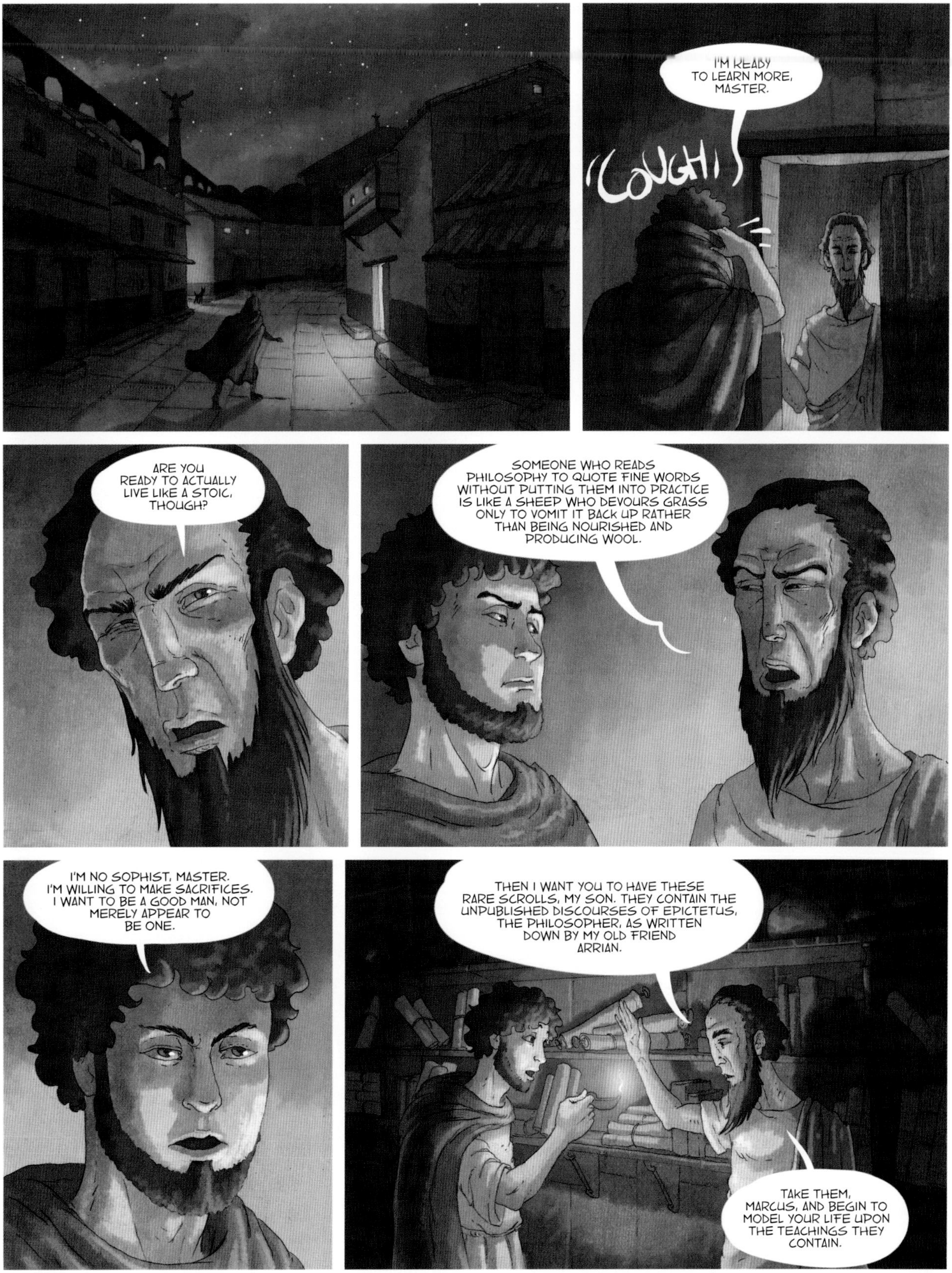
I'M READY TO LEARN MORE, MASTER.
COUGH!
ARE YOU READY TO ACTUALLY LIVE LIKE A STOIC, THOUGH?
SOMEONE WHO READS PHILOSOPHY TO QUOTE FINE WORDS WITHOUT PUTTING THEM INTO PRACTICE IS LIKE A SHEEP WHO DEVOURS GRASS ONLY TO VOMIT IT BACK UP RATHER THAN BEING NOURISHED AND PRODUCING WOOL.
I'M NO SOPHIST, MASTER. I'M WILLING TO MAKE SACRIFICES. I WANT TO BE A GOOD MAN, NOT MERELY APPEAR TO BE ONE.
THEN I WANT YOU TO HAVE THESE RARE SCROLLS, MY SON. THEY CONTAIN THE UNPUBLISHED DISCOURSES OF EPICTETUS, THE PHILOSOPHER, AS WRITTEN DOWN BY MY OLD FRIEND ARRIAN.
TAKE THEM, MARCUS, AND BEGIN TO MODEL YOUR LIFE UPON THE TEACHINGS THEY CONTAIN.

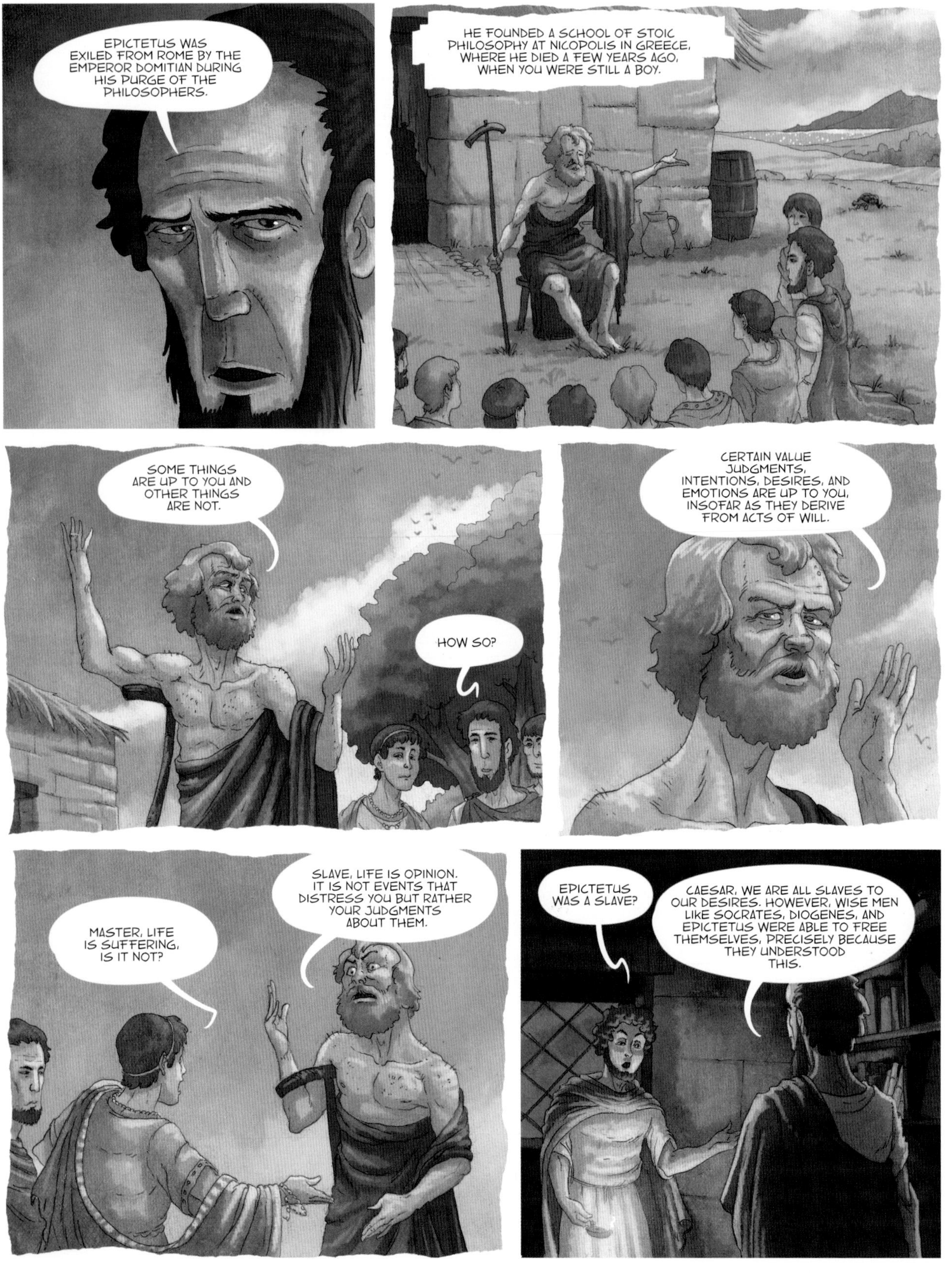
EPICTETUS WAS EXILED FROM ROME BY THE EMPEROR DOMITIAN DURING HIS PURGE OF THE PHILOSOPHERS.
HE FOUNDED A SCHOOL OF STOIC PHILOSOPHY AT NICOPOLIS IN GREECE, WHERE HE DIED A FEW YEARS AGO, WHEN YOU WERE STILL A BOY.
SOME THINGS ARE UP TO YOU AND OTHER THINGS ARE NOT.
HOW SO?
CERTAIN VALUE JUDGMENTS, INTENTIONS, DESIRES, AND EMOTIONS ARE UP TO YOU, INSOFAR AS THEY DERIVE FROM ACTS OF WILL.
MASTER, LIFE IS SUFFERING, IS IT NOT?
SLAVE, LIFE IS OPINION. IT IS NOT EVENTS THAT DISTRESS YOU BUT RATHER YOUR JUDGMENTS ABOUT THEM.
EPICTETUS WAS A SLAVE?
CAESAR, WE ARE ALL SLAVES TO OUR DESIRES. HOWEVER, WISE MEN LIKE SOCRATES, DIOGENES, AND EPICTETUS WERE ABLE TO FREE THEMSELVES, PRECISELY BECAUSE THEY UNDERSTOOD THIS.

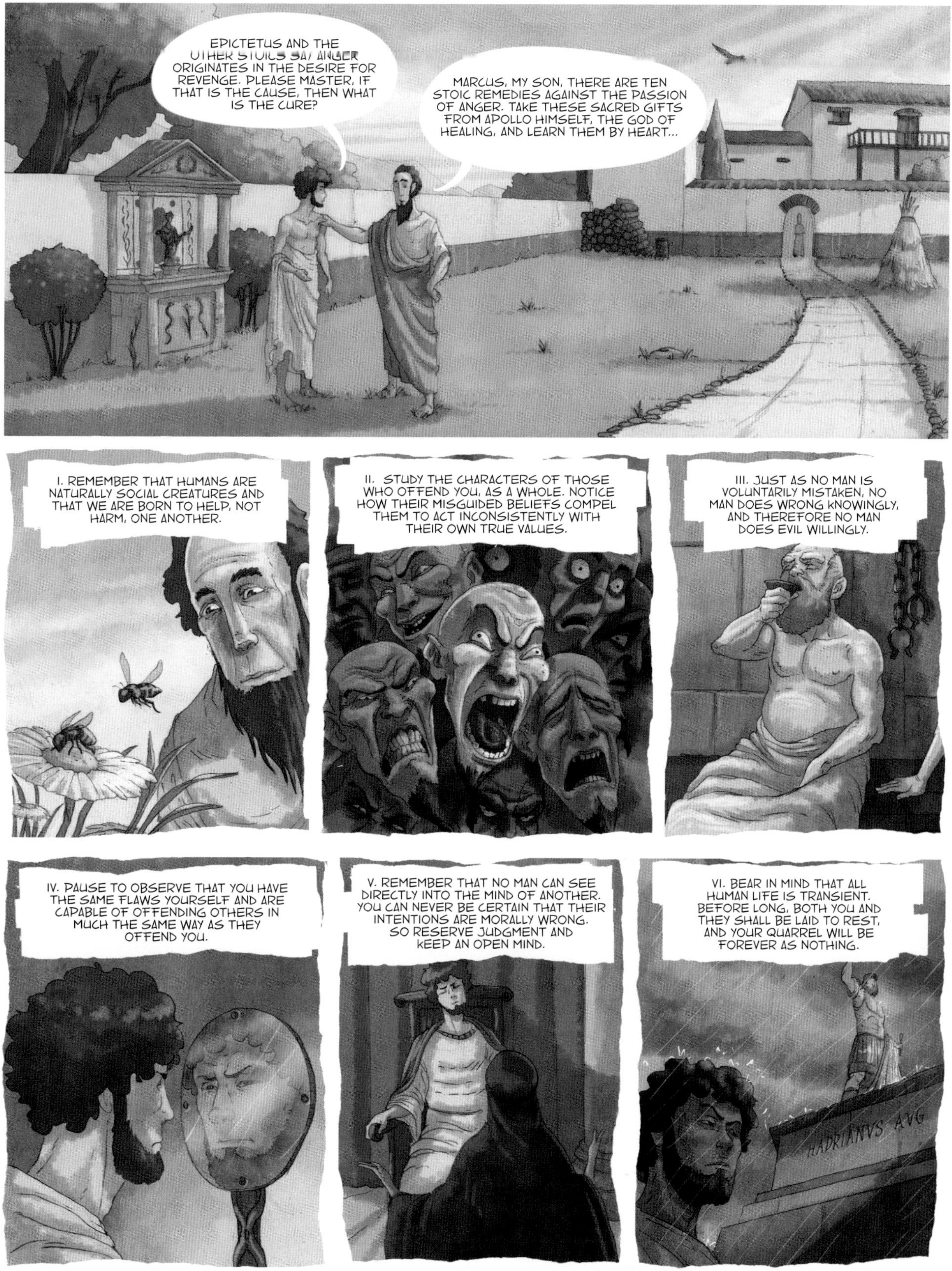
EPICTETUS AND THE OTHER STOICS SAY ANGER ORIGINATES IN THE DESIRE FOR REVENGE. PLEASE MASTER, IF THAT IS THE CAUSE, THEN WHAT IS THE CURE?
MARCUS, MY SON, THERE ARE TEN STOIC REMEDIES AGAINST THE PASSION OF ANGER. TAKE THESE SACRED GIFTS FROM APOLLO HIMSELF, THE GOD OF HEALING, AND LEARN THEM BY HEART...
I. REMEMBER THAT HUMANS ARE NATURALLY SOCIAL CREATURES AND THAT WE ARE BORN TO HELP, NOT HARM, ONE ANOTHER.
II. STUDY THE CHARACTERS OF THOSE WHO OFFEND YOU, AS A WHOLE. NOTICE HOW THEIR MISGUIDED BELIEFS COMPEL THEM TO ACT INCONSISTENTLY WITH THEIR OWN TRUE VALUES.
III. JUST AS NO MAN IS VOLUNTARILY MISTAKEN, NO MAN DOES WRONG KNOWINGLY, AND THEREFORE NO MAN DOES EVIL WILLINGLY.
IV. PAUSE TO OBSERVE THAT YOU HAVE THE SAME FLAWS YOURSELF AND ARE CAPABLE OF OFFENDING OTHERS IN MUCH THE SAME WAY AS THEY OFFEND YOU.
V. REMEMBER THAT NO MAN CAN SEE DIRECTLY INTO THE MIND OF ANOTHER. YOU CAN NEVER BE CERTAIN THAT THEIR INTENTIONS ARE MORALLY WRONG. SO RESERVE JUDGMENT AND KEEP AN OPEN MIND.
VI. BEAR IN MIND THAT ALL HUMAN LIFE IS TRANSIENT. BEFORE LONG, BOTH YOU AND THEY SHALL BE LAID TO REST, AND YOUR QUARREL WILL BE FOREVER AS NOTHING.
HADRIANVS AVG

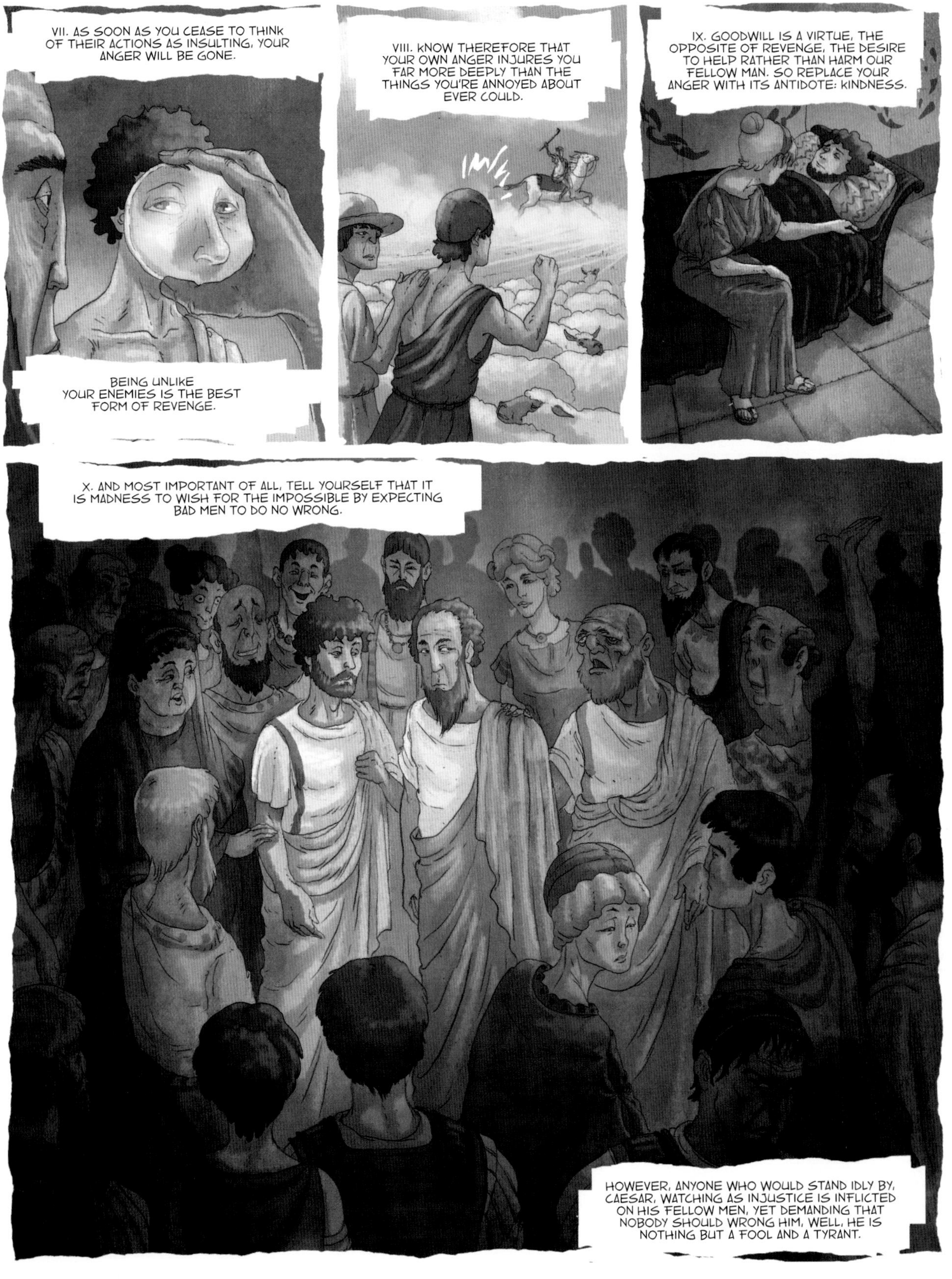
VII. AS SOON AS YOU CEASE TO THINK OF THEIR ACTIONS AS INSULTING, YOUR ANGER WILL BE GONE.
BEING UNLIKE YOUR ENEMIES IS THE BEST FORM OF REVENGE.
VIII. KNOW THEREFORE THAT YOUR OWN ANGER INJURES YOU FAR MORE DEEPLY THAN THE THINGS YOU'RE ANNOYED ABOUT EVER COULD.
IX. GOODWILL IS A VIRTUE, THE OPPOSITE OF REVENGE, THE DESIRE TO HELP RATHER THAN HARM OUR FELLOW MAN. SO REPLACE YOUR ANGER WITH ITS ANTIDOTE: KINDNESS.
X. AND MOST IMPORTANT OF ALL, TELL YOURSELF THAT IT IS MADNESS TO WISH FOR THE IMPOSSIBLE BY EXPECTING BAD MEN TO DO NO WRONG.
HOWEVER, ANYONE WHO WOULD STAND IDLY BY, CAESAR, WATCHING AS INJUSTICE IS INFLICTED ON HIS FELLOW MEN, YET DEMANDING THAT NOBODY SHOULD WRONG HIM, WELL, HE IS NOTHING BUT A FOOL AND A TYRANT.

THE
EMPRESS
FAUSTINA

The heavens love to rain down and the earth to receive showers. The whole universe loves to create whatever is to be. So I will say to it: "Your love is my love too."

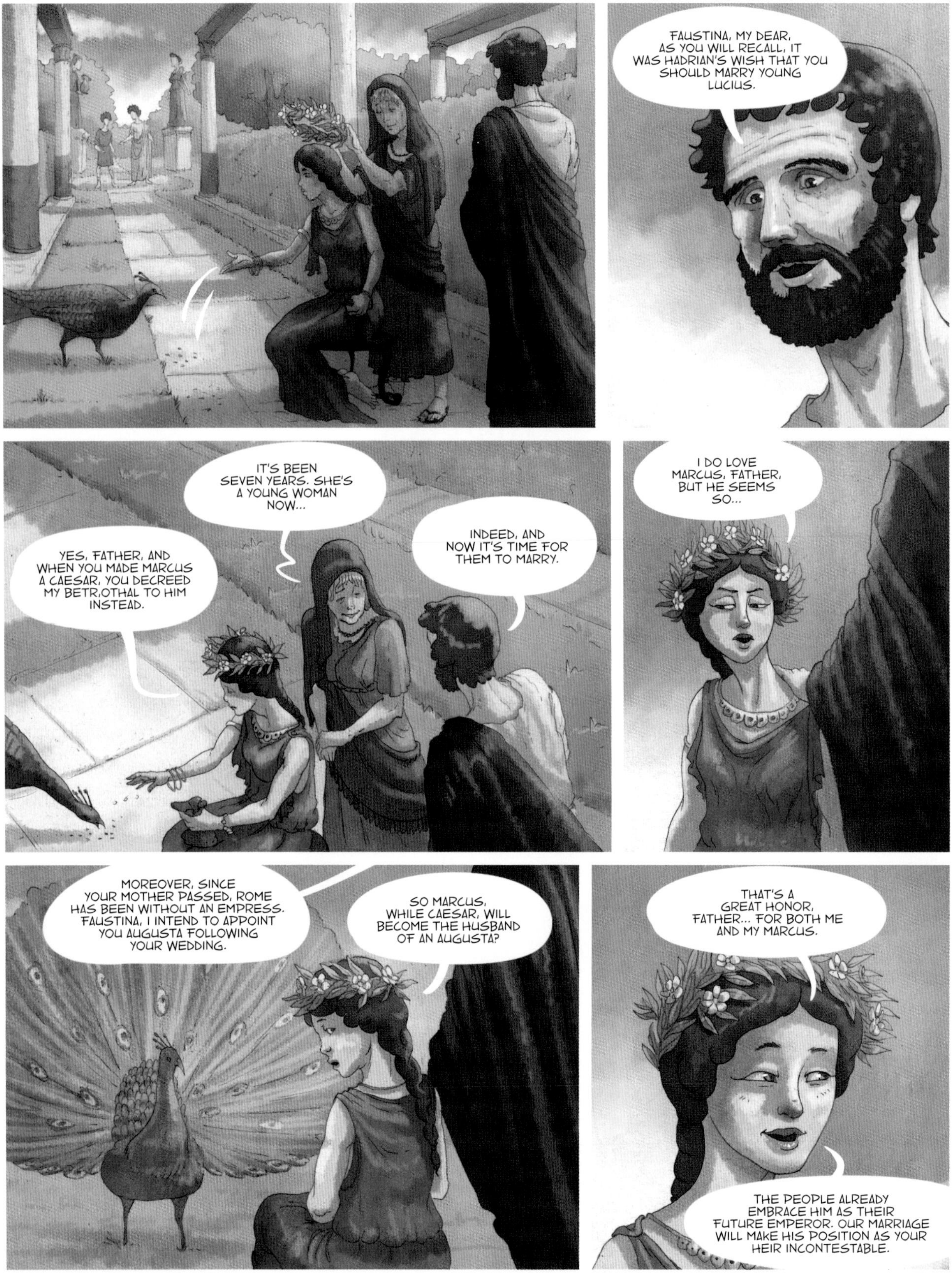
FAUSTINA, MY DEAR, AS YOU WILL RECALL, IT WAS HADRIAN'S WISH THAT YOU SHOULD MARRY YOUNG LUCIUS.
IT'S BEEN SEVEN YEARS. SHE'S A YOUNG WOMAN NOW...
YES, FATHER, AND WHEN YOU MADE MARCUS A CAESAR, YOU DECREED MY BETROTHAL TO HIM INSTEAD.
INDEED, AND NOW IT'S TIME FOR THEM TO MARRY.
I DO LOVE MARCUS, FATHER, BUT HE SEEMS SO...
MOREOVER, SINCE YOUR MOTHER PASSED, ROME HAS BEEN WITHOUT AN EMPRESS. FAUSTINA, I INTEND TO APPOINT YOU AUGUSTA FOLLOWING YOUR WEDDING.
SO MARCUS, WHILE CAESAR, WILL BECOME THE HUSBAND OF AN AUGUSTA?
THAT'S A GREAT HONOR, FATHER... FOR BOTH ME AND MY MARCUS.
THE PEOPLE ALREADY EMBRACE HIM AS THEIR FUTURE EMPEROR. OUR MARRIAGE WILL MAKE HIS POSITION AS YOUR HEIR INCONTESTABLE.

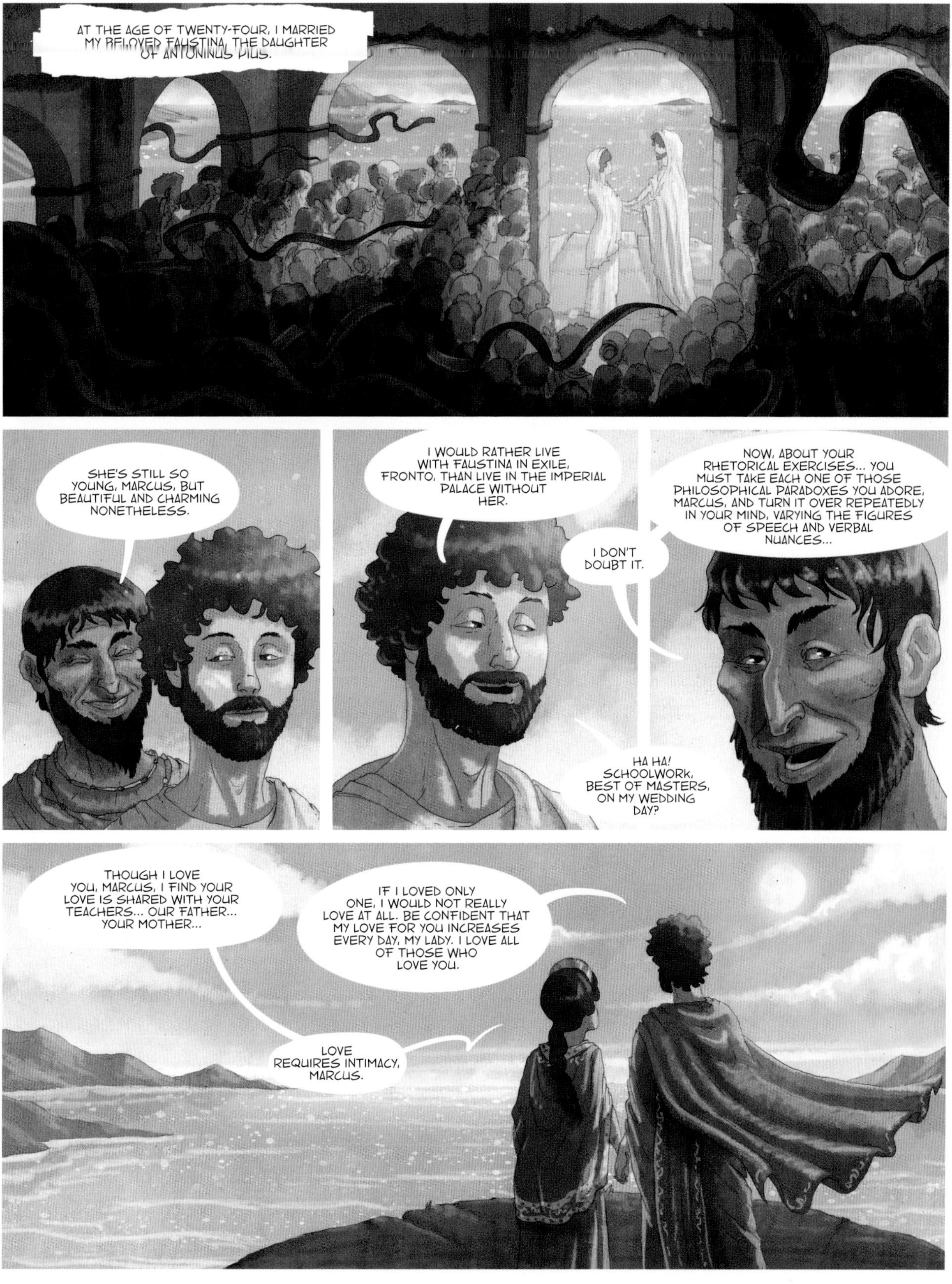
AT THE AGE OF TWENTY-FOUR, I MARRIED MY BELOVED FAUSTINA, THE DAUGHTER OF ANTONINUS PIUS.
SHE'S STILL SO YOUNG, MARCUS, BUT BEAUTIFUL AND CHARMING NONETHELESS.
I WOULD RATHER LIVE WITH FAUSTINA IN EXILE, FRONTO, THAN LIVE IN THE IMPERIAL PALACE WITHOUT HER.
I DON'T DOUBT IT.
NOW, ABOUT YOUR RHETORICAL EXERCISES... YOU MUST TAKE EACH ONE OF THOSE PHILOSOPHICAL PARADOXES YOU ADORE, MARCUS, AND TURN IT OVER REPEATEDLY IN YOUR MIND, VARYING THE FIGURES OF SPEECH AND VERBAL NUANCES...
HA HA! SCHOOLWORK, BEST OF MASTERS, ON MY WEDDING DAY?
THOUGH I LOVE YOU, MARCUS, I FIND YOUR LOVE IS SHARED WITH YOUR TEACHERS... OUR FATHER... YOUR MOTHER...
IF I LOVED ONLY ONE, I WOULD NOT REALLY LOVE AT ALL. BE CONFIDENT THAT MY LOVE FOR YOU INCREASES EVERY DAY, MY LADY. I LOVE ALL OF THOSE WHO LOVE YOU.
LOVE REQUIRES INTIMACY, MARCUS.

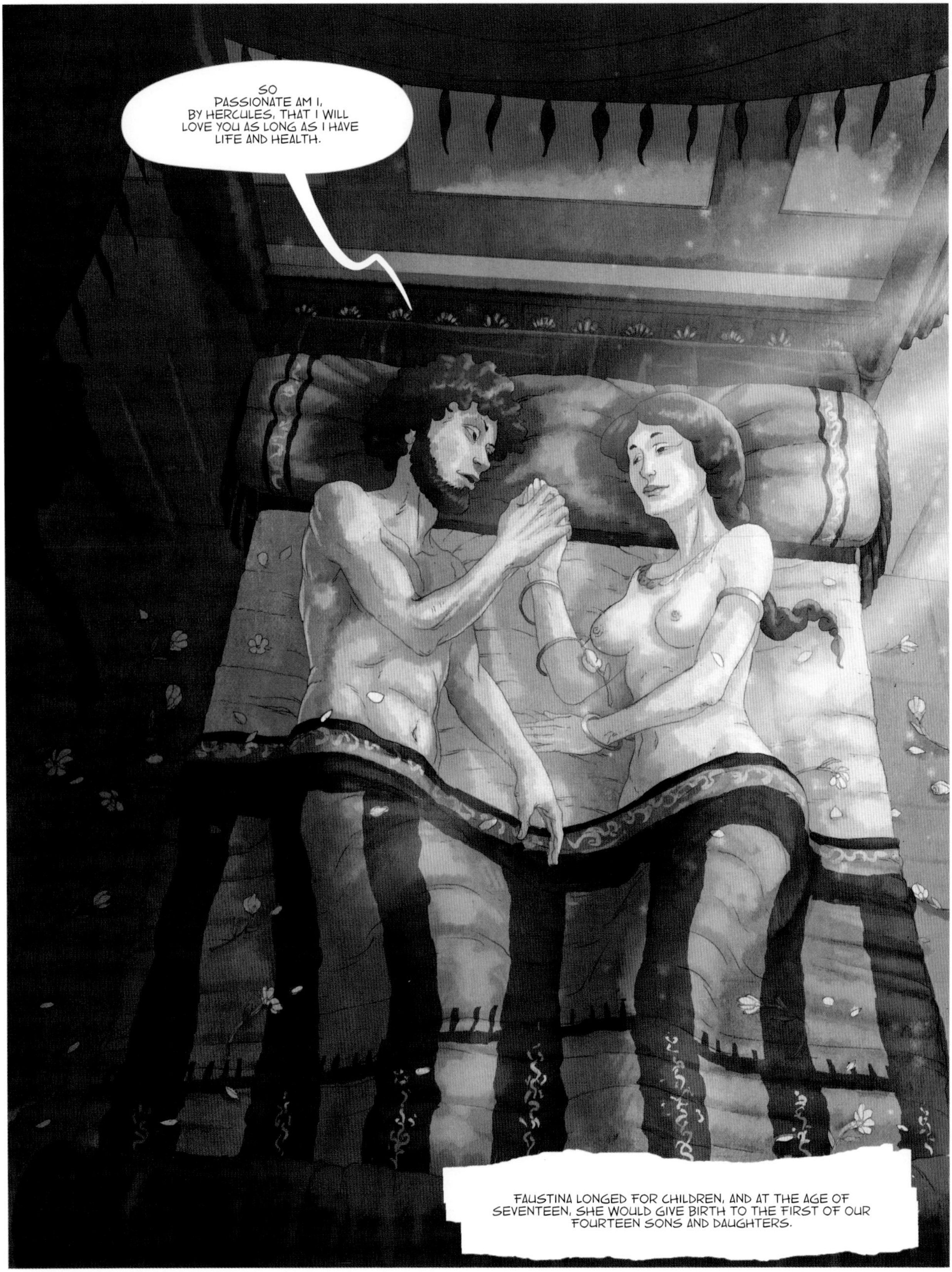
SO PASSIONATE AM I, BY HERCULES, THAT I WILL LOVE YOU AS LONG AS I HAVE LIFE AND HEALTH.
FAUSTINA LONGED FOR CHILDREN, AND AT THE AGE OF SEVENTEEN, SHE WOULD GIVE BIRTH TO THE FIRST OF OUR FOURTEEN SONS AND DAUGHTERS.

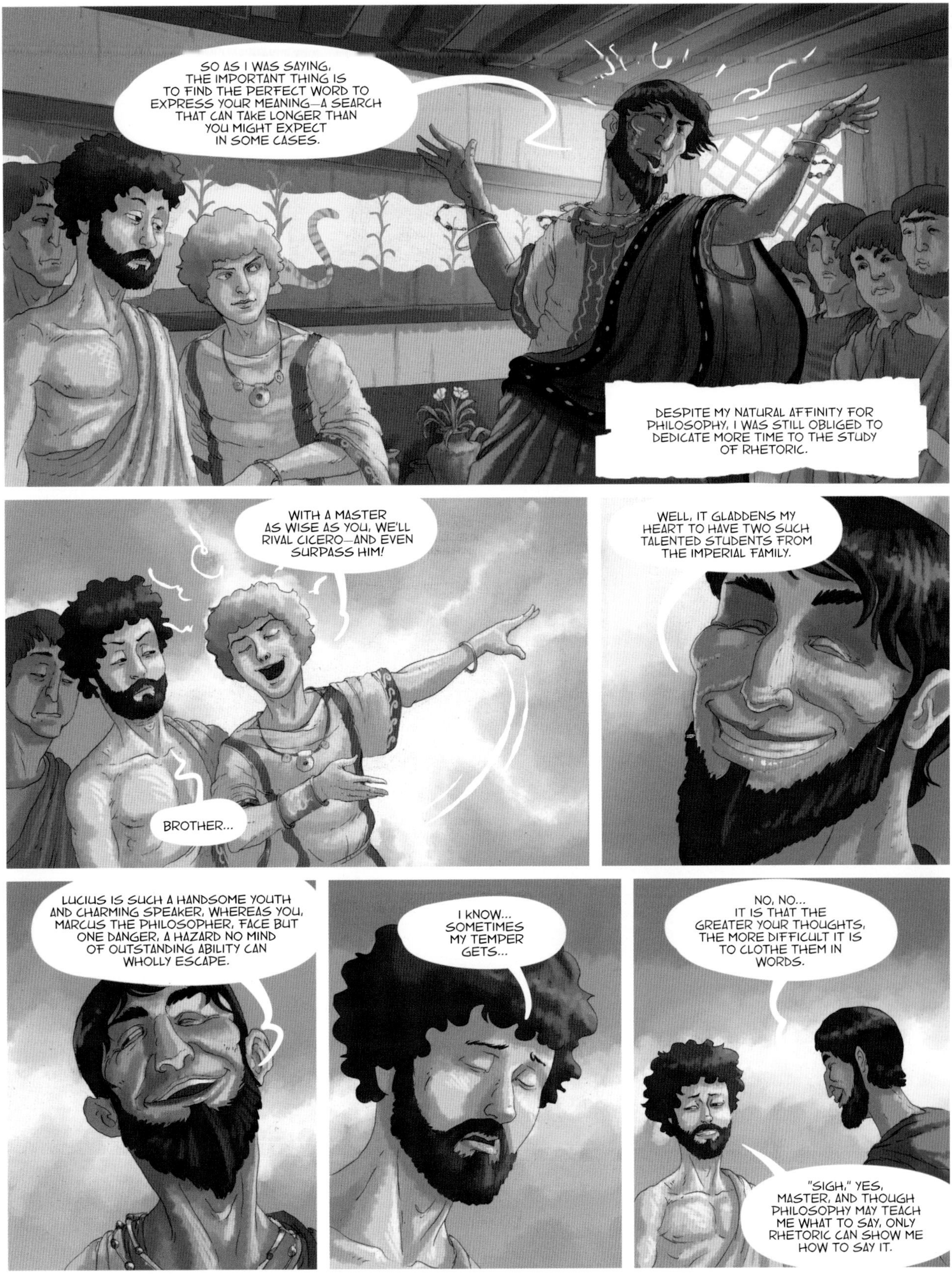
SO AS I WAS SAYING, THE IMPORTANT THING IS TO FIND THE PERFECT WORD TO EXPRESS YOUR MEANING—A SEARCH THAT CAN TAKE LONGER THAN YOU MIGHT EXPECT IN SOME CASES.
DESPITE MY NATURAL AFFINITY FOR PHILOSOPHY, I WAS STILL OBLIGED TO DEDICATE MORE TIME TO THE STUDY OF RHETORIC.
WITH A MASTER AS WISE AS YOU, WE'LL RIVAL CICERO—AND EVEN SURPASS HIM!
BROTHER...
WELL, IT GLADDENS MY HEART TO HAVE TWO SUCH TALENTED STUDENTS FROM THE IMPERIAL FAMILY.
LUCIUS IS SUCH A HANDSOME YOUTH AND CHARMING SPEAKER, WHEREAS YOU, MARCUS THE PHILOSOPHER, FACE BUT ONE DANGER, A HAZARD NO MIND OF OUTSTANDING ABILITY CAN WHOLLY ESCAPE.
I KNOW... SOMETIMES MY TEMPER GETS...
NO, NO... IT IS THAT THE GREATER YOUR THOUGHTS, THE MORE DIFFICULT IT IS TO CLOTHE THEM IN WORDS.
"SIGH," YES, MASTER, AND THOUGH PHILOSOPHY MAY TEACH ME WHAT TO SAY, ONLY RHETORIC CAN SHOW ME HOW TO SAY IT.

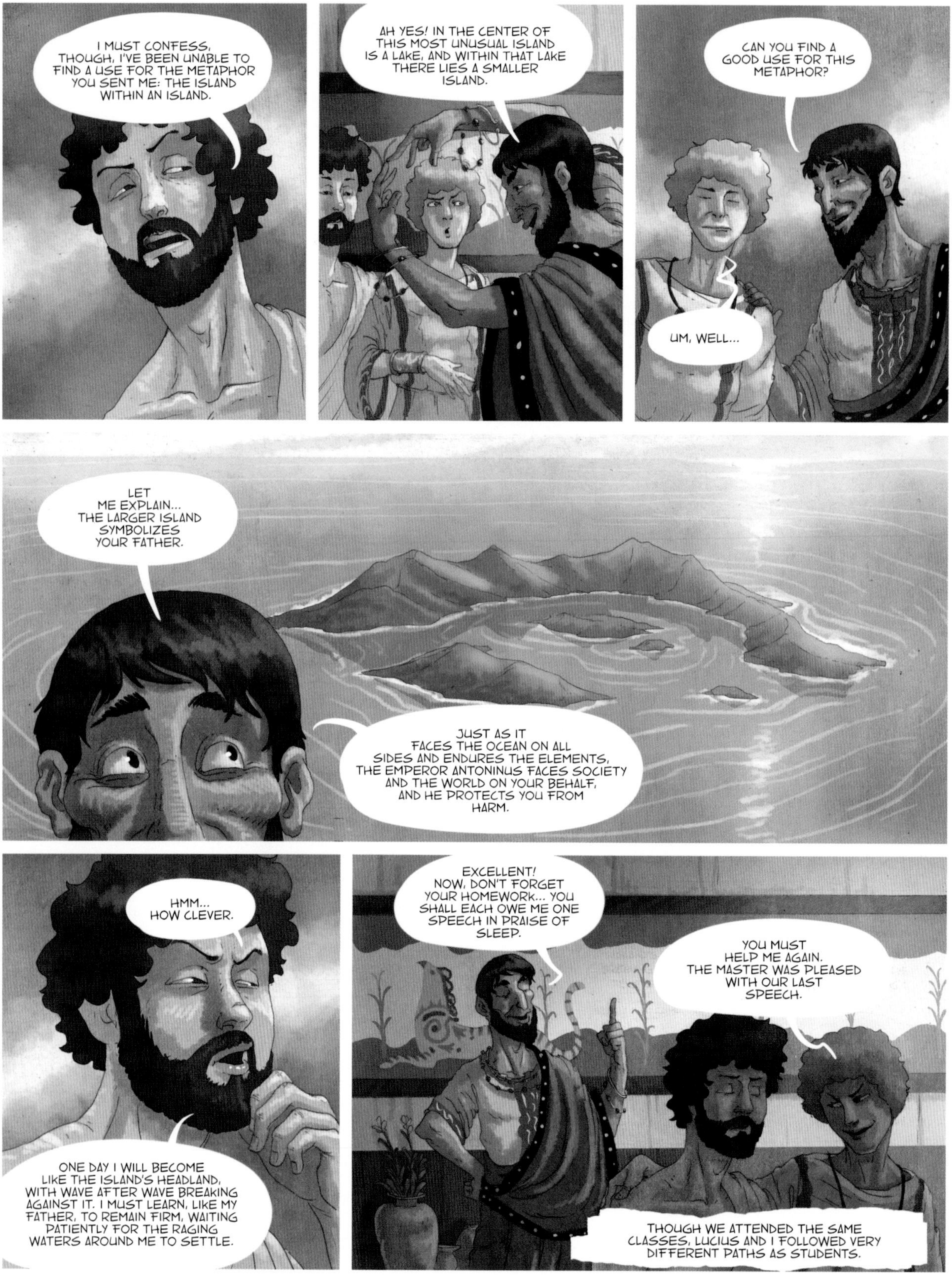
I MUST CONFESS, THOUGH, I'VE BEEN UNABLE TO FIND A USE FOR THE METAPHOR YOU SENT ME: THE ISLAND WITHIN AN ISLAND.
AH YES! IN THE CENTER OF THIS MOST UNUSUAL ISLAND IS A LAKE, AND WITHIN THAT LAKE THERE LIES A SMALLER ISLAND.
CAN YOU FIND A GOOD USE FOR THIS METAPHOR?
UM, WELL...
LET ME EXPLAIN... THE LARGER ISLAND SYMBOLIZES YOUR FATHER.
JUST AS IT FACES THE OCEAN ON ALL SIDES AND ENDURES THE ELEMENTS, THE EMPEROR ANTONINUS FACES SOCIETY AND THE WORLD ON YOUR BEHALF, AND HE PROTECTS YOU FROM HARM.
HMM... HOW CLEVER.
ONE DAY I WILL BECOME LIKE THE ISLAND'S HEADLAND, WITH WAVE AFTER WAVE BREAKING AGAINST IT. I MUST LEARN, LIKE MY FATHER, TO REMAIN FIRM, WAITING PATIENTLY FOR THE RAGING WATERS AROUND ME TO SETTLE.
EXCELLENT! NOW, DON'T FORGET YOUR HOMEWORK... YOU SHALL EACH OWE ME ONE SPEECH IN PRAISE OF SLEEP.
YOU MUST HELP ME AGAIN. THE MASTER WAS PLEASED WITH OUR LAST SPEECH.
THOUGH WE ATTENDED THE SAME CLASSES, LUCIUS AND I FOLLOWED VERY DIFFERENT PATHS AS STUDENTS.

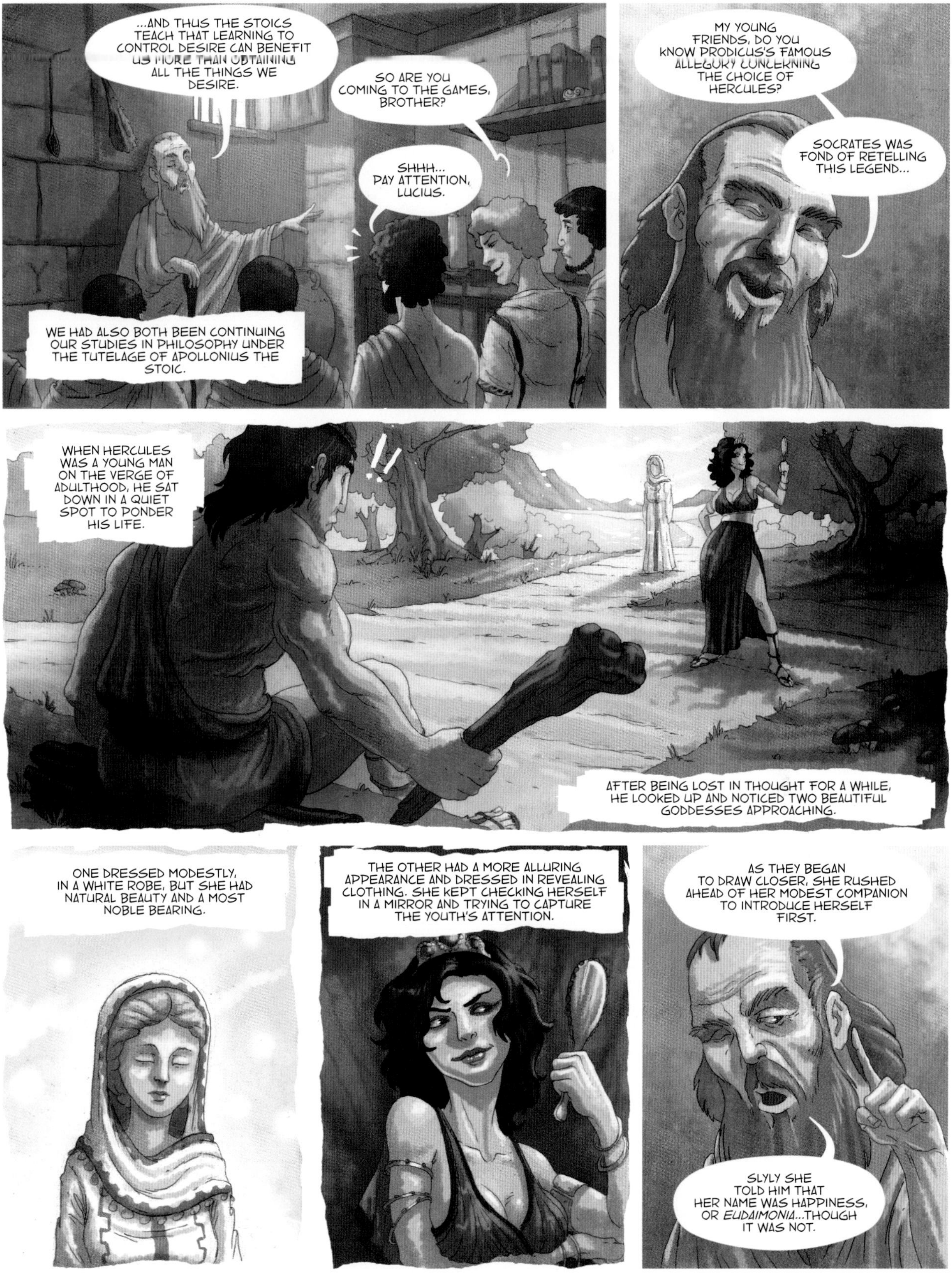
...AND THUS THE STOICS TEACH THAT LEARNING TO CONTROL DESIRE CAN BENEFIT US MORE THAN OBTAINING ALL THE THINGS WE DESIRE.
SO ARE YOU COMING TO THE GAMES, BROTHER?
SHHH... PAY ATTENTION, LUCIUS.
WE HAD ALSO BOTH BEEN CONTINUING OUR STUDIES IN PHILOSOPHY UNDER THE TUTELAGE OF APOLLONIUS THE STOIC.
MY YOUNG FRIENDS, DO YOU KNOW PRODICUS'S FAMOUS ALLEGORY CONCERNING THE CHOICE OF HERCULES?
SOCRATES WAS FOND OF RETELLING THIS LEGEND...
WHEN HERCULES WAS A YOUNG MAN ON THE VERGE OF ADULTHOOD, HE SAT DOWN IN A QUIET SPOT TO PONDER HIS LIFE.
!!
AFTER BEING LOST IN THOUGHT FOR A WHILE, HE LOOKED UP AND NOTICED TWO BEAUTIFUL GODDESSES APPROACHING.
ONE DRESSED MODESTLY, IN A WHITE ROBE, BUT SHE HAD NATURAL BEAUTY AND A MOST NOBLE BEARING.
THE OTHER HAD A MORE ALLURING APPEARANCE AND DRESSED IN REVEALING CLOTHING. SHE KEPT CHECKING HERSELF IN A MIRROR AND TRYING TO CAPTURE THE YOUTH'S ATTENTION.
AS THEY BEGAN TO DRAW CLOSER, SHE RUSHED AHEAD OF HER MODEST COMPANION TO INTRODUCE HERSELF FIRST.
SLYLY SHE TOLD HIM THAT HER NAME WAS HAPPINESS, OR *EUDAIMONIA*...THOUGH IT WAS NOT.

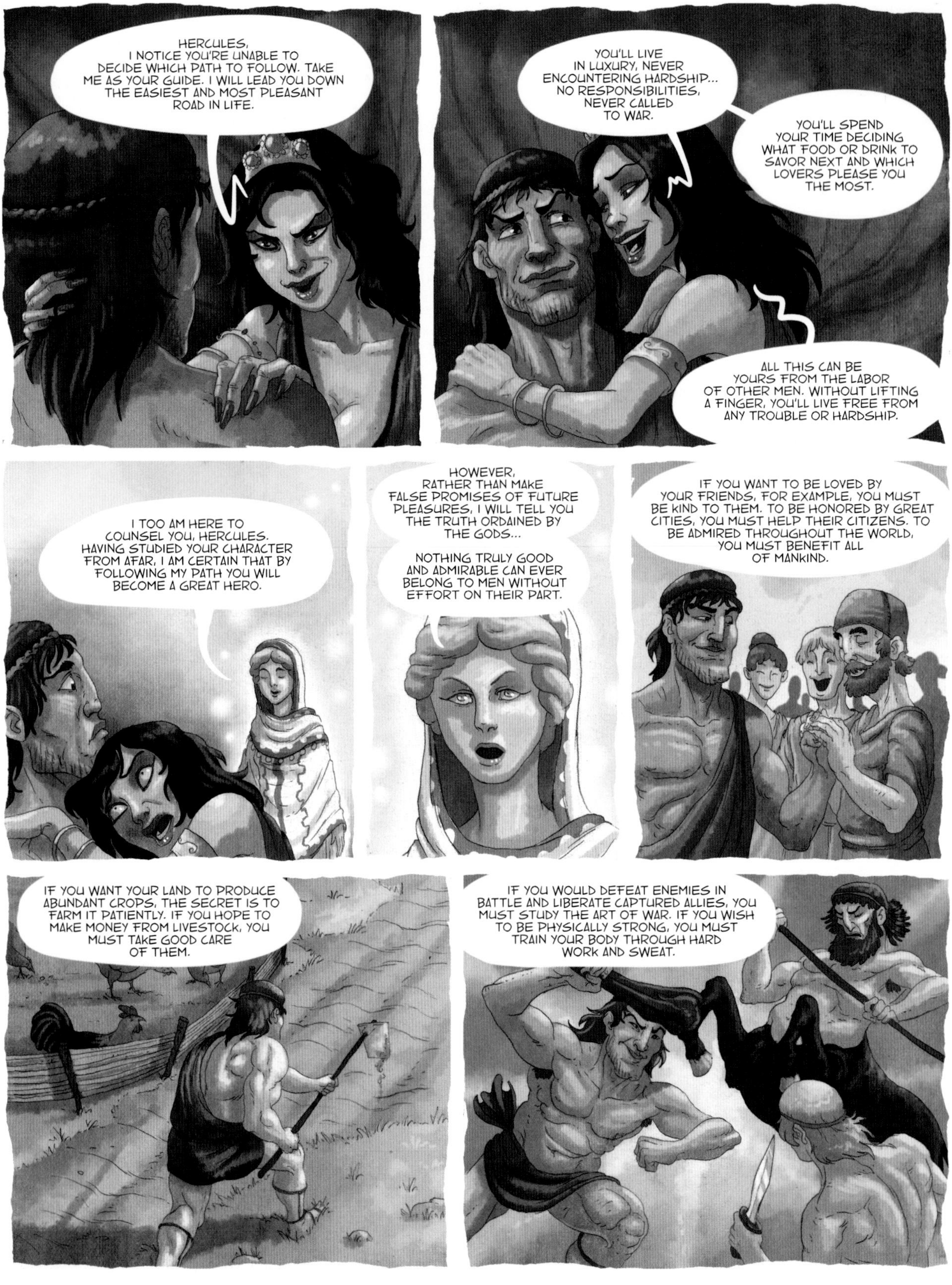
HERCULES, I NOTICE YOU'RE UNABLE TO DECIDE WHICH PATH TO FOLLOW. TAKE ME AS YOUR GUIDE. I WILL LEAD YOU DOWN THE EASIEST AND MOST PLEASANT ROAD IN LIFE.
YOU'LL LIVE IN LUXURY, NEVER ENCOUNTERING HARDSHIP... NO RESPONSIBILITIES, NEVER CALLED TO WAR.
YOU'LL SPEND YOUR TIME DECIDING WHAT FOOD OR DRINK TO SAVOR NEXT AND WHICH LOVERS PLEASE YOU THE MOST.
ALL THIS CAN BE YOURS FROM THE LABOR OF OTHER MEN. WITHOUT LIFTING A FINGER, YOU'LL LIVE FREE FROM ANY TROUBLE OR HARDSHIP.
I TOO AM HERE TO COUNSEL YOU, HERCULES. HAVING STUDIED YOUR CHARACTER FROM AFAR, I AM CERTAIN THAT BY FOLLOWING MY PATH YOU WILL BECOME A GREAT HERO.
HOWEVER, RATHER THAN MAKE FALSE PROMISES OF FUTURE PLEASURES, I WILL TELL YOU THE TRUTH ORDAINED BY THE GODS...
NOTHING TRULY GOOD AND ADMIRABLE CAN EVER BELONG TO MEN WITHOUT EFFORT ON THEIR PART.
IF YOU WANT TO BE LOVED BY YOUR FRIENDS, FOR EXAMPLE, YOU MUST BE KIND TO THEM. TO BE HONORED BY GREAT CITIES, YOU MUST HELP THEIR CITIZENS. TO BE ADMIRED THROUGHOUT THE WORLD, YOU MUST BENEFIT ALL OF MANKIND.
IF YOU WANT YOUR LAND TO PRODUCE ABUNDANT CROPS, THE SECRET IS TO FARM IT PATIENTLY. IF YOU HOPE TO MAKE MONEY FROM LIVESTOCK, YOU MUST TAKE GOOD CARE OF THEM.
IF YOU WOULD DEFEAT ENEMIES IN BATTLE AND LIBERATE CAPTURED ALLIES, YOU MUST STUDY THE ART OF WAR. IF YOU WISH TO BE PHYSICALLY STRONG, YOU MUST TRAIN YOUR BODY THROUGH HARD WORK AND SWEAT.

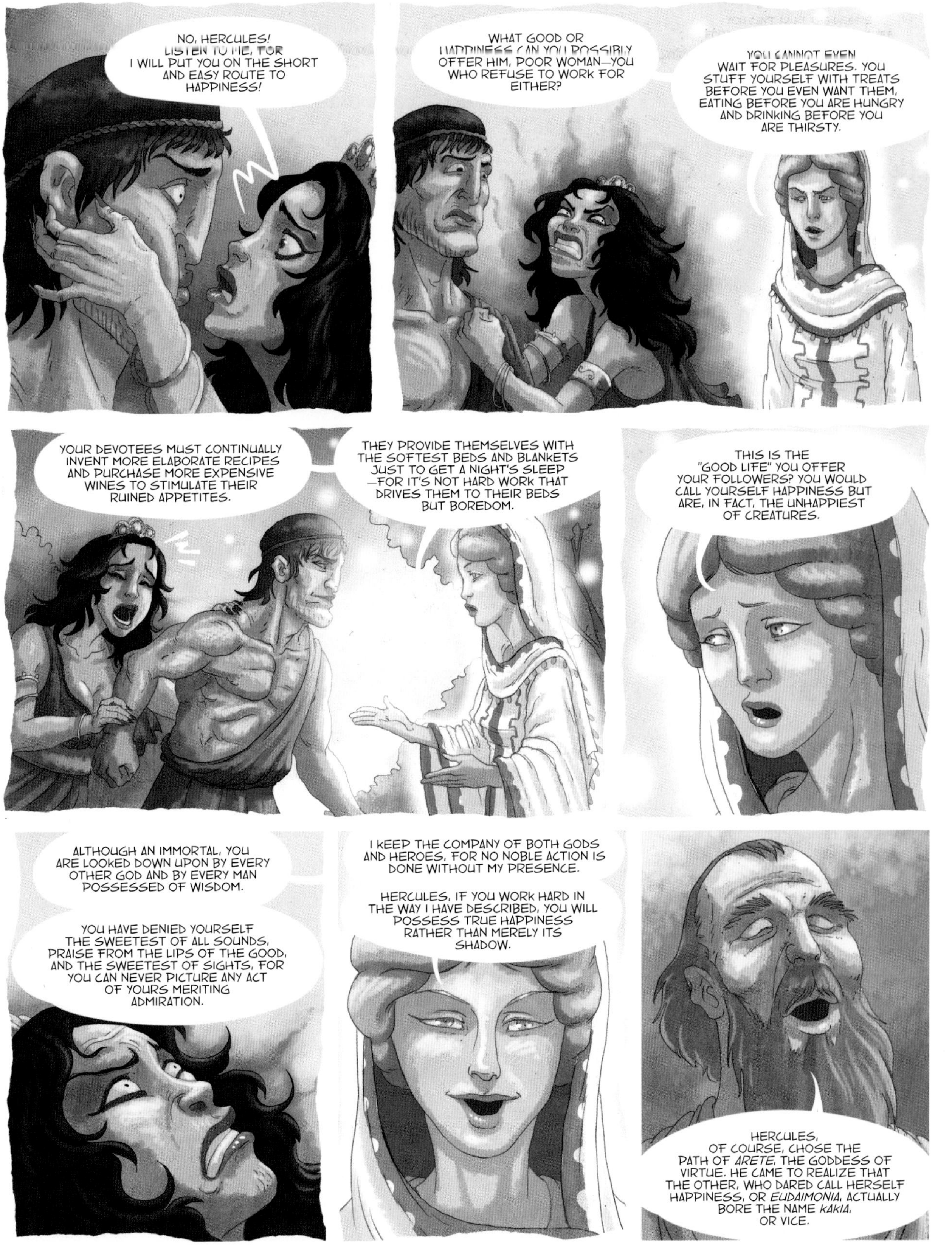
NO, HERCULES! LISTEN TO ME, FOR I WILL PUT YOU ON THE SHORT AND EASY ROUTE TO HAPPINESS!
WHAT GOOD OR HAPPINESS CAN YOU POSSIBLY OFFER HIM, POOR WOMAN—YOU WHO REFUSE TO WORK FOR EITHER?
YOU CANNOT EVEN WAIT FOR PLEASURES. YOU STUFF YOURSELF WITH TREATS BEFORE YOU EVEN WANT THEM, EATING BEFORE YOU ARE HUNGRY AND DRINKING BEFORE YOU ARE THIRSTY.
YOUR DEVOTEES MUST CONTINUALLY INVENT MORE ELABORATE RECIPES AND PURCHASE MORE EXPENSIVE WINES TO STIMULATE THEIR RUINED APPETITES.
THEY PROVIDE THEMSELVES WITH THE SOFTEST BEDS AND BLANKETS JUST TO GET A NIGHT'S SLEEP —FOR IT'S NOT HARD WORK THAT DRIVES THEM TO THEIR BEDS BUT BOREDOM.
THIS IS THE "GOOD LIFE" YOU OFFER YOUR FOLLOWERS? YOU WOULD CALL YOURSELF HAPPINESS BUT ARE, IN FACT, THE UNHAPPIEST OF CREATURES.
ALTHOUGH AN IMMORTAL, YOU ARE LOOKED DOWN UPON BY EVERY OTHER GOD AND BY EVERY MAN POSSESSED OF WISDOM.
YOU HAVE DENIED YOURSELF THE SWEETEST OF ALL SOUNDS, PRAISE FROM THE LIPS OF THE GOOD, AND THE SWEETEST OF SIGHTS, FOR YOU CAN NEVER PICTURE ANY ACT OF YOURS MERITING ADMIRATION.
I KEEP THE COMPANY OF BOTH GODS AND HEROES, FOR NO NOBLE ACTION IS DONE WITHOUT MY PRESENCE.
HERCULES, IF YOU WORK HARD IN THE WAY I HAVE DESCRIBED, YOU WILL POSSESS TRUE HAPPINESS RATHER THAN MERELY ITS SHADOW.
HERCULES, OF COURSE, CHOSE THE PATH OF *ARETE*, THE GODDESS OF VIRTUE. HE CAME TO REALIZE THAT THE OTHER, WHO DARED CALL HERSELF HAPPINESS, OR *EUDAIMONIA*, ACTUALLY BORE THE NAME *KAKIA*, OR VICE.

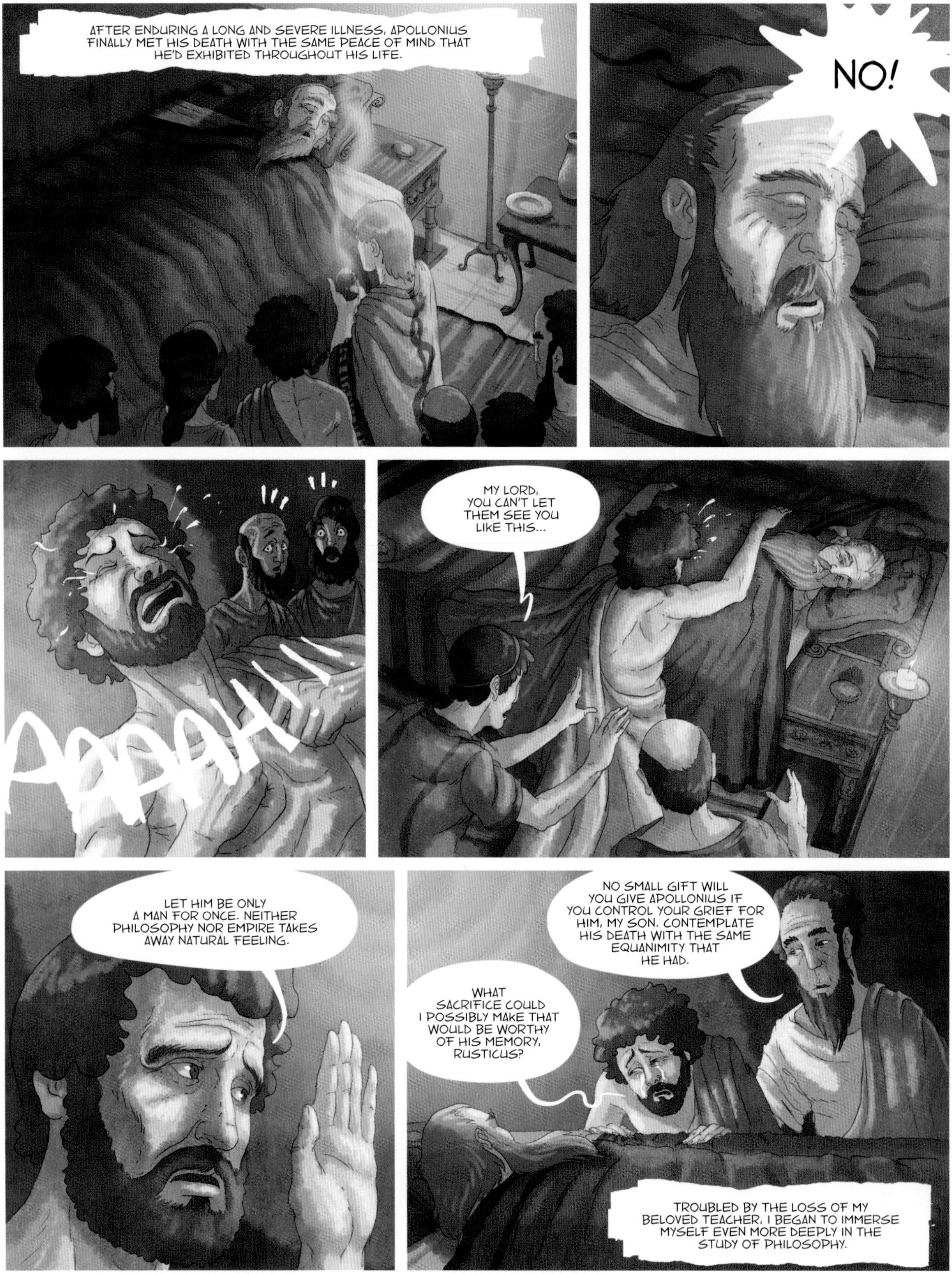
AFTER ENDURING A LONG AND SEVERE ILLNESS, APOLLONIUS FINALLY MET HIS DEATH WITH THE SAME PEACE OF MIND THAT HE'D EXHIBITED THROUGHOUT HIS LIFE.
NO!
AAAAH!!
MY LORD, YOU CAN'T LET THEM SEE YOU LIKE THIS...
LET HIM BE ONLY A MAN FOR ONCE. NEITHER PHILOSOPHY NOR EMPIRE TAKES AWAY NATURAL FEELING.
NO SMALL GIFT WILL YOU GIVE APOLLONIUS IF YOU CONTROL YOUR GRIEF FOR HIM, MY SON. CONTEMPLATE HIS DEATH WITH THE SAME EQUANIMITY THAT HE HAD.
WHAT SACRIFICE COULD I POSSIBLY MAKE THAT WOULD BE WORTHY OF HIS MEMORY, RUSTICUS?
TROUBLED BY THE LOSS OF MY BELOVED TEACHER, I BEGAN TO IMMERSE MYSELF EVEN MORE DEEPLY IN THE STUDY OF PHILOSOPHY.

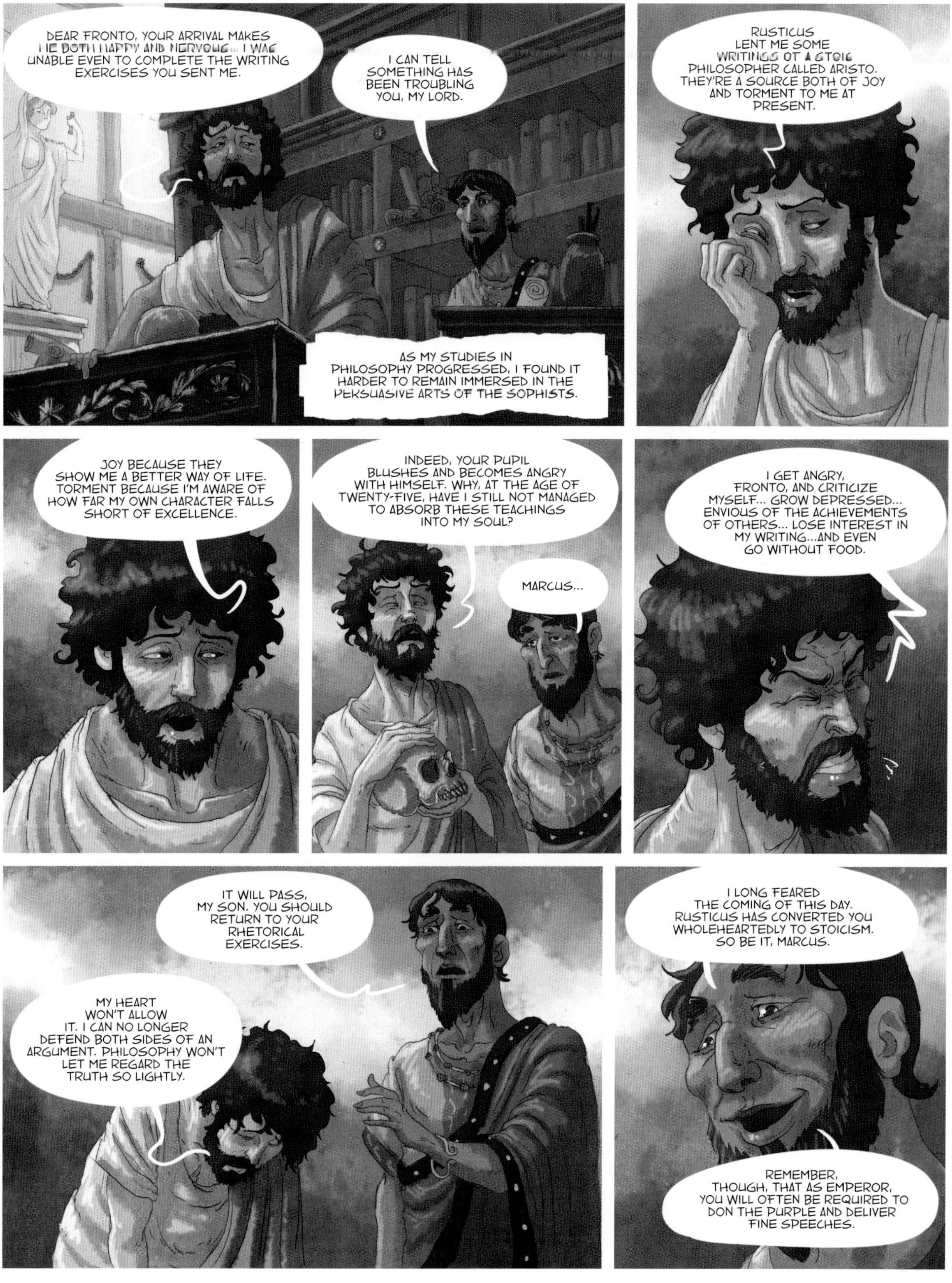
DEAR FRONTO, YOUR ARRIVAL MAKES ME BOTH HAPPY AND NERVOUS... I WAS UNABLE EVEN TO COMPLETE THE WRITING EXERCISES YOU SENT ME.
I CAN TELL SOMETHING HAS BEEN TROUBLING YOU, MY LORD.
AS MY STUDIES IN PHILOSOPHY PROGRESSED, I FOUND IT HARDER TO REMAIN IMMERSED IN THE PERSUASIVE ARTS OF THE SOPHISTS.
RUSTICUS LENT ME SOME WRITINGS OF A STOIC PHILOSOPHER CALLED ARISTO. THEY'RE A SOURCE BOTH OF JOY AND TORMENT TO ME AT PRESENT.
JOY BECAUSE THEY SHOW ME A BETTER WAY OF LIFE. TORMENT BECAUSE I'M AWARE OF HOW FAR MY OWN CHARACTER FALLS SHORT OF EXCELLENCE.
INDEED, YOUR PUPIL BLUSHES AND BECOMES ANGRY WITH HIMSELF. WHY, AT THE AGE OF TWENTY-FIVE, HAVE I STILL NOT MANAGED TO ABSORB THESE TEACHINGS INTO MY SOUL?
MARCUS...
I GET ANGRY, FRONTO, AND CRITICIZE MYSELF... GROW DEPRESSED... ENVIOUS OF THE ACHIEVEMENTS OF OTHERS... LOSE INTEREST IN MY WRITING...AND EVEN GO WITHOUT FOOD.
IT WILL PASS, MY SON. YOU SHOULD RETURN TO YOUR RHETORICAL EXERCISES.
MY HEART WON'T ALLOW IT. I CAN NO LONGER DEFEND BOTH SIDES OF AN ARGUMENT. PHILOSOPHY WON'T LET ME REGARD THE TRUTH SO LIGHTLY.
I LONG FEARED THE COMING OF THIS DAY. RUSTICUS HAS CONVERTED YOU WHOLEHEARTEDLY TO STOICISM. SO BE IT, MARCUS.
REMEMBER, THOUGH, THAT AS EMPEROR, YOU WILL OFTEN BE REQUIRED TO DON THE PURPLE AND DELIVER FINE SPEECHES.

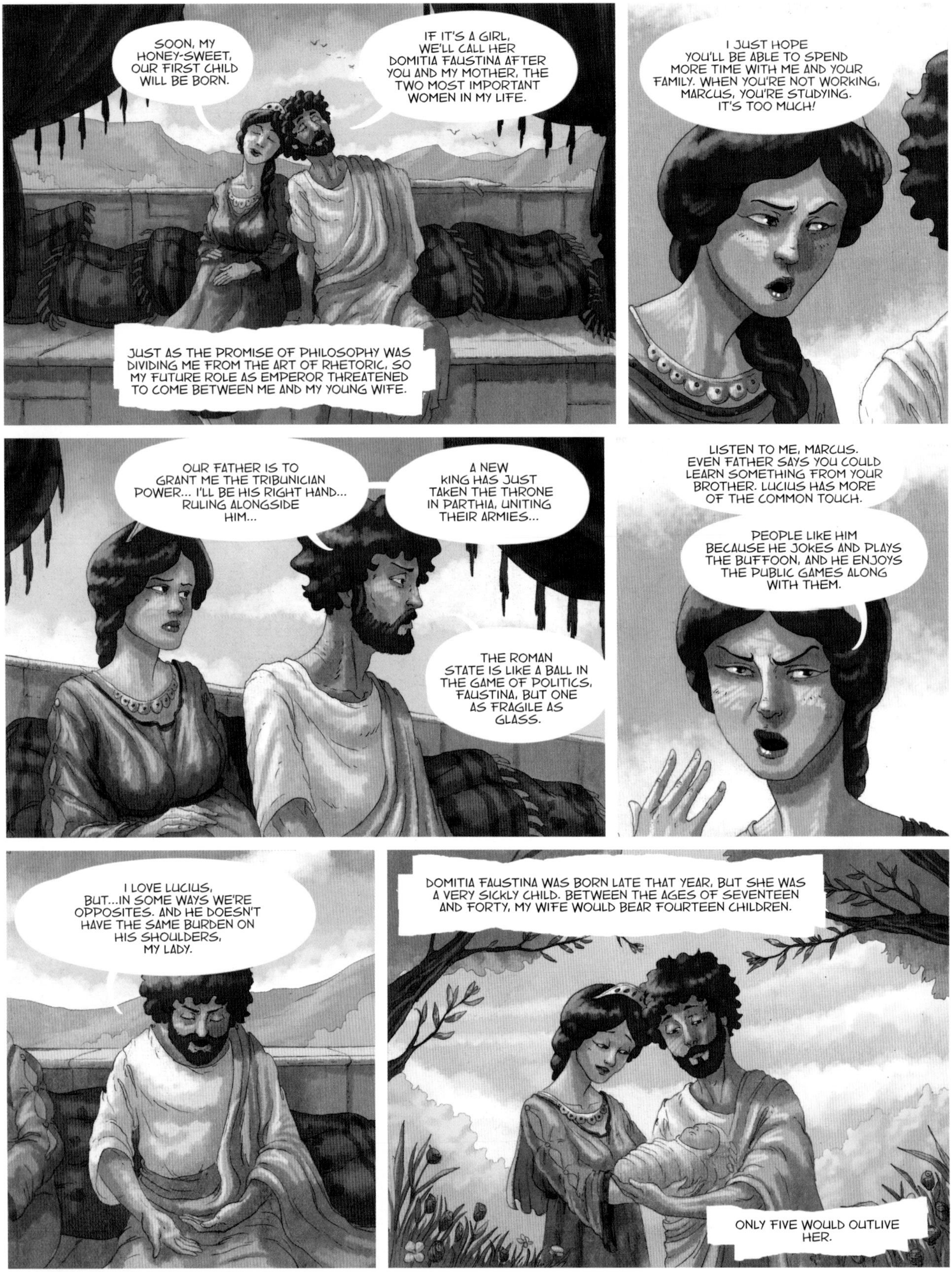

SOON, MY HONEY-SWEET, OUR FIRST CHILD WILL BE BORN.
IF IT'S A GIRL, WE'LL CALL HER DOMITIA FAUSTINA AFTER YOU AND MY MOTHER, THE TWO MOST IMPORTANT WOMEN IN MY LIFE.
JUST AS THE PROMISE OF PHILOSOPHY WAS DIVIDING ME FROM THE ART OF RHETORIC, SO MY FUTURE ROLE AS EMPEROR THREATENED TO COME BETWEEN ME AND MY YOUNG WIFE.
I JUST HOPE YOU'LL BE ABLE TO SPEND MORE TIME WITH ME AND YOUR FAMILY. WHEN YOU'RE NOT WORKING, MARCUS, YOU'RE STUDYING. IT'S TOO MUCH!
OUR FATHER IS TO GRANT ME THE TRIBUNICIAN POWER... I'LL BE HIS RIGHT HAND... RULING ALONGSIDE HIM...
A NEW KING HAS JUST TAKEN THE THRONE IN PARTHIA, UNITING THEIR ARMIES...
THE ROMAN STATE IS LIKE A BALL IN THE GAME OF POLITICS, FAUSTINA, BUT ONE AS FRAGILE AS GLASS.
LISTEN TO ME, MARCUS. EVEN FATHER SAYS YOU COULD LEARN SOMETHING FROM YOUR BROTHER. LUCIUS HAS MORE OF THE COMMON TOUCH.
PEOPLE LIKE HIM BECAUSE HE JOKES AND PLAYS THE BUFFOON, AND HE ENJOYS THE PUBLIC GAMES ALONG WITH THEM.
I LOVE LUCIUS, BUT...IN SOME WAYS WE'RE OPPOSITES. AND HE DOESN'T HAVE THE SAME BURDEN ON HIS SHOULDERS, MY LADY.
DOMITIA FAUSTINA WAS BORN LATE THAT YEAR, BUT SHE WAS A VERY SICKLY CHILD. BETWEEN THE AGES OF SEVENTEEN AND FORTY, MY WIFE WOULD BEAR FOURTEEN CHILDREN.
ONLY FIVE WOULD OUTLIVE HER.

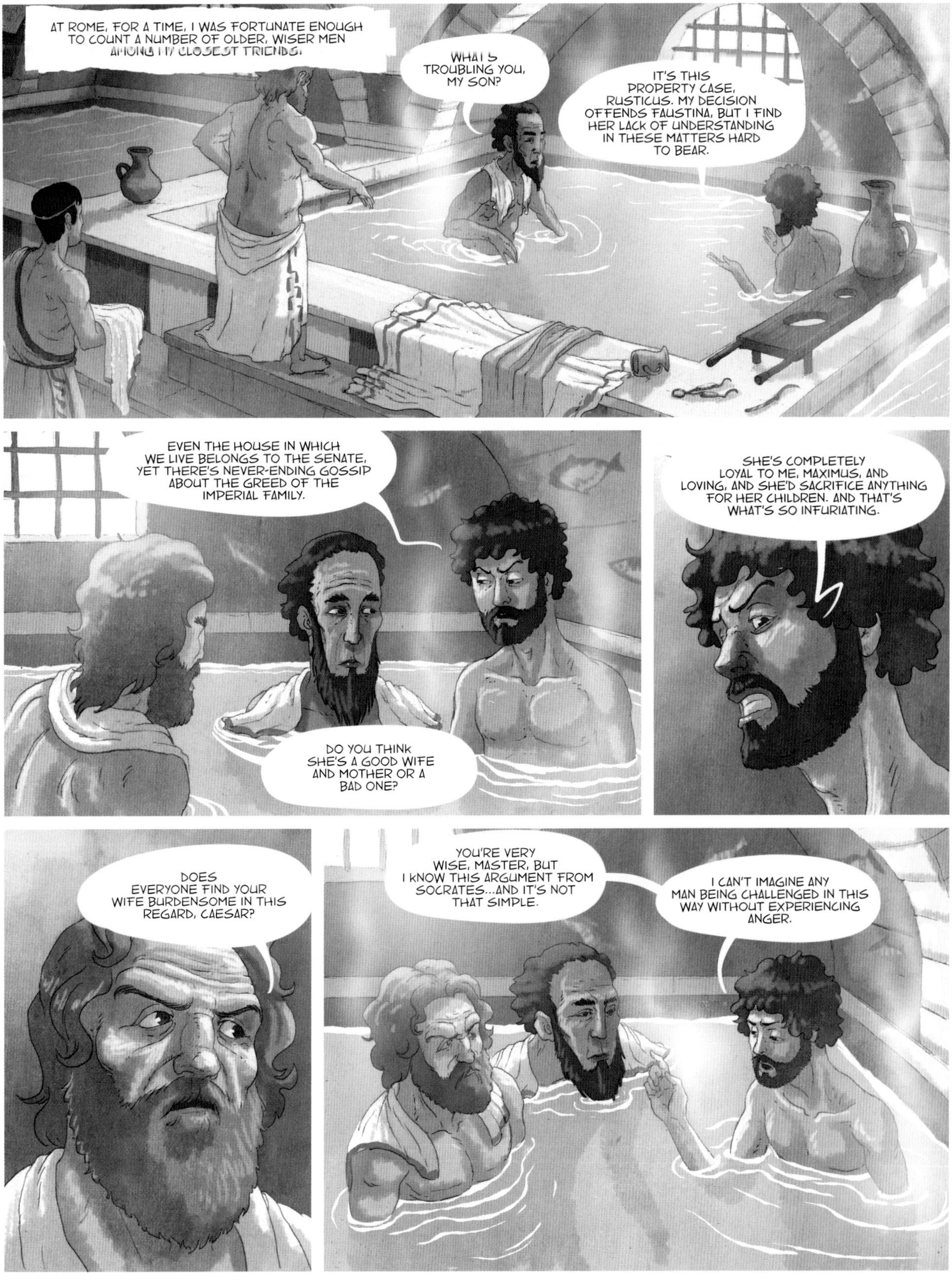
AT ROME, FOR A TIME, I WAS FORTUNATE ENOUGH TO COUNT A NUMBER OF OLDER, WISER MEN AMONG MY CLOSEST FRIENDS.
WHAT'S TROUBLING YOU, MY SON?
IT'S THIS PROPERTY CASE, RUSTICUS. MY DECISION OFFENDS FAUSTINA, BUT I FIND HER LACK OF UNDERSTANDING IN THESE MATTERS HARD TO BEAR.
EVEN THE HOUSE IN WHICH WE LIVE BELONGS TO THE SENATE, YET THERE'S NEVER-ENDING GOSSIP ABOUT THE GREED OF THE IMPERIAL FAMILY.
DO YOU THINK SHE'S A GOOD WIFE AND MOTHER OR A BAD ONE?
SHE'S COMPLETELY LOYAL TO ME, MAXIMUS, AND LOVING, AND SHE'D SACRIFICE ANYTHING FOR HER CHILDREN. AND THAT'S WHAT'S SO INFURIATING.
DOES EVERYONE FIND YOUR WIFE BURDENSOME IN THIS REGARD, CAESAR?
YOU'RE VERY WISE, MASTER, BUT I KNOW THIS ARGUMENT FROM SOCRATES...AND IT'S NOT THAT SIMPLE.
I CAN'T IMAGINE ANY MAN BEING CHALLENGED IN THIS WAY WITHOUT EXPERIENCING ANGER.

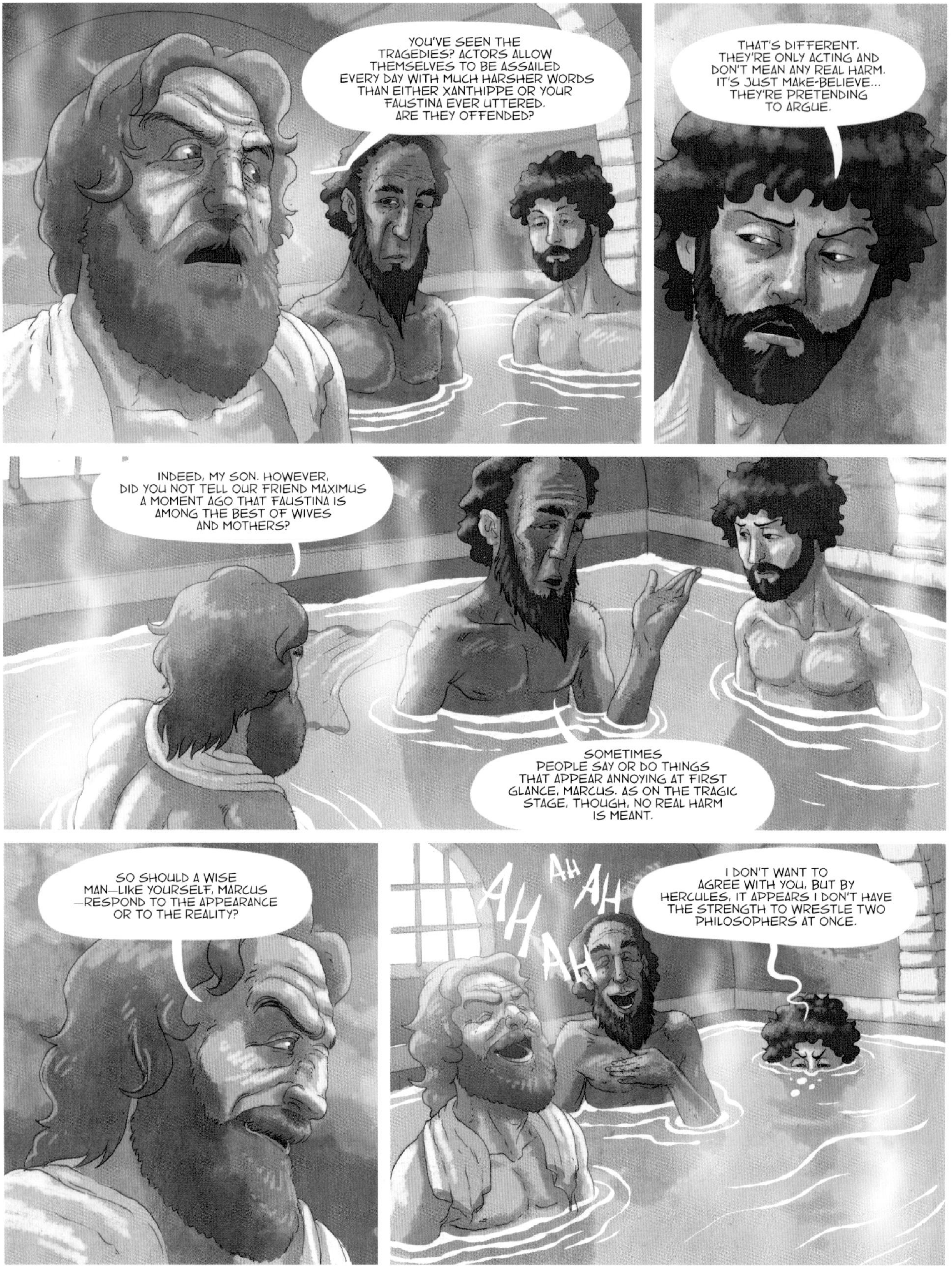
YOU'VE SEEN THE TRAGEDIES? ACTORS ALLOW THEMSELVES TO BE ASSAILED EVERY DAY WITH MUCH HARSHER WORDS THAN EITHER XANTHIPPE OR YOUR FAUSTINA EVER UTTERED. ARE THEY OFFENDED?
THAT'S DIFFERENT. THEY'RE ONLY ACTING AND DON'T MEAN ANY REAL HARM. IT'S JUST MAKE-BELIEVE... THEY'RE PRETENDING TO ARGUE.
INDEED, MY SON. HOWEVER, DID YOU NOT TELL OUR FRIEND MAXIMUS A MOMENT AGO THAT FAUSTINA IS AMONG THE BEST OF WIVES AND MOTHERS?
SOMETIMES PEOPLE SAY OR DO THINGS THAT APPEAR ANNOYING AT FIRST GLANCE, MARCUS. AS ON THE TRAGIC STAGE, THOUGH, NO REAL HARM IS MEANT.
SO SHOULD A WISE MAN—LIKE YOURSELF, MARCUS —RESPOND TO THE APPEARANCE OR TO THE REALITY?
AH AH AH AH AH
I DON'T WANT TO AGREE WITH YOU, BUT BY HERCULES, IT APPEARS I DON'T HAVE THE STRENGTH TO WRESTLE TWO PHILOSOPHERS AT ONCE.

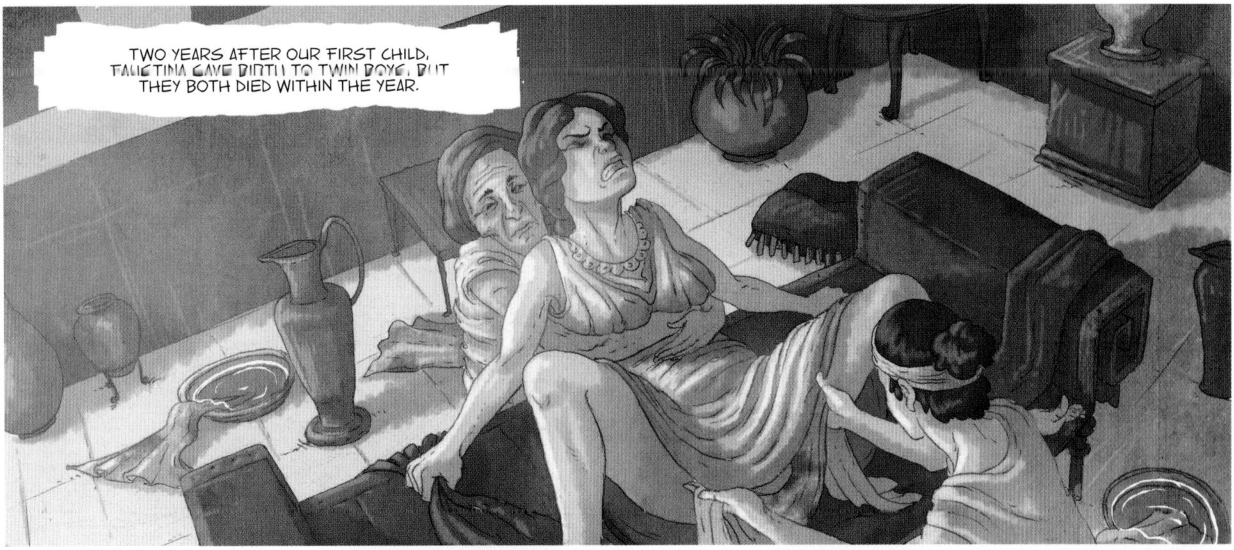
TWO YEARS AFTER OUR FIRST CHILD, FAUSTINA GAVE BIRTH TO TWIN BOYS, BUT THEY BOTH DIED WITHIN THE YEAR.

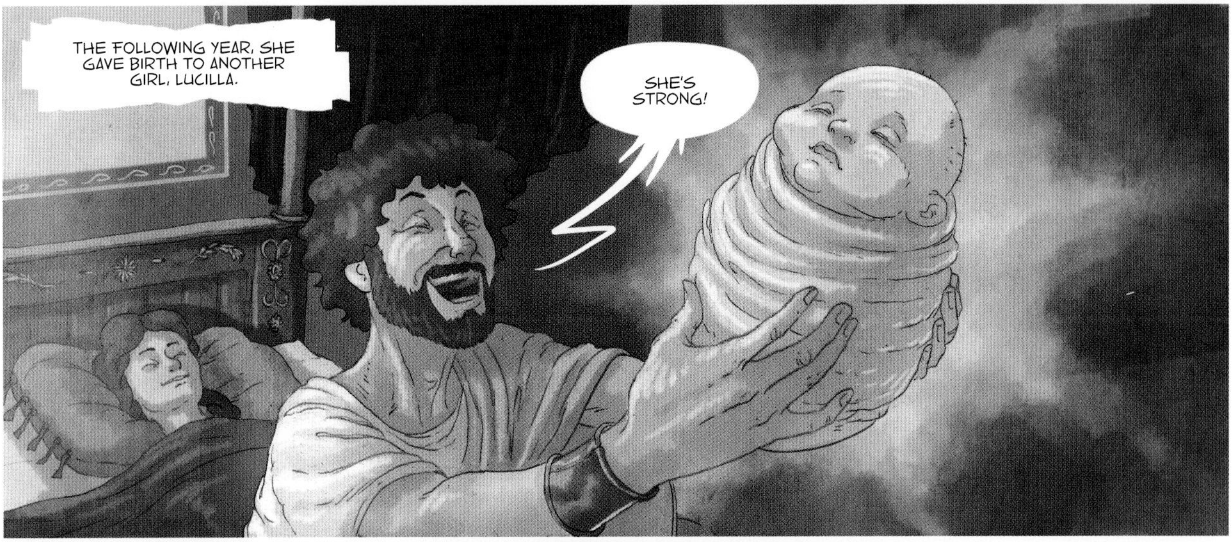
THE FOLLOWING YEAR, SHE GAVE BIRTH TO ANOTHER GIRL, LUCILLA.
SHE'S STRONG!

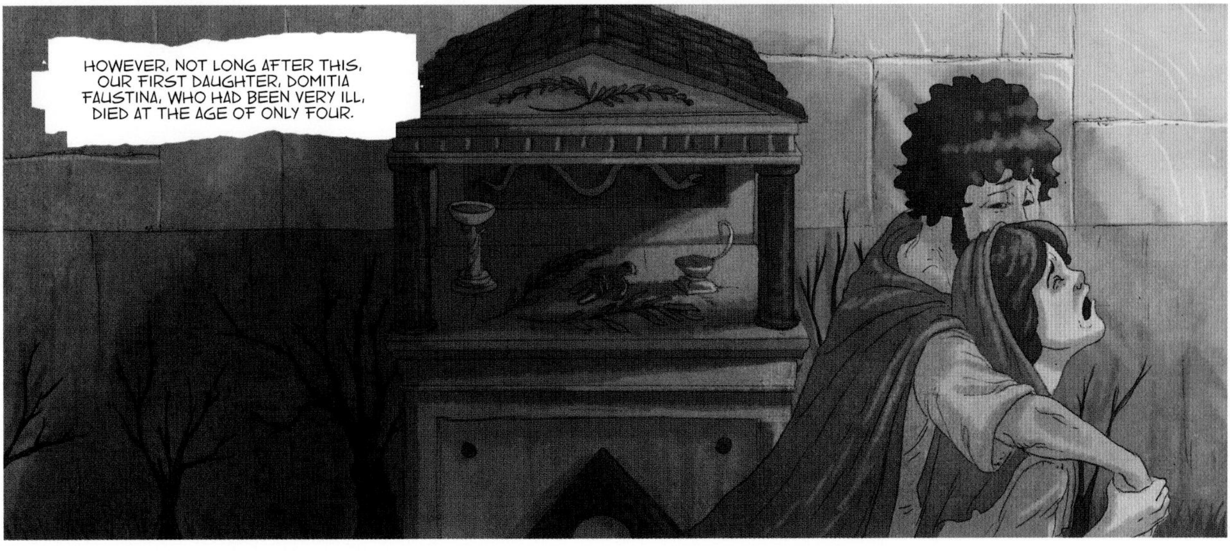
HOWEVER, NOT LONG AFTER THIS, OUR FIRST DAUGHTER, DOMITIA FAUSTINA, WHO HAD BEEN VERY ILL, DIED AT THE AGE OF ONLY FOUR.

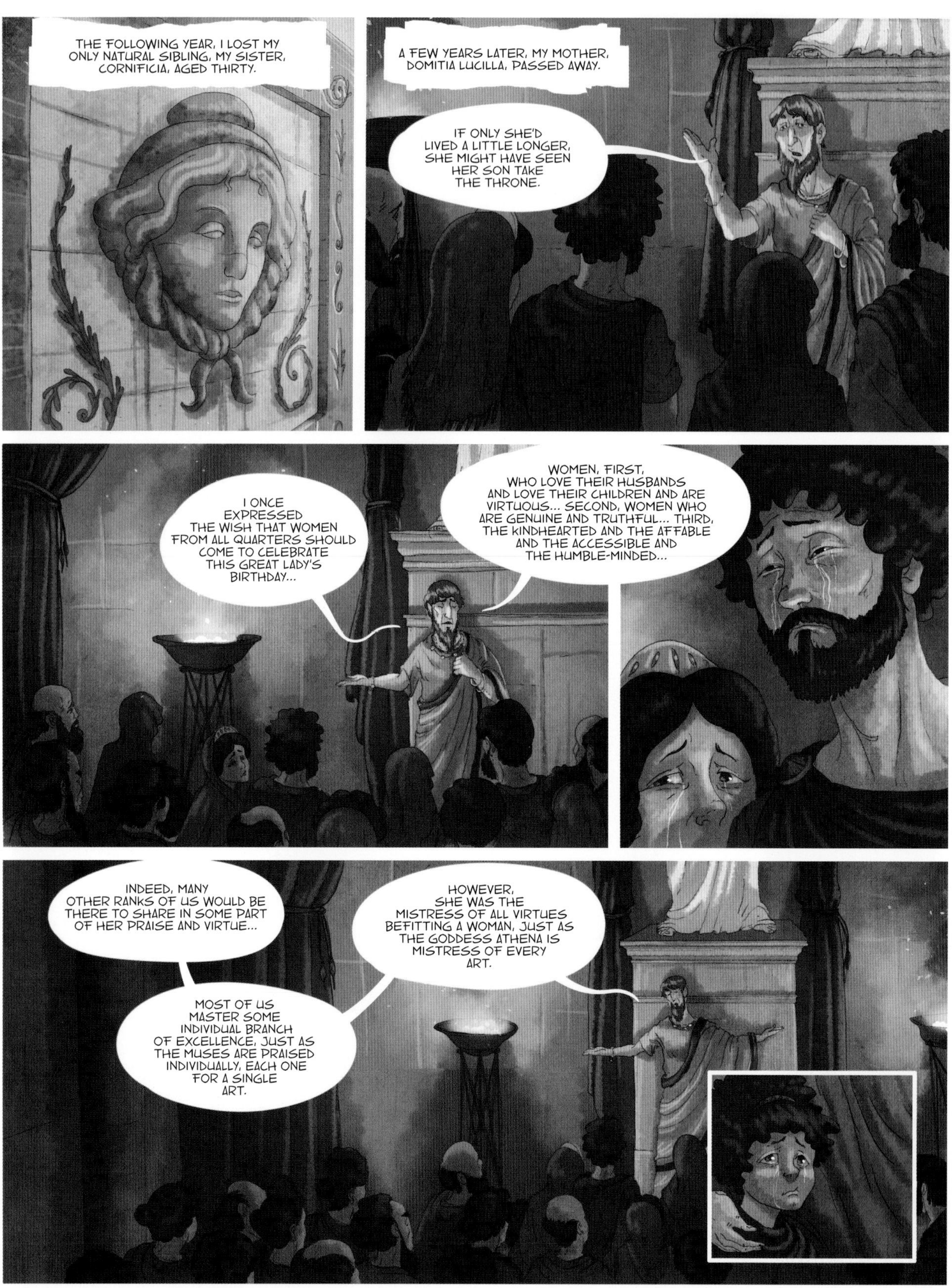
THE FOLLOWING YEAR, I LOST MY ONLY NATURAL SIBLING, MY SISTER, CORNIFICIA, AGED THIRTY.
A FEW YEARS LATER, MY MOTHER, DOMITIA LUCILLA, PASSED AWAY.
IF ONLY SHE'D LIVED A LITTLE LONGER, SHE MIGHT HAVE SEEN HER SON TAKE THE THRONE.
I ONCE EXPRESSED THE WISH THAT WOMEN FROM ALL QUARTERS SHOULD COME TO CELEBRATE THIS GREAT LADY'S BIRTHDAY...
WOMEN, FIRST, WHO LOVE THEIR HUSBANDS AND LOVE THEIR CHILDREN AND ARE VIRTUOUS... SECOND, WOMEN WHO ARE GENUINE AND TRUTHFUL... THIRD, THE KINDHEARTED AND THE AFFABLE AND THE ACCESSIBLE AND THE HUMBLE-MINDED...
INDEED, MANY OTHER RANKS OF US WOULD BE THERE TO SHARE IN SOME PART OF HER PRAISE AND VIRTUE...
MOST OF US MASTER SOME INDIVIDUAL BRANCH OF EXCELLENCE, JUST AS THE MUSES ARE PRAISED INDIVIDUALLY, EACH ONE FOR A SINGLE ART.
HOWEVER, SHE WAS THE MISTRESS OF ALL VIRTUES BEFITTING A WOMAN, JUST AS THE GODDESS ATHENA IS MISTRESS OF EVERY ART.

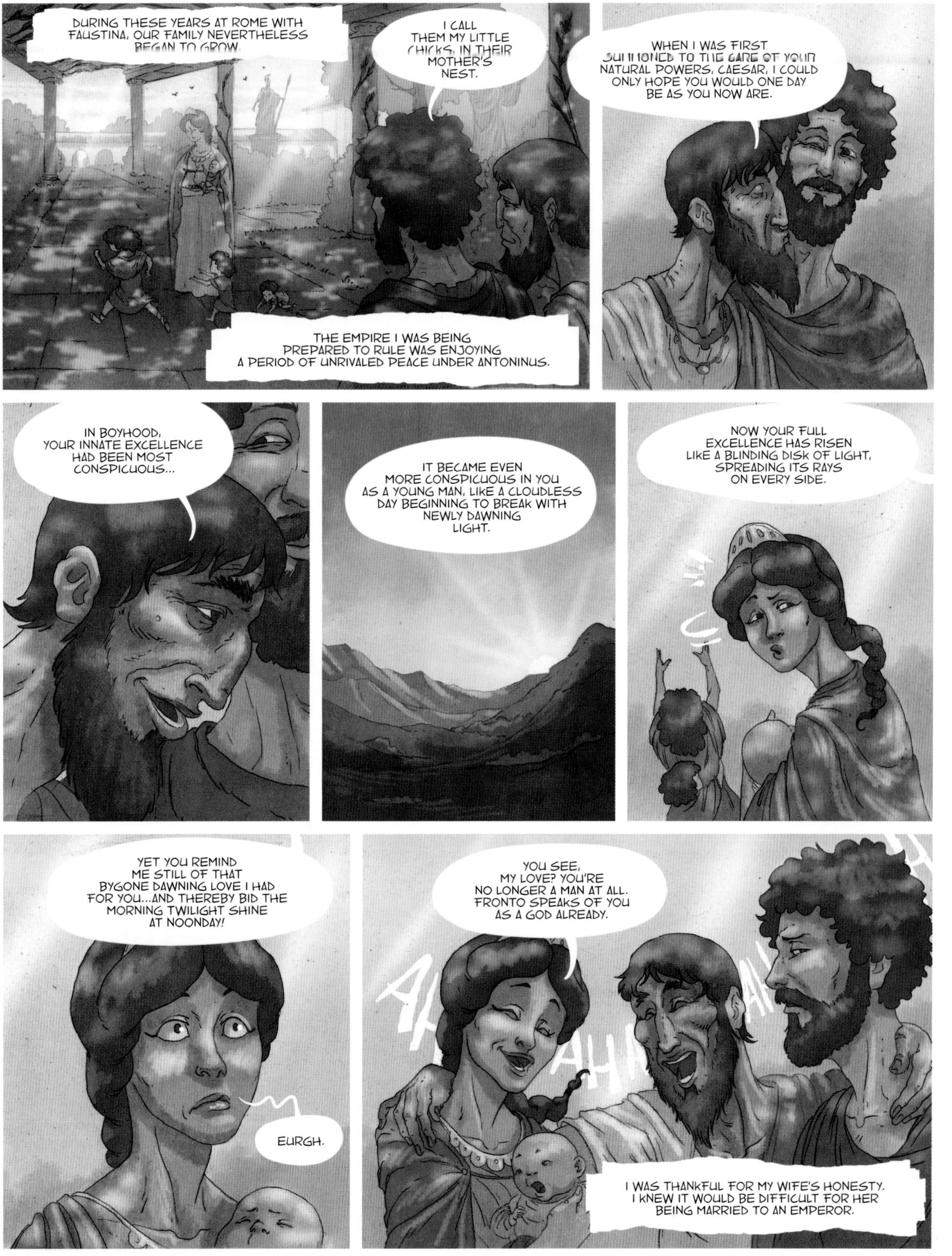
DURING THESE YEARS AT ROME WITH FAUSTINA, OUR FAMILY NEVERTHELESS BEGAN TO GROW.
I CALL THEM MY LITTLE CHICKS, IN THEIR MOTHER'S NEST.
THE EMPIRE I WAS BEING PREPARED TO RULE WAS ENJOYING A PERIOD OF UNRIVALED PEACE UNDER ANTONINUS.
WHEN I WAS FIRST SUMMONED TO THE CARE OF YOUR NATURAL POWERS, CAESAR, I COULD ONLY HOPE YOU WOULD ONE DAY BE AS YOU NOW ARE.
IN BOYHOOD, YOUR INNATE EXCELLENCE HAD BEEN MOST CONSPICUOUS...
IT BECAME EVEN MORE CONSPICUOUS IN YOU AS A YOUNG MAN, LIKE A CLOUDLESS DAY BEGINNING TO BREAK WITH NEWLY DAWNING LIGHT.
NOW YOUR FULL EXCELLENCE HAS RISEN LIKE A BLINDING DISK OF LIGHT, SPREADING ITS RAYS ON EVERY SIDE.
YET YOU REMIND ME STILL OF THAT BYGONE DAWNING LOVE I HAD FOR YOU...AND THEREBY BID THE MORNING TWILIGHT SHINE AT NOONDAY!
EURGH.
YOU SEE, MY LOVE? YOU'RE NO LONGER A MAN AT ALL. FRONTO SPEAKS OF YOU AS A GOD ALREADY.
I WAS THANKFUL FOR MY WIFE'S HONESTY. I KNEW IT WOULD BE DIFFICULT FOR HER BEING MARRIED TO AN EMPEROR.

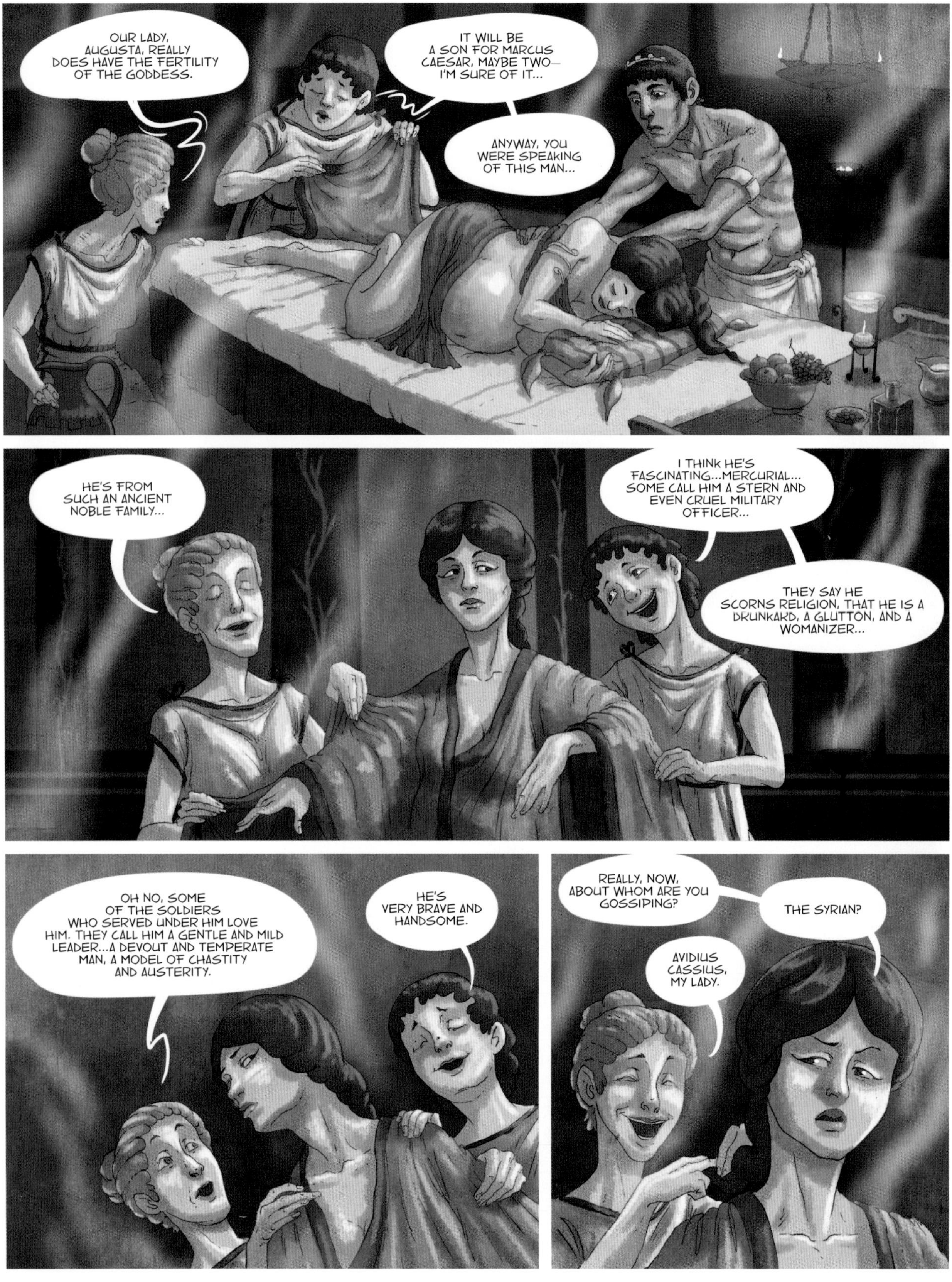
OUR LADY, AUGUSTA, REALLY DOES HAVE THE FERTILITY OF THE GODDESS.
IT WILL BE A SON FOR MARCUS CAESAR, MAYBE TWO— I'M SURE OF IT...
ANYWAY, YOU WERE SPEAKING OF THIS MAN...
HE'S FROM SUCH AN ANCIENT NOBLE FAMILY...
I THINK HE'S FASCINATING...MERCURIAL... SOME CALL HIM A STERN AND EVEN CRUEL MILITARY OFFICER...
THEY SAY HE SCORNS RELIGION, THAT HE IS A DRUNKARD, A GLUTTON, AND A WOMANIZER...
OH NO, SOME OF THE SOLDIERS WHO SERVED UNDER HIM LOVE HIM. THEY CALL HIM A GENTLE AND MILD LEADER...A DEVOUT AND TEMPERATE MAN, A MODEL OF CHASTITY AND AUSTERITY.
HE'S VERY BRAVE AND HANDSOME.
REALLY, NOW, ABOUT WHOM ARE YOU GOSSIPING?
THE SYRIAN?
AVIDIUS CASSIUS, MY LADY.

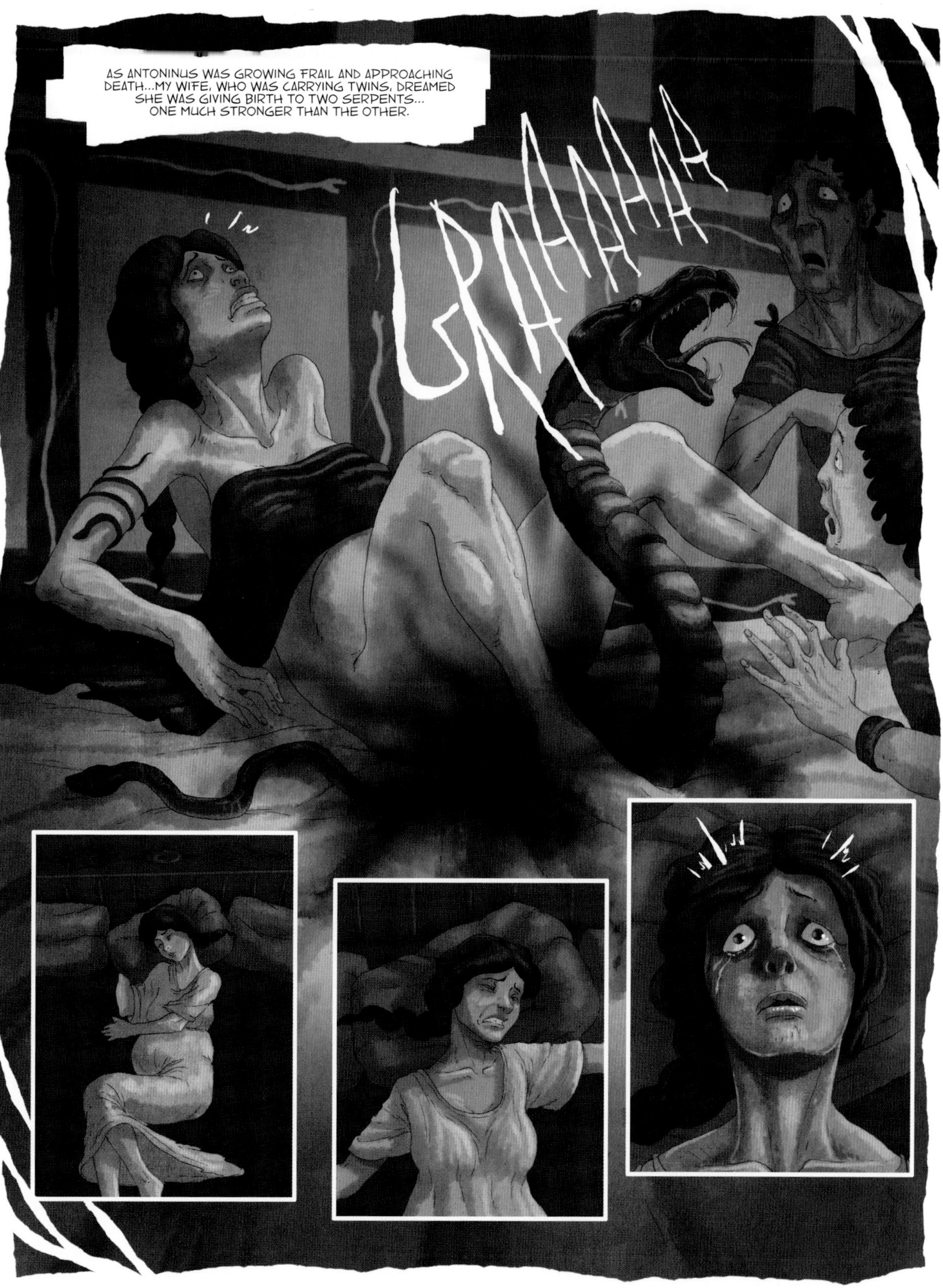
AS ANTONINUS WAS GROWING FRAIL AND APPROACHING DEATH...MY WIFE, WHO WAS CARRYING TWINS, DREAMED SHE WAS GIVING BIRTH TO TWO SERPENTS... ONE MUCH STRONGER THAN THE OTHER.
GRAAAAAA

CAVE CANEM

THE
LEGIONARY
LEGATE

*Alexander the Great, Julius Caesar,
and Pompey ... how many things they
had to worry about, and by how many
such cares were they enslaved!*

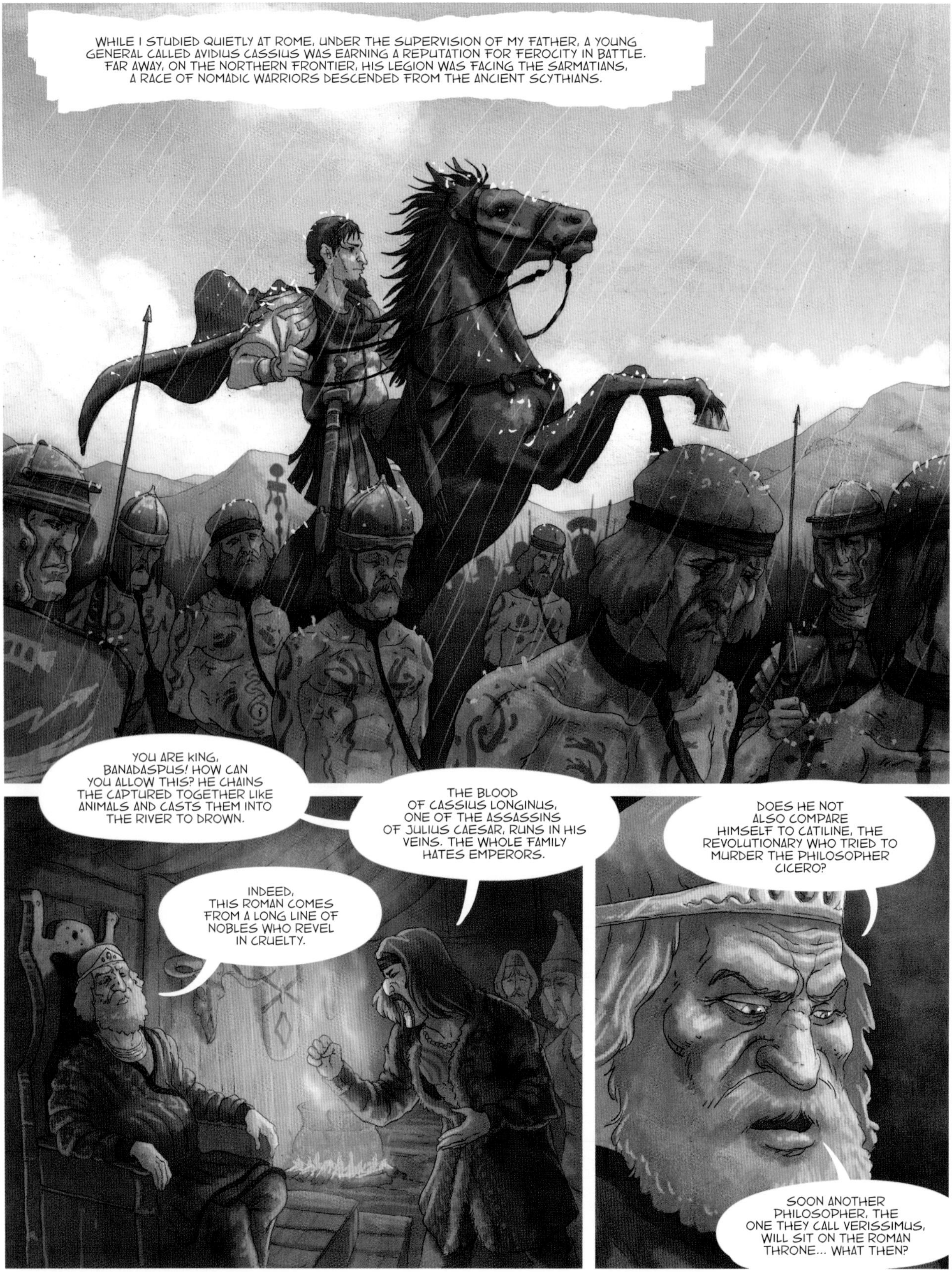
WHILE I STUDIED QUIETLY AT ROME, UNDER THE SUPERVISION OF MY FATHER, A YOUNG GENERAL CALLED AVIDIUS CASSIUS WAS EARNING A REPUTATION FOR FEROCITY IN BATTLE. FAR AWAY, ON THE NORTHERN FRONTIER, HIS LEGION WAS FACING THE SARMATIANS, A RACE OF NOMADIC WARRIORS DESCENDED FROM THE ANCIENT SCYTHIANS.
YOU ARE KING, BANADASPUS! HOW CAN YOU ALLOW THIS? HE CHAINS THE CAPTURED TOGETHER LIKE ANIMALS AND CASTS THEM INTO THE RIVER TO DROWN.
INDEED, THIS ROMAN COMES FROM A LONG LINE OF NOBLES WHO REVEL IN CRUELTY.
THE BLOOD OF CASSIUS LONGINUS, ONE OF THE ASSASSINS OF JULIUS CAESAR, RUNS IN HIS VEINS. THE WHOLE FAMILY HATES EMPERORS.
DOES HE NOT ALSO COMPARE HIMSELF TO CATILINE, THE REVOLUTIONARY WHO TRIED TO MURDER THE PHILOSOPHER CICERO?
SOON ANOTHER PHILOSOPHER, THE ONE THEY CALL VERISSIMUS, WILL SIT ON THE ROMAN THRONE... WHAT THEN?

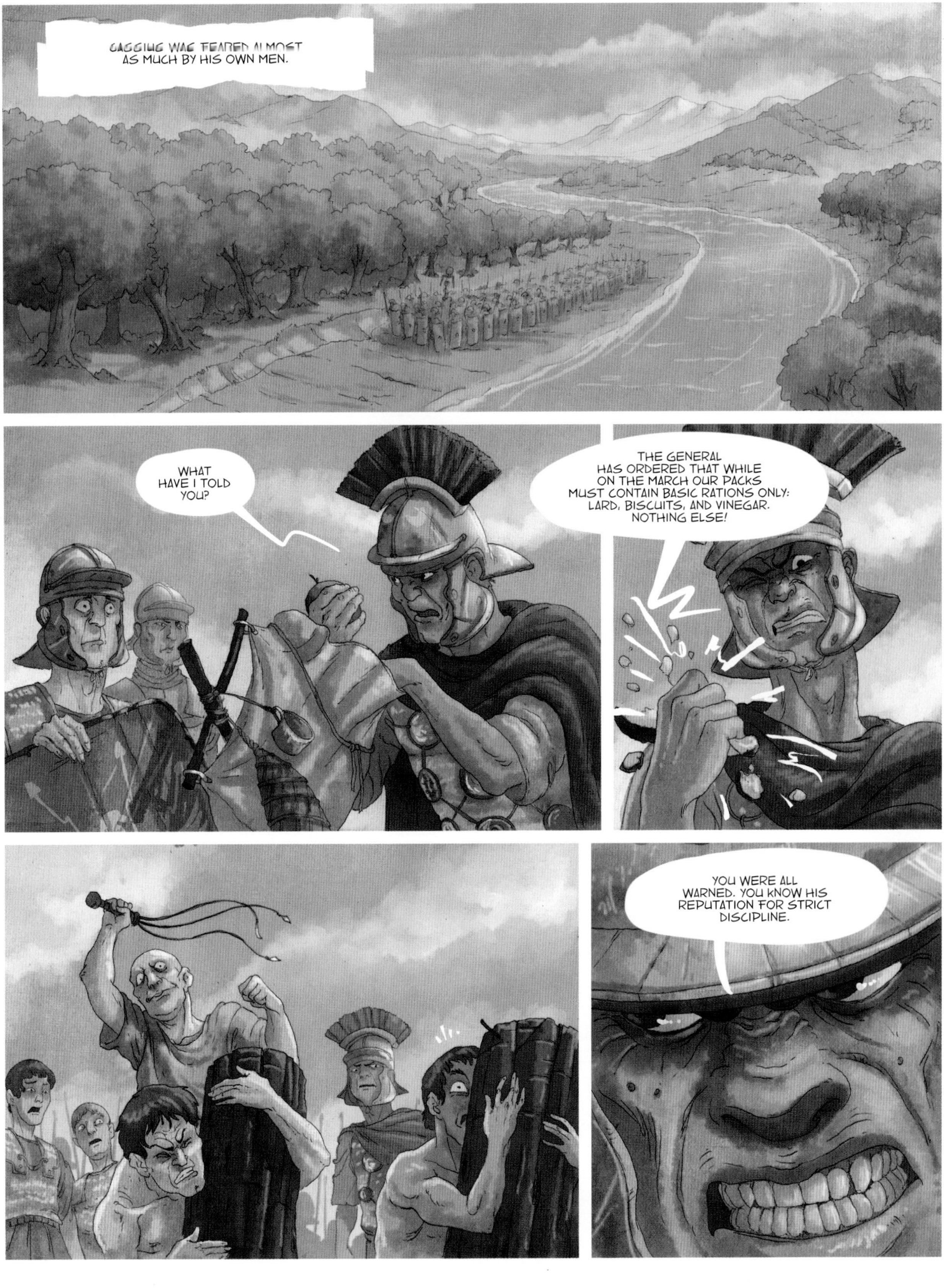
CASSIUS WAS FEARED ALMOST
AS MUCH BY HIS OWN MEN.
WHAT HAVE I TOLD YOU?
THE GENERAL HAS ORDERED THAT WHILE ON THE MARCH OUR PACKS MUST CONTAIN BASIC RATIONS ONLY: LARD, BISCUITS, AND VINEGAR. NOTHING ELSE!
YOU WERE ALL WARNED. YOU KNOW HIS REPUTATION FOR STRICT DISCIPLINE.

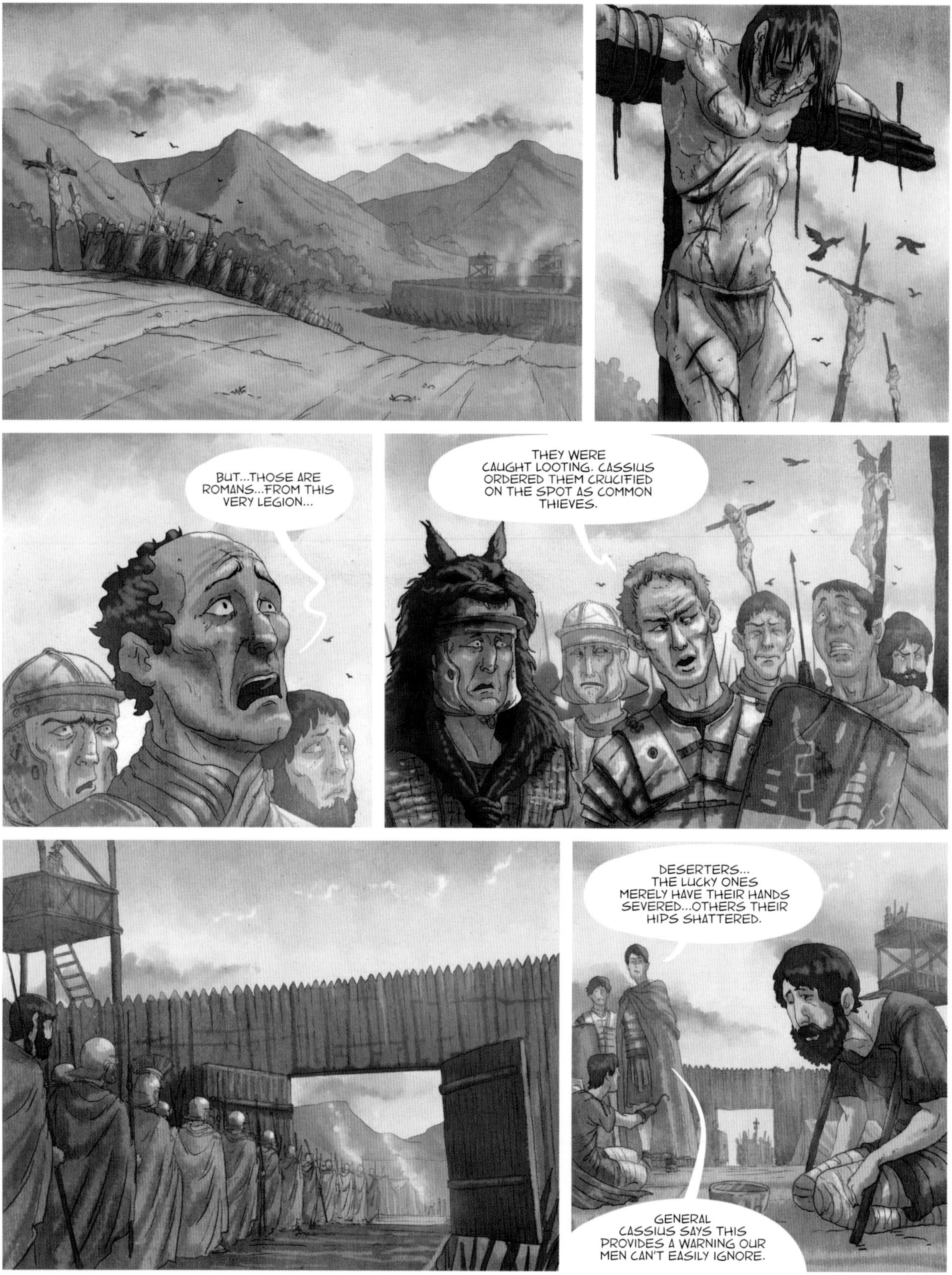
BUT...THOSE ARE ROMANS...FROM THIS VERY LEGION...
THEY WERE CAUGHT LOOTING. CASSIUS ORDERED THEM CRUCIFIED ON THE SPOT AS COMMON THIEVES.
DESERTERS... THE LUCKY ONES MERELY HAVE THEIR HANDS SEVERED...OTHERS THEIR HIPS SHATTERED.
GENERAL CASSIUS SAYS THIS PROVIDES A WARNING OUR MEN CAN'T EASILY IGNORE.

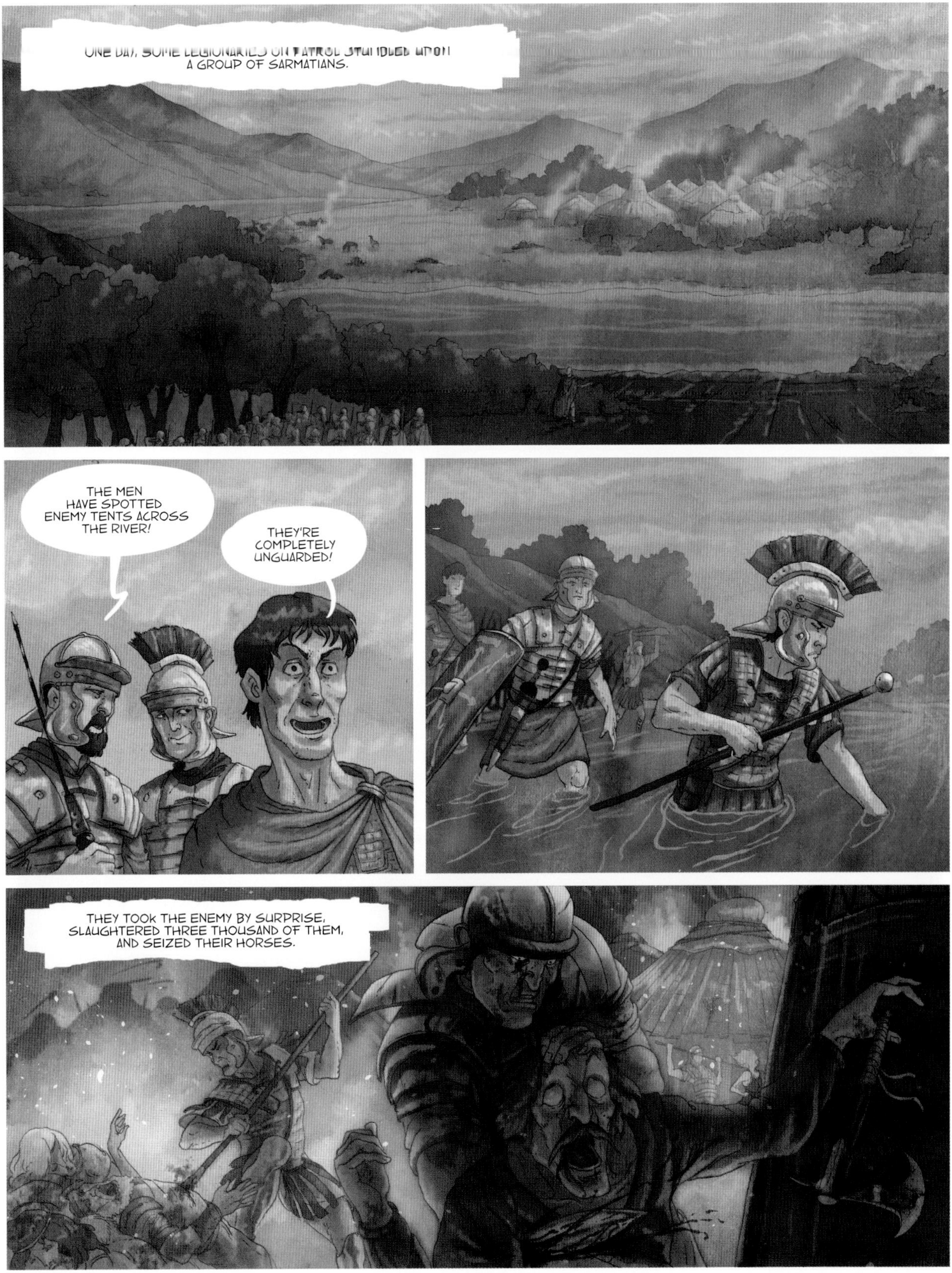
ONE DAY, SOME LEGIONARIES ON PATROL STUMBLED UPON A GROUP OF SARMATIANS.
THE MEN HAVE SPOTTED ENEMY TENTS ACROSS THE RIVER!
THEY'RE COMPLETELY UNGUARDED!
THEY TOOK THE ENEMY BY SURPRISE, SLAUGHTERED THREE THOUSAND OF THEM, AND SEIZED THEIR HORSES.

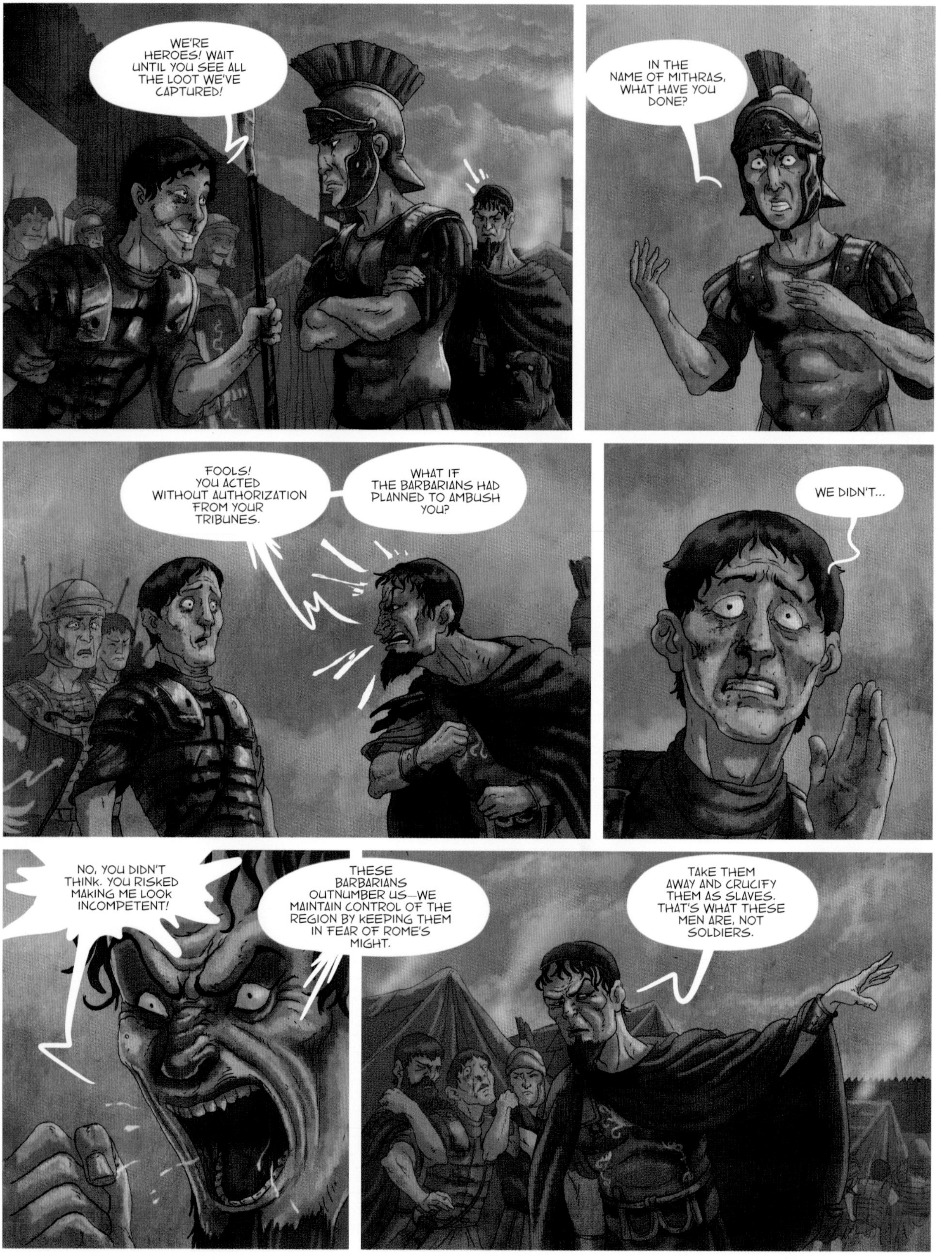
WE'RE HEROES! WAIT UNTIL YOU SEE ALL THE LOOT WE'VE CAPTURED!
IN THE NAME OF MITHRAS, WHAT HAVE YOU DONE?
FOOLS! YOU ACTED WITHOUT AUTHORIZATION FROM YOUR TRIBUNES.
WHAT IF THE BARBARIANS HAD PLANNED TO AMBUSH YOU?
WE DIDN'T...
NO, YOU DIDN'T THINK. YOU RISKED MAKING ME LOOK INCOMPETENT!
THESE BARBARIANS OUTNUMBER US—WE MAINTAIN CONTROL OF THE REGION BY KEEPING THEM IN FEAR OF ROME'S MIGHT.
TAKE THEM AWAY AND CRUCIFY THEM AS SLAVES. THAT'S WHAT THESE MEN ARE, NOT SOLDIERS.

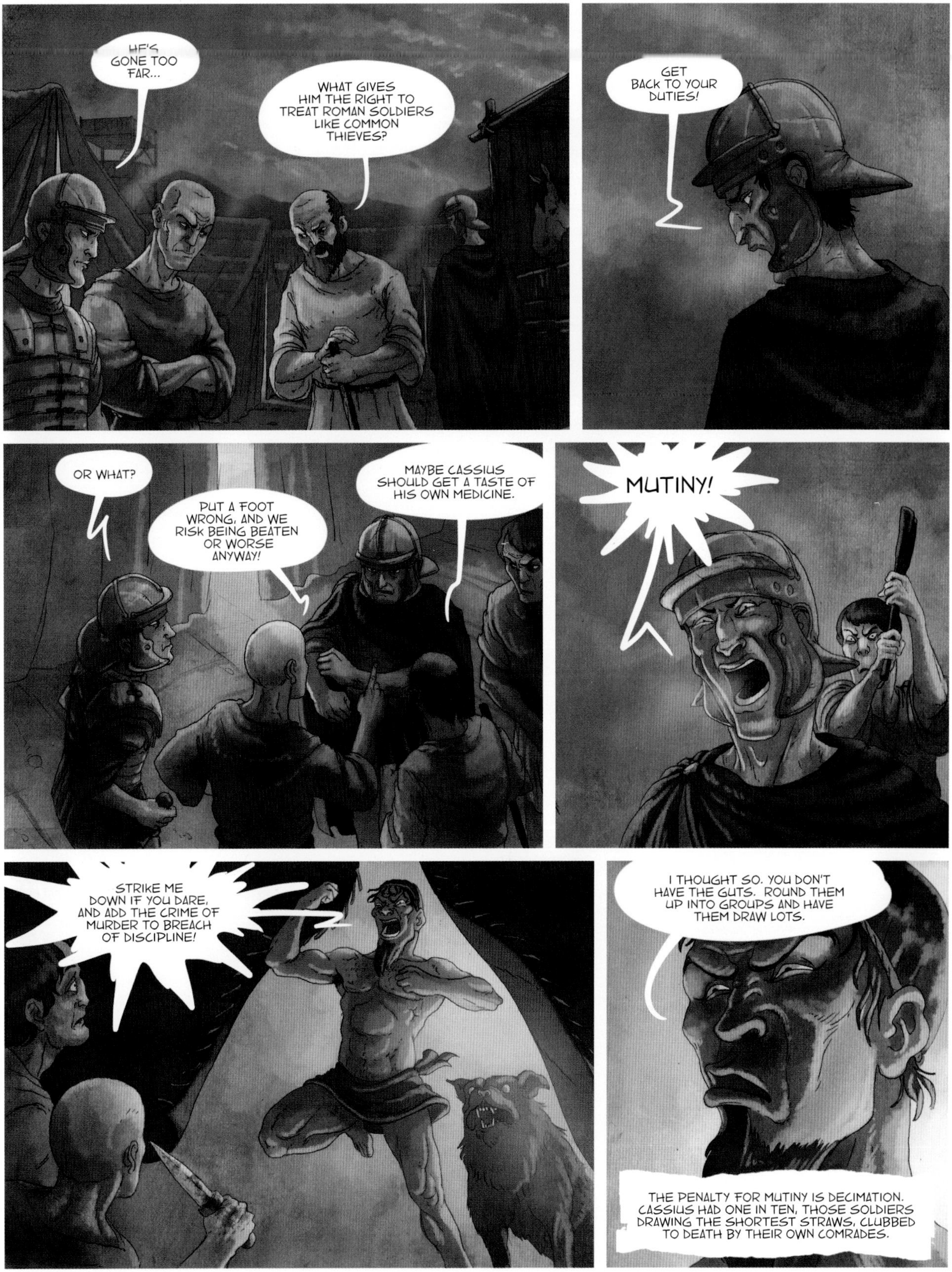
HE'S GONE TOO FAR...
WHAT GIVES HIM THE RIGHT TO TREAT ROMAN SOLDIERS LIKE COMMON THIEVES?
GET BACK TO YOUR DUTIES!
OR WHAT?
PUT A FOOT WRONG, AND WE RISK BEING BEATEN OR WORSE ANYWAY!
MAYBE CASSIUS SHOULD GET A TASTE OF HIS OWN MEDICINE.
MUTINY!
STRIKE ME DOWN IF YOU DARE, AND ADD THE CRIME OF MURDER TO BREACH OF DISCIPLINE!
I THOUGHT SO. YOU DON'T HAVE THE GUTS. ROUND THEM UP INTO GROUPS AND HAVE THEM DRAW LOTS.
THE PENALTY FOR MUTINY IS DECIMATION. CASSIUS HAD ONE IN TEN, THOSE SOLDIERS DRAWING THE SHORTEST STRAWS, CLUBBED TO DEATH BY THEIR OWN COMRADES.

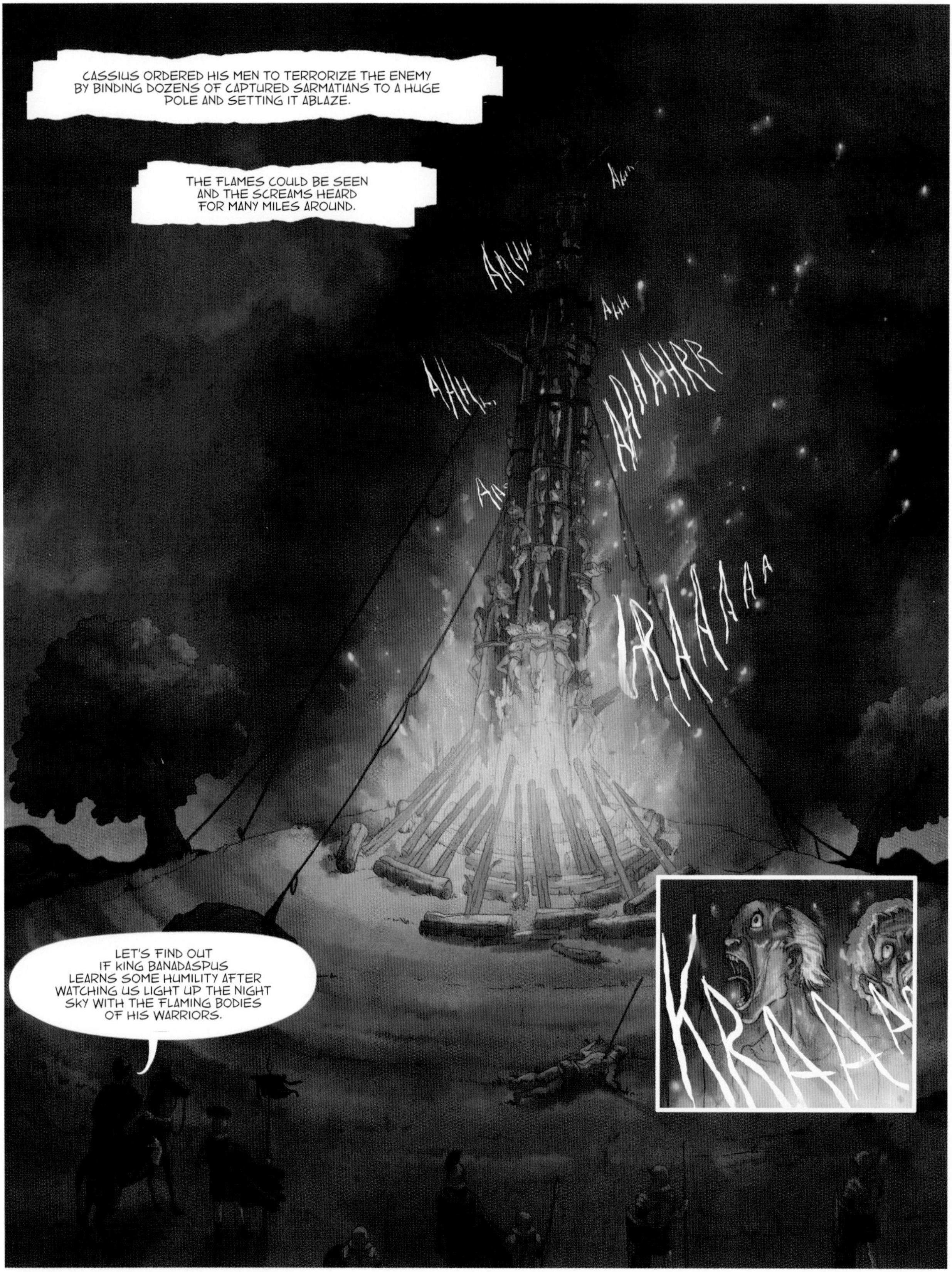
CASSIUS ORDERED HIS MEN TO TERRORIZE THE ENEMY BY BINDING DOZENS OF CAPTURED SARMATIANS TO A HUGE POLE AND SETTING IT ABLAZE.
THE FLAMES COULD BE SEEN AND THE SCREAMS HEARD FOR MANY MILES AROUND.
AAHH
AHH
AHH...
AAAAAHRR
AAAAAAA
LET'S FIND OUT IF KING BANADASPUS LEARNS SOME HUMILITY AFTER WATCHING US LIGHT UP THE NIGHT SKY WITH THE FLAMING BODIES OF HIS WARRIORS.
KRAAA

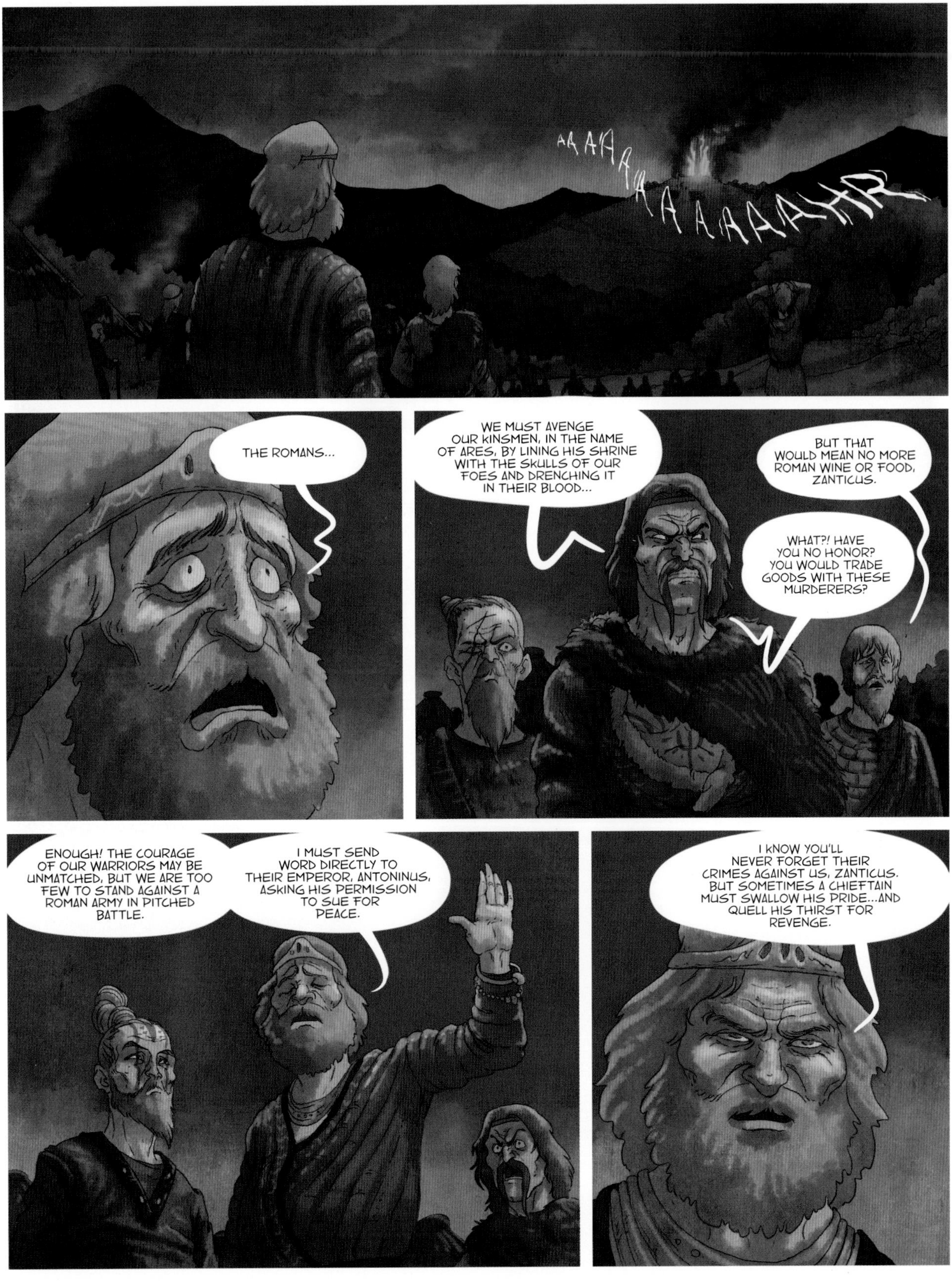

AAAAAAAAAAAAAAAHR
THE ROMANS...
WE MUST AVENGE OUR KINSMEN, IN THE NAME OF ARES, BY LINING HIS SHRINE WITH THE SKULLS OF OUR FOES AND DRENCHING IT IN THEIR BLOOD...
BUT THAT WOULD MEAN NO MORE ROMAN WINE OR FOOD, ZANTICUS.
WHAT?! HAVE YOU NO HONOR? YOU WOULD TRADE GOODS WITH THESE MURDERERS?
ENOUGH! THE COURAGE OF OUR WARRIORS MAY BE UNMATCHED, BUT WE ARE TOO FEW TO STAND AGAINST A ROMAN ARMY IN PITCHED BATTLE.
I MUST SEND WORD DIRECTLY TO THEIR EMPEROR, ANTONINUS, ASKING HIS PERMISSION TO SUE FOR PEACE.
I KNOW YOU'LL NEVER FORGET THEIR CRIMES AGAINST US, ZANTICUS. BUT SOMETIMES A CHIEFTAIN MUST SWALLOW HIS PRIDE...AND QUELL HIS THIRST FOR REVENGE.

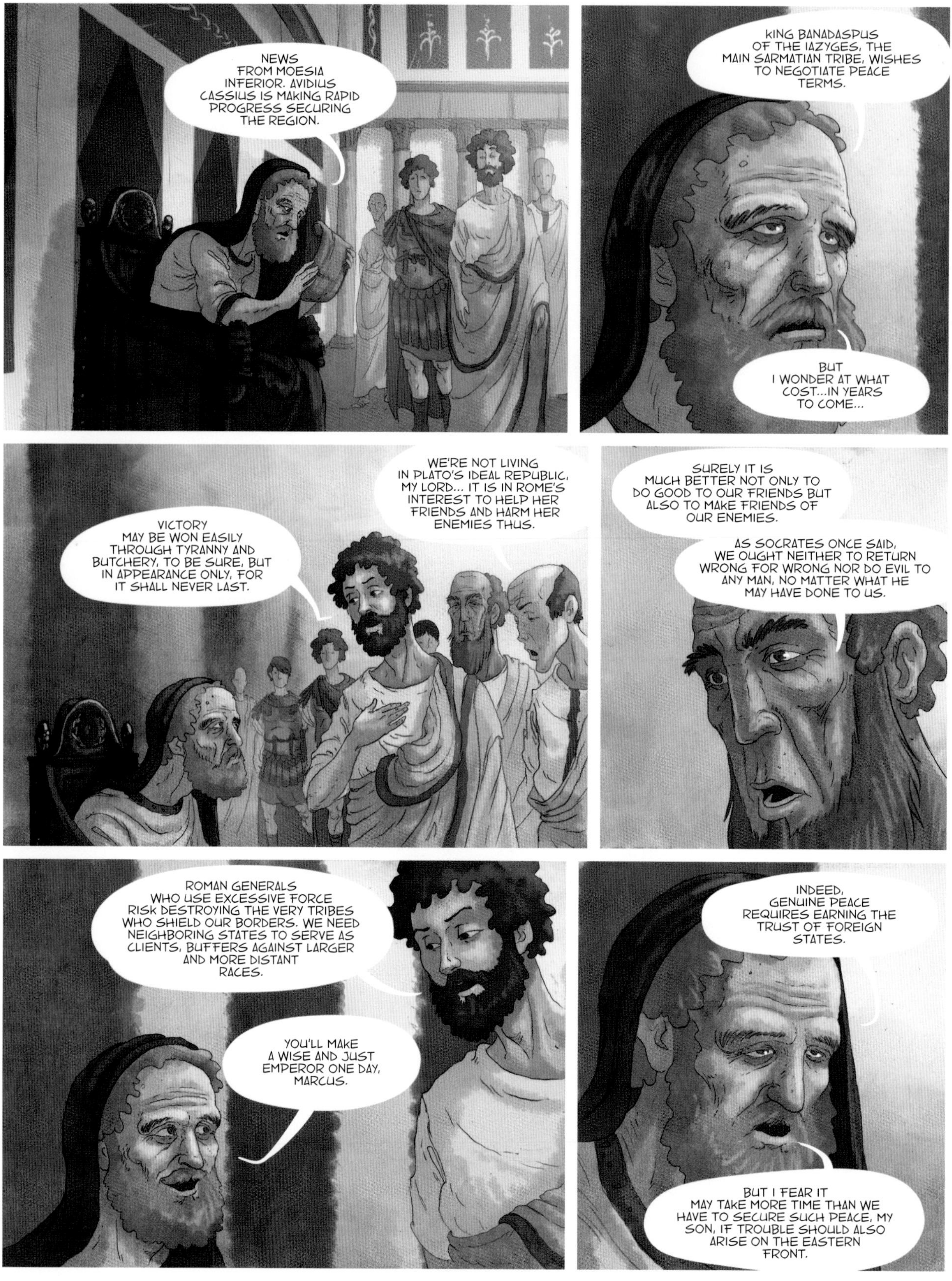
NEWS FROM MOESIA INFERIOR. AVIDIUS CASSIUS IS MAKING RAPID PROGRESS SECURING THE REGION.
KING BANADASPUS OF THE IAZYGES, THE MAIN SARMATIAN TRIBE, WISHES TO NEGOTIATE PEACE TERMS.
BUT I WONDER AT WHAT COST...IN YEARS TO COME...
VICTORY MAY BE WON EASILY THROUGH TYRANNY AND BUTCHERY, TO BE SURE, BUT IN APPEARANCE ONLY, FOR IT SHALL NEVER LAST.
WE'RE NOT LIVING IN PLATO'S IDEAL REPUBLIC, MY LORD... IT IS IN ROME'S INTEREST TO HELP HER FRIENDS AND HARM HER ENEMIES THUS.
SURELY IT IS MUCH BETTER NOT ONLY TO DO GOOD TO OUR FRIENDS BUT ALSO TO MAKE FRIENDS OF OUR ENEMIES.
AS SOCRATES ONCE SAID, WE OUGHT NEITHER TO RETURN WRONG FOR WRONG NOR DO EVIL TO ANY MAN, NO MATTER WHAT HE MAY HAVE DONE TO US.
ROMAN GENERALS WHO USE EXCESSIVE FORCE RISK DESTROYING THE VERY TRIBES WHO SHIELD OUR BORDERS. WE NEED NEIGHBORING STATES TO SERVE AS CLIENTS, BUFFERS AGAINST LARGER AND MORE DISTANT RACES.
YOU'LL MAKE A WISE AND JUST EMPEROR ONE DAY, MARCUS.
INDEED, GENUINE PEACE REQUIRES EARNING THE TRUST OF FOREIGN STATES.
BUT I FEAR IT MAY TAKE MORE TIME THAN WE HAVE TO SECURE SUCH PEACE, MY SON, IF TROUBLE SHOULD ALSO ARISE ON THE EASTERN FRONT.

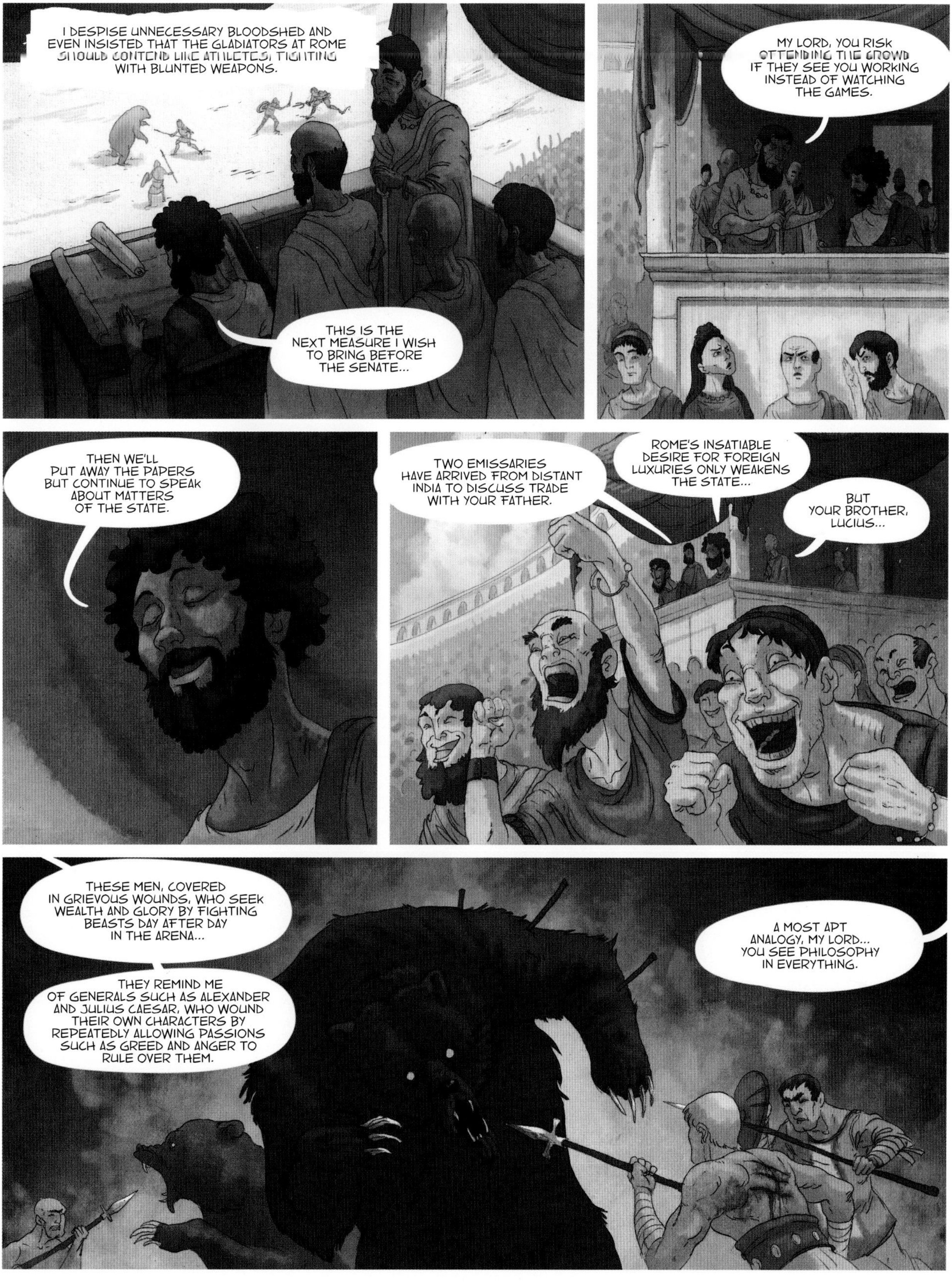
I DESPISE UNNECESSARY BLOODSHED AND EVEN INSISTED THAT THE GLADIATORS AT ROME SHOULD CONTEND LIKE ATHLETES, FIGHTING WITH BLUNTED WEAPONS.
THIS IS THE NEXT MEASURE I WISH TO BRING BEFORE THE SENATE...
MY LORD, YOU RISK OFFENDING THE CROWD IF THEY SEE YOU WORKING INSTEAD OF WATCHING THE GAMES.
THEN WE'LL PUT AWAY THE PAPERS BUT CONTINUE TO SPEAK ABOUT MATTERS OF THE STATE.
TWO EMISSARIES HAVE ARRIVED FROM DISTANT INDIA TO DISCUSS TRADE WITH YOUR FATHER.
ROME'S INSATIABLE DESIRE FOR FOREIGN LUXURIES ONLY WEAKENS THE STATE...
BUT YOUR BROTHER, LUCIUS...
THESE MEN, COVERED IN GRIEVOUS WOUNDS, WHO SEEK WEALTH AND GLORY BY FIGHTING BEASTS DAY AFTER DAY IN THE ARENA...
THEY REMIND ME OF GENERALS SUCH AS ALEXANDER AND JULIUS CAESAR, WHO WOUND THEIR OWN CHARACTERS BY REPEATEDLY ALLOWING PASSIONS SUCH AS GREED AND ANGER TO RULE OVER THEM.
A MOST APT ANALOGY, MY LORD... YOU SEE PHILOSOPHY IN EVERYTHING.

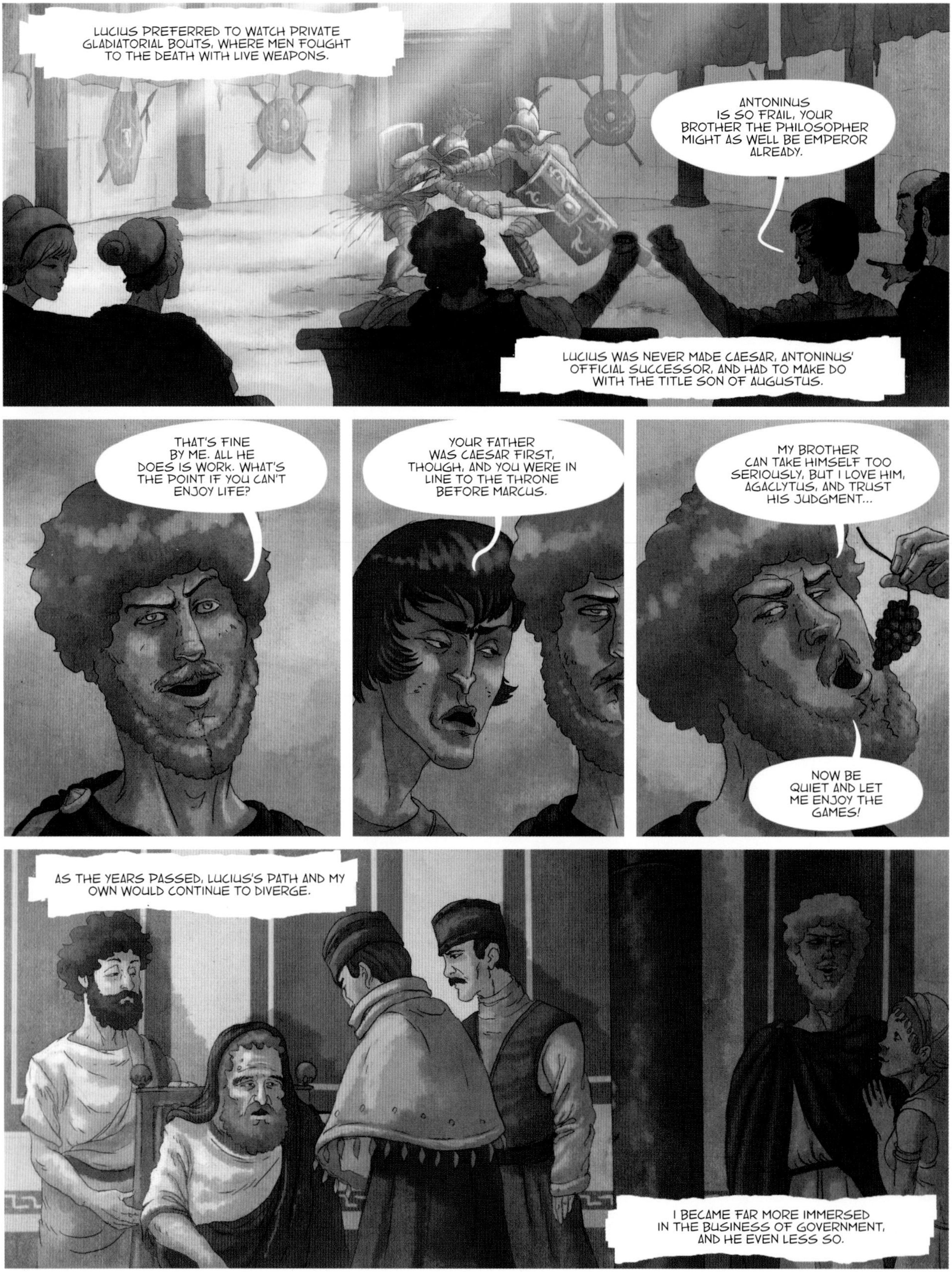
LUCIUS PREFERRED TO WATCH PRIVATE GLADIATORIAL BOUTS, WHERE MEN FOUGHT TO THE DEATH WITH LIVE WEAPONS.
ANTONINUS IS SO FRAIL, YOUR BROTHER THE PHILOSOPHER MIGHT AS WELL BE EMPEROR ALREADY.
LUCIUS WAS NEVER MADE CAESAR, ANTONINUS' OFFICIAL SUCCESSOR, AND HAD TO MAKE DO WITH THE TITLE SON OF AUGUSTUS.
THAT'S FINE BY ME. ALL HE DOES IS WORK. WHAT'S THE POINT IF YOU CAN'T ENJOY LIFE?
YOUR FATHER WAS CAESAR FIRST, THOUGH, AND YOU WERE IN LINE TO THE THRONE BEFORE MARCUS.
MY BROTHER CAN TAKE HIMSELF TOO SERIOUSLY, BUT I LOVE HIM, AGACLYTUS, AND TRUST HIS JUDGMENT...
NOW BE QUIET AND LET ME ENJOY THE GAMES!
AS THE YEARS PASSED, LUCIUS'S PATH AND MY OWN WOULD CONTINUE TO DIVERGE.
I BECAME FAR MORE IMMERSED IN THE BUSINESS OF GOVERNMENT, AND HE EVEN LESS SO.

ANTONINUS HAD A LONG LIFE.
HE WAS SEVENTY-FOUR.

NOT SINCE THE REIGN OF KING NUMA,
THEY SAY, HAD ROME ENJOYED SUCH
A PERIOD OF PEACE AND STABILITY.

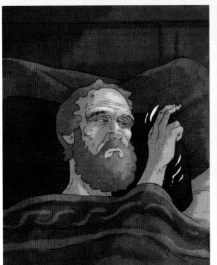

AEQUANIMITAS.

THE SENATE IMMEDIATELY ASKED
ME TO SUCCEED MY ADOPTIVE
FATHER AS EMPEROR...

FOLLOW HIS
EXAMPLE, THEN,
SO THAT YOU MAY HAVE
AS CLEAR A CONSCIENCE AS
HE WHEN YOUR FINAL
HOUR ARRIVES.

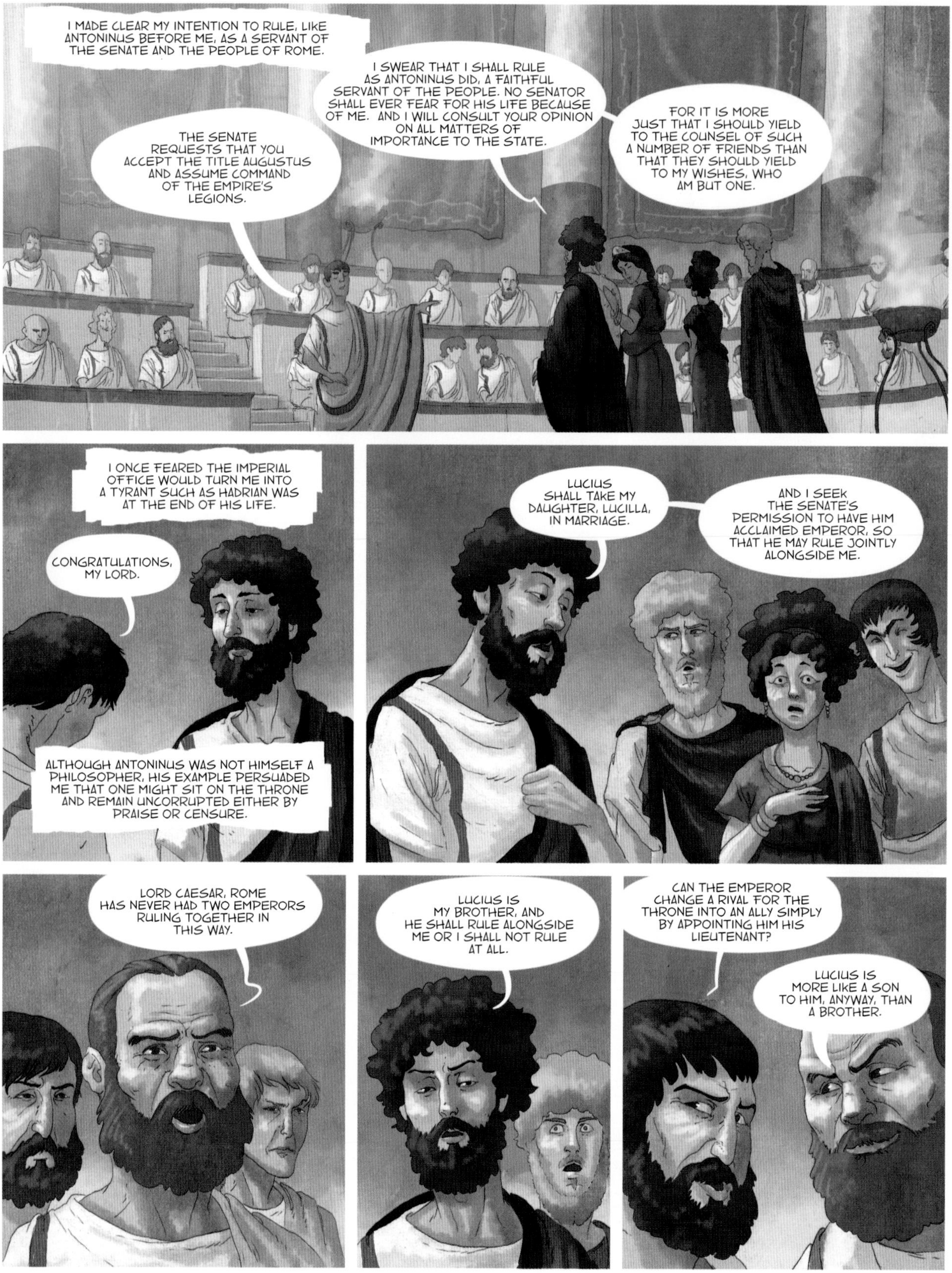
I MADE CLEAR MY INTENTION TO RULE, LIKE ANTONINUS BEFORE ME, AS A SERVANT OF THE SENATE AND THE PEOPLE OF ROME.
THE SENATE REQUESTS THAT YOU ACCEPT THE TITLE AUGUSTUS AND ASSUME COMMAND OF THE EMPIRE'S LEGIONS.
I SWEAR THAT I SHALL RULE AS ANTONINUS DID, A FAITHFUL SERVANT OF THE PEOPLE. NO SENATOR SHALL EVER FEAR FOR HIS LIFE BECAUSE OF ME. AND I WILL CONSULT YOUR OPINION ON ALL MATTERS OF IMPORTANCE TO THE STATE.
FOR IT IS MORE JUST THAT I SHOULD YIELD TO THE COUNSEL OF SUCH A NUMBER OF FRIENDS THAN THAT THEY SHOULD YIELD TO MY WISHES, WHO AM BUT ONE.
I ONCE FEARED THE IMPERIAL OFFICE WOULD TURN ME INTO A TYRANT SUCH AS HADRIAN WAS AT THE END OF HIS LIFE.
CONGRATULATIONS, MY LORD.
ALTHOUGH ANTONINUS WAS NOT HIMSELF A PHILOSOPHER, HIS EXAMPLE PERSUADED ME THAT ONE MIGHT SIT ON THE THRONE AND REMAIN UNCORRUPTED EITHER BY PRAISE OR CENSURE.
LUCIUS SHALL TAKE MY DAUGHTER, LUCILLA, IN MARRIAGE.
AND I SEEK THE SENATE'S PERMISSION TO HAVE HIM ACCLAIMED EMPEROR, SO THAT HE MAY RULE JOINTLY ALONGSIDE ME.
LORD CAESAR, ROME HAS NEVER HAD TWO EMPERORS RULING TOGETHER IN THIS WAY.
LUCIUS IS MY BROTHER, AND HE SHALL RULE ALONGSIDE ME OR I SHALL NOT RULE AT ALL.
CAN THE EMPEROR CHANGE A RIVAL FOR THE THRONE INTO AN ALLY SIMPLY BY APPOINTING HIM HIS LIEUTENANT?
LUCIUS IS MORE LIKE A SON TO HIM, ANYWAY, THAN A BROTHER.

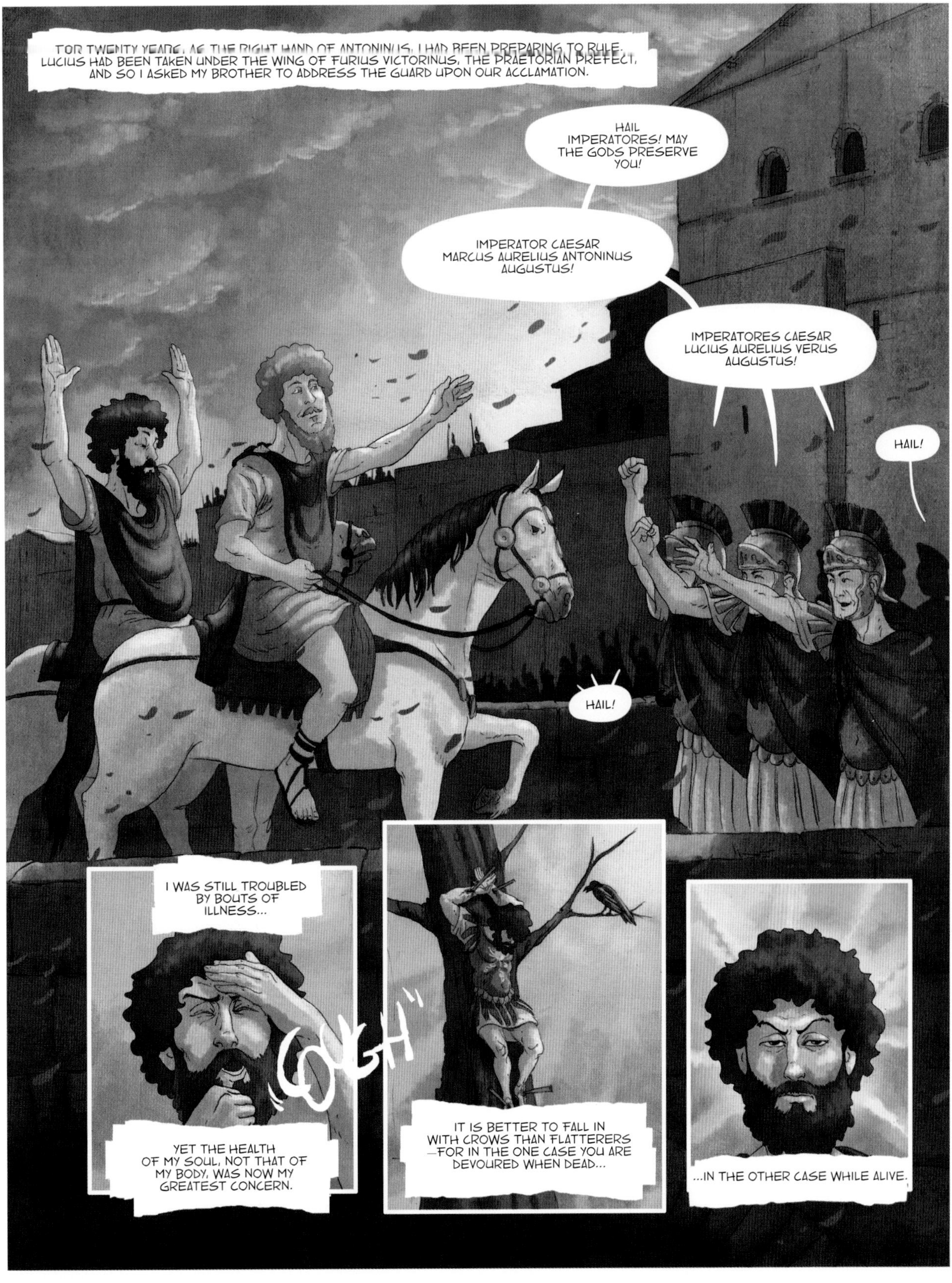
FOR TWENTY YEARS, AS THE RIGHT HAND OF ANTONINUS, I HAD BEEN PREPARING TO RULE. LUCIUS HAD BEEN TAKEN UNDER THE WING OF FURIUS VICTORINUS, THE PRAETORIAN PREFECT, AND SO I ASKED MY BROTHER TO ADDRESS THE GUARD UPON OUR ACCLAMATION.
HAIL IMPERATORES! MAY THE GODS PRESERVE YOU!
IMPERATOR CAESAR MARCUS AURELIUS ANTONINUS AUGUSTUS!
IMPERATORES CAESAR LUCIUS AURELIUS VERUS AUGUSTUS!
HAIL!
HAIL!
I WAS STILL TROUBLED BY BOUTS OF ILLNESS...
COUGH
YET THE HEALTH OF MY SOUL, NOT THAT OF MY BODY, WAS NOW MY GREATEST CONCERN.
IT IS BETTER TO FALL IN WITH CROWS THAN FLATTERERS —FOR IN THE ONE CASE YOU ARE DEVOURED WHEN DEAD...
...IN THE OTHER CASE WHILE ALIVE.

THE
PARTHIAN
WAR

*Asia and Europe, mere corners of the universe…
and the lion's gaping jaws, and every harmful
thing, mere by-products of the grand and
beautiful whole which you venerate.*

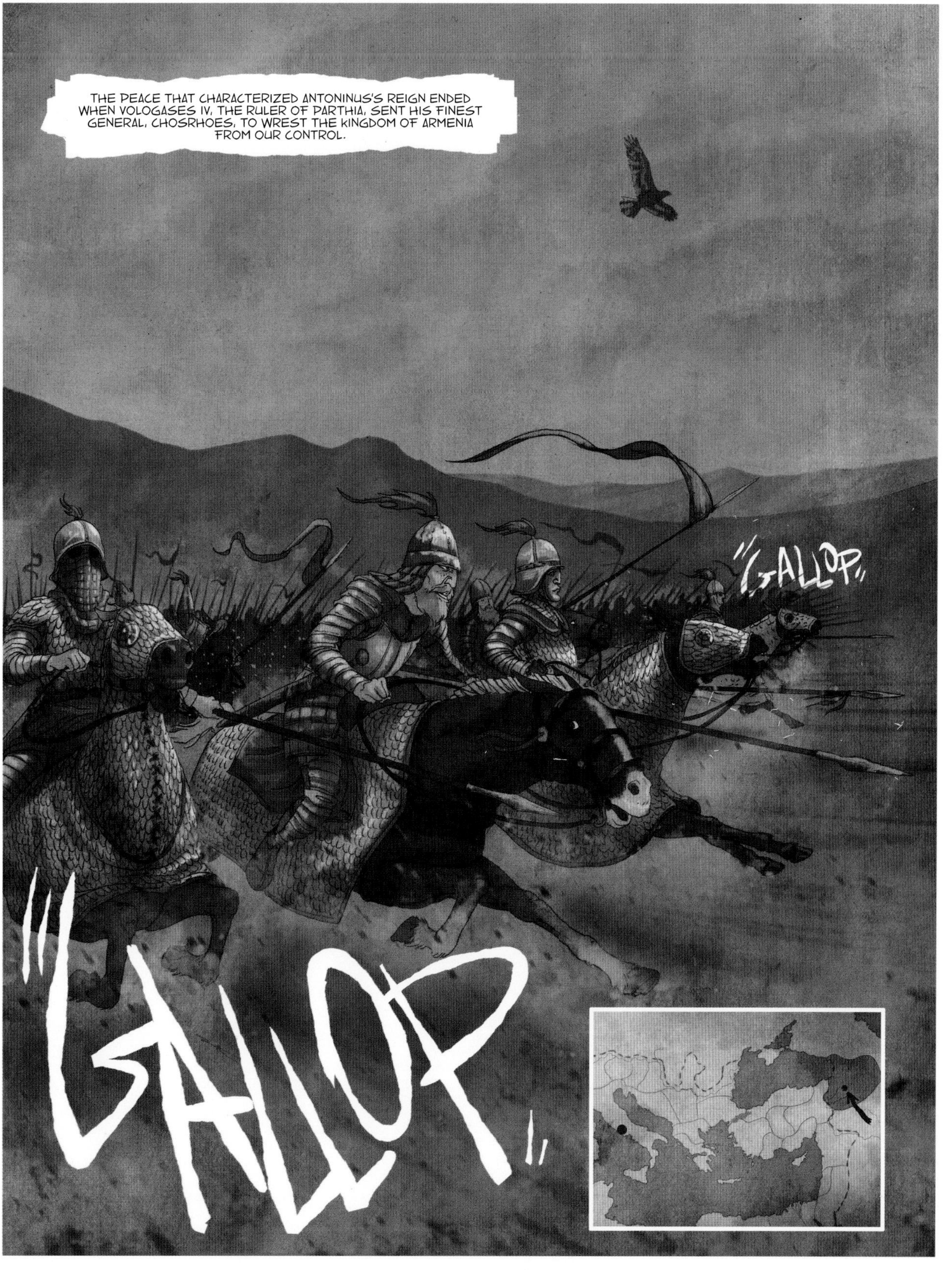
THE PEACE THAT CHARACTERIZED ANTONINUS'S REIGN ENDED WHEN VOLOGASES IV, THE RULER OF PARTHIA, SENT HIS FINEST GENERAL, CHOSRHOES, TO WREST THE KINGDOM OF ARMENIA FROM OUR CONTROL.
"GALLOP"
"GALLOP"

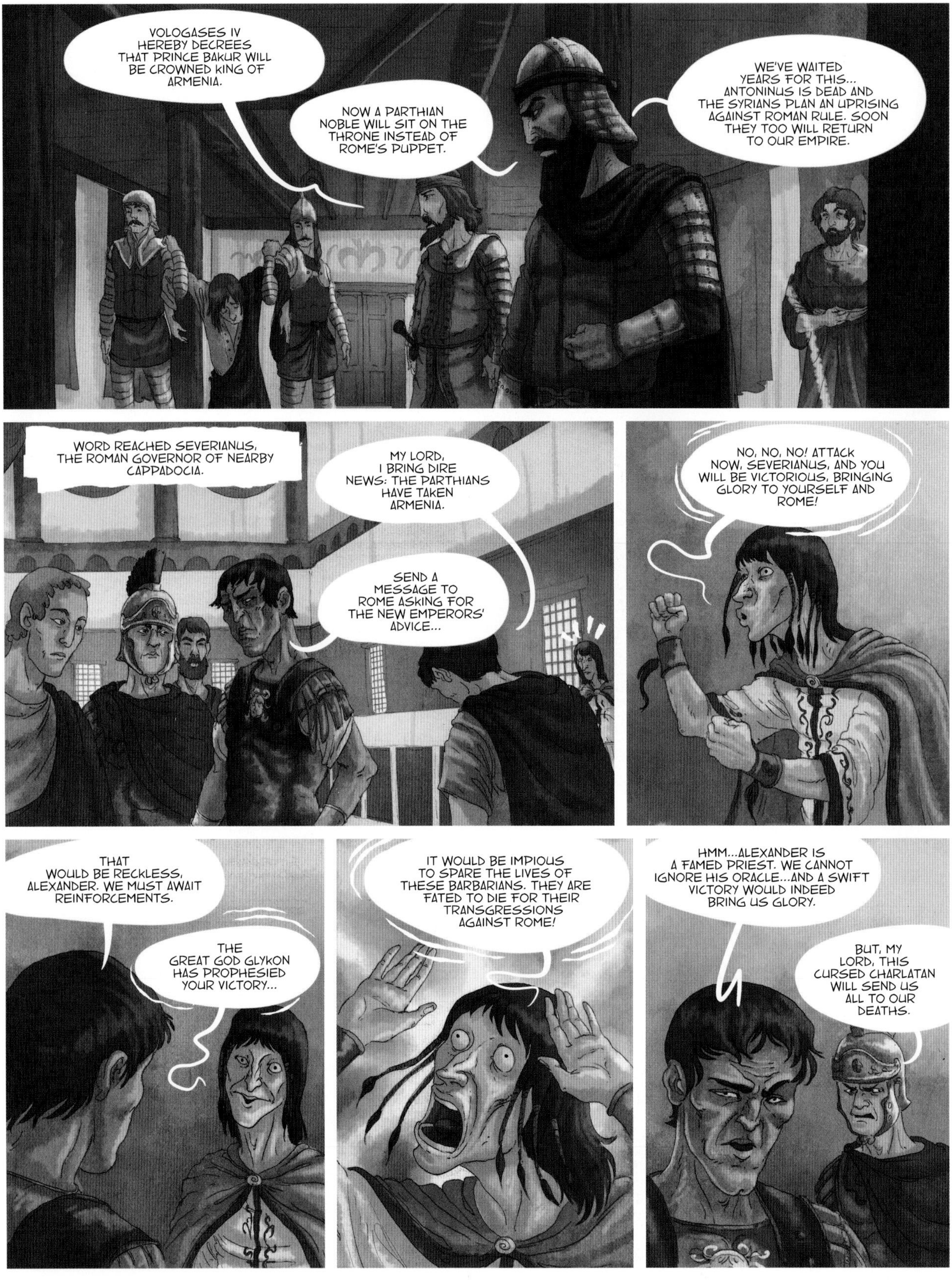
VOLOGASES IV HEREBY DECREES THAT PRINCE BAKUR WILL BE CROWNED KING OF ARMENIA.
NOW A PARTHIAN NOBLE WILL SIT ON THE THRONE INSTEAD OF ROME'S PUPPET.
WE'VE WAITED YEARS FOR THIS... ANTONINUS IS DEAD AND THE SYRIANS PLAN AN UPRISING AGAINST ROMAN RULE. SOON THEY TOO WILL RETURN TO OUR EMPIRE.
WORD REACHED SEVERIANUS, THE ROMAN GOVERNOR OF NEARBY CAPPADOCIA.
MY LORD, I BRING DIRE NEWS: THE PARTHIANS HAVE TAKEN ARMENIA.
SEND A MESSAGE TO ROME ASKING FOR THE NEW EMPERORS' ADVICE...
NO, NO, NO! ATTACK NOW, SEVERIANUS, AND YOU WILL BE VICTORIOUS, BRINGING GLORY TO YOURSELF AND ROME!
THAT WOULD BE RECKLESS, ALEXANDER. WE MUST AWAIT REINFORCEMENTS.
THE GREAT GOD GLYKON HAS PROPHESIED YOUR VICTORY...
IT WOULD BE IMPIOUS TO SPARE THE LIVES OF THESE BARBARIANS. THEY ARE FATED TO DIE FOR THEIR TRANSGRESSIONS AGAINST ROME!
HMM...ALEXANDER IS A FAMED PRIEST. WE CANNOT IGNORE HIS ORACLE...AND A SWIFT VICTORY WOULD INDEED BRING US GLORY.
BUT, MY LORD, THIS CURSED CHARLATAN WILL SEND US ALL TO OUR DEATHS.

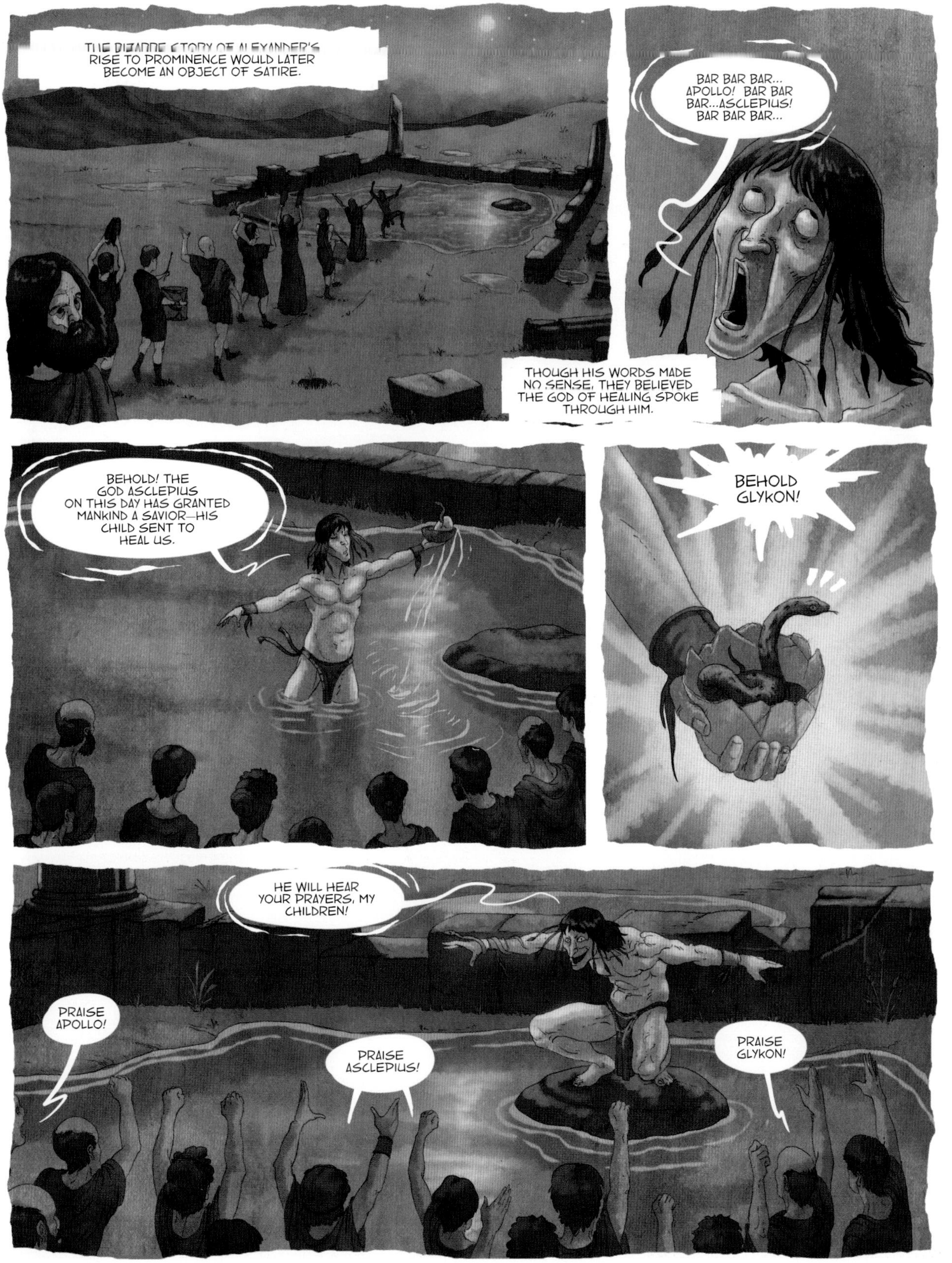
THE BIZARRE STORY OF ALEXANDER'S RISE TO PROMINENCE WOULD LATER BECOME AN OBJECT OF SATIRE.
BAR BAR BAR... APOLLO! BAR BAR BAR...ASCLEPIUS! BAR BAR BAR...
THOUGH HIS WORDS MADE NO SENSE, THEY BELIEVED THE GOD OF HEALING SPOKE THROUGH HIM.
BEHOLD! THE GOD ASCLEPIUS ON THIS DAY HAS GRANTED MANKIND A SAVIOR—HIS CHILD SENT TO HEAL US.
BEHOLD GLYKON!
HE WILL HEAR YOUR PRAYERS, MY CHILDREN!
PRAISE APOLLO!
PRAISE ASCLEPIUS!
PRAISE GLYKON!

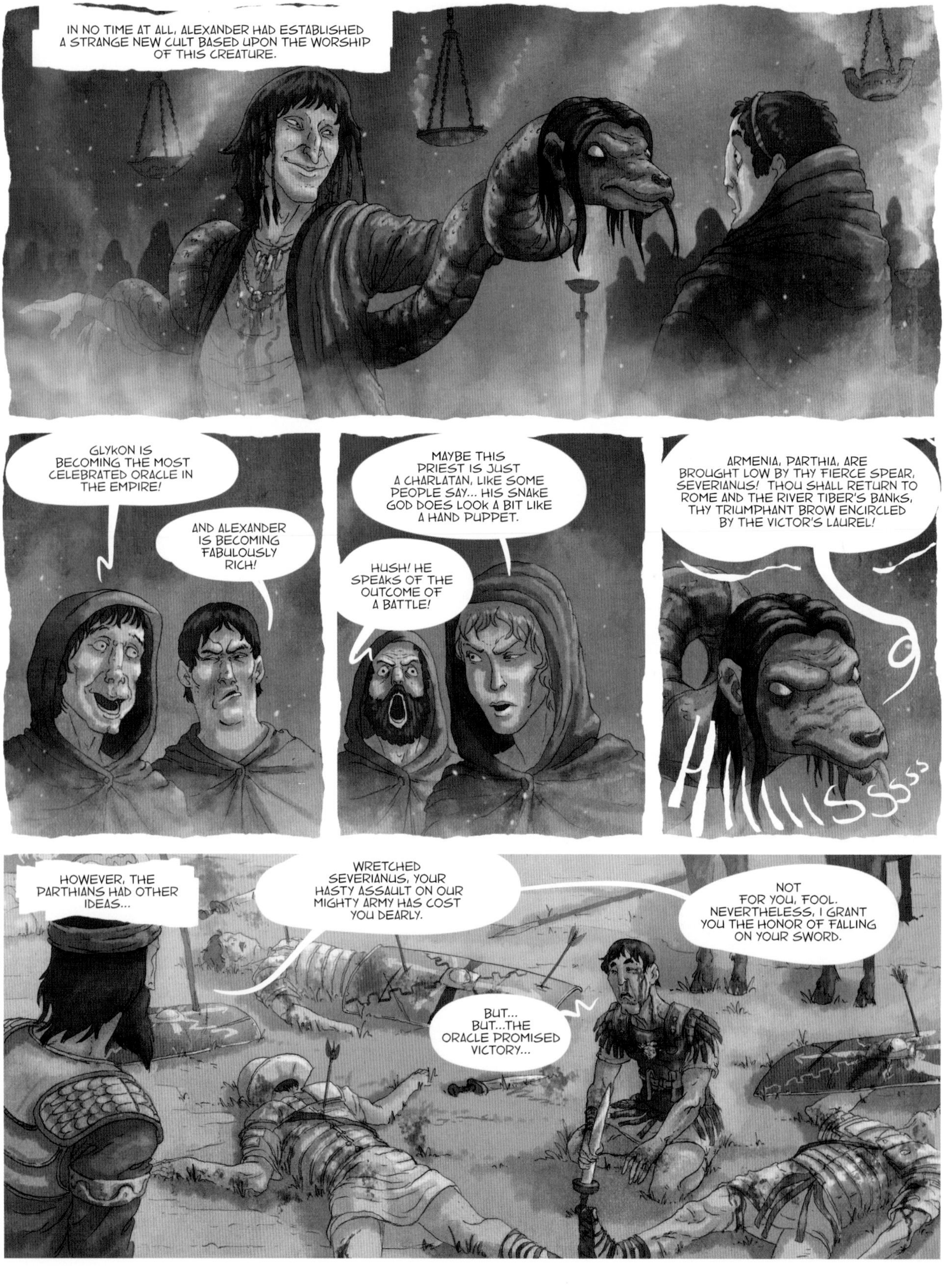
IN NO TIME AT ALL, ALEXANDER HAD ESTABLISHED A STRANGE NEW CULT BASED UPON THE WORSHIP OF THIS CREATURE.
GLYKON IS BECOMING THE MOST CELEBRATED ORACLE IN THE EMPIRE!
AND ALEXANDER IS BECOMING FABULOUSLY RICH!
MAYBE THIS PRIEST IS JUST A CHARLATAN, LIKE SOME PEOPLE SAY... HIS SNAKE GOD DOES LOOK A BIT LIKE A HAND PUPPET.
HUSH! HE SPEAKS OF THE OUTCOME OF A BATTLE!
ARMENIA, PARTHIA, ARE BROUGHT LOW BY THY FIERCE SPEAR, SEVERIANUS! THOU SHALL RETURN TO ROME AND THE RIVER TIBER'S BANKS, THY TRIUMPHANT BROW ENCIRCLED BY THE VICTOR'S LAUREL!
HISSSSS
HOWEVER, THE PARTHIANS HAD OTHER IDEAS...
WRETCHED SEVERIANUS, YOUR HASTY ASSAULT ON OUR MIGHTY ARMY HAS COST YOU DEARLY.
BUT... BUT...THE ORACLE PROMISED VICTORY...
NOT FOR YOU, FOOL. NEVERTHELESS, I GRANT YOU THE HONOR OF FALLING ON YOUR SWORD.

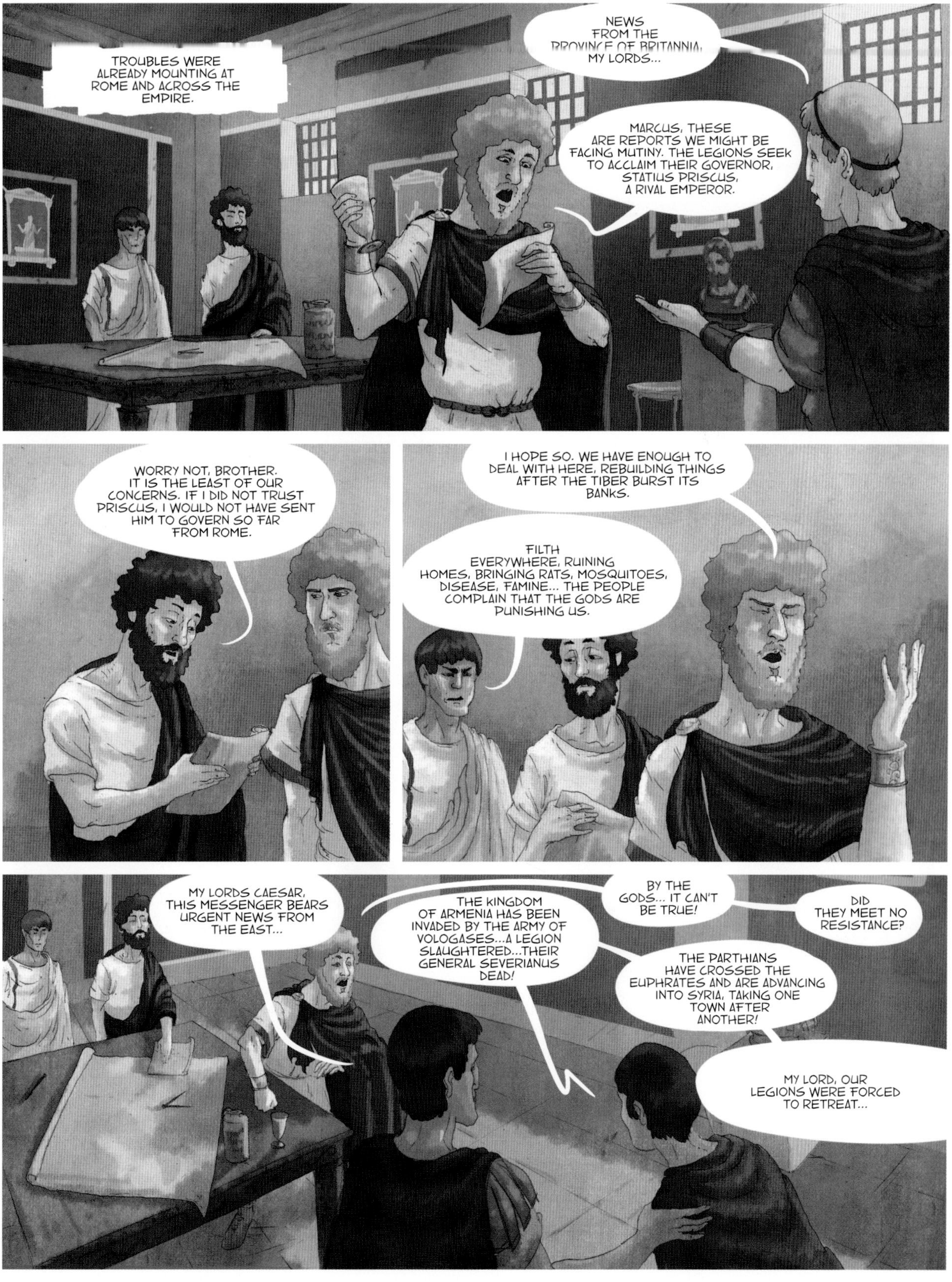
TROUBLES WERE ALREADY MOUNTING AT ROME AND ACROSS THE EMPIRE.
NEWS FROM THE PROVINCE OF BRITANNIA, MY LORDS...
MARCUS, THESE ARE REPORTS WE MIGHT BE FACING MUTINY. THE LEGIONS SEEK TO ACCLAIM THEIR GOVERNOR, STATIUS PRISCUS, A RIVAL EMPEROR.
WORRY NOT, BROTHER. IT IS THE LEAST OF OUR CONCERNS. IF I DID NOT TRUST PRISCUS, I WOULD NOT HAVE SENT HIM TO GOVERN SO FAR FROM ROME.
I HOPE SO. WE HAVE ENOUGH TO DEAL WITH HERE, REBUILDING THINGS AFTER THE TIBER BURST ITS BANKS.
FILTH EVERYWHERE, RUINING HOMES, BRINGING RATS, MOSQUITOES, DISEASE, FAMINE... THE PEOPLE COMPLAIN THAT THE GODS ARE PUNISHING US.
MY LORDS CAESAR, THIS MESSENGER BEARS URGENT NEWS FROM THE EAST...
THE KINGDOM OF ARMENIA HAS BEEN INVADED BY THE ARMY OF VOLOGASES...A LEGION SLAUGHTERED...THEIR GENERAL SEVERIANUS DEAD!
BY THE GODS... IT CAN'T BE TRUE!
DID THEY MEET NO RESISTANCE?
THE PARTHIANS HAVE CROSSED THE EUPHRATES AND ARE ADVANCING INTO SYRIA, TAKING ONE TOWN AFTER ANOTHER!
MY LORD, OUR LEGIONS WERE FORCED TO RETREAT...

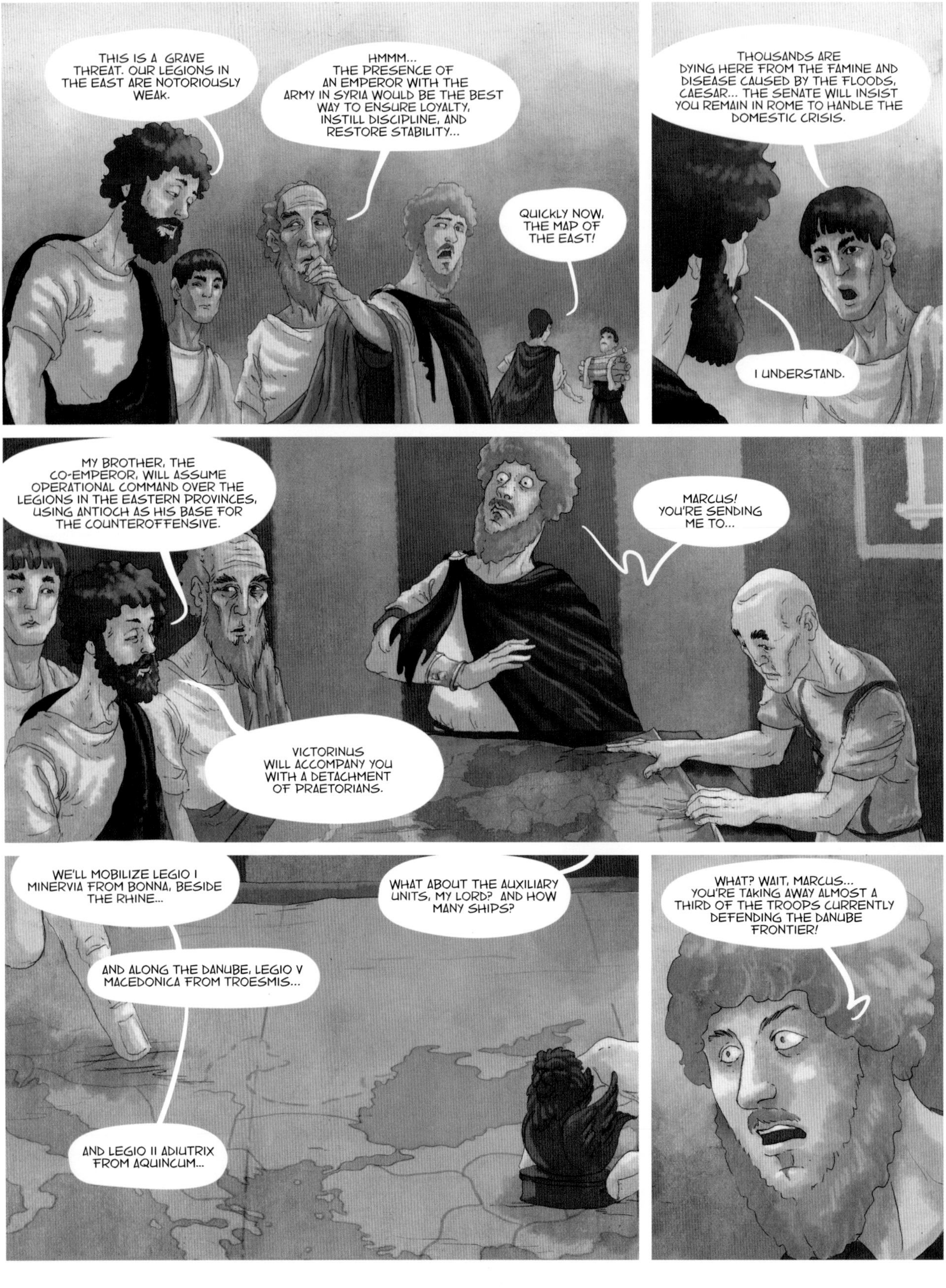
THIS IS A GRAVE THREAT. OUR LEGIONS IN THE EAST ARE NOTORIOUSLY WEAK.
HMMM... THE PRESENCE OF AN EMPEROR WITH THE ARMY IN SYRIA WOULD BE THE BEST WAY TO ENSURE LOYALTY, INSTILL DISCIPLINE, AND RESTORE STABILITY...
QUICKLY NOW, THE MAP OF THE EAST!
THOUSANDS ARE DYING HERE FROM THE FAMINE AND DISEASE CAUSED BY THE FLOODS, CAESAR... THE SENATE WILL INSIST YOU REMAIN IN ROME TO HANDLE THE DOMESTIC CRISIS.
I UNDERSTAND.
MY BROTHER, THE CO-EMPEROR, WILL ASSUME OPERATIONAL COMMAND OVER THE LEGIONS IN THE EASTERN PROVINCES, USING ANTIOCH AS HIS BASE FOR THE COUNTEROFFENSIVE.
MARCUS! YOU'RE SENDING ME TO...
VICTORINUS WILL ACCOMPANY YOU WITH A DETACHMENT OF PRAETORIANS.
WE'LL MOBILIZE LEGIO I MINERVIA FROM BONNA, BESIDE THE RHINE...
WHAT ABOUT THE AUXILIARY UNITS, MY LORD? AND HOW MANY SHIPS?
AND ALONG THE DANUBE, LEGIO V MACEDONICA FROM TROESMIS...
AND LEGIO II ADIUTRIX FROM AQUINCUM...
WHAT? WAIT, MARCUS... YOU'RE TAKING AWAY ALMOST A THIRD OF THE TROOPS CURRENTLY DEFENDING THE DANUBE FRONTIER!

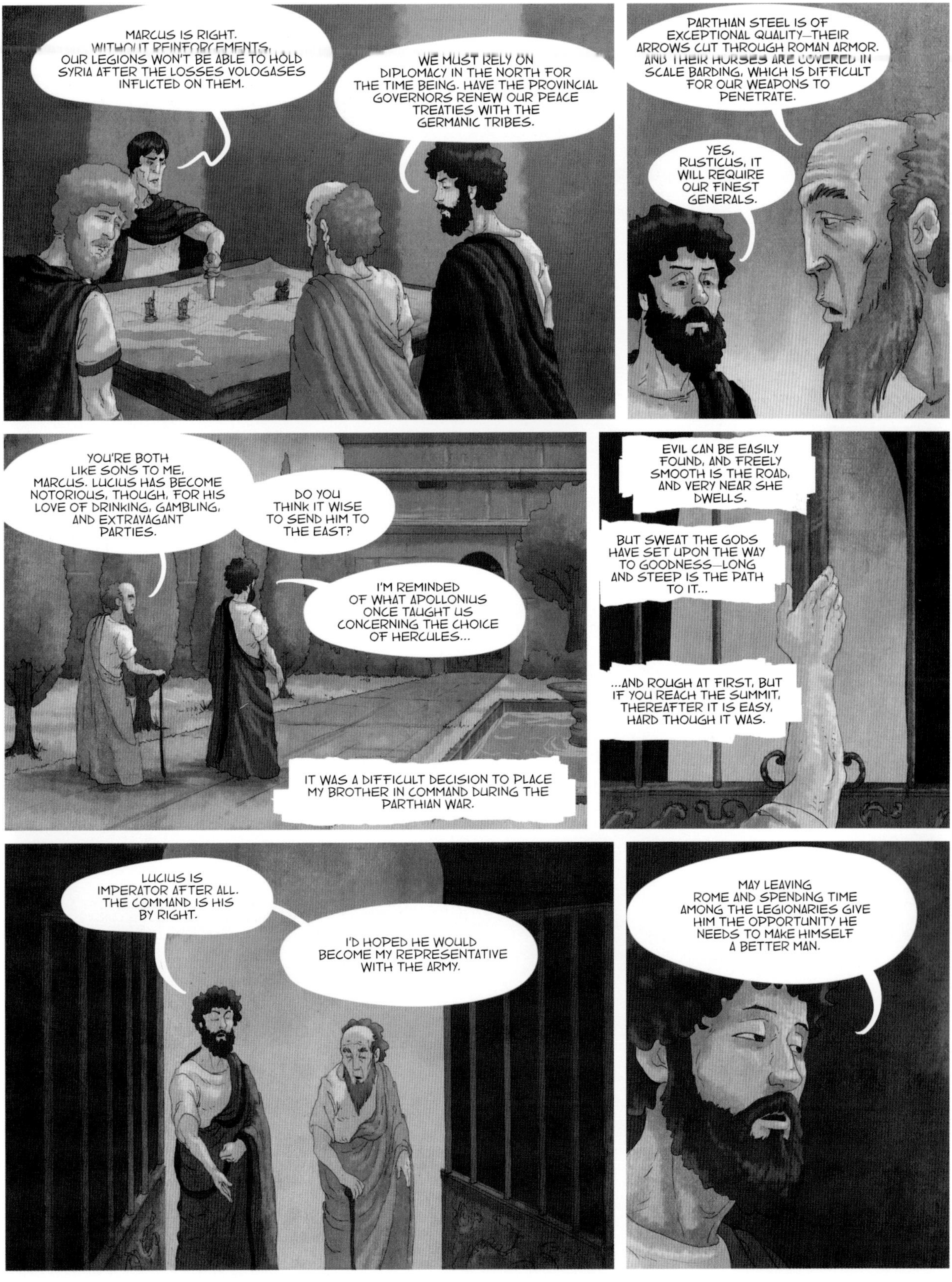
MARCUS IS RIGHT. WITHOUT REINFORCEMENTS, OUR LEGIONS WON'T BE ABLE TO HOLD SYRIA AFTER THE LOSSES VOLOGASES INFLICTED ON THEM.
WE MUST RELY ON DIPLOMACY IN THE NORTH FOR THE TIME BEING. HAVE THE PROVINCIAL GOVERNORS RENEW OUR PEACE TREATIES WITH THE GERMANIC TRIBES.
PARTHIAN STEEL IS OF EXCEPTIONAL QUALITY—THEIR ARROWS CUT THROUGH ROMAN ARMOR. AND THEIR HORSES ARE COVERED IN SCALE BARDING, WHICH IS DIFFICULT FOR OUR WEAPONS TO PENETRATE.
YES, RUSTICUS, IT WILL REQUIRE OUR FINEST GENERALS.
YOU'RE BOTH LIKE SONS TO ME, MARCUS. LUCIUS HAS BECOME NOTORIOUS, THOUGH, FOR HIS LOVE OF DRINKING, GAMBLING, AND EXTRAVAGANT PARTIES.
DO YOU THINK IT WISE TO SEND HIM TO THE EAST?
I'M REMINDED OF WHAT APOLLONIUS ONCE TAUGHT US CONCERNING THE CHOICE OF HERCULES...
IT WAS A DIFFICULT DECISION TO PLACE MY BROTHER IN COMMAND DURING THE PARTHIAN WAR.
EVIL CAN BE EASILY FOUND, AND FREELY SMOOTH IS THE ROAD, AND VERY NEAR SHE DWELLS.
BUT SWEAT THE GODS HAVE SET UPON THE WAY TO GOODNESS—LONG AND STEEP IS THE PATH TO IT...
...AND ROUGH AT FIRST, BUT IF YOU REACH THE SUMMIT, THEREAFTER IT IS EASY, HARD THOUGH IT WAS.
LUCIUS IS IMPERATOR AFTER ALL. THE COMMAND IS HIS BY RIGHT.
I'D HOPED HE WOULD BECOME MY REPRESENTATIVE WITH THE ARMY.
MAY LEAVING ROME AND SPENDING TIME AMONG THE LEGIONARIES GIVE HIM THE OPPORTUNITY HE NEEDS TO MAKE HIMSELF A BETTER MAN.

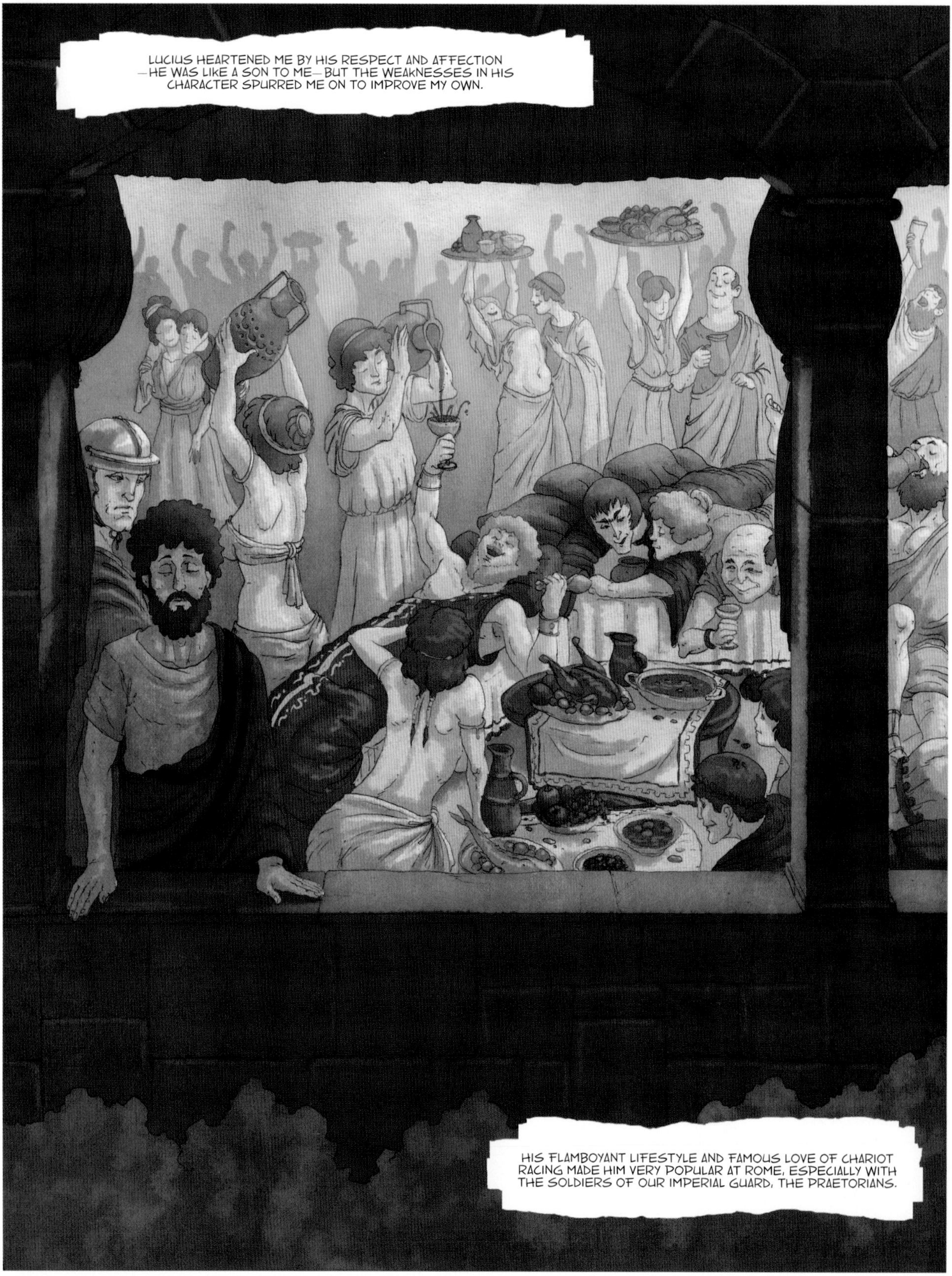
LUCIUS HEARTENED ME BY HIS RESPECT AND AFFECTION —HE WAS LIKE A SON TO ME— BUT THE WEAKNESSES IN HIS CHARACTER SPURRED ME ON TO IMPROVE MY OWN.
HIS FLAMBOYANT LIFESTYLE AND FAMOUS LOVE OF CHARIOT RACING MADE HIM VERY POPULAR AT ROME, ESPECIALLY WITH THE SOLDIERS OF OUR IMPERIAL GUARD, THE PRAETORIANS.

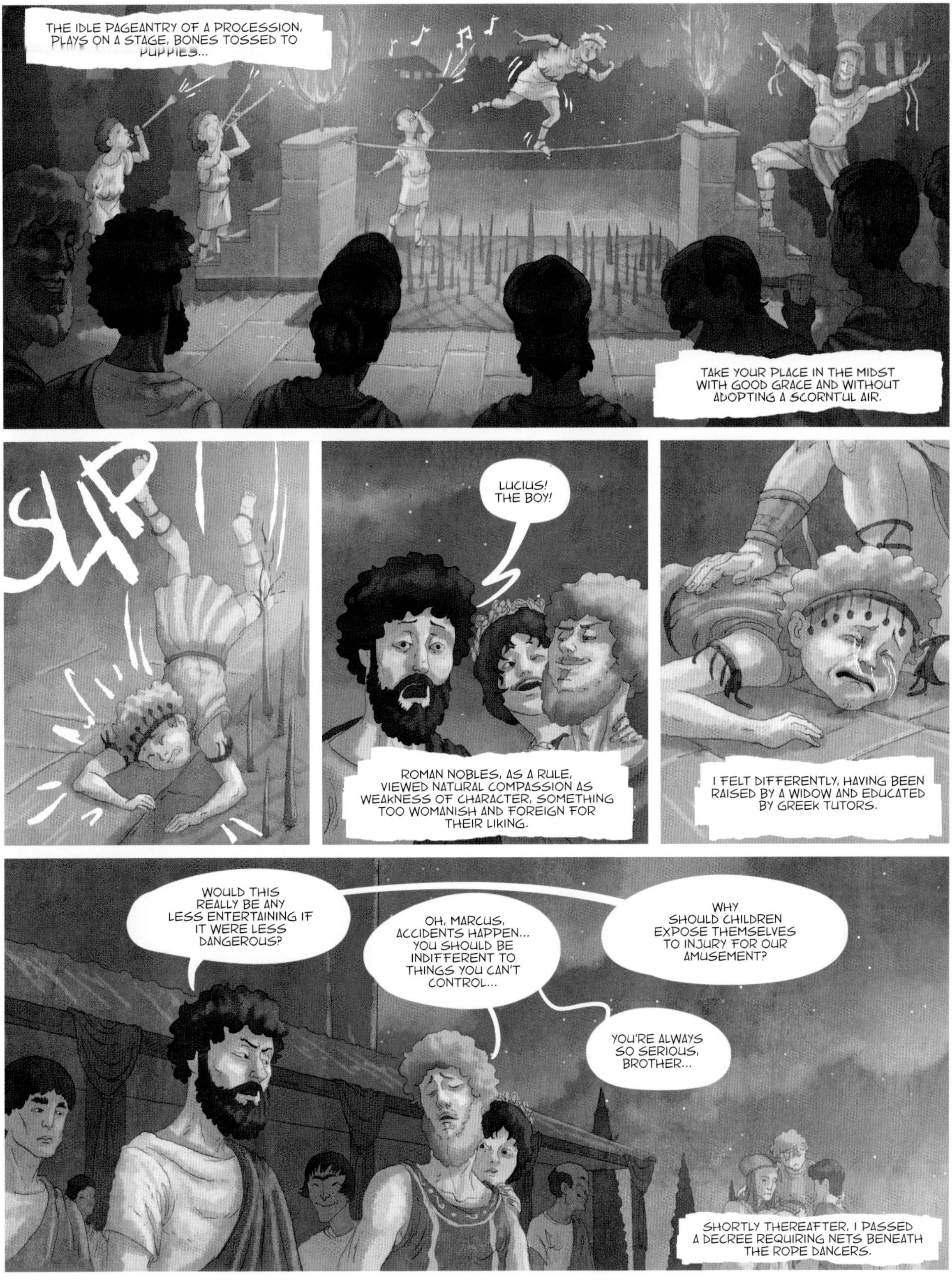
THE IDLE PAGEANTRY OF A PROCESSION, PLAYS ON A STAGE, BONES TOSSED TO PUPPIES...
TAKE YOUR PLACE IN THE MIDST WITH GOOD GRACE AND WITHOUT ADOPTING A SCORNFUL AIR.
SLIP
LUCIUS! THE BOY!
ROMAN NOBLES, AS A RULE, VIEWED NATURAL COMPASSION AS WEAKNESS OF CHARACTER, SOMETHING TOO WOMANISH AND FOREIGN FOR THEIR LIKING.
I FELT DIFFERENTLY, HAVING BEEN RAISED BY A WIDOW AND EDUCATED BY GREEK TUTORS.
WOULD THIS REALLY BE ANY LESS ENTERTAINING IF IT WERE LESS DANGEROUS?
WHY SHOULD CHILDREN EXPOSE THEMSELVES TO INJURY FOR OUR AMUSEMENT?
OH, MARCUS, ACCIDENTS HAPPEN... YOU SHOULD BE INDIFFERENT TO THINGS YOU CAN'T CONTROL...
YOU'RE ALWAYS SO SERIOUS, BROTHER...
SHORTLY THEREAFTER, I PASSED A DECREE REQUIRING NETS BENEATH THE ROPE DANCERS.

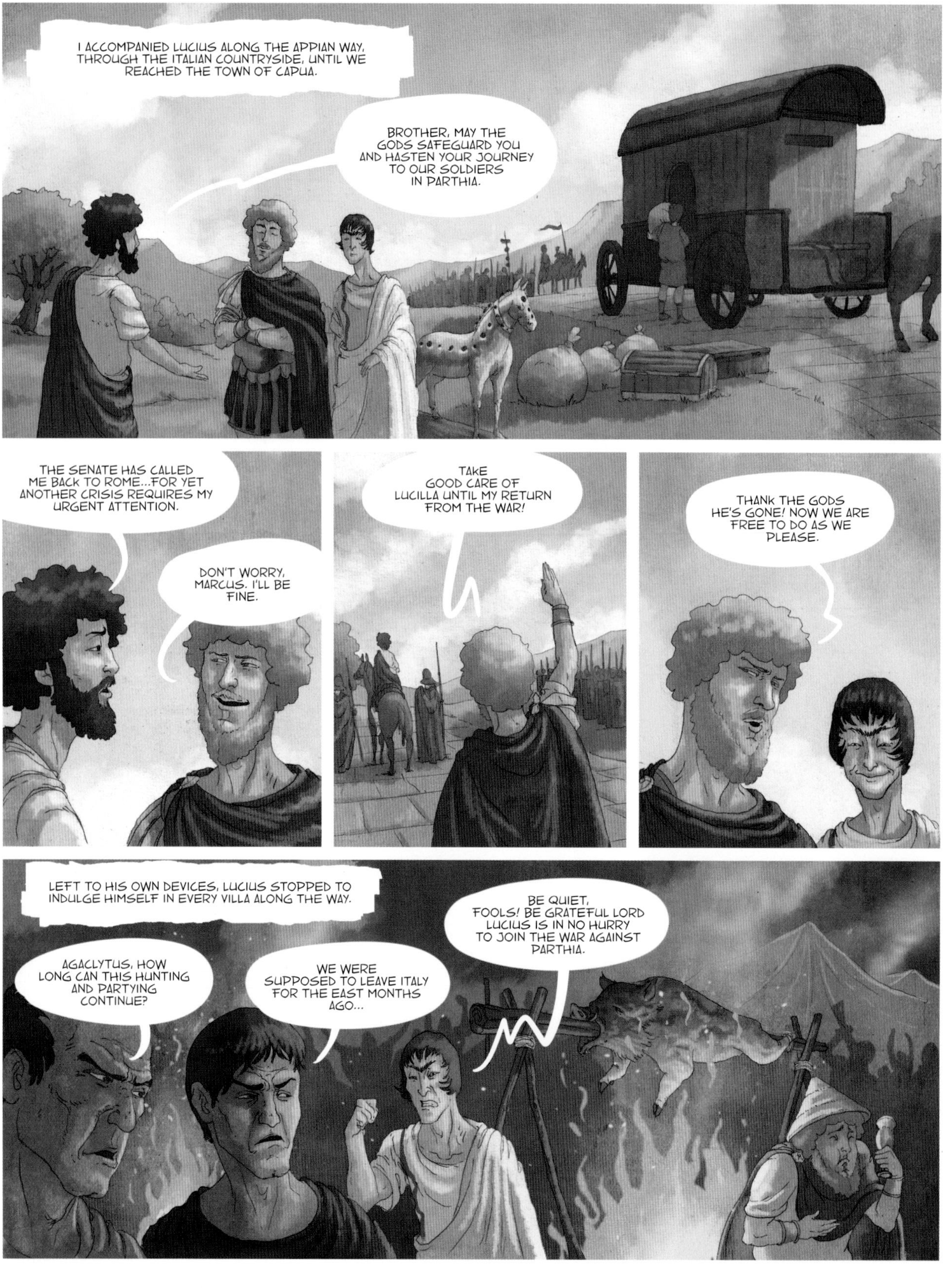
I ACCOMPANIED LUCIUS ALONG THE APPIAN WAY, THROUGH THE ITALIAN COUNTRYSIDE, UNTIL WE REACHED THE TOWN OF CAPUA.
BROTHER, MAY THE GODS SAFEGUARD YOU AND HASTEN YOUR JOURNEY TO OUR SOLDIERS IN PARTHIA.
THE SENATE HAS CALLED ME BACK TO ROME...FOR YET ANOTHER CRISIS REQUIRES MY URGENT ATTENTION.
DON'T WORRY, MARCUS. I'LL BE FINE.
TAKE GOOD CARE OF LUCILLA UNTIL MY RETURN FROM THE WAR!
THANK THE GODS HE'S GONE! NOW WE ARE FREE TO DO AS WE PLEASE.
LEFT TO HIS OWN DEVICES, LUCIUS STOPPED TO INDULGE HIMSELF IN EVERY VILLA ALONG THE WAY.
AGACLYTUS, HOW LONG CAN THIS HUNTING AND PARTYING CONTINUE?
WE WERE SUPPOSED TO LEAVE ITALY FOR THE EAST MONTHS AGO...
BE QUIET, FOOLS! BE GRATEFUL LORD LUCIUS IS IN NO HURRY TO JOIN THE WAR AGAINST PARTHIA.

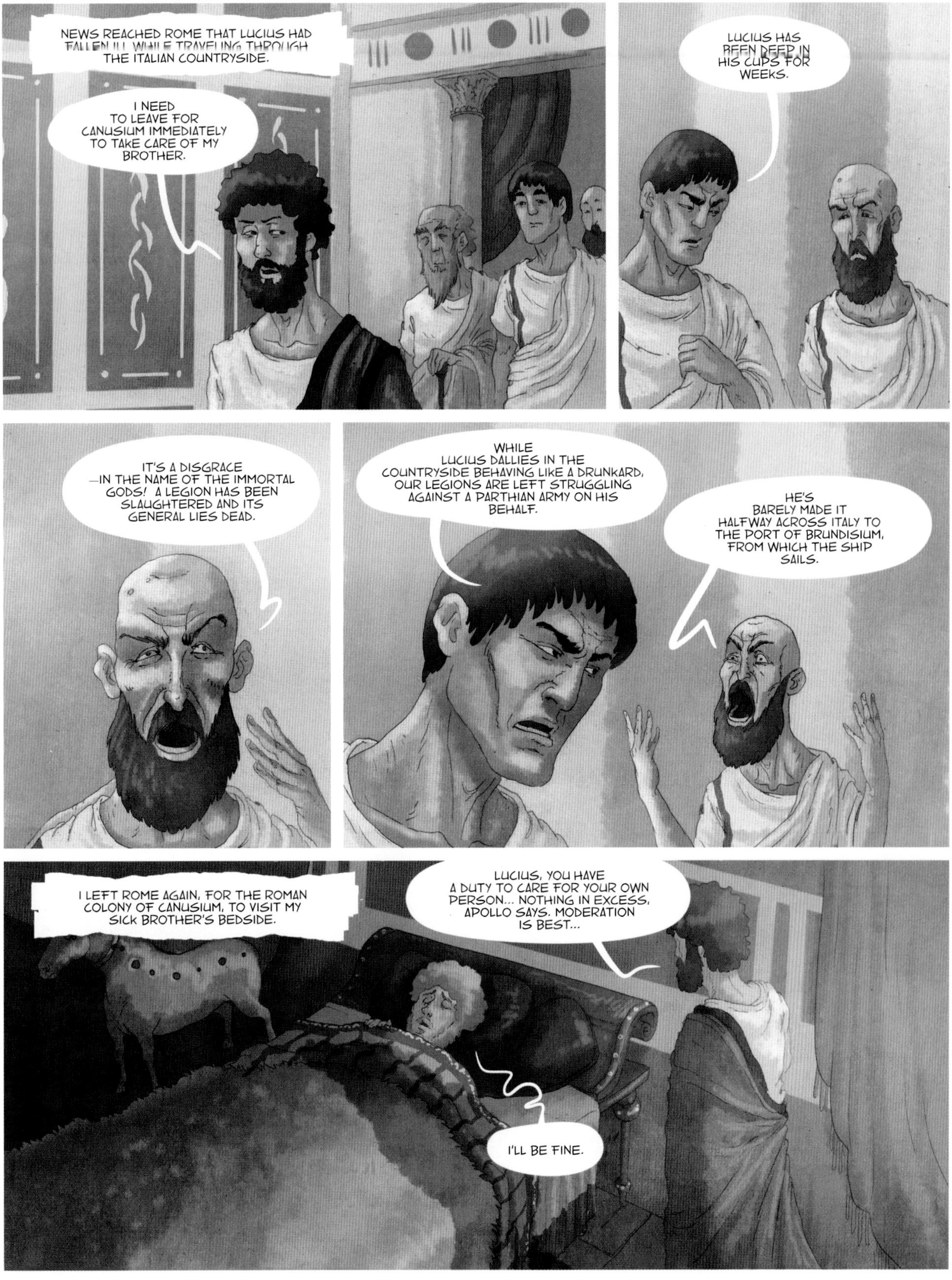
NEWS REACHED ROME THAT LUCIUS HAD FALLEN ILL WHILE TRAVELING THROUGH THE ITALIAN COUNTRYSIDE.
I NEED TO LEAVE FOR CANUSIUM IMMEDIATELY TO TAKE CARE OF MY BROTHER.
LUCIUS HAS BEEN DEEP IN HIS CUPS FOR WEEKS.
IT'S A DISGRACE —IN THE NAME OF THE IMMORTAL GODS! A LEGION HAS BEEN SLAUGHTERED AND ITS GENERAL LIES DEAD.
WHILE LUCIUS DALLIES IN THE COUNTRYSIDE BEHAVING LIKE A DRUNKARD, OUR LEGIONS ARE LEFT STRUGGLING AGAINST A PARTHIAN ARMY ON HIS BEHALF.
HE'S BARELY MADE IT HALFWAY ACROSS ITALY TO THE PORT OF BRUNDISIUM, FROM WHICH THE SHIP SAILS.
I LEFT ROME AGAIN, FOR THE ROMAN COLONY OF CANUSIUM, TO VISIT MY SICK BROTHER'S BEDSIDE.
LUCIUS, YOU HAVE A DUTY TO CARE FOR YOUR OWN PERSON... NOTHING IN EXCESS, APOLLO SAYS. MODERATION IS BEST...
I'LL BE FINE.

SATIRISTS AT ROME WERE FREE TO RIDICULE EVEN THE IMPERIAL FAMILY.

POUR ME ANOTHER, DAD... I MEAN, BROTHER!

ALAS!

EMPRESS!

YOU'RE SO STRONG... AND HANDSOME TOO!

AHAH AH AH AH AHAH AH AH AH

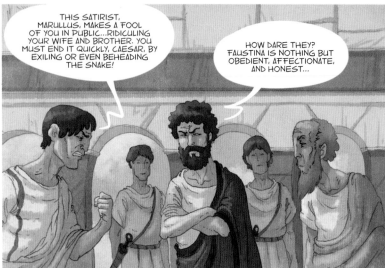

THIS SATIRIST, MARULLUS, MAKES A FOOL OF YOU IN PUBLIC...RIDICULING YOUR WIFE AND BROTHER. YOU MUST END IT QUICKLY, CAESAR, BY EXILING OR EVEN BEHEADING THE SNAKE!

HOW DARE THEY? FAUSTINA IS NOTHING BUT OBEDIENT, AFFECTIONATE, AND HONEST...

REMEMBER WHAT YOU'VE LEARNED... SET ASIDE THE OPINION THAT YOU'VE BEEN HARMED, MY SON, AND NOTHING CAN HARM YOU.

AND WHAT, MASTER, ABOUT MY WIFE'S REPUTATION?

ON THE ONE HAND, IF WHAT THEY SAY IS TRUE, THEN YOU SHOULD LISTEN TO THEM.

ON THE OTHER, IF IT IS FALSE, AND THEY'RE MERELY ACTING OUT OF IGNORANCE, FAUSTINA HERSELF SUFFERS NOTHING BY IT.

EITHER WAY YOU SHOULD TAKE NO NOTICE.

INDEED. MY LADY'S ACTIONS SPEAK FOR THEMSELVES. THE PEOPLE WILL LEARN TO LOVE HER IN DUE COURSE.

I FELT MY BLOOD BOIL AND WANTED TO DEFEND MY WIFE'S HONOR, BUT INSTEAD I ASKED MYSELF WHAT A WISER AND MORE TEMPERATE MAN WOULD DO.

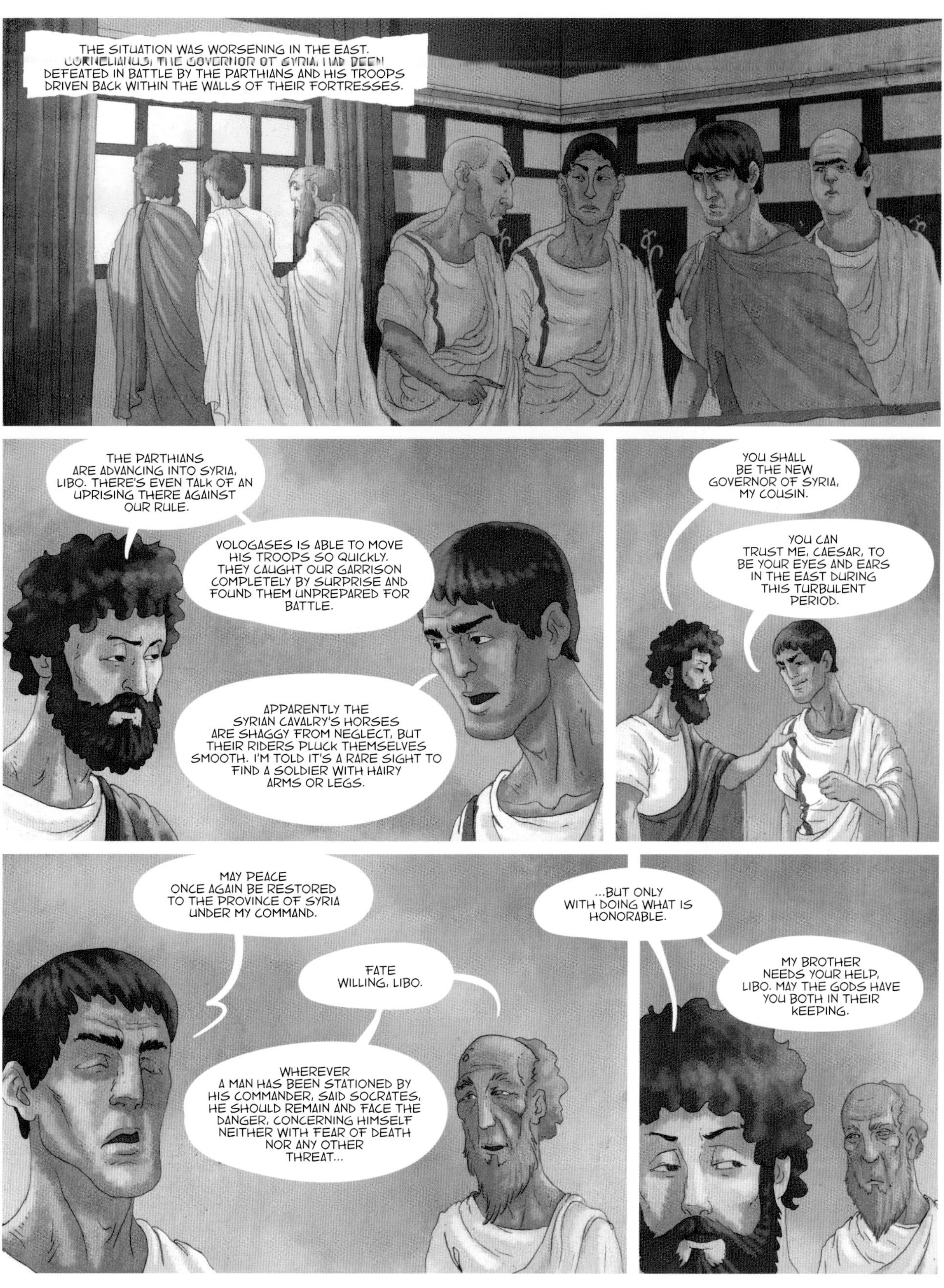
THE SITUATION WAS WORSENING IN THE EAST. CORNELIANUS, THE GOVERNOR OF SYRIA, HAD BEEN DEFEATED IN BATTLE BY THE PARTHIANS AND HIS TROOPS DRIVEN BACK WITHIN THE WALLS OF THEIR FORTRESSES.
THE PARTHIANS ARE ADVANCING INTO SYRIA, LIBO. THERE'S EVEN TALK OF AN UPRISING THERE AGAINST OUR RULE.
VOLOGASES IS ABLE TO MOVE HIS TROOPS SO QUICKLY. THEY CAUGHT OUR GARRISON COMPLETELY BY SURPRISE AND FOUND THEM UNPREPARED FOR BATTLE.
APPARENTLY THE SYRIAN CAVALRY'S HORSES ARE SHAGGY FROM NEGLECT, BUT THEIR RIDERS PLUCK THEMSELVES SMOOTH. I'M TOLD IT'S A RARE SIGHT TO FIND A SOLDIER WITH HAIRY ARMS OR LEGS.
YOU SHALL BE THE NEW GOVERNOR OF SYRIA, MY COUSIN.
YOU CAN TRUST ME, CAESAR, TO BE YOUR EYES AND EARS IN THE EAST DURING THIS TURBULENT PERIOD.
MAY PEACE ONCE AGAIN BE RESTORED TO THE PROVINCE OF SYRIA UNDER MY COMMAND.
FATE WILLING, LIBO.
WHEREVER A MAN HAS BEEN STATIONED BY HIS COMMANDER, SAID SOCRATES, HE SHOULD REMAIN AND FACE THE DANGER, CONCERNING HIMSELF NEITHER WITH FEAR OF DEATH NOR ANY OTHER THREAT...
...BUT ONLY WITH DOING WHAT IS HONORABLE.
MY BROTHER NEEDS YOUR HELP, LIBO. MAY THE GODS HAVE YOU BOTH IN THEIR KEEPING.

MY LORD, AN OFFICER WITH EXPERIENCE SUPPRESSING MUTINOUS PASSIONS COULD BE OF GREAT ASSISTANCE TO LIBO.

IN THE EAST, OUR LEGIONS GET THEIR WATER BY BEING STATIONED IN CITIES, WHICH INEVITABLY LEADS TO PROBLEMS WITH DISCIPLINE.

THEY'VE BECOME HOPELESSLY GRECIANIZED, RUSTICUS. SOLDIERS ARE OUT THERE SOAKING THEIR DAINTY BODIES IN WARM BATHWATER. IT'S A DISGRACE!

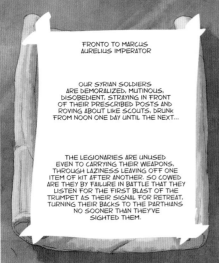

FRONTO TO MARCUS AURELIUS IMPERATOR

OUR SYRIAN SOLDIERS ARE DEMORALIZED, MUTINOUS, DISOBEDIENT, STRAYING IN FRONT OF THEIR PRESCRIBED POSTS AND ROVING ABOUT LIKE SCOUTS, DRUNK FROM NOON ONE DAY UNTIL THE NEXT...

THE LEGIONARIES ARE UNUSED EVEN TO CARRYING THEIR WEAPONS, THROUGH LAZINESS LEAVING OFF ONE ITEM OF KIT AFTER ANOTHER. SO COWED ARE THEY BY FAILURE IN BATTLE THAT THEY LISTEN FOR THE FIRST BLAST OF THE TRUMPET AS THEIR SIGNAL FOR RETREAT, TURNING THEIR BACKS TO THE PARTHIANS NO SOONER THAN THEY'VE SIGHTED THEM.

THE LEGATE AVIDIUS CASSIUS SHALL BE TRANSFERRED IMMEDIATELY FROM THE DANUBE REGION TO TAKE COMMAND OF A SYRIAN LEGION, UNDER YOUR SUPERVISION, LIBO.

WE COULD USE THE OLD-FASHIONED STRICTNESS FOR WHICH HIS FAMILY IS RENOWNED. CASSIUS SHALL KNOCK THE FLOWERS FROM THEIR HAIR AND DRAG THESE SOLDIERS OUT OF THE BROTHELS AND DRINKING HOLES!

MY LORD CAESAR, THIS CASSIAN OFFICER DOES NOT SHARE THE VALUES BY WHICH YOU GOVERN. HIS SOUL IS THAT OF A WOLF...

NO MAN IS PERFECT, RUSTICUS.

WE MUST EMPLOY THE OFFICERS WE HAVE FOR WHATEVER SERVICE THEY MAY RENDER TO THE STATE. ROME REQUIRES CASSIUS TO DO WHAT LUCIUS COULD NOT.

CASSIUS IS A SYRIAN OF ROYAL BLOOD. BE CAREFUL YOU DO NOT GRANT HIM TOO MUCH AUTHORITY IN HIS OWN HOMELAND, MY SON, AND GIVE HIM THOUGHTS OF BECOMING A KING.

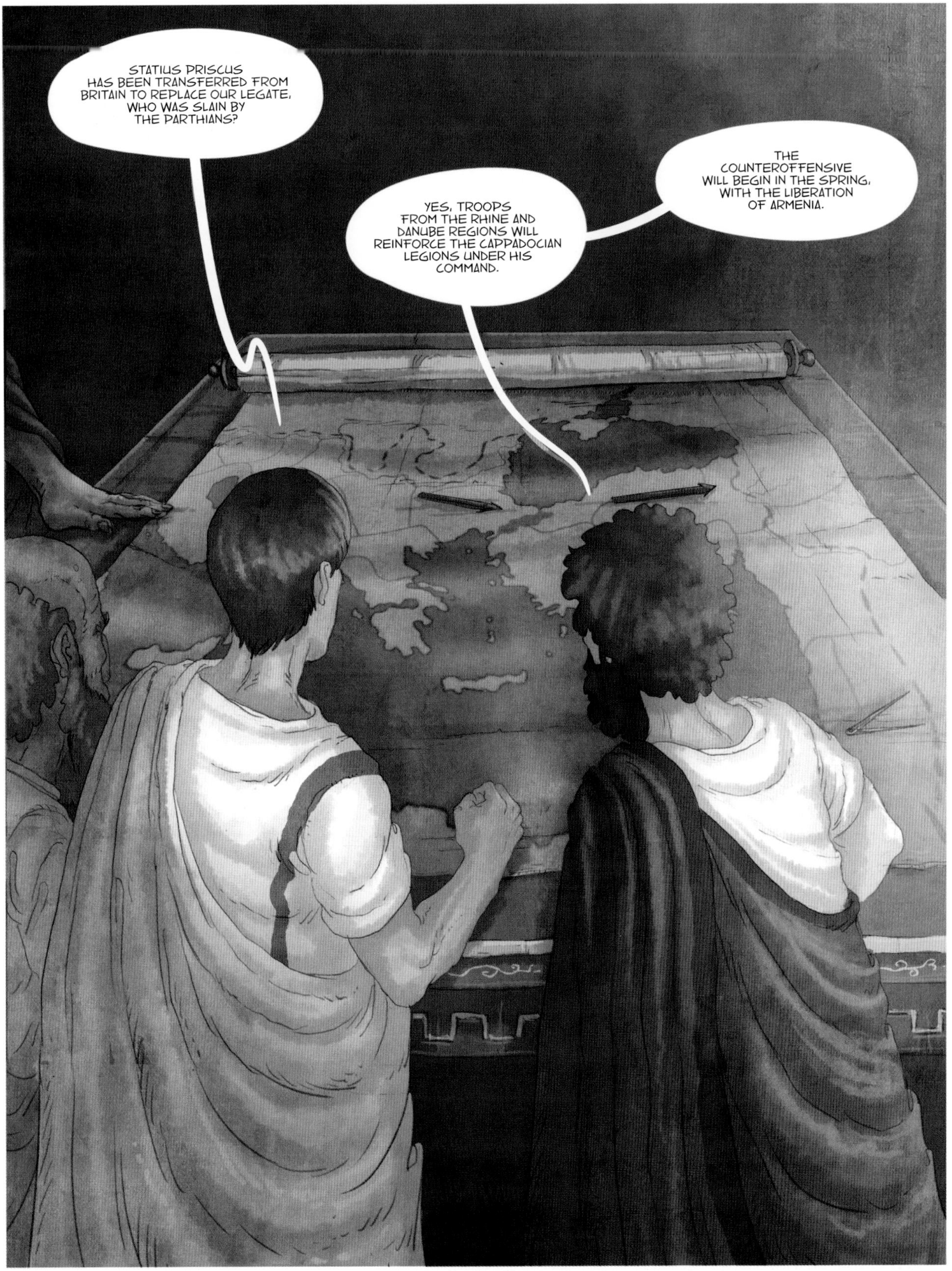
STATIUS PRISCUS HAS BEEN TRANSFERRED FROM BRITAIN TO REPLACE OUR LEGATE, WHO WAS SLAIN BY THE PARTHIANS?
YES, TROOPS FROM THE RHINE AND DANUBE REGIONS WILL REINFORCE THE CAPPADOCIAN LEGIONS UNDER HIS COMMAND.
THE COUNTEROFFENSIVE WILL BEGIN IN THE SPRING, WITH THE LIBERATION OF ARMENIA.

THE
TEMPLE OF APOLLO

To be pulled by the strings of desire belongs both to wild beasts and to men who have made themselves into tyrants.

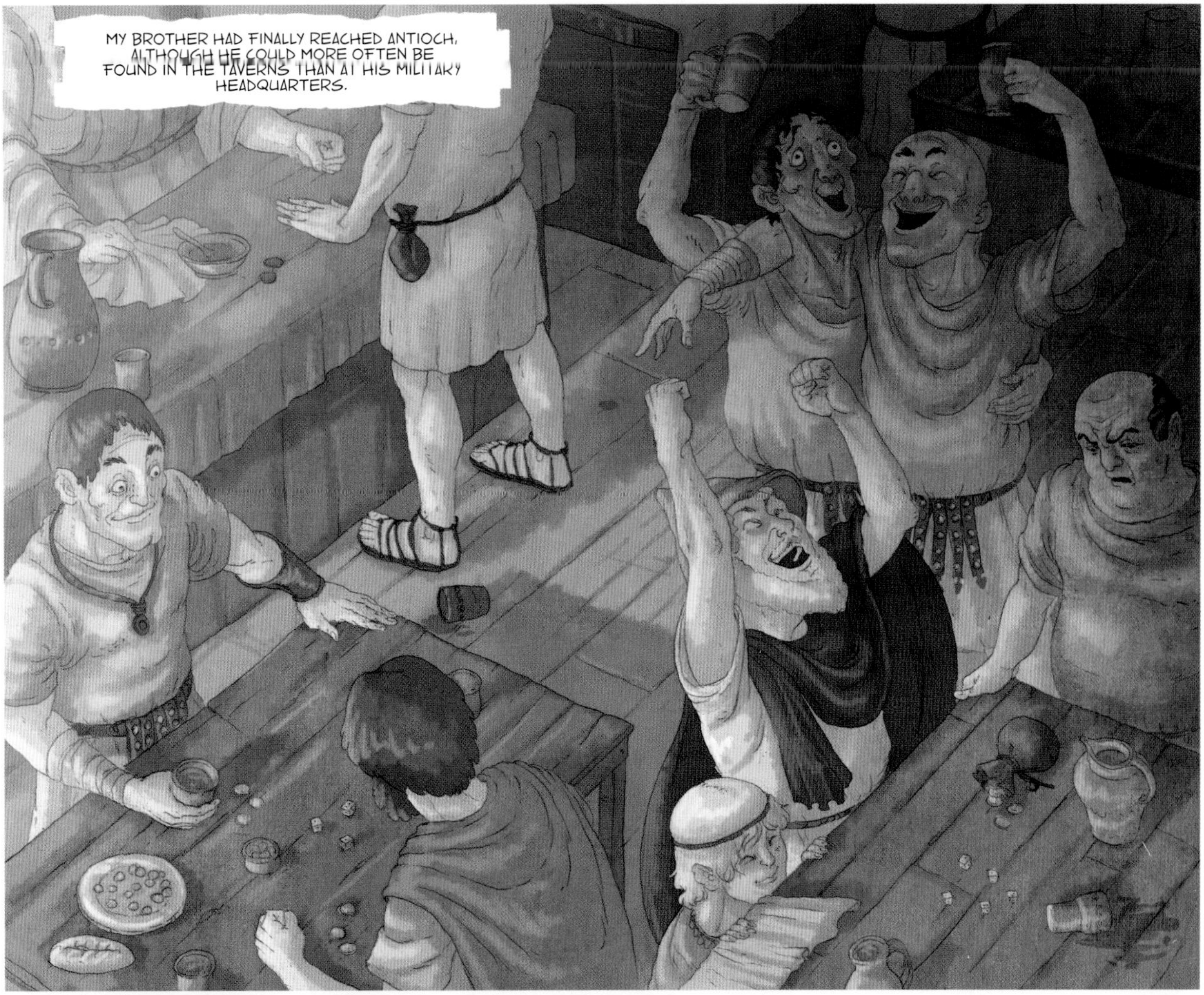
MY BROTHER HAD FINALLY REACHED ANTIOCH, ALTHOUGH HE COULD MORE OFTEN BE FOUND IN THE TAVERNS THAN AT HIS MILITARY HEADQUARTERS.

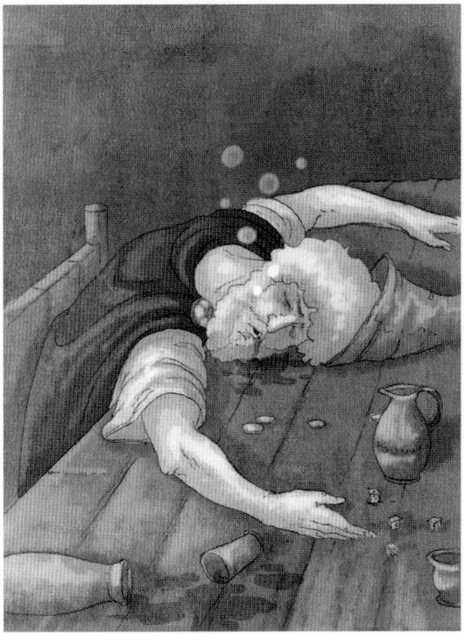

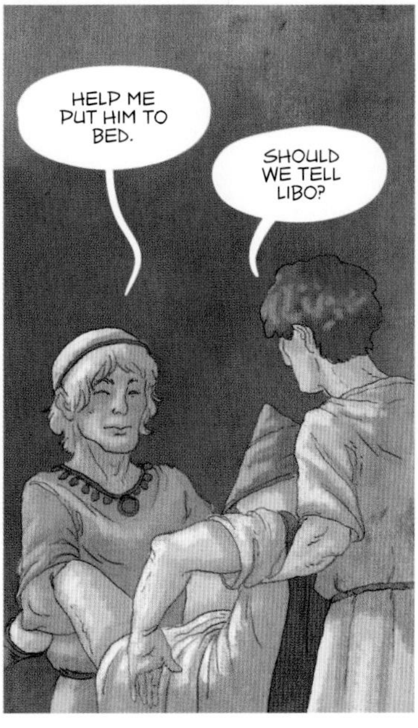
HELP ME PUT HIM TO BED.
SHOULD WE TELL LIBO?

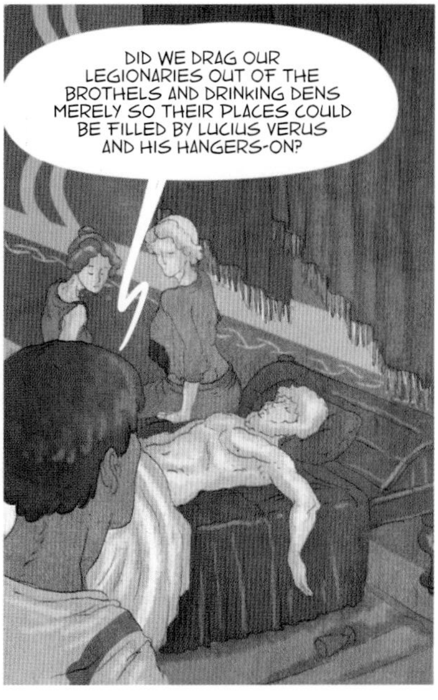
DID WE DRAG OUR LEGIONARIES OUT OF THE BROTHELS AND DRINKING DENS MERELY SO THEIR PLACES COULD BE FILLED BY LUCIUS VERUS AND HIS HANGERS-ON?

ALTHOUGH LUCIUS'S ARRIVAL WAS MET AT FIRST WITH CELEBRATION, HE SOON BEGAN TO IRRITATE THE GOVERNOR OF SYRIA.

OUR AMBASSADORS HAVE RETURNED EMPTY-HANDED FROM THEIR MEETING WITH THE PARTHIAN KING.

MAYBE WE SHOULD SEND VOLOGASES SOME OF THIS SYRIAN WINE NEXT TIME, LIBO.

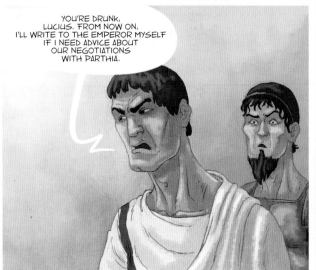

YOU'RE DRUNK, LUCIUS. FROM NOW ON, I'LL WRITE TO THE EMPEROR MYSELF IF I NEED ADVICE ABOUT OUR NEGOTIATIONS WITH PARTHIA.

HOW DARE YOU, LIBO! I AM IN COMMAND HERE, NOT MY BROTHER!

I AM YOUR EMPEROR!

GET OUT OF MY SIGHT BEFORE I DO SOMETHING I'LL REGRET!

THIS DRUNK'S PRESENCE WAS MEANT TO QUELL UNREST? IT'S DANGEROUS TO SEND LEGIONS AGAINST THE PARTHIANS WHILE THERE'S STILL TALK OF AN UPRISING HERE IN SYRIA...

HE'S NO CAESAR AND HE'S A WORTHLESS GENERAL... HE'S NOTHING, BY HERCULES, BUT A...

COUGH

MASTER, WHAT'S HAPPENING?

GASP

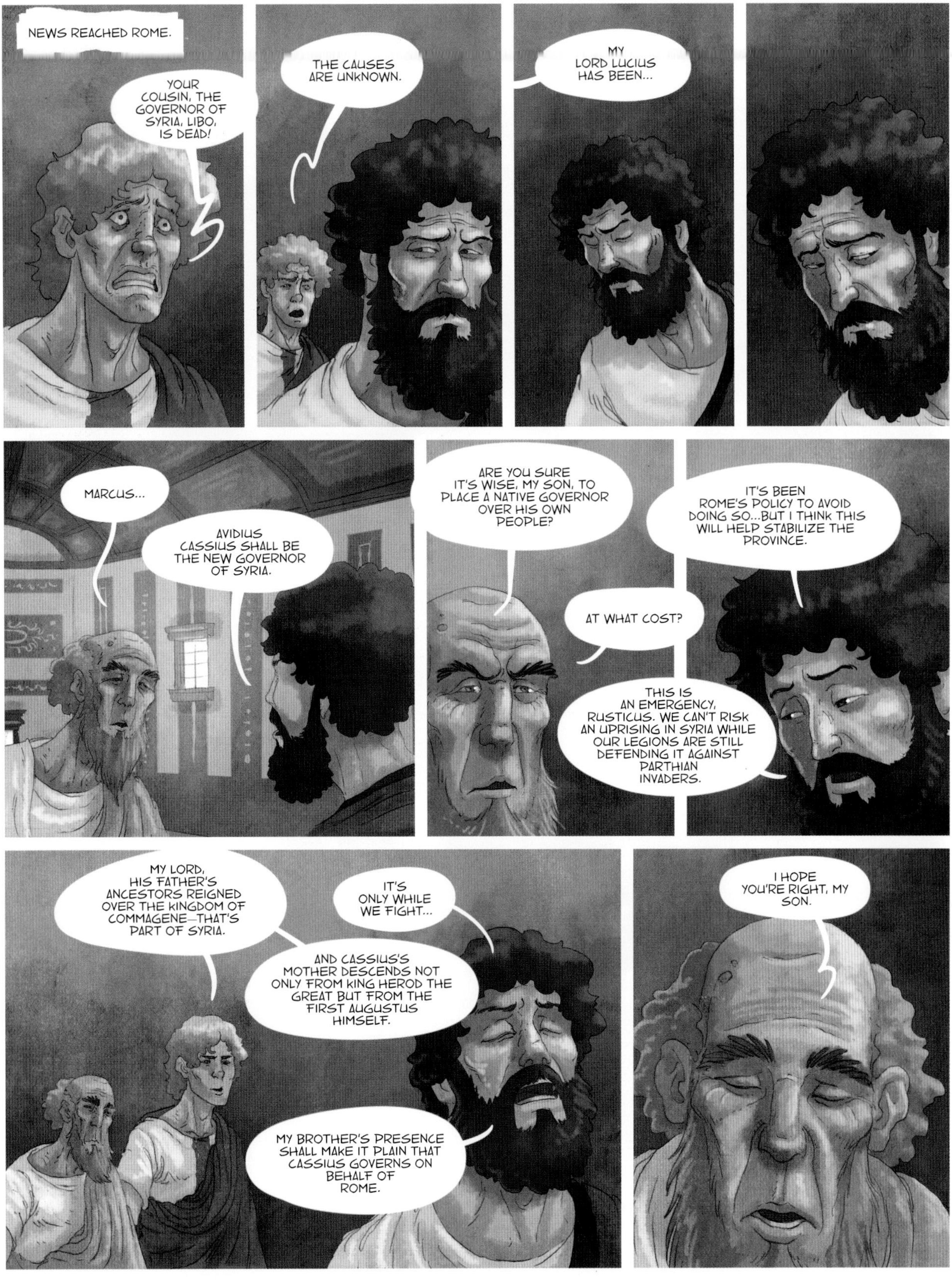
NEWS REACHED ROME.
YOUR COUSIN, THE GOVERNOR OF SYRIA, LIBO, IS DEAD!
THE CAUSES ARE UNKNOWN.
MY LORD LUCIUS HAS BEEN...
MARCUS...
AVIDIUS CASSIUS SHALL BE THE NEW GOVERNOR OF SYRIA.
ARE YOU SURE IT'S WISE, MY SON, TO PLACE A NATIVE GOVERNOR OVER HIS OWN PEOPLE?
IT'S BEEN ROME'S POLICY TO AVOID DOING SO...BUT I THINK THIS WILL HELP STABILIZE THE PROVINCE.
AT WHAT COST?
THIS IS AN EMERGENCY, RUSTICUS. WE CAN'T RISK AN UPRISING IN SYRIA WHILE OUR LEGIONS ARE STILL DEFENDING IT AGAINST PARTHIAN INVADERS.
MY LORD, HIS FATHER'S ANCESTORS REIGNED OVER THE KINGDOM OF COMMAGENE—THAT'S PART OF SYRIA.
IT'S ONLY WHILE WE FIGHT...
AND CASSIUS'S MOTHER DESCENDS NOT ONLY FROM KING HEROD THE GREAT BUT FROM THE FIRST AUGUSTUS HIMSELF.
MY BROTHER'S PRESENCE SHALL MAKE IT PLAIN THAT CASSIUS GOVERNS ON BEHALF OF ROME.
I HOPE YOU'RE RIGHT, MY SON.

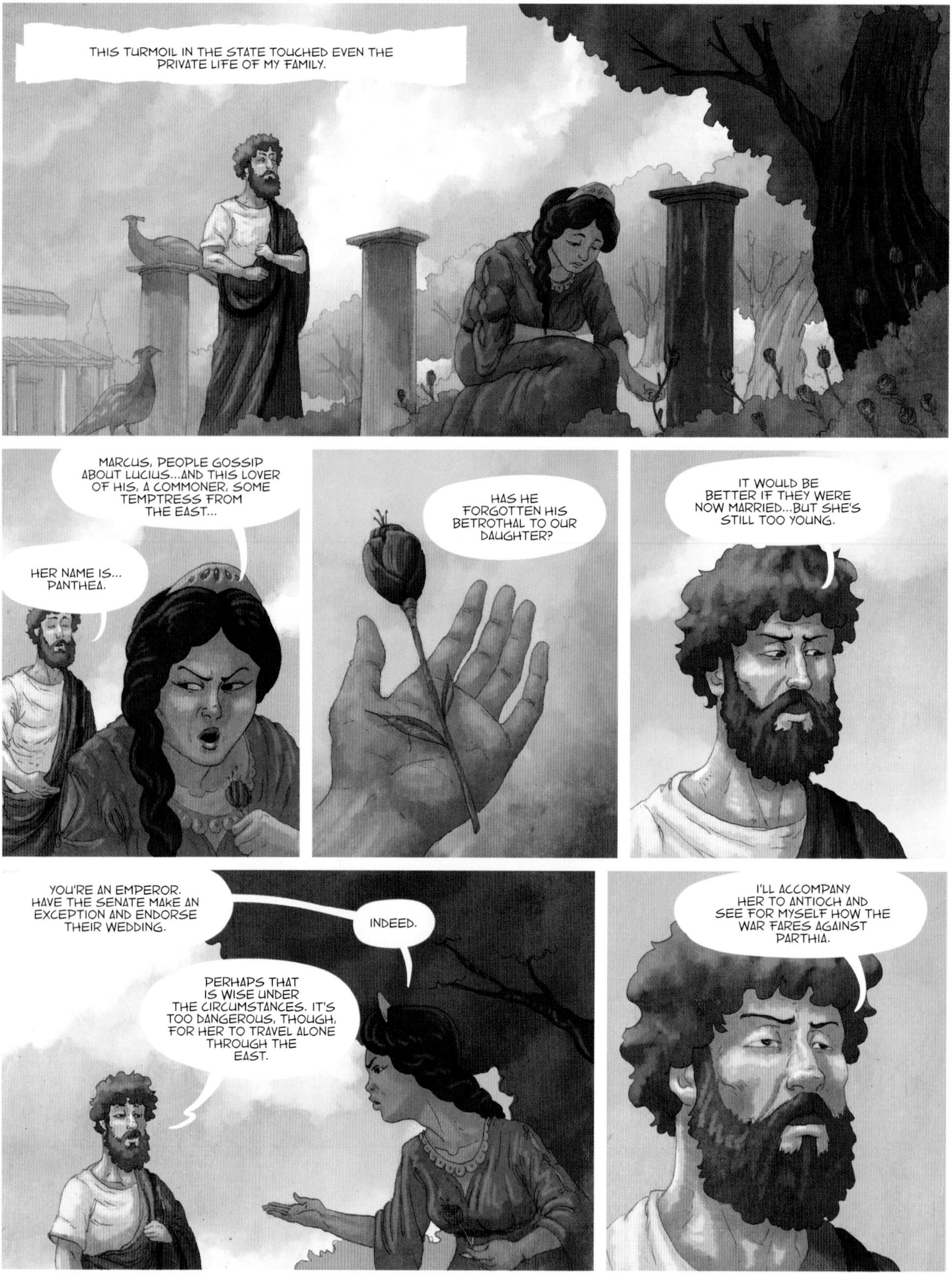
THIS TURMOIL IN THE STATE TOUCHED EVEN THE PRIVATE LIFE OF MY FAMILY.
MARCUS, PEOPLE GOSSIP ABOUT LUCIUS...AND THIS LOVER OF HIS, A COMMONER, SOME TEMPTRESS FROM THE EAST...
HER NAME IS... PANTHEA.
HAS HE FORGOTTEN HIS BETROTHAL TO OUR DAUGHTER?
IT WOULD BE BETTER IF THEY WERE NOW MARRIED...BUT SHE'S STILL TOO YOUNG.
YOU'RE AN EMPEROR. HAVE THE SENATE MAKE AN EXCEPTION AND ENDORSE THEIR WEDDING.
INDEED.
PERHAPS THAT IS WISE UNDER THE CIRCUMSTANCES. IT'S TOO DANGEROUS, THOUGH, FOR HER TO TRAVEL ALONE THROUGH THE EAST.
I'LL ACCOMPANY HER TO ANTIOCH AND SEE FOR MYSELF HOW THE WAR FARES AGAINST PARTHIA.

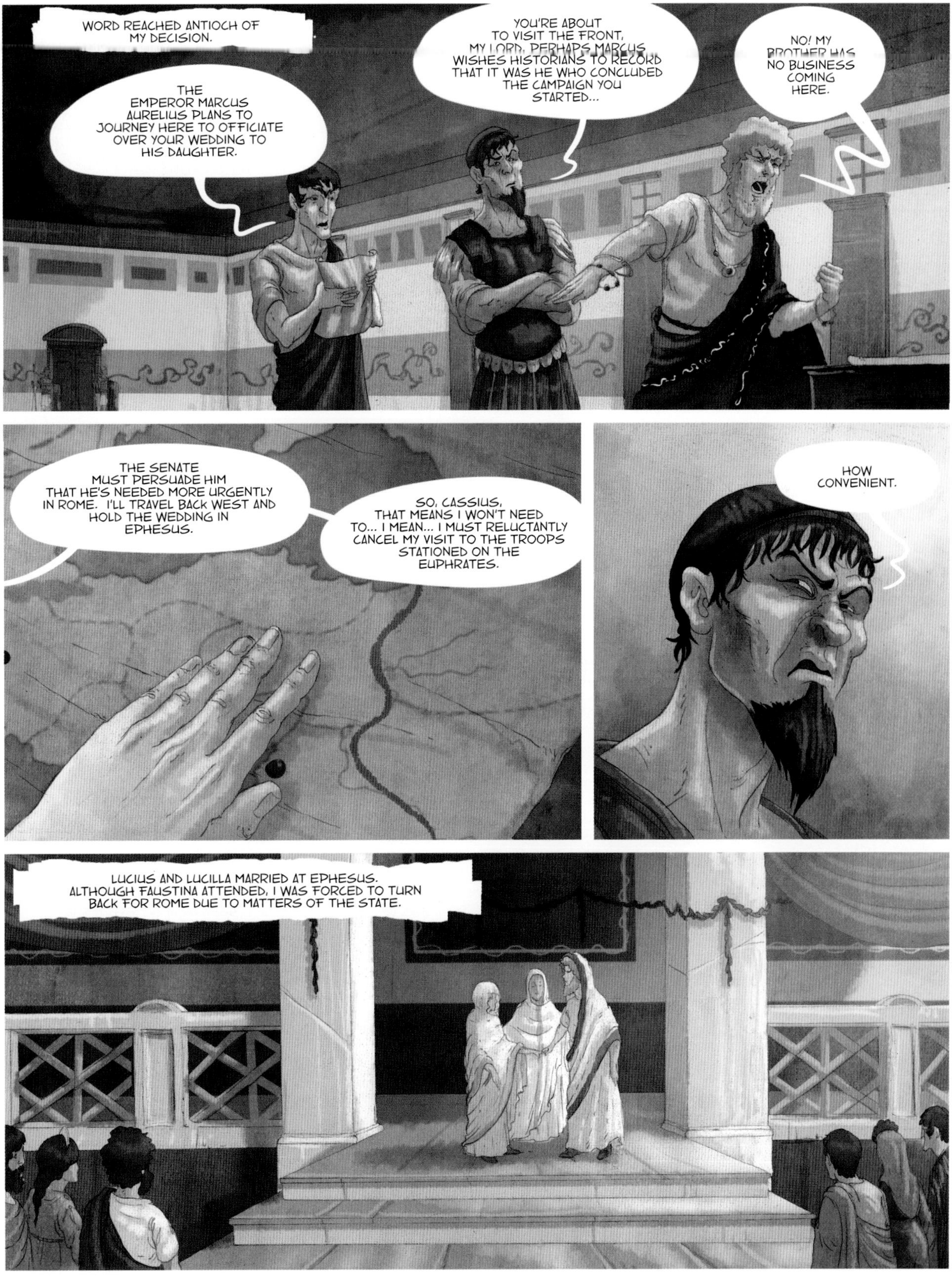
WORD REACHED ANTIOCH OF MY DECISION.
THE EMPEROR MARCUS AURELIUS PLANS TO JOURNEY HERE TO OFFICIATE OVER YOUR WEDDING TO HIS DAUGHTER.
YOU'RE ABOUT TO VISIT THE FRONT, MY LORD. PERHAPS MARCUS WISHES HISTORIANS TO RECORD THAT IT WAS HE WHO CONCLUDED THE CAMPAIGN YOU STARTED...
NO! MY BROTHER HAS NO BUSINESS COMING HERE.
THE SENATE MUST PERSUADE HIM THAT HE'S NEEDED MORE URGENTLY IN ROME. I'LL TRAVEL BACK WEST AND HOLD THE WEDDING IN EPHESUS.
SO, CASSIUS, THAT MEANS I WON'T NEED TO... I MEAN... I MUST RELUCTANTLY CANCEL MY VISIT TO THE TROOPS STATIONED ON THE EUPHRATES.
HOW CONVENIENT.
LUCIUS AND LUCILLA MARRIED AT EPHESUS. ALTHOUGH FAUSTINA ATTENDED, I WAS FORCED TO TURN BACK FOR ROME DUE TO MATTERS OF THE STATE.

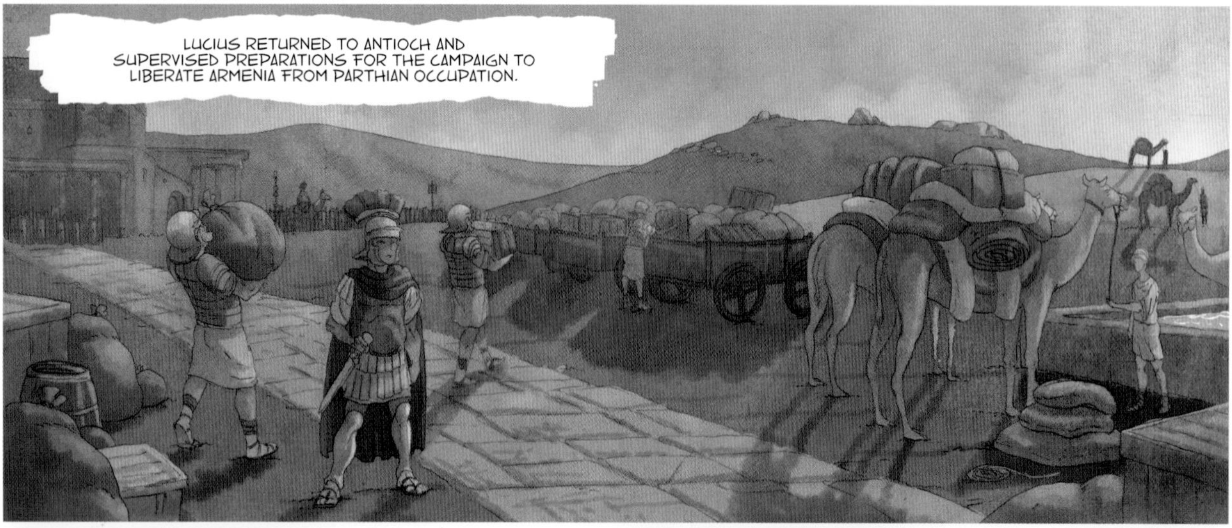
LUCIUS RETURNED TO ANTIOCH AND SUPERVISED PREPARATIONS FOR THE CAMPAIGN TO LIBERATE ARMENIA FROM PARTHIAN OCCUPATION.

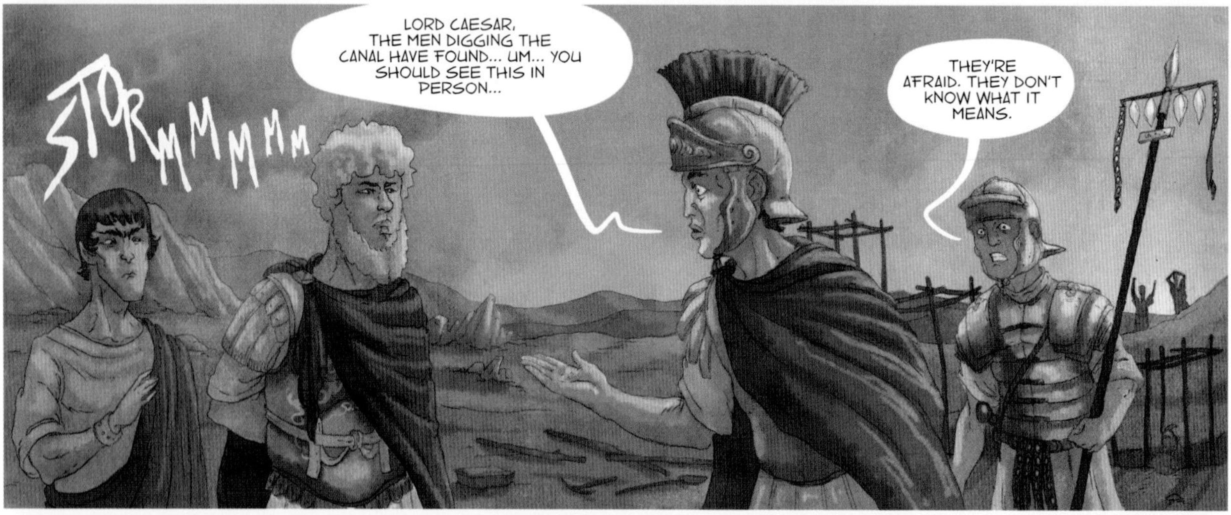
STORMMMMM
LORD CAESAR, THE MEN DIGGING THE CANAL HAVE FOUND... UM... YOU SHOULD SEE THIS IN PERSON...
THEY'RE AFRAID. THEY DON'T KNOW WHAT IT MEANS.

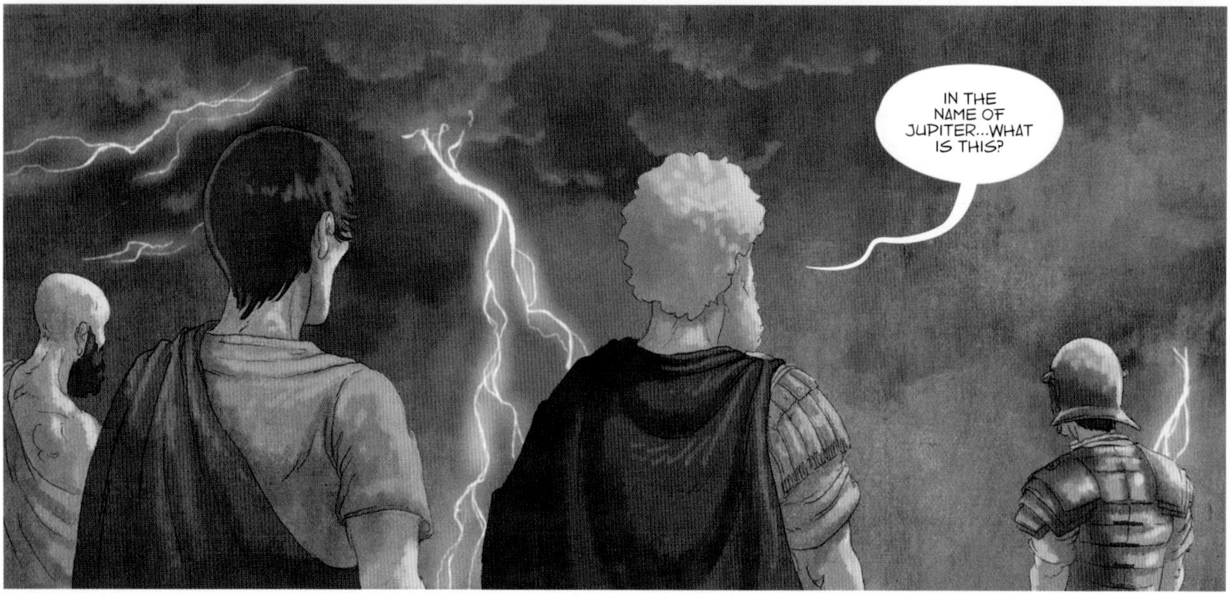
IN THE NAME OF JUPITER...WHAT IS THIS?

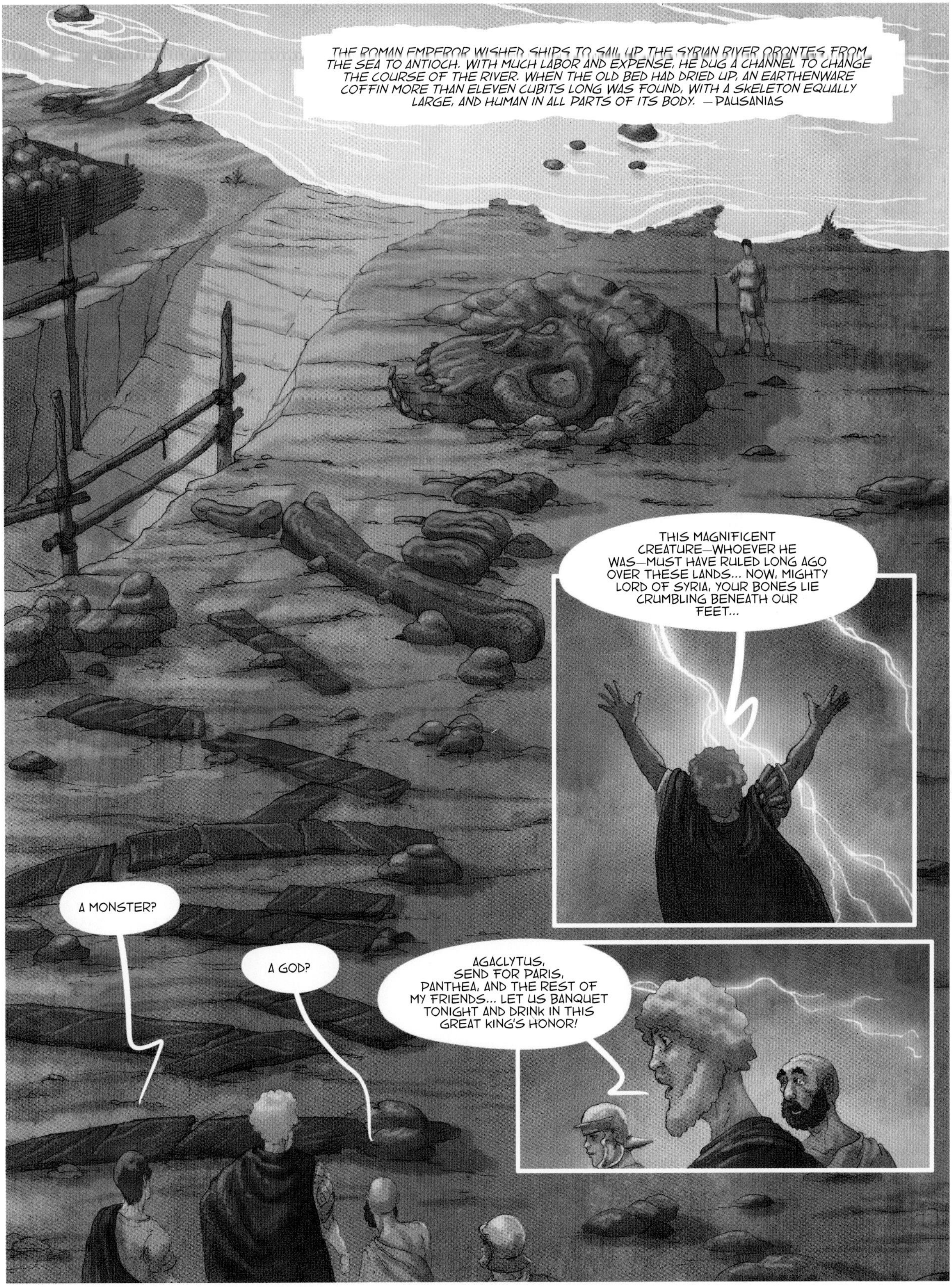
THE ROMAN EMPEROR WISHED SHIPS TO SAIL UP THE SYRIAN RIVER ORONTES FROM THE SEA TO ANTIOCH. WITH MUCH LABOR AND EXPENSE, HE DUG A CHANNEL TO CHANGE THE COURSE OF THE RIVER. WHEN THE OLD BED HAD DRIED UP, AN EARTHENWARE COFFIN MORE THAN ELEVEN CUBITS LONG WAS FOUND, WITH A SKELETON EQUALLY LARGE, AND HUMAN IN ALL PARTS OF ITS BODY. —PAUSANIAS
A MONSTER?
A GOD?
THIS MAGNIFICENT CREATURE—WHOEVER HE WAS—MUST HAVE RULED LONG AGO OVER THESE LANDS... NOW, MIGHTY LORD OF SYRIA, YOUR BONES LIE CRUMBLING BENEATH OUR FEET...
AGACLYTUS, SEND FOR PARIS, PANTHEA, AND THE REST OF MY FRIENDS... LET US BANQUET TONIGHT AND DRINK IN THIS GREAT KING'S HONOR!

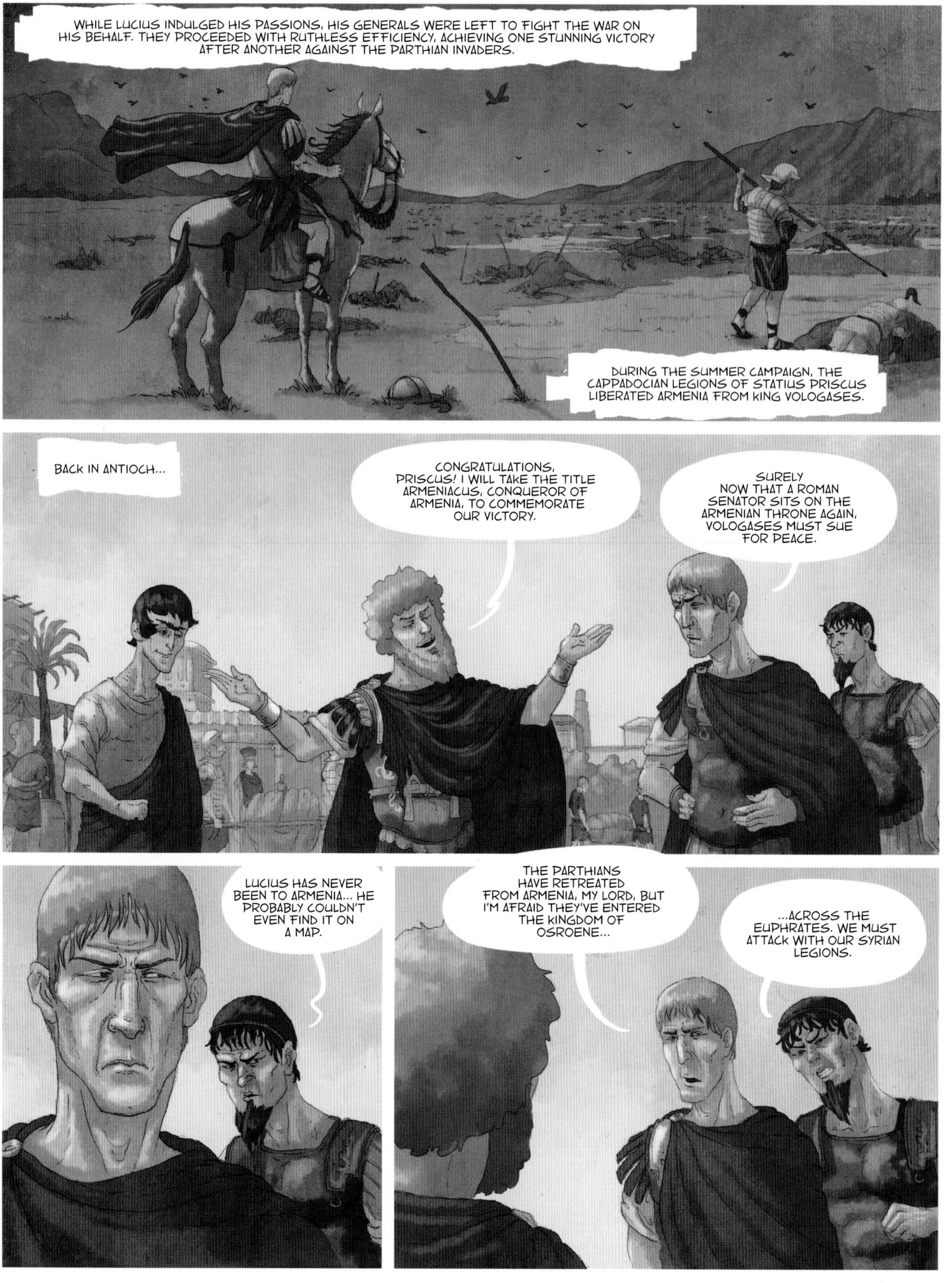
WHILE LUCIUS INDULGED HIS PASSIONS, HIS GENERALS WERE LEFT TO FIGHT THE WAR ON HIS BEHALF. THEY PROCEEDED WITH RUTHLESS EFFICIENCY, ACHIEVING ONE STUNNING VICTORY AFTER ANOTHER AGAINST THE PARTHIAN INVADERS.
DURING THE SUMMER CAMPAIGN, THE CAPPADOCIAN LEGIONS OF STATIUS PRISCUS LIBERATED ARMENIA FROM KING VOLOGASES.
BACK IN ANTIOCH...
CONGRATULATIONS, PRISCUS! I WILL TAKE THE TITLE ARMENIACUS, CONQUEROR OF ARMENIA, TO COMMEMORATE OUR VICTORY.
SURELY NOW THAT A ROMAN SENATOR SITS ON THE ARMENIAN THRONE AGAIN, VOLOGASES MUST SUE FOR PEACE.
LUCIUS HAS NEVER BEEN TO ARMENIA... HE PROBABLY COULDN'T EVEN FIND IT ON A MAP.
THE PARTHIANS HAVE RETREATED FROM ARMENIA, MY LORD, BUT I'M AFRAID THEY'VE ENTERED THE KINGDOM OF OSROENE...
...ACROSS THE EUPHRATES. WE MUST ATTACK WITH OUR SYRIAN LEGIONS.

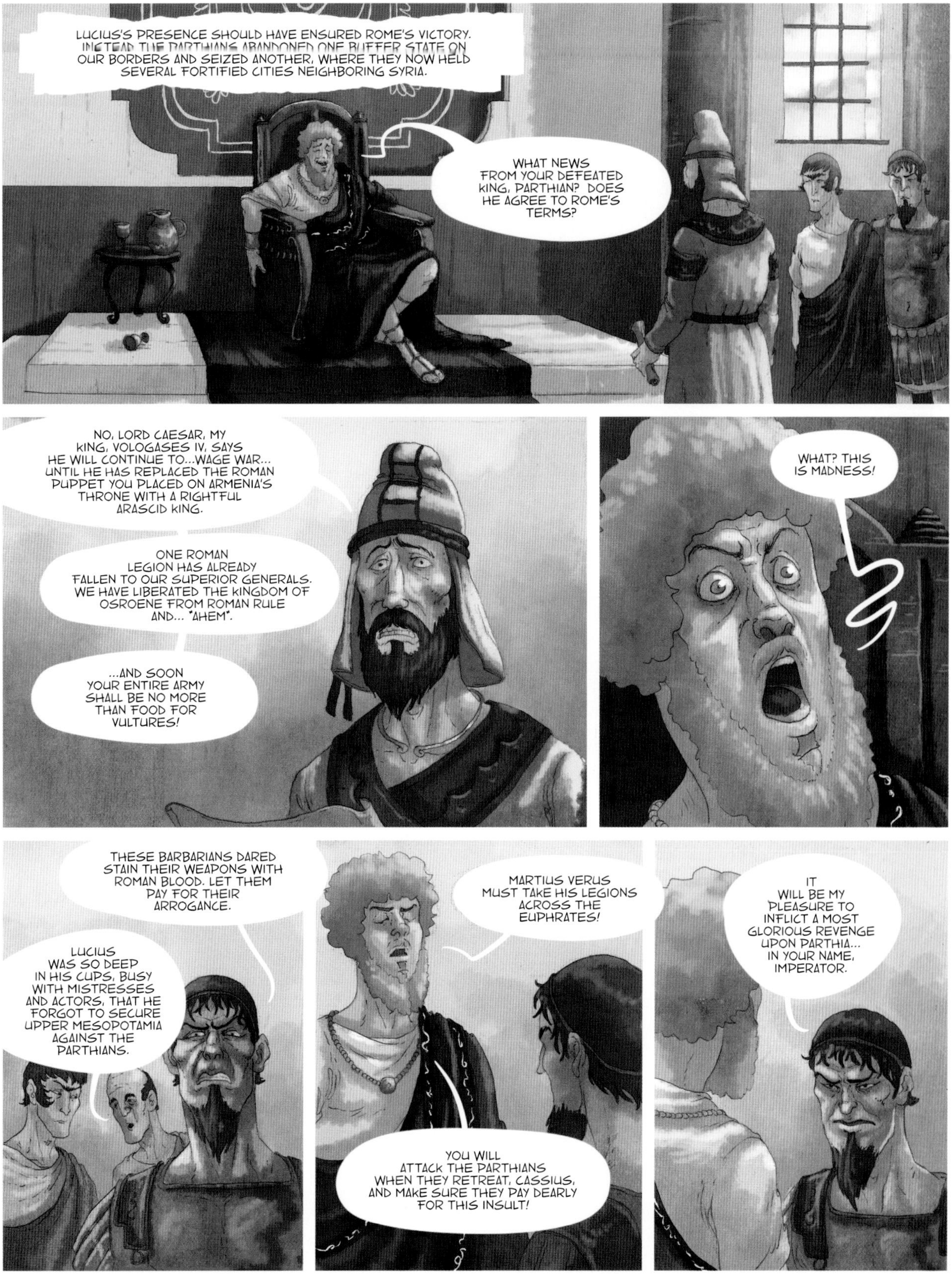
LUCIUS'S PRESENCE SHOULD HAVE ENSURED ROME'S VICTORY. INSTEAD THE PARTHIANS ABANDONED ONE BUFFER STATE ON OUR BORDERS AND SEIZED ANOTHER, WHERE THEY NOW HELD SEVERAL FORTIFIED CITIES NEIGHBORING SYRIA.
WHAT NEWS FROM YOUR DEFEATED KING, PARTHIAN? DOES HE AGREE TO ROME'S TERMS?
NO, LORD CAESAR, MY KING, VOLOGASES IV, SAYS HE WILL CONTINUE TO...WAGE WAR... UNTIL HE HAS REPLACED THE ROMAN PUPPET YOU PLACED ON ARMENIA'S THRONE WITH A RIGHTFUL ARASCID KING.
ONE ROMAN LEGION HAS ALREADY FALLEN TO OUR SUPERIOR GENERALS. WE HAVE LIBERATED THE KINGDOM OF OSROENE FROM ROMAN RULE AND... *AHEM*.
...AND SOON YOUR ENTIRE ARMY SHALL BE NO MORE THAN FOOD FOR VULTURES!
WHAT? THIS IS MADNESS!
THESE BARBARIANS DARED STAIN THEIR WEAPONS WITH ROMAN BLOOD. LET THEM PAY FOR THEIR ARROGANCE.
LUCIUS WAS SO DEEP IN HIS CUPS, BUSY WITH MISTRESSES AND ACTORS, THAT HE FORGOT TO SECURE UPPER MESOPOTAMIA AGAINST THE PARTHIANS.
MARTIUS VERUS MUST TAKE HIS LEGIONS ACROSS THE EUPHRATES!
YOU WILL ATTACK THE PARTHIANS WHEN THEY RETREAT, CASSIUS, AND MAKE SURE THEY PAY DEARLY FOR THIS INSULT!
IT WILL BE MY PLEASURE TO INFLICT A MOST GLORIOUS REVENGE UPON PARTHIA... IN YOUR NAME, IMPERATOR.

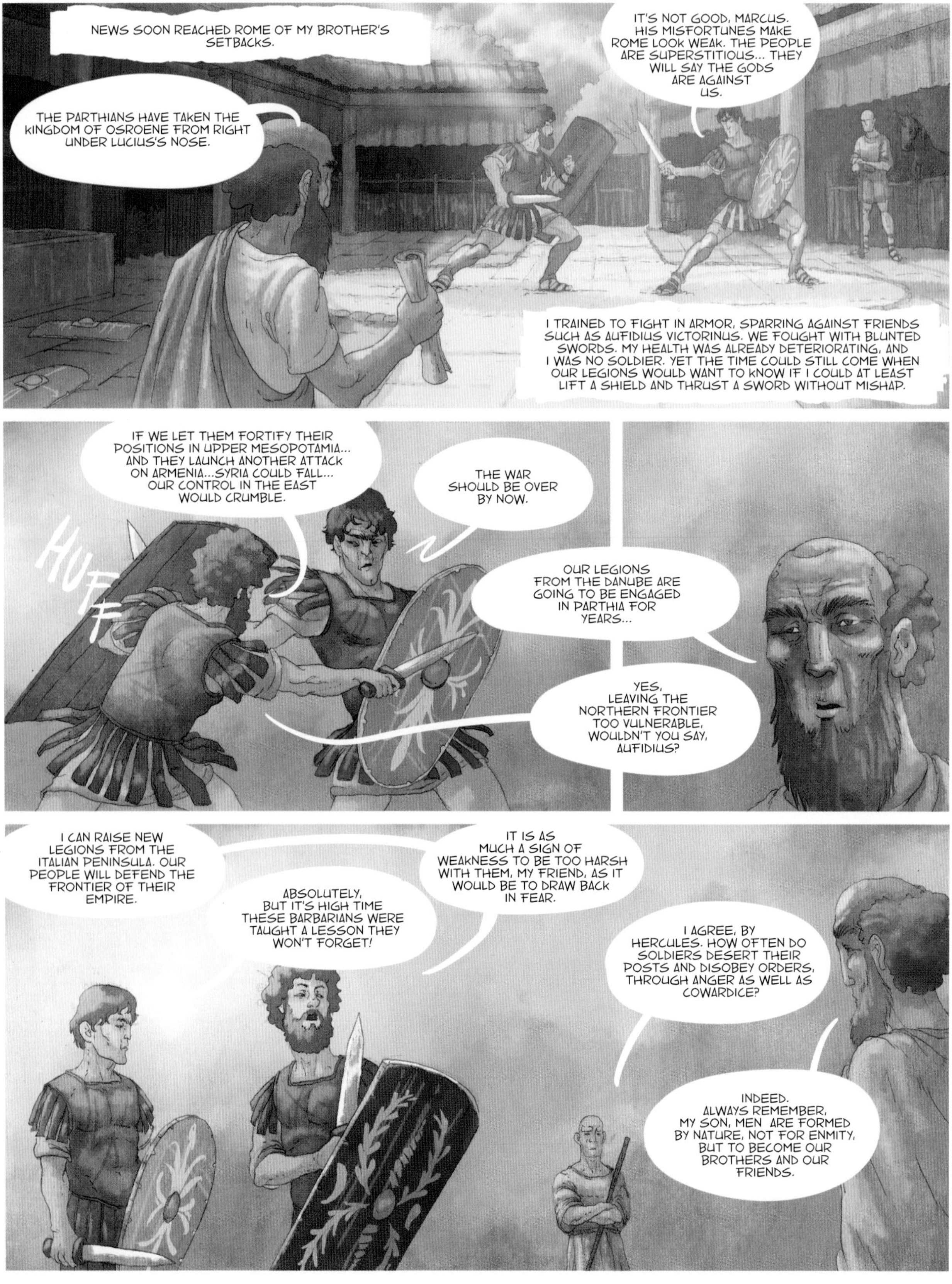
NEWS SOON REACHED ROME OF MY BROTHER'S SETBACKS.
THE PARTHIANS HAVE TAKEN THE KINGDOM OF OSROENE FROM RIGHT UNDER LUCIUS'S NOSE.
IT'S NOT GOOD, MARCUS. HIS MISFORTUNES MAKE ROME LOOK WEAK. THE PEOPLE ARE SUPERSTITIOUS... THEY WILL SAY THE GODS ARE AGAINST US.
I TRAINED TO FIGHT IN ARMOR, SPARRING AGAINST FRIENDS SUCH AS AUFIDIUS VICTORINUS. WE FOUGHT WITH BLUNTED SWORDS. MY HEALTH WAS ALREADY DETERIORATING, AND I WAS NO SOLDIER. YET THE TIME COULD STILL COME WHEN OUR LEGIONS WOULD WANT TO KNOW IF I COULD AT LEAST LIFT A SHIELD AND THRUST A SWORD WITHOUT MISHAP.
IF WE LET THEM FORTIFY THEIR POSITIONS IN UPPER MESOPOTAMIA... AND THEY LAUNCH ANOTHER ATTACK ON ARMENIA...SYRIA COULD FALL... OUR CONTROL IN THE EAST WOULD CRUMBLE.
THE WAR SHOULD BE OVER BY NOW.
HUFF
OUR LEGIONS FROM THE DANUBE ARE GOING TO BE ENGAGED IN PARTHIA FOR YEARS...
YES, LEAVING THE NORTHERN FRONTIER TOO VULNERABLE, WOULDN'T YOU SAY, AUFIDIUS?
I CAN RAISE NEW LEGIONS FROM THE ITALIAN PENINSULA. OUR PEOPLE WILL DEFEND THE FRONTIER OF THEIR EMPIRE.
ABSOLUTELY, BUT IT'S HIGH TIME THESE BARBARIANS WERE TAUGHT A LESSON THEY WON'T FORGET!
IT IS AS MUCH A SIGN OF WEAKNESS TO BE TOO HARSH WITH THEM, MY FRIEND, AS IT WOULD BE TO DRAW BACK IN FEAR.
I AGREE, BY HERCULES. HOW OFTEN DO SOLDIERS DESERT THEIR POSTS AND DISOBEY ORDERS, THROUGH ANGER AS WELL AS COWARDICE?
INDEED. ALWAYS REMEMBER, MY SON, MEN ARE FORMED BY NATURE, NOT FOR ENMITY, BUT TO BECOME OUR BROTHERS AND OUR FRIENDS.

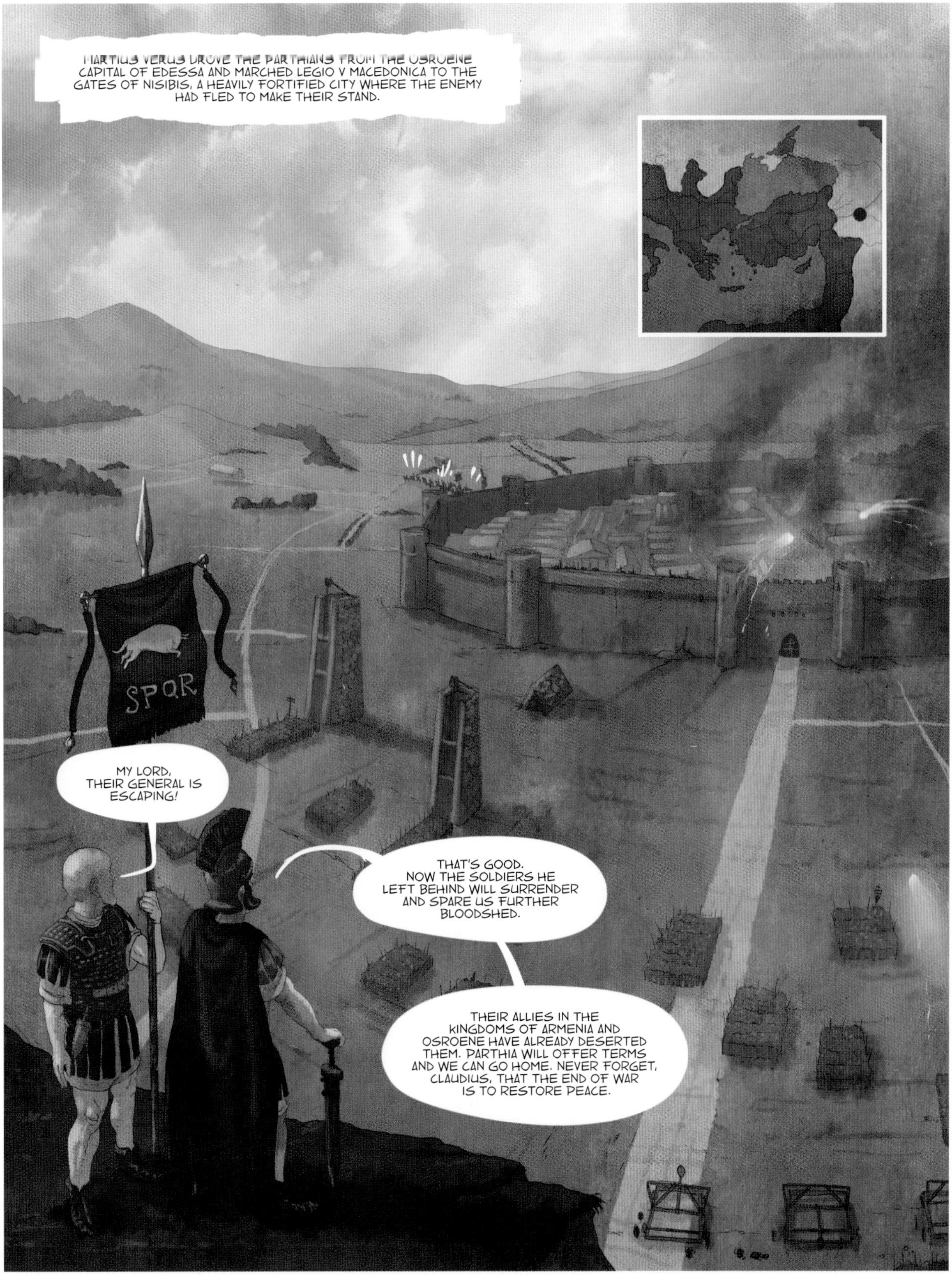
MARTIUS VERUS DROVE THE PARTHIANS FROM THE OSROENE CAPITAL OF EDESSA AND MARCHED LEGIO V MACEDONICA TO THE GATES OF NISIBIS, A HEAVILY FORTIFIED CITY WHERE THE ENEMY HAD FLED TO MAKE THEIR STAND.
SPQR
MY LORD, THEIR GENERAL IS ESCAPING!
THAT'S GOOD. NOW THE SOLDIERS HE LEFT BEHIND WILL SURRENDER AND SPARE US FURTHER BLOODSHED.
THEIR ALLIES IN THE KINGDOMS OF ARMENIA AND OSROENE HAVE ALREADY DESERTED THEM. PARTHIA WILL OFFER TERMS AND WE CAN GO HOME. NEVER FORGET, CLAUDIUS, THAT THE END OF WAR IS TO RESTORE PEACE.

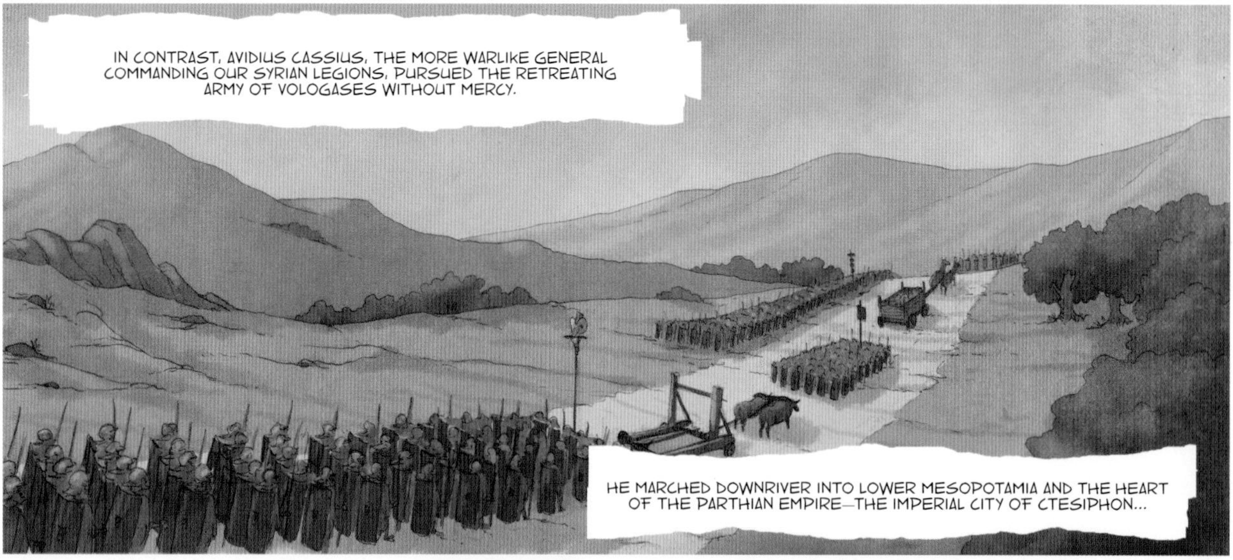
IN CONTRAST, AVIDIUS CASSIUS, THE MORE WARLIKE GENERAL COMMANDING OUR SYRIAN LEGIONS, PURSUED THE RETREATING ARMY OF VOLOGASES WITHOUT MERCY.
HE MARCHED DOWNRIVER INTO LOWER MESOPOTAMIA AND THE HEART OF THE PARTHIAN EMPIRE—THE IMPERIAL CITY OF CTESIPHON...

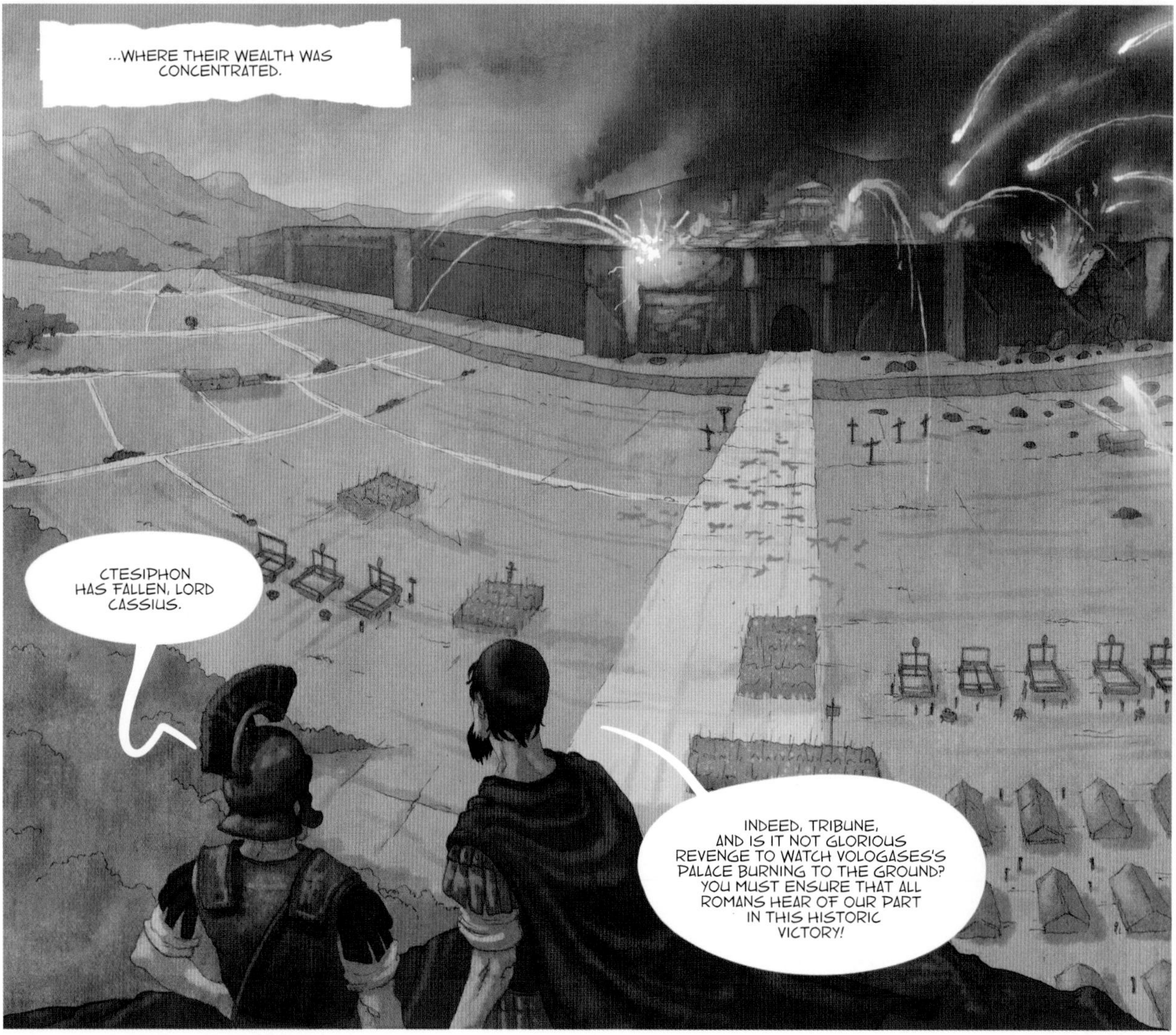
...WHERE THEIR WEALTH WAS CONCENTRATED.
CTESIPHON HAS FALLEN, LORD CASSIUS.
INDEED, TRIBUNE, AND IS IT NOT GLORIOUS REVENGE TO WATCH VOLOGASES'S PALACE BURNING TO THE GROUND? YOU MUST ENSURE THAT ALL ROMANS HEAR OF OUR PART IN THIS HISTORIC VICTORY!

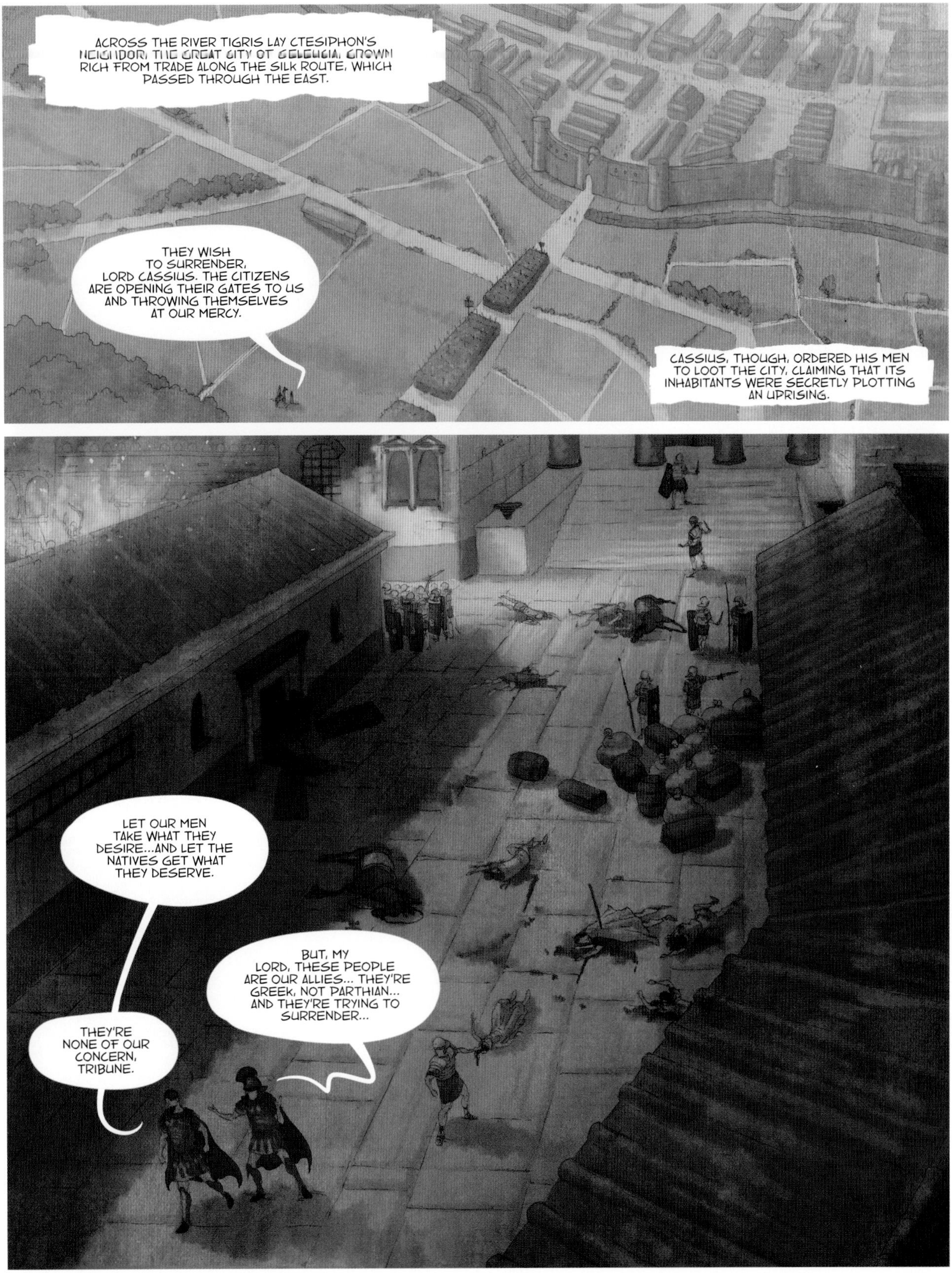
ACROSS THE RIVER TIGRIS LAY CTESIPHON'S NEIGHBOR, THE GREAT CITY OF SELEUCIA, GROWN RICH FROM TRADE ALONG THE SILK ROUTE, WHICH PASSED THROUGH THE EAST.
THEY WISH TO SURRENDER, LORD CASSIUS. THE CITIZENS ARE OPENING THEIR GATES TO US AND THROWING THEMSELVES AT OUR MERCY.
CASSIUS, THOUGH, ORDERED HIS MEN TO LOOT THE CITY, CLAIMING THAT ITS INHABITANTS WERE SECRETLY PLOTTING AN UPRISING.
LET OUR MEN TAKE WHAT THEY DESIRE...AND LET THE NATIVES GET WHAT THEY DESERVE.
BUT, MY LORD, THESE PEOPLE ARE OUR ALLIES... THEY'RE GREEK, NOT PARTHIAN... AND THEY'RE TRYING TO SURRENDER...
THEY'RE NONE OF OUR CONCERN, TRIBUNE.

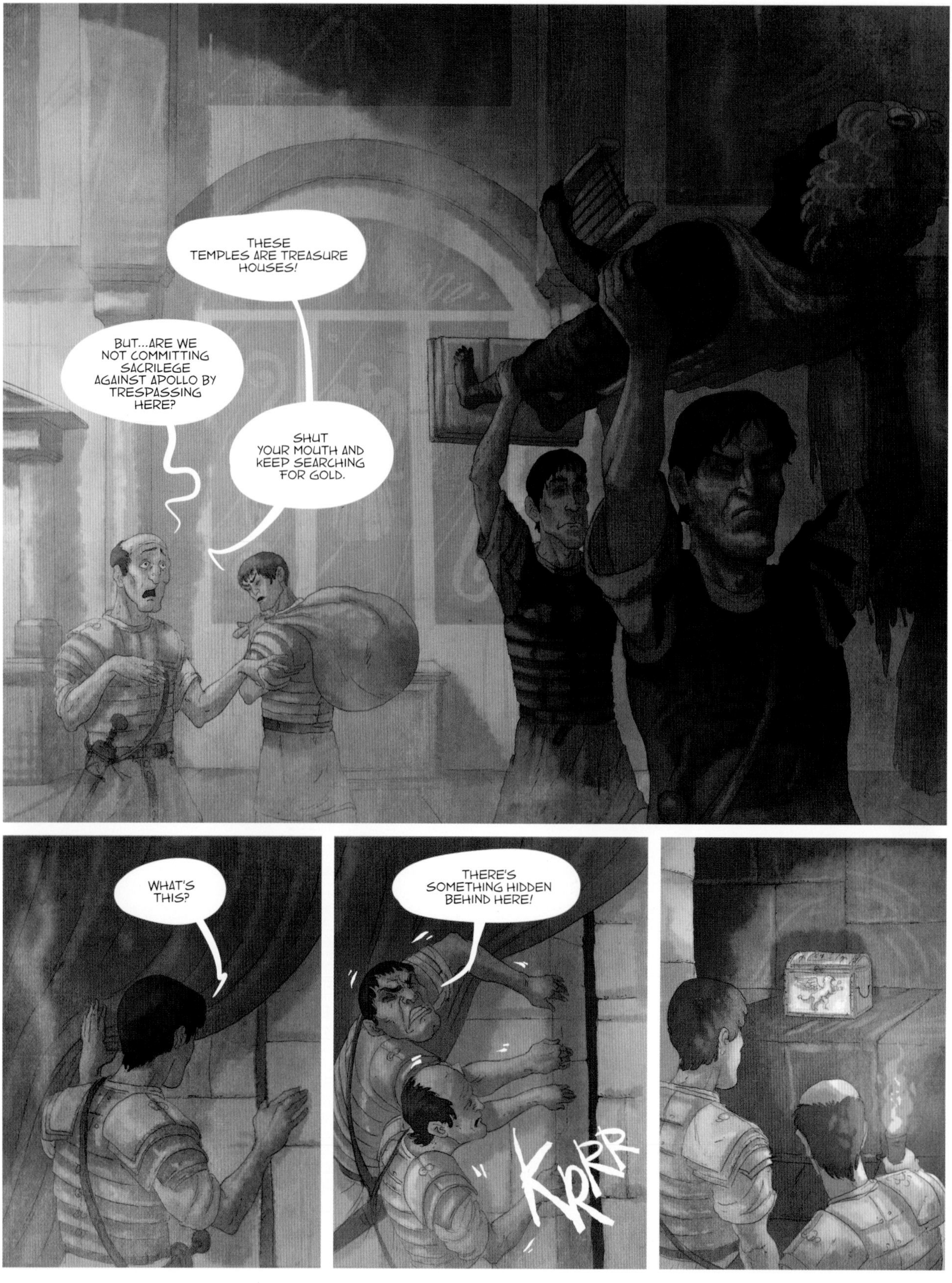
THESE TEMPLES ARE TREASURE HOUSES!
BUT...ARE WE NOT COMMITTING SACRILEGE AGAINST APOLLO BY TRESPASSING HERE?
SHUT YOUR MOUTH AND KEEP SEARCHING FOR GOLD.
WHAT'S THIS?
THERE'S SOMETHING HIDDEN BEHIND HERE!
KRRR

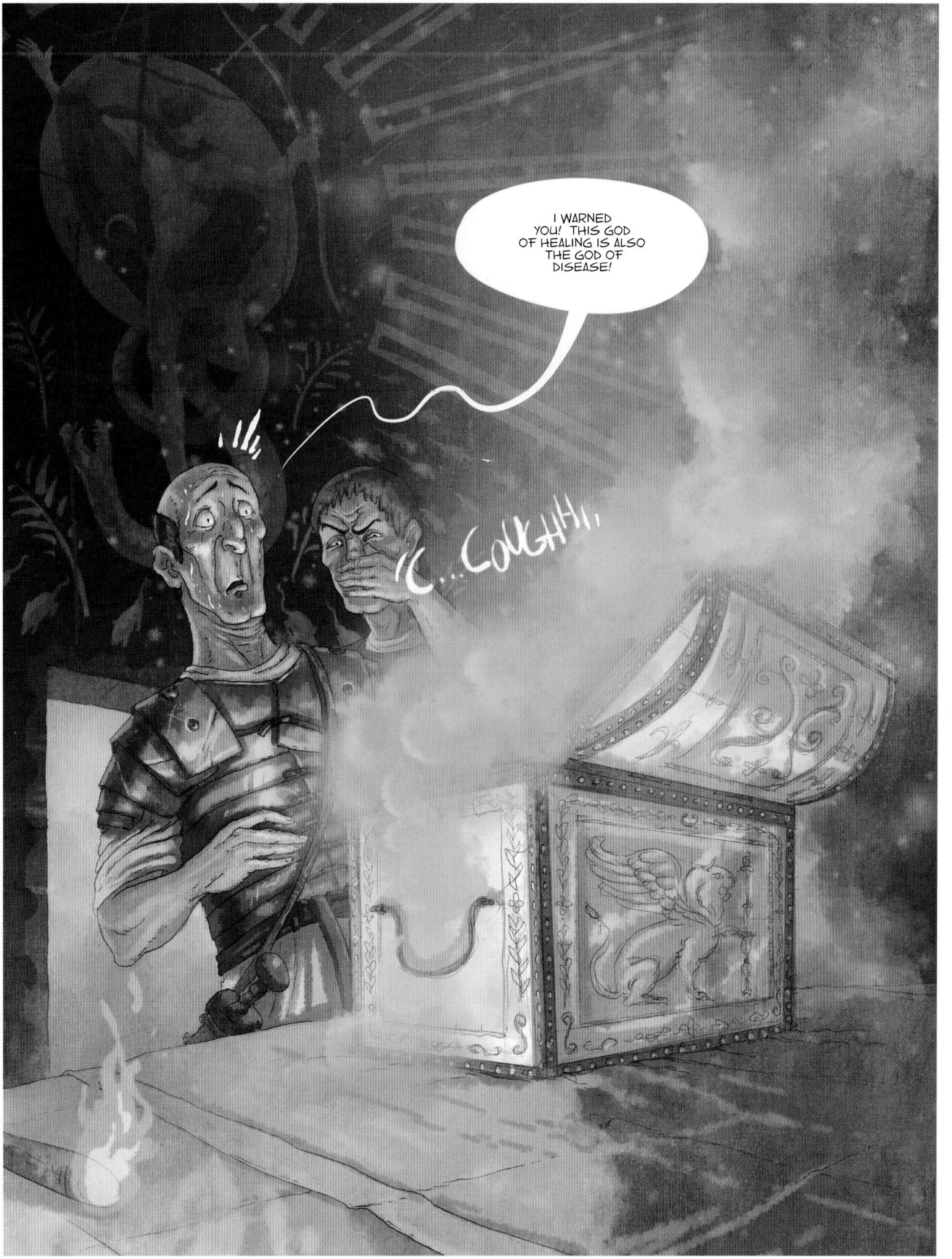
I WARNED YOU! THIS GOD OF HEALING IS ALSO THE GOD OF DISEASE!
C... COUGH!

THE HISTORY OF THE PARTHIAN WAR, WHICH LUCIUS INSTRUCTED FRONTO TO COMPOSE, DID NOT MENTION THE LOSS OF OSROENE, WHICH HAD STALLED ROME'S EARLY HOPES FOR VICTORY, OR THE LOOTING OF SELEUCIA BY CASSIUS'S LEGIONS.

SEND FRONTO SOME MORE NOTES FOR THAT HISTORY OF THE PARTHIAN WAR HE PROMISED TO WRITE...

YES, MY LORD, HE MUST STRESS THAT OUR FORTUNES ONLY IMPROVED AFTER YOU ASSUMED COMMAND...

AND REMIND HIM NOT TO RUSH PAST THE FIRST YEAR OR TWO OF THE WAR, WHEN THE PARTHIANS WERE WINNING...

MANY OF HIS FELLOW SOLDIERS WOULD THE EMPEROR CALL BY NAME, AYE, AND EVEN BY THEIR HUMOROUS CAMP NICKNAMES.

EXCELLENT, LORD CAESAR.

LUCIUS MARCHED TIRELESSLY IN PERSON AT THE HEAD OF HIS ARMY, TRUDGING ON FOOT AS OFTEN AS RIDING ON HORSEBACK. BARING HIS HEAD IN THE BLAZING DESERT AS HE NONCHALANTLY BRUSHED ASIDE THE CHOKING DUST.

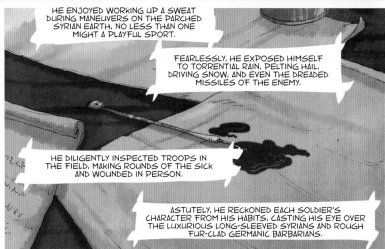

HE ENJOYED WORKING UP A SWEAT DURING MANEUVERS ON THE PARCHED SYRIAN EARTH, NO LESS THAN ONE MIGHT A PLAYFUL SPORT.

FEARLESSLY, HE EXPOSED HIMSELF TO TORRENTIAL RAIN, PELTING HAIL, DRIVING SNOW, AND EVEN THE DREADED MISSILES OF THE ENEMY.

HE DILIGENTLY INSPECTED TROOPS IN THE FIELD, MAKING ROUNDS OF THE SICK AND WOUNDED IN PERSON.

ASTUTELY, HE RECKONED EACH SOLDIER'S CHARACTER FROM HIS HABITS, CASTING HIS EYE OVER THE LUXURIOUS LONG-SLEEVED SYRIANS AND ROUGH FUR-CLAD GERMANIC BARBARIANS.

THE EMPEROR'S TABLE WAS SPREAD WITH COMMON CAMP FARE. MODEST LOCAL WINES AND LUKEWARM WATER WERE ENOUGH TO SLAKE HIS THIRST.

WHILE ON CAMPAIGN, HE SLEPT UPON THE EARTH, WITH LEAVES AND BRANCHES FOR HIS BEDDING.

PREFERRING, BY HIS NATURE, WORK TO LEISURE, WHAT TIME LUCIUS HAD FREE FROM MILITARY DUTIES, HE DEVOTED TIRELESSLY TO CIVIC ONES.

PUNISHING SERIOUS OFFENSES WITH A FIRM HAND AND YET SHOWING MERCY IN TRIFLING ONES, HE IMPROVED MANY MEN BY OPENING THE DOOR TO THEIR REPENTANCE.

OH...AND LIKE HERCULES, IN PRODICUS'S TALE, INDEED, SLEEP OVERTOOK HIM, EARNED BY HARDEST TOIL—HE WAS NOT LULLED TO SLEEP BY PLEASANT LUXURY!

THE REALITY OF WAR WAS OFTEN COMPLEX, AND FAR CRUELER THAN HISTORIES RECORD.

CASSIUS MARCHED HIS TROOPS, LADEN WITH TREASURE, HUNDREDS OF MILES FROM PARTHIA BACK TO ROMAN SYRIA, BUT MANY SUCCUMBED TO FATIGUE AND ILLNESS ALONG THE WAY.

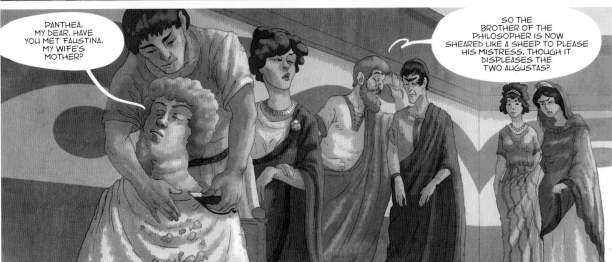

PANTHEA, MY DEAR, HAVE YOU MET FAUSTINA, MY WIFE'S MOTHER?

SO THE BROTHER OF THE PHILOSOPHER IS NOW SHEARED LIKE A SHEEP TO PLEASE HIS MISTRESS, THOUGH IT DISPLEASES THE TWO AUGUSTAS?

EPICTETUS ONCE SAID THAT IF THE EMPEROR DOMITIAN, WHO PERSECUTED THE STOICS, WANTED TO SHAVE OFF THE PHILOSOPHER'S BEARD, HE'D HAVE TO CUT OFF HIS HEAD FIRST.

I MAY BE THE DAUGHTER OF MARCUS AURELIUS, BUT MY HUSBAND HAS NEVER BEEN A PHILOSOPHER. HE'S QUITE THE OPPOSITE OF FATHER.

CASSIUS, WHAT ARE YOU DOING HERE?

MY LORD IMPERATOR, AS CTESIPHON, SELEUCIA, AND BABYLON HAVE ALL FALLEN TO OUR LEGIONS, KING VOLOGASES NOW SUES FOR PEACE.

IT'S HIM, MOTHER, THE SYRIAN IN WHOSE VEINS, THEY SAY, RUNS THE BLOOD OF OUR FIRST AUGUSTUS.

HE HAS NO OPTION BUT TO CEDE MESOPOTAMIA TO US, AT LEAST FOR THE TIME BEING.

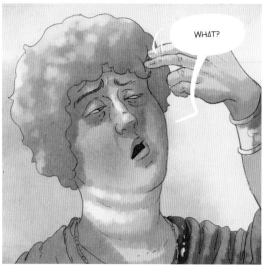

WHAT?

YOUR HUSBAND IS AN EMPEROR OF ROME, BUT HE ACTS MORE LIKE A KING OF SYRIA...

HE MAY HAVE CONQUERED THE PARTHIANS, BUT HE HAS FAILED TO CONQUER HIMSELF.

MOTHER, HE'S RELUCTANT TO RETURN HOME SO LONG AS HE CAN INDULGE HIMSELF HERE...

NO, WE'RE NOT FINISHED HERE, CASSIUS! PREPARE YOUR MEN FOR ANOTHER OFFENSIVE ACROSS THE TIGRIS.

GO AND DRIVE THE PARTHIANS OUT OF MEDIA AS WELL. WE WILL TAKE THE CITY OF ECBATANA AND CLEAR A PATH ALONG THE SILK ROUTE.

IT WILL BE MY PLEASURE, IMPERATOR.

HOW WOULD WE EVER HOLD ON TO A CITY THAT FAR EAST?

IF ONLY IT WASN'T AT THE BEHEST OF THIS BUFFOON...

LUCIUS TO MY BROTHER, MARCUS. AVIDIUS CASSIUS IS HUNGRY FOR THE THRONE...

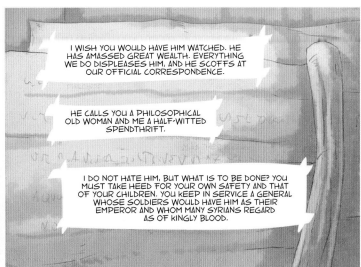

I WISH YOU WOULD HAVE HIM WATCHED. HE HAS AMASSED GREAT WEALTH. EVERYTHING WE DO DISPLEASES HIM, AND HE SCOFFS AT OUR OFFICIAL CORRESPONDENCE.

HE CALLS YOU A PHILOSOPHICAL OLD WOMAN AND ME A HALF-WITTED SPENDTHRIFT.

I DO NOT HATE HIM, BUT WHAT IS TO BE DONE? YOU MUST TAKE HEED FOR YOUR OWN SAFETY AND THAT OF YOUR CHILDREN. YOU KEEP IN SERVICE A GENERAL WHOSE SOLDIERS WOULD HAVE HIM AS THEIR EMPEROR AND WHOM MANY SYRIANS REGARD AS OF KINGLY BLOOD.

LUCIUS, YOUR LETTER IS THAT OF A DISQUIETED MAN RATHER THAN A GENERAL, AND IT IS NOT WORTHY OF OUR STATION.

FOR IF THE GODS HAVE DECREED THAT THE EMPIRE SHOULD FALL INTO SOME USURPER'S HANDS, WE CANNOT SLAY HIM EVEN SHOULD WE SO DESIRE. NO ONE EVER KILLS HIS SUCCESSOR.

YET IF A REBELLION IS DOOMED TO FAIL, BY THE GODS, ITS INSTIGATOR WILL FALL INTO MISFORTUNE WITHOUT ANY ACT OF VIOLENCE ON OUR PART.

IN ANY CASE, WE CANNOT JUDGE A MAN GUILTY WHOM NO ONE HAS ACCUSED AND, AS YOU SAY, THE SOLDIERS REVERE.

INDEED, IN CASES OF TREASON, EVEN THOSE PROVED GUILTY MAY SEEM TO THE PEOPLE TO HAVE SUFFERED AN INJUSTICE.

YOU REMEMBER WHAT OUR GRANDFATHER HADRIAN LIKED TO SAY: "UNHAPPY IS THE LOT OF EMPERORS, FOR THEY ARE NEVER BELIEVED WHEN THEY ACCUSE ANYONE OF PRETENDING TO THE THRONE UNTIL AFTER THEY ARE SLAIN."

SO LET CASSIUS BE ALONE, AS HE IS AN ABLE GENERAL AND A STERN AND BRAVE MAN, OF WHOM ROME CURRENTLY HAS NEED.

AS FOR YOUR STATEMENT THAT I SHOULD TAKE HEED FOR MY CHILDREN'S LIVES BY TAKING HIS...

IF CASSIUS IS MORE DESERVING OF LOVE AND IF IT BENEFITS ROME FOR HIM TO LIVE RATHER THAN THEM, BY ALL MEANS LET MY CHILDREN PERISH.

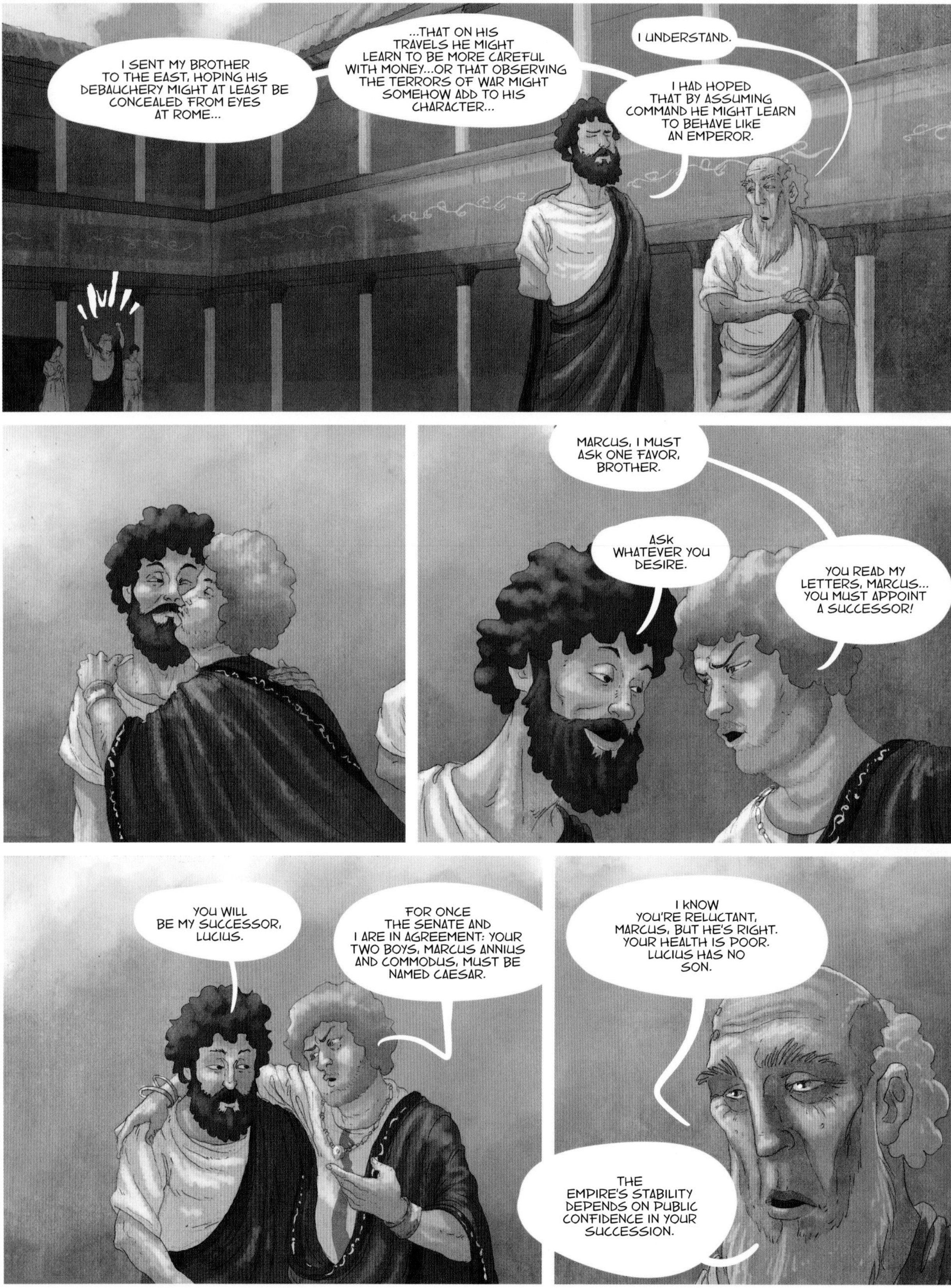
I SENT MY BROTHER TO THE EAST, HOPING HIS DEBAUCHERY MIGHT AT LEAST BE CONCEALED FROM EYES AT ROME...
...THAT ON HIS TRAVELS HE MIGHT LEARN TO BE MORE CAREFUL WITH MONEY...OR THAT OBSERVING THE TERRORS OF WAR MIGHT SOMEHOW ADD TO HIS CHARACTER...
I HAD HOPED THAT BY ASSUMING COMMAND HE MIGHT LEARN TO BEHAVE LIKE AN EMPEROR.
I UNDERSTAND.
MARCUS, I MUST ASK ONE FAVOR, BROTHER.
ASK WHATEVER YOU DESIRE.
YOU READ MY LETTERS, MARCUS... YOU MUST APPOINT A SUCCESSOR!
YOU WILL BE MY SUCCESSOR, LUCIUS.
FOR ONCE THE SENATE AND I ARE IN AGREEMENT: YOUR TWO BOYS, MARCUS ANNIUS AND COMMODUS, MUST BE NAMED CAESAR.
I KNOW YOU'RE RELUCTANT, MARCUS, BUT HE'S RIGHT. YOUR HEALTH IS POOR. LUCIUS HAS NO SON.
THE EMPIRE'S STABILITY DEPENDS ON PUBLIC CONFIDENCE IN YOUR SUCCESSION.

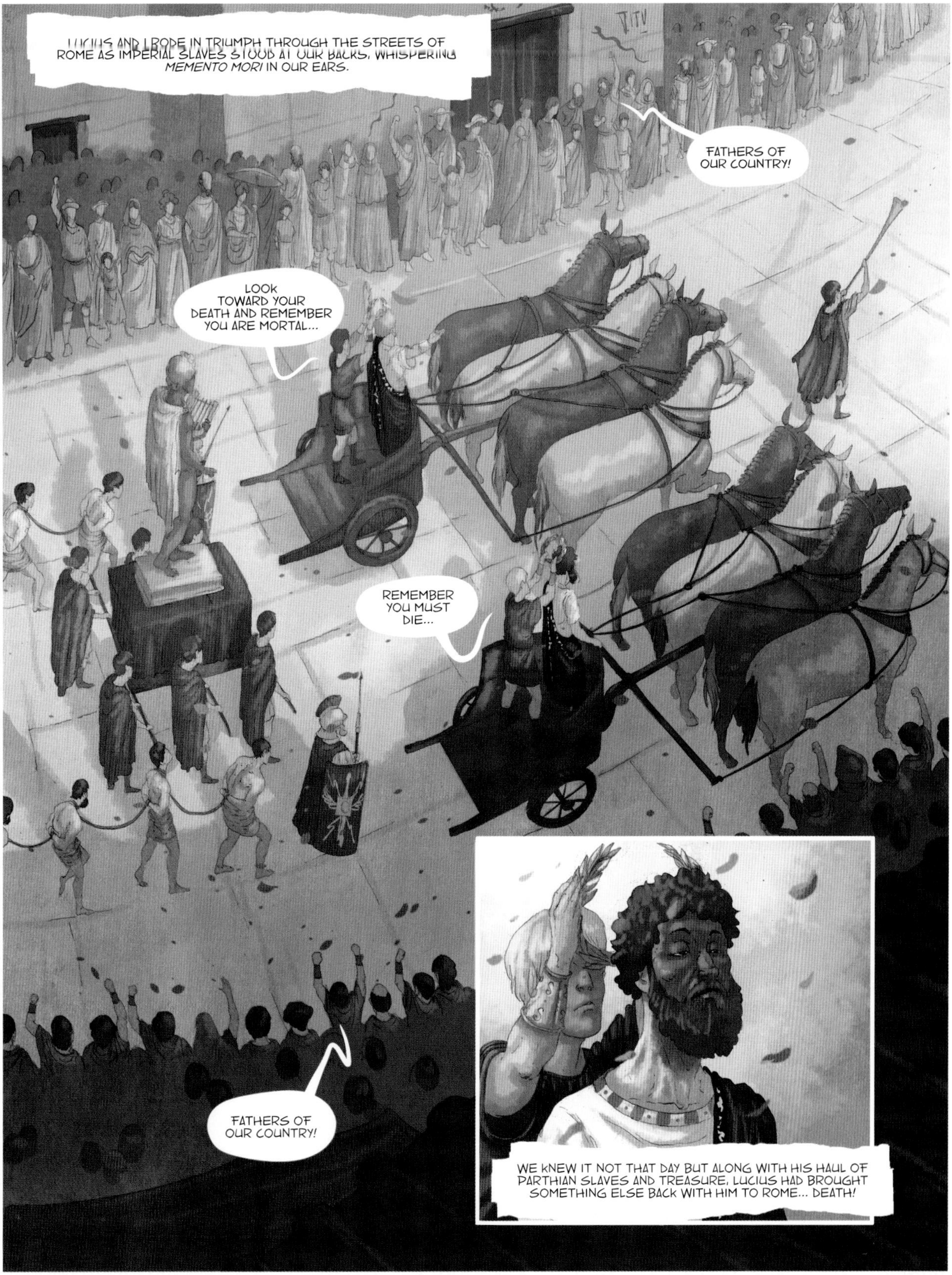

LUCIUS AND I RODE IN TRIUMPH THROUGH THE STREETS OF ROME AS IMPERIAL SLAVES STOOD AT OUR BACKS, WHISPERING *MEMENTO MORI* IN OUR EARS.
FATHERS OF OUR COUNTRY!
LOOK TOWARD YOUR DEATH AND REMEMBER YOU ARE MORTAL...
REMEMBER YOU MUST DIE...
FATHERS OF OUR COUNTRY!
WE KNEW IT NOT THAT DAY BUT ALONG WITH HIS HAUL OF PARTHIAN SLAVES AND TREASURE, LUCIUS HAD BROUGHT SOMETHING ELSE BACK WITH HIM TO ROME... DEATH!

THE
ANTONINE
PLAGUE

*For the destruction of the soul is a
more serious pestilence, indeed, than
the corruption of the air which
surrounds us.*

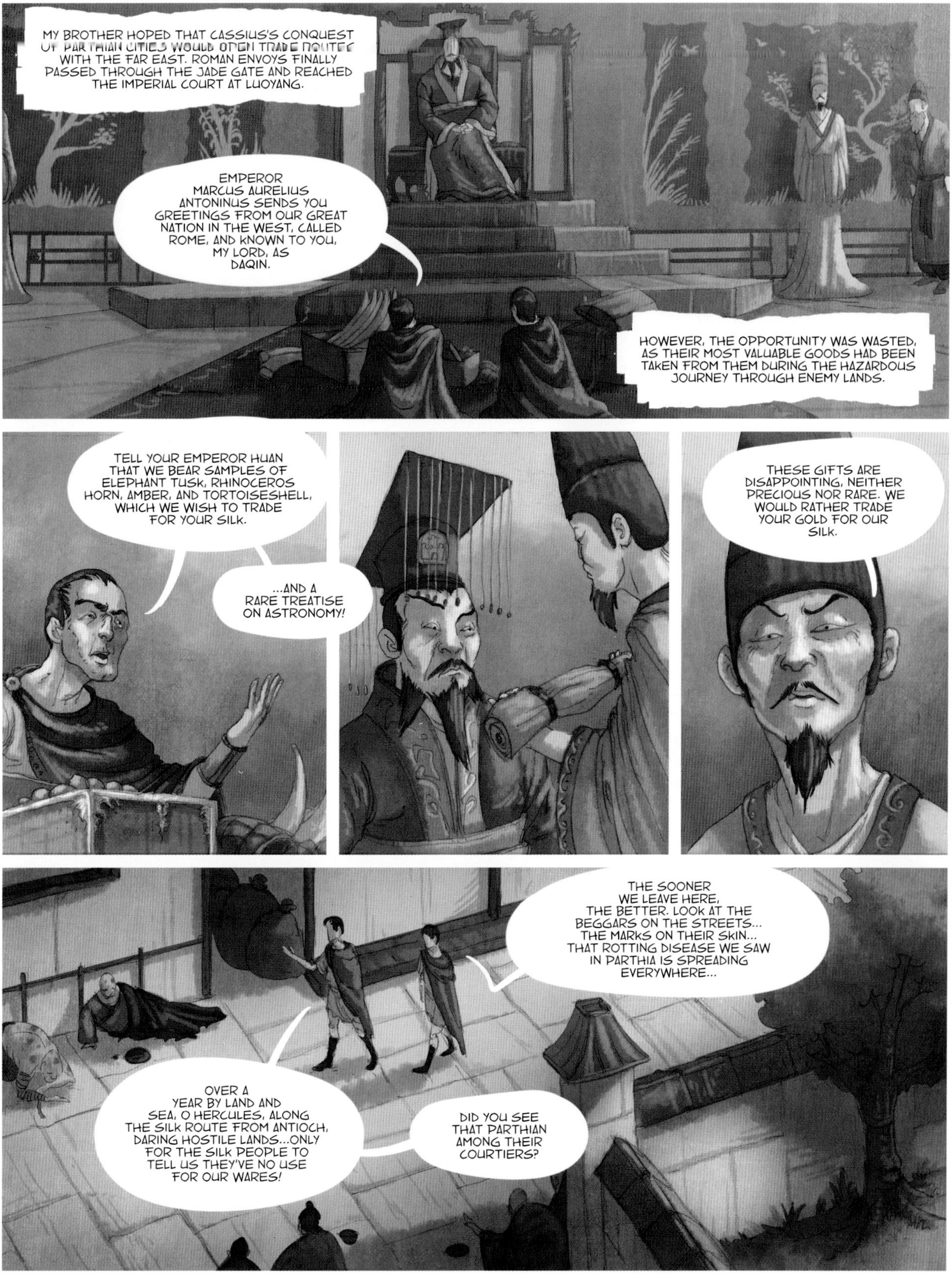
MY BROTHER HOPED THAT CASSIUS'S CONQUEST OF PARTHIAN CITIES WOULD OPEN TRADE ROUTES WITH THE FAR EAST. ROMAN ENVOYS FINALLY PASSED THROUGH THE JADE GATE AND REACHED THE IMPERIAL COURT AT LUOYANG.
EMPEROR MARCUS AURELIUS ANTONINUS SENDS YOU GREETINGS FROM OUR GREAT NATION IN THE WEST, CALLED ROME, AND KNOWN TO YOU, MY LORD, AS DAQIN.
HOWEVER, THE OPPORTUNITY WAS WASTED, AS THEIR MOST VALUABLE GOODS HAD BEEN TAKEN FROM THEM DURING THE HAZARDOUS JOURNEY THROUGH ENEMY LANDS.
TELL YOUR EMPEROR HUAN THAT WE BEAR SAMPLES OF ELEPHANT TUSK, RHINOCEROS HORN, AMBER, AND TORTOISESHELL, WHICH WE WISH TO TRADE FOR YOUR SILK.
...AND A RARE TREATISE ON ASTRONOMY!
THESE GIFTS ARE DISAPPOINTING, NEITHER PRECIOUS NOR RARE. WE WOULD RATHER TRADE YOUR GOLD FOR OUR SILK.
THE SOONER WE LEAVE HERE, THE BETTER. LOOK AT THE BEGGARS ON THE STREETS... THE MARKS ON THEIR SKIN... THAT ROTTING DISEASE WE SAW IN PARTHIA IS SPREADING EVERYWHERE...
OVER A YEAR BY LAND AND SEA, O HERCULES, ALONG THE SILK ROUTE FROM ANTIOCH, DARING HOSTILE LANDS...ONLY FOR THE SILK PEOPLE TO TELL US THEY'VE NO USE FOR OUR WARES!
DID YOU SEE THAT PARTHIAN AMONG THEIR COURTIERS?

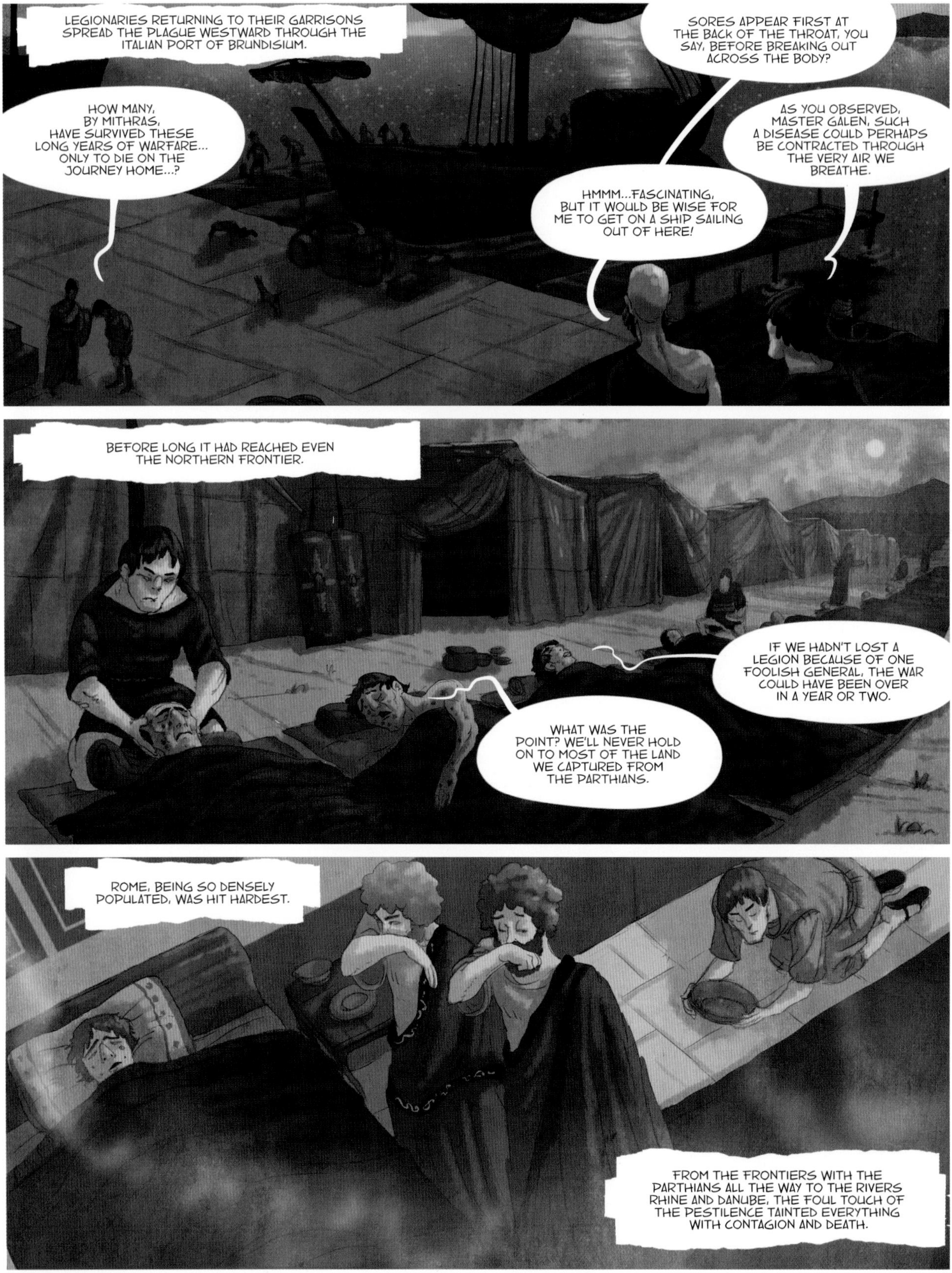

LEGIONARIES RETURNING TO THEIR GARRISONS SPREAD THE PLAGUE WESTWARD THROUGH THE ITALIAN PORT OF BRUNDISIUM.
HOW MANY, BY MITHRAS, HAVE SURVIVED THESE LONG YEARS OF WARFARE... ONLY TO DIE ON THE JOURNEY HOME...?
SORES APPEAR FIRST AT THE BACK OF THE THROAT, YOU SAY, BEFORE BREAKING OUT ACROSS THE BODY?
AS YOU OBSERVED, MASTER GALEN, SUCH A DISEASE COULD PERHAPS BE CONTRACTED THROUGH THE VERY AIR WE BREATHE.
HMMM...FASCINATING, BUT IT WOULD BE WISE FOR ME TO GET ON A SHIP SAILING OUT OF HERE!
BEFORE LONG IT HAD REACHED EVEN THE NORTHERN FRONTIER.
IF WE HADN'T LOST A LEGION BECAUSE OF ONE FOOLISH GENERAL, THE WAR COULD HAVE BEEN OVER IN A YEAR OR TWO.
WHAT WAS THE POINT? WE'LL NEVER HOLD ON TO MOST OF THE LAND WE CAPTURED FROM THE PARTHIANS.
ROME, BEING SO DENSELY POPULATED, WAS HIT HARDEST.
FROM THE FRONTIERS WITH THE PARTHIANS ALL THE WAY TO THE RIVERS RHINE AND DANUBE, THE FOUL TOUCH OF THE PESTILENCE TAINTED EVERYTHING WITH CONTAGION AND DEATH.

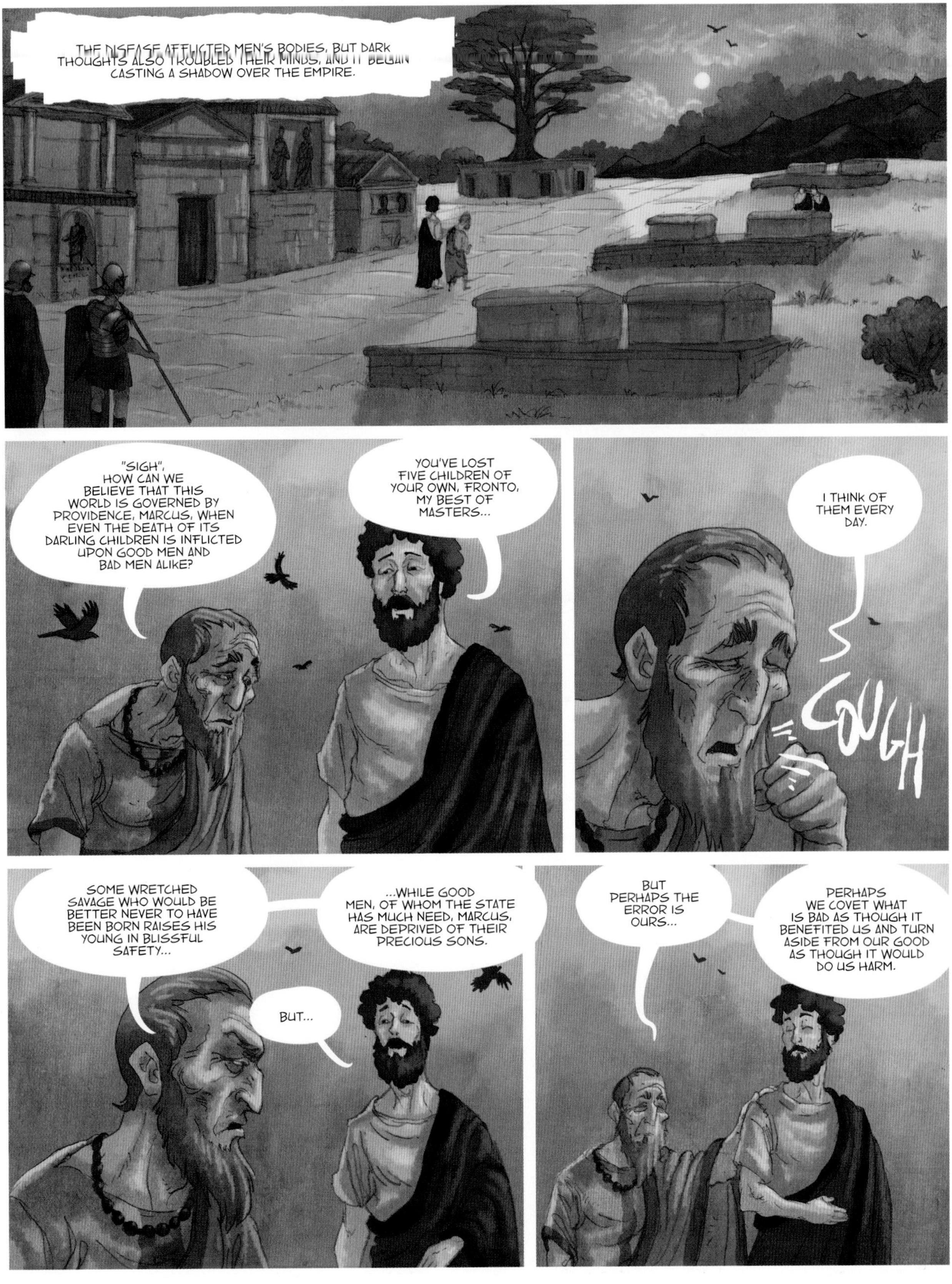
THE DISEASE AFFLICTED MEN'S BODIES, BUT DARK THOUGHTS ALSO TROUBLED THEIR MINDS, AND IT BEGAN CASTING A SHADOW OVER THE EMPIRE.
"SIGH", HOW CAN WE BELIEVE THAT THIS WORLD IS GOVERNED BY PROVIDENCE, MARCUS, WHEN EVEN THE DEATH OF ITS DARLING CHILDREN IS INFLICTED UPON GOOD MEN AND BAD MEN ALIKE?
YOU'VE LOST FIVE CHILDREN OF YOUR OWN, FRONTO, MY BEST OF MASTERS...
I THINK OF THEM EVERY DAY.
COUGH
SOME WRETCHED SAVAGE WHO WOULD BE BETTER NEVER TO HAVE BEEN BORN RAISES HIS YOUNG IN BLISSFUL SAFETY...
...WHILE GOOD MEN, OF WHOM THE STATE HAS MUCH NEED, MARCUS, ARE DEPRIVED OF THEIR PRECIOUS SONS.
BUT...
BUT PERHAPS THE ERROR IS OURS...
PERHAPS WE COVET WHAT IS BAD AS THOUGH IT BENEFITED US AND TURN ASIDE FROM OUR GOOD AS THOUGH IT WOULD DO US HARM.

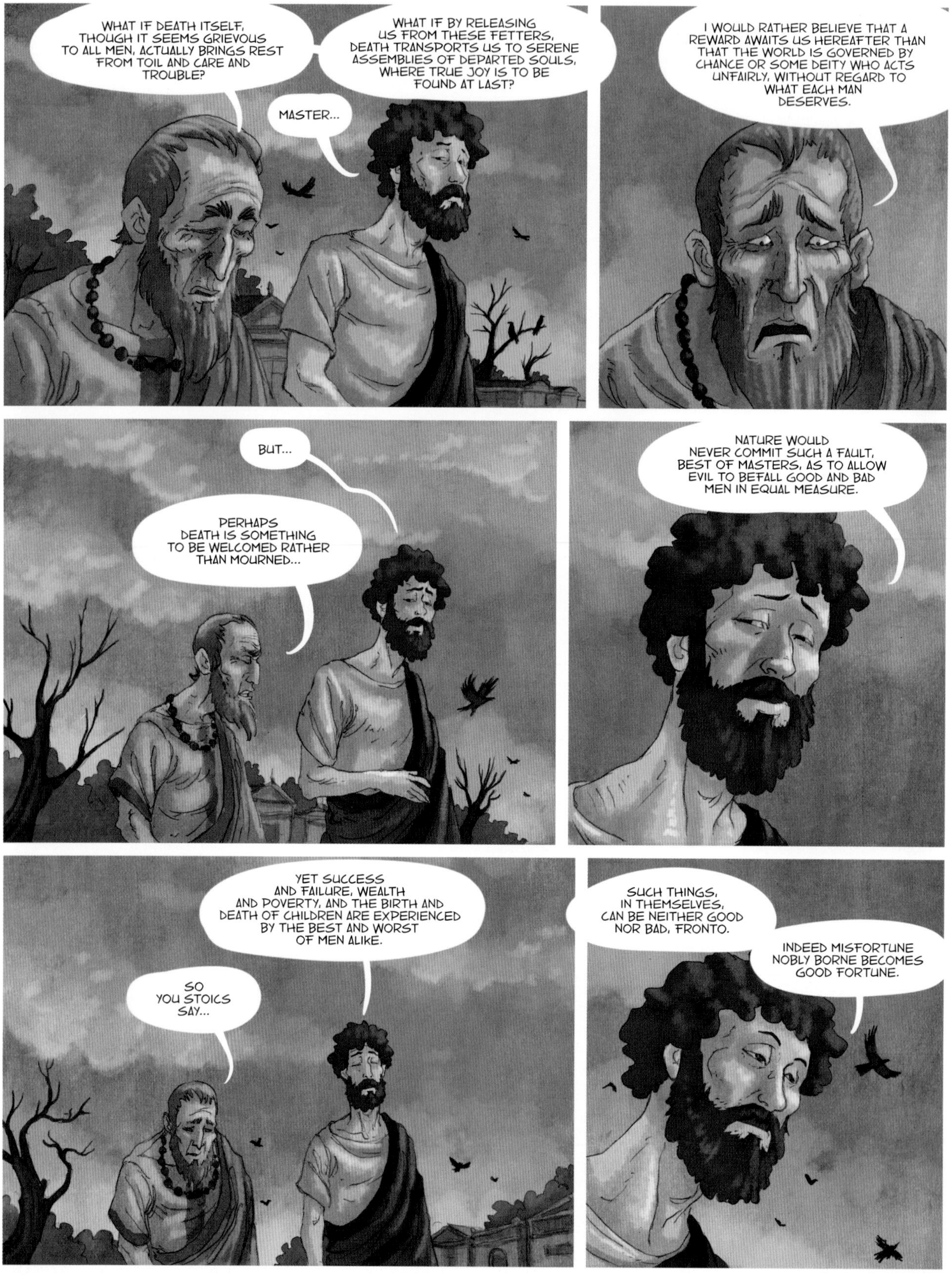
WHAT IF DEATH ITSELF, THOUGH IT SEEMS GRIEVOUS TO ALL MEN, ACTUALLY BRINGS REST FROM TOIL AND CARE AND TROUBLE?
WHAT IF BY RELEASING US FROM THESE FETTERS, DEATH TRANSPORTS US TO SERENE ASSEMBLIES OF DEPARTED SOULS, WHERE TRUE JOY IS TO BE FOUND AT LAST?
MASTER...
I WOULD RATHER BELIEVE THAT A REWARD AWAITS US HEREAFTER THAN THAT THE WORLD IS GOVERNED BY CHANCE OR SOME DEITY WHO ACTS UNFAIRLY, WITHOUT REGARD TO WHAT EACH MAN DESERVES.
BUT...
PERHAPS DEATH IS SOMETHING TO BE WELCOMED RATHER THAN MOURNED...
NATURE WOULD NEVER COMMIT SUCH A FAULT, BEST OF MASTERS, AS TO ALLOW EVIL TO BEFALL GOOD AND BAD MEN IN EQUAL MEASURE.
YET SUCCESS AND FAILURE, WEALTH AND POVERTY, AND THE BIRTH AND DEATH OF CHILDREN ARE EXPERIENCED BY THE BEST AND WORST OF MEN ALIKE.
SO YOU STOICS SAY...
SUCH THINGS, IN THEMSELVES, CAN BE NEITHER GOOD NOR BAD, FRONTO.
INDEED MISFORTUNE NOBLY BORNE BECOMES GOOD FORTUNE.

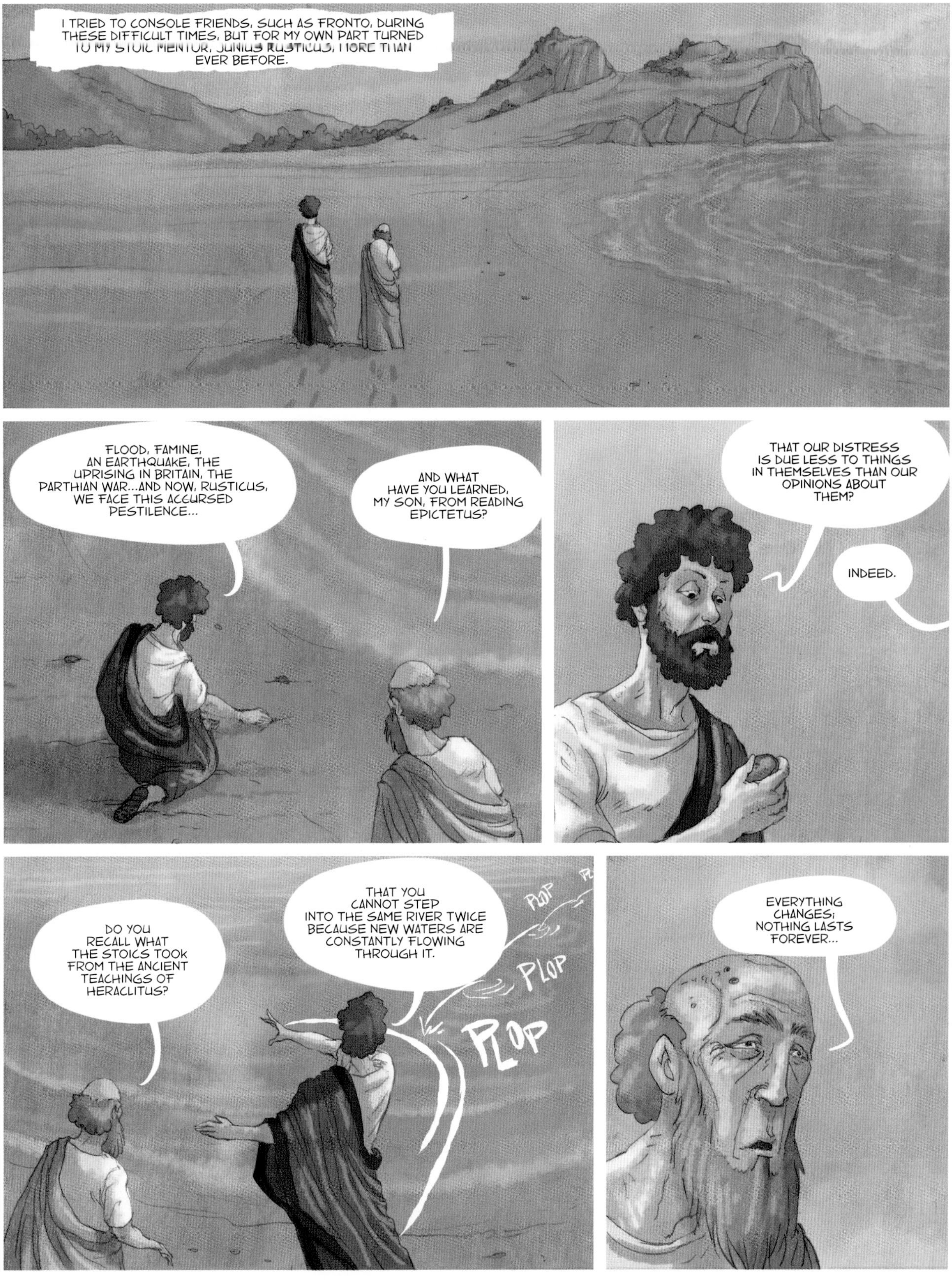
I TRIED TO CONSOLE FRIENDS, SUCH AS FRONTO, DURING THESE DIFFICULT TIMES, BUT FOR MY OWN PART TURNED TO MY STOIC MENTOR, JUNIUS RUSTICUS, MORE THAN EVER BEFORE.
FLOOD, FAMINE, AN EARTHQUAKE, THE UPRISING IN BRITAIN, THE PARTHIAN WAR...AND NOW, RUSTICUS, WE FACE THIS ACCURSED PESTILENCE...
AND WHAT HAVE YOU LEARNED, MY SON, FROM READING EPICTETUS?
THAT OUR DISTRESS IS DUE LESS TO THINGS IN THEMSELVES THAN OUR OPINIONS ABOUT THEM?
INDEED.
DO YOU RECALL WHAT THE STOICS TOOK FROM THE ANCIENT TEACHINGS OF HERACLITUS?
THAT YOU CANNOT STEP INTO THE SAME RIVER TWICE BECAUSE NEW WATERS ARE CONSTANTLY FLOWING THROUGH IT.
PLOP
PLOP
PLOP
EVERYTHING CHANGES; NOTHING LASTS FOREVER...

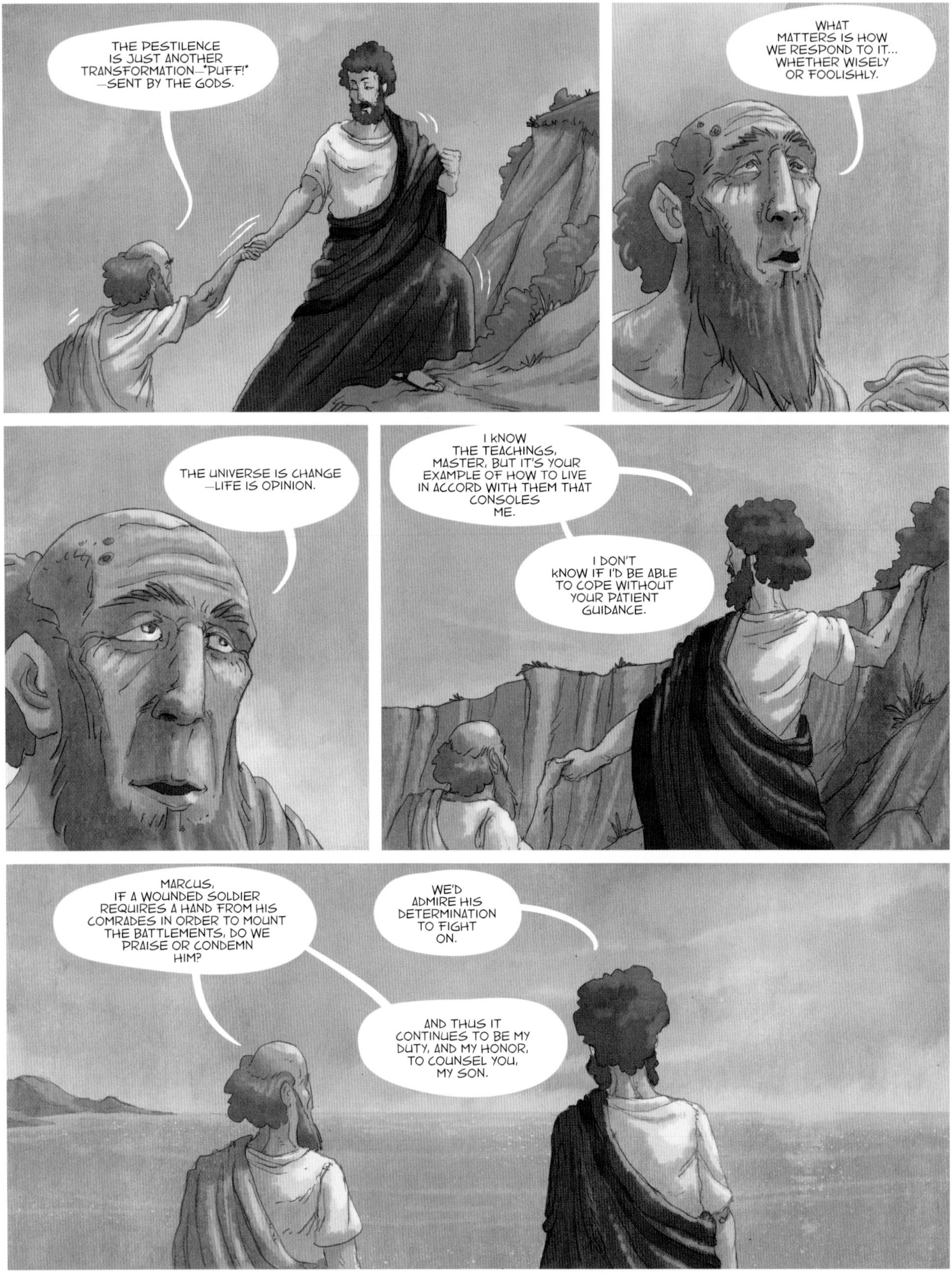
THE PESTILENCE IS JUST ANOTHER TRANSFORMATION—"PUFF!" —SENT BY THE GODS.
WHAT MATTERS IS HOW WE RESPOND TO IT... WHETHER WISELY OR FOOLISHLY.
THE UNIVERSE IS CHANGE —LIFE IS OPINION.
I KNOW THE TEACHINGS, MASTER, BUT IT'S YOUR EXAMPLE OF HOW TO LIVE IN ACCORD WITH THEM THAT CONSOLES ME.
I DON'T KNOW IF I'D BE ABLE TO COPE WITHOUT YOUR PATIENT GUIDANCE.
MARCUS, IF A WOUNDED SOLDIER REQUIRES A HAND FROM HIS COMRADES IN ORDER TO MOUNT THE BATTLEMENTS, DO WE PRAISE OR CONDEMN HIM?
WE'D ADMIRE HIS DETERMINATION TO FIGHT ON.
AND THUS IT CONTINUES TO BE MY DUTY, AND MY HONOR, TO COUNSEL YOU, MY SON.

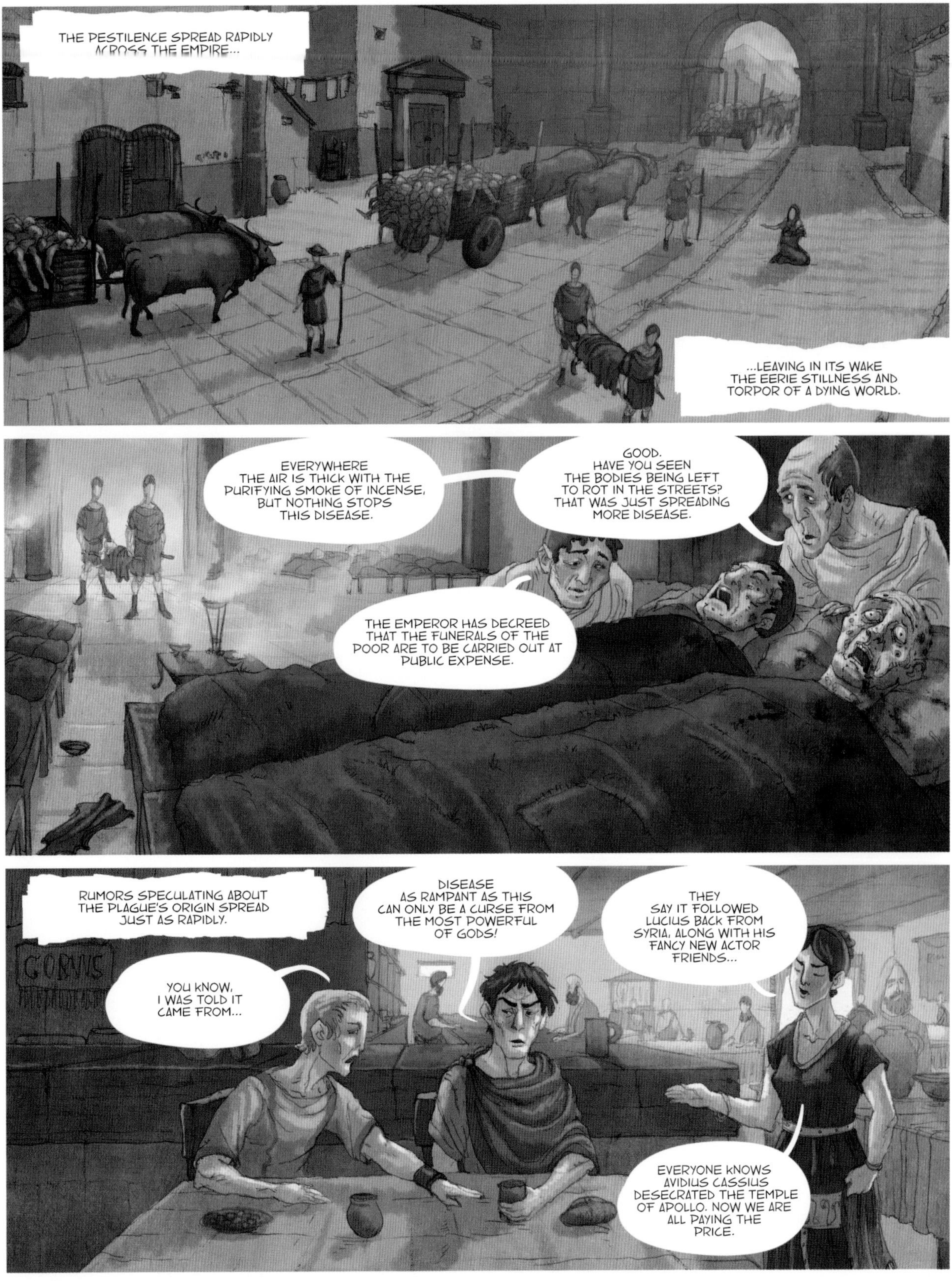
THE PESTILENCE SPREAD RAPIDLY ACROSS THE EMPIRE...
...LEAVING IN ITS WAKE THE EERIE STILLNESS AND TORPOR OF A DYING WORLD.
EVERYWHERE THE AIR IS THICK WITH THE PURIFYING SMOKE OF INCENSE, BUT NOTHING STOPS THIS DISEASE.
GOOD. HAVE YOU SEEN THE BODIES BEING LEFT TO ROT IN THE STREETS? THAT WAS JUST SPREADING MORE DISEASE.
THE EMPEROR HAS DECREED THAT THE FUNERALS OF THE POOR ARE TO BE CARRIED OUT AT PUBLIC EXPENSE.
RUMORS SPECULATING ABOUT THE PLAGUE'S ORIGIN SPREAD JUST AS RAPIDLY.
CORVUS
YOU KNOW, I WAS TOLD IT CAME FROM...
DISEASE AS RAMPANT AS THIS CAN ONLY BE A CURSE FROM THE MOST POWERFUL OF GODS!
THEY SAY IT FOLLOWED LUCIUS BACK FROM SYRIA, ALONG WITH HIS FANCY NEW ACTOR FRIENDS...
EVERYONE KNOWS AVIDIUS CASSIUS DESECRATED THE TEMPLE OF APOLLO. NOW WE ARE ALL PAYING THE PRICE.

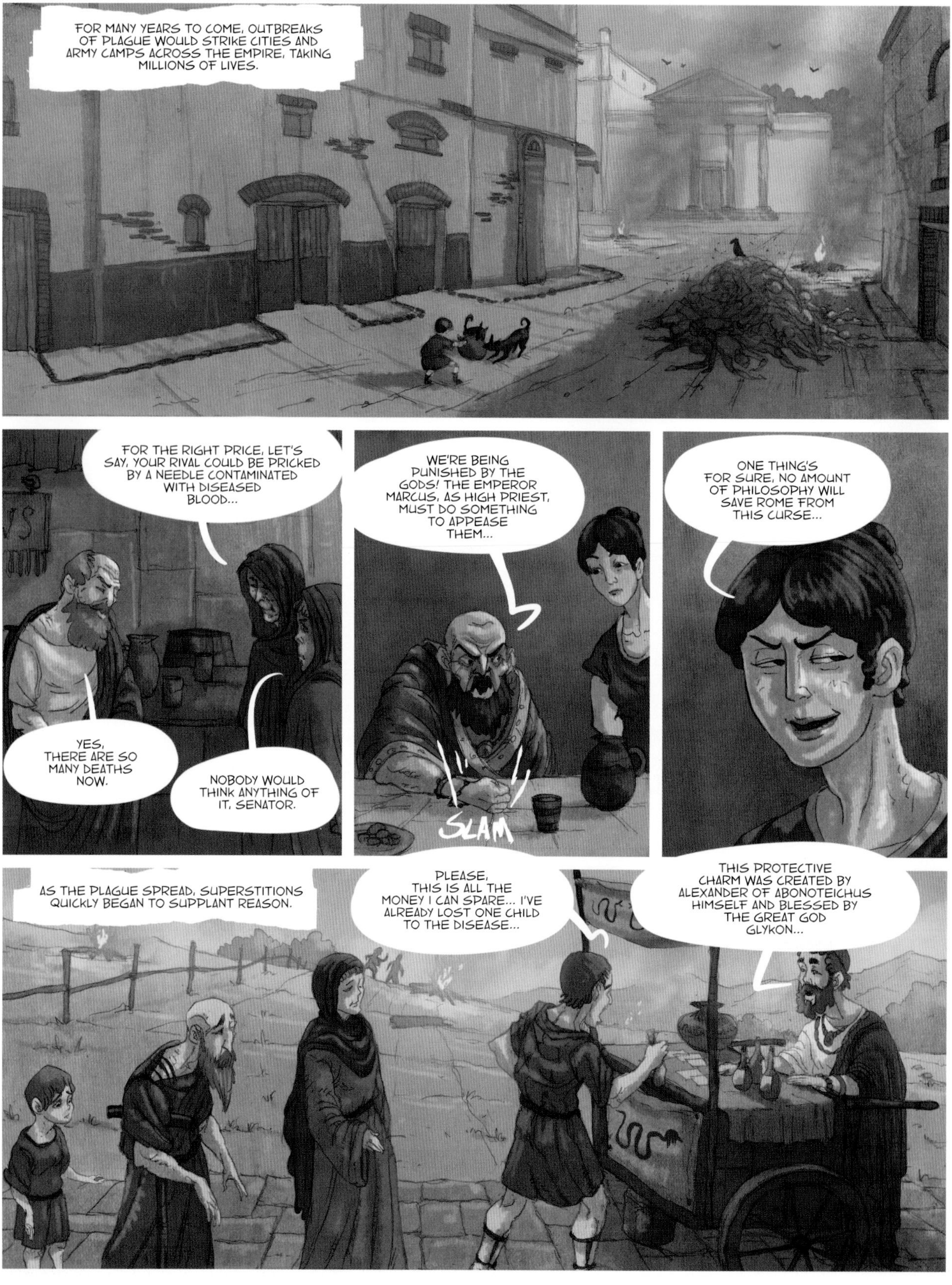

FOR MANY YEARS TO COME, OUTBREAKS OF PLAGUE WOULD STRIKE CITIES AND ARMY CAMPS ACROSS THE EMPIRE, TAKING MILLIONS OF LIVES.
FOR THE RIGHT PRICE, LET'S SAY, YOUR RIVAL COULD BE PRICKED BY A NEEDLE CONTAMINATED WITH DISEASED BLOOD...
YES, THERE ARE SO MANY DEATHS NOW.
NOBODY WOULD THINK ANYTHING OF IT, SENATOR.
WE'RE BEING PUNISHED BY THE GODS! THE EMPEROR MARCUS, AS HIGH PRIEST, MUST DO SOMETHING TO APPEASE THEM...
SLAM
ONE THING'S FOR SURE, NO AMOUNT OF PHILOSOPHY WILL SAVE ROME FROM THIS CURSE...
AS THE PLAGUE SPREAD, SUPERSTITIONS QUICKLY BEGAN TO SUPPLANT REASON.
PLEASE, THIS IS ALL THE MONEY I CAN SPARE... I'VE ALREADY LOST ONE CHILD TO THE DISEASE...
THIS PROTECTIVE CHARM WAS CREATED BY ALEXANDER OF ABONOTEICHUS HIMSELF AND BLESSED BY THE GREAT GOD GLYKON...

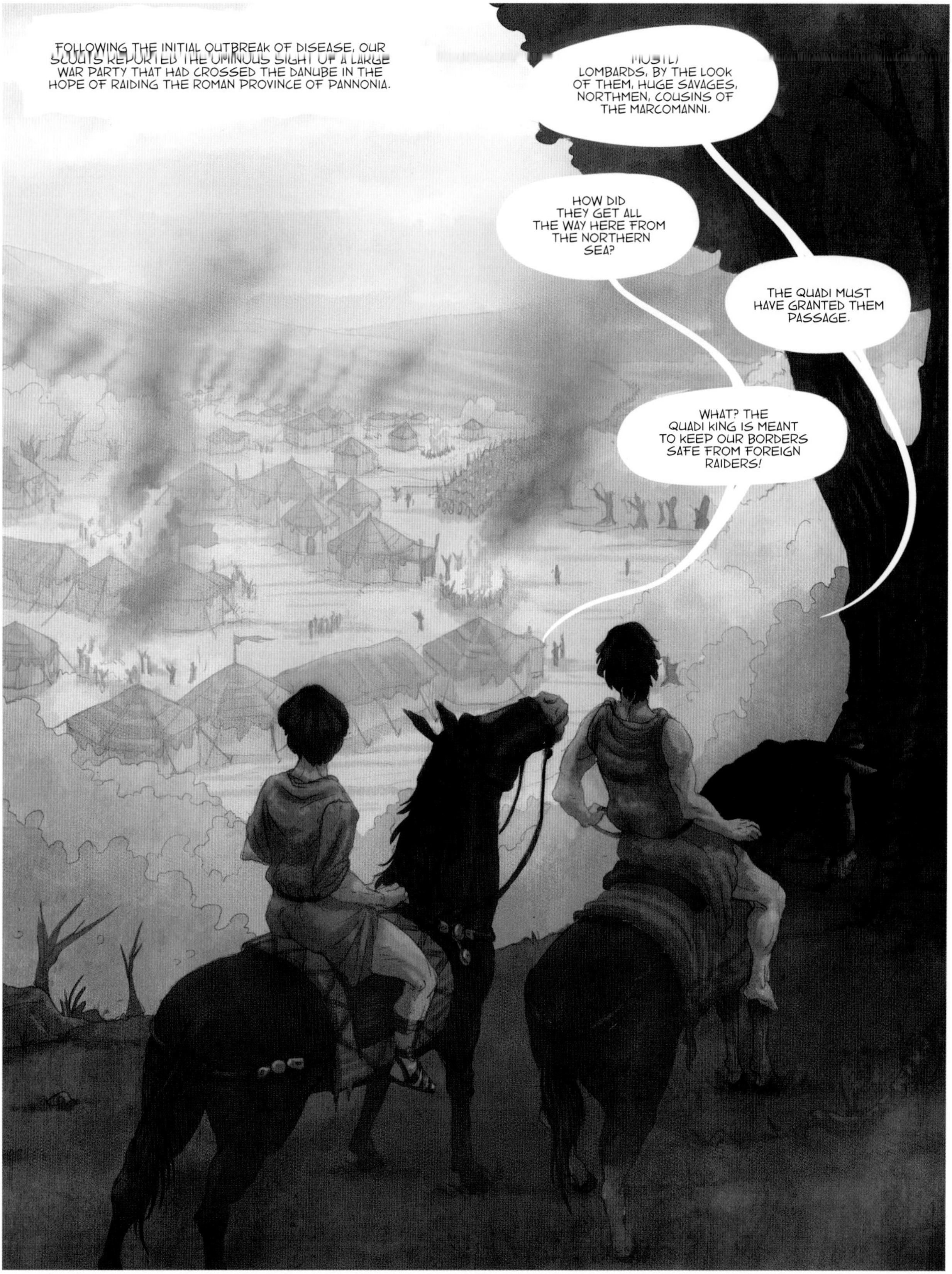

FOLLOWING THE INITIAL OUTBREAK OF DISEASE, OUR SCOUTS REPORTED THE OMINOUS SIGHT OF A LARGE WAR PARTY THAT HAD CROSSED THE DANUBE IN THE HOPE OF RAIDING THE ROMAN PROVINCE OF PANNONIA.
MOSTLY LOMBARDS, BY THE LOOK OF THEM, HUGE SAVAGES, NORTHMEN, COUSINS OF THE MARCOMANNI.
HOW DID THEY GET ALL THE WAY HERE FROM THE NORTHERN SEA?
THE QUADI MUST HAVE GRANTED THEM PASSAGE.
WHAT? THE QUADI KING IS MEANT TO KEEP OUR BORDERS SAFE FROM FOREIGN RAIDERS!

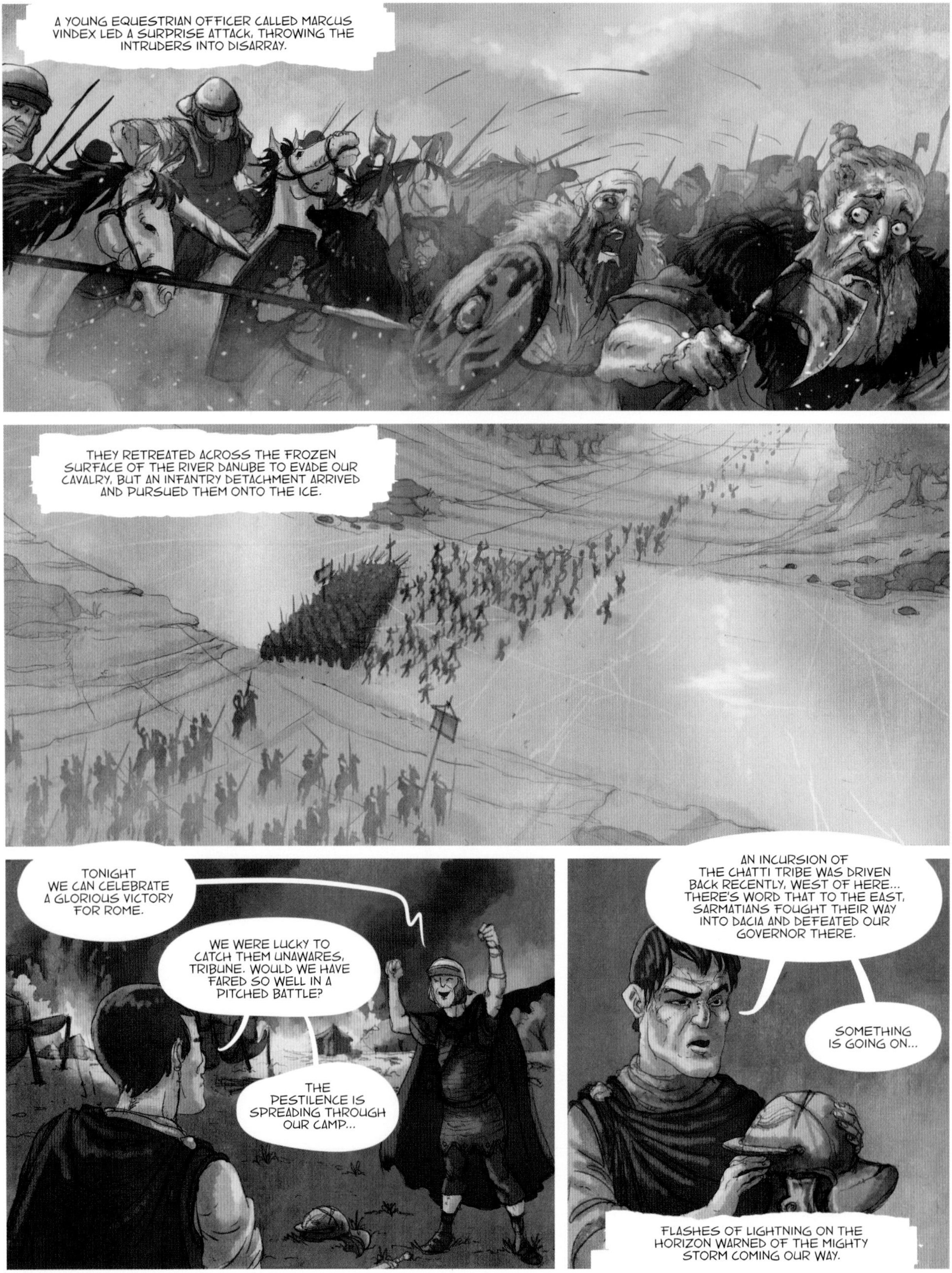
A YOUNG EQUESTRIAN OFFICER CALLED MARCUS VINDEX LED A SURPRISE ATTACK, THROWING THE INTRUDERS INTO DISARRAY.
THEY RETREATED ACROSS THE FROZEN SURFACE OF THE RIVER DANUBE TO EVADE OUR CAVALRY, BUT AN INFANTRY DETACHMENT ARRIVED AND PURSUED THEM ONTO THE ICE.
TONIGHT WE CAN CELEBRATE A GLORIOUS VICTORY FOR ROME.
WE WERE LUCKY TO CATCH THEM UNAWARES, TRIBUNE. WOULD WE HAVE FARED SO WELL IN A PITCHED BATTLE?
THE PESTILENCE IS SPREADING THROUGH OUR CAMP...
AN INCURSION OF THE CHATTI TRIBE WAS DRIVEN BACK RECENTLY, WEST OF HERE... THERE'S WORD THAT TO THE EAST, SARMATIANS FOUGHT THEIR WAY INTO DACIA AND DEFEATED OUR GOVERNOR THERE.
SOMETHING IS GOING ON...
FLASHES OF LIGHTNING ON THE HORIZON WARNED OF THE MIGHTY STORM COMING OUR WAY.

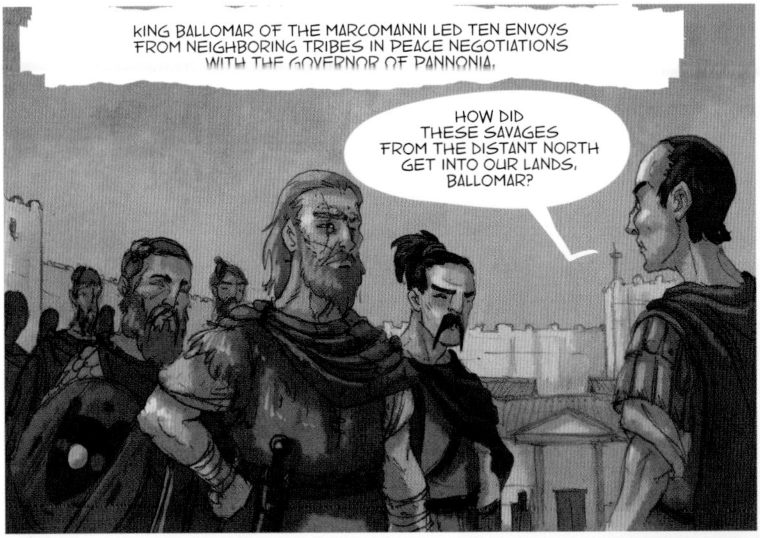
KING BALLOMAR OF THE MARCOMANNI LED TEN ENVOYS FROM NEIGHBORING TRIBES IN PEACE NEGOTIATIONS WITH THE GOVERNOR OF PANNONIA.
HOW DID THESE SAVAGES FROM THE DISTANT NORTH GET INTO OUR LANDS, BALLOMAR?

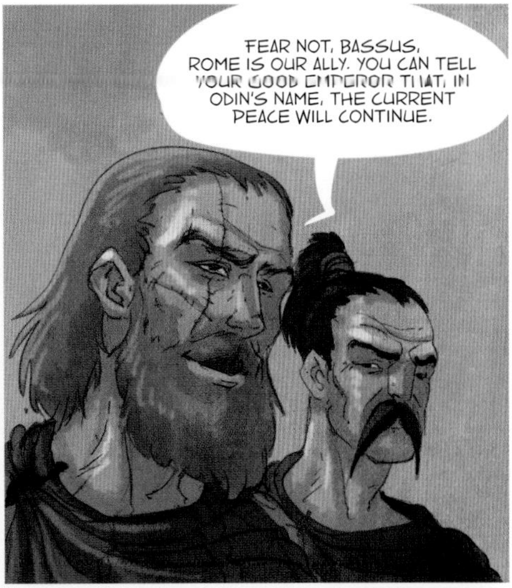
FEAR NOT, BASSUS, ROME IS OUR ALLY. YOU CAN TELL YOUR GOOD EMPEROR THAT, IN ODIN'S NAME, THE CURRENT PEACE WILL CONTINUE.

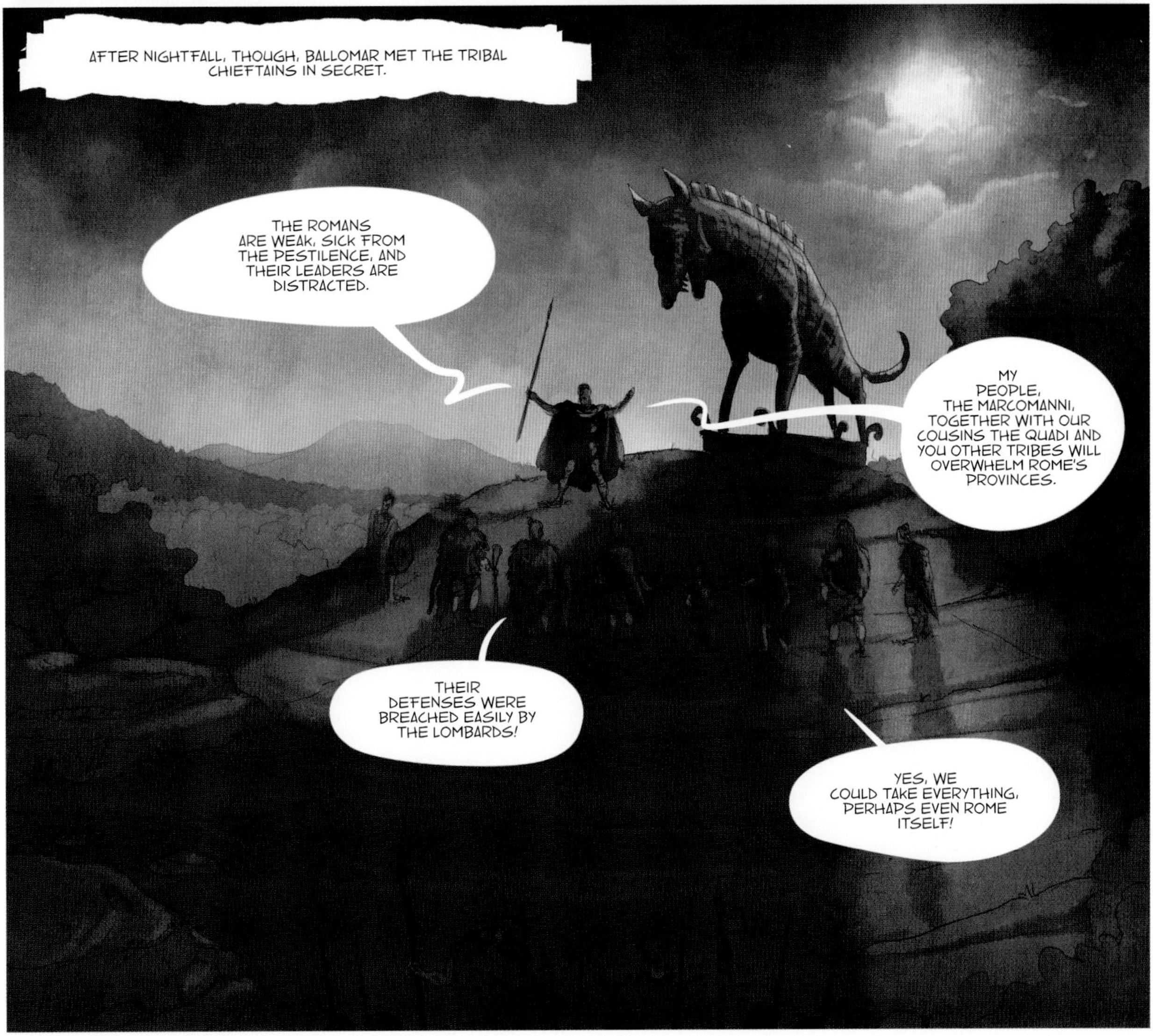
AFTER NIGHTFALL, THOUGH, BALLOMAR MET THE TRIBAL CHIEFTAINS IN SECRET.
THE ROMANS ARE WEAK, SICK FROM THE PESTILENCE, AND THEIR LEADERS ARE DISTRACTED.
MY PEOPLE, THE MARCOMANNI, TOGETHER WITH OUR COUSINS THE QUADI AND YOU OTHER TRIBES WILL OVERWHELM ROME'S PROVINCES.
THEIR DEFENSES WERE BREACHED EASILY BY THE LOMBARDS!
YES, WE COULD TAKE EVERYTHING, PERHAPS EVEN ROME ITSELF!

AS VIRULENT DISEASE ENGULFED THE EMPIRE, ROME WAS INCREASINGLY TROUBLED BY RUMORS, CONSPIRACIES, AND SUPERSTITIOUS FEVER.

THERE'S GROWING UNREST AMONG THE PEOPLE.

I'M ISSUING A RESCRIPT. ANYONE FOUND GUILTY OF ALARMING FICKLE MINDS WITH SUPERNATURAL DREAD IS TO BE EXILED.

IN THE DISTANT PAST, WHEN ROME WAS YOUNG, KING NUMA GAVE OUR PEOPLE SOLEMN AND CONTEMPLATIVE RITES.

MY FATHER, ANTONINUS, HELPED RESTORE THE GRAVITY OF THAT TRADITION. HE NEVER ENTERTAINED RELIGIOUS CHARLATANS...

IN DESPERATION, THOUGH, ROMANS WERE TURNING TO THE SUPERNATURAL.

WHO WILL JOIN ME? THE GODS HAVE SPOKEN! THE MIGHTY ARE CORRUPT! A STORM IS COMING, AND WE MUST TAKE BACK ROME FOR THE PEOPLE!

ON THIS DAY, AS FORETOLD, FIRE SHALL COME FROM HEAVEN AND END THE WORLD. MY DISCIPLES AND I SHALL ALONE BE SAVED. BEHOLD! I SHALL FALL FROM THIS TREE AND ARISE TRANSFORMED INTO A STORK!

THE BIRD HAD CLEARLY BEEN TUCKED UNDER HIS CLOAK. ITS APPEARANCE FOOLED NO ONE.

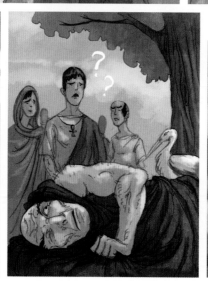

A FEW DAYS LATER, HE WAS BROUGHT BEFORE MY COURT.

THIS MAN IS PARDONED, BUT HE IS NOT OF SOUND MIND. WE THEREFORE HOLD HIS FAMILY ACCOUNTABLE FOR ENSURING HE CAUSES NO MORE DISTURBANCE.

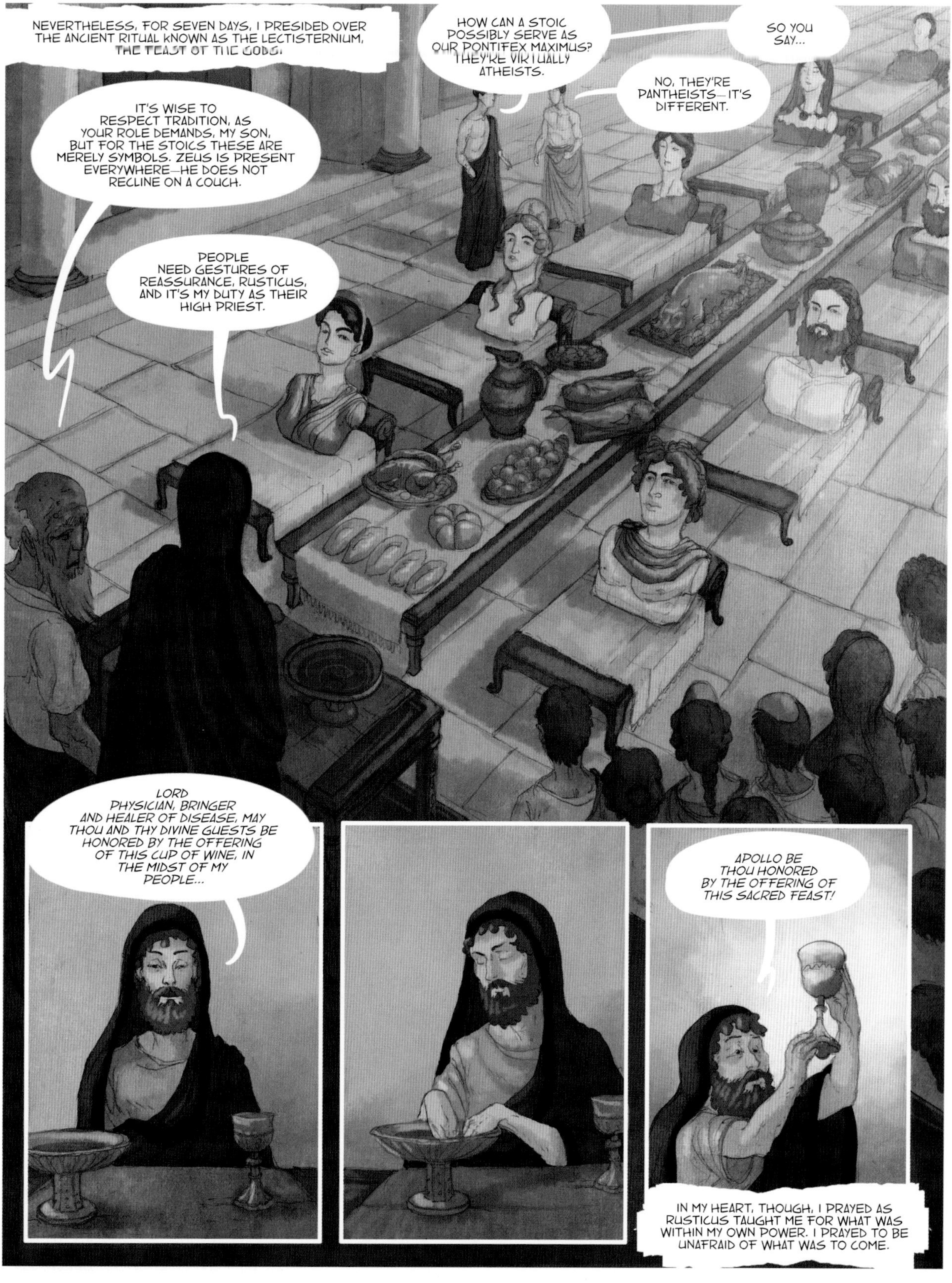
NEVERTHELESS, FOR SEVEN DAYS, I PRESIDED OVER THE ANCIENT RITUAL KNOWN AS THE LECTISTERNIUM, THE FEAST OF THE GODS.
HOW CAN A STOIC POSSIBLY SERVE AS OUR PONTIFEX MAXIMUS? THEY'RE VIRTUALLY ATHEISTS.
SO YOU SAY...
NO, THEY'RE PANTHEISTS—IT'S DIFFERENT.
IT'S WISE TO RESPECT TRADITION, AS YOUR ROLE DEMANDS, MY SON, BUT FOR THE STOICS THESE ARE MERELY SYMBOLS. ZEUS IS PRESENT EVERYWHERE—HE DOES NOT RECLINE ON A COUCH.
PEOPLE NEED GESTURES OF REASSURANCE, RUSTICUS, AND IT'S MY DUTY AS THEIR HIGH PRIEST.
LORD PHYSICIAN, BRINGER AND HEALER OF DISEASE, MAY THOU AND THY DIVINE GUESTS BE HONORED BY THE OFFERING OF THIS CUP OF WINE, IN THE MIDST OF MY PEOPLE...
APOLLO BE THOU HONORED BY THE OFFERING OF THIS SACRED FEAST!
IN MY HEART, THOUGH, I PRAYED AS RUSTICUS TAUGHT ME FOR WHAT WAS WITHIN MY OWN POWER. I PRAYED TO BE UNAFRAID OF WHAT WAS TO COME.

THE
MARCOMANNIC
INVASION

When a storm from the gods blows down upon us,
Man must toil and endure and not complain.

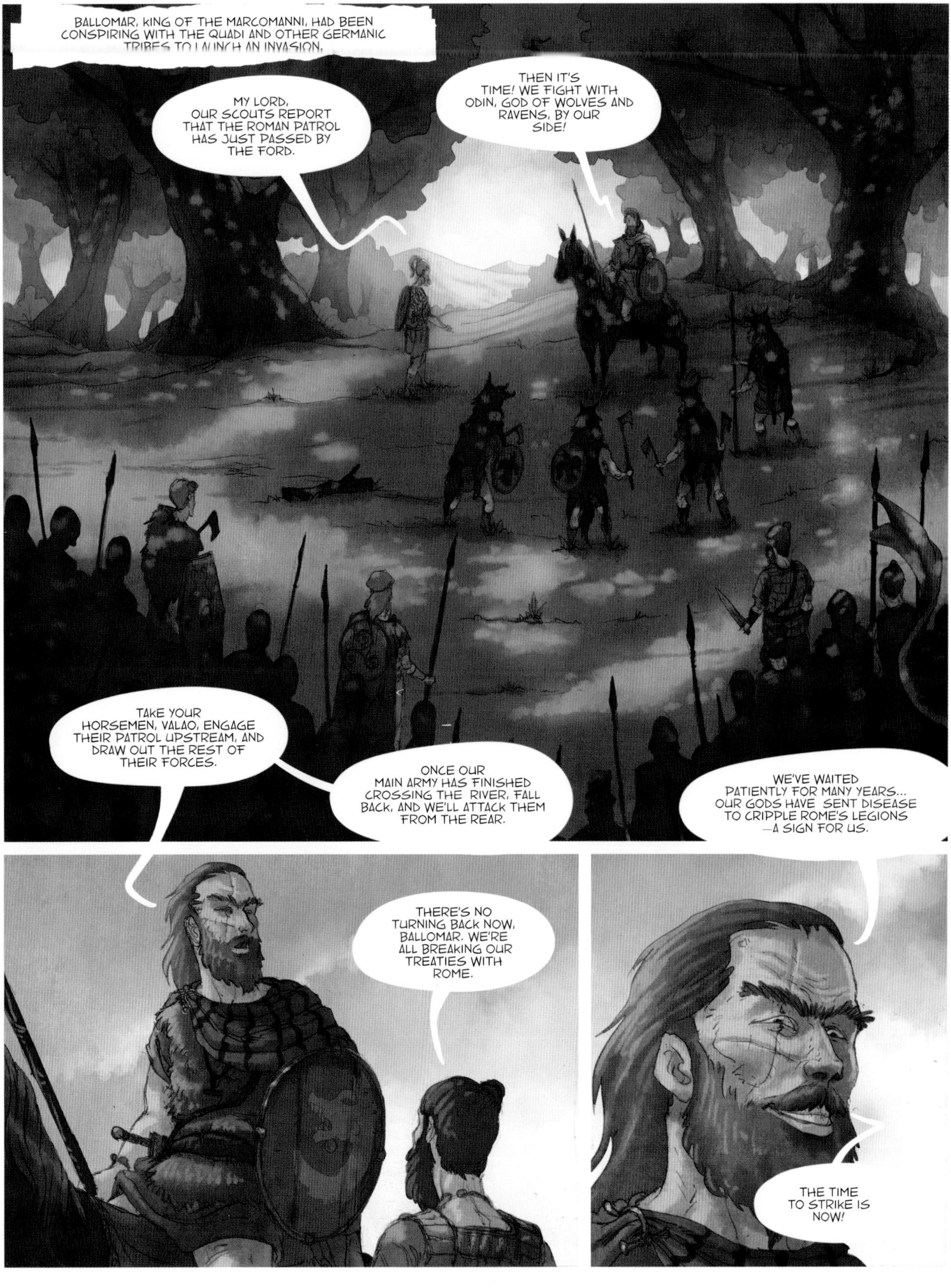
BALLOMAR, KING OF THE MARCOMANNI, HAD BEEN CONSPIRING WITH THE QUADI AND OTHER GERMANIC TRIBES TO LAUNCH AN INVASION.
MY LORD, OUR SCOUTS REPORT THAT THE ROMAN PATROL HAS JUST PASSED BY THE FORD.
THEN IT'S TIME! WE FIGHT WITH ODIN, GOD OF WOLVES AND RAVENS, BY OUR SIDE!
TAKE YOUR HORSEMEN, VALAO, ENGAGE THEIR PATROL UPSTREAM, AND DRAW OUT THE REST OF THEIR FORCES.
ONCE OUR MAIN ARMY HAS FINISHED CROSSING THE RIVER, FALL BACK, AND WE'LL ATTACK THEM FROM THE REAR.
THERE'S NO TURNING BACK NOW, BALLOMAR. WE'RE ALL BREAKING OUR TREATIES WITH ROME.
WE'VE WAITED PATIENTLY FOR MANY YEARS... OUR GODS HAVE SENT DISEASE TO CRIPPLE ROME'S LEGIONS —A SIGN FOR US.
THE TIME TO STRIKE IS NOW!

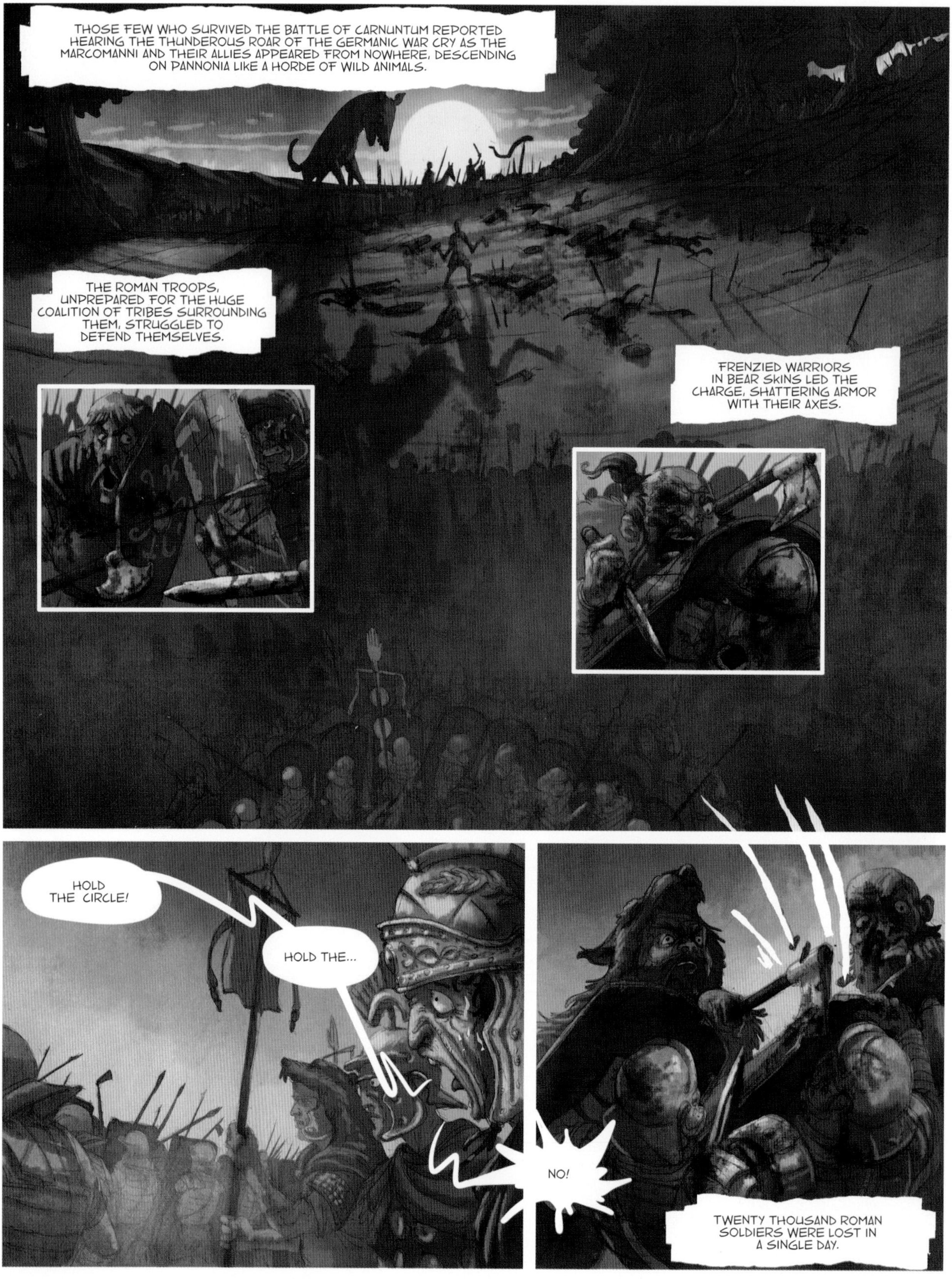
THOSE FEW WHO SURVIVED THE BATTLE OF CARNUNTUM REPORTED HEARING THE THUNDEROUS ROAR OF THE GERMANIC WAR CRY AS THE MARCOMANNI AND THEIR ALLIES APPEARED FROM NOWHERE, DESCENDING ON PANNONIA LIKE A HORDE OF WILD ANIMALS.
THE ROMAN TROOPS, UNPREPARED FOR THE HUGE COALITION OF TRIBES SURROUNDING THEM, STRUGGLED TO DEFEND THEMSELVES.
FRENZIED WARRIORS IN BEAR SKINS LED THE CHARGE, SHATTERING ARMOR WITH THEIR AXES.
HOLD THE CIRCLE!
HOLD THE...
NO!
TWENTY THOUSAND ROMAN SOLDIERS WERE LOST IN A SINGLE DAY.

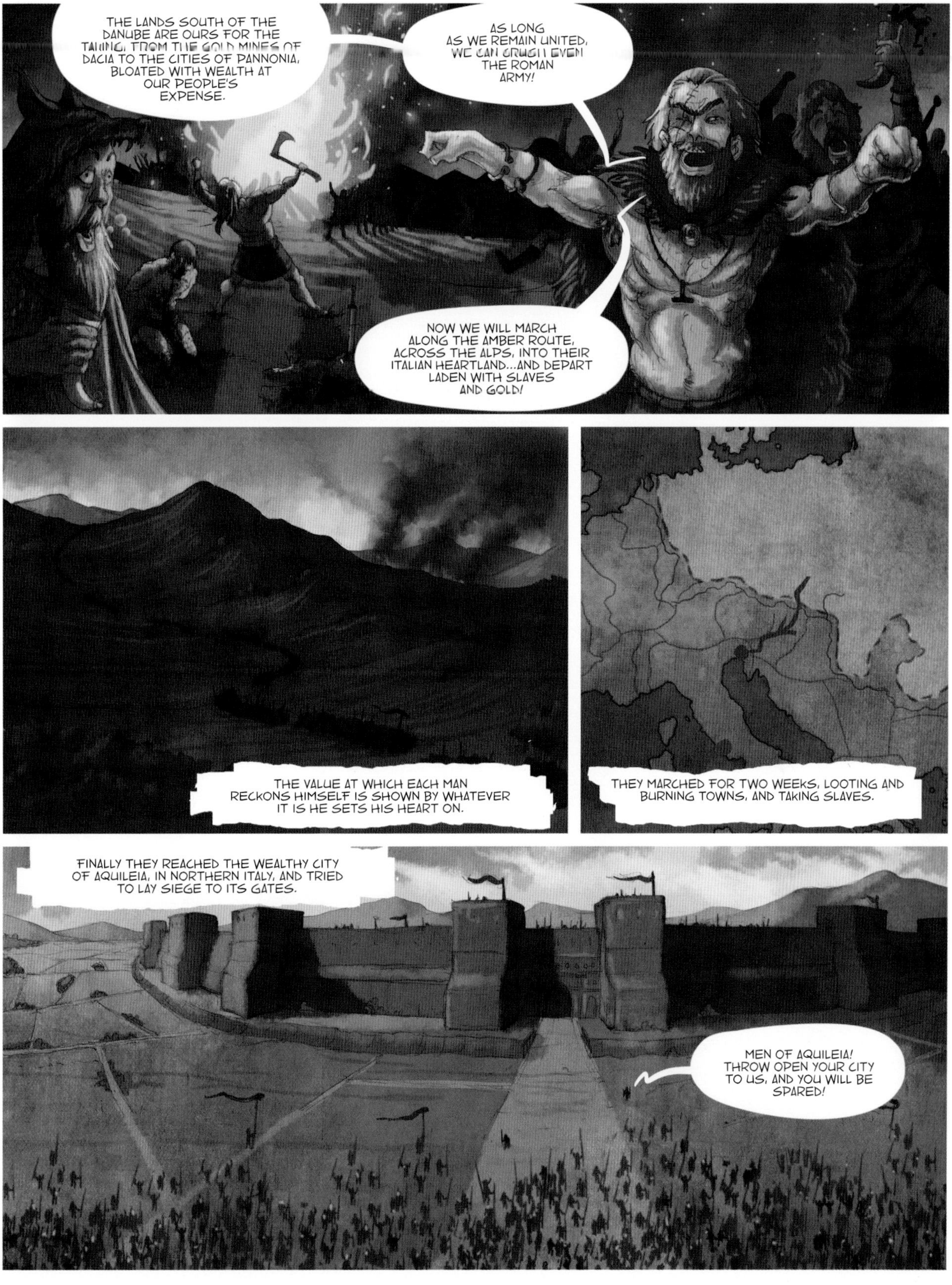
THE LANDS SOUTH OF THE DANUBE ARE OURS FOR THE TAKING, FROM THE GOLD MINES OF DACIA TO THE CITIES OF PANNONIA, BLOATED WITH WEALTH AT OUR PEOPLE'S EXPENSE.
AS LONG AS WE REMAIN UNITED, WE CAN CRUSH EVEN THE ROMAN ARMY!
NOW WE WILL MARCH ALONG THE AMBER ROUTE, ACROSS THE ALPS, INTO THEIR ITALIAN HEARTLAND...AND DEPART LADEN WITH SLAVES AND GOLD!
THE VALUE AT WHICH EACH MAN RECKONS HIMSELF IS SHOWN BY WHATEVER IT IS HE SETS HIS HEART ON.
THEY MARCHED FOR TWO WEEKS, LOOTING AND BURNING TOWNS, AND TAKING SLAVES.
FINALLY THEY REACHED THE WEALTHY CITY OF AQUILEIA, IN NORTHERN ITALY, AND TRIED TO LAY SIEGE TO ITS GATES.
MEN OF AQUILEIA! THROW OPEN YOUR CITY TO US, AND YOU WILL BE SPARED!

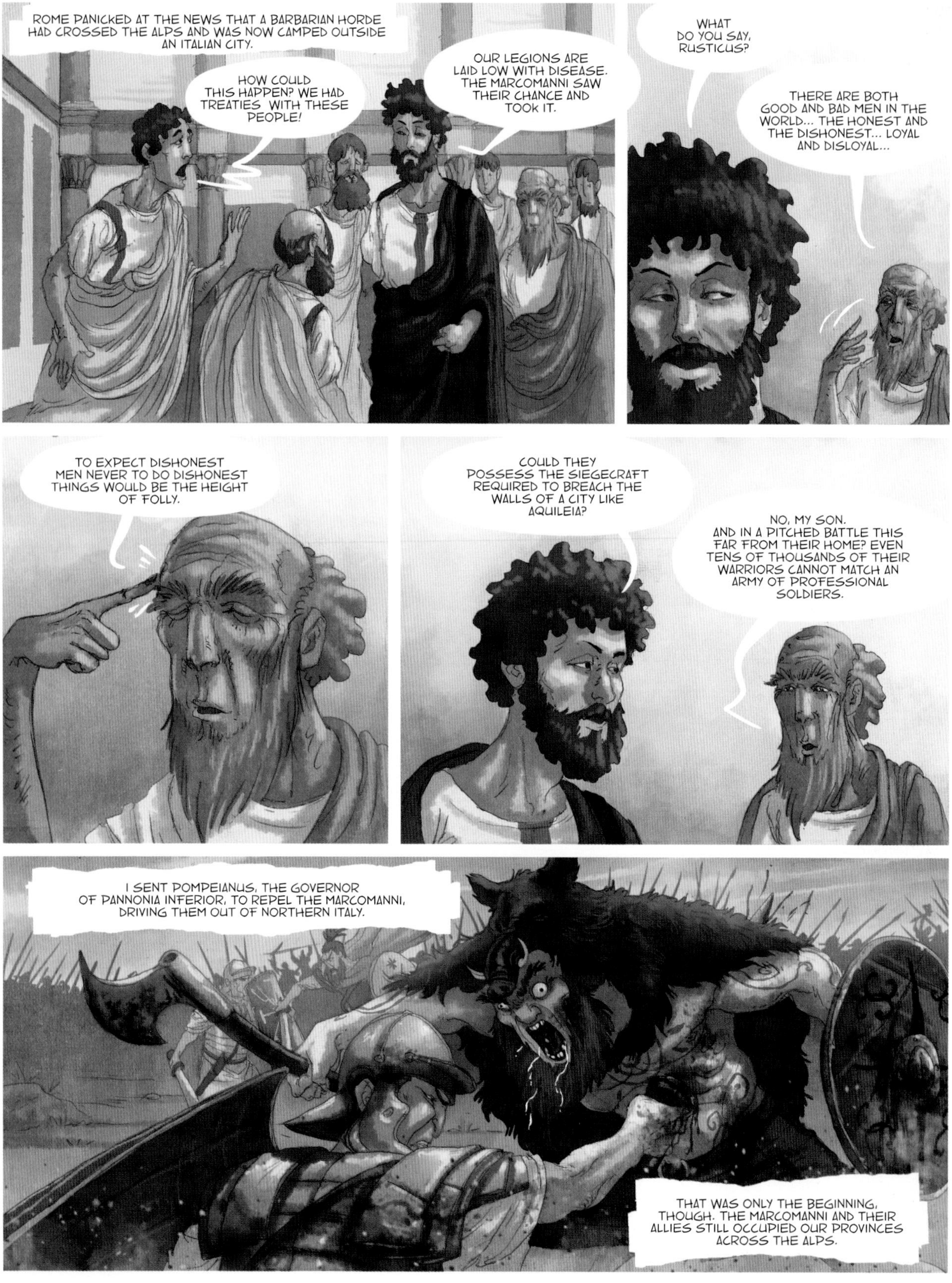
ROME PANICKED AT THE NEWS THAT A BARBARIAN HORDE HAD CROSSED THE ALPS AND WAS NOW CAMPED OUTSIDE AN ITALIAN CITY.
HOW COULD THIS HAPPEN? WE HAD TREATIES WITH THESE PEOPLE!
OUR LEGIONS ARE LAID LOW WITH DISEASE. THE MARCOMANNI SAW THEIR CHANCE AND TOOK IT.
WHAT DO YOU SAY, RUSTICUS?
THERE ARE BOTH GOOD AND BAD MEN IN THE WORLD... THE HONEST AND THE DISHONEST... LOYAL AND DISLOYAL...
TO EXPECT DISHONEST MEN NEVER TO DO DISHONEST THINGS WOULD BE THE HEIGHT OF FOLLY.
COULD THEY POSSESS THE SIEGECRAFT REQUIRED TO BREACH THE WALLS OF A CITY LIKE AQUILEIA?
NO, MY SON. AND IN A PITCHED BATTLE THIS FAR FROM THEIR HOME? EVEN TENS OF THOUSANDS OF THEIR WARRIORS CANNOT MATCH AN ARMY OF PROFESSIONAL SOLDIERS.
I SENT POMPEIANUS, THE GOVERNOR OF PANNONIA INFERIOR, TO REPEL THE MARCOMANNI, DRIVING THEM OUT OF NORTHERN ITALY.
THAT WAS ONLY THE BEGINNING, THOUGH. THE MARCOMANNI AND THEIR ALLIES STILL OCCUPIED OUR PROVINCES ACROSS THE ALPS.

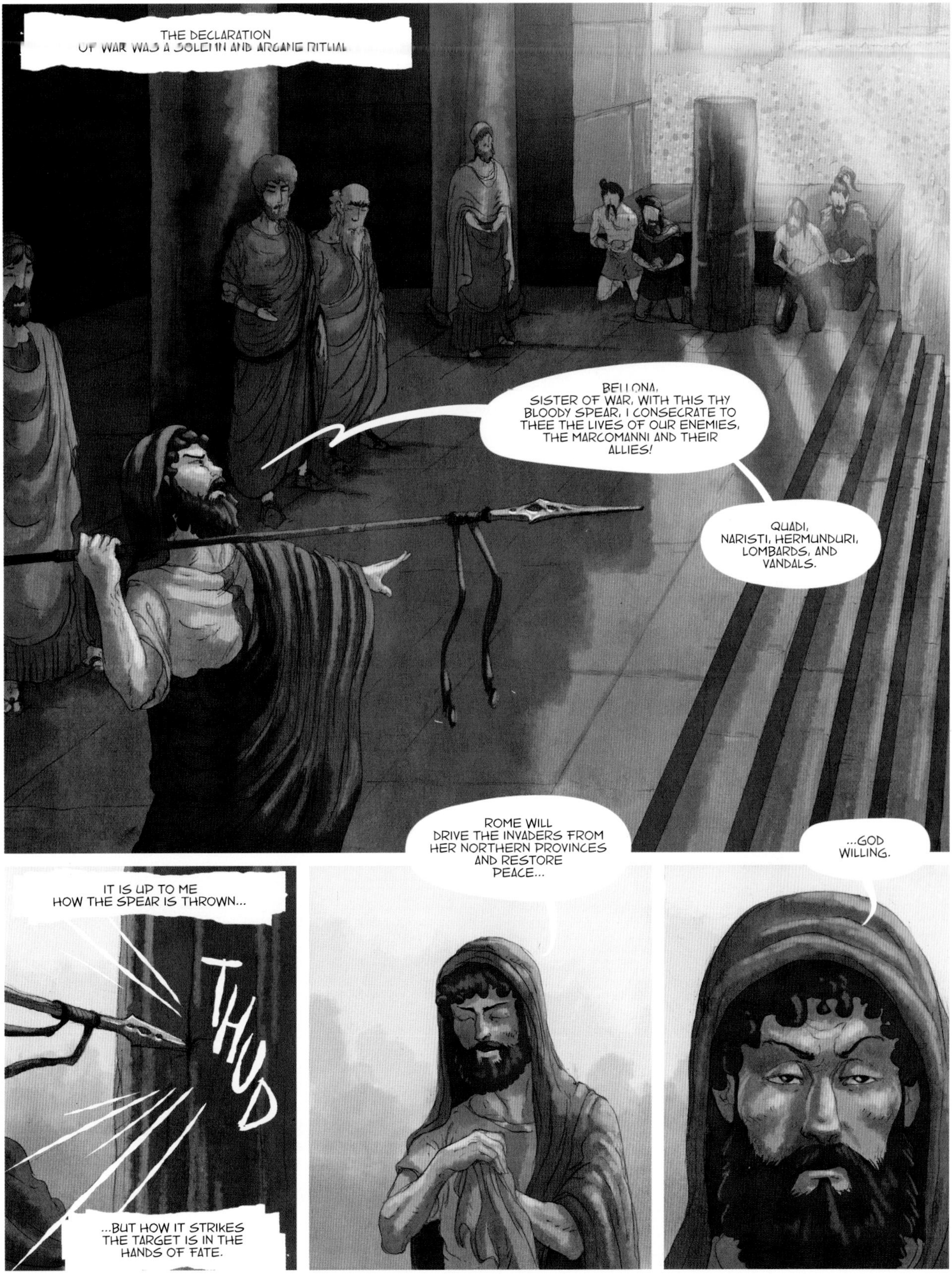
THE DECLARATION OF WAR WAS A SOLEMN AND ARCANE RITUAL
BELLONA, SISTER OF WAR, WITH THIS THY BLOODY SPEAR, I CONSECRATE TO THEE THE LIVES OF OUR ENEMIES, THE MARCOMANNI AND THEIR ALLIES!
QUADI, NARISTI, HERMUNDURI, LOMBARDS, AND VANDALS.
IT IS UP TO ME HOW THE SPEAR IS THROWN...
THUD
...BUT HOW IT STRIKES THE TARGET IS IN THE HANDS OF FATE.
ROME WILL DRIVE THE INVADERS FROM HER NORTHERN PROVINCES AND RESTORE PEACE...
...GOD WILLING.

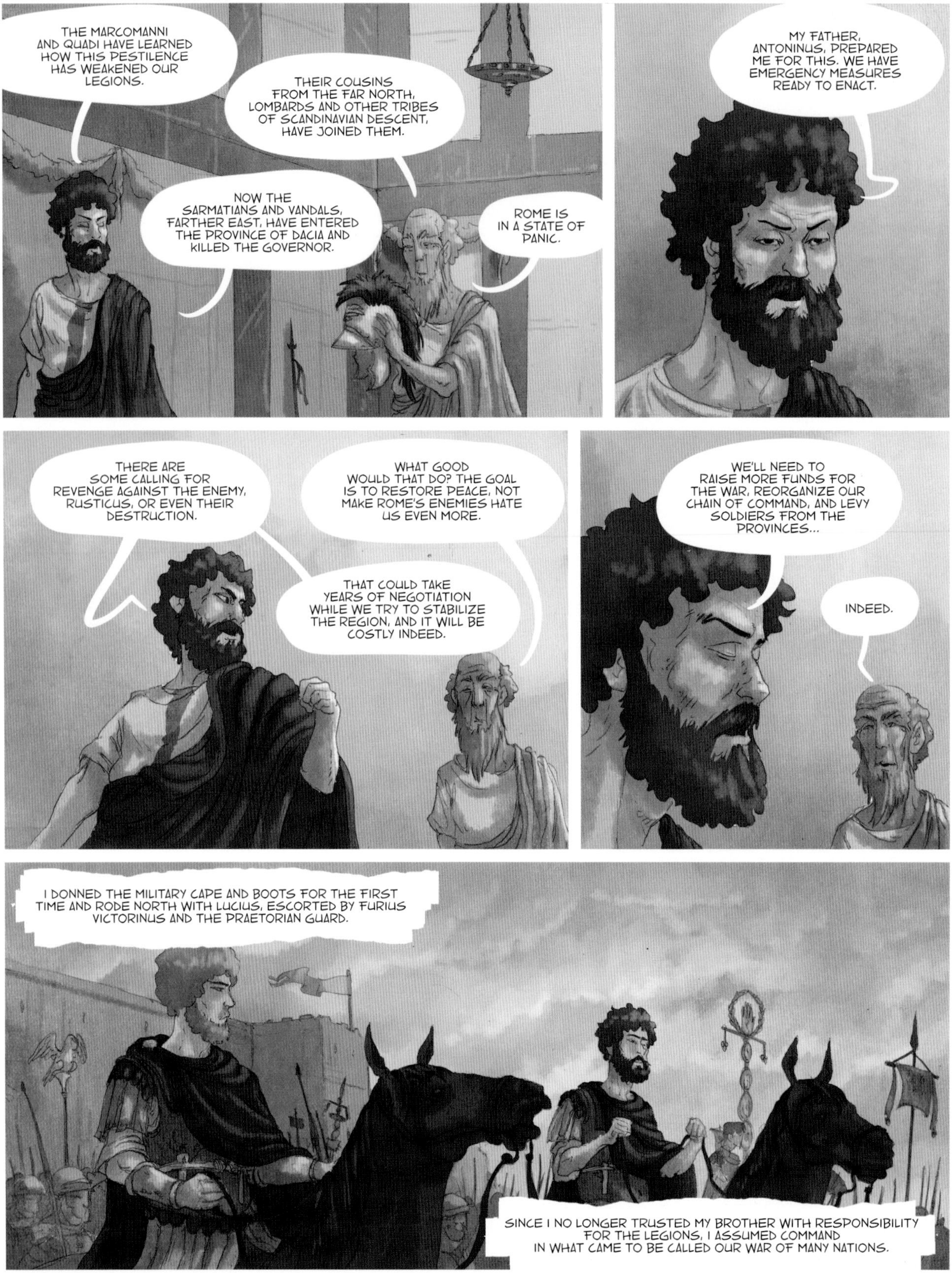

THE MARCOMANNI AND QUADI HAVE LEARNED HOW THIS PESTILENCE HAS WEAKENED OUR LEGIONS.
THEIR COUSINS FROM THE FAR NORTH, LOMBARDS AND OTHER TRIBES OF SCANDINAVIAN DESCENT, HAVE JOINED THEM.
NOW THE SARMATIANS AND VANDALS, FARTHER EAST, HAVE ENTERED THE PROVINCE OF DACIA AND KILLED THE GOVERNOR.
ROME IS IN A STATE OF PANIC.
MY FATHER, ANTONINUS, PREPARED ME FOR THIS. WE HAVE EMERGENCY MEASURES READY TO ENACT.
THERE ARE SOME CALLING FOR REVENGE AGAINST THE ENEMY, RUSTICUS, OR EVEN THEIR DESTRUCTION.
WHAT GOOD WOULD THAT DO? THE GOAL IS TO RESTORE PEACE, NOT MAKE ROME'S ENEMIES HATE US EVEN MORE.
THAT COULD TAKE YEARS OF NEGOTIATION WHILE WE TRY TO STABILIZE THE REGION, AND IT WILL BE COSTLY INDEED.
WE'LL NEED TO RAISE MORE FUNDS FOR THE WAR, REORGANIZE OUR CHAIN OF COMMAND, AND LEVY SOLDIERS FROM THE PROVINCES...
INDEED.
I DONNED THE MILITARY CAPE AND BOOTS FOR THE FIRST TIME AND RODE NORTH WITH LUCIUS, ESCORTED BY FURIUS VICTORINUS AND THE PRAETORIAN GUARD.
SINCE I NO LONGER TRUSTED MY BROTHER WITH RESPONSIBILITY FOR THE LEGIONS, I ASSUMED COMMAND IN WHAT CAME TO BE CALLED OUR WAR OF MANY NATIONS.

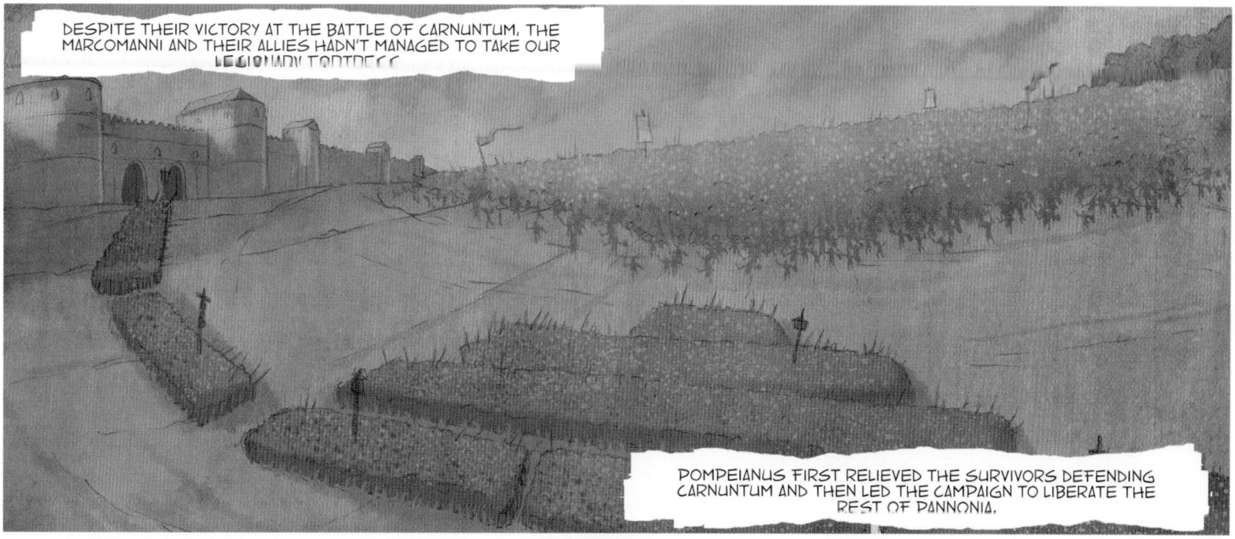
DESPITE THEIR VICTORY AT THE BATTLE OF CARNUNTUM, THE MARCOMANNI AND THEIR ALLIES HADN'T MANAGED TO TAKE OUR LEGIONARY FORTRESS.
POMPEIANUS FIRST RELIEVED THE SURVIVORS DEFENDING CARNUNTUM AND THEN LED THE CAMPAIGN TO LIBERATE THE REST OF PANNONIA.

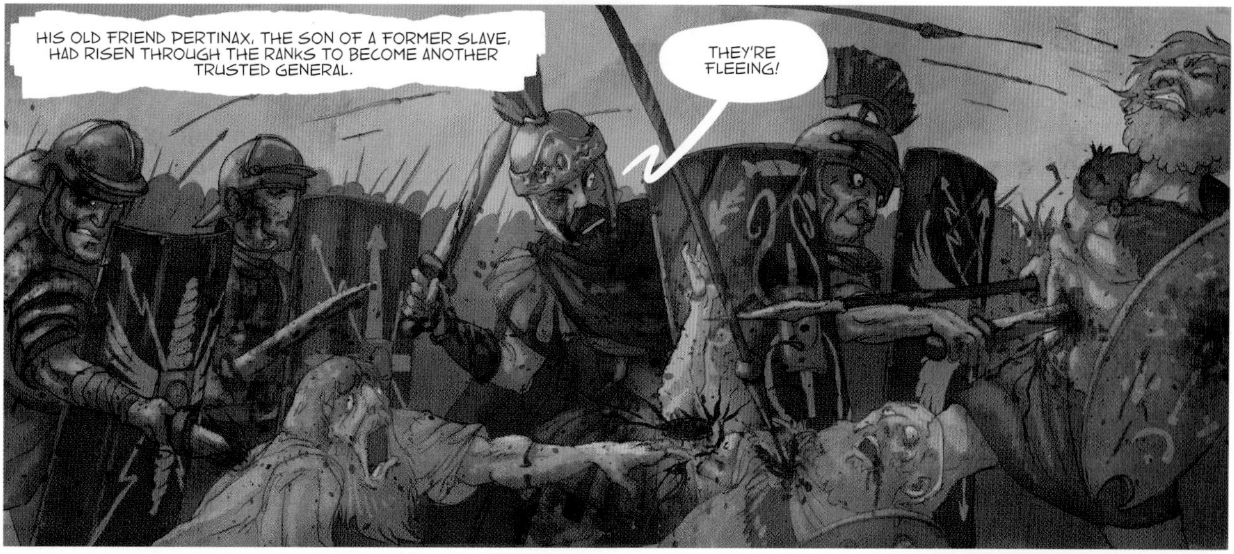
HIS OLD FRIEND PERTINAX, THE SON OF A FORMER SLAVE, HAD RISEN THROUGH THE RANKS TO BECOME ANOTHER TRUSTED GENERAL.
THEY'RE FLEEING!

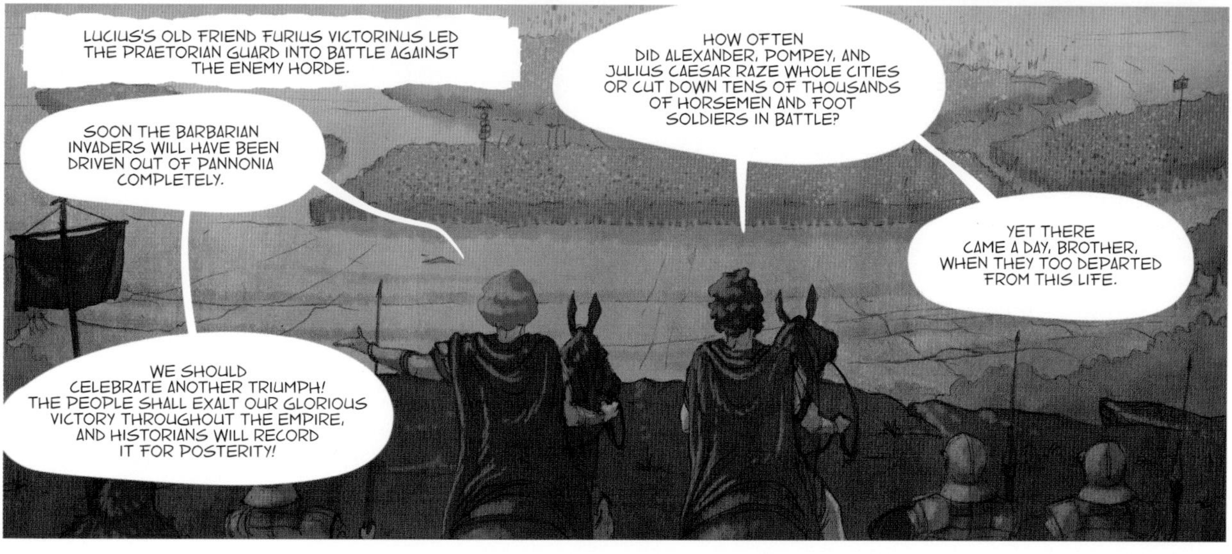
LUCIUS'S OLD FRIEND FURIUS VICTORINUS LED THE PRAETORIAN GUARD INTO BATTLE AGAINST THE ENEMY HORDE.
SOON THE BARBARIAN INVADERS WILL HAVE BEEN DRIVEN OUT OF PANNONIA COMPLETELY.
WE SHOULD CELEBRATE ANOTHER TRIUMPH! THE PEOPLE SHALL EXALT OUR GLORIOUS VICTORY THROUGHOUT THE EMPIRE, AND HISTORIANS WILL RECORD IT FOR POSTERITY!
HOW OFTEN DID ALEXANDER, POMPEY, AND JULIUS CAESAR RAZE WHOLE CITIES OR CUT DOWN TENS OF THOUSANDS OF HORSEMEN AND FOOT SOLDIERS IN BATTLE?
YET THERE CAME A DAY, BROTHER, WHEN THEY TOO DEPARTED FROM THIS LIFE.

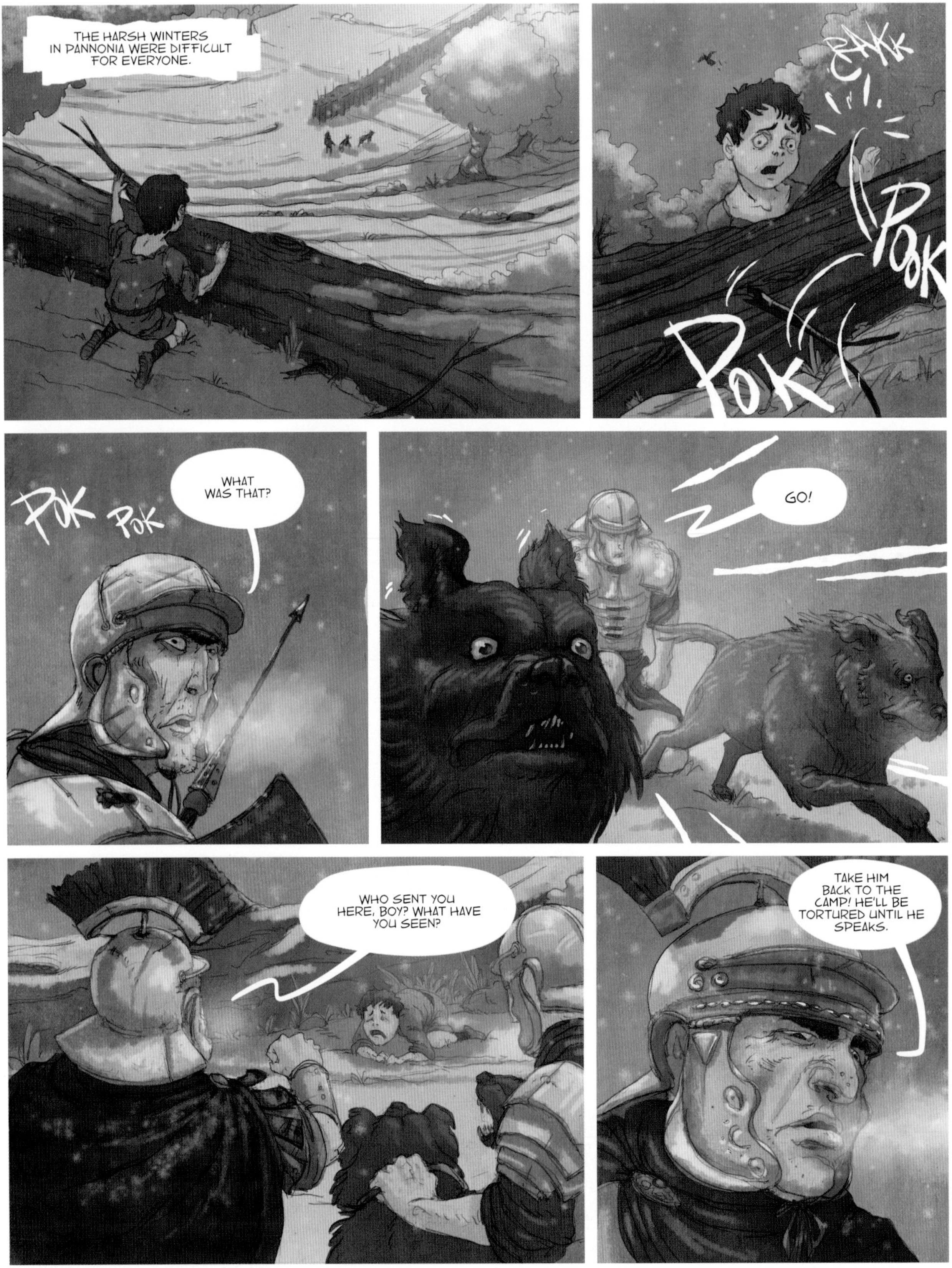
THE HARSH WINTERS IN PANNONIA WERE DIFFICULT FOR EVERYONE.
CRAKK
POOK
POK
POK
POK
WHAT WAS THAT?
GO!
WHO SENT YOU HERE, BOY? WHAT HAVE YOU SEEN?
TAKE HIM BACK TO THE CAMP! HE'LL BE TORTURED UNTIL HE SPEAKS.

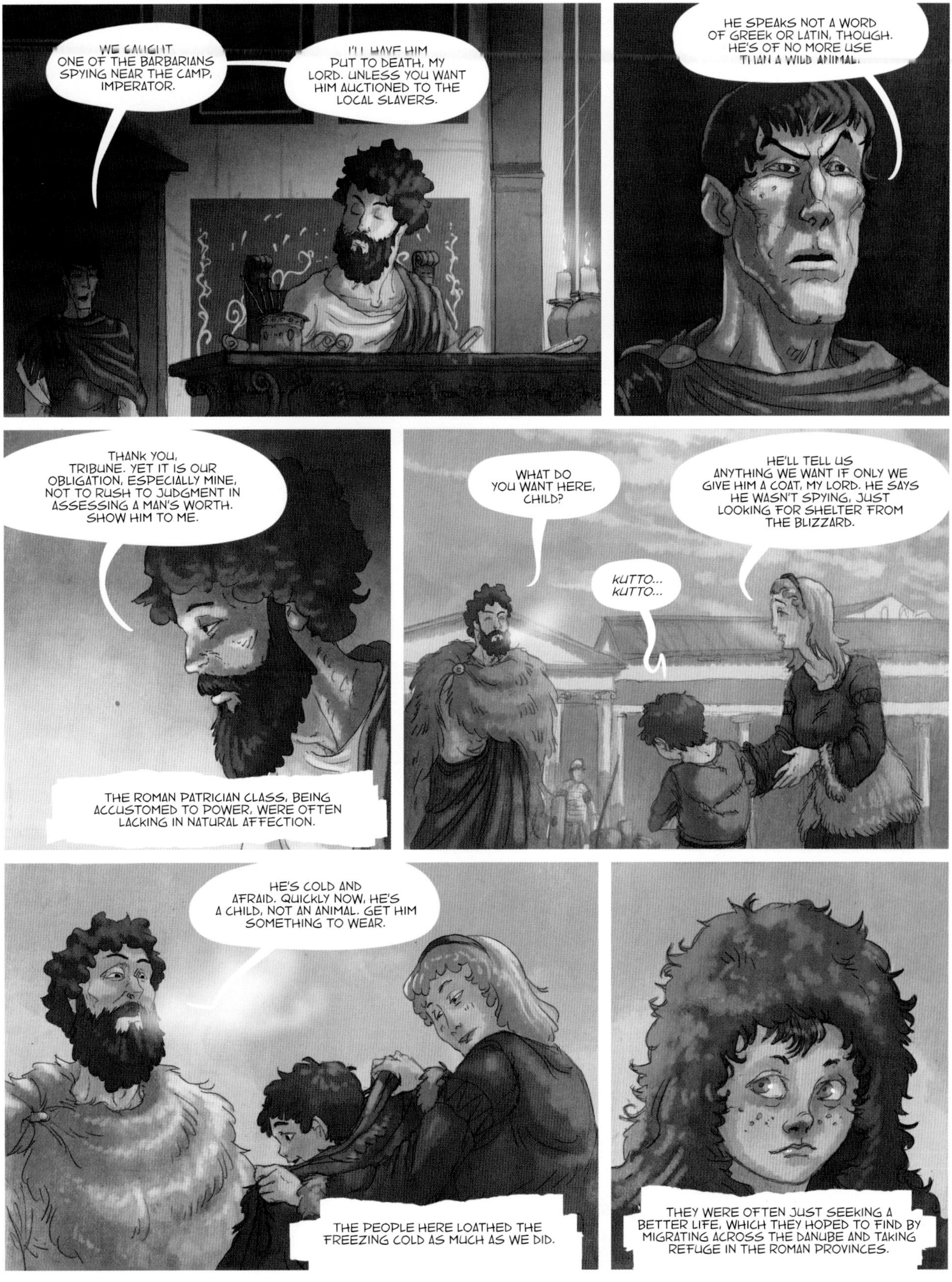
WE CAUGHT ONE OF THE BARBARIANS SPYING NEAR THE CAMP, IMPERATOR.
I'LL HAVE HIM PUT TO DEATH, MY LORD. UNLESS YOU WANT HIM AUCTIONED TO THE LOCAL SLAVERS.
HE SPEAKS NOT A WORD OF GREEK OR LATIN, THOUGH. HE'S OF NO MORE USE THAN A WILD ANIMAL.
THANK YOU, TRIBUNE. YET IT IS OUR OBLIGATION, ESPECIALLY MINE, NOT TO RUSH TO JUDGMENT IN ASSESSING A MAN'S WORTH. SHOW HIM TO ME.
THE ROMAN PATRICIAN CLASS, BEING ACCUSTOMED TO POWER, WERE OFTEN LACKING IN NATURAL AFFECTION.
WHAT DO YOU WANT HERE, CHILD?
HE'LL TELL US ANYTHING WE WANT IF ONLY WE GIVE HIM A COAT, MY LORD. HE SAYS HE WASN'T SPYING, JUST LOOKING FOR SHELTER FROM THE BLIZZARD.
KUTTO... KUTTO...
HE'S COLD AND AFRAID. QUICKLY NOW, HE'S A CHILD, NOT AN ANIMAL. GET HIM SOMETHING TO WEAR.
THE PEOPLE HERE LOATHED THE FREEZING COLD AS MUCH AS WE DID.
THEY WERE OFTEN JUST SEEKING A BETTER LIFE, WHICH THEY HOPED TO FIND BY MIGRATING ACROSS THE DANUBE AND TAKING REFUGE IN THE ROMAN PROVINCES.

MARCUS AURELIUS
TO JUNIUS RUSTICUS

I HOPE YOU ARE WELL, MY BELOVED MASTER, AND I DAILY LONG FOR THE SIGHT OF YOU ONCE AGAIN.

PANNONIA IS INDEED A FOREIGN LAND, AND LIFE IN THE MILITARY COULDN'T BE MORE DIFFERENT FROM AT THE HOUSE OF TIBERIUS OR MY BELOVED CAELIAN HILL.

THE HARSH WINTERS TAKE THEIR TOLL ON ME. I STRUGGLE TO BREATHE IN THE FRIGID AIR WHEN ADDRESSING MY FELLOW SOLDIERS.

THE PESTILENCE RAGES MORE AMONG THE ARMY CAMPS DURING THE WINTER MONTHS. NOW THE DISEASE ALSO AFFLICTS THE ENEMY, OR RATHER OUR FELLOW CITIZENS, FOR AS YOU WOULD SAY, DEAR MASTER, WE ALL DWELL IN THE SAME UNIVERSAL CITY UNDER ZEUS.

THOSE WHO WOULD BE OUR ENEMIES ARE OUR KINSMEN AND PARTNERS, ALTHOUGH THEY MAY APPEAR IGNORANT OF MAN'S RATIONAL AND SOCIAL NATURE.

BUT I KNOW ENOUGH TO UNDERSTAND THAT I SHOULD BEHAVE TOWARD ALL MEN ACCORDING TO THE NATURAL LAW OF FELLOWSHIP, BENEVOLENCE, AND JUSTICE.

NEVERTHELESS, THESE PEOPLE ARE BOTH FEARED AND HATED BY OTHER ROMANS IN EQUAL MEASURE.

JUNIUS RUSTICUS
TO MARCUS AURELIUS

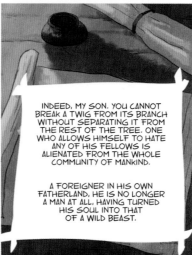

INDEED, MY SON. YOU CANNOT BREAK A TWIG FROM ITS BRANCH WITHOUT SEPARATING IT FROM THE REST OF THE TREE. ONE WHO ALLOWS HIMSELF TO HATE ANY OF HIS FELLOWS IS ALIENATED FROM THE WHOLE COMMUNITY OF MANKIND.

A FOREIGNER IN HIS OWN FATHERLAND, HE IS NO LONGER A MAN AT ALL, HAVING TURNED HIS SOUL INTO THAT OF A WILD BEAST.

REMEMBER THAT HE WHO YIELDS TO ANGER HAS BEEN WOUNDED MOST OF ALL AND HAS SURRENDERED TO OUR TRUE ENEMY.

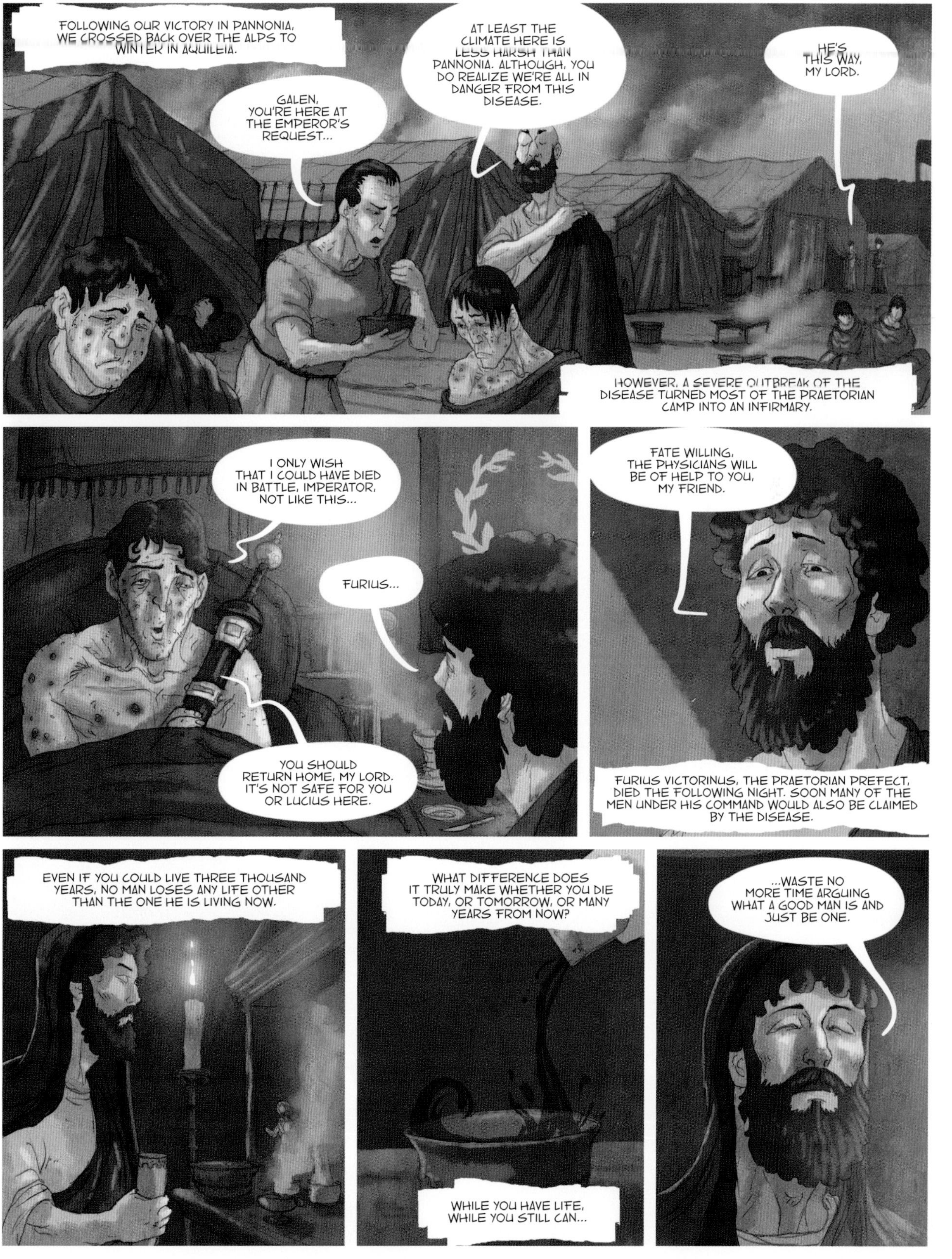
FOLLOWING OUR VICTORY IN PANNONIA, WE CROSSED BACK OVER THE ALPS TO WINTER IN AQUILEIA.
GALEN, YOU'RE HERE AT THE EMPEROR'S REQUEST...
AT LEAST THE CLIMATE HERE IS LESS HARSH THAN PANNONIA. ALTHOUGH, YOU DO REALIZE WE'RE ALL IN DANGER FROM THIS DISEASE.
HE'S THIS WAY, MY LORD.
HOWEVER, A SEVERE OUTBREAK OF THE DISEASE TURNED MOST OF THE PRAETORIAN CAMP INTO AN INFIRMARY.
I ONLY WISH THAT I COULD HAVE DIED IN BATTLE, IMPERATOR, NOT LIKE THIS...
FURIUS...
YOU SHOULD RETURN HOME, MY LORD. IT'S NOT SAFE FOR YOU OR LUCIUS HERE.
FATE WILLING, THE PHYSICIANS WILL BE OF HELP TO YOU, MY FRIEND.
FURIUS VICTORINUS, THE PRAETORIAN PREFECT, DIED THE FOLLOWING NIGHT. SOON MANY OF THE MEN UNDER HIS COMMAND WOULD ALSO BE CLAIMED BY THE DISEASE.
EVEN IF YOU COULD LIVE THREE THOUSAND YEARS, NO MAN LOSES ANY LIFE OTHER THAN THE ONE HE IS LIVING NOW.
WHAT DIFFERENCE DOES IT TRULY MAKE WHETHER YOU DIE TODAY, OR TOMORROW, OR MANY YEARS FROM NOW?
WHILE YOU HAVE LIFE, WHILE YOU STILL CAN...
...WASTE NO MORE TIME ARGUING WHAT A GOOD MAN IS AND JUST BE ONE.

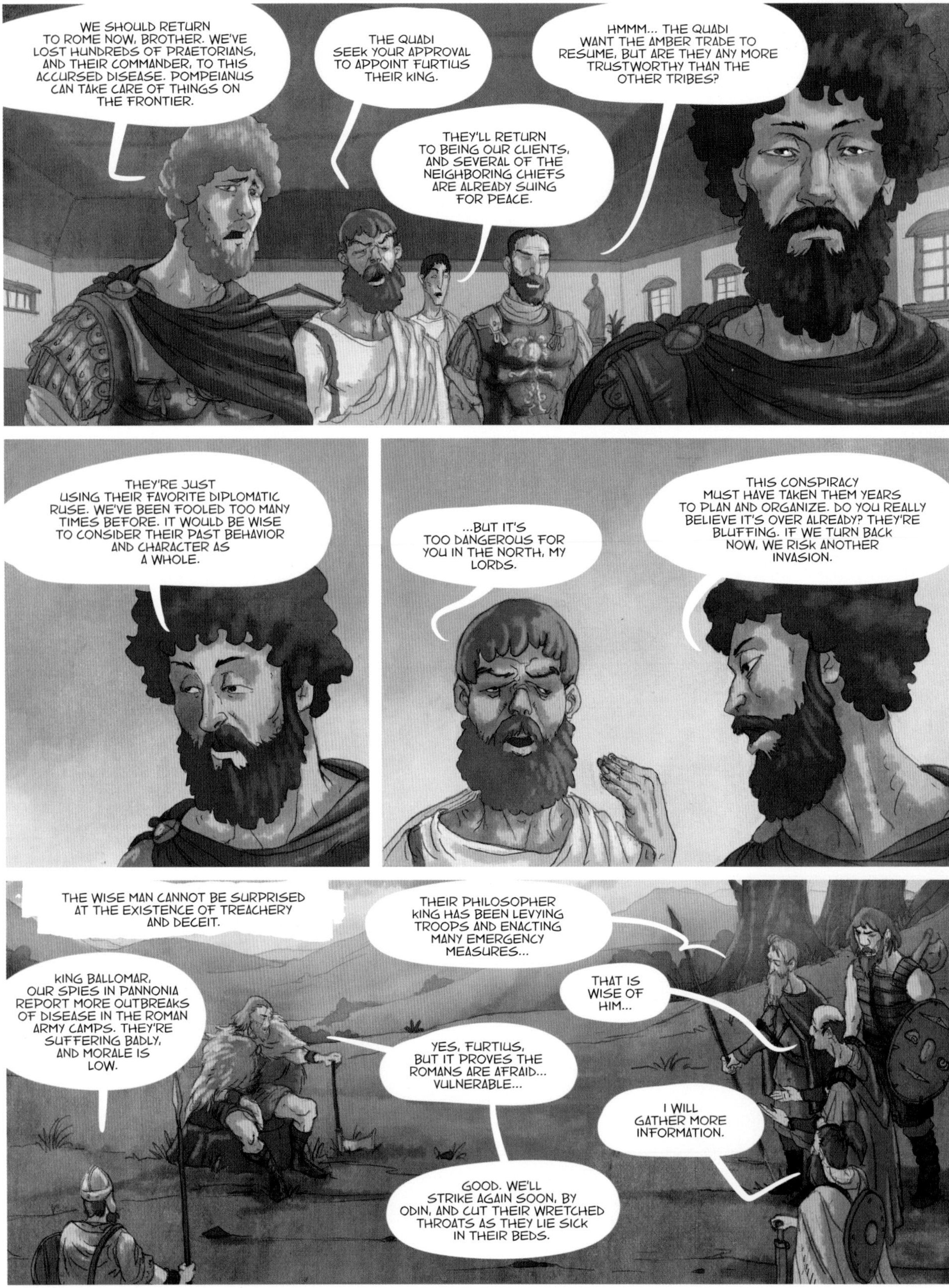
WE SHOULD RETURN TO ROME NOW, BROTHER. WE'VE LOST HUNDREDS OF PRAETORIANS, AND THEIR COMMANDER, TO THIS ACCURSED DISEASE. POMPEIANUS CAN TAKE CARE OF THINGS ON THE FRONTIER.
THE QUADI SEEK YOUR APPROVAL TO APPOINT FURTIUS THEIR KING.
THEY'LL RETURN TO BEING OUR CLIENTS, AND SEVERAL OF THE NEIGHBORING CHIEFS ARE ALREADY SUING FOR PEACE.
HMMM... THE QUADI WANT THE AMBER TRADE TO RESUME, BUT ARE THEY ANY MORE TRUSTWORTHY THAN THE OTHER TRIBES?
THEY'RE JUST USING THEIR FAVORITE DIPLOMATIC RUSE. WE'VE BEEN FOOLED TOO MANY TIMES BEFORE. IT WOULD BE WISE TO CONSIDER THEIR PAST BEHAVIOR AND CHARACTER AS A WHOLE.
...BUT IT'S TOO DANGEROUS FOR YOU IN THE NORTH, MY LORDS.
THIS CONSPIRACY MUST HAVE TAKEN THEM YEARS TO PLAN AND ORGANIZE. DO YOU REALLY BELIEVE IT'S OVER ALREADY? THEY'RE BLUFFING. IF WE TURN BACK NOW, WE RISK ANOTHER INVASION.
THE WISE MAN CANNOT BE SURPRISED AT THE EXISTENCE OF TREACHERY AND DECEIT.
KING BALLOMAR, OUR SPIES IN PANNONIA REPORT MORE OUTBREAKS OF DISEASE IN THE ROMAN ARMY CAMPS. THEY'RE SUFFERING BADLY, AND MORALE IS LOW.
THEIR PHILOSOPHER KING HAS BEEN LEVYING TROOPS AND ENACTING MANY EMERGENCY MEASURES...
THAT IS WISE OF HIM...
YES, FURTIUS, BUT IT PROVES THE ROMANS ARE AFRAID... VULNERABLE...
I WILL GATHER MORE INFORMATION.
GOOD. WE'LL STRIKE AGAIN SOON, BY ODIN, AND CUT THEIR WRETCHED THROATS AS THEY LIE SICK IN THEIR BEDS.

LUCIUS BEGAN TO SHOW SIGNS OF ILLNESS, AND I AGREED HE SHOULD RETURN TO THE SAFETY OF ROME.

MARCUS, I FEEL WEAK...

LUCIUS!

ON THE ROAD THROUGH NORTHERN ITALY, HE HAD AN ALARMING SEIZURE.

ARE YOU HURT, CAESAR?

QUICKLY! I MUST TRY BLEEDING HIM.

MY LORD!

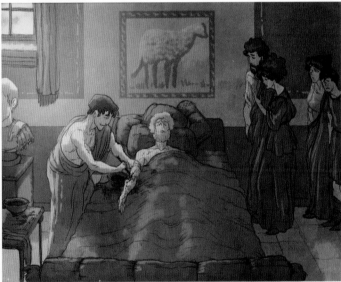

I RETURNED TO ROME TO OFFICIATE AT MY BROTHER'S FUNERAL.

EVERYONE EXPECTED MY LORD LUCIUS TO OUTLIVE HIS BROTHER AND REIGN AFTER HIM...

NOW WHO WILL DISCOURAGE THE PHILOSOPHER FROM TAKING MORE TROOPS TO DIE IN THE NORTH? WE SHOULD BE EXPANDING OUR EMPIRE TO THE EAST.

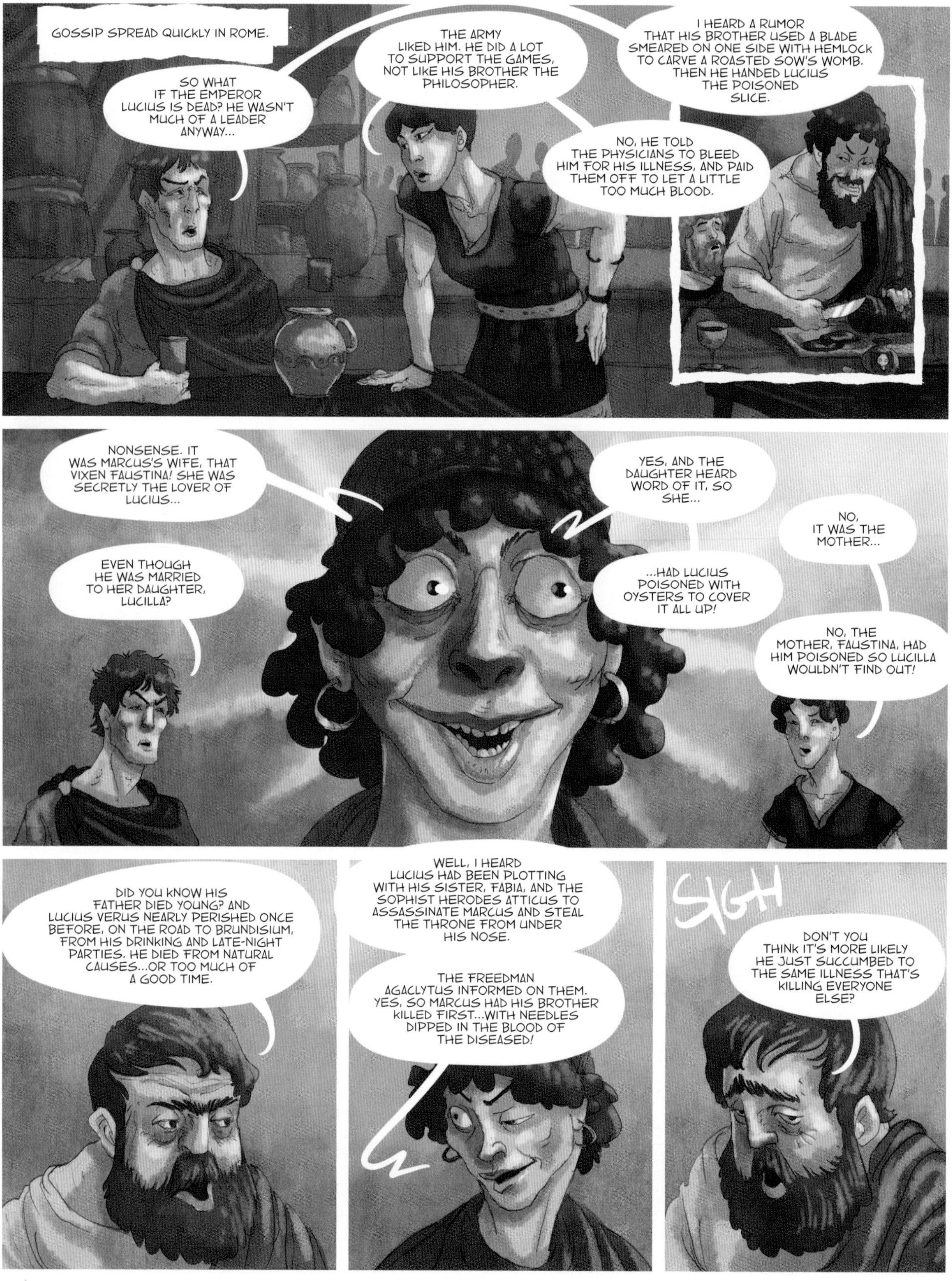
GOSSIP SPREAD QUICKLY IN ROME.
SO WHAT IF THE EMPEROR LUCIUS IS DEAD? HE WASN'T MUCH OF A LEADER ANYWAY...
THE ARMY LIKED HIM. HE DID A LOT TO SUPPORT THE GAMES, NOT LIKE HIS BROTHER THE PHILOSOPHER.
I HEARD A RUMOR THAT HIS BROTHER USED A BLADE SMEARED ON ONE SIDE WITH HEMLOCK TO CARVE A ROASTED SOW'S WOMB. THEN HE HANDED LUCIUS THE POISONED SLICE.
NO, HE TOLD THE PHYSICIANS TO BLEED HIM FOR HIS ILLNESS, AND PAID THEM OFF TO LET A LITTLE TOO MUCH BLOOD.
NONSENSE. IT WAS MARCUS'S WIFE, THAT VIXEN FAUSTINA! SHE WAS SECRETLY THE LOVER OF LUCIUS...
EVEN THOUGH HE WAS MARRIED TO HER DAUGHTER, LUCILLA?
YES, AND THE DAUGHTER HEARD WORD OF IT, SO SHE...
...HAD LUCIUS POISONED WITH OYSTERS TO COVER IT ALL UP!
NO, IT WAS THE MOTHER...
NO, THE MOTHER, FAUSTINA, HAD HIM POISONED SO LUCILLA WOULDN'T FIND OUT!
DID YOU KNOW HIS FATHER DIED YOUNG? AND LUCIUS VERUS NEARLY PERISHED ONCE BEFORE, ON THE ROAD TO BRUNDISIUM, FROM HIS DRINKING AND LATE-NIGHT PARTIES. HE DIED FROM NATURAL CAUSES...OR TOO MUCH OF A GOOD TIME.
WELL, I HEARD LUCIUS HAD BEEN PLOTTING WITH HIS SISTER, FABIA, AND THE SOPHIST HERODES ATTICUS TO ASSASSINATE MARCUS AND STEAL THE THRONE FROM UNDER HIS NOSE.
THE FREEDMAN AGACLYTUS INFORMED ON THEM. YES, SO MARCUS HAD HIS BROTHER KILLED FIRST...WITH NEEDLES DIPPED IN THE BLOOD OF THE DISEASED!
SIGH
DON'T YOU THINK IT'S MORE LIKELY HE JUST SUCCUMBED TO THE SAME ILLNESS THAT'S KILLING EVERYONE ELSE?

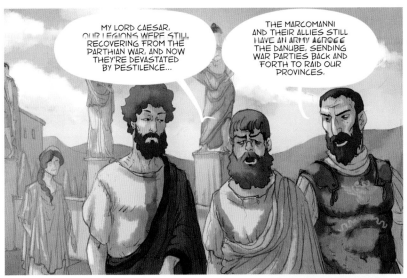

MY LORD CAESAR, OUR LEGIONS WERE STILL RECOVERING FROM THE PARTHIAN WAR, AND NOW THEY'RE DEVASTATED BY PESTILENCE...

THE MARCOMANNI AND THEIR ALLIES STILL HAVE AN ARMY ACROSS THE DANUBE, SENDING WAR PARTIES BACK AND FORTH TO RAID OUR PROVINCES.

WE NEED TO STOP THEM, BUT THE CAMPAIGN WILL HAVE TO WAIT UNTIL WE'VE MADE PREPARATIONS, IMPROVED OUR DEFENSES, AND REBUILT OUR ARMY.

WE'LL BEGIN RECRUITING SLAVES AND GLADIATORS INTO THE ARMY, AS ROME DID DURING THE PUNIC WARS, IN THE TIME OF THE REPUBLIC. THESE MEN SHALL HAVE THE CHANCE TO EARN THEIR OWN FREEDOM.

THE BANDITS TROUBLING DALMATIA AND MOESIA WILL BE OFFERED THE CHANCE TO REDEEM THEMSELVES AND AVOID PUNISHMENT, THROUGH MILITARY SERVICE.

SOME OF THE EXISTING BORDER GUARDS WILL NO LONGER BE REQUIRED, AND THEY CAN BE TRANSFERRED TO THE ARMY.

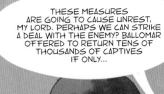

THESE MEASURES ARE GOING TO CAUSE UNREST, MY LORD. PERHAPS WE CAN STRIKE A DEAL WITH THE ENEMY? BALLOMAR OFFERED TO RETURN TENS OF THOUSANDS OF CAPTIVES IF ONLY...

NO, THEY'RE BLUFFING TO DELAY US. MY DUTY IS TO PROTECT THE STATE EVEN IF THE STEPS REQUIRED TO DO SO MAY PROVE UNPOPULAR.

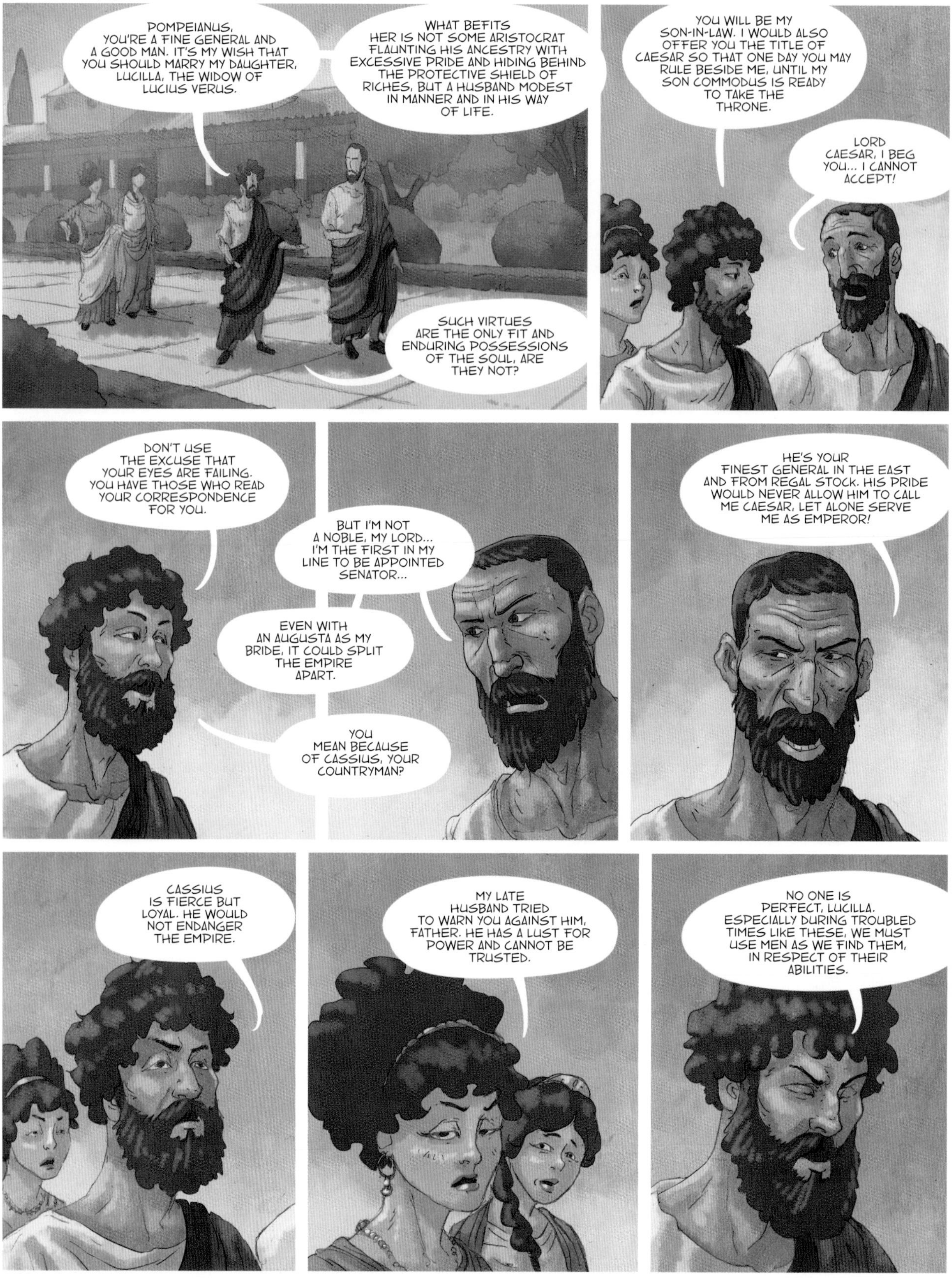
POMPEIANUS, YOU'RE A FINE GENERAL AND A GOOD MAN. IT'S MY WISH THAT YOU SHOULD MARRY MY DAUGHTER, LUCILLA, THE WIDOW OF LUCIUS VERUS.
WHAT BEFITS HER IS NOT SOME ARISTOCRAT FLAUNTING HIS ANCESTRY WITH EXCESSIVE PRIDE AND HIDING BEHIND THE PROTECTIVE SHIELD OF RICHES, BUT A HUSBAND MODEST IN MANNER AND IN HIS WAY OF LIFE.
SUCH VIRTUES ARE THE ONLY FIT AND ENDURING POSSESSIONS OF THE SOUL, ARE THEY NOT?
YOU WILL BE MY SON-IN-LAW. I WOULD ALSO OFFER YOU THE TITLE OF CAESAR SO THAT ONE DAY YOU MAY RULE BESIDE ME, UNTIL MY SON COMMODUS IS READY TO TAKE THE THRONE.
LORD CAESAR, I BEG YOU... I CANNOT ACCEPT!
DON'T USE THE EXCUSE THAT YOUR EYES ARE FAILING. YOU HAVE THOSE WHO READ YOUR CORRESPONDENCE FOR YOU.
BUT I'M NOT A NOBLE, MY LORD... I'M THE FIRST IN MY LINE TO BE APPOINTED SENATOR...
EVEN WITH AN AUGUSTA AS MY BRIDE, IT COULD SPLIT THE EMPIRE APART.
YOU MEAN BECAUSE OF CASSIUS, YOUR COUNTRYMAN?
HE'S YOUR FINEST GENERAL IN THE EAST AND FROM REGAL STOCK. HIS PRIDE WOULD NEVER ALLOW HIM TO CALL ME CAESAR, LET ALONE SERVE ME AS EMPEROR!
CASSIUS IS FIERCE BUT LOYAL. HE WOULD NOT ENDANGER THE EMPIRE.
MY LATE HUSBAND TRIED TO WARN YOU AGAINST HIM, FATHER. HE HAS A LUST FOR POWER AND CANNOT BE TRUSTED.
NO ONE IS PERFECT, LUCILLA. ESPECIALLY DURING TROUBLED TIMES LIKE THESE, WE MUST USE MEN AS WE FIND THEM, IN RESPECT OF THEIR ABILITIES.

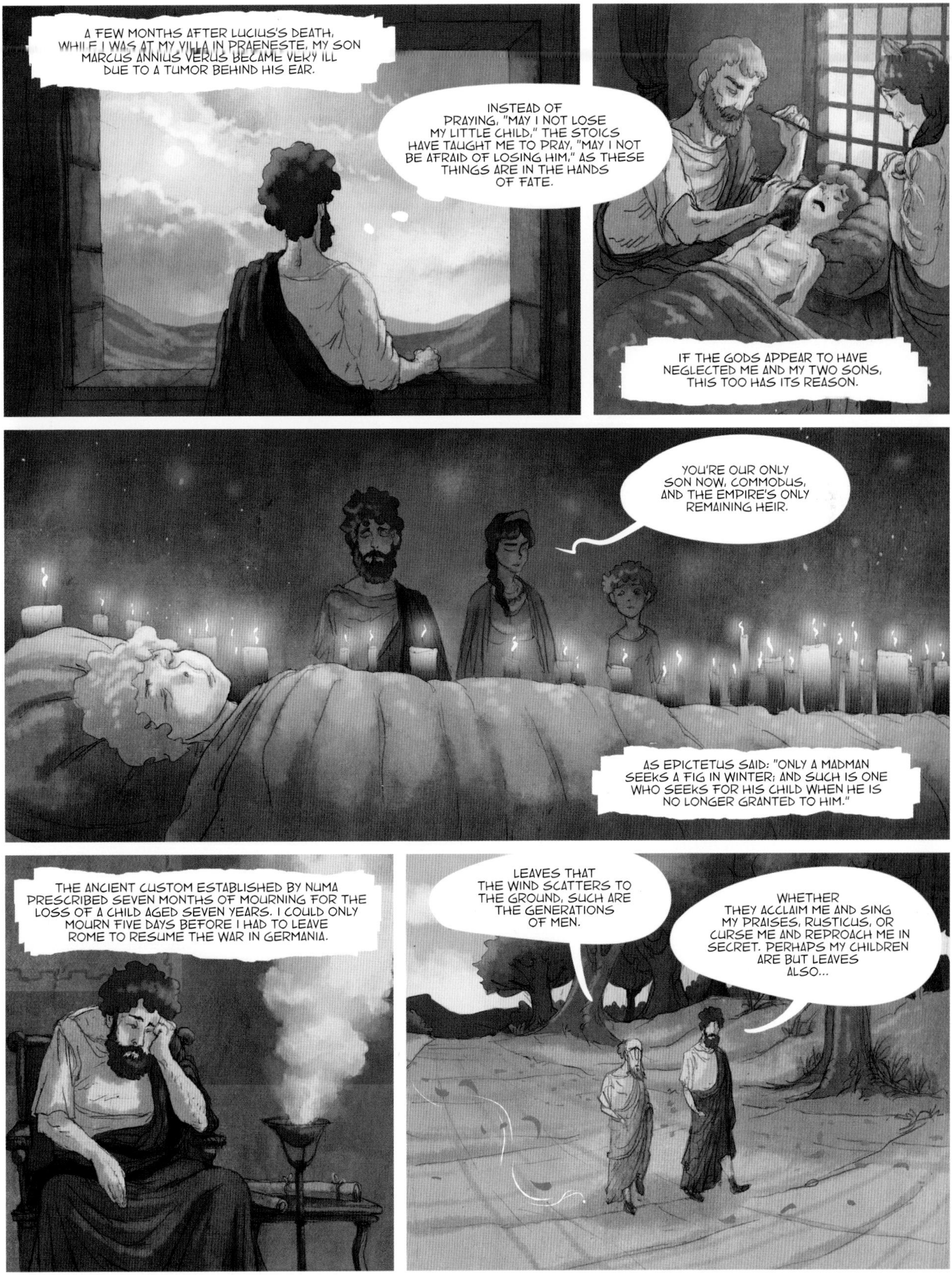
A FEW MONTHS AFTER LUCIUS'S DEATH, WHILE I WAS AT MY VILLA IN PRAENESTE, MY SON MARCUS ANNIUS VERUS BECAME VERY ILL DUE TO A TUMOR BEHIND HIS EAR.
INSTEAD OF PRAYING, "MAY I NOT LOSE MY LITTLE CHILD," THE STOICS HAVE TAUGHT ME TO PRAY, "MAY I NOT BE AFRAID OF LOSING HIM," AS THESE THINGS ARE IN THE HANDS OF FATE.
IF THE GODS APPEAR TO HAVE NEGLECTED ME AND MY TWO SONS, THIS TOO HAS ITS REASON.
YOU'RE OUR ONLY SON NOW, COMMODUS, AND THE EMPIRE'S ONLY REMAINING HEIR.
AS EPICTETUS SAID: "ONLY A MADMAN SEEKS A FIG IN WINTER; AND SUCH IS ONE WHO SEEKS FOR HIS CHILD WHEN HE IS NO LONGER GRANTED TO HIM."
THE ANCIENT CUSTOM ESTABLISHED BY NUMA PRESCRIBED SEVEN MONTHS OF MOURNING FOR THE LOSS OF A CHILD AGED SEVEN YEARS. I COULD ONLY MOURN FIVE DAYS BEFORE I HAD TO LEAVE ROME TO RESUME THE WAR IN GERMANIA.
LEAVES THAT THE WIND SCATTERS TO THE GROUND, SUCH ARE THE GENERATIONS OF MEN.
WHETHER THEY ACCLAIM ME AND SING MY PRAISES, RUSTICUS, OR CURSE ME AND REPROACH ME IN SECRET. PERHAPS MY CHILDREN ARE BUT LEAVES ALSO...

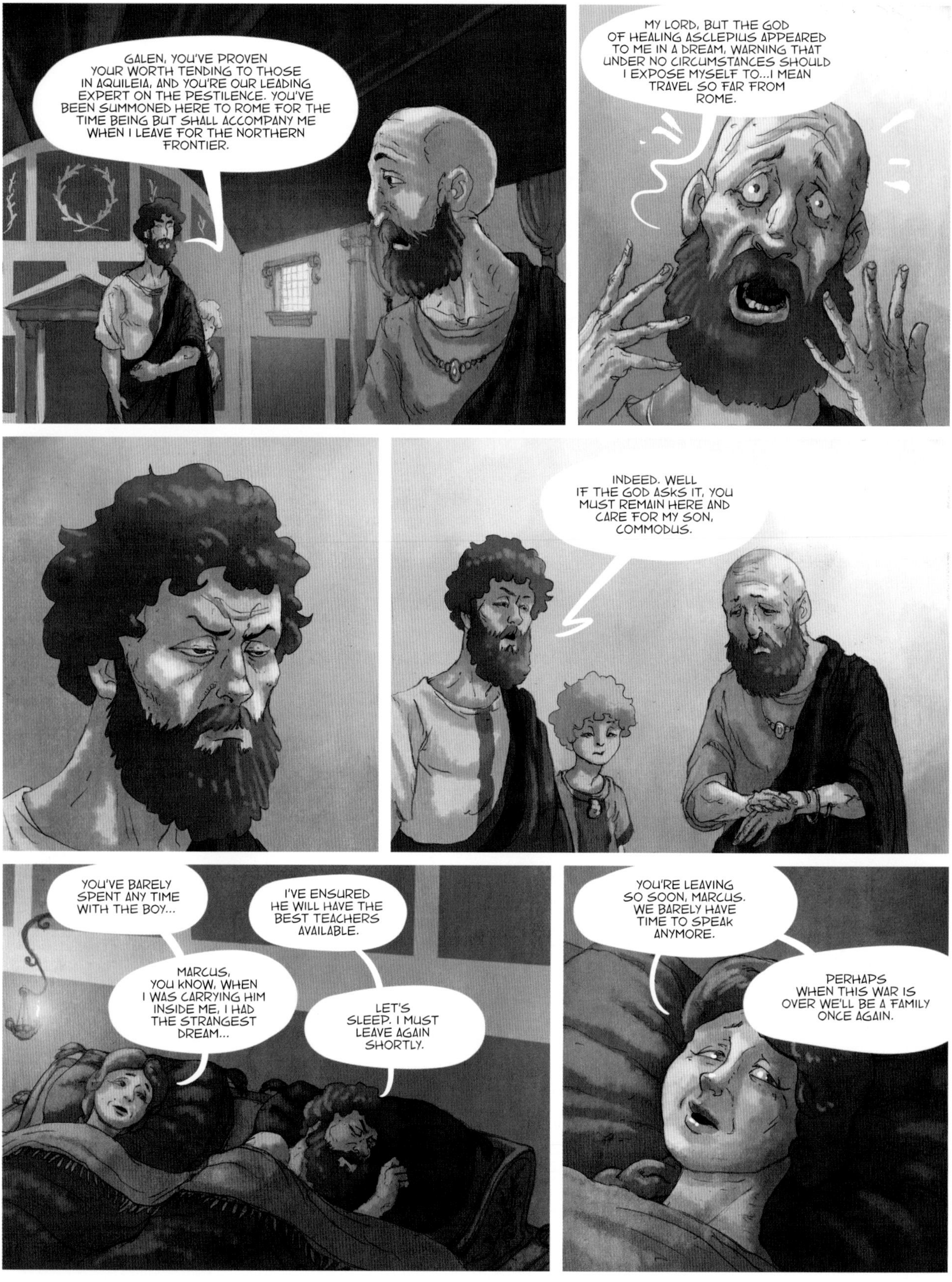

GALEN, YOU'VE PROVEN YOUR WORTH TENDING TO THOSE IN AQUILEIA, AND YOU'RE OUR LEADING EXPERT ON THE PESTILENCE. YOU'VE BEEN SUMMONED HERE TO ROME FOR THE TIME BEING BUT SHALL ACCOMPANY ME WHEN I LEAVE FOR THE NORTHERN FRONTIER.
MY LORD, BUT THE GOD OF HEALING ASCLEPIUS APPEARED TO ME IN A DREAM, WARNING THAT UNDER NO CIRCUMSTANCES SHOULD I EXPOSE MYSELF TO...I MEAN TRAVEL SO FAR FROM ROME.
INDEED. WELL IF THE GOD ASKS IT, YOU MUST REMAIN HERE AND CARE FOR MY SON, COMMODUS.
YOU'VE BARELY SPENT ANY TIME WITH THE BOY...
I'VE ENSURED HE WILL HAVE THE BEST TEACHERS AVAILABLE.
MARCUS, YOU KNOW, WHEN I WAS CARRYING HIM INSIDE ME, I HAD THE STRANGEST DREAM...
LET'S SLEEP. I MUST LEAVE AGAIN SHORTLY.
YOU'RE LEAVING SO SOON, MARCUS. WE BARELY HAVE TIME TO SPEAK ANYMORE.
PERHAPS WHEN THIS WAR IS OVER WE'LL BE A FAMILY ONCE AGAIN.

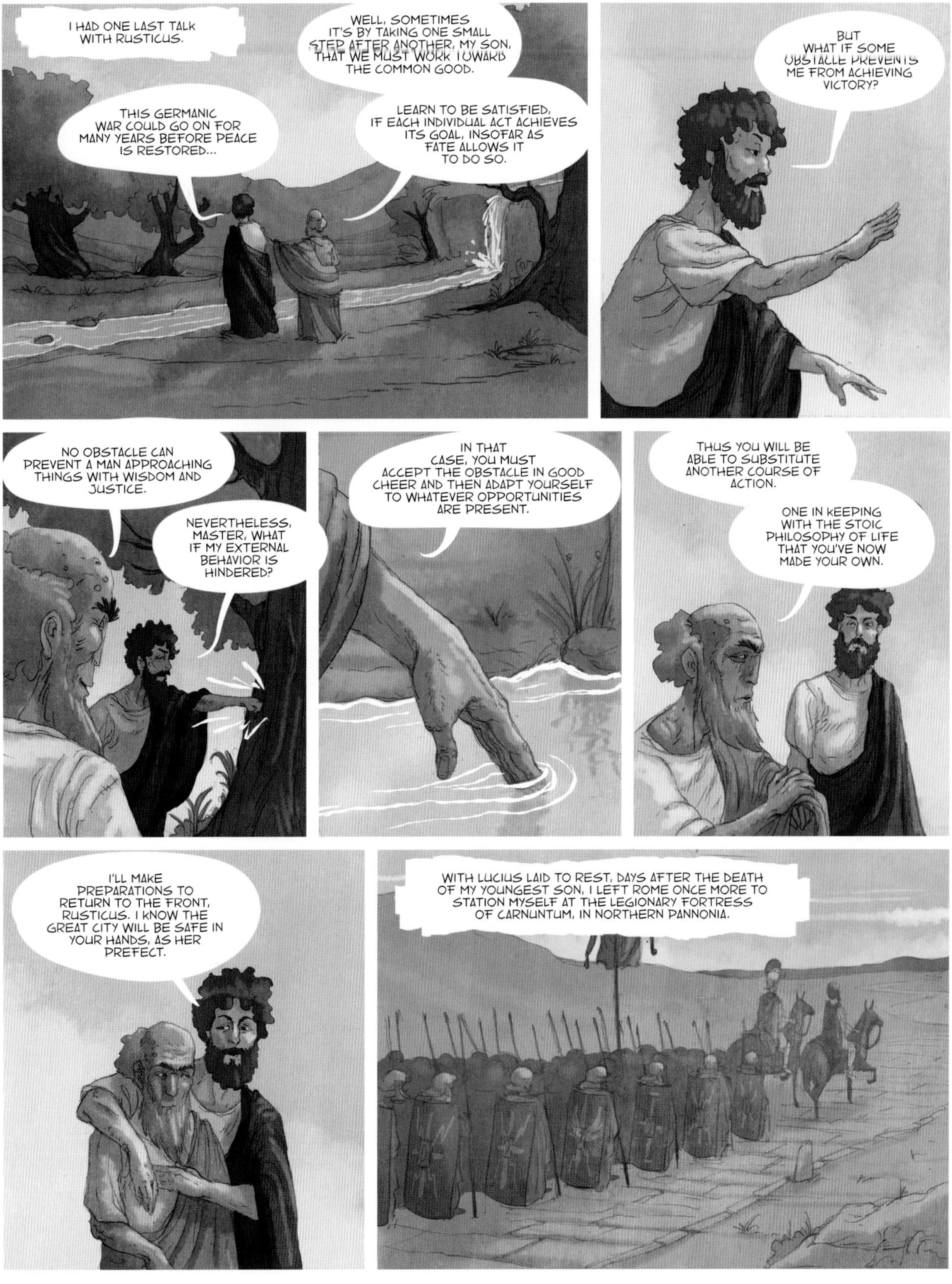

I HAD ONE LAST TALK WITH RUSTICUS.
THIS GERMANIC WAR COULD GO ON FOR MANY YEARS BEFORE PEACE IS RESTORED...
WELL, SOMETIMES IT'S BY TAKING ONE SMALL STEP AFTER ANOTHER, MY SON, THAT WE MUST WORK TOWARD THE COMMON GOOD.
LEARN TO BE SATISFIED, IF EACH INDIVIDUAL ACT ACHIEVES ITS GOAL, INSOFAR AS FATE ALLOWS IT TO DO SO.
BUT WHAT IF SOME OBSTACLE PREVENTS ME FROM ACHIEVING VICTORY?
NO OBSTACLE CAN PREVENT A MAN APPROACHING THINGS WITH WISDOM AND JUSTICE.
NEVERTHELESS, MASTER, WHAT IF MY EXTERNAL BEHAVIOR IS HINDERED?
IN THAT CASE, YOU MUST ACCEPT THE OBSTACLE IN GOOD CHEER AND THEN ADAPT YOURSELF TO WHATEVER OPPORTUNITIES ARE PRESENT.
THUS YOU WILL BE ABLE TO SUBSTITUTE ANOTHER COURSE OF ACTION.
ONE IN KEEPING WITH THE STOIC PHILOSOPHY OF LIFE THAT YOU'VE NOW MADE YOUR OWN.
I'LL MAKE PREPARATIONS TO RETURN TO THE FRONT, RUSTICUS. I KNOW THE GREAT CITY WILL BE SAFE IN YOUR HANDS, AS HER PREFECT.
WITH LUCIUS LAID TO REST, DAYS AFTER THE DEATH OF MY YOUNGEST SON, I LEFT ROME ONCE MORE TO STATION MYSELF AT THE LEGIONARY FORTRESS OF CARNUNTUM, IN NORTHERN PANNONIA.

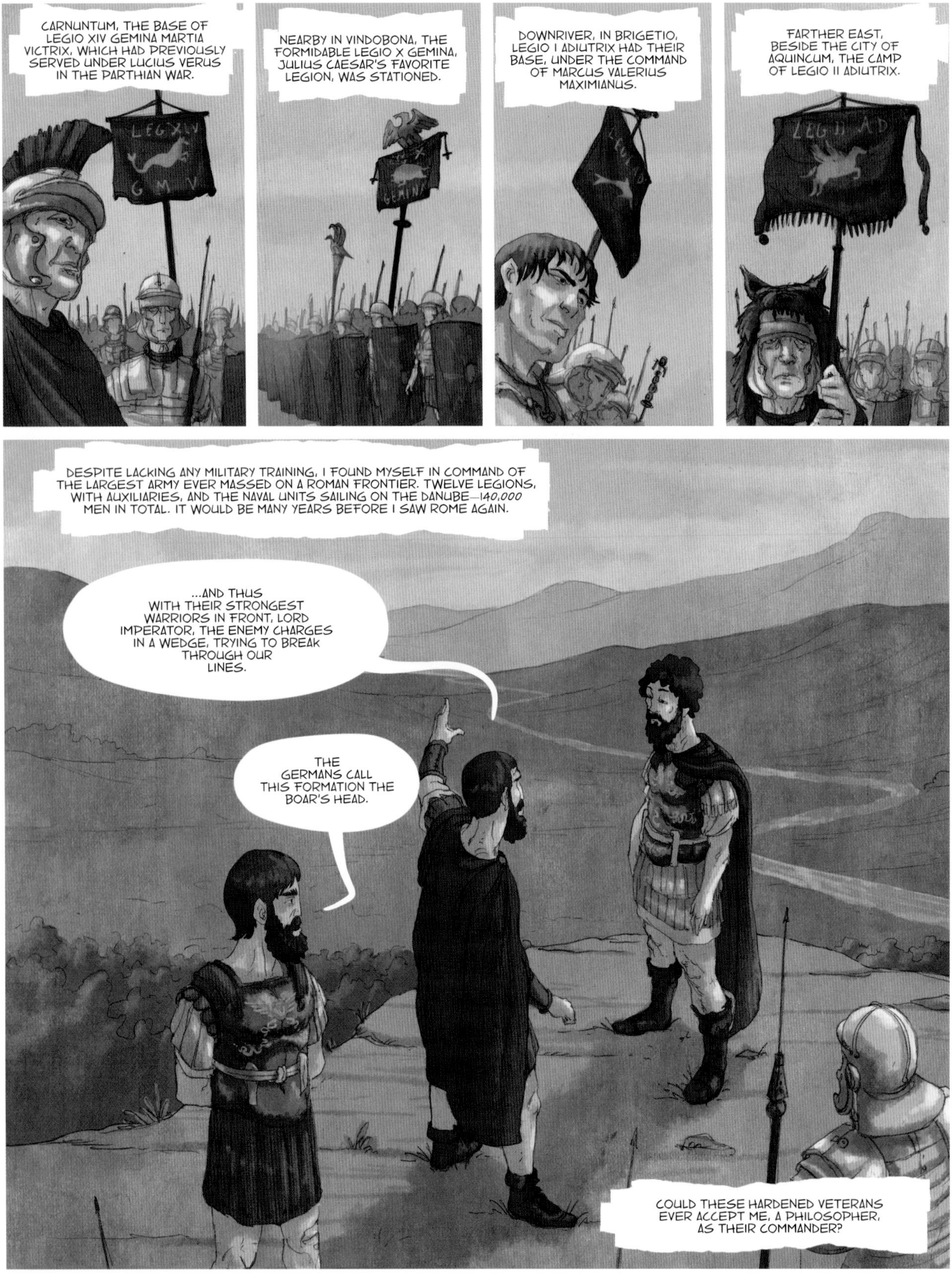
CARNUNTUM, THE BASE OF LEGIO XIV GEMINA MARTIA VICTRIX, WHICH HAD PREVIOUSLY SERVED UNDER LUCIUS VERUS IN THE PARTHIAN WAR.
NEARBY IN VINDOBONA, THE FORMIDABLE LEGIO X GEMINA, JULIUS CAESAR'S FAVORITE LEGION, WAS STATIONED.
DOWNRIVER, IN BRIGETIO, LEGIO I ADIUTRIX HAD THEIR BASE, UNDER THE COMMAND OF MARCUS VALERIUS MAXIMIANUS.
FARTHER EAST, BESIDE THE CITY OF AQUINCUM, THE CAMP OF LEGIO II ADIUTRIX.
DESPITE LACKING ANY MILITARY TRAINING, I FOUND MYSELF IN COMMAND OF THE LARGEST ARMY EVER MASSED ON A ROMAN FRONTIER. TWELVE LEGIONS, WITH AUXILIARIES, AND THE NAVAL UNITS SAILING ON THE DANUBE—140,000 MEN IN TOTAL. IT WOULD BE MANY YEARS BEFORE I SAW ROME AGAIN.
...AND THUS WITH THEIR STRONGEST WARRIORS IN FRONT, LORD IMPERATOR, THE ENEMY CHARGES IN A WEDGE, TRYING TO BREAK THROUGH OUR LINES.
THE GERMANS CALL THIS FORMATION THE BOAR'S HEAD.
COULD THESE HARDENED VETERANS EVER ACCEPT ME, A PHILOSOPHER, AS THEIR COMMANDER?

THE
WAR of MANY
NATIONS

Time is like a river, a violent stream, made up of the events which befall us. For as soon as a thing has been seen, it is carried away, and another comes in its place, and this will be carried away too.

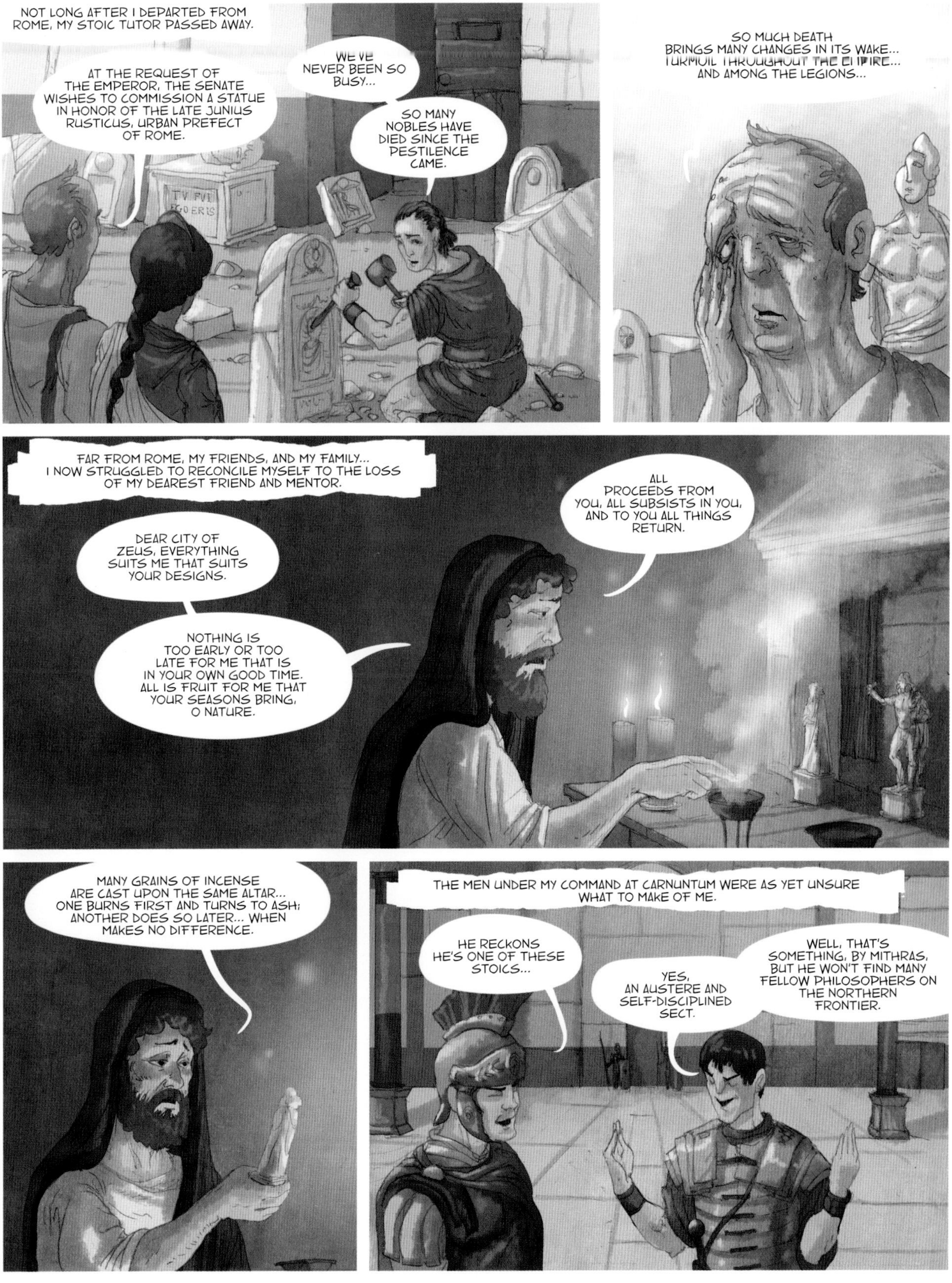

NOT LONG AFTER I DEPARTED FROM ROME, MY STOIC TUTOR PASSED AWAY.
AT THE REQUEST OF THE EMPEROR, THE SENATE WISHES TO COMMISSION A STATUE IN HONOR OF THE LATE JUNIUS RUSTICUS, URBAN PREFECT OF ROME.
WE'VE NEVER BEEN SO BUSY...
SO MANY NOBLES HAVE DIED SINCE THE PESTILENCE CAME.
TV FVI EGO ERIS
SO MUCH DEATH BRINGS MANY CHANGES IN ITS WAKE... TURMOIL THROUGHOUT THE EMPIRE... AND AMONG THE LEGIONS...
FAR FROM ROME, MY FRIENDS, AND MY FAMILY... I NOW STRUGGLED TO RECONCILE MYSELF TO THE LOSS OF MY DEAREST FRIEND AND MENTOR.
DEAR CITY OF ZEUS, EVERYTHING SUITS ME THAT SUITS YOUR DESIGNS.
NOTHING IS TOO EARLY OR TOO LATE FOR ME THAT IS IN YOUR OWN GOOD TIME. ALL IS FRUIT FOR ME THAT YOUR SEASONS BRING, O NATURE.
ALL PROCEEDS FROM YOU, ALL SUBSISTS IN YOU, AND TO YOU ALL THINGS RETURN.
MANY GRAINS OF INCENSE ARE CAST UPON THE SAME ALTAR... ONE BURNS FIRST AND TURNS TO ASH; ANOTHER DOES SO LATER... WHEN MAKES NO DIFFERENCE.
THE MEN UNDER MY COMMAND AT CARNUNTUM WERE AS YET UNSURE WHAT TO MAKE OF ME.
HE RECKONS HE'S ONE OF THESE STOICS...
YES, AN AUSTERE AND SELF-DISCIPLINED SECT.
WELL, THAT'S SOMETHING, BY MITHRAS, BUT HE WON'T FIND MANY FELLOW PHILOSOPHERS ON THE NORTHERN FRONTIER.

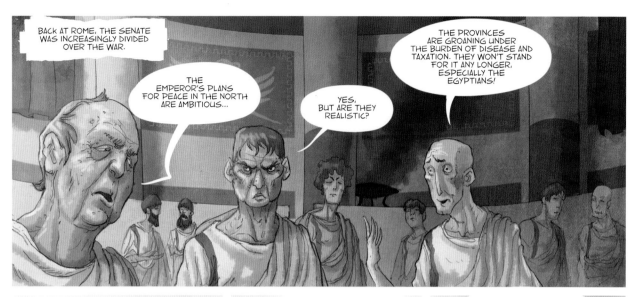

BACK AT ROME, THE SENATE WAS INCREASINGLY DIVIDED OVER THE WAR.

THE EMPEROR'S PLANS FOR PEACE IN THE NORTH ARE AMBITIOUS...

YES, BUT ARE THEY REALISTIC?

THE PROVINCES ARE GROANING UNDER THE BURDEN OF DISEASE AND TAXATION. THEY WON'T STAND FOR IT ANY LONGER, ESPECIALLY THE EGYPTIANS!

WE LOSE MORE SOLDIERS EVERY DAY. AT LEAST LUCIUS BROUGHT BACK GOLD FROM PARTHIA. THESE GERMANIC TRIBES HAVE NOTHING WORTH SEIZING.

MY SON-IN-LAW, CASSIUS, DEALT SWIFTLY WITH ROME'S BARBAROUS ENEMIES. WE NEED MORE SWORDS IN THE NORTH, NOT MORE DIPLOMACY...

REMARKABLE! THE EMPEROR SENDS A LIST OF GOODS TO BE STRIPPED FROM HIS PALACE AND AUCTIONED FOR THE WAR EFFORT.

THE AUCTION WENT ON FOR TWO MONTHS, AS WE SOLD OFF COUNTLESS IMPERIAL TREASURES, INCLUDING HORDES OF GEMS ACCUMULATED IN SECRET BY HADRIAN.

IT SEEMS THE EMPEROR MEANT WHAT HE ALWAYS SAYS—PROPERTY IS MERELY ON LOAN FROM NATURE!

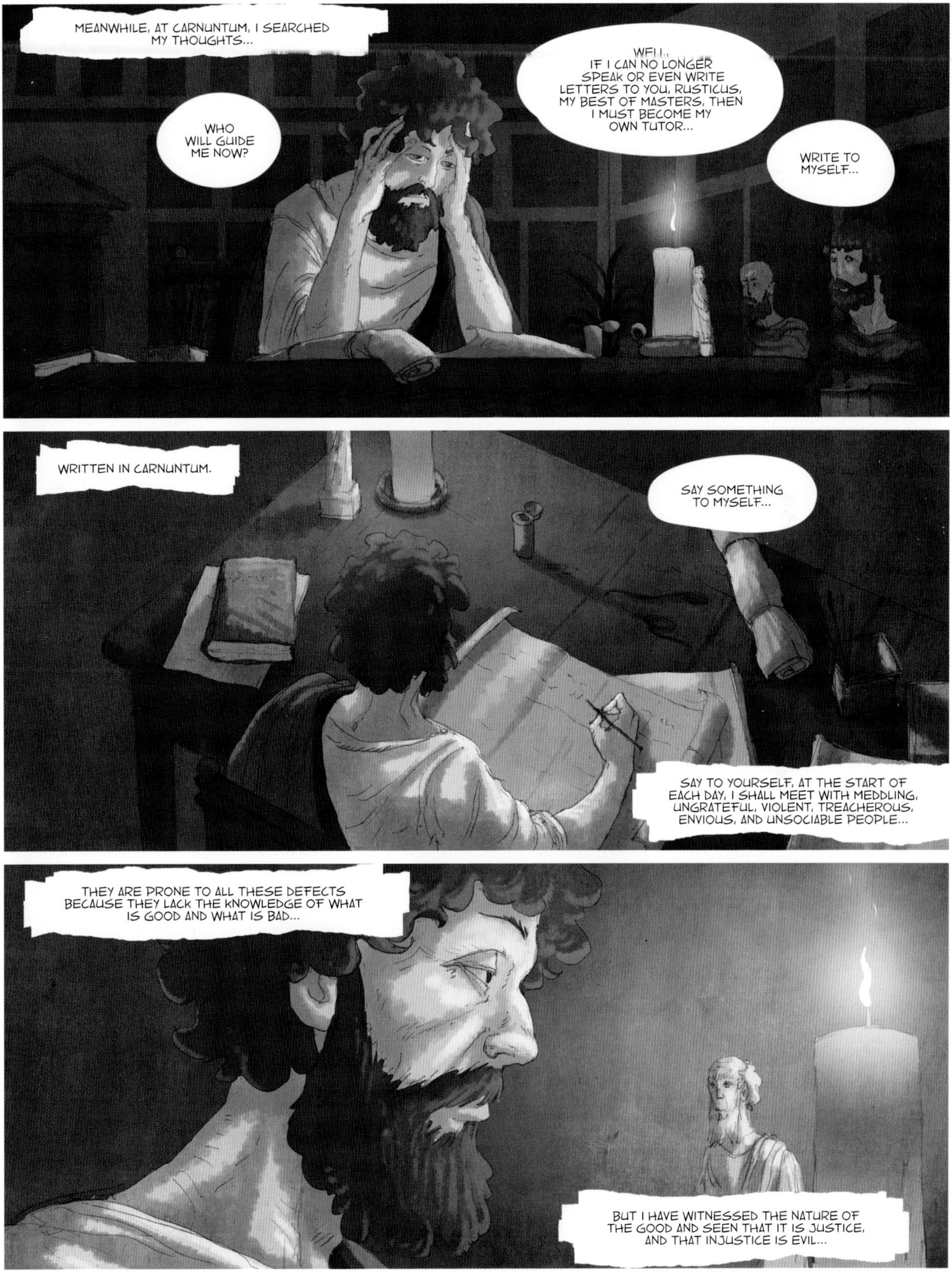
MEANWHILE, AT CARNUNTUM, I SEARCHED MY THOUGHTS...
WHO WILL GUIDE ME NOW?
WELL, IF I CAN NO LONGER SPEAK OR EVEN WRITE LETTERS TO YOU, RUSTICUS, MY BEST OF MASTERS, THEN I MUST BECOME MY OWN TUTOR...
WRITE TO MYSELF...
WRITTEN IN CARNUNTUM.
SAY SOMETHING TO MYSELF...
SAY TO YOURSELF, AT THE START OF EACH DAY, I SHALL MEET WITH MEDDLING, UNGRATEFUL, VIOLENT, TREACHEROUS, ENVIOUS, AND UNSOCIABLE PEOPLE...
THEY ARE PRONE TO ALL THESE DEFECTS BECAUSE THEY LACK THE KNOWLEDGE OF WHAT IS GOOD AND WHAT IS BAD...
BUT I HAVE WITNESSED THE NATURE OF THE GOOD AND SEEN THAT IT IS JUSTICE, AND THAT INJUSTICE IS EVIL...

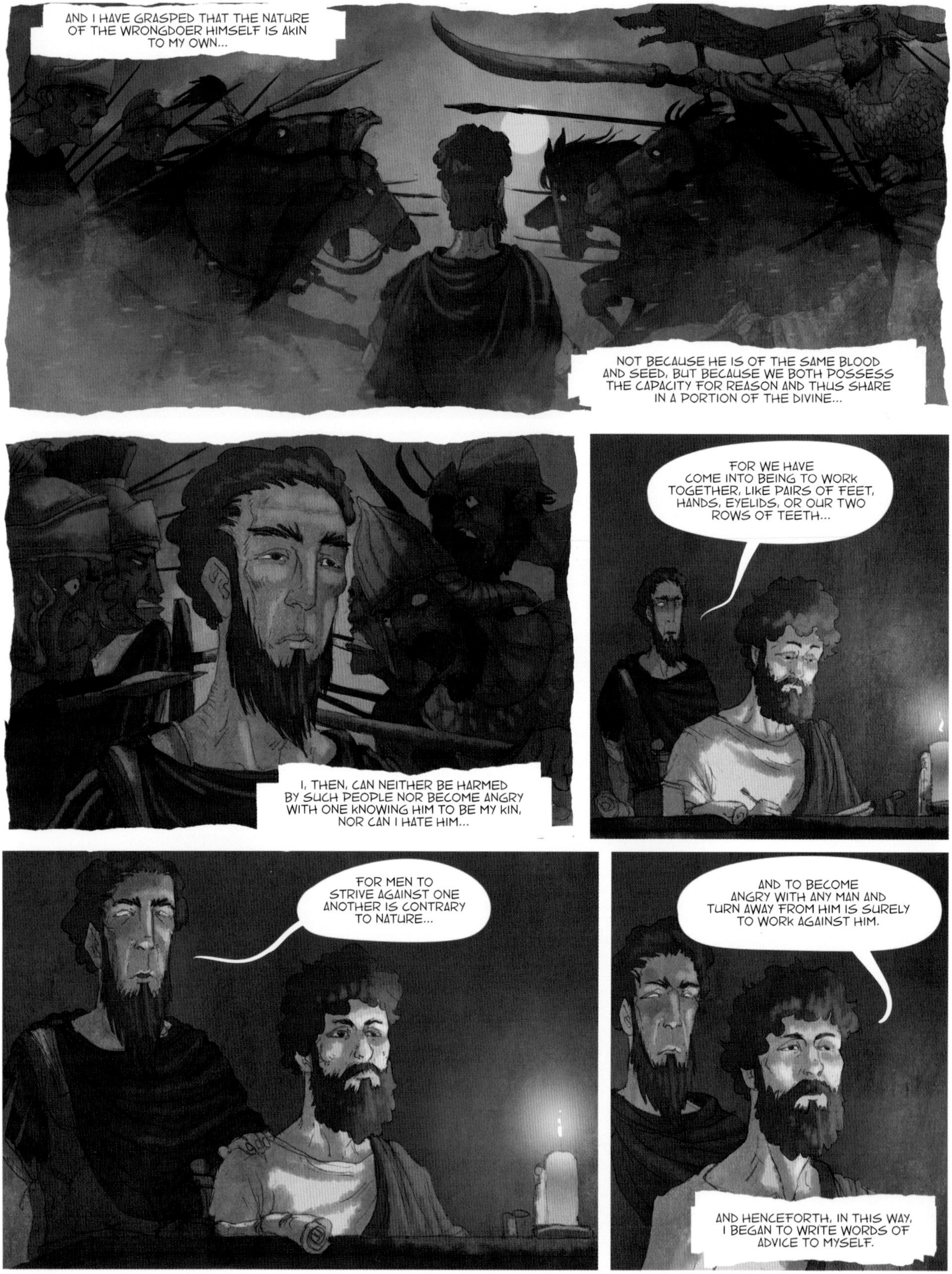
AND I HAVE GRASPED THAT THE NATURE OF THE WRONGDOER HIMSELF IS AKIN TO MY OWN...
NOT BECAUSE HE IS OF THE SAME BLOOD AND SEED, BUT BECAUSE WE BOTH POSSESS THE CAPACITY FOR REASON AND THUS SHARE IN A PORTION OF THE DIVINE...
I, THEN, CAN NEITHER BE HARMED BY SUCH PEOPLE NOR BECOME ANGRY WITH ONE KNOWING HIM TO BE MY KIN, NOR CAN I HATE HIM...
FOR WE HAVE COME INTO BEING TO WORK TOGETHER, LIKE PAIRS OF FEET, HANDS, EYELIDS, OR OUR TWO ROWS OF TEETH...
FOR MEN TO STRIVE AGAINST ONE ANOTHER IS CONTRARY TO NATURE...
AND TO BECOME ANGRY WITH ANY MAN AND TURN AWAY FROM HIM IS SURELY TO WORK AGAINST HIM.
AND HENCEFORTH, IN THIS WAY, I BEGAN TO WRITE WORDS OF ADVICE TO MYSELF.

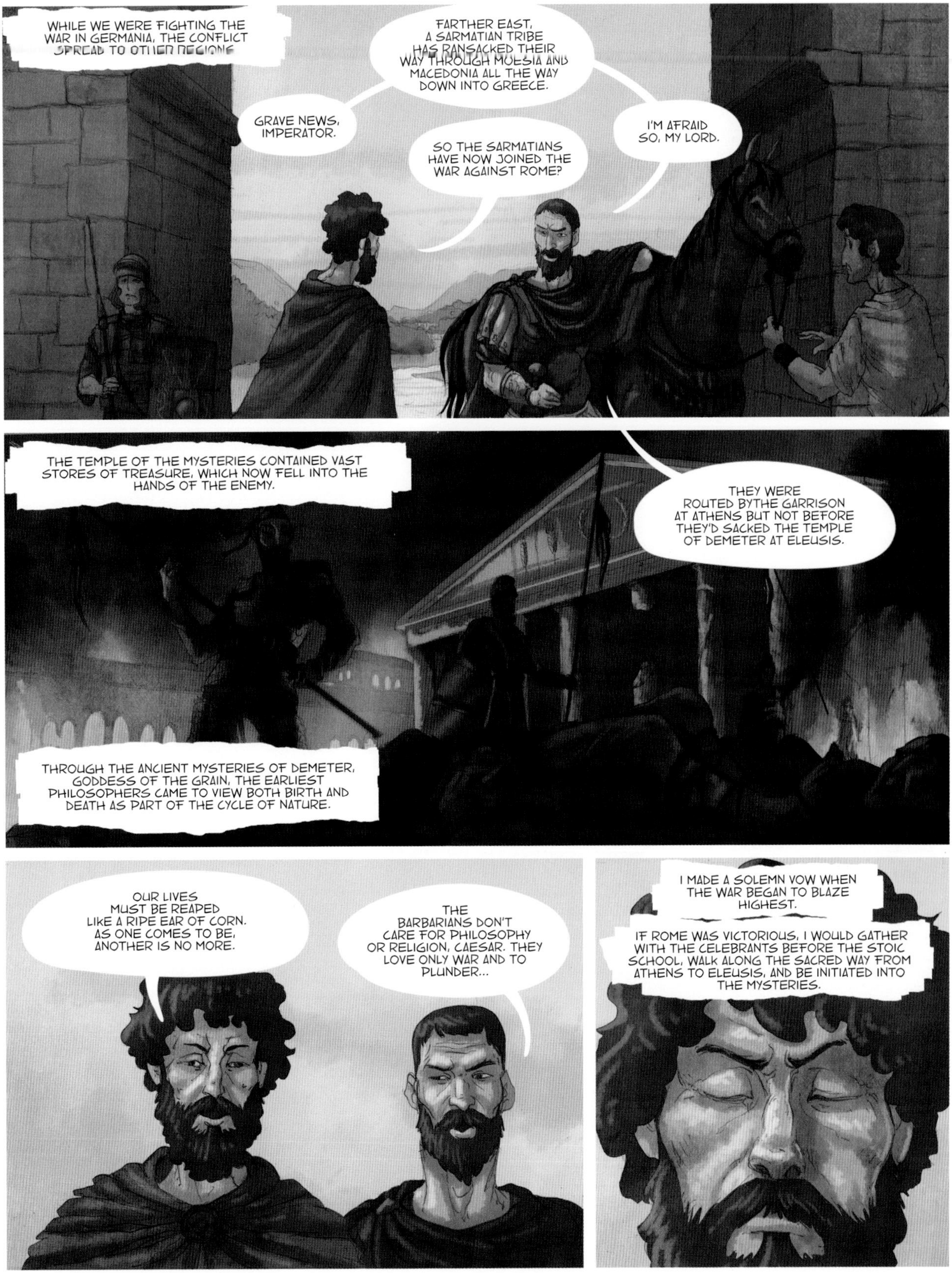
WHILE WE WERE FIGHTING THE WAR IN GERMANIA, THE CONFLICT SPREAD TO OTHER REGIONS
GRAVE NEWS, IMPERATOR.
FARTHER EAST, A SARMATIAN TRIBE HAS RANSACKED THEIR WAY THROUGH MOESIA AND MACEDONIA ALL THE WAY DOWN INTO GREECE.
SO THE SARMATIANS HAVE NOW JOINED THE WAR AGAINST ROME?
I'M AFRAID SO, MY LORD.
THEY WERE ROUTED BYTHE GARRISON AT ATHENS BUT NOT BEFORE THEY'D SACKED THE TEMPLE OF DEMETER AT ELEUSIS.
THE TEMPLE OF THE MYSTERIES CONTAINED VAST STORES OF TREASURE, WHICH NOW FELL INTO THE HANDS OF THE ENEMY.
THROUGH THE ANCIENT MYSTERIES OF DEMETER, GODDESS OF THE GRAIN, THE EARLIEST PHILOSOPHERS CAME TO VIEW BOTH BIRTH AND DEATH AS PART OF THE CYCLE OF NATURE.
OUR LIVES MUST BE REAPED LIKE A RIPE EAR OF CORN. AS ONE COMES TO BE, ANOTHER IS NO MORE.
THE BARBARIANS DON'T CARE FOR PHILOSOPHY OR RELIGION, CAESAR. THEY LOVE ONLY WAR AND TO PLUNDER...
I MADE A SOLEMN VOW WHEN THE WAR BEGAN TO BLAZE HIGHEST.
IF ROME WAS VICTORIOUS, I WOULD GATHER WITH THE CELEBRANTS BEFORE THE STOIC SCHOOL, WALK ALONG THE SACRED WAY FROM ATHENS TO ELEUSIS, AND BE INITIATED INTO THE MYSTERIES.

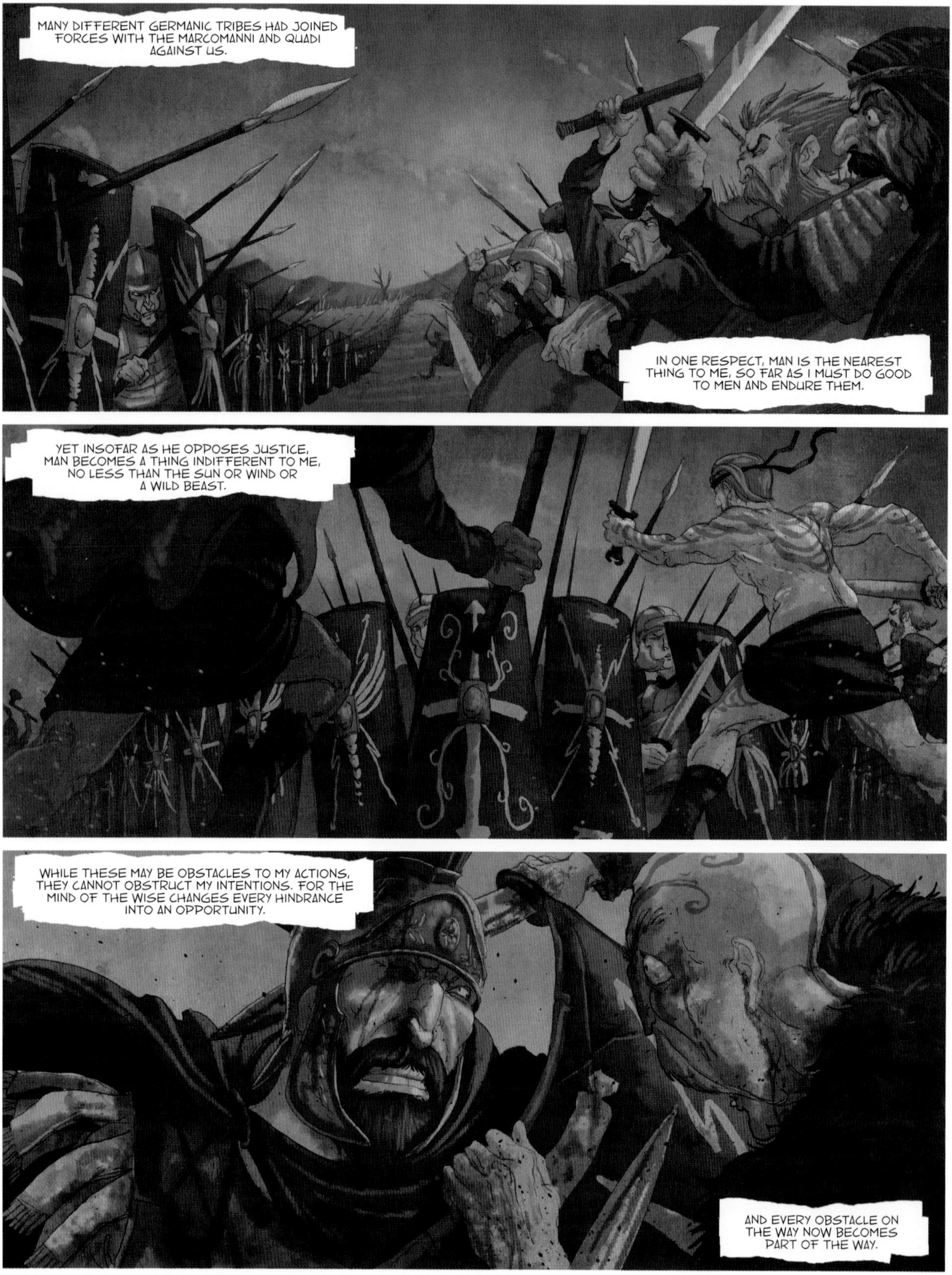
MANY DIFFERENT GERMANIC TRIBES HAD JOINED FORCES WITH THE MARCOMANNI AND QUADI AGAINST US.
IN ONE RESPECT, MAN IS THE NEAREST THING TO ME, SO FAR AS I MUST DO GOOD TO MEN AND ENDURE THEM.
YET INSOFAR AS HE OPPOSES JUSTICE, MAN BECOMES A THING INDIFFERENT TO ME, NO LESS THAN THE SUN OR WIND OR A WILD BEAST.
WHILE THESE MAY BE OBSTACLES TO MY ACTIONS, THEY CANNOT OBSTRUCT MY INTENTIONS. FOR THE MIND OF THE WISE CHANGES EVERY HINDRANCE INTO AN OPPORTUNITY.
AND EVERY OBSTACLE ON THE WAY NOW BECOMES PART OF THE WAY.

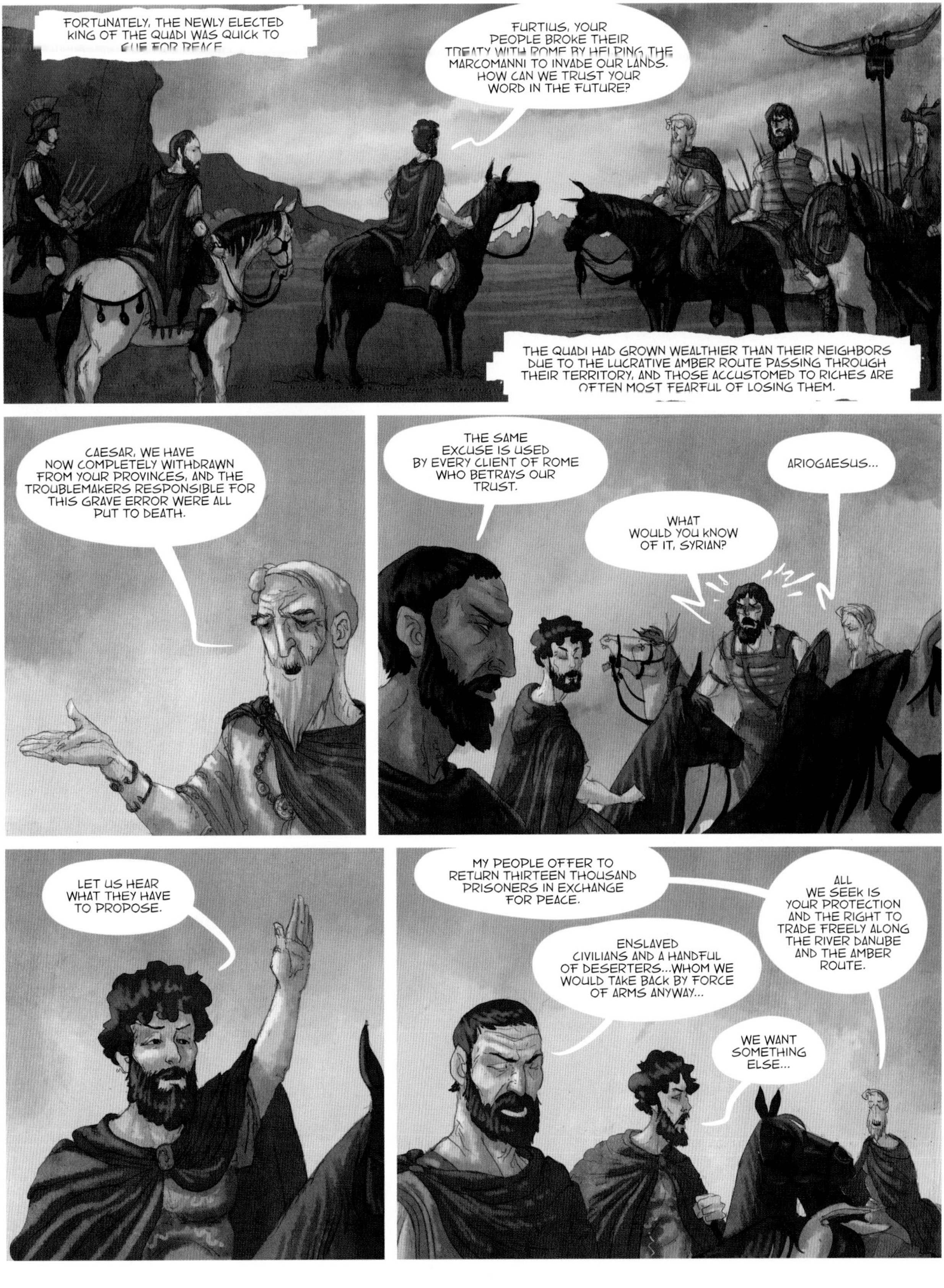
FORTUNATELY, THE NEWLY ELECTED KING OF THE QUADI WAS QUICK TO SUE FOR PEACE.
FURTIUS, YOUR PEOPLE BROKE THEIR TREATY WITH ROME BY HELPING THE MARCOMANNI TO INVADE OUR LANDS. HOW CAN WE TRUST YOUR WORD IN THE FUTURE?
THE QUADI HAD GROWN WEALTHIER THAN THEIR NEIGHBORS DUE TO THE LUCRATIVE AMBER ROUTE PASSING THROUGH THEIR TERRITORY, AND THOSE ACCUSTOMED TO RICHES ARE OFTEN MOST FEARFUL OF LOSING THEM.
CAESAR, WE HAVE NOW COMPLETELY WITHDRAWN FROM YOUR PROVINCES, AND THE TROUBLEMAKERS RESPONSIBLE FOR THIS GRAVE ERROR WERE ALL PUT TO DEATH.
THE SAME EXCUSE IS USED BY EVERY CLIENT OF ROME WHO BETRAYS OUR TRUST.
ARIOGAESUS...
WHAT WOULD YOU KNOW OF IT, SYRIAN?
LET US HEAR WHAT THEY HAVE TO PROPOSE.
MY PEOPLE OFFER TO RETURN THIRTEEN THOUSAND PRISONERS IN EXCHANGE FOR PEACE.
ALL WE SEEK IS YOUR PROTECTION AND THE RIGHT TO TRADE FREELY ALONG THE RIVER DANUBE AND THE AMBER ROUTE.
ENSLAVED CIVILIANS AND A HANDFUL OF DESERTERS...WHOM WE WOULD TAKE BACK BY FORCE OF ARMS ANYWAY...
WE WANT SOMETHING ELSE...

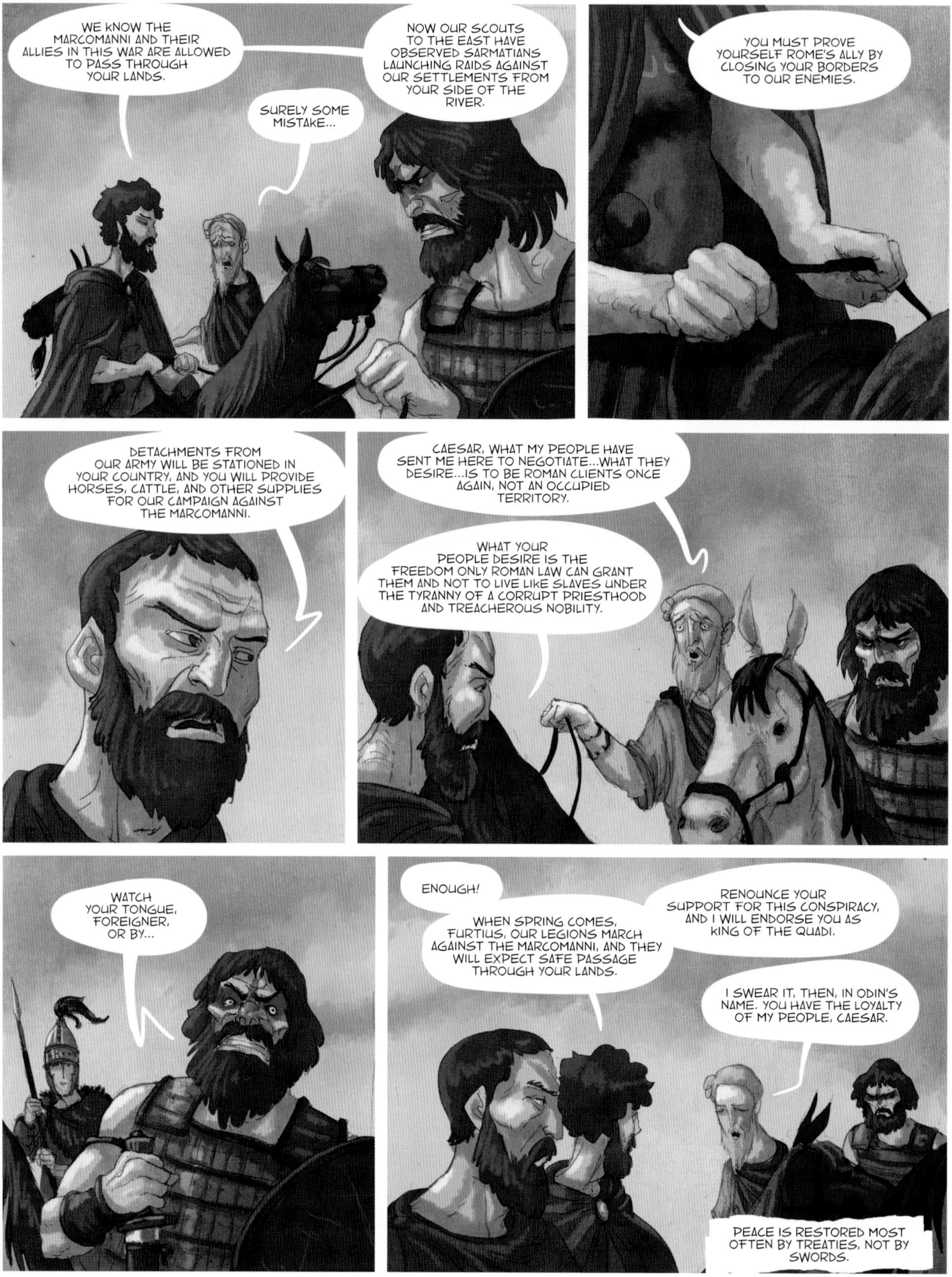
WE KNOW THE MARCOMANNI AND THEIR ALLIES IN THIS WAR ARE ALLOWED TO PASS THROUGH YOUR LANDS.
NOW OUR SCOUTS TO THE EAST HAVE OBSERVED SARMATIANS LAUNCHING RAIDS AGAINST OUR SETTLEMENTS FROM YOUR SIDE OF THE RIVER.
SURELY SOME MISTAKE...
YOU MUST PROVE YOURSELF ROME'S ALLY BY CLOSING YOUR BORDERS TO OUR ENEMIES.
DETACHMENTS FROM OUR ARMY WILL BE STATIONED IN YOUR COUNTRY, AND YOU WILL PROVIDE HORSES, CATTLE, AND OTHER SUPPLIES FOR OUR CAMPAIGN AGAINST THE MARCOMANNI.
CAESAR, WHAT MY PEOPLE HAVE SENT ME HERE TO NEGOTIATE...WHAT THEY DESIRE...IS TO BE ROMAN CLIENTS ONCE AGAIN, NOT AN OCCUPIED TERRITORY.
WHAT YOUR PEOPLE DESIRE IS THE FREEDOM ONLY ROMAN LAW CAN GRANT THEM AND NOT TO LIVE LIKE SLAVES UNDER THE TYRANNY OF A CORRUPT PRIESTHOOD AND TREACHEROUS NOBILITY.
WATCH YOUR TONGUE, FOREIGNER, OR BY...
ENOUGH!
WHEN SPRING COMES, FURTIUS, OUR LEGIONS MARCH AGAINST THE MARCOMANNI, AND THEY WILL EXPECT SAFE PASSAGE THROUGH YOUR LANDS.
RENOUNCE YOUR SUPPORT FOR THIS CONSPIRACY, AND I WILL ENDORSE YOU AS KING OF THE QUADI.
I SWEAR IT, THEN, IN ODIN'S NAME. YOU HAVE THE LOYALTY OF MY PEOPLE, CAESAR.
PEACE IS RESTORED MOST OFTEN BY TREATIES, NOT BY SWORDS.

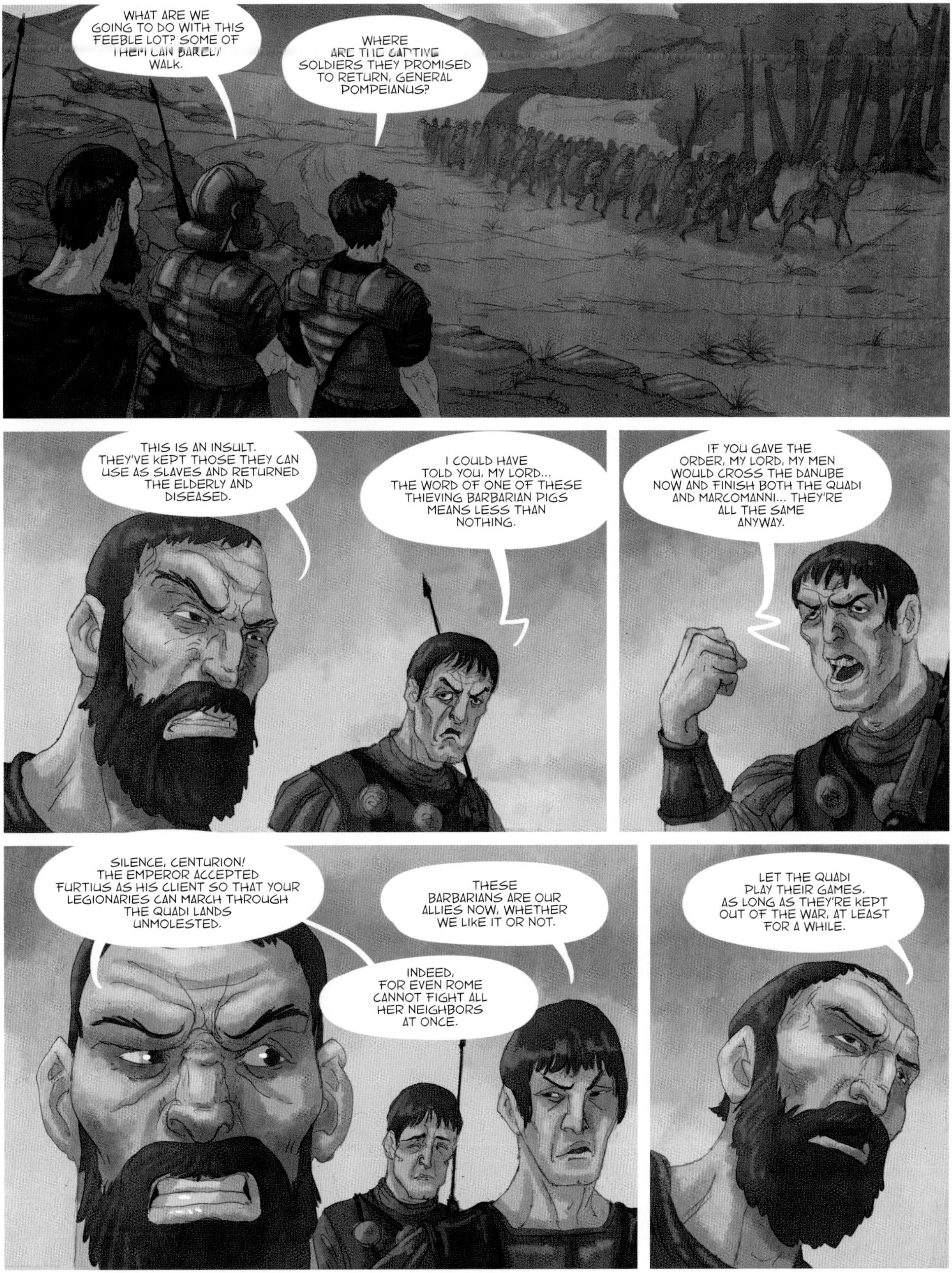
WHAT ARE WE GOING TO DO WITH THIS FEEBLE LOT? SOME OF THEM CAN BARELY WALK.
WHERE ARE THE CAPTIVE SOLDIERS THEY PROMISED TO RETURN, GENERAL POMPEIANUS?
THIS IS AN INSULT. THEY'VE KEPT THOSE THEY CAN USE AS SLAVES AND RETURNED THE ELDERLY AND DISEASED.
I COULD HAVE TOLD YOU, MY LORD... THE WORD OF ONE OF THESE THIEVING BARBARIAN PIGS MEANS LESS THAN NOTHING.
IF YOU GAVE THE ORDER, MY LORD, MY MEN WOULD CROSS THE DANUBE NOW AND FINISH BOTH THE QUADI AND MARCOMANNI... THEY'RE ALL THE SAME ANYWAY.
SILENCE, CENTURION! THE EMPEROR ACCEPTED FURTIUS AS HIS CLIENT SO THAT YOUR LEGIONARIES CAN MARCH THROUGH THE QUADI LANDS UNMOLESTED.
THESE BARBARIANS ARE OUR ALLIES NOW, WHETHER WE LIKE IT OR NOT.
INDEED, FOR EVEN ROME CANNOT FIGHT ALL HER NEIGHBORS AT ONCE.
LET THE QUADI PLAY THEIR GAMES. AS LONG AS THEY'RE KEPT OUT OF THE WAR, AT LEAST FOR A WHILE.

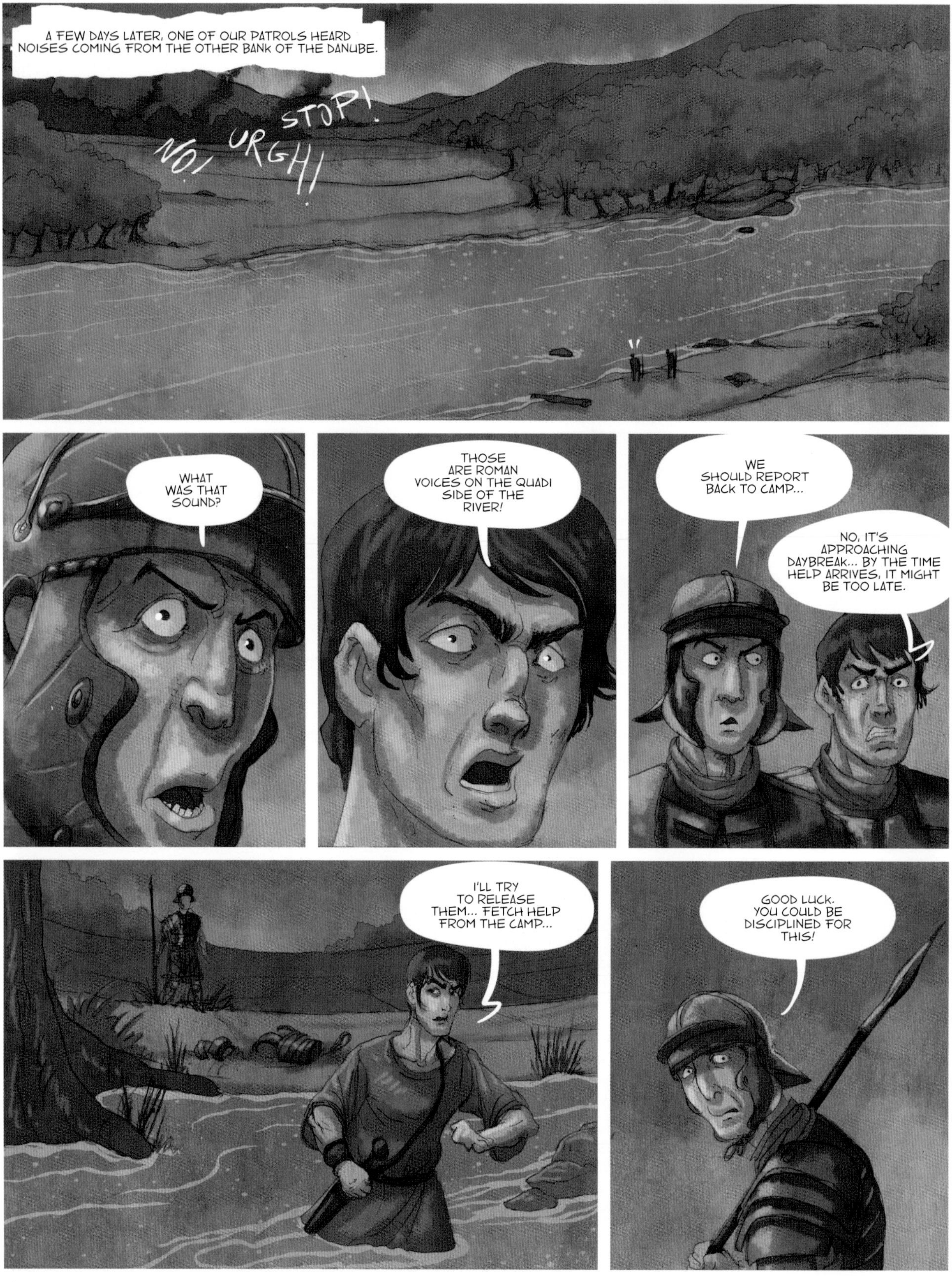
A FEW DAYS LATER, ONE OF OUR PATROLS HEARD NOISES COMING FROM THE OTHER BANK OF THE DANUBE.
NO!
URGH!
STOP!
WHAT WAS THAT SOUND?
THOSE ARE ROMAN VOICES ON THE QUADI SIDE OF THE RIVER!
WE SHOULD REPORT BACK TO CAMP...
NO, IT'S APPROACHING DAYBREAK... BY THE TIME HELP ARRIVES, IT MIGHT BE TOO LATE.
I'LL TRY TO RELEASE THEM... FETCH HELP FROM THE CAMP...
GOOD LUCK. YOU COULD BE DISCIPLINED FOR THIS!

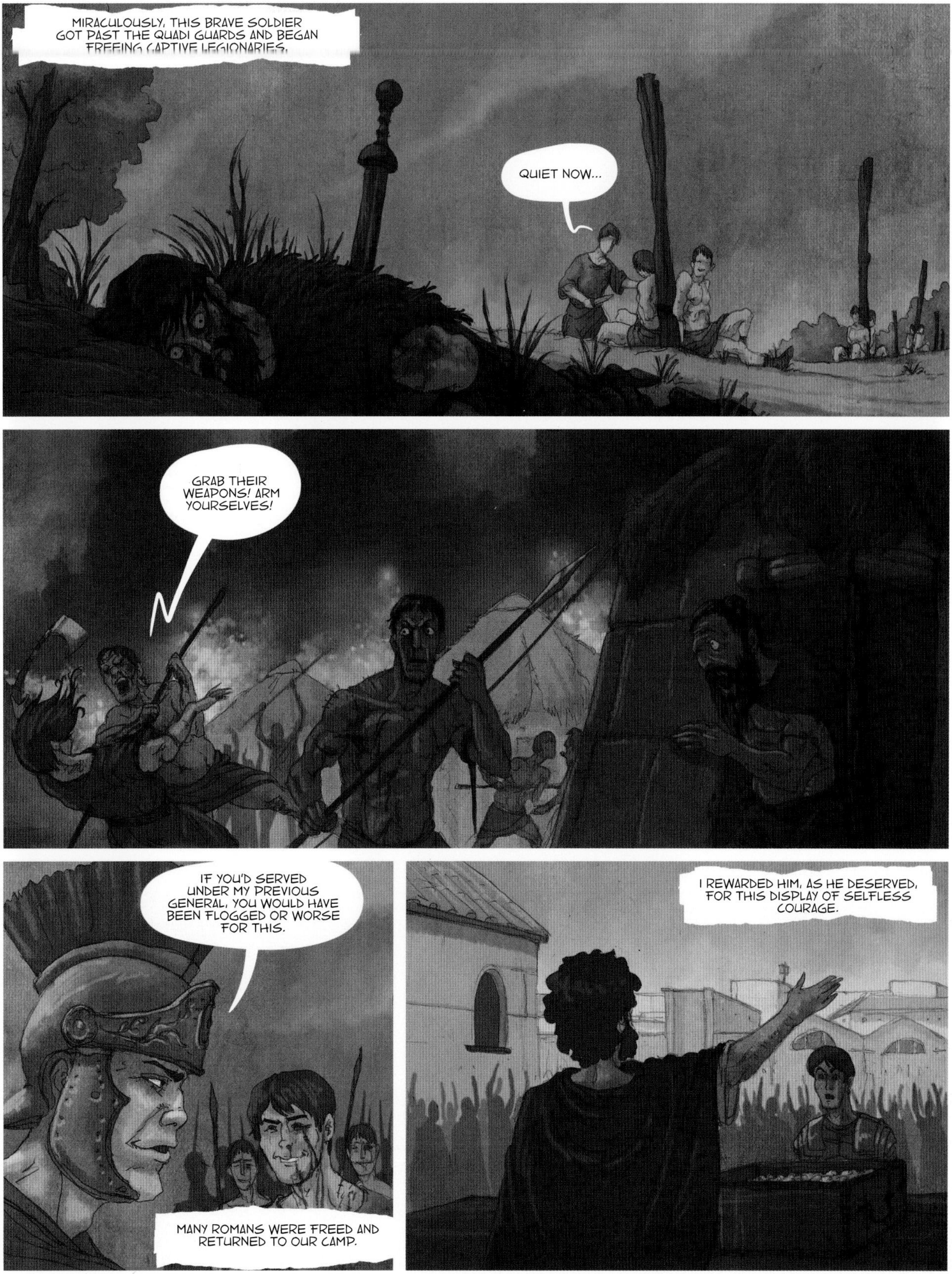
MIRACULOUSLY, THIS BRAVE SOLDIER GOT PAST THE QUADI GUARDS AND BEGAN FREEING CAPTIVE LEGIONARIES.
QUIET NOW...
GRAB THEIR WEAPONS! ARM YOURSELVES!
IF YOU'D SERVED UNDER MY PREVIOUS GENERAL, YOU WOULD HAVE BEEN FLOGGED OR WORSE FOR THIS.
MANY ROMANS WERE FREED AND RETURNED TO OUR CAMP.
I REWARDED HIM, AS HE DESERVED, FOR THIS DISPLAY OF SELFLESS COURAGE.

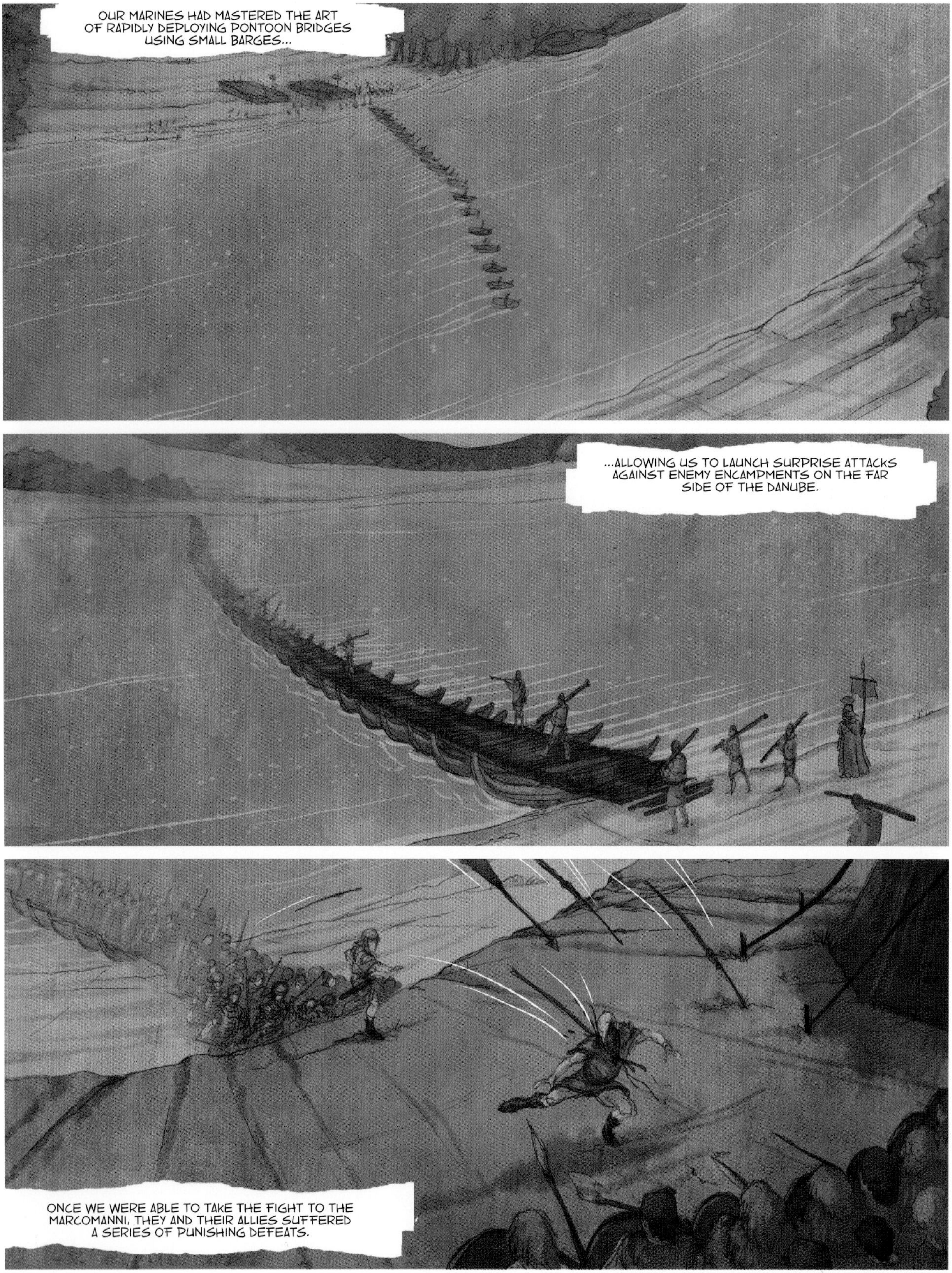
OUR MARINES HAD MASTERED THE ART OF RAPIDLY DEPLOYING PONTOON BRIDGES USING SMALL BARGES...
...ALLOWING US TO LAUNCH SURPRISE ATTACKS AGAINST ENEMY ENCAMPMENTS ON THE FAR SIDE OF THE DANUBE.
ONCE WE WERE ABLE TO TAKE THE FIGHT TO THE MARCOMANNI, THEY AND THEIR ALLIES SUFFERED A SERIES OF PUNISHING DEFEATS.

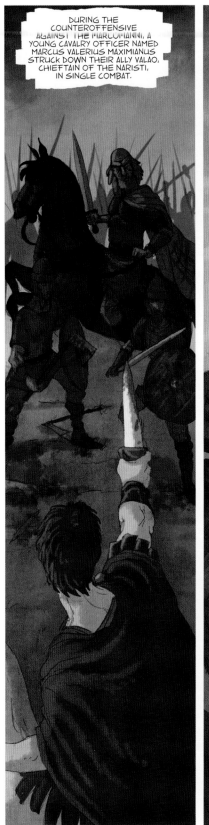

DURING THE
COUNTEROFFENSIVE
AGAINST THE MARCOMANNI, A
YOUNG CAVALRY OFFICER NAMED
MARCUS VALERIUS MAXIMIANUS
STRUCK DOWN THEIR ALLY VALAO,
CHIEFTAIN OF THE NARISTI,
IN SINGLE COMBAT.

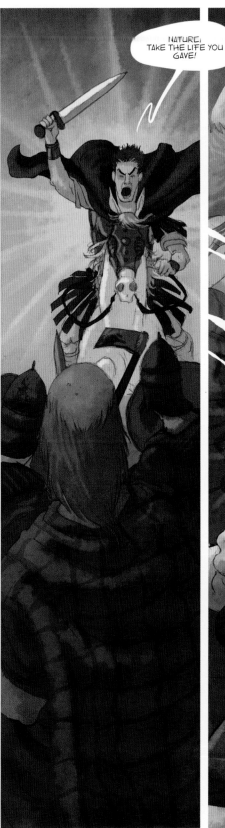

NATURE,
TAKE THE LIFE YOU
GAVE!

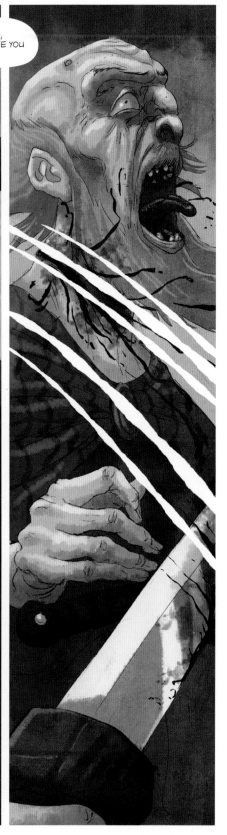

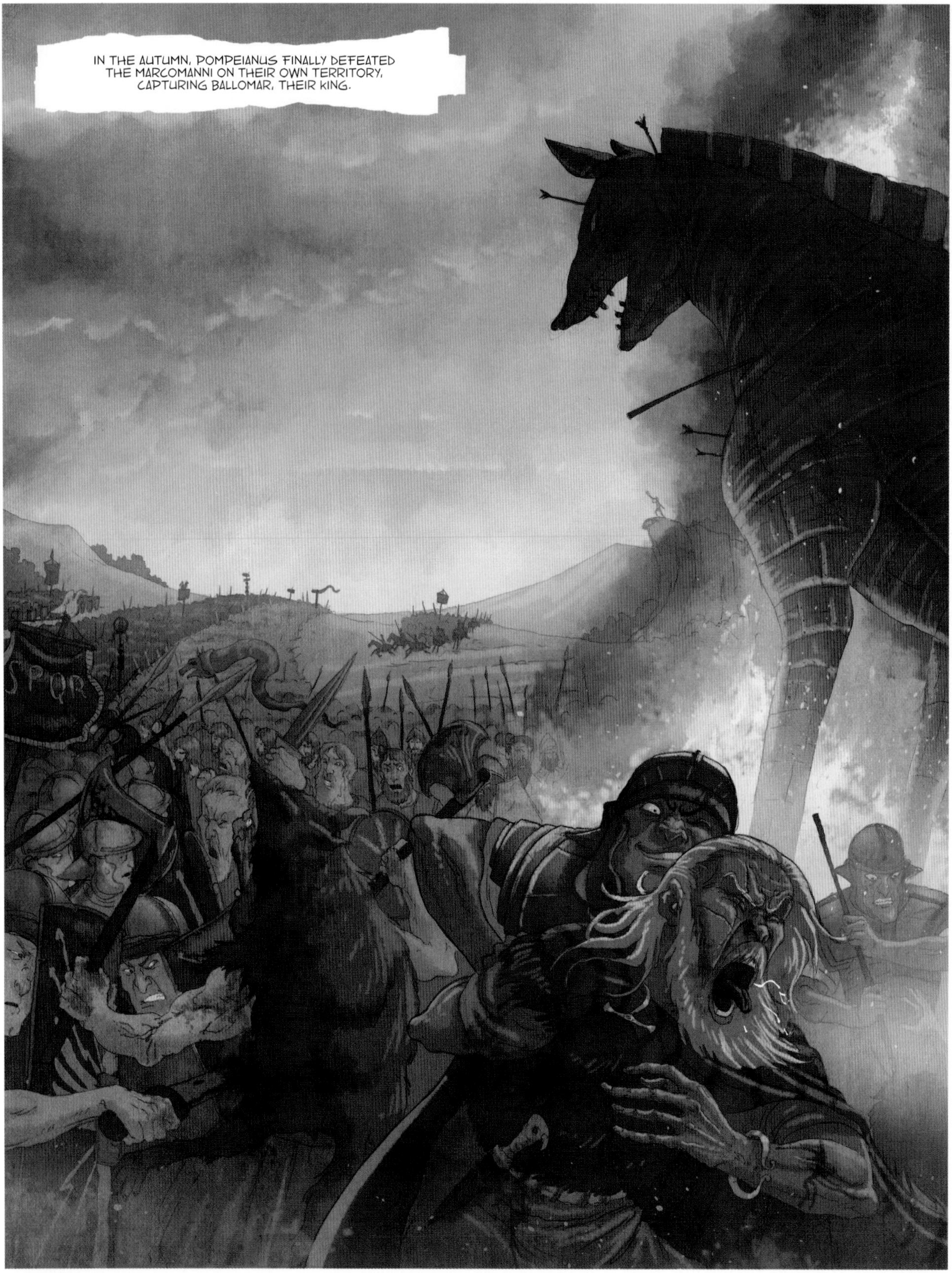
IN THE AUTUMN, POMPEIANUS FINALLY DEFEATED THE MARCOMANNI ON THEIR OWN TERRITORY, CAPTURING BALLOMAR, THEIR KING.
SPQR

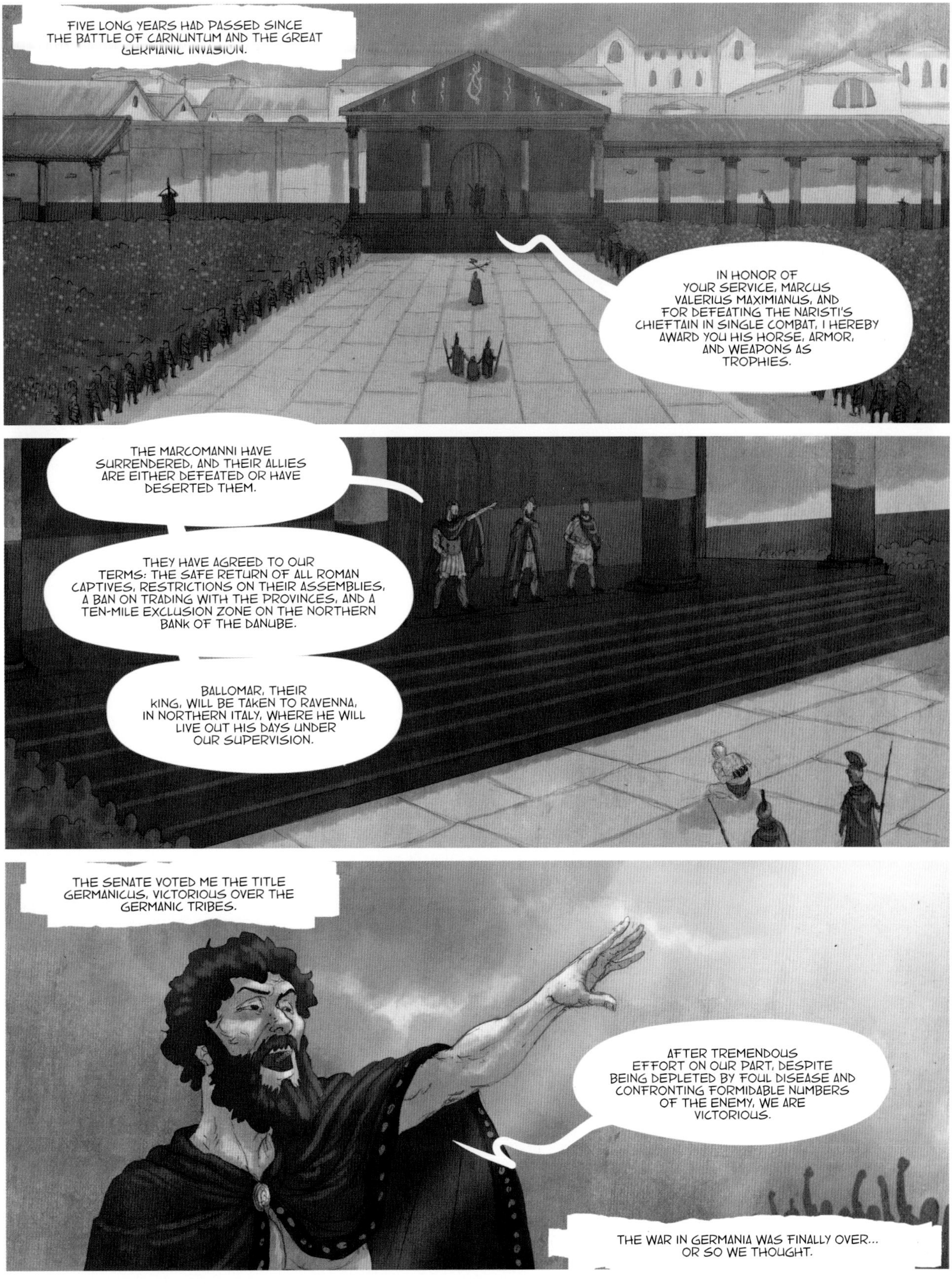
FIVE LONG YEARS HAD PASSED SINCE THE BATTLE OF CARNUNTUM AND THE GREAT GERMANIC INVASION.
IN HONOR OF YOUR SERVICE, MARCUS VALERIUS MAXIMIANUS, AND FOR DEFEATING THE NARISTI'S CHIEFTAIN IN SINGLE COMBAT, I HEREBY AWARD YOU HIS HORSE, ARMOR, AND WEAPONS AS TROPHIES.
THE MARCOMANNI HAVE SURRENDERED, AND THEIR ALLIES ARE EITHER DEFEATED OR HAVE DESERTED THEM.
THEY HAVE AGREED TO OUR TERMS: THE SAFE RETURN OF ALL ROMAN CAPTIVES, RESTRICTIONS ON THEIR ASSEMBLIES, A BAN ON TRADING WITH THE PROVINCES, AND A TEN-MILE EXCLUSION ZONE ON THE NORTHERN BANK OF THE DANUBE.
BALLOMAR, THEIR KING, WILL BE TAKEN TO RAVENNA, IN NORTHERN ITALY, WHERE HE WILL LIVE OUT HIS DAYS UNDER OUR SUPERVISION.
THE SENATE VOTED ME THE TITLE GERMANICUS, VICTORIOUS OVER THE GERMANIC TRIBES.
AFTER TREMENDOUS EFFORT ON OUR PART, DESPITE BEING DEPLETED BY FOUL DISEASE AND CONFRONTING FORMIDABLE NUMBERS OF THE ENEMY, WE ARE VICTORIOUS.
THE WAR IN GERMANIA WAS FINALLY OVER... OR SO WE THOUGHT.

THE
EGYPTIAN
UPRISING

The clashing of spears, a bone tossed to some pups … every man is worth just so much as the things to which he attaches his desire.

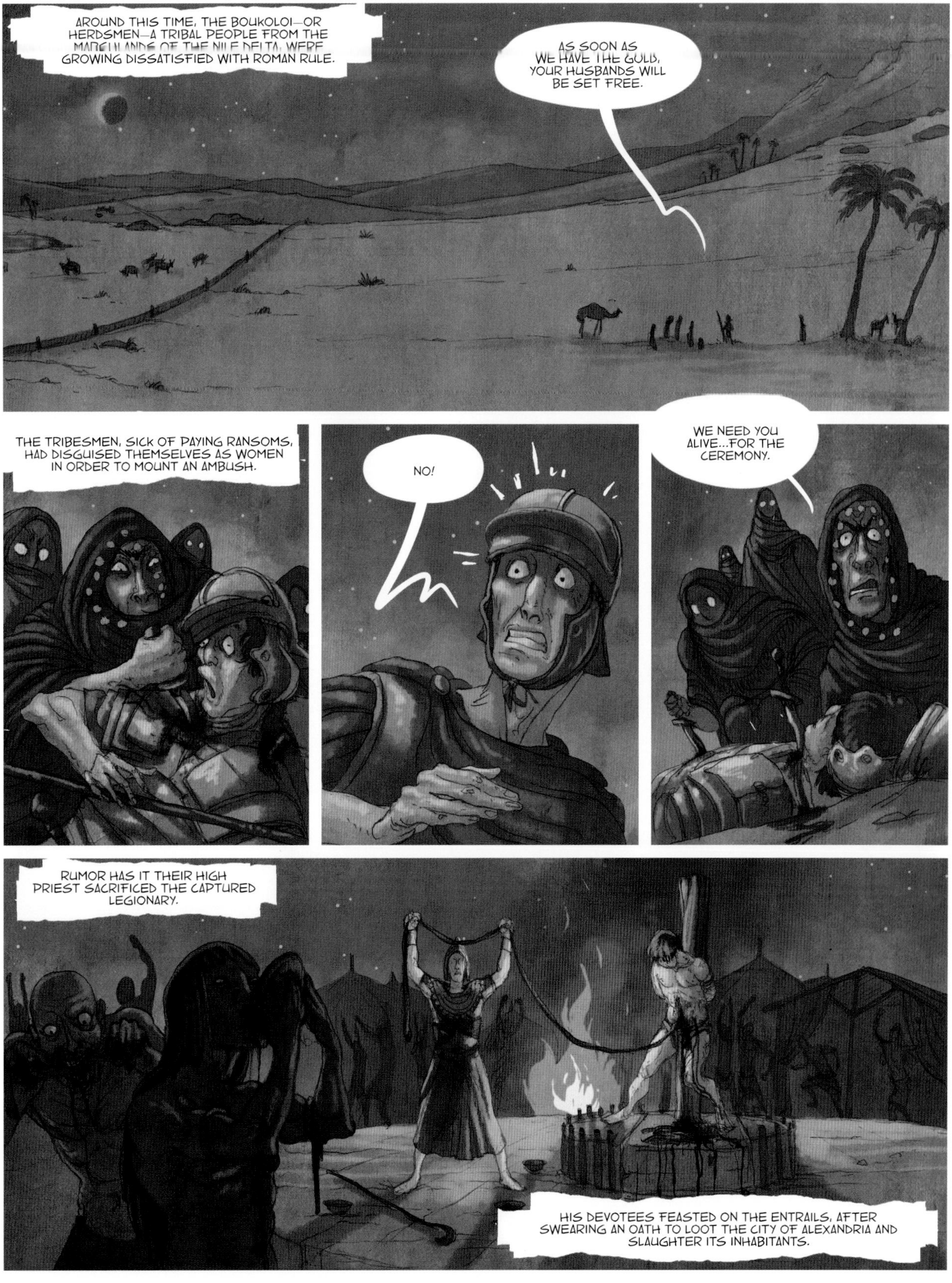
AROUND THIS TIME, THE BOUKOLOI—OR HERDSMEN—A TRIBAL PEOPLE FROM THE MARSHLANDS OF THE NILE DELTA, WERE GROWING DISSATISFIED WITH ROMAN RULE.
AS SOON AS WE HAVE THE GOLD, YOUR HUSBANDS WILL BE SET FREE.
THE TRIBESMEN, SICK OF PAYING RANSOMS, HAD DISGUISED THEMSELVES AS WOMEN IN ORDER TO MOUNT AN AMBUSH.
NO!
WE NEED YOU ALIVE...FOR THE CEREMONY.
RUMOR HAS IT THEIR HIGH PRIEST SACRIFICED THE CAPTURED LEGIONARY.
HIS DEVOTEES FEASTED ON THE ENTRAILS, AFTER SWEARING AN OATH TO LOOT THE CITY OF ALEXANDRIA AND SLAUGHTER ITS INHABITANTS.

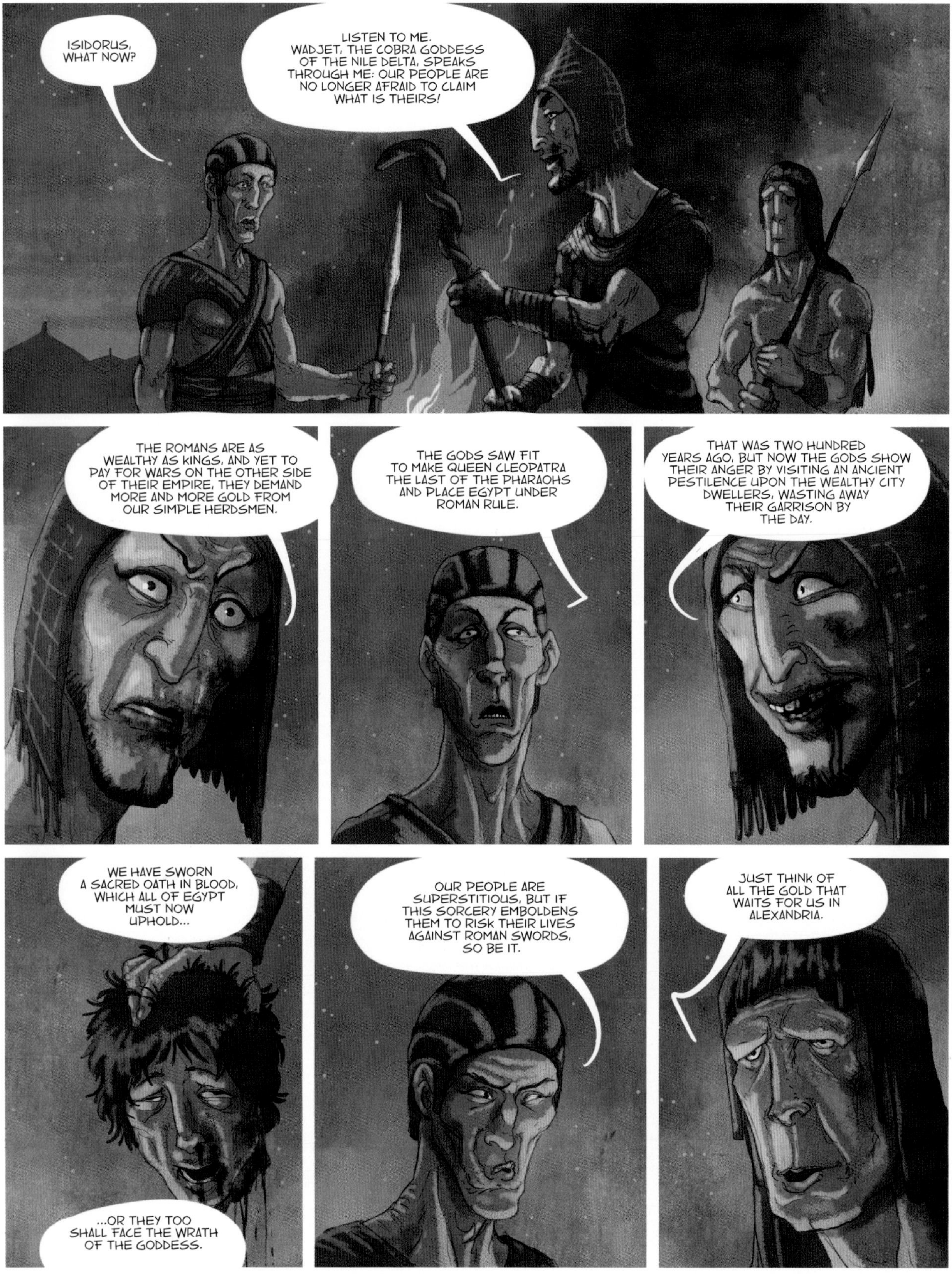
ISIDORUS, WHAT NOW?
LISTEN TO ME. WADJET, THE COBRA GODDESS OF THE NILE DELTA, SPEAKS THROUGH ME: OUR PEOPLE ARE NO LONGER AFRAID TO CLAIM WHAT IS THEIRS!
THE ROMANS ARE AS WEALTHY AS KINGS, AND YET TO PAY FOR WARS ON THE OTHER SIDE OF THEIR EMPIRE, THEY DEMAND MORE AND MORE GOLD FROM OUR SIMPLE HERDSMEN.
THE GODS SAW FIT TO MAKE QUEEN CLEOPATRA THE LAST OF THE PHARAOHS AND PLACE EGYPT UNDER ROMAN RULE.
THAT WAS TWO HUNDRED YEARS AGO, BUT NOW THE GODS SHOW THEIR ANGER BY VISITING AN ANCIENT PESTILENCE UPON THE WEALTHY CITY DWELLERS, WASTING AWAY THEIR GARRISON BY THE DAY.
WE HAVE SWORN A SACRED OATH IN BLOOD, WHICH ALL OF EGYPT MUST NOW UPHOLD...
...OR THEY TOO SHALL FACE THE WRATH OF THE GODDESS.
OUR PEOPLE ARE SUPERSTITIOUS, BUT IF THIS SORCERY EMBOLDENS THEM TO RISK THEIR LIVES AGAINST ROMAN SWORDS, SO BE IT.
JUST THINK OF ALL THE GOLD THAT WAITS FOR US IN ALEXANDRIA.

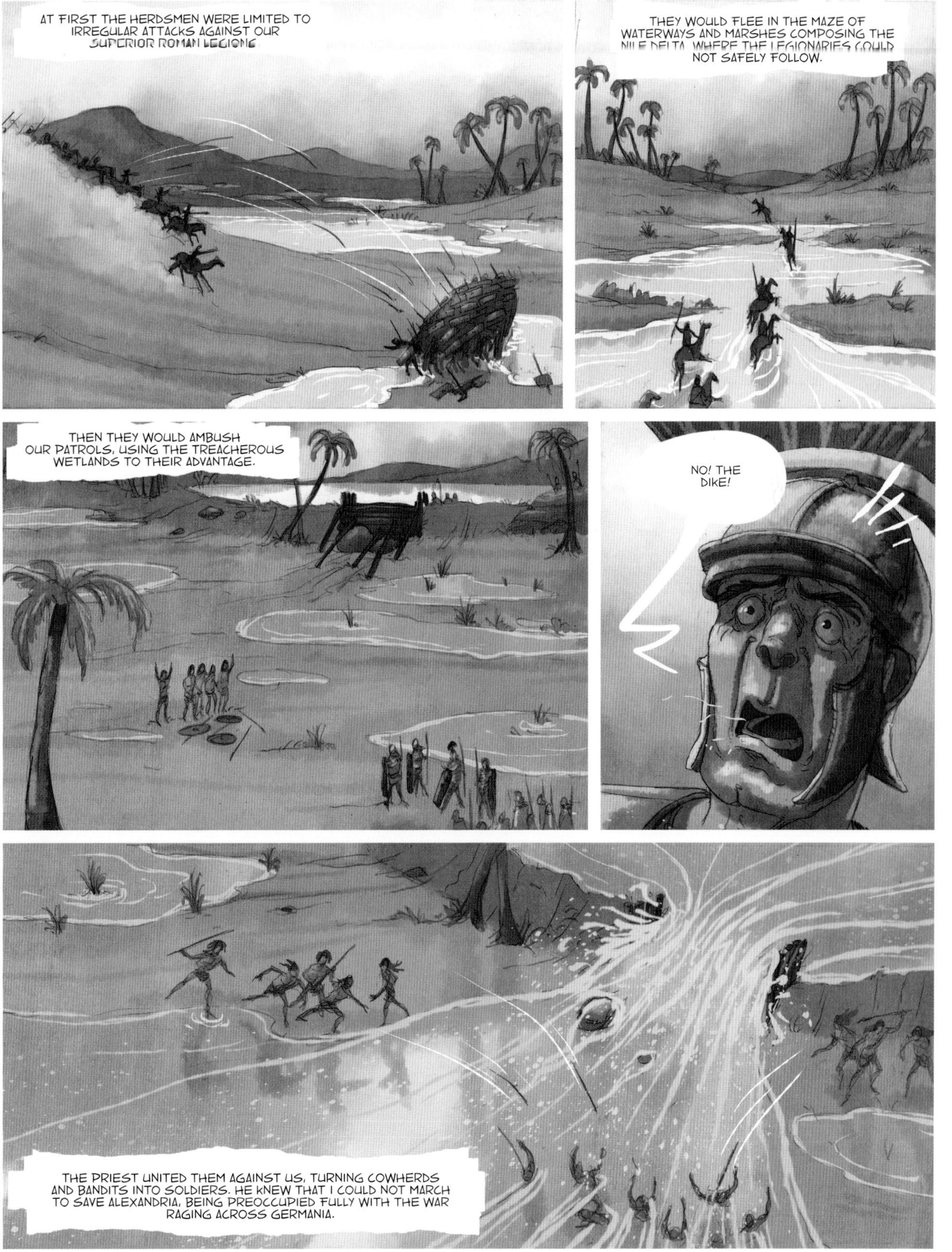
AT FIRST THE HERDSMEN WERE LIMITED TO IRREGULAR ATTACKS AGAINST OUR SUPERIOR ROMAN LEGIONS.
THEY WOULD FLEE IN THE MAZE OF WATERWAYS AND MARSHES COMPOSING THE NILE DELTA, WHERE THE LEGIONARIES COULD NOT SAFELY FOLLOW.
THEN THEY WOULD AMBUSH OUR PATROLS, USING THE TREACHEROUS WETLANDS TO THEIR ADVANTAGE.
NO! THE DIKE!
THE PRIEST UNITED THEM AGAINST US, TURNING COWHERDS AND BANDITS INTO SOLDIERS. HE KNEW THAT I COULD NOT MARCH TO SAVE ALEXANDRIA, BEING PREOCCUPIED FULLY WITH THE WAR RAGING ACROSS GERMANIA.

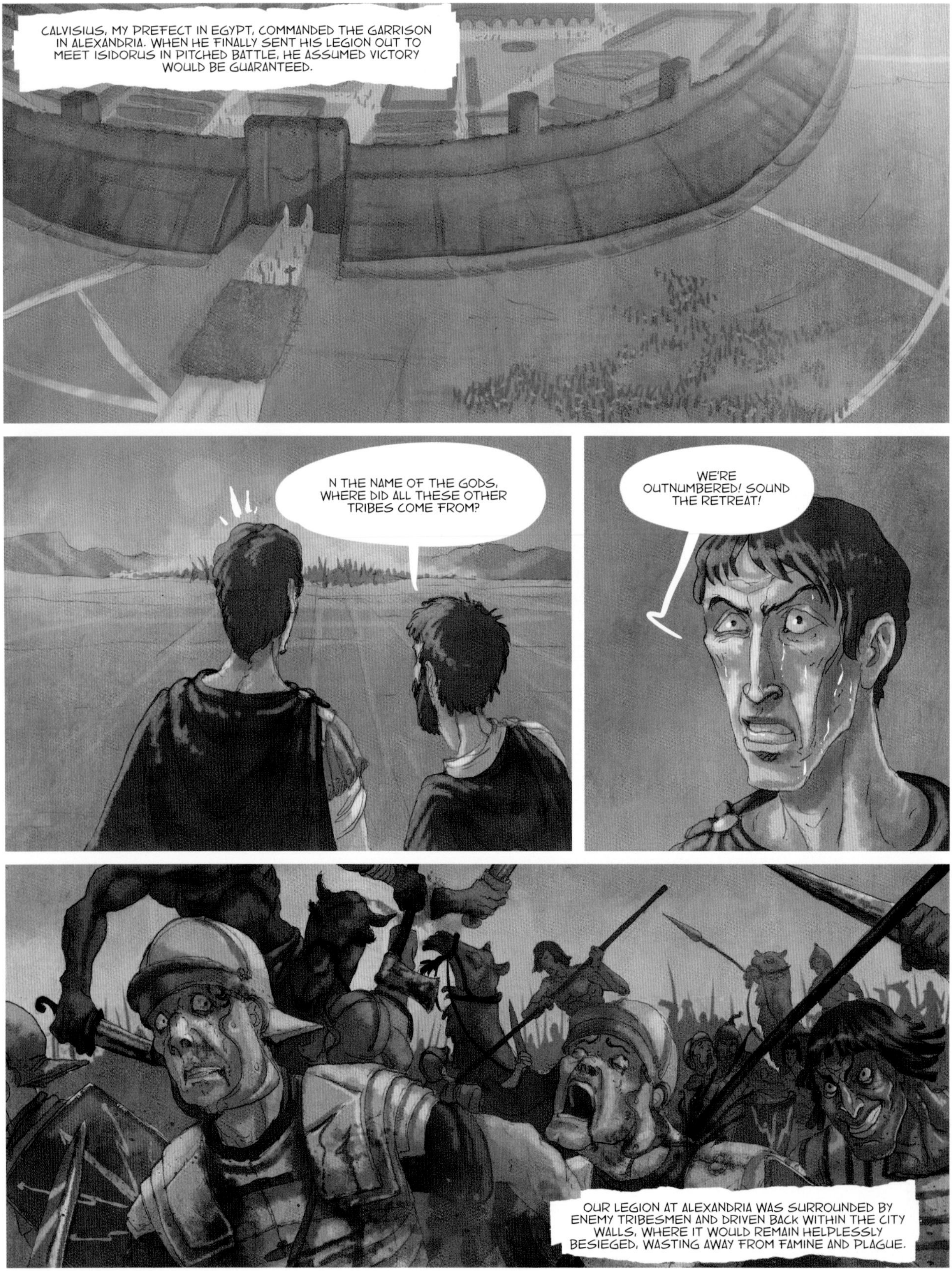
CALVISIUS, MY PREFECT IN EGYPT, COMMANDED THE GARRISON IN ALEXANDRIA. WHEN HE FINALLY SENT HIS LEGION OUT TO MEET ISIDORUS IN PITCHED BATTLE, HE ASSUMED VICTORY WOULD BE GUARANTEED.
N THE NAME OF THE GODS, WHERE DID ALL THESE OTHER TRIBES COME FROM?
WE'RE OUTNUMBERED! SOUND THE RETREAT!
OUR LEGION AT ALEXANDRIA WAS SURROUNDED BY ENEMY TRIBESMEN AND DRIVEN BACK WITHIN THE CITY WALLS, WHERE IT WOULD REMAIN HELPLESSLY BESIEGED, WASTING AWAY FROM FAMINE AND PLAGUE.

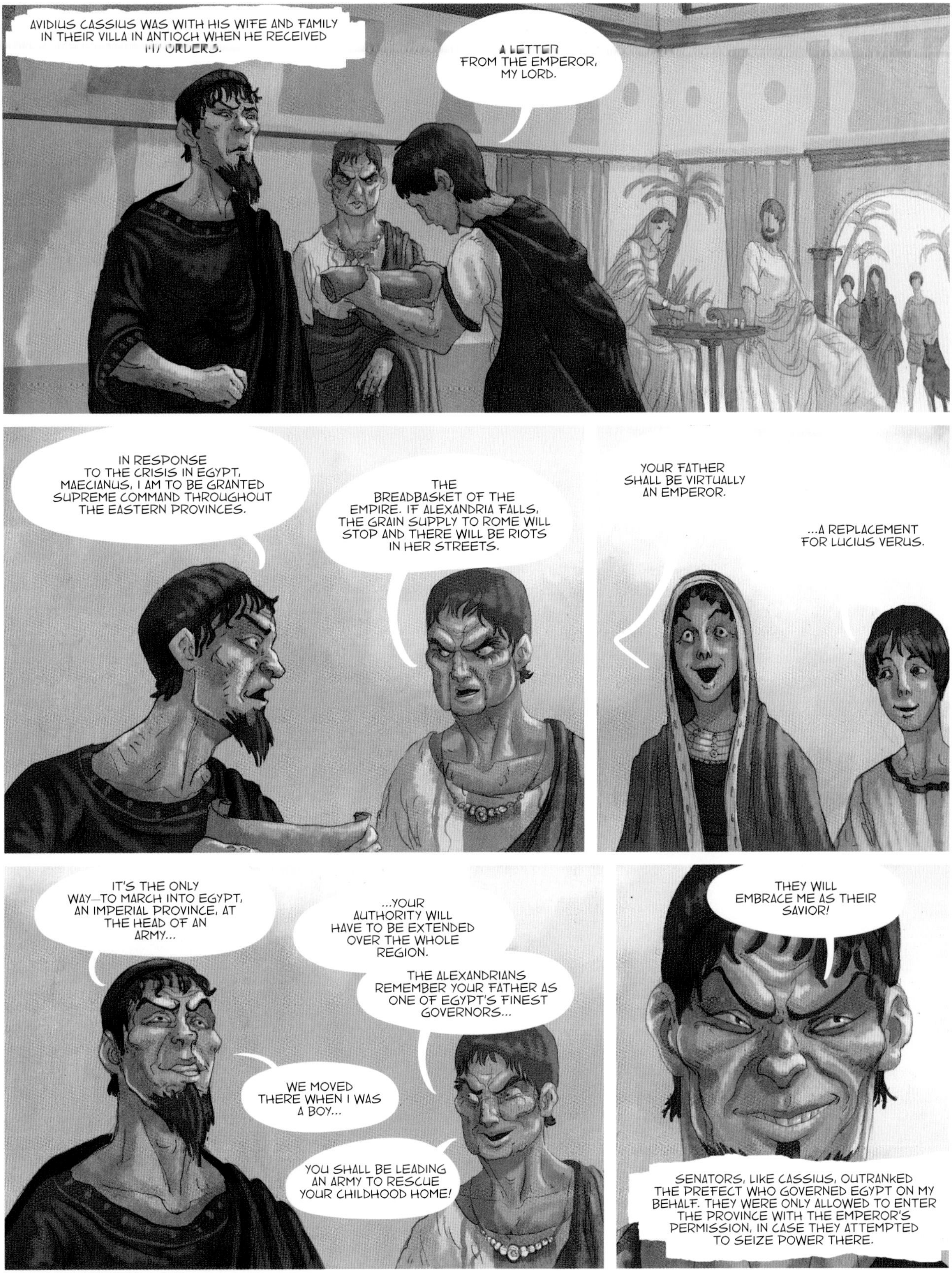
AVIDIUS CASSIUS WAS WITH HIS WIFE AND FAMILY IN THEIR VILLA IN ANTIOCH WHEN HE RECEIVED MY ORDERS.
A LETTER FROM THE EMPEROR, MY LORD.
IN RESPONSE TO THE CRISIS IN EGYPT, MAECIANUS, I AM TO BE GRANTED SUPREME COMMAND THROUGHOUT THE EASTERN PROVINCES.
THE BREADBASKET OF THE EMPIRE. IF ALEXANDRIA FALLS, THE GRAIN SUPPLY TO ROME WILL STOP AND THERE WILL BE RIOTS IN HER STREETS.
YOUR FATHER SHALL BE VIRTUALLY AN EMPEROR.
...A REPLACEMENT FOR LUCIUS VERUS.
IT'S THE ONLY WAY—TO MARCH INTO EGYPT, AN IMPERIAL PROVINCE, AT THE HEAD OF AN ARMY...
...YOUR AUTHORITY WILL HAVE TO BE EXTENDED OVER THE WHOLE REGION.
THE ALEXANDRIANS REMEMBER YOUR FATHER AS ONE OF EGYPT'S FINEST GOVERNORS...
WE MOVED THERE WHEN I WAS A BOY...
YOU SHALL BE LEADING AN ARMY TO RESCUE YOUR CHILDHOOD HOME!
THEY WILL EMBRACE ME AS THEIR SAVIOR!
SENATORS, LIKE CASSIUS, OUTRANKED THE PREFECT WHO GOVERNED EGYPT ON MY BEHALF. THEY WERE ONLY ALLOWED TO ENTER THE PROVINCE WITH THE EMPEROR'S PERMISSION, IN CASE THEY ATTEMPTED TO SEIZE POWER THERE.

CASSIUS'S LEGIONS ARRIVED JUST IN TIME TO LIBERATE ALEXANDRIA FROM THE TRIBESMEN LAYING SIEGE TO THE CITY.

ALEXANDRIA AND ITS LEGIONARY CAMP HAVE BEEN RAVAGED BY THE PESTILENCE, BUT THESE ACCURSED NOMADS SEEM RELATIVELY UNTOUCHED BY THE DISEASE.

NOW OTHER TRIBES HAVE JOINED THE BOUKOLOI. THEY'RE FAR TOO NUMEROUS TO ENGAGE IN PITCHED BATTLE.

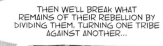

THEN WE'LL BREAK WHAT REMAINS OF THEIR REBELLION BY DIVIDING THEM, TURNING ONE TRIBE AGAINST ANOTHER...

WE'LL BUY OFF THEIR CHIEFTAINS WITH ROMAN GOLD...

...TAKE THEIR FAMILIES HOSTAGE...

...AND IF THAT DOESN'T WORK, WE'LL SEND THEM A MESSAGE EVEN THESE BARBARIANS UNDERSTAND.

AND THUS ISIDORUS'S REBELLION WAS DEFEATED, MAKING CASSIUS A HERO IN EGYPT.

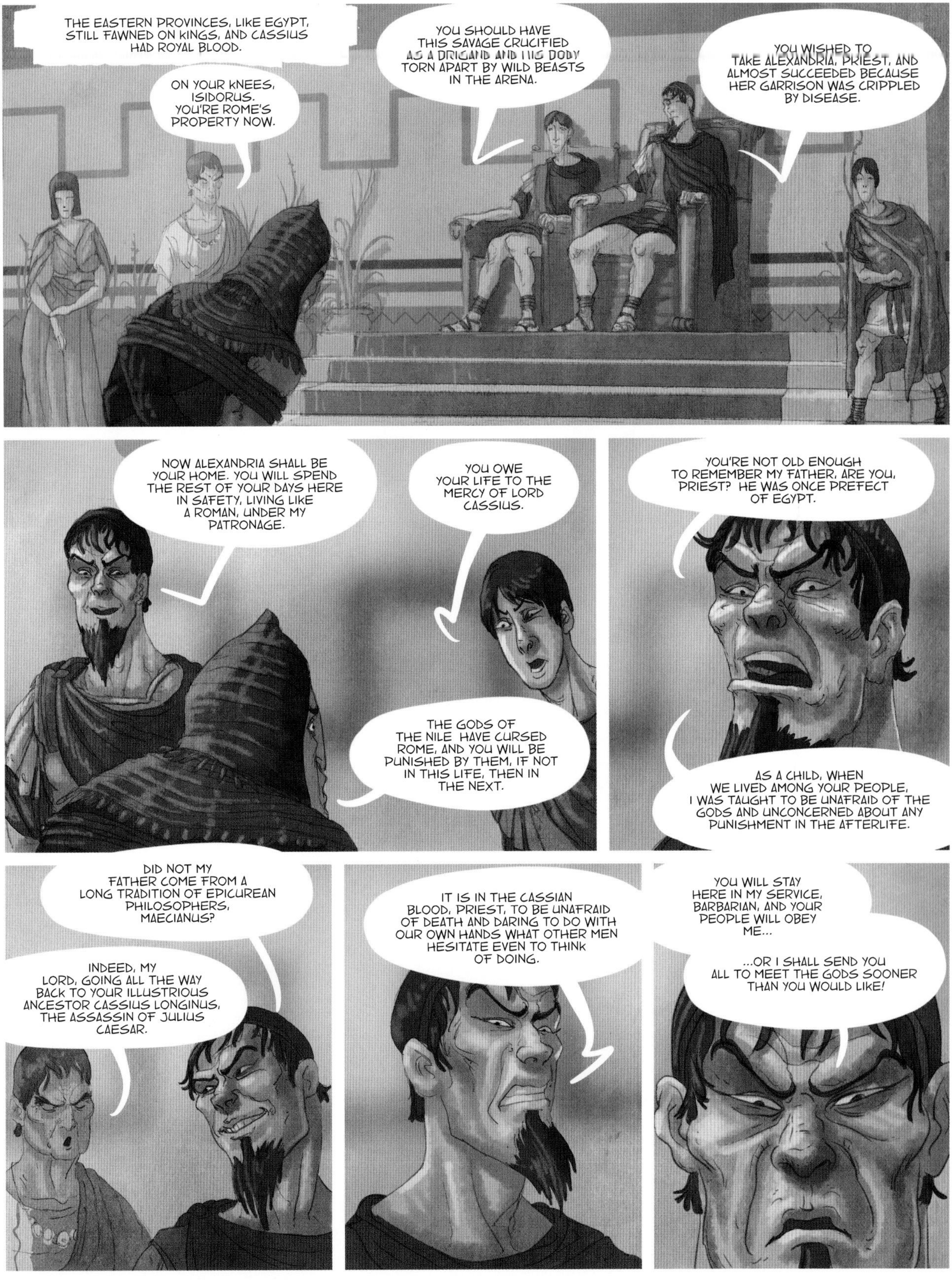
THE EASTERN PROVINCES, LIKE EGYPT, STILL FAWNED ON KINGS, AND CASSIUS HAD ROYAL BLOOD.
ON YOUR KNEES, ISIDORUS. YOU'RE ROME'S PROPERTY NOW.
YOU SHOULD HAVE THIS SAVAGE CRUCIFIED AS A BRIGAND AND HIS BODY TORN APART BY WILD BEASTS IN THE ARENA.
YOU WISHED TO TAKE ALEXANDRIA, PRIEST, AND ALMOST SUCCEEDED BECAUSE HER GARRISON WAS CRIPPLED BY DISEASE.
NOW ALEXANDRIA SHALL BE YOUR HOME. YOU WILL SPEND THE REST OF YOUR DAYS HERE IN SAFETY, LIVING LIKE A ROMAN, UNDER MY PATRONAGE.
YOU OWE YOUR LIFE TO THE MERCY OF LORD CASSIUS.
THE GODS OF THE NILE HAVE CURSED ROME, AND YOU WILL BE PUNISHED BY THEM, IF NOT IN THIS LIFE, THEN IN THE NEXT.
YOU'RE NOT OLD ENOUGH TO REMEMBER MY FATHER, ARE YOU, PRIEST? HE WAS ONCE PREFECT OF EGYPT.
AS A CHILD, WHEN WE LIVED AMONG YOUR PEOPLE, I WAS TAUGHT TO BE UNAFRAID OF THE GODS AND UNCONCERNED ABOUT ANY PUNISHMENT IN THE AFTERLIFE.
DID NOT MY FATHER COME FROM A LONG TRADITION OF EPICUREAN PHILOSOPHERS, MAECIANUS?
INDEED, MY LORD, GOING ALL THE WAY BACK TO YOUR ILLUSTRIOUS ANCESTOR CASSIUS LONGINUS, THE ASSASSIN OF JULIUS CAESAR.
IT IS IN THE CASSIAN BLOOD, PRIEST, TO BE UNAFRAID OF DEATH AND DARING TO DO WITH OUR OWN HANDS WHAT OTHER MEN HESITATE EVEN TO THINK OF DOING.
YOU WILL STAY HERE IN MY SERVICE, BARBARIAN, AND YOUR PEOPLE WILL OBEY ME...
...OR I SHALL SEND YOU ALL TO MEET THE GODS SOONER THAN YOU WOULD LIKE!

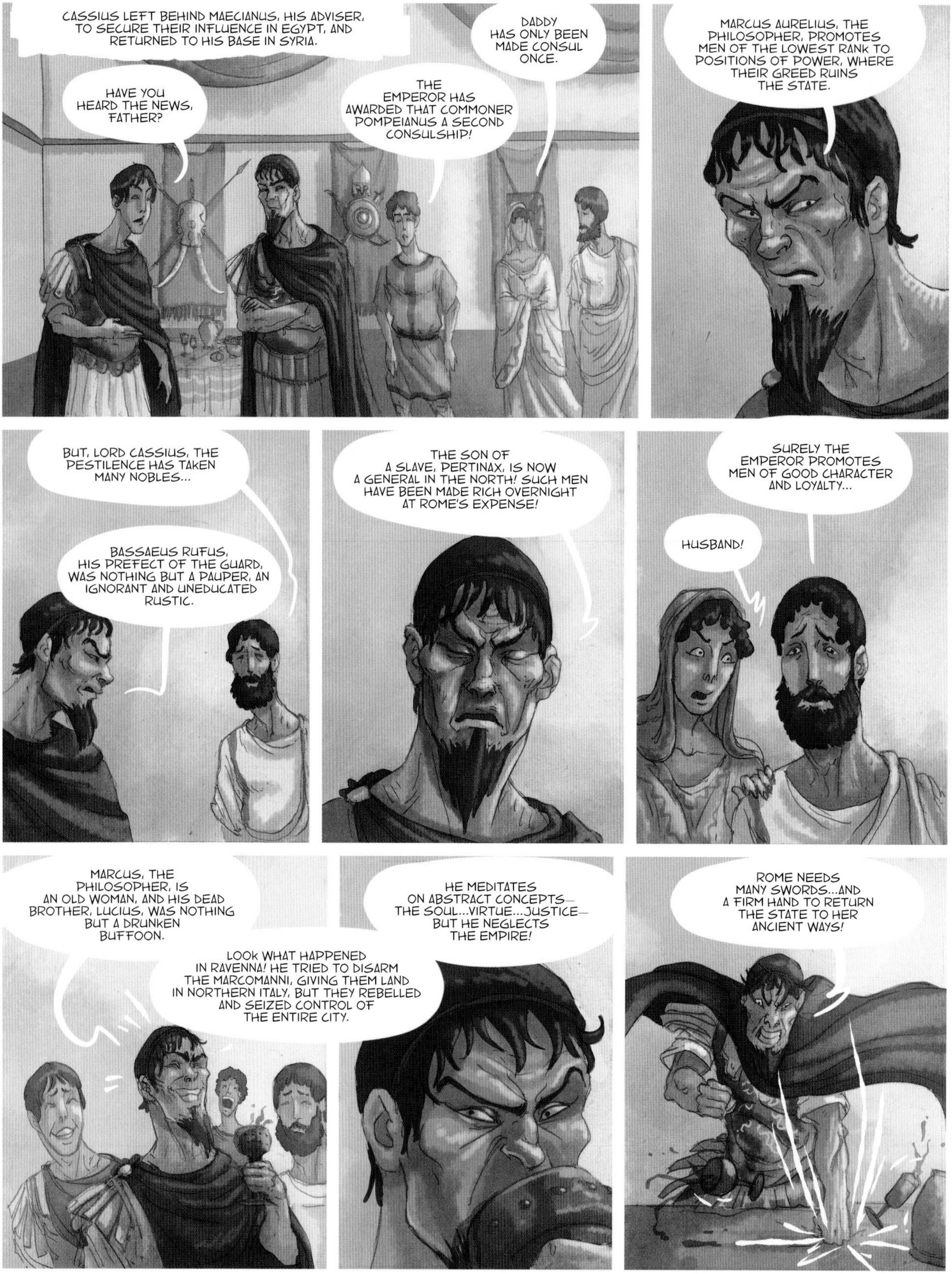
CASSIUS LEFT BEHIND MAECIANUS, HIS ADVISER, TO SECURE THEIR INFLUENCE IN EGYPT, AND RETURNED TO HIS BASE IN SYRIA.
HAVE YOU HEARD THE NEWS, FATHER?
THE EMPEROR HAS AWARDED THAT COMMONER POMPEIANUS A SECOND CONSULSHIP!
DADDY HAS ONLY BEEN MADE CONSUL ONCE.
MARCUS AURELIUS, THE PHILOSOPHER, PROMOTES MEN OF THE LOWEST RANK TO POSITIONS OF POWER, WHERE THEIR GREED RUINS THE STATE.
BUT, LORD CASSIUS, THE PESTILENCE HAS TAKEN MANY NOBLES...
BASSAEUS RUFUS, HIS PREFECT OF THE GUARD, WAS NOTHING BUT A PAUPER, AN IGNORANT AND UNEDUCATED RUSTIC.
THE SON OF A SLAVE, PERTINAX, IS NOW A GENERAL IN THE NORTH! SUCH MEN HAVE BEEN MADE RICH OVERNIGHT AT ROME'S EXPENSE!
SURELY THE EMPEROR PROMOTES MEN OF GOOD CHARACTER AND LOYALTY...
HUSBAND!
MARCUS, THE PHILOSOPHER, IS AN OLD WOMAN, AND HIS DEAD BROTHER, LUCIUS, WAS NOTHING BUT A DRUNKEN BUFFOON.
LOOK WHAT HAPPENED IN RAVENNA! HE TRIED TO DISARM THE MARCOMANNI, GIVING THEM LAND IN NORTHERN ITALY, BUT THEY REBELLED AND SEIZED CONTROL OF THE ENTIRE CITY.
HE MEDITATES ON ABSTRACT CONCEPTS—THE SOUL...VIRTUE...JUSTICE—BUT HE NEGLECTS THE EMPIRE!
ROME NEEDS MANY SWORDS...AND A FIRM HAND TO RETURN THE STATE TO HER ANCIENT WAYS!

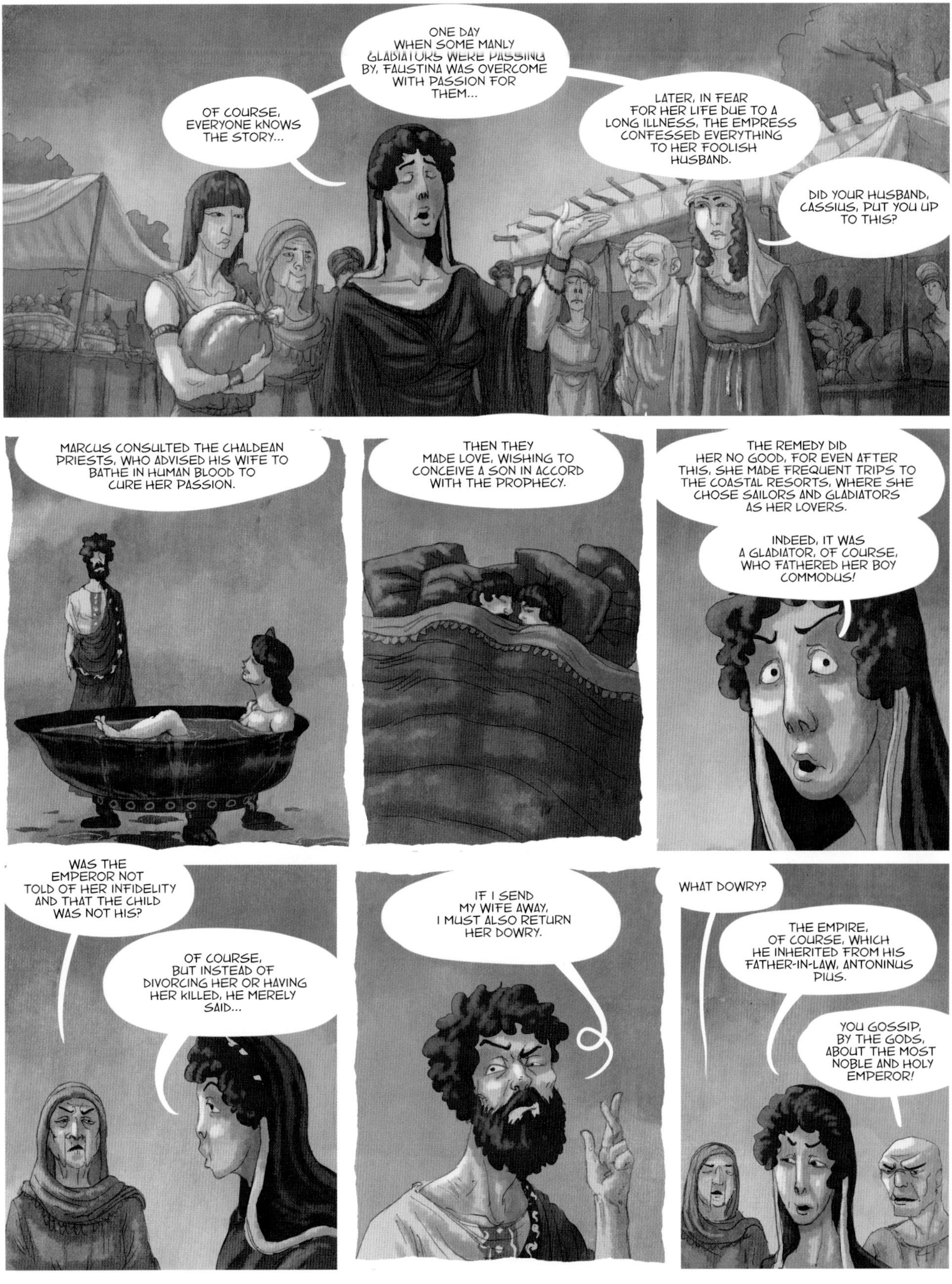

OF COURSE, EVERYONE KNOWS THE STORY...
ONE DAY WHEN SOME MANLY GLADIATORS WERE PASSING BY, FAUSTINA WAS OVERCOME WITH PASSION FOR THEM...
LATER, IN FEAR FOR HER LIFE DUE TO A LONG ILLNESS, THE EMPRESS CONFESSED EVERYTHING TO HER FOOLISH HUSBAND.
DID YOUR HUSBAND, CASSIUS, PUT YOU UP TO THIS?
MARCUS CONSULTED THE CHALDEAN PRIESTS, WHO ADVISED HIS WIFE TO BATHE IN HUMAN BLOOD TO CURE HER PASSION.
THEN THEY MADE LOVE, WISHING TO CONCEIVE A SON IN ACCORD WITH THE PROPHECY.
THE REMEDY DID HER NO GOOD, FOR EVEN AFTER THIS, SHE MADE FREQUENT TRIPS TO THE COASTAL RESORTS, WHERE SHE CHOSE SAILORS AND GLADIATORS AS HER LOVERS.
INDEED, IT WAS A GLADIATOR, OF COURSE, WHO FATHERED HER BOY COMMODUS!
WAS THE EMPEROR NOT TOLD OF HER INFIDELITY AND THAT THE CHILD WAS NOT HIS?
OF COURSE, BUT INSTEAD OF DIVORCING HER OR HAVING HER KILLED, HE MERELY SAID...
IF I SEND MY WIFE AWAY, I MUST ALSO RETURN HER DOWRY.
WHAT DOWRY?
THE EMPIRE, OF COURSE, WHICH HE INHERITED FROM HIS FATHER-IN-LAW, ANTONINUS PIUS.
YOU GOSSIP, BY THE GODS, ABOUT THE MOST NOBLE AND HOLY EMPEROR!

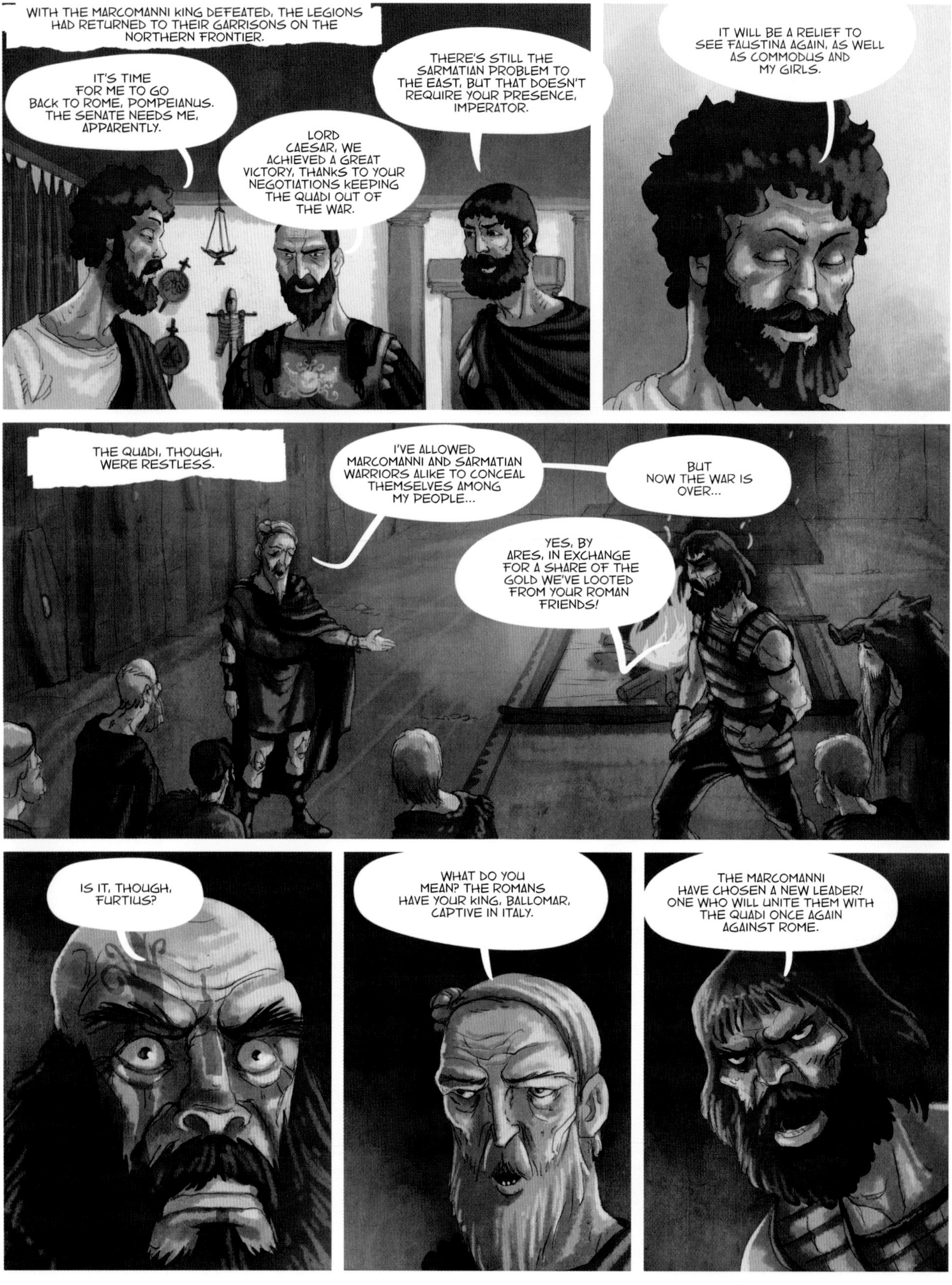
WITH THE MARCOMANNI KING DEFEATED, THE LEGIONS HAD RETURNED TO THEIR GARRISONS ON THE NORTHERN FRONTIER.
IT'S TIME FOR ME TO GO BACK TO ROME, POMPEIANUS. THE SENATE NEEDS ME, APPARENTLY.
LORD CAESAR, WE ACHIEVED A GREAT VICTORY, THANKS TO YOUR NEGOTIATIONS KEEPING THE QUADI OUT OF THE WAR.
THERE'S STILL THE SARMATIAN PROBLEM TO THE EAST, BUT THAT DOESN'T REQUIRE YOUR PRESENCE, IMPERATOR.
IT WILL BE A RELIEF TO SEE FAUSTINA AGAIN, AS WELL AS COMMODUS AND MY GIRLS.
THE QUADI, THOUGH, WERE RESTLESS.
I'VE ALLOWED MARCOMANNI AND SARMATIAN WARRIORS ALIKE TO CONCEAL THEMSELVES AMONG MY PEOPLE...
BUT NOW THE WAR IS OVER...
YES, BY ARES, IN EXCHANGE FOR A SHARE OF THE GOLD WE'VE LOOTED FROM YOUR ROMAN FRIENDS!
IS IT, THOUGH, FURTIUS?
WHAT DO YOU MEAN? THE ROMANS HAVE YOUR KING, BALLOMAR, CAPTIVE IN ITALY.
THE MARCOMANNI HAVE CHOSEN A NEW LEADER! ONE WHO WILL UNITE THEM WITH THE QUADI ONCE AGAIN AGAINST ROME.

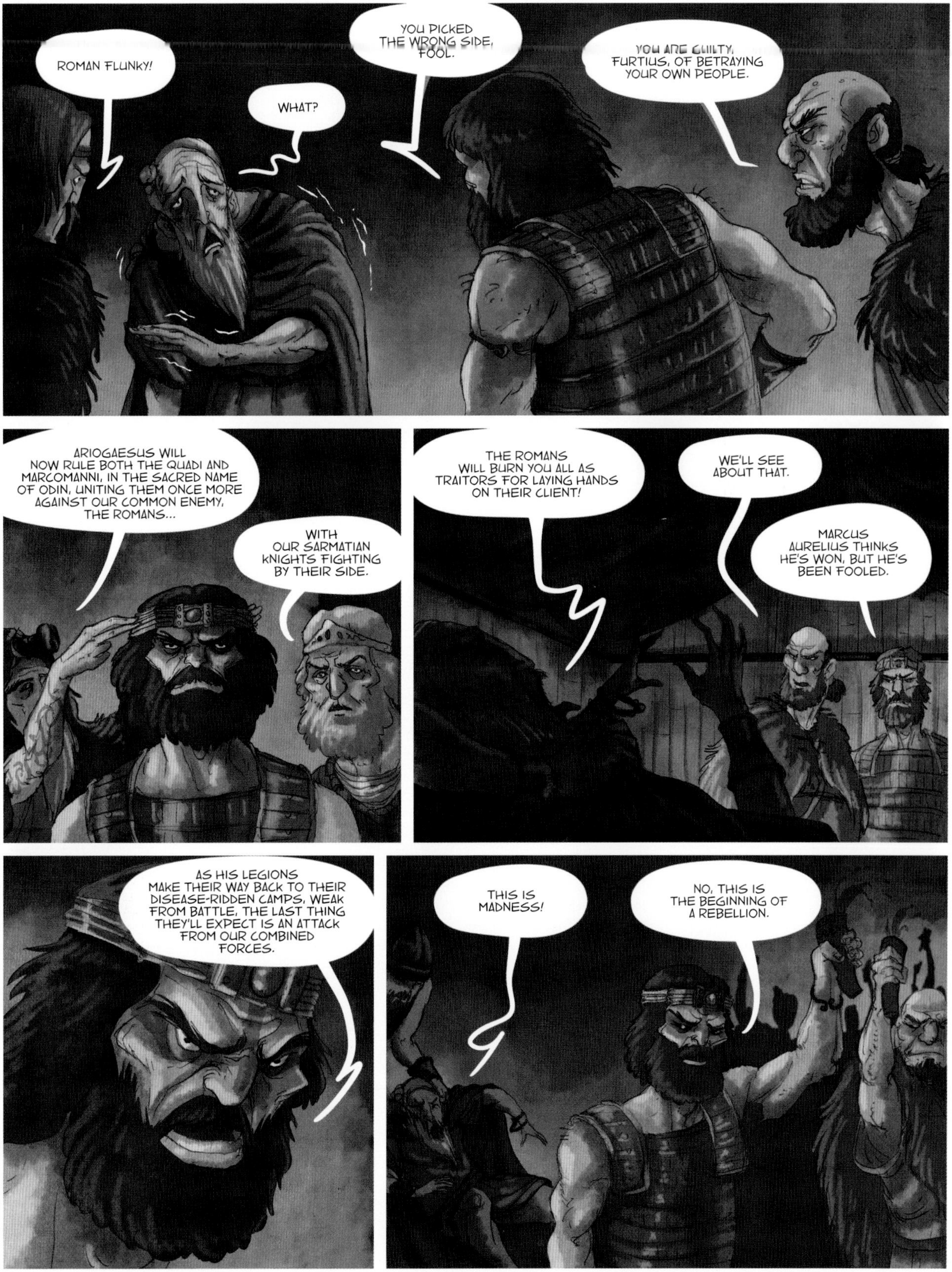
ROMAN FLUNKY!
WHAT?
YOU PICKED THE WRONG SIDE, FOOL.
YOU ARE GUILTY, FURTIUS, OF BETRAYING YOUR OWN PEOPLE.
ARIOGAESUS WILL NOW RULE BOTH THE QUADI AND MARCOMANNI, IN THE SACRED NAME OF ODIN, UNITING THEM ONCE MORE AGAINST OUR COMMON ENEMY, THE ROMANS...
WITH OUR SARMATIAN KNIGHTS FIGHTING BY THEIR SIDE.
THE ROMANS WILL BURN YOU ALL AS TRAITORS FOR LAYING HANDS ON THEIR CLIENT!
WE'LL SEE ABOUT THAT.
MARCUS AURELIUS THINKS HE'S WON, BUT HE'S BEEN FOOLED.
AS HIS LEGIONS MAKE THEIR WAY BACK TO THEIR DISEASE-RIDDEN CAMPS, WEAK FROM BATTLE, THE LAST THING THEY'LL EXPECT IS AN ATTACK FROM OUR COMBINED FORCES.
THIS IS MADNESS!
NO, THIS IS THE BEGINNING OF A REBELLION.

THE
SARMATIAN WAR

Love the art, simple as it may be, which you have learned, and find therein your contentment ... trusting everything to the gods, making yourself neither the tyrant nor the slave of any man.

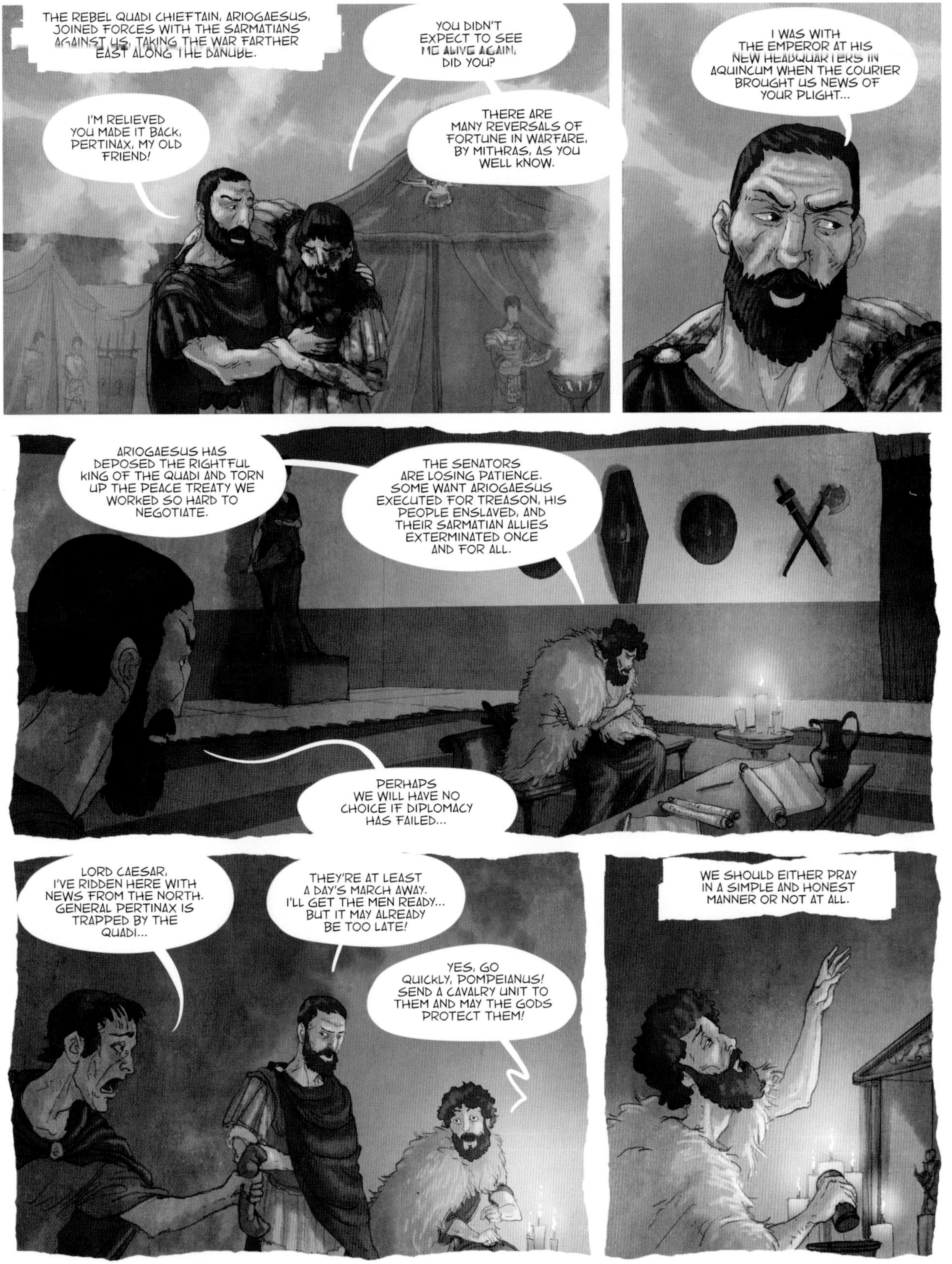
THE REBEL QUADI CHIEFTAIN, ARIOGAESUS, JOINED FORCES WITH THE SARMATIANS AGAINST US, TAKING THE WAR FARTHER EAST ALONG THE DANUBE.
I'M RELIEVED YOU MADE IT BACK, PERTINAX, MY OLD FRIEND!
YOU DIDN'T EXPECT TO SEE ME ALIVE AGAIN, DID YOU?
THERE ARE MANY REVERSALS OF FORTUNE IN WARFARE, BY MITHRAS, AS YOU WELL KNOW.
I WAS WITH THE EMPEROR AT HIS NEW HEADQUARTERS IN AQUINCUM WHEN THE COURIER BROUGHT US NEWS OF YOUR PLIGHT...
ARIOGAESUS HAS DEPOSED THE RIGHTFUL KING OF THE QUADI AND TORN UP THE PEACE TREATY WE WORKED SO HARD TO NEGOTIATE.
THE SENATORS ARE LOSING PATIENCE. SOME WANT ARIOGAESUS EXECUTED FOR TREASON, HIS PEOPLE ENSLAVED, AND THEIR SARMATIAN ALLIES EXTERMINATED ONCE AND FOR ALL.
PERHAPS WE WILL HAVE NO CHOICE IF DIPLOMACY HAS FAILED...
LORD CAESAR, I'VE RIDDEN HERE WITH NEWS FROM THE NORTH. GENERAL PERTINAX IS TRAPPED BY THE QUADI...
THEY'RE AT LEAST A DAY'S MARCH AWAY. I'LL GET THE MEN READY... BUT IT MAY ALREADY BE TOO LATE!
YES, GO QUICKLY, POMPEIANUS! SEND A CAVALRY UNIT TO THEM AND MAY THE GODS PROTECT THEM!
WE SHOULD EITHER PRAY IN A SIMPLE AND HONEST MANNER OR NOT AT ALL.

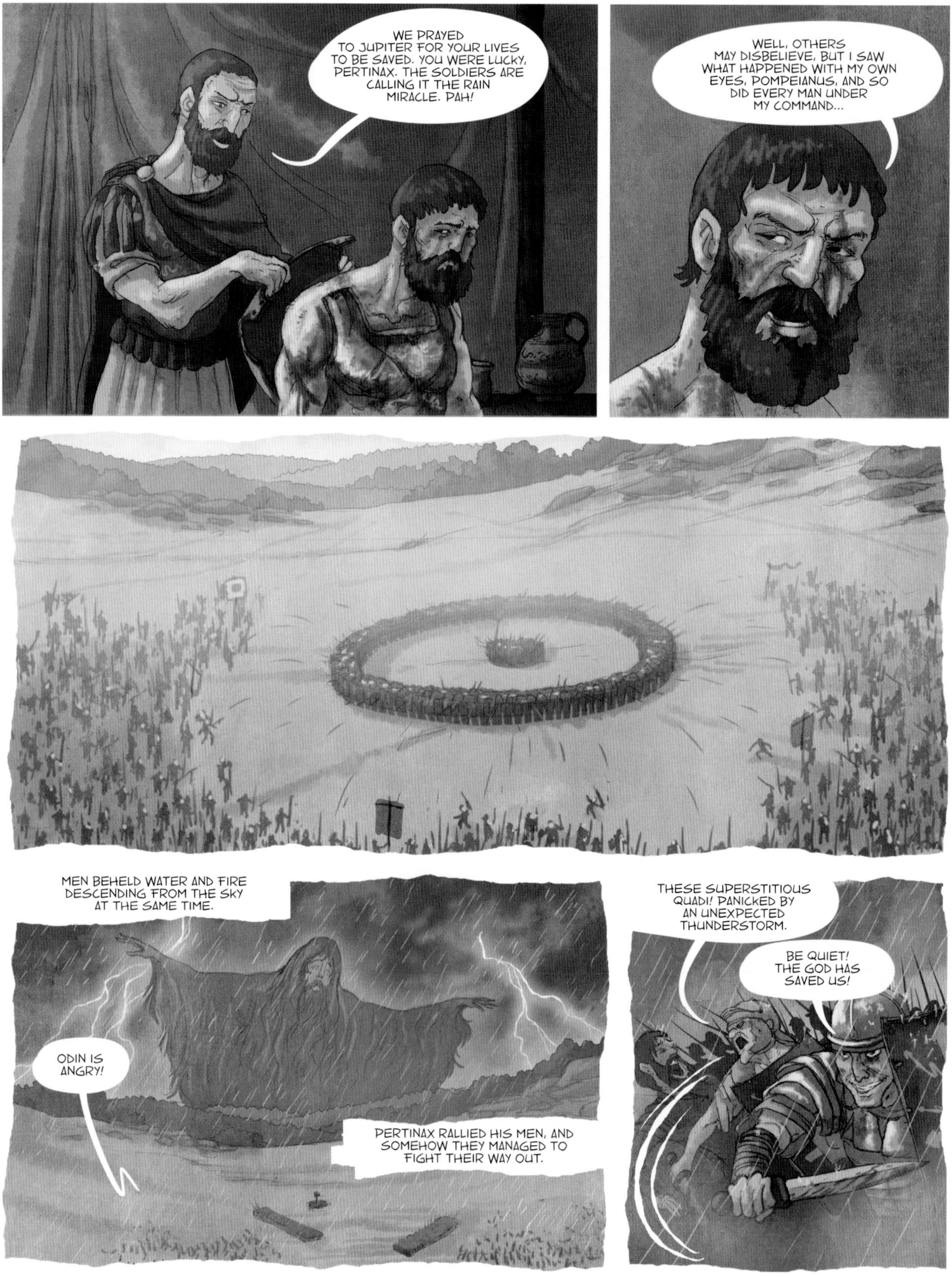
WE PRAYED TO JUPITER FOR YOUR LIVES TO BE SAVED. YOU WERE LUCKY, PERTINAX. THE SOLDIERS ARE CALLING IT THE RAIN MIRACLE. PAH!
WELL, OTHERS MAY DISBELIEVE, BUT I SAW WHAT HAPPENED WITH MY OWN EYES, POMPEIANUS, AND SO DID EVERY MAN UNDER MY COMMAND...
MEN BEHELD WATER AND FIRE DESCENDING FROM THE SKY AT THE SAME TIME.
ODIN IS ANGRY!
PERTINAX RALLIED HIS MEN, AND SOMEHOW THEY MANAGED TO FIGHT THEIR WAY OUT.
THESE SUPERSTITIOUS QUADI! PANICKED BY AN UNEXPECTED THUNDERSTORM.
BE QUIET! THE GOD HAS SAVED US!

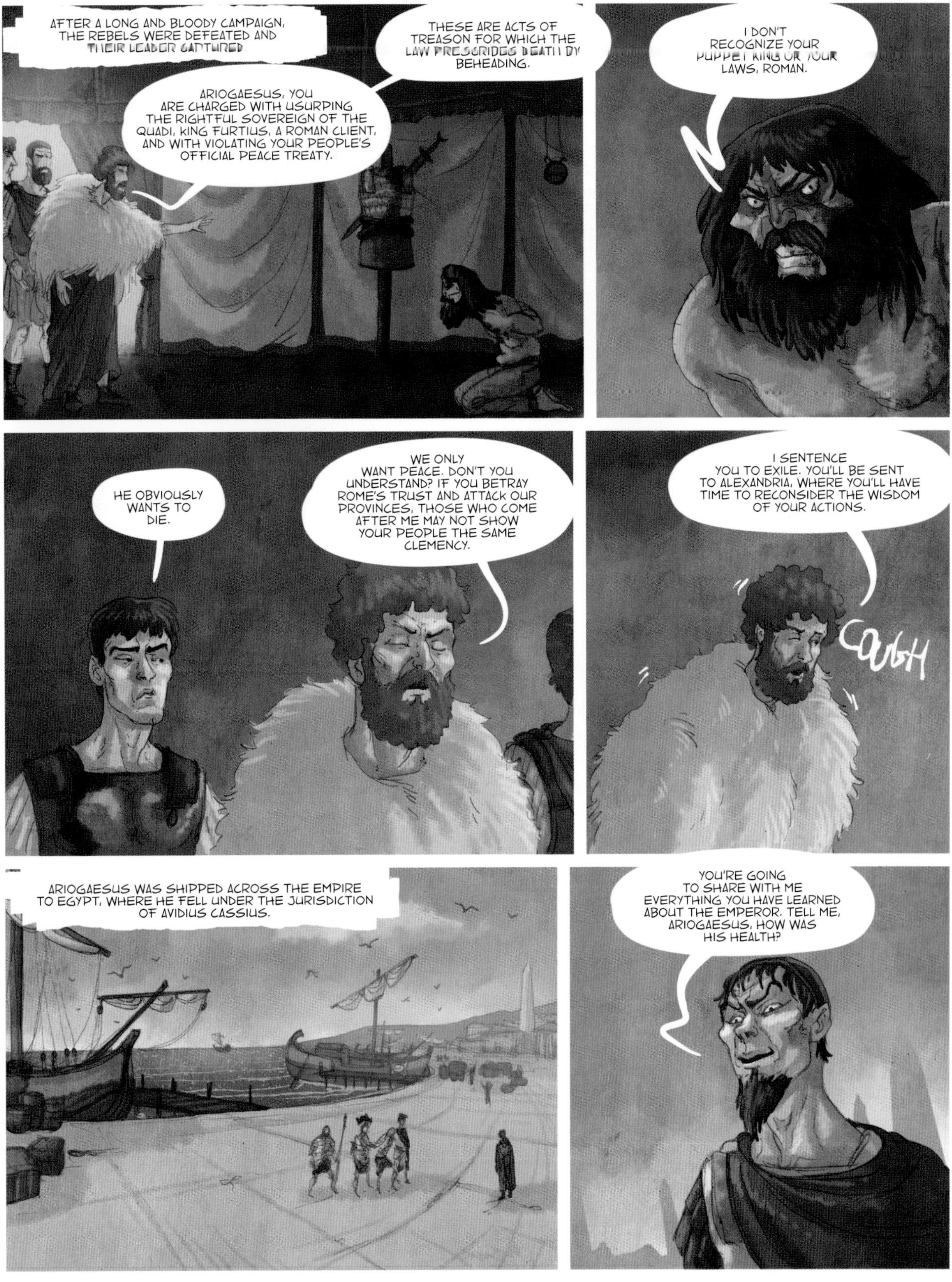
AFTER A LONG AND BLOODY CAMPAIGN, THE REBELS WERE DEFEATED AND THEIR LEADER CAPTURED.
ARIOGAESUS, YOU ARE CHARGED WITH USURPING THE RIGHTFUL SOVEREIGN OF THE QUADI, KING FURTIUS, A ROMAN CLIENT, AND WITH VIOLATING YOUR PEOPLE'S OFFICIAL PEACE TREATY.
THESE ARE ACTS OF TREASON FOR WHICH THE LAW PRESCRIBES DEATH BY BEHEADING.
I DON'T RECOGNIZE YOUR PUPPET KING OR YOUR LAWS, ROMAN.
HE OBVIOUSLY WANTS TO DIE.
WE ONLY WANT PEACE. DON'T YOU UNDERSTAND? IF YOU BETRAY ROME'S TRUST AND ATTACK OUR PROVINCES, THOSE WHO COME AFTER ME MAY NOT SHOW YOUR PEOPLE THE SAME CLEMENCY.
I SENTENCE YOU TO EXILE. YOU'LL BE SENT TO ALEXANDRIA, WHERE YOU'LL HAVE TIME TO RECONSIDER THE WISDOM OF YOUR ACTIONS.
COUGH
ARIOGAESUS WAS SHIPPED ACROSS THE EMPIRE TO EGYPT, WHERE HE FELL UNDER THE JURISDICTION OF AVIDIUS CASSIUS.
YOU'RE GOING TO SHARE WITH ME EVERYTHING YOU HAVE LEARNED ABOUT THE EMPEROR. TELL ME, ARIOGAESUS, HOW WAS HIS HEALTH?

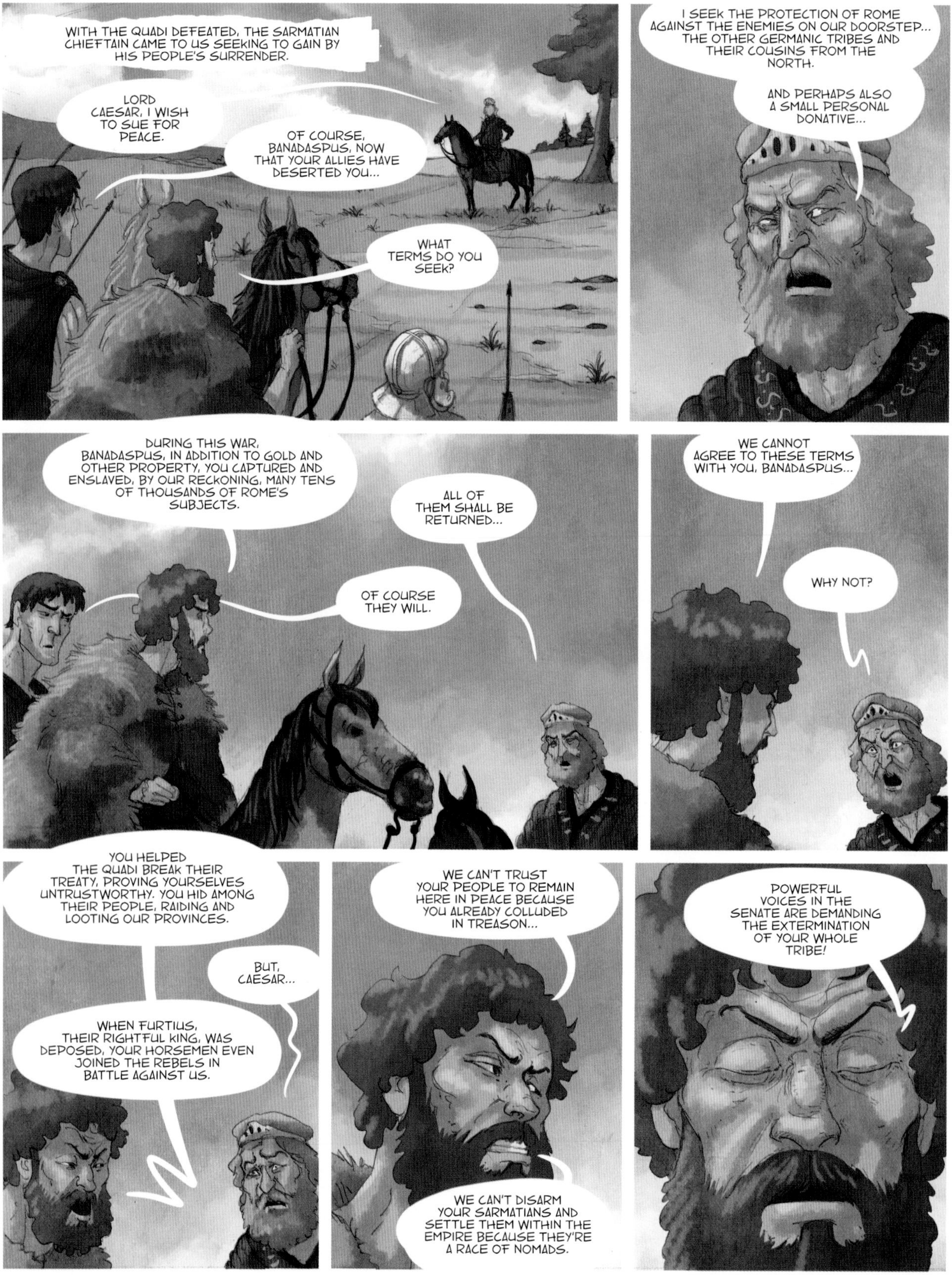
WITH THE QUADI DEFEATED, THE SARMATIAN CHIEFTAIN CAME TO US SEEKING TO GAIN BY HIS PEOPLE'S SURRENDER.
LORD CAESAR, I WISH TO SUE FOR PEACE.
OF COURSE, BANADASPUS, NOW THAT YOUR ALLIES HAVE DESERTED YOU...
WHAT TERMS DO YOU SEEK?
I SEEK THE PROTECTION OF ROME AGAINST THE ENEMIES ON OUR DOORSTEP... THE OTHER GERMANIC TRIBES AND THEIR COUSINS FROM THE NORTH.
AND PERHAPS ALSO A SMALL PERSONAL DONATIVE...
DURING THIS WAR, BANADASPUS, IN ADDITION TO GOLD AND OTHER PROPERTY, YOU CAPTURED AND ENSLAVED, BY OUR RECKONING, MANY TENS OF THOUSANDS OF ROME'S SUBJECTS.
ALL OF THEM SHALL BE RETURNED...
OF COURSE THEY WILL.
WE CANNOT AGREE TO THESE TERMS WITH YOU, BANADASPUS...
WHY NOT?
YOU HELPED THE QUADI BREAK THEIR TREATY, PROVING YOURSELVES UNTRUSTWORTHY. YOU HID AMONG THEIR PEOPLE, RAIDING AND LOOTING OUR PROVINCES.
BUT, CAESAR...
WHEN FURTIUS, THEIR RIGHTFUL KING, WAS DEPOSED, YOUR HORSEMEN EVEN JOINED THE REBELS IN BATTLE AGAINST US.
WE CAN'T TRUST YOUR PEOPLE TO REMAIN HERE IN PEACE BECAUSE YOU ALREADY COLLUDED IN TREASON...
WE CAN'T DISARM YOUR SARMATIANS AND SETTLE THEM WITHIN THE EMPIRE BECAUSE THEY'RE A RACE OF NOMADS.
POWERFUL VOICES IN THE SENATE ARE DEMANDING THE EXTERMINATION OF YOUR WHOLE TRIBE!

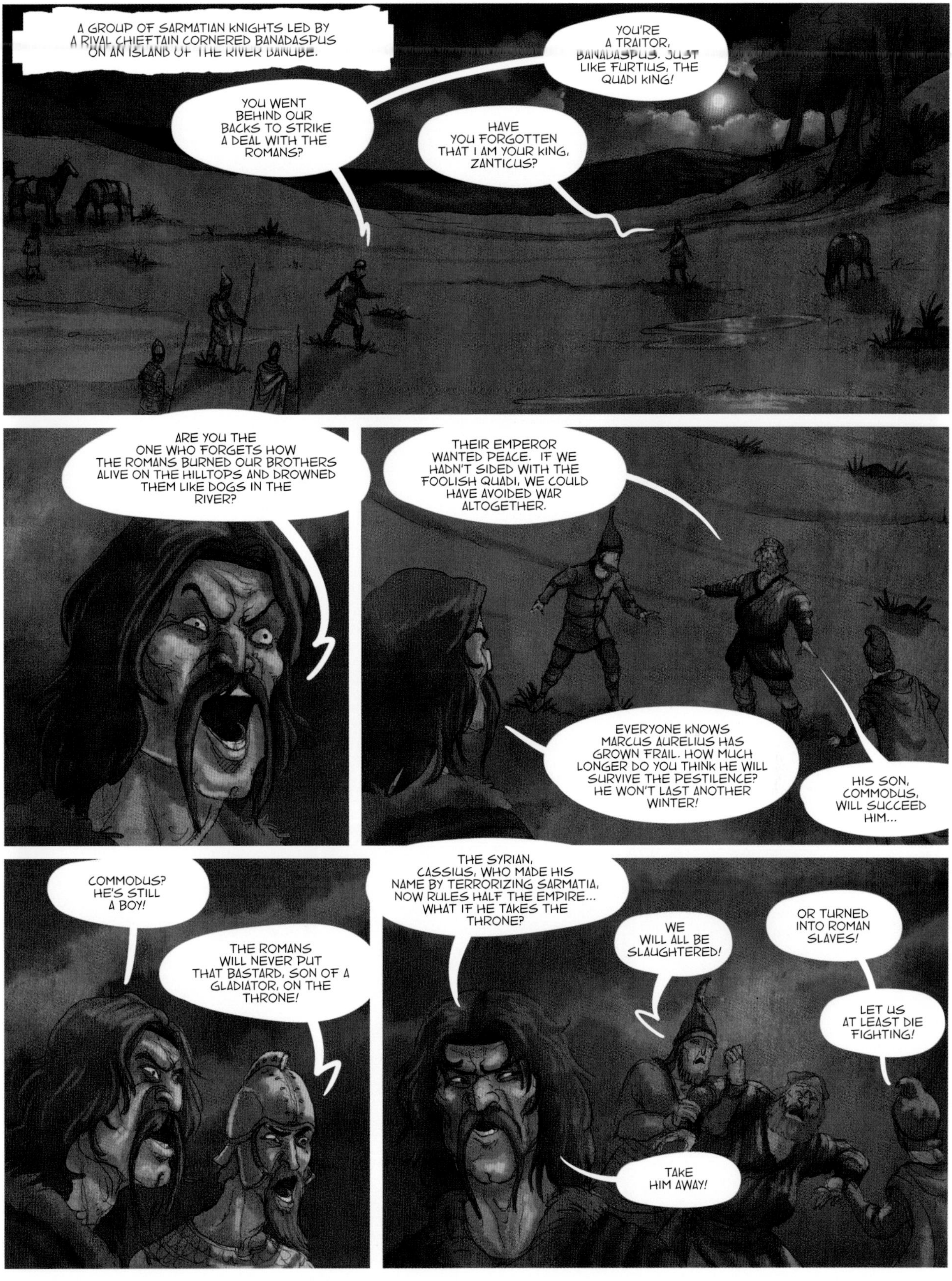
A GROUP OF SARMATIAN KNIGHTS LED BY A RIVAL CHIEFTAIN CORNERED BANADASPUS ON AN ISLAND OF THE RIVER DANUBE.
YOU WENT BEHIND OUR BACKS TO STRIKE A DEAL WITH THE ROMANS?
YOU'RE A TRAITOR, BANADASPUS. JUST LIKE FURTIUS, THE QUADI KING!
HAVE YOU FORGOTTEN THAT I AM YOUR KING, ZANTICUS?
ARE YOU THE ONE WHO FORGETS HOW THE ROMANS BURNED OUR BROTHERS ALIVE ON THE HILLTOPS AND DROWNED THEM LIKE DOGS IN THE RIVER?
THEIR EMPEROR WANTED PEACE. IF WE HADN'T SIDED WITH THE FOOLISH QUADI, WE COULD HAVE AVOIDED WAR ALTOGETHER.
EVERYONE KNOWS MARCUS AURELIUS HAS GROWN FRAIL. HOW MUCH LONGER DO YOU THINK HE WILL SURVIVE THE PESTILENCE? HE WON'T LAST ANOTHER WINTER!
HIS SON, COMMODUS, WILL SUCCEED HIM...
COMMODUS? HE'S STILL A BOY!
THE ROMANS WILL NEVER PUT THAT BASTARD, SON OF A GLADIATOR, ON THE THRONE!
THE SYRIAN, CASSIUS, WHO MADE HIS NAME BY TERRORIZING SARMATIA, NOW RULES HALF THE EMPIRE... WHAT IF HE TAKES THE THRONE?
WE WILL ALL BE SLAUGHTERED!
OR TURNED INTO ROMAN SLAVES!
LET US AT LEAST DIE FIGHTING!
TAKE HIM AWAY!

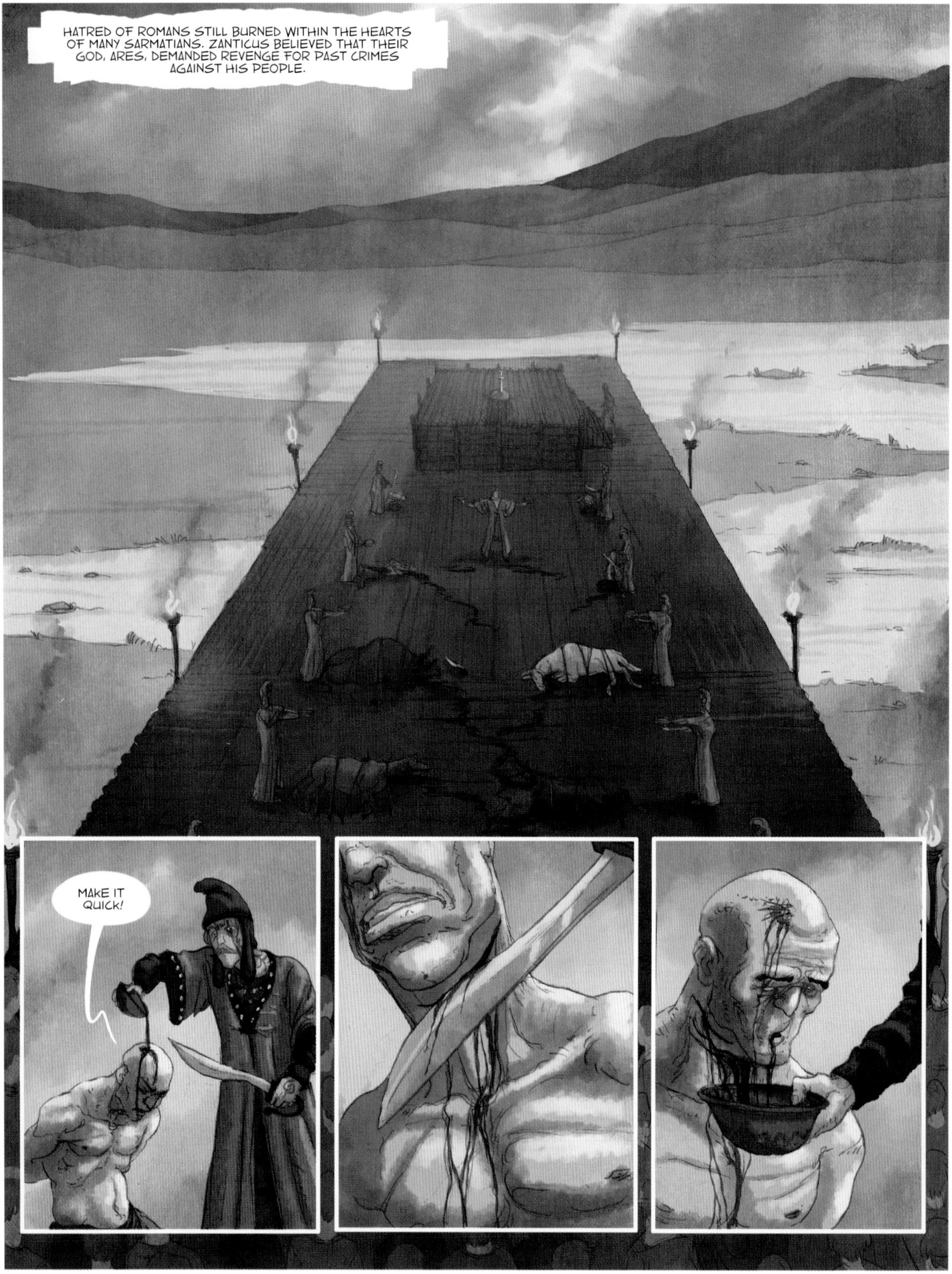
HATRED OF ROMANS STILL BURNED WITHIN THE HEARTS OF MANY SARMATIANS. ZANTICUS BELIEVED THAT THEIR GOD, ARES, DEMANDED REVENGE FOR PAST CRIMES AGAINST HIS PEOPLE.
MAKE IT QUICK!

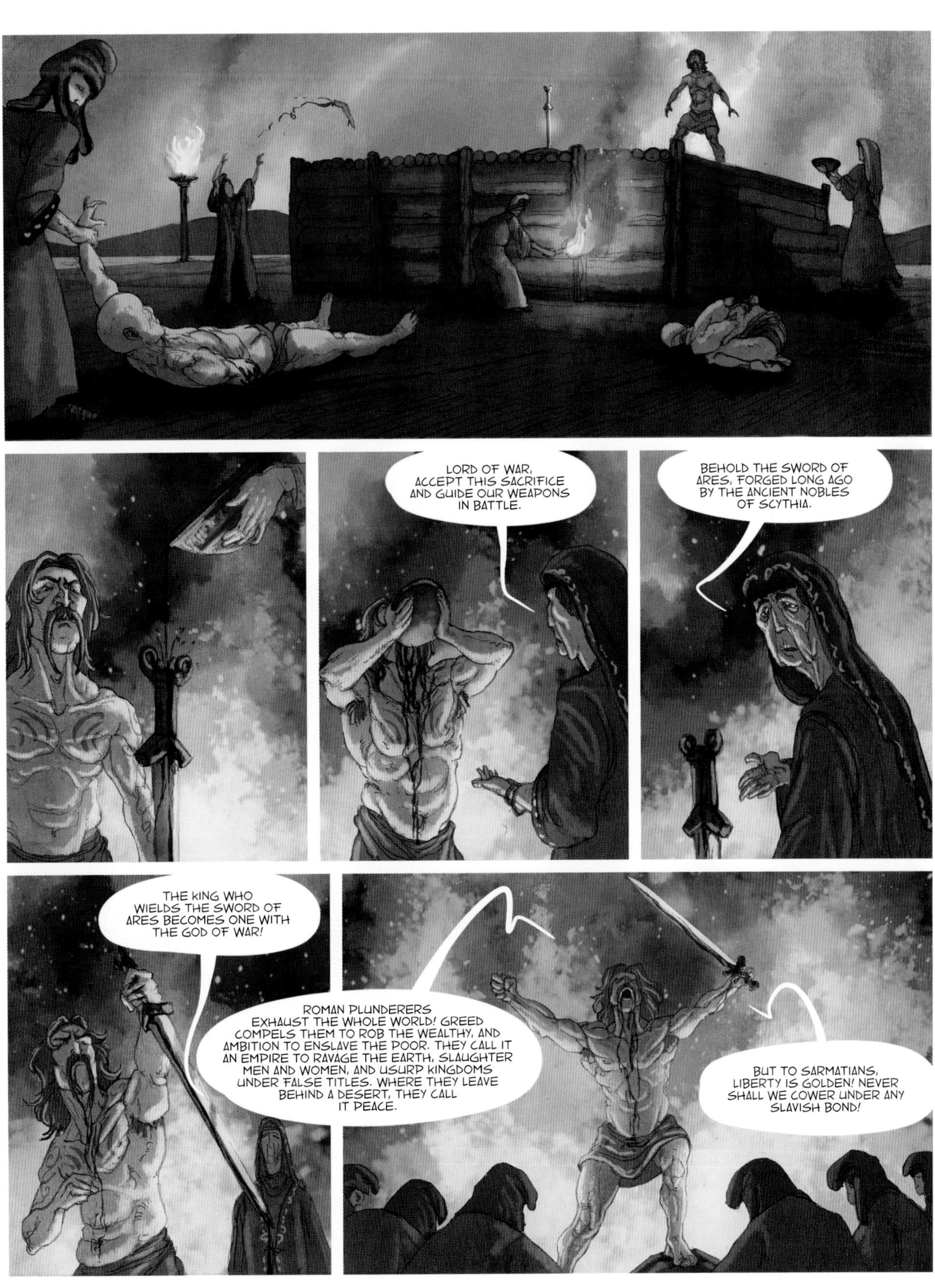
LORD OF WAR, ACCEPT THIS SACRIFICE AND GUIDE OUR WEAPONS IN BATTLE.
BEHOLD THE SWORD OF ARES, FORGED LONG AGO BY THE ANCIENT NOBLES OF SCYTHIA.
THE KING WHO WIELDS THE SWORD OF ARES BECOMES ONE WITH THE GOD OF WAR!
ROMAN PLUNDERERS EXHAUST THE WHOLE WORLD! GREED COMPELS THEM TO ROB THE WEALTHY, AND AMBITION TO ENSLAVE THE POOR. THEY CALL IT AN EMPIRE TO RAVAGE THE EARTH, SLAUGHTER MEN AND WOMEN, AND USURP KINGDOMS UNDER FALSE TITLES. WHERE THEY LEAVE BEHIND A DESERT, THEY CALL IT PEACE.
BUT TO SARMATIANS, LIBERTY IS GOLDEN! NEVER SHALL WE COWER UNDER ANY SLAVISH BOND!

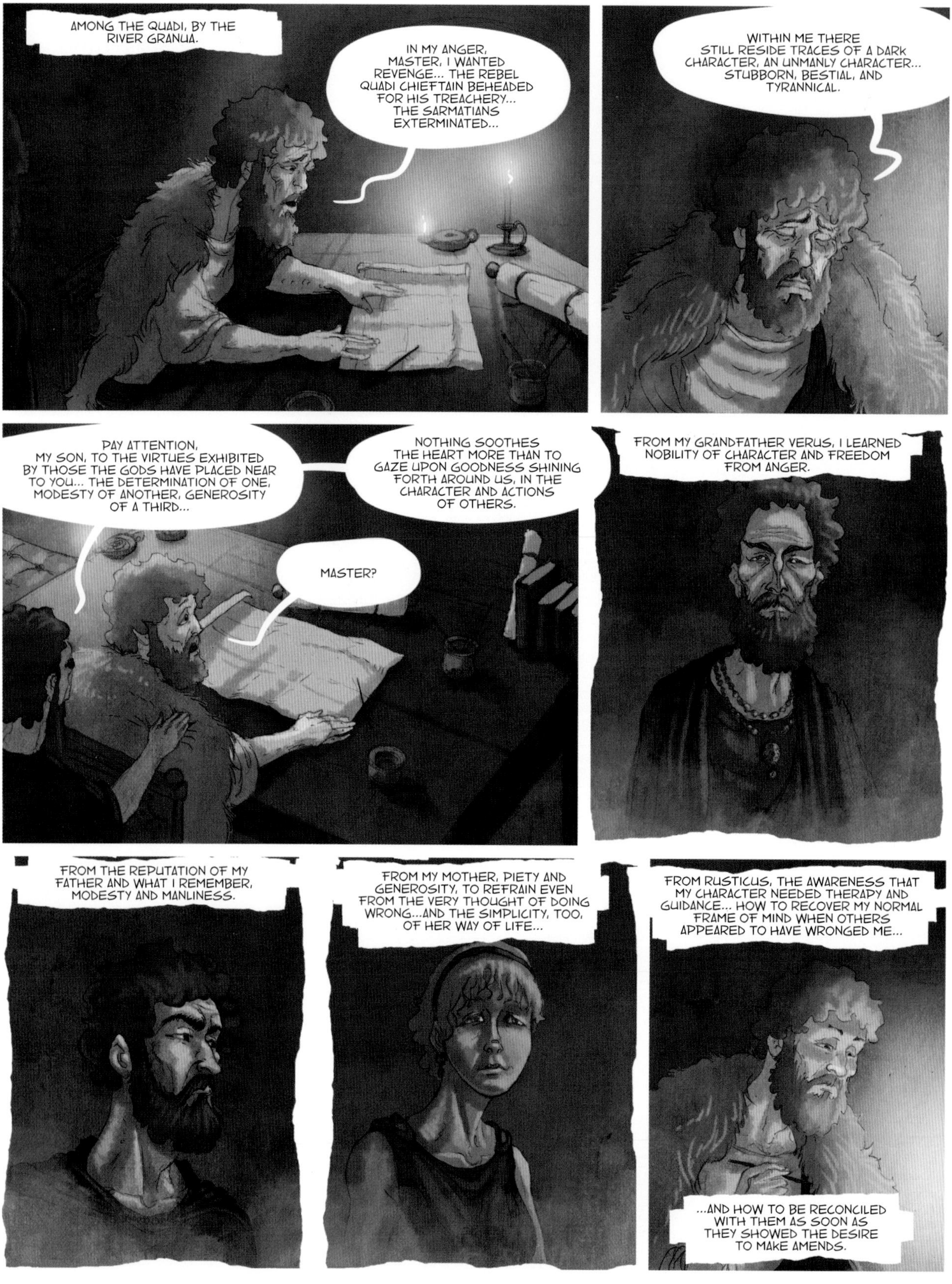
AMONG THE QUADI, BY THE RIVER GRANUA.
IN MY ANGER, MASTER, I WANTED REVENGE... THE REBEL QUADI CHIEFTAIN BEHEADED FOR HIS TREACHERY... THE SARMATIANS EXTERMINATED...
WITHIN ME THERE STILL RESIDE TRACES OF A DARK CHARACTER, AN UNMANLY CHARACTER... STUBBORN, BESTIAL, AND TYRANNICAL.
PAY ATTENTION, MY SON, TO THE VIRTUES EXHIBITED BY THOSE THE GODS HAVE PLACED NEAR TO YOU... THE DETERMINATION OF ONE, MODESTY OF ANOTHER, GENEROSITY OF A THIRD...
NOTHING SOOTHES THE HEART MORE THAN TO GAZE UPON GOODNESS SHINING FORTH AROUND US, IN THE CHARACTER AND ACTIONS OF OTHERS.
MASTER?
FROM MY GRANDFATHER VERUS, I LEARNED NOBILITY OF CHARACTER AND FREEDOM FROM ANGER.
FROM THE REPUTATION OF MY FATHER AND WHAT I REMEMBER, MODESTY AND MANLINESS.
FROM MY MOTHER, PIETY AND GENEROSITY, TO REFRAIN EVEN FROM THE VERY THOUGHT OF DOING WRONG...AND THE SIMPLICITY, TOO, OF HER WAY OF LIFE...
FROM RUSTICUS, THE AWARENESS THAT MY CHARACTER NEEDED THERAPY AND GUIDANCE... HOW TO RECOVER MY NORMAL FRAME OF MIND WHEN OTHERS APPEARED TO HAVE WRONGED ME...
...AND HOW TO BE RECONCILED WITH THEM AS SOON AS THEY SHOWED THE DESIRE TO MAKE AMENDS.

MOVING SOUTH, WE FOLLOWED THE TURN IN THE DANUBE, RELOCATING OUR HEADQUARTERS TO THE CITY OF SIRMIUM.

WITH VICTORY OVER THE MARCOMANNI AND QUADI, LORD CAESAR, IT IS THE SENATE'S WISH THAT YOU SHOULD RETURN TO ROME TO CELEBRATE YOUR TRIUMPH.

ZANTICUS AND HIS SARMATIAN RAIDERS HAVE LOOTED ANOTHER SETTLEMENT NEAR AQUINCUM.

FATE PERMITTING, WE SHALL LIVE IN PEACE ONCE AGAIN.

MY LORD, THE WAR HAS BECOME SO VERY COSTLY... WOULDN'T IT BE WISE TO BRING IT TO AN END QUICKLY BY USING MORE FORCEFUL MEASURES AGAINST THESE BARBARIANS?

THE SARMATIANS ARE A CATTLE-DRIVING RACE, EXPERT HORSEMEN AND LANCERS, WHO LIVE BY AN ANCIENT CODE OF HONOR.

AHAH EHEH

THEY OCCUPY THE LAND DIVIDING OUR TWO PROVINCES OF DACIA AND PANNONIA, MAKING THE FRONTIER VULNERABLE AND COSTLY TO MAINTAIN.

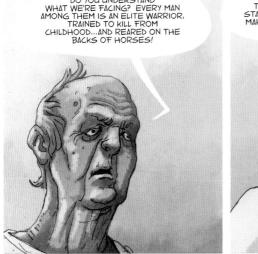

DO YOU UNDERSTAND WHAT WE'RE FACING? EVERY MAN AMONG THEM IS AN ELITE WARRIOR, TRAINED TO KILL FROM CHILDHOOD...AND REARED ON THE BACKS OF HORSES!

AVIDIUS CASSIUS CAPTURED THOUSANDS WHEN HE WAS STATIONED IN THE NORTH. THEY MAKE FINE SLAVES, ESPECIALLY THE WOMEN.

THOSE WHO TAKE PRIDE IN CAPTURING SARMATIANS, LIKE FISH HAULED UP IN NETS, ARE NO BETTER THAN BRIGANDS THEMSELVES.

A JUST RULER VALUES THE FREEDOM OF HIS SUBJECTS ABOVE ALL ELSE.

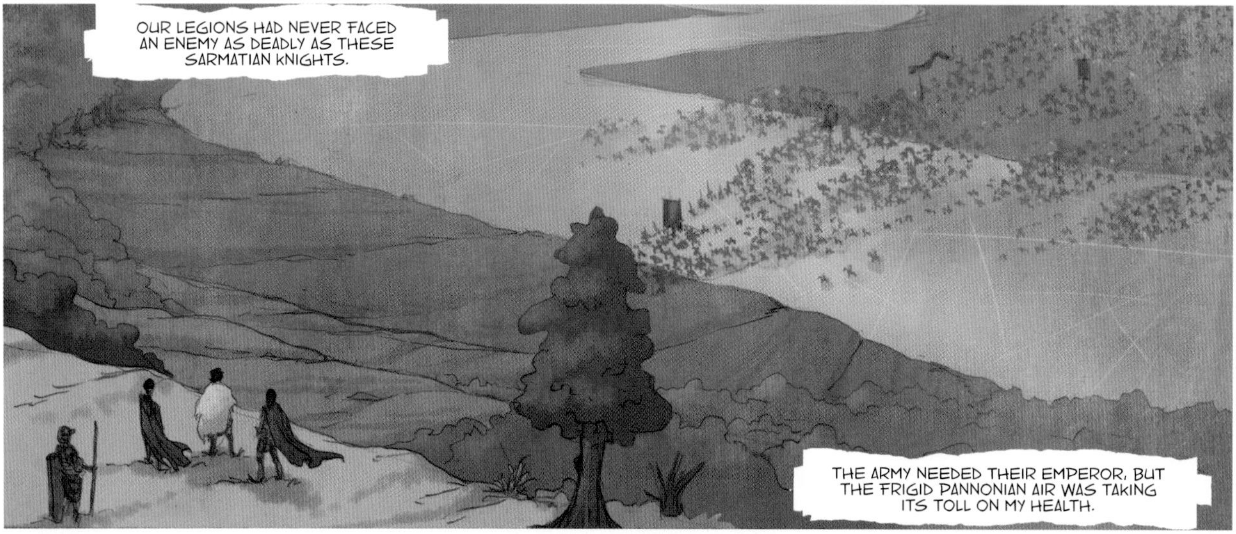
OUR LEGIONS HAD NEVER FACED AN ENEMY AS DEADLY AS THESE SARMATIAN KNIGHTS.
THE ARMY NEEDED THEIR EMPEROR, BUT THE FRIGID PANNONIAN AIR WAS TAKING ITS TOLL ON MY HEALTH.

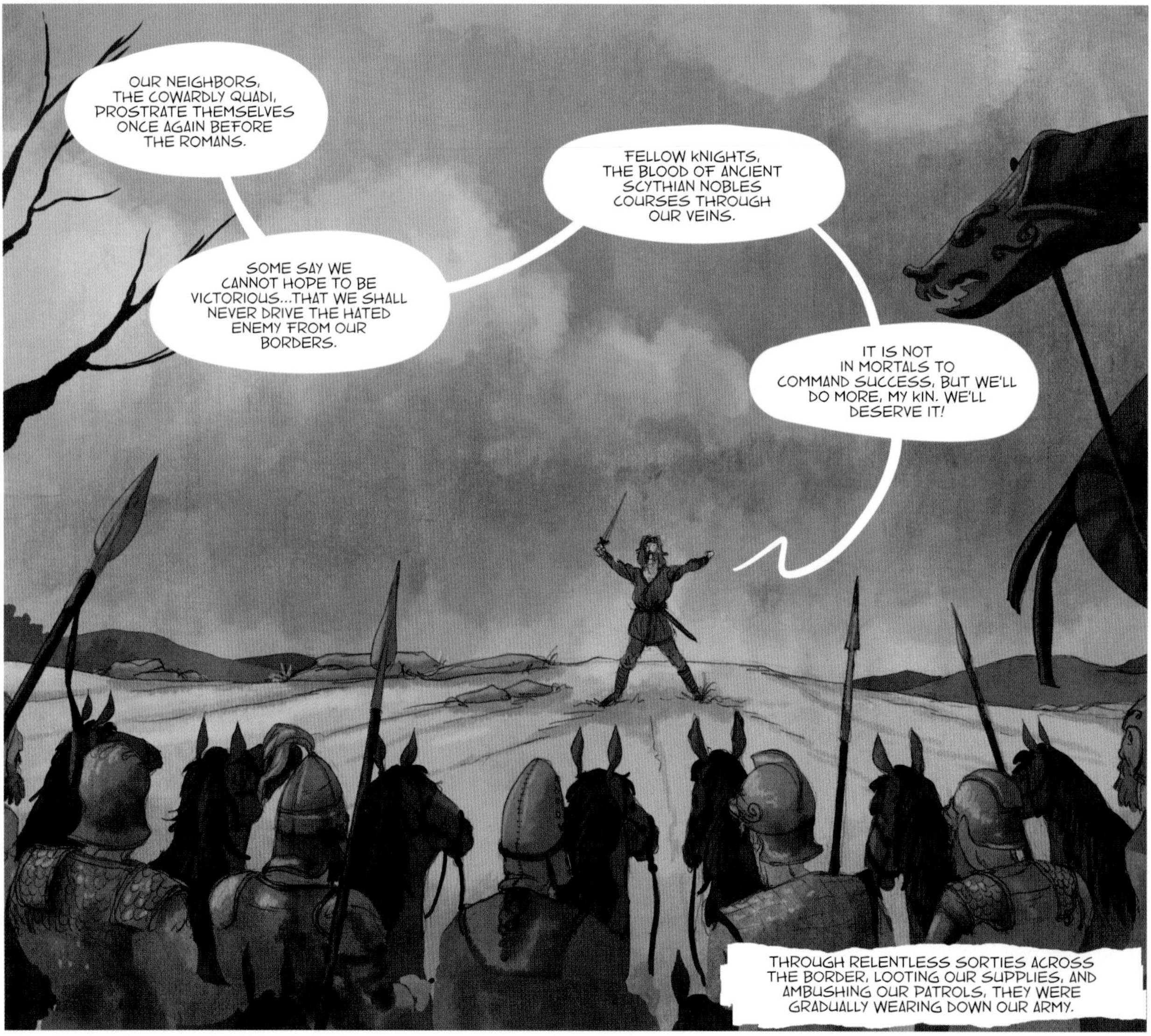
OUR NEIGHBORS, THE COWARDLY QUADI, PROSTRATE THEMSELVES ONCE AGAIN BEFORE THE ROMANS.
SOME SAY WE CANNOT HOPE TO BE VICTORIOUS...THAT WE SHALL NEVER DRIVE THE HATED ENEMY FROM OUR BORDERS.
FELLOW KNIGHTS, THE BLOOD OF ANCIENT SCYTHIAN NOBLES COURSES THROUGH OUR VEINS.
IT IS NOT IN MORTALS TO COMMAND SUCCESS, BUT WE'LL DO MORE, MY KIN. WE'LL DESERVE IT!
THROUGH RELENTLESS SORTIES ACROSS THE BORDER, LOOTING OUR SUPPLIES, AND AMBUSHING OUR PATROLS, THEY WERE GRADUALLY WEARING DOWN OUR ARMY.

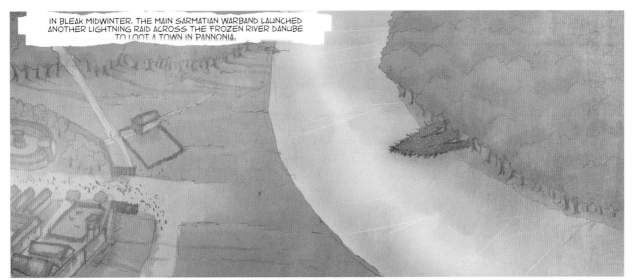

IN BLEAK MIDWINTER, THE MAIN SARMATIAN WARBAND LAUNCHED ANOTHER LIGHTNING RAID ACROSS THE FROZEN RIVER DANUBE TO LOOT A TOWN IN PANNONIA.

THEY'RE ON THE MOVE...

GIVE THE SIGNAL!

AFTER THEM, QUICK MARCH! WE'LL CATCH UP WHEN THEY SLOW TO CROSS THE RIVER.

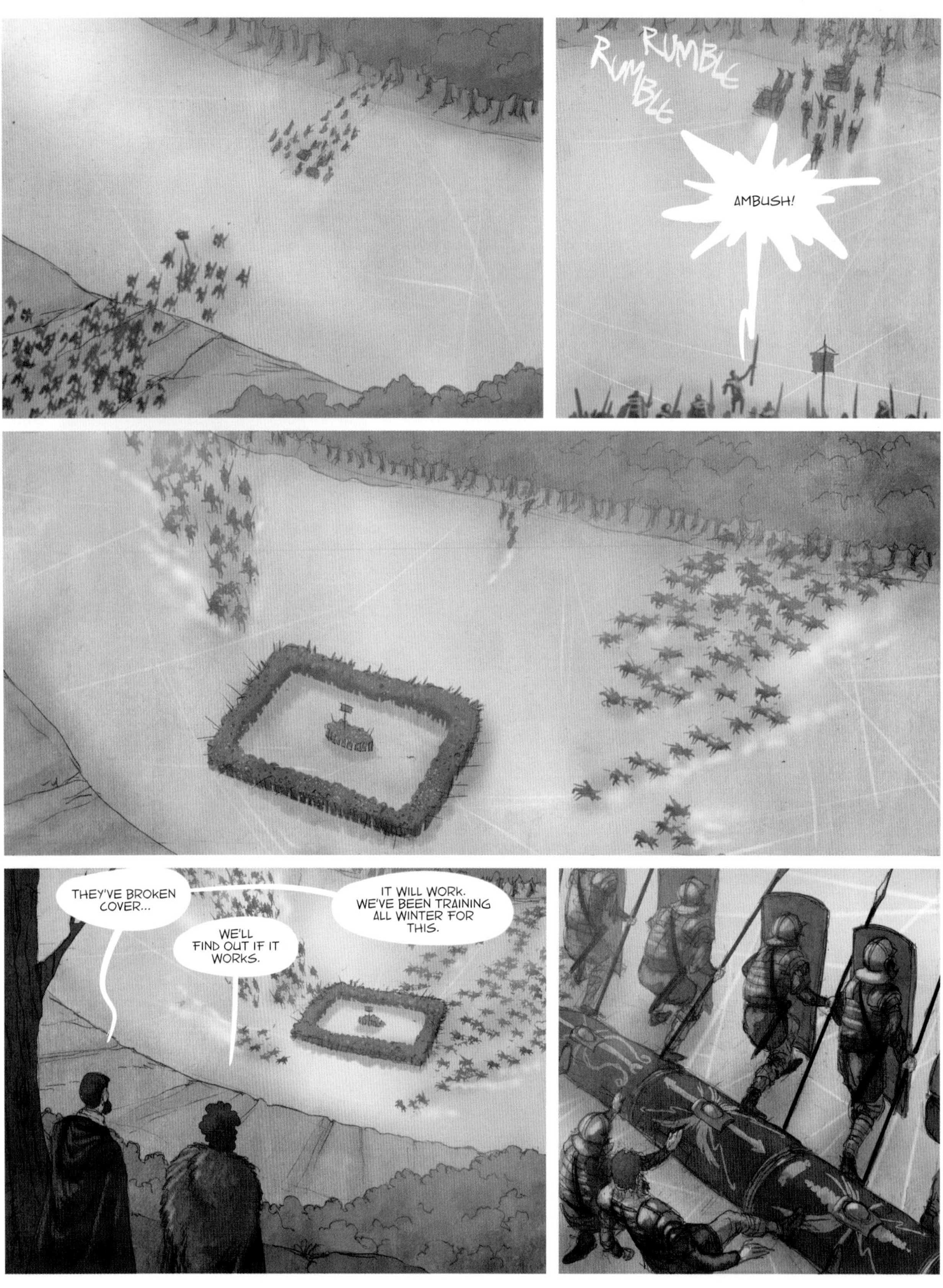
RUMBLE
RUMBLE
AMBUSH!
THEY'VE BROKEN COVER...
WE'LL FIND OUT IF IT WORKS.
IT WILL WORK. WE'VE BEEN TRAINING ALL WINTER FOR THIS.

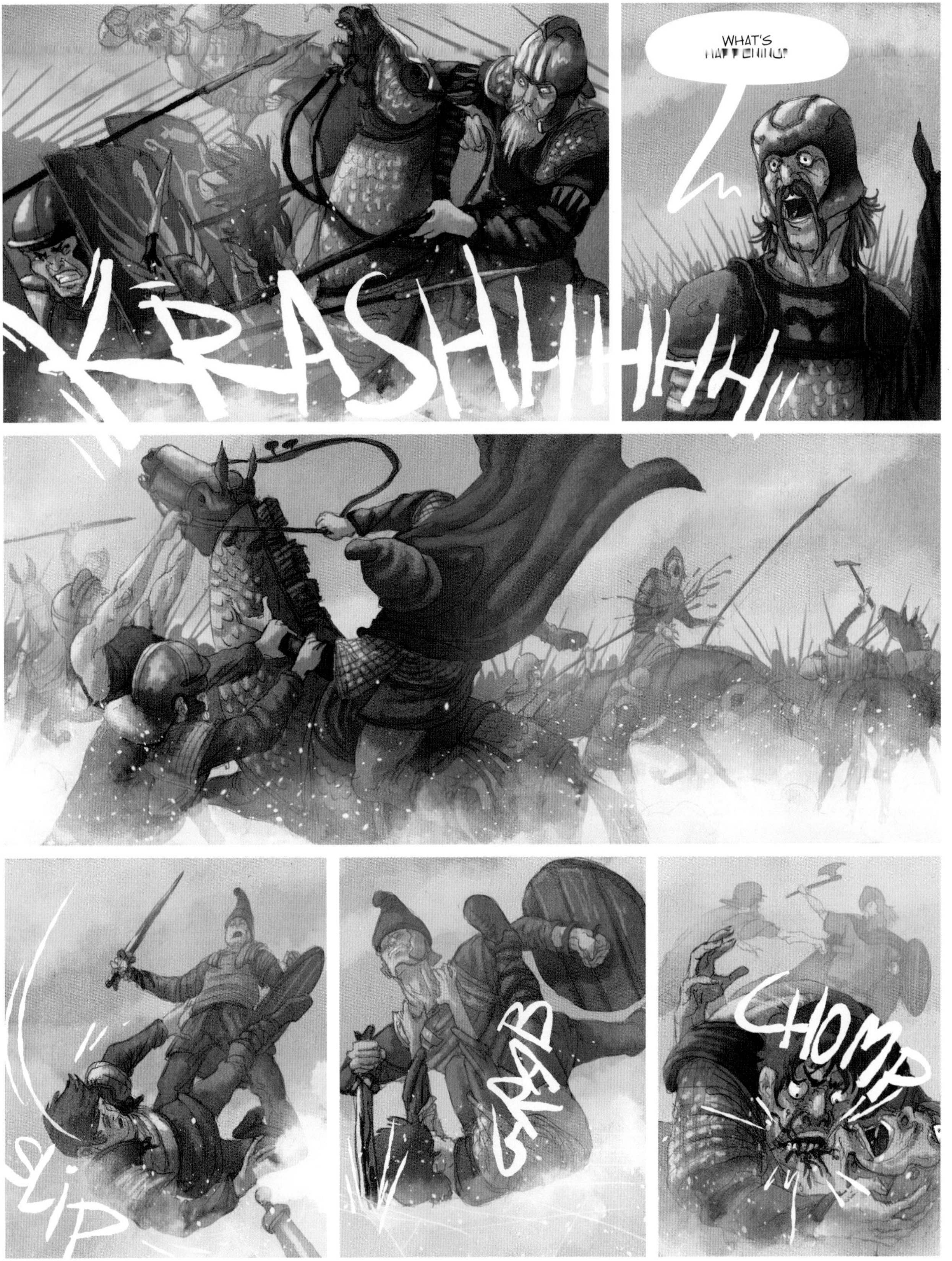
KRASHHHHHH
WHAT'S
HAPPENING!
SLIP
GRAB
CHOMP

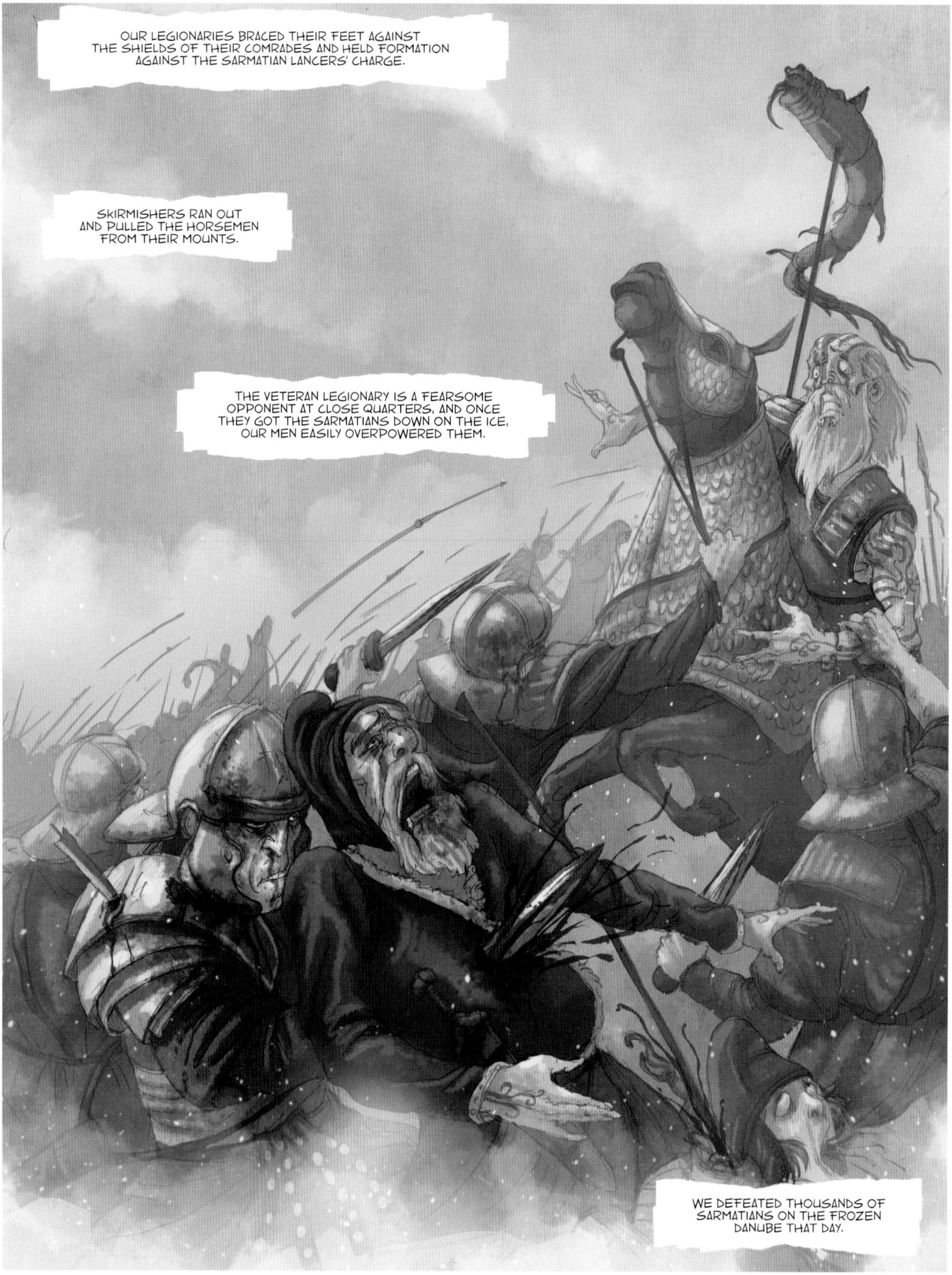
OUR LEGIONARIES BRACED THEIR FEET AGAINST THE SHIELDS OF THEIR COMRADES AND HELD FORMATION AGAINST THE SARMATIAN LANCERS' CHARGE.
SKIRMISHERS RAN OUT AND PULLED THE HORSEMEN FROM THEIR MOUNTS.
THE VETERAN LEGIONARY IS A FEARSOME OPPONENT AT CLOSE QUARTERS, AND ONCE THEY GOT THE SARMATIANS DOWN ON THE ICE, OUR MEN EASILY OVERPOWERED THEM.
WE DEFEATED THOUSANDS OF SARMATIANS ON THE FROZEN DANUBE THAT DAY.

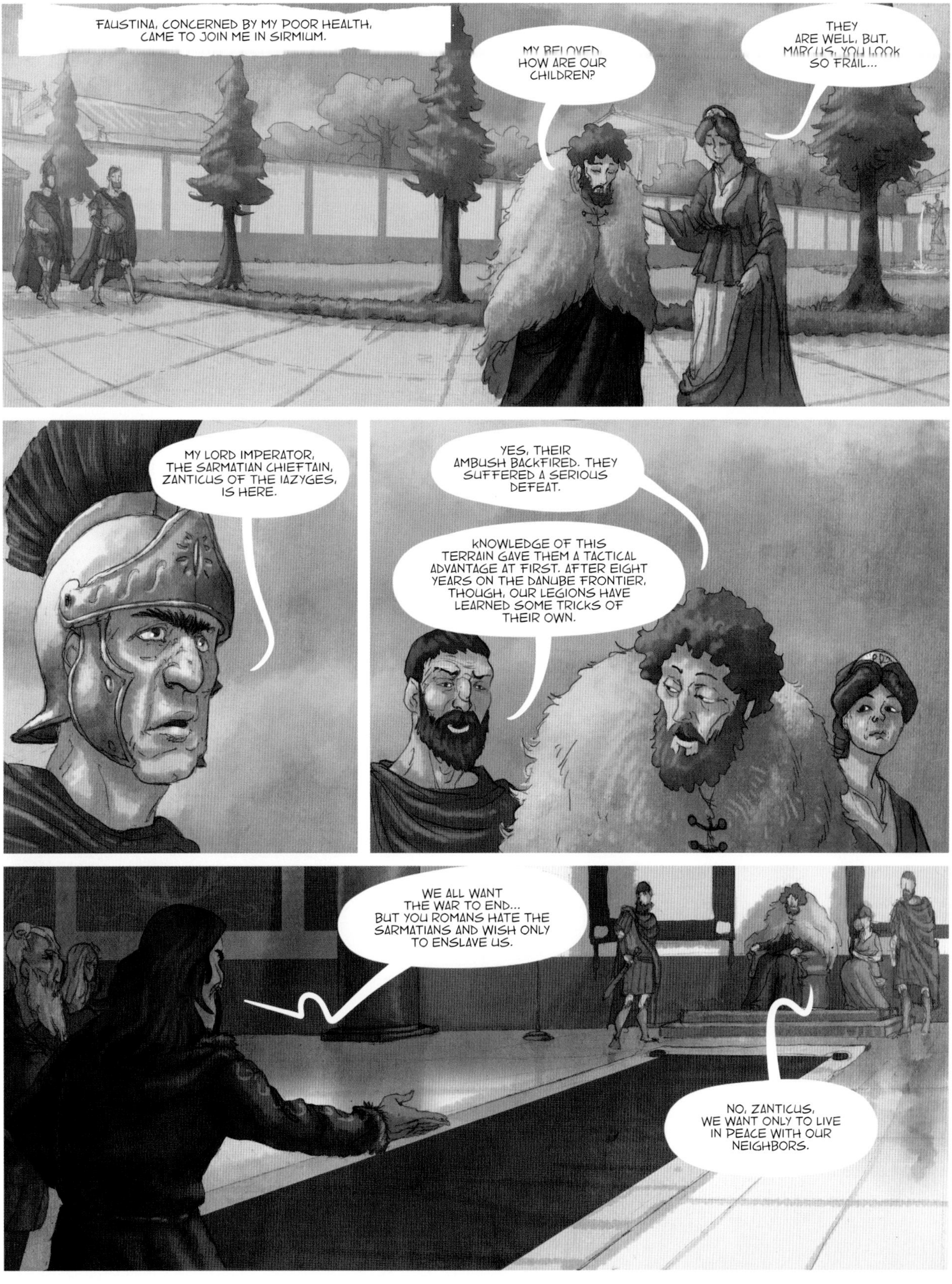
FAUSTINA, CONCERNED BY MY POOR HEALTH, CAME TO JOIN ME IN SIRMIUM.
MY BELOVED, HOW ARE OUR CHILDREN?
THEY ARE WELL, BUT, MARCUS, YOU LOOK SO FRAIL...
MY LORD IMPERATOR, THE SARMATIAN CHIEFTAIN, ZANTICUS OF THE IAZYGES, IS HERE.
YES, THEIR AMBUSH BACKFIRED. THEY SUFFERED A SERIOUS DEFEAT.
KNOWLEDGE OF THIS TERRAIN GAVE THEM A TACTICAL ADVANTAGE AT FIRST. AFTER EIGHT YEARS ON THE DANUBE FRONTIER, THOUGH, OUR LEGIONS HAVE LEARNED SOME TRICKS OF THEIR OWN.
WE ALL WANT THE WAR TO END... BUT YOU ROMANS HATE THE SARMATIANS AND WISH ONLY TO ENSLAVE US.
NO, ZANTICUS, WE WANT ONLY TO LIVE IN PEACE WITH OUR NEIGHBORS.

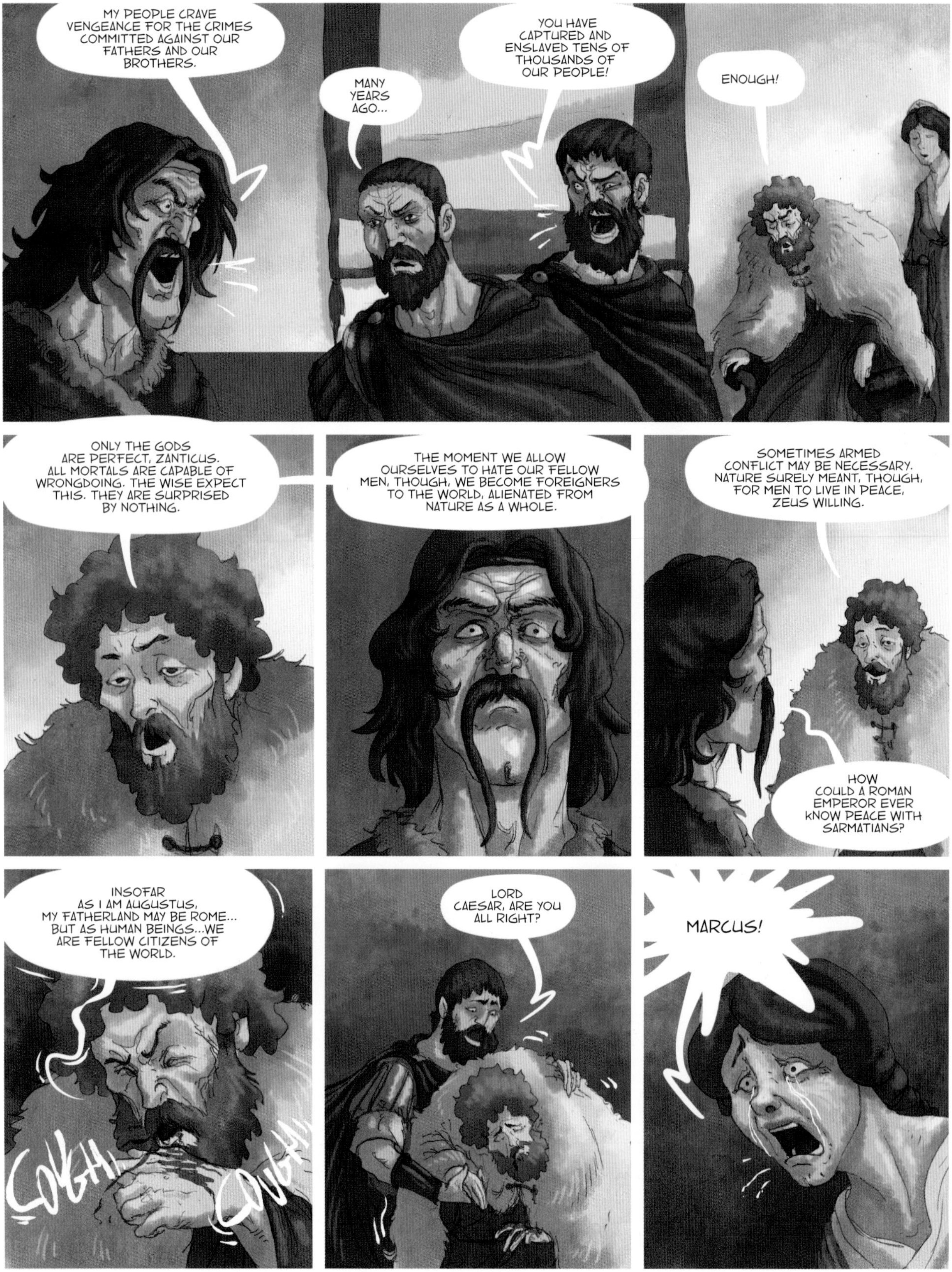
MY PEOPLE CRAVE VENGEANCE FOR THE CRIMES COMMITTED AGAINST OUR FATHERS AND OUR BROTHERS.
MANY YEARS AGO...
YOU HAVE CAPTURED AND ENSLAVED TENS OF THOUSANDS OF OUR PEOPLE!
ENOUGH!
ONLY THE GODS ARE PERFECT, ZANTICUS. ALL MORTALS ARE CAPABLE OF WRONGDOING. THE WISE EXPECT THIS. THEY ARE SURPRISED BY NOTHING.
THE MOMENT WE ALLOW OURSELVES TO HATE OUR FELLOW MEN, THOUGH, WE BECOME FOREIGNERS TO THE WORLD, ALIENATED FROM NATURE AS A WHOLE.
SOMETIMES ARMED CONFLICT MAY BE NECESSARY. NATURE SURELY MEANT, THOUGH, FOR MEN TO LIVE IN PEACE, ZEUS WILLING.
HOW COULD A ROMAN EMPEROR EVER KNOW PEACE WITH SARMATIANS?
INSOFAR AS I AM AUGUSTUS, MY FATHERLAND MAY BE ROME... BUT AS HUMAN BEINGS...WE ARE FELLOW CITIZENS OF THE WORLD.
COUGH!
COUGH!
LORD CAESAR, ARE YOU ALL RIGHT?
MARCUS!

THE
CIVIL
WAR

It is uniquely human to love even those who do us wrong. It happens naturally, if you realize that they are your kinsmen, that they do wrong through ignorance, that soon both of you will die, and above all that the wrongdoer has done you no harm.

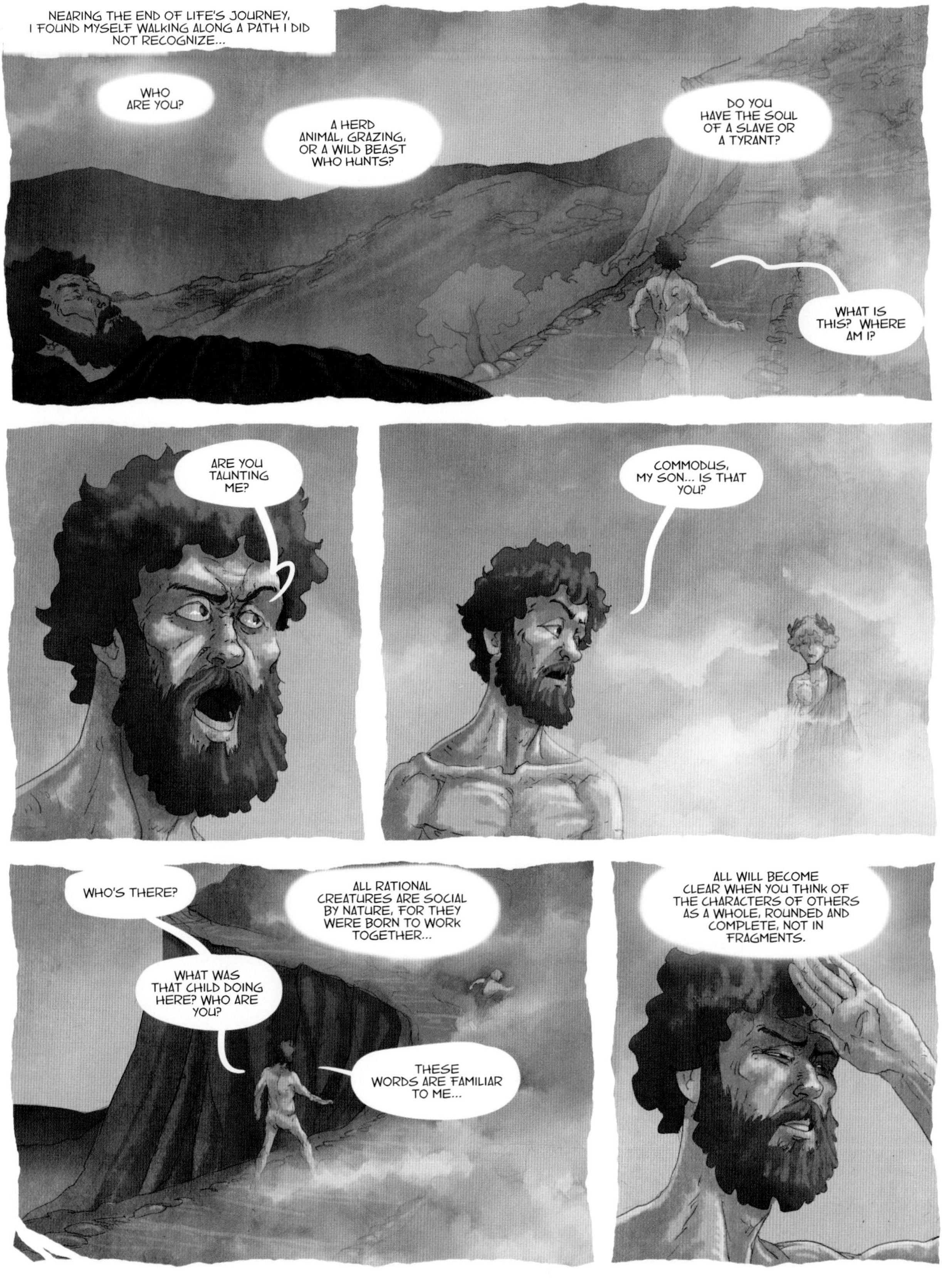
NEARING THE END OF LIFE'S JOURNEY, I FOUND MYSELF WALKING ALONG A PATH I DID NOT RECOGNIZE...
WHO ARE YOU?
A HERD ANIMAL, GRAZING, OR A WILD BEAST WHO HUNTS?
DO YOU HAVE THE SOUL OF A SLAVE OR A TYRANT?
WHAT IS THIS? WHERE AM I?
ARE YOU TAUNTING ME?
COMMODUS, MY SON... IS THAT YOU?
WHO'S THERE?
ALL RATIONAL CREATURES ARE SOCIAL BY NATURE, FOR THEY WERE BORN TO WORK TOGETHER...
WHAT WAS THAT CHILD DOING HERE? WHO ARE YOU?
THESE WORDS ARE FAMILIAR TO ME...
ALL WILL BECOME CLEAR WHEN YOU THINK OF THE CHARACTERS OF OTHERS AS A WHOLE, ROUNDED AND COMPLETE, NOT IN FRAGMENTS.

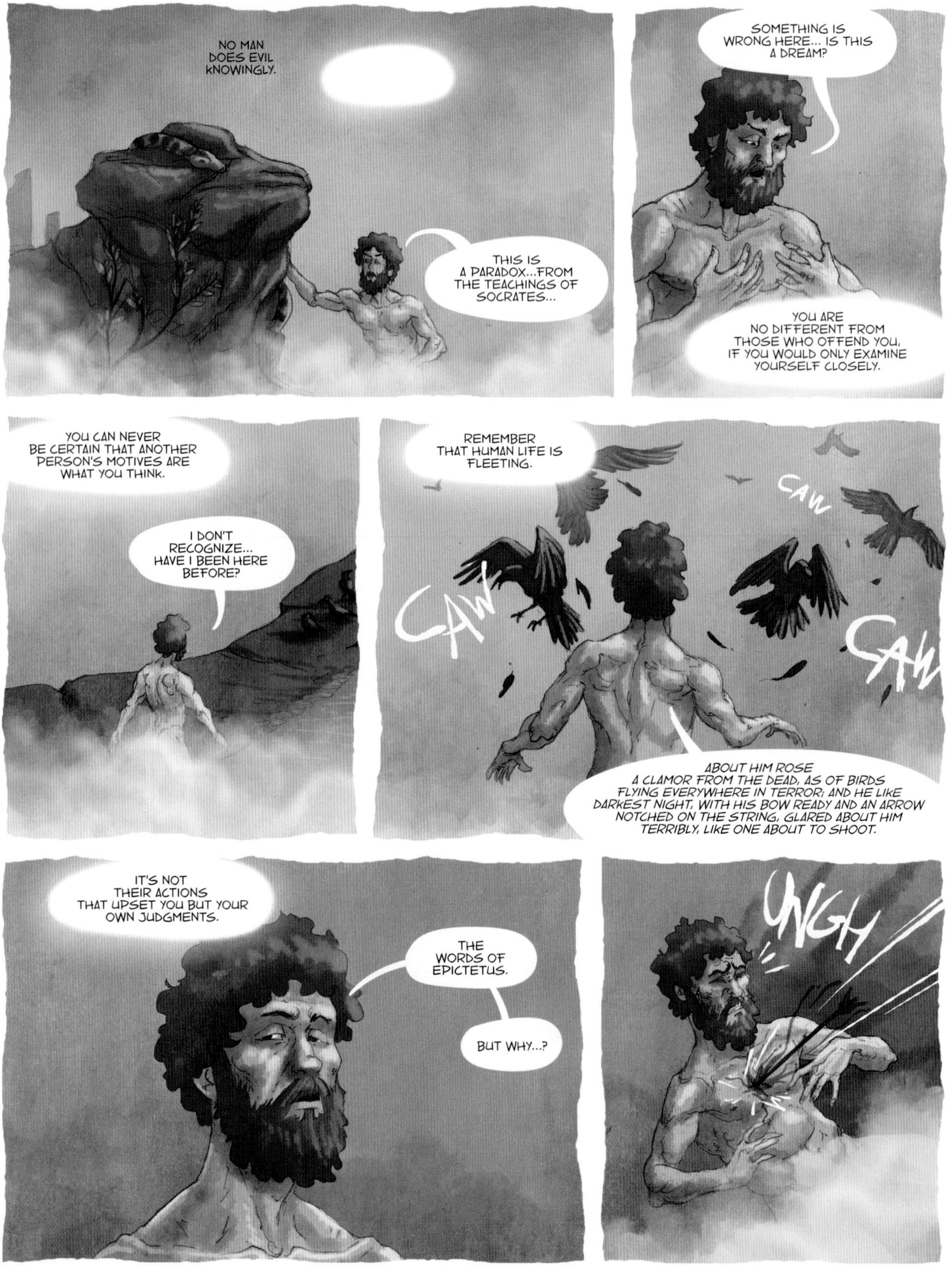
NO MAN DOES EVIL KNOWINGLY.
THIS IS A PARADOX...FROM THE TEACHINGS OF SOCRATES...
SOMETHING IS WRONG HERE... IS THIS A DREAM?
YOU ARE NO DIFFERENT FROM THOSE WHO OFFEND YOU, IF YOU WOULD ONLY EXAMINE YOURSELF CLOSELY.
YOU CAN NEVER BE CERTAIN THAT ANOTHER PERSON'S MOTIVES ARE WHAT YOU THINK.
I DON'T RECOGNIZE... HAVE I BEEN HERE BEFORE?
REMEMBER THAT HUMAN LIFE IS FLEETING.
CAW
CAW
CAW
ABOUT HIM ROSE A CLAMOR FROM THE DEAD, AS OF BIRDS FLYING EVERYWHERE IN TERROR; AND HE LIKE DARKEST NIGHT, WITH HIS BOW READY AND AN ARROW NOTCHED ON THE STRING, GLARED ABOUT HIM TERRIBLY, LIKE ONE ABOUT TO SHOOT.
IT'S NOT THEIR ACTIONS THAT UPSET YOU BUT YOUR OWN JUDGMENTS.
THE WORDS OF EPICTETUS.
BUT WHY...?
UNGH

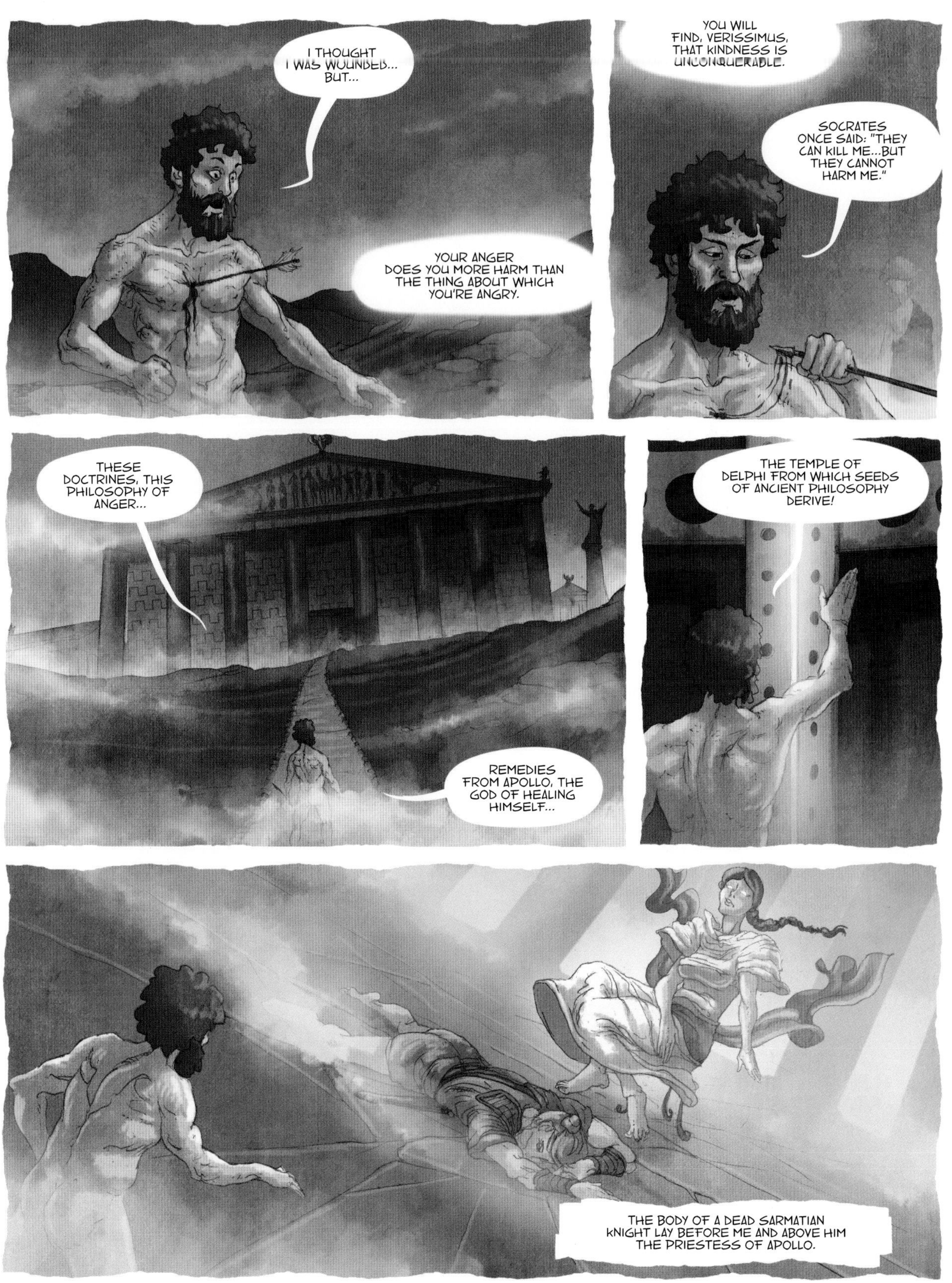
I THOUGHT I WAS WOUNDED... BUT...
YOUR ANGER DOES YOU MORE HARM THAN THE THING ABOUT WHICH YOU'RE ANGRY.
YOU WILL FIND, VERISSIMUS, THAT KINDNESS IS UNCONQUERABLE.
SOCRATES ONCE SAID: "THEY CAN KILL ME...BUT THEY CANNOT HARM ME."
THESE DOCTRINES, THIS PHILOSOPHY OF ANGER...
REMEDIES FROM APOLLO, THE GOD OF HEALING HIMSELF...
THE TEMPLE OF DELPHI FROM WHICH SEEDS OF ANCIENT PHILOSOPHY DERIVE!
THE BODY OF A DEAD SARMATIAN KNIGHT LAY BEFORE ME AND ABOVE HIM THE PRIESTESS OF APOLLO.

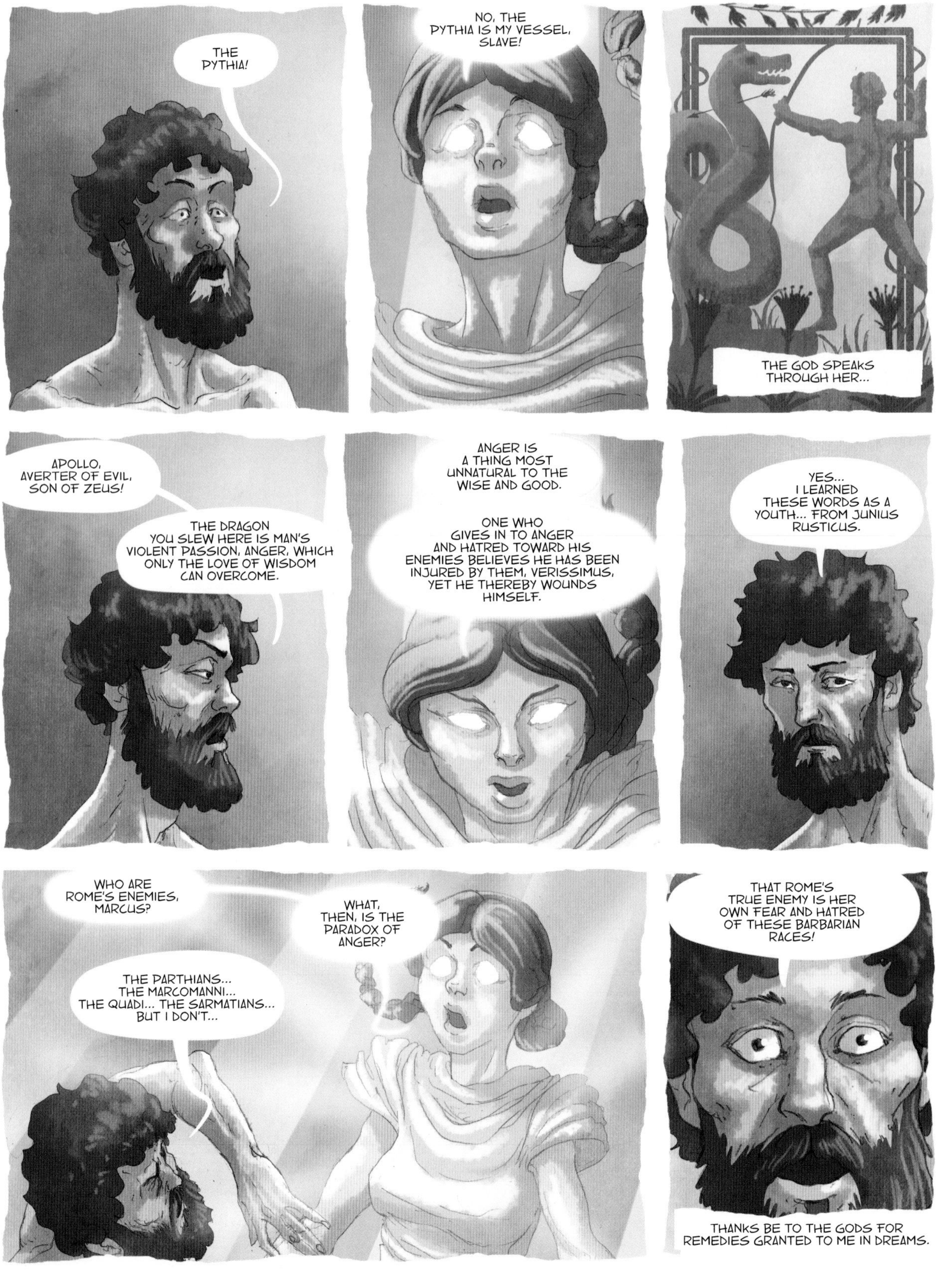
THE PYTHIA!
NO, THE PYTHIA IS MY VESSEL, SLAVE!
THE GOD SPEAKS THROUGH HER...
APOLLO, AVERTER OF EVIL, SON OF ZEUS!
THE DRAGON YOU SLEW HERE IS MAN'S VIOLENT PASSION, ANGER, WHICH ONLY THE LOVE OF WISDOM CAN OVERCOME.
ANGER IS A THING MOST UNNATURAL TO THE WISE AND GOOD.
ONE WHO GIVES IN TO ANGER AND HATRED TOWARD HIS ENEMIES BELIEVES HE HAS BEEN INJURED BY THEM, VERISSIMUS, YET HE THEREBY WOUNDS HIMSELF.
YES... I LEARNED THESE WORDS AS A YOUTH... FROM JUNIUS RUSTICUS.
WHO ARE ROME'S ENEMIES, MARCUS?
THE PARTHIANS... THE MARCOMANNI... THE QUADI... THE SARMATIANS... BUT I DON'T...
WHAT, THEN, IS THE PARADOX OF ANGER?
THAT ROME'S TRUE ENEMY IS HER OWN FEAR AND HATRED OF THESE BARBARIAN RACES!
THANKS BE TO THE GODS FOR REMEDIES GRANTED TO ME IN DREAMS.

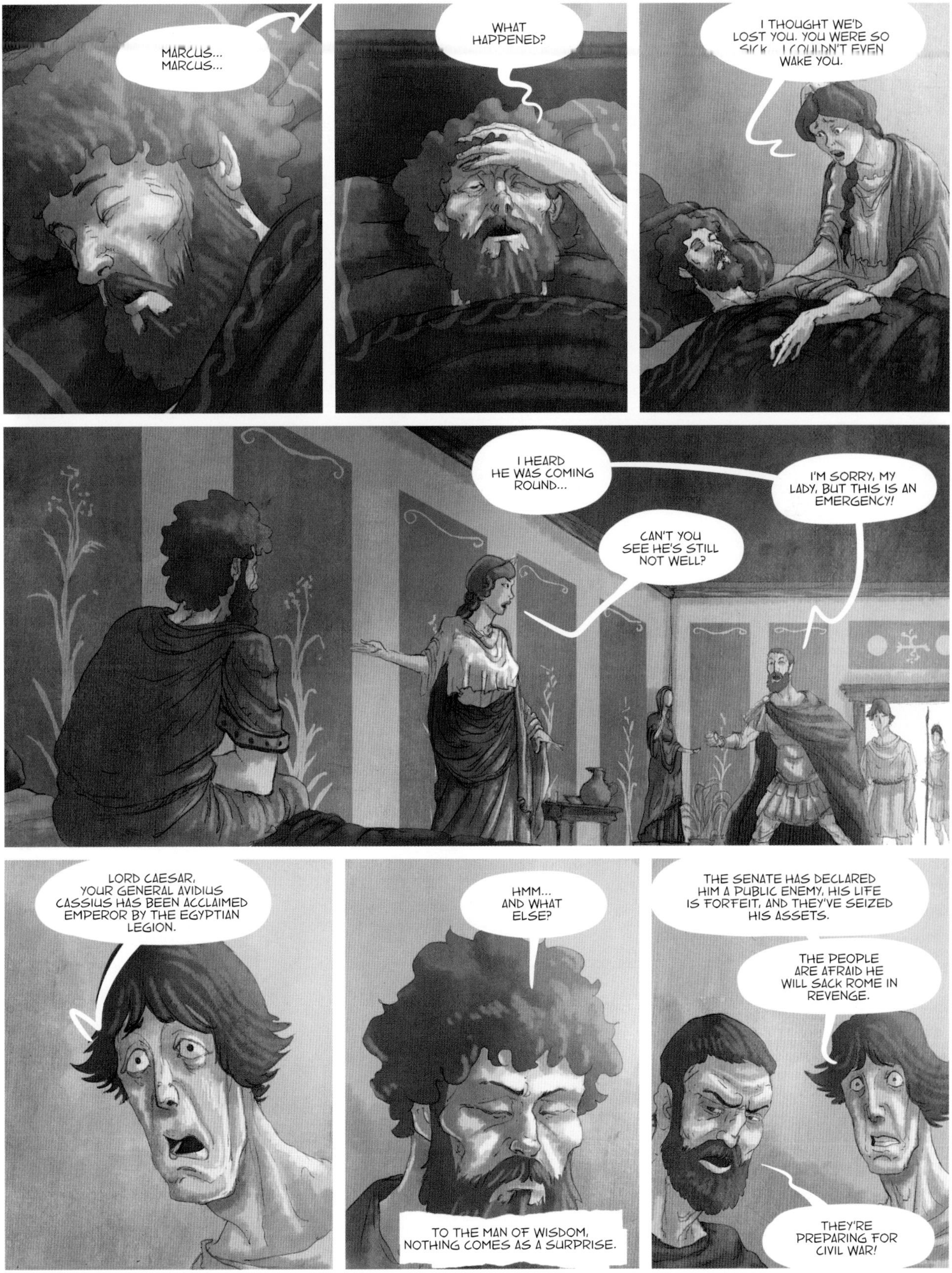
MARCUS... MARCUS...
WHAT HAPPENED?
I THOUGHT WE'D LOST YOU. YOU WERE SO SICK... I COULDN'T EVEN WAKE YOU.
I HEARD HE WAS COMING ROUND...
I'M SORRY, MY LADY, BUT THIS IS AN EMERGENCY!
CAN'T YOU SEE HE'S STILL NOT WELL?
LORD CAESAR, YOUR GENERAL AVIDIUS CASSIUS HAS BEEN ACCLAIMED EMPEROR BY THE EGYPTIAN LEGION.
HMM... AND WHAT ELSE?
TO THE MAN OF WISDOM, NOTHING COMES AS A SURPRISE.
THE SENATE HAS DECLARED HIM A PUBLIC ENEMY, HIS LIFE IS FORFEIT, AND THEY'VE SEIZED HIS ASSETS.
THE PEOPLE ARE AFRAID HE WILL SACK ROME IN REVENGE.
THEY'RE PREPARING FOR CIVIL WAR!

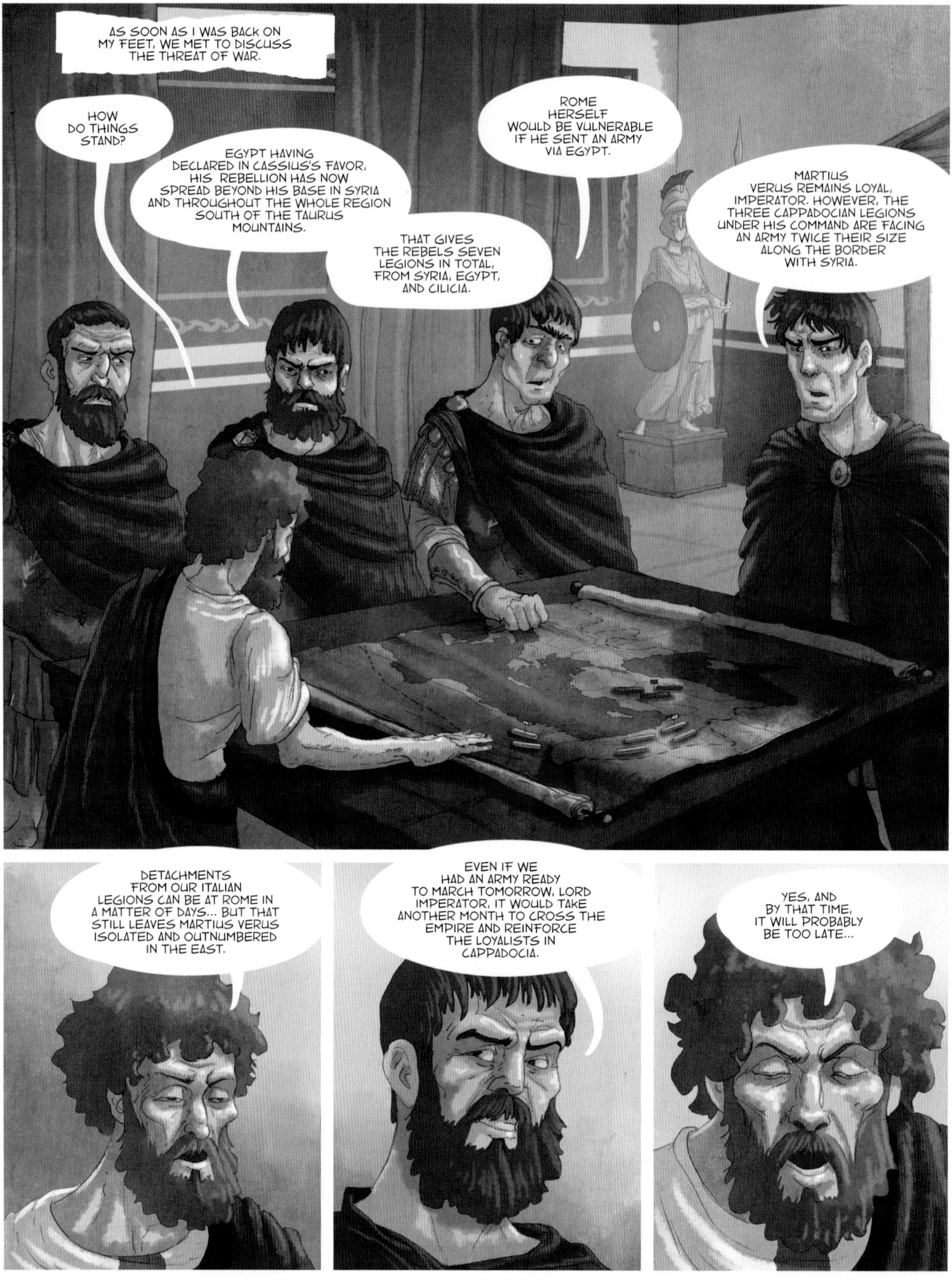
AS SOON AS I WAS BACK ON MY FEET, WE MET TO DISCUSS THE THREAT OF WAR.
HOW DO THINGS STAND?
EGYPT HAVING DECLARED IN CASSIUS'S FAVOR, HIS REBELLION HAS NOW SPREAD BEYOND HIS BASE IN SYRIA AND THROUGHOUT THE WHOLE REGION SOUTH OF THE TAURUS MOUNTAINS.
THAT GIVES THE REBELS SEVEN LEGIONS IN TOTAL, FROM SYRIA, EGYPT, AND CILICIA.
ROME HERSELF WOULD BE VULNERABLE IF HE SENT AN ARMY VIA EGYPT.
MARTIUS VERUS REMAINS LOYAL, IMPERATOR. HOWEVER, THE THREE CAPPADOCIAN LEGIONS UNDER HIS COMMAND ARE FACING AN ARMY TWICE THEIR SIZE ALONG THE BORDER WITH SYRIA.
DETACHMENTS FROM OUR ITALIAN LEGIONS CAN BE AT ROME IN A MATTER OF DAYS... BUT THAT STILL LEAVES MARTIUS VERUS ISOLATED AND OUTNUMBERED IN THE EAST.
EVEN IF WE HAD AN ARMY READY TO MARCH TOMORROW, LORD IMPERATOR, IT WOULD TAKE ANOTHER MONTH TO CROSS THE EMPIRE AND REINFORCE THE LOYALISTS IN CAPPADOCIA.
YES, AND BY THAT TIME, IT WILL PROBABLY BE TOO LATE...

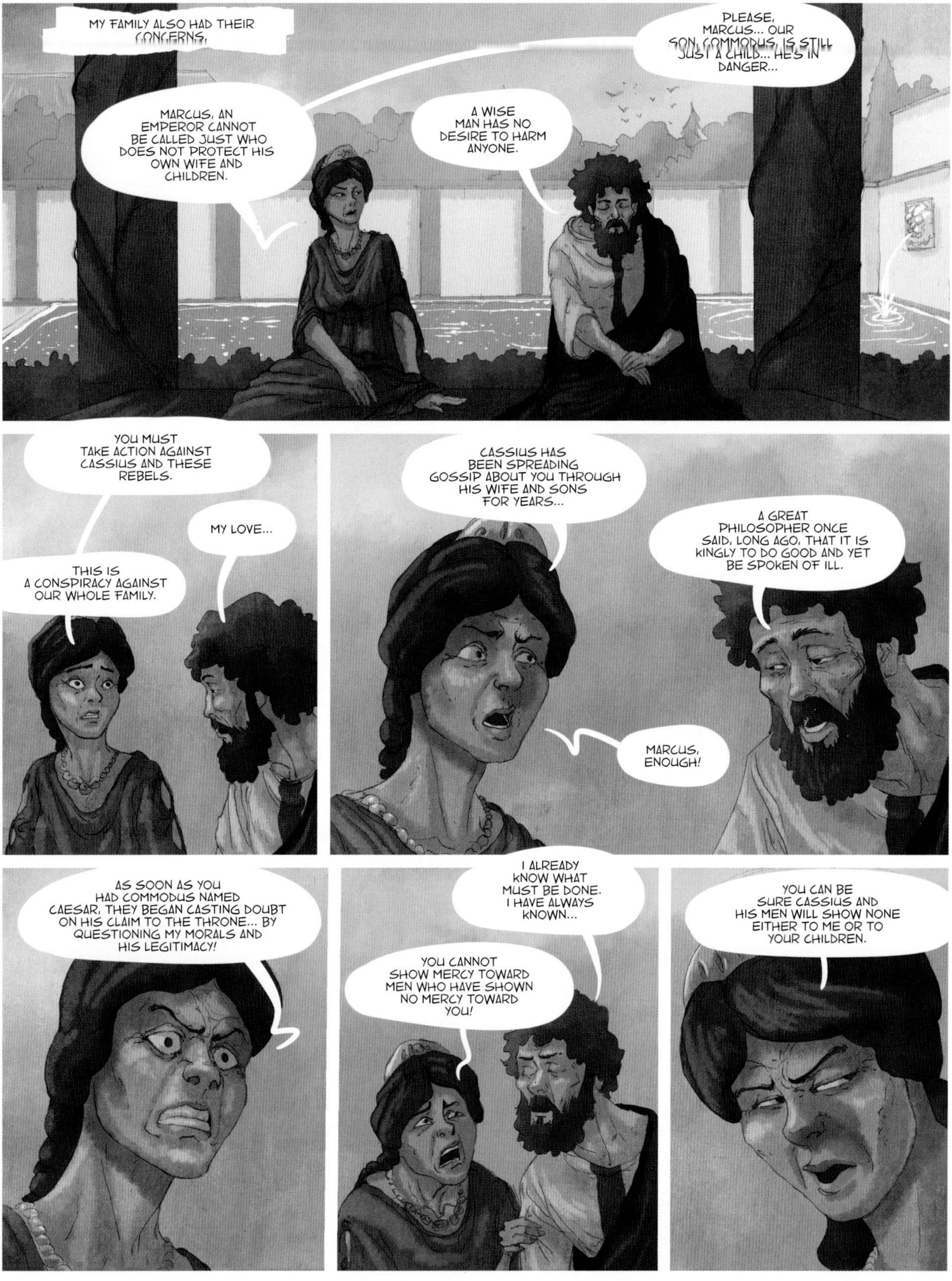
MY FAMILY ALSO HAD THEIR CONCERNS.
MARCUS, AN EMPEROR CANNOT BE CALLED JUST WHO DOES NOT PROTECT HIS OWN WIFE AND CHILDREN.
PLEASE, MARCUS... OUR SON, COMMODUS, IS STILL JUST A CHILD... HE'S IN DANGER...
A WISE MAN HAS NO DESIRE TO HARM ANYONE.
YOU MUST TAKE ACTION AGAINST CASSIUS AND THESE REBELS.
THIS IS A CONSPIRACY AGAINST OUR WHOLE FAMILY.
MY LOVE...
CASSIUS HAS BEEN SPREADING GOSSIP ABOUT YOU THROUGH HIS WIFE AND SONS FOR YEARS...
A GREAT PHILOSOPHER ONCE SAID, LONG AGO, THAT IT IS KINGLY TO DO GOOD AND YET BE SPOKEN OF ILL.
MARCUS, ENOUGH!
AS SOON AS YOU HAD COMMODUS NAMED CAESAR, THEY BEGAN CASTING DOUBT ON HIS CLAIM TO THE THRONE... BY QUESTIONING MY MORALS AND HIS LEGITIMACY!
YOU CANNOT SHOW MERCY TOWARD MEN WHO HAVE SHOWN NO MERCY TOWARD YOU!
I ALREADY KNOW WHAT MUST BE DONE. I HAVE ALWAYS KNOWN...
YOU CAN BE SURE CASSIUS AND HIS MEN WILL SHOW NONE EITHER TO ME OR TO YOUR CHILDREN.

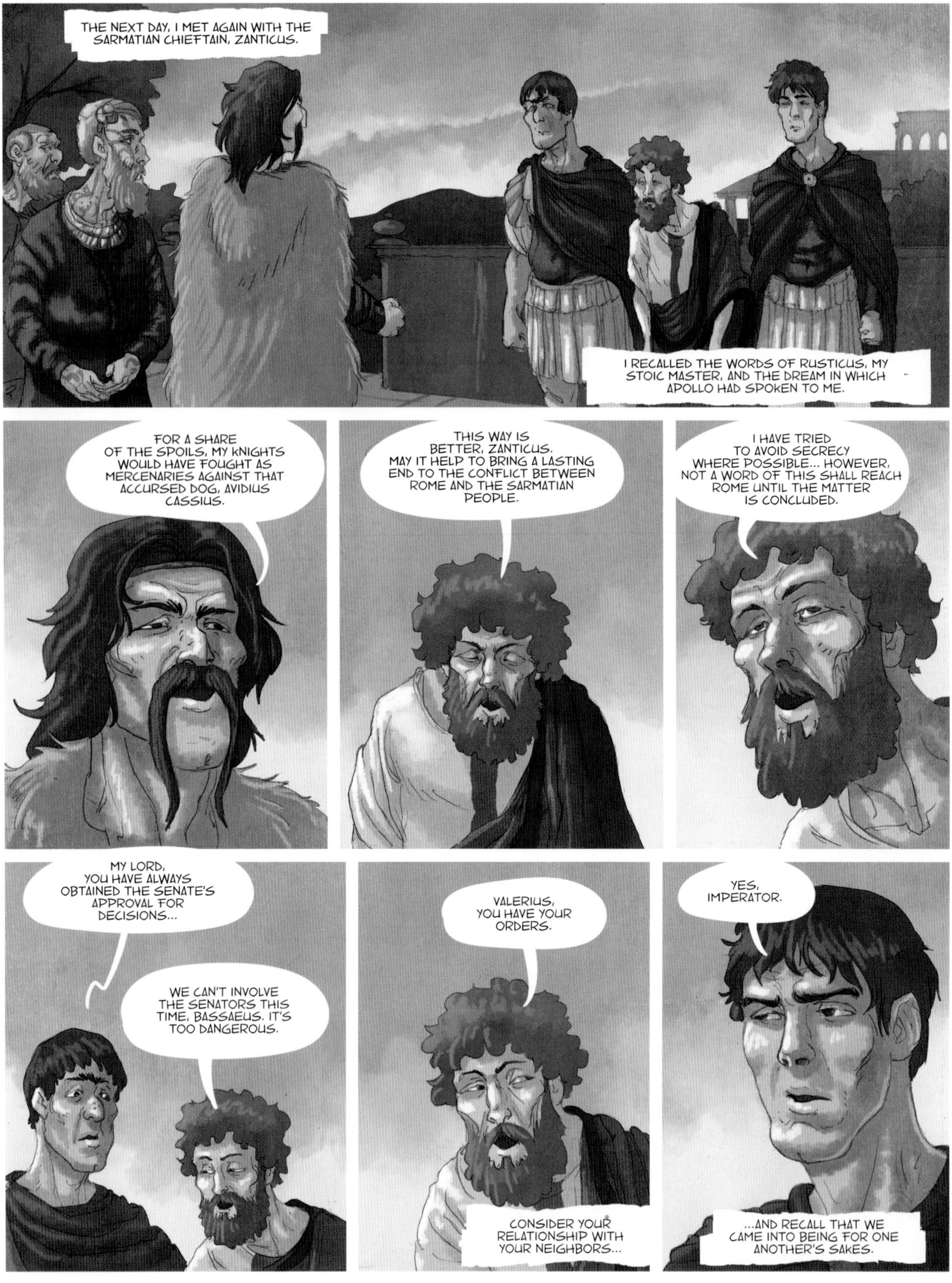
THE NEXT DAY, I MET AGAIN WITH THE SARMATIAN CHIEFTAIN, ZANTICUS.
I RECALLED THE WORDS OF RUSTICUS, MY STOIC MASTER, AND THE DREAM IN WHICH APOLLO HAD SPOKEN TO ME.
FOR A SHARE OF THE SPOILS, MY KNIGHTS WOULD HAVE FOUGHT AS MERCENARIES AGAINST THAT ACCURSED DOG, AVIDIUS CASSIUS.
THIS WAY IS BETTER, ZANTICUS. MAY IT HELP TO BRING A LASTING END TO THE CONFLICT BETWEEN ROME AND THE SARMATIAN PEOPLE.
I HAVE TRIED TO AVOID SECRECY WHERE POSSIBLE... HOWEVER, NOT A WORD OF THIS SHALL REACH ROME UNTIL THE MATTER IS CONCLUDED.
MY LORD, YOU HAVE ALWAYS OBTAINED THE SENATE'S APPROVAL FOR DECISIONS...
WE CAN'T INVOLVE THE SENATORS THIS TIME, BASSAEUS. IT'S TOO DANGEROUS.
VALERIUS, YOU HAVE YOUR ORDERS.
CONSIDER YOUR RELATIONSHIP WITH YOUR NEIGHBORS...
YES, IMPERATOR.
...AND RECALL THAT WE CAME INTO BEING FOR ONE ANOTHER'S SAKES.

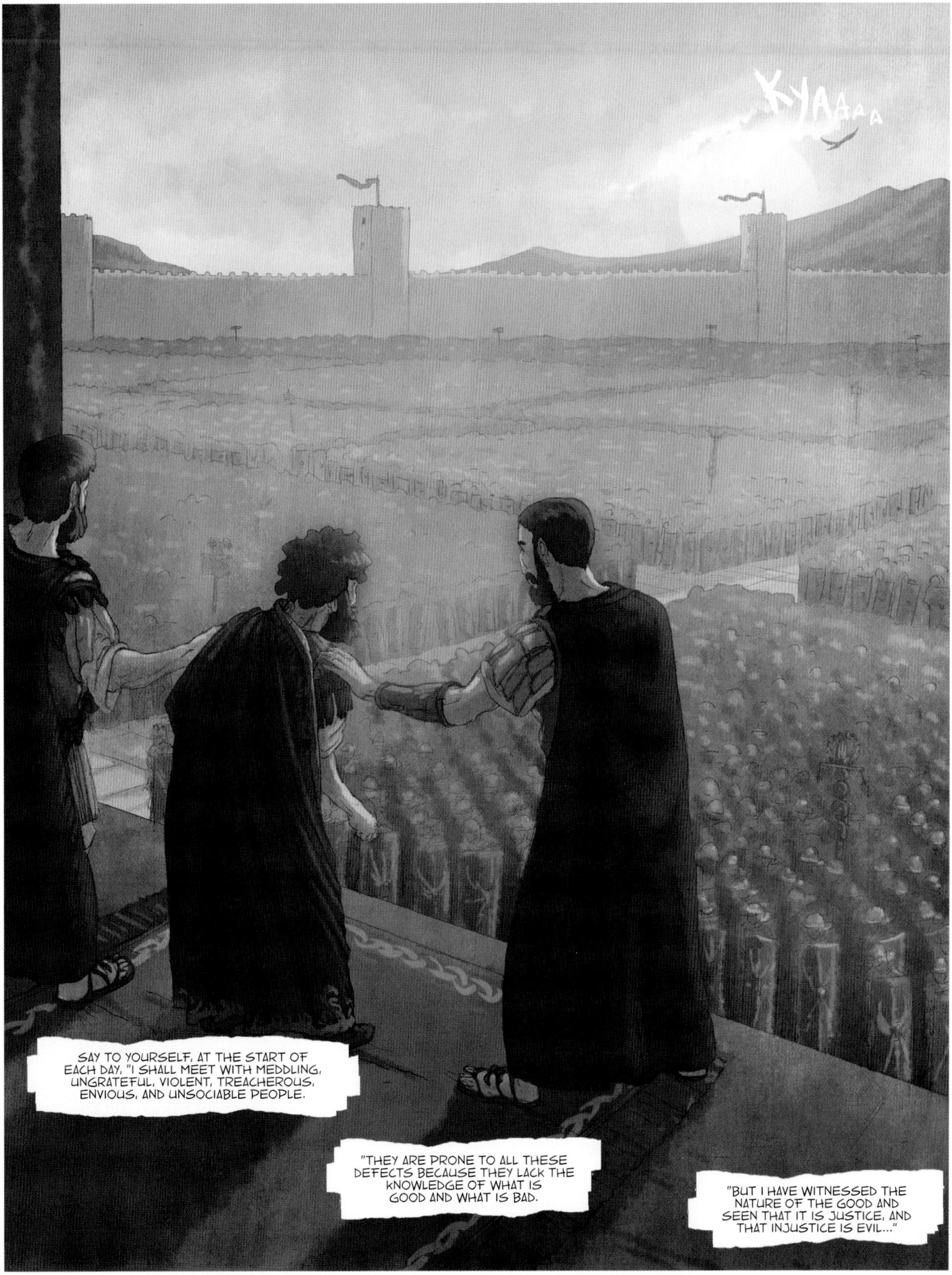
KYAAAAA
SAY TO YOURSELF, AT THE START OF EACH DAY, "I SHALL MEET WITH MEDDLING, UNGRATEFUL, VIOLENT, TREACHEROUS, ENVIOUS, AND UNSOCIABLE PEOPLE.
"THEY ARE PRONE TO ALL THESE DEFECTS BECAUSE THEY LACK THE KNOWLEDGE OF WHAT IS GOOD AND WHAT IS BAD.
"BUT I HAVE WITNESSED THE NATURE OF THE GOOD AND SEEN THAT IT IS JUSTICE, AND THAT INJUSTICE IS EVIL..."

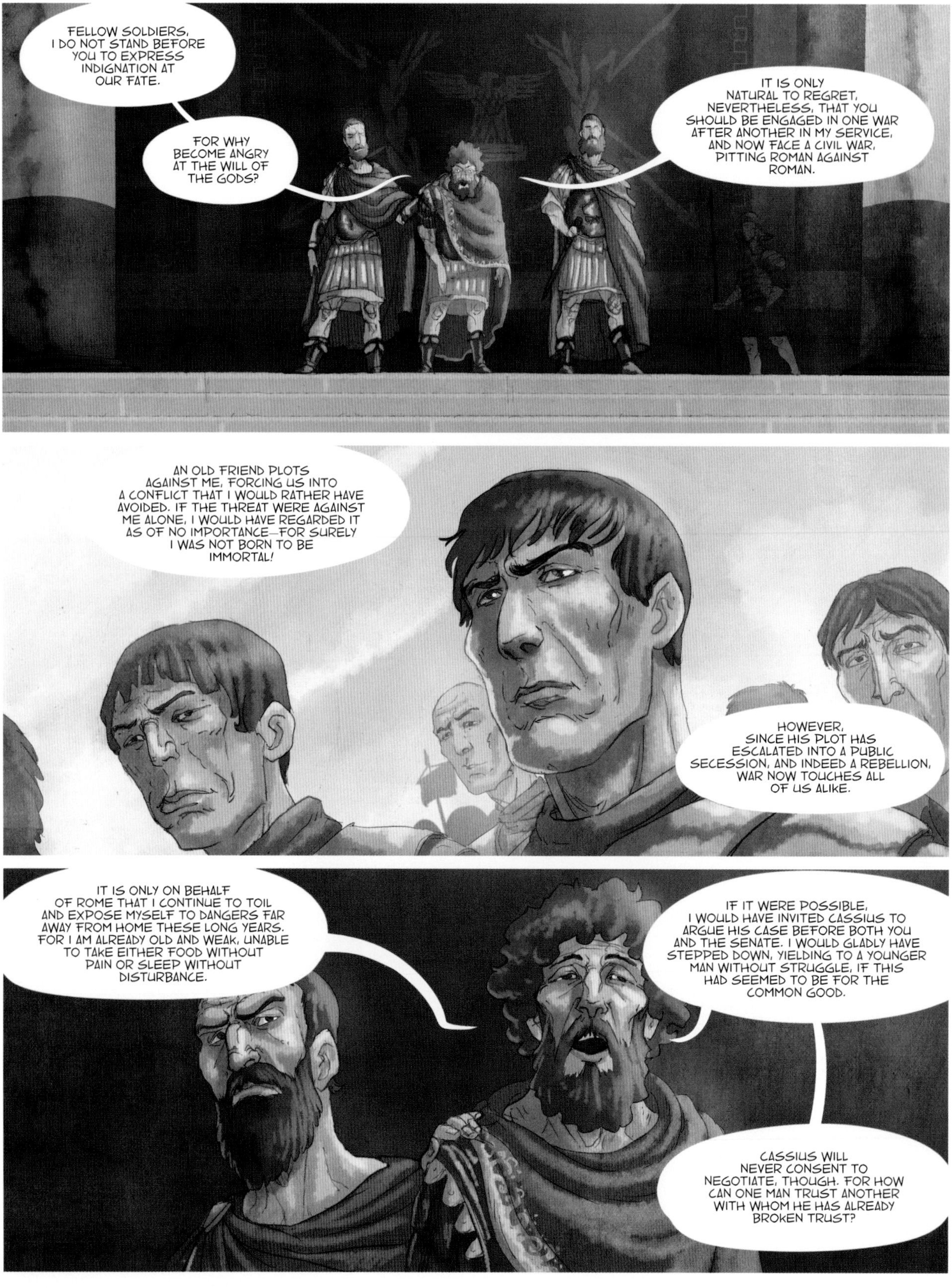
FELLOW SOLDIERS, I DO NOT STAND BEFORE YOU TO EXPRESS INDIGNATION AT OUR FATE.
FOR WHY BECOME ANGRY AT THE WILL OF THE GODS?
IT IS ONLY NATURAL TO REGRET, NEVERTHELESS, THAT YOU SHOULD BE ENGAGED IN ONE WAR AFTER ANOTHER IN MY SERVICE, AND NOW FACE A CIVIL WAR, PITTING ROMAN AGAINST ROMAN.
AN OLD FRIEND PLOTS AGAINST ME, FORCING US INTO A CONFLICT THAT I WOULD RATHER HAVE AVOIDED. IF THE THREAT WERE AGAINST ME ALONE, I WOULD HAVE REGARDED IT AS OF NO IMPORTANCE—FOR SURELY I WAS NOT BORN TO BE IMMORTAL!
HOWEVER, SINCE HIS PLOT HAS ESCALATED INTO A PUBLIC SECESSION, AND INDEED A REBELLION, WAR NOW TOUCHES ALL OF US ALIKE.
IT IS ONLY ON BEHALF OF ROME THAT I CONTINUE TO TOIL AND EXPOSE MYSELF TO DANGERS FAR AWAY FROM HOME THESE LONG YEARS. FOR I AM ALREADY OLD AND WEAK, UNABLE TO TAKE EITHER FOOD WITHOUT PAIN OR SLEEP WITHOUT DISTURBANCE.
IF IT WERE POSSIBLE, I WOULD HAVE INVITED CASSIUS TO ARGUE HIS CASE BEFORE BOTH YOU AND THE SENATE. I WOULD GLADLY HAVE STEPPED DOWN, YIELDING TO A YOUNGER MAN WITHOUT STRUGGLE, IF THIS HAD SEEMED TO BE FOR THE COMMON GOOD.
CASSIUS WILL NEVER CONSENT TO NEGOTIATE, THOUGH. FOR HOW CAN ONE MAN TRUST ANOTHER WITH WHOM HE HAS ALREADY BROKEN TRUST?

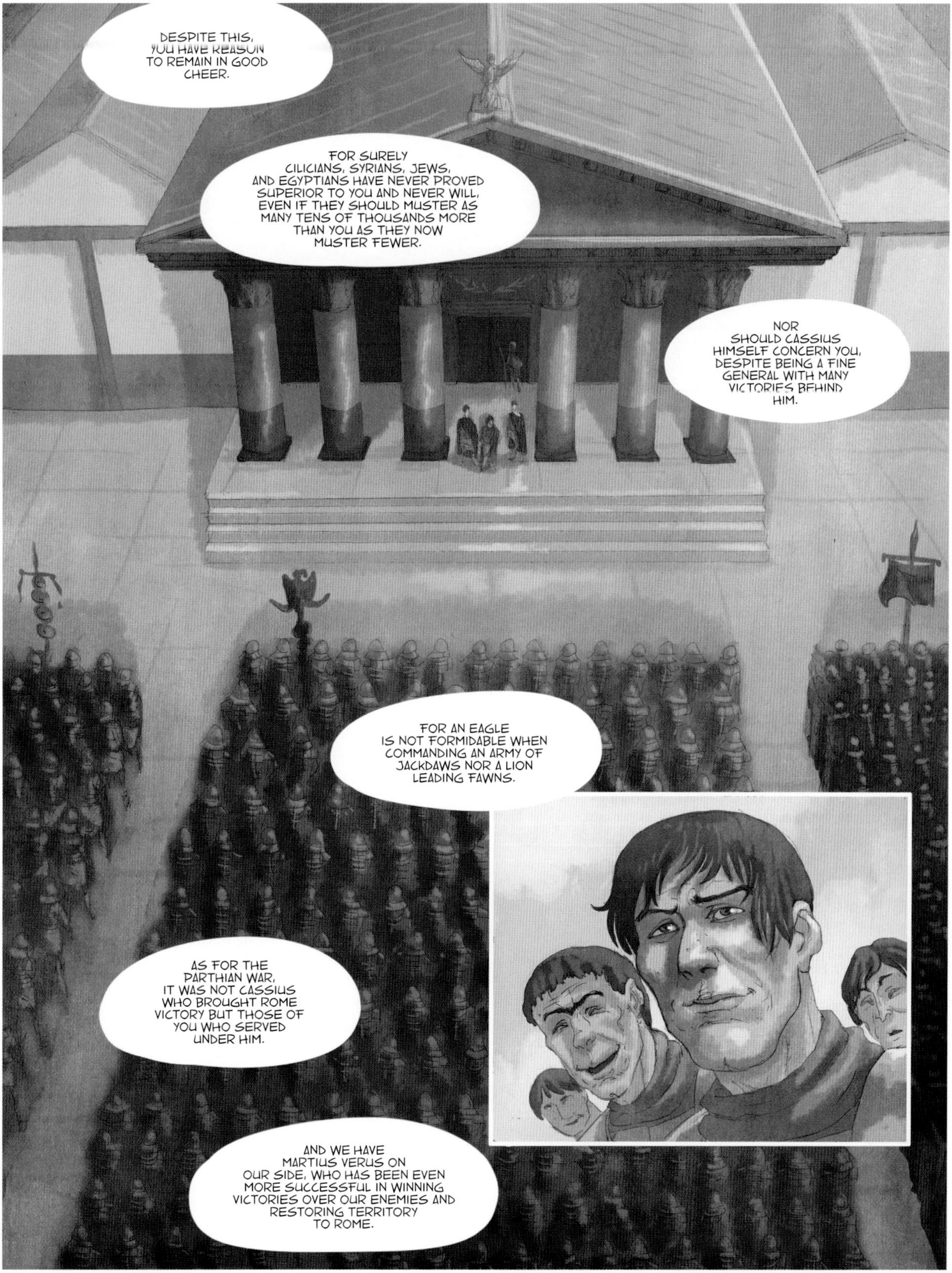
DESPITE THIS, YOU HAVE REASON TO REMAIN IN GOOD CHEER.
FOR SURELY CILICIANS, SYRIANS, JEWS, AND EGYPTIANS HAVE NEVER PROVED SUPERIOR TO YOU AND NEVER WILL, EVEN IF THEY SHOULD MUSTER AS MANY TENS OF THOUSANDS MORE THAN YOU AS THEY NOW MUSTER FEWER.
NOR SHOULD CASSIUS HIMSELF CONCERN YOU, DESPITE BEING A FINE GENERAL WITH MANY VICTORIES BEHIND HIM.
FOR AN EAGLE IS NOT FORMIDABLE WHEN COMMANDING AN ARMY OF JACKDAWS NOR A LION LEADING FAWNS.
AS FOR THE PARTHIAN WAR, IT WAS NOT CASSIUS WHO BROUGHT ROME VICTORY BUT THOSE OF YOU WHO SERVED UNDER HIM.
AND WE HAVE MARTIUS VERUS ON OUR SIDE, WHO HAS BEEN EVEN MORE SUCCESSFUL IN WINNING VICTORIES OVER OUR ENEMIES AND RESTORING TERRITORY TO ROME.

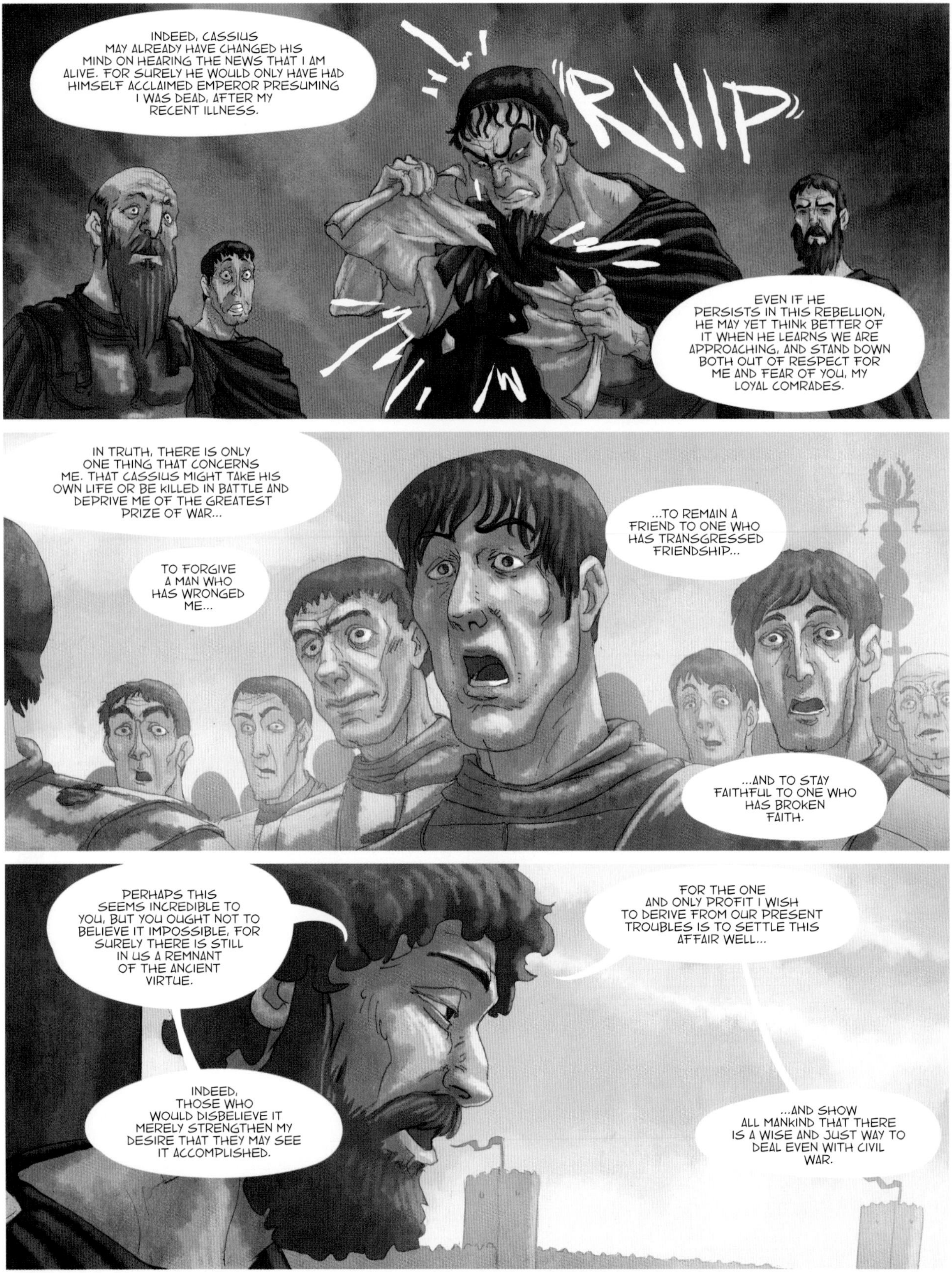
INDEED, CASSIUS MAY ALREADY HAVE CHANGED HIS MIND ON HEARING THE NEWS THAT I AM ALIVE. FOR SURELY HE WOULD ONLY HAVE HAD HIMSELF ACCLAIMED EMPEROR PRESUMING I WAS DEAD, AFTER MY RECENT ILLNESS.
RIIIP
EVEN IF HE PERSISTS IN THIS REBELLION, HE MAY YET THINK BETTER OF IT WHEN HE LEARNS WE ARE APPROACHING, AND STAND DOWN BOTH OUT OF RESPECT FOR ME AND FEAR OF YOU, MY LOYAL COMRADES.
IN TRUTH, THERE IS ONLY ONE THING THAT CONCERNS ME. THAT CASSIUS MIGHT TAKE HIS OWN LIFE OR BE KILLED IN BATTLE AND DEPRIVE ME OF THE GREATEST PRIZE OF WAR...
TO FORGIVE A MAN WHO HAS WRONGED ME...
...TO REMAIN A FRIEND TO ONE WHO HAS TRANSGRESSED FRIENDSHIP...
...AND TO STAY FAITHFUL TO ONE WHO HAS BROKEN FAITH.
PERHAPS THIS SEEMS INCREDIBLE TO YOU, BUT YOU OUGHT NOT TO BELIEVE IT IMPOSSIBLE, FOR SURELY THERE IS STILL IN US A REMNANT OF THE ANCIENT VIRTUE.
INDEED, THOSE WHO WOULD DISBELIEVE IT MERELY STRENGTHEN MY DESIRE THAT THEY MAY SEE IT ACCOMPLISHED.
FOR THE ONE AND ONLY PROFIT I WISH TO DERIVE FROM OUR PRESENT TROUBLES IS TO SETTLE THIS AFFAIR WELL...
...AND SHOW ALL MANKIND THAT THERE IS A WISE AND JUST WAY TO DEAL EVEN WITH CIVIL WAR.

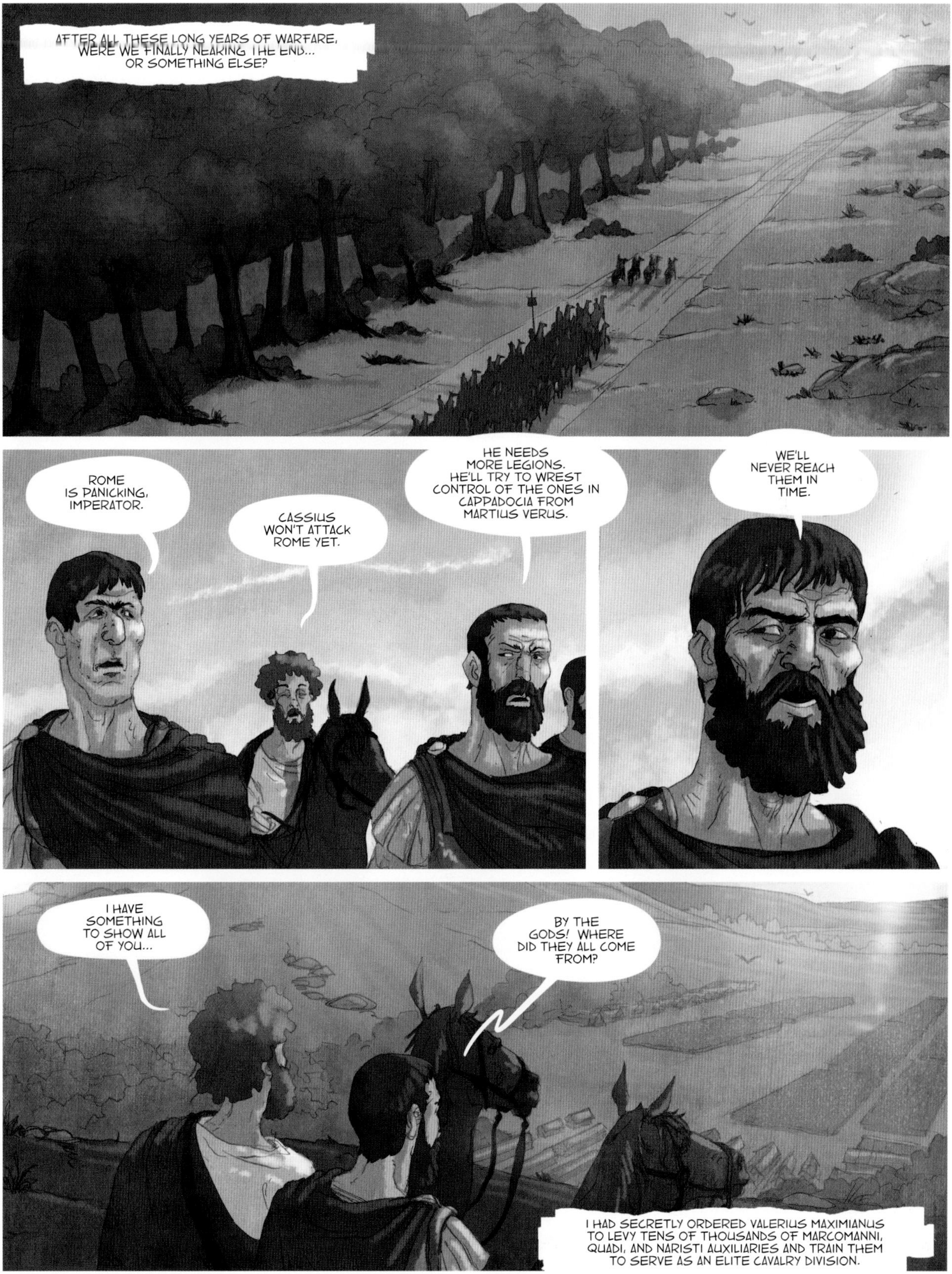
AFTER ALL THESE LONG YEARS OF WARFARE, WERE WE FINALLY NEARING THE END... OR SOMETHING ELSE?
ROME IS PANICKING, IMPERATOR.
CASSIUS WON'T ATTACK ROME YET.
HE NEEDS MORE LEGIONS. HE'LL TRY TO WREST CONTROL OF THE ONES IN CAPPADOCIA FROM MARTIUS VERUS.
WE'LL NEVER REACH THEM IN TIME.
I HAVE SOMETHING TO SHOW ALL OF YOU...
BY THE GODS! WHERE DID THEY ALL COME FROM?
I HAD SECRETLY ORDERED VALERIUS MAXIMIANUS TO LEVY TENS OF THOUSANDS OF MARCOMANNI, QUADI, AND NARISTI AUXILIARIES AND TRAIN THEM TO SERVE AS AN ELITE CAVALRY DIVISION.

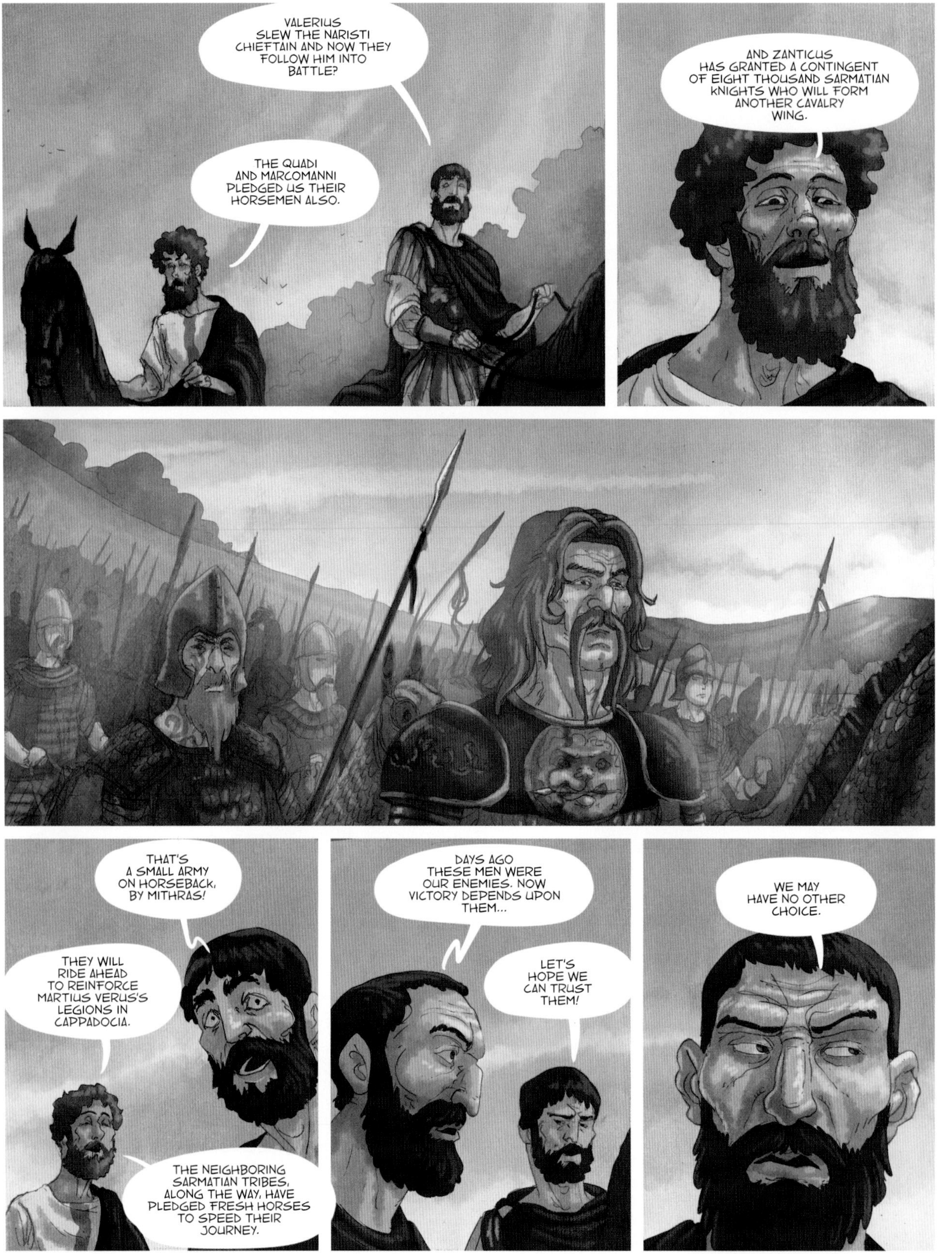
VALERIUS SLEW THE NARISTI CHIEFTAIN AND NOW THEY FOLLOW HIM INTO BATTLE?
THE QUADI AND MARCOMANNI PLEDGED US THEIR HORSEMEN ALSO.
AND ZANTICUS HAS GRANTED A CONTINGENT OF EIGHT THOUSAND SARMATIAN KNIGHTS WHO WILL FORM ANOTHER CAVALRY WING.
THAT'S A SMALL ARMY ON HORSEBACK, BY MITHRAS!
THEY WILL RIDE AHEAD TO REINFORCE MARTIUS VERUS'S LEGIONS IN CAPPADOCIA.
THE NEIGHBORING SARMATIAN TRIBES, ALONG THE WAY, HAVE PLEDGED FRESH HORSES TO SPEED THEIR JOURNEY.
DAYS AGO THESE MEN WERE OUR ENEMIES. NOW VICTORY DEPENDS UPON THEM...
LET'S HOPE WE CAN TRUST THEM!
WE MAY HAVE NO OTHER CHOICE.

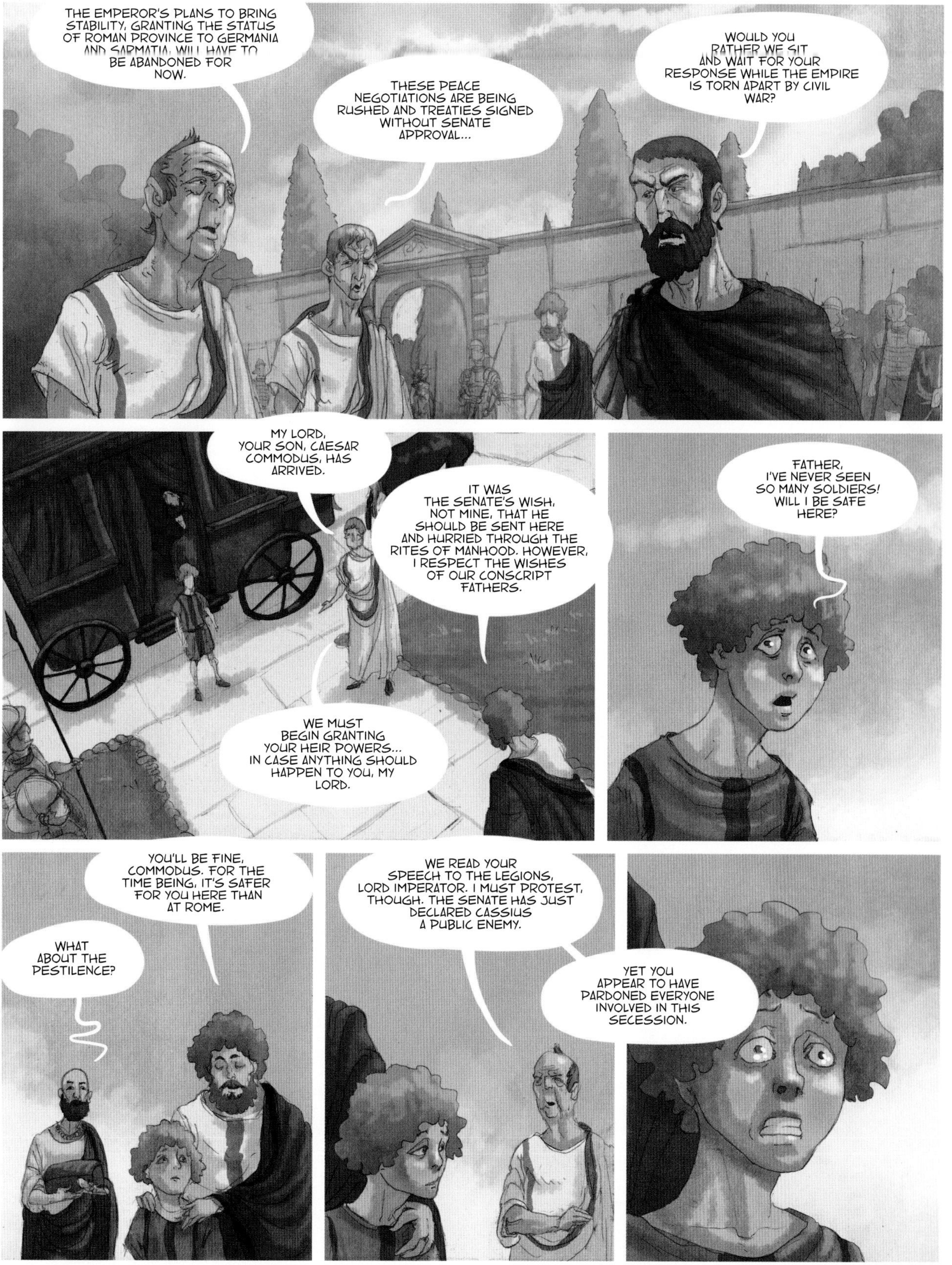
THE EMPEROR'S PLANS TO BRING STABILITY, GRANTING THE STATUS OF ROMAN PROVINCE TO GERMANIA AND SARMATIA, WILL HAVE TO BE ABANDONED FOR NOW.
THESE PEACE NEGOTIATIONS ARE BEING RUSHED AND TREATIES SIGNED WITHOUT SENATE APPROVAL...
WOULD YOU RATHER WE SIT AND WAIT FOR YOUR RESPONSE WHILE THE EMPIRE IS TORN APART BY CIVIL WAR?
MY LORD, YOUR SON, CAESAR COMMODUS, HAS ARRIVED.
IT WAS THE SENATE'S WISH, NOT MINE, THAT HE SHOULD BE SENT HERE AND HURRIED THROUGH THE RITES OF MANHOOD. HOWEVER, I RESPECT THE WISHES OF OUR CONSCRIPT FATHERS.
WE MUST BEGIN GRANTING YOUR HEIR POWERS... IN CASE ANYTHING SHOULD HAPPEN TO YOU, MY LORD.
FATHER, I'VE NEVER SEEN SO MANY SOLDIERS! WILL I BE SAFE HERE?
YOU'LL BE FINE, COMMODUS. FOR THE TIME BEING, IT'S SAFER FOR YOU HERE THAN AT ROME.
WHAT ABOUT THE PESTILENCE?
WE READ YOUR SPEECH TO THE LEGIONS, LORD IMPERATOR. I MUST PROTEST, THOUGH. THE SENATE HAS JUST DECLARED CASSIUS A PUBLIC ENEMY.
YET YOU APPEAR TO HAVE PARDONED EVERYONE INVOLVED IN THIS SECESSION.

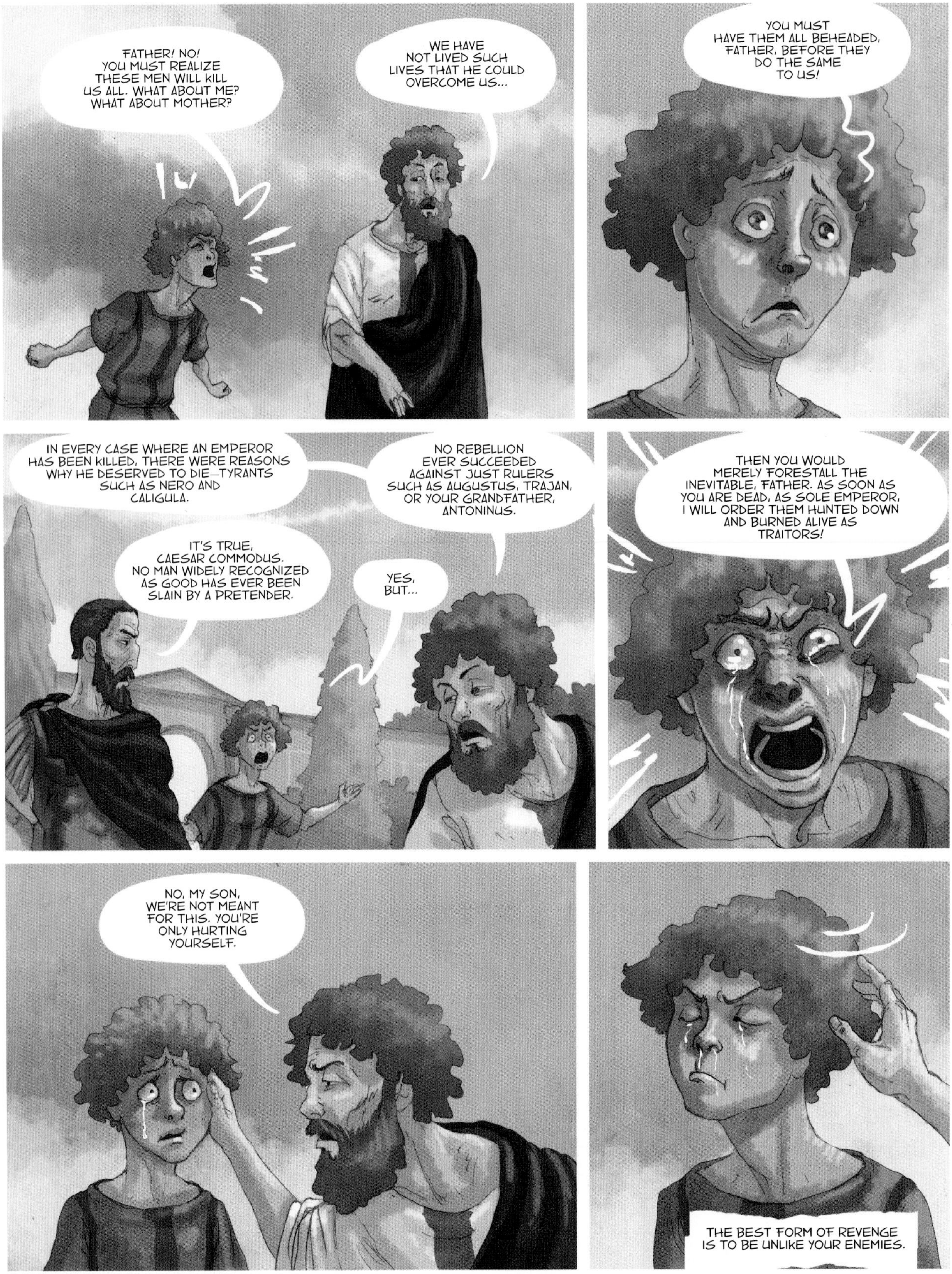
FATHER! NO! YOU MUST REALIZE THESE MEN WILL KILL US ALL. WHAT ABOUT ME? WHAT ABOUT MOTHER?
WE HAVE NOT LIVED SUCH LIVES THAT HE COULD OVERCOME US...
YOU MUST HAVE THEM ALL BEHEADED, FATHER, BEFORE THEY DO THE SAME TO US!
IN EVERY CASE WHERE AN EMPEROR HAS BEEN KILLED, THERE WERE REASONS WHY HE DESERVED TO DIE—TYRANTS SUCH AS NERO AND CALIGULA.
NO REBELLION EVER SUCCEEDED AGAINST JUST RULERS SUCH AS AUGUSTUS, TRAJAN, OR YOUR GRANDFATHER, ANTONINUS.
IT'S TRUE, CAESAR COMMODUS. NO MAN WIDELY RECOGNIZED AS GOOD HAS EVER BEEN SLAIN BY A PRETENDER.
YES, BUT...
THEN YOU WOULD MERELY FORESTALL THE INEVITABLE, FATHER. AS SOON AS YOU ARE DEAD, AS SOLE EMPEROR, I WILL ORDER THEM HUNTED DOWN AND BURNED ALIVE AS TRAITORS!
NO, MY SON, WE'RE NOT MEANT FOR THIS. YOU'RE ONLY HURTING YOURSELF.
THE BEST FORM OF REVENGE IS TO BE UNLIKE YOUR ENEMIES.

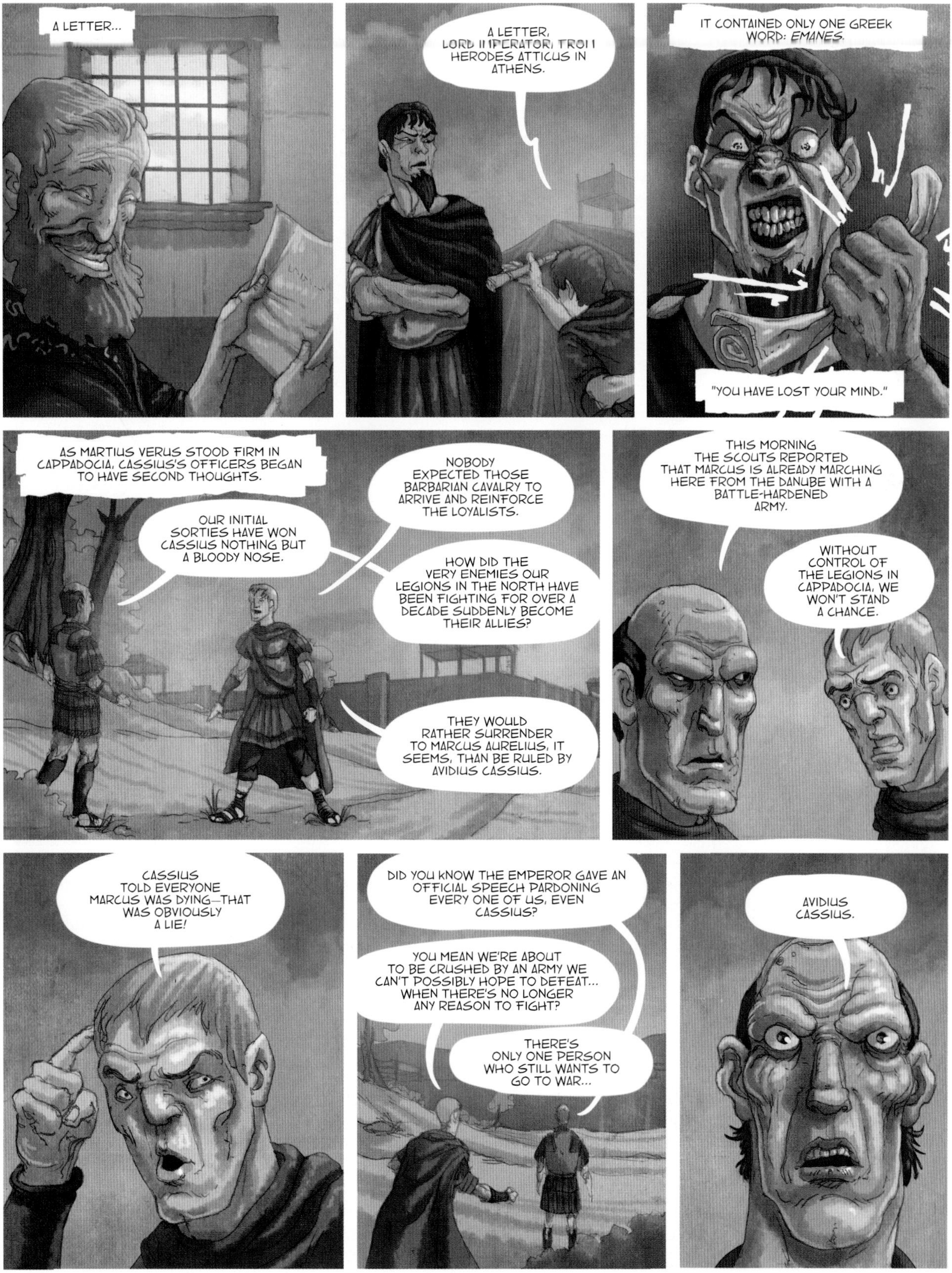
A LETTER...
A LETTER, LORD IMPERATOR, FROM HERODES ATTICUS IN ATHENS.
IT CONTAINED ONLY ONE GREEK WORD: *EMANES*.
"YOU HAVE LOST YOUR MIND."
AS MARTIUS VERUS STOOD FIRM IN CAPPADOCIA, CASSIUS'S OFFICERS BEGAN TO HAVE SECOND THOUGHTS.
OUR INITIAL SORTIES HAVE WON CASSIUS NOTHING BUT A BLOODY NOSE.
NOBODY EXPECTED THOSE BARBARIAN CAVALRY TO ARRIVE AND REINFORCE THE LOYALISTS.
HOW DID THE VERY ENEMIES OUR LEGIONS IN THE NORTH HAVE BEEN FIGHTING FOR OVER A DECADE SUDDENLY BECOME THEIR ALLIES?
THEY WOULD RATHER SURRENDER TO MARCUS AURELIUS, IT SEEMS, THAN BE RULED BY AVIDIUS CASSIUS.
THIS MORNING THE SCOUTS REPORTED THAT MARCUS IS ALREADY MARCHING HERE FROM THE DANUBE WITH A BATTLE-HARDENED ARMY.
WITHOUT CONTROL OF THE LEGIONS IN CAPPADOCIA, WE WON'T STAND A CHANCE.
CASSIUS TOLD EVERYONE MARCUS WAS DYING—THAT WAS OBVIOUSLY A LIE!
DID YOU KNOW THE EMPEROR GAVE AN OFFICIAL SPEECH PARDONING EVERY ONE OF US, EVEN CASSIUS?
YOU MEAN WE'RE ABOUT TO BE CRUSHED BY AN ARMY WE CAN'T POSSIBLY HOPE TO DEFEAT... WHEN THERE'S NO LONGER ANY REASON TO FIGHT?
THERE'S ONLY ONE PERSON WHO STILL WANTS TO GO TO WAR...
AVIDIUS CASSIUS.

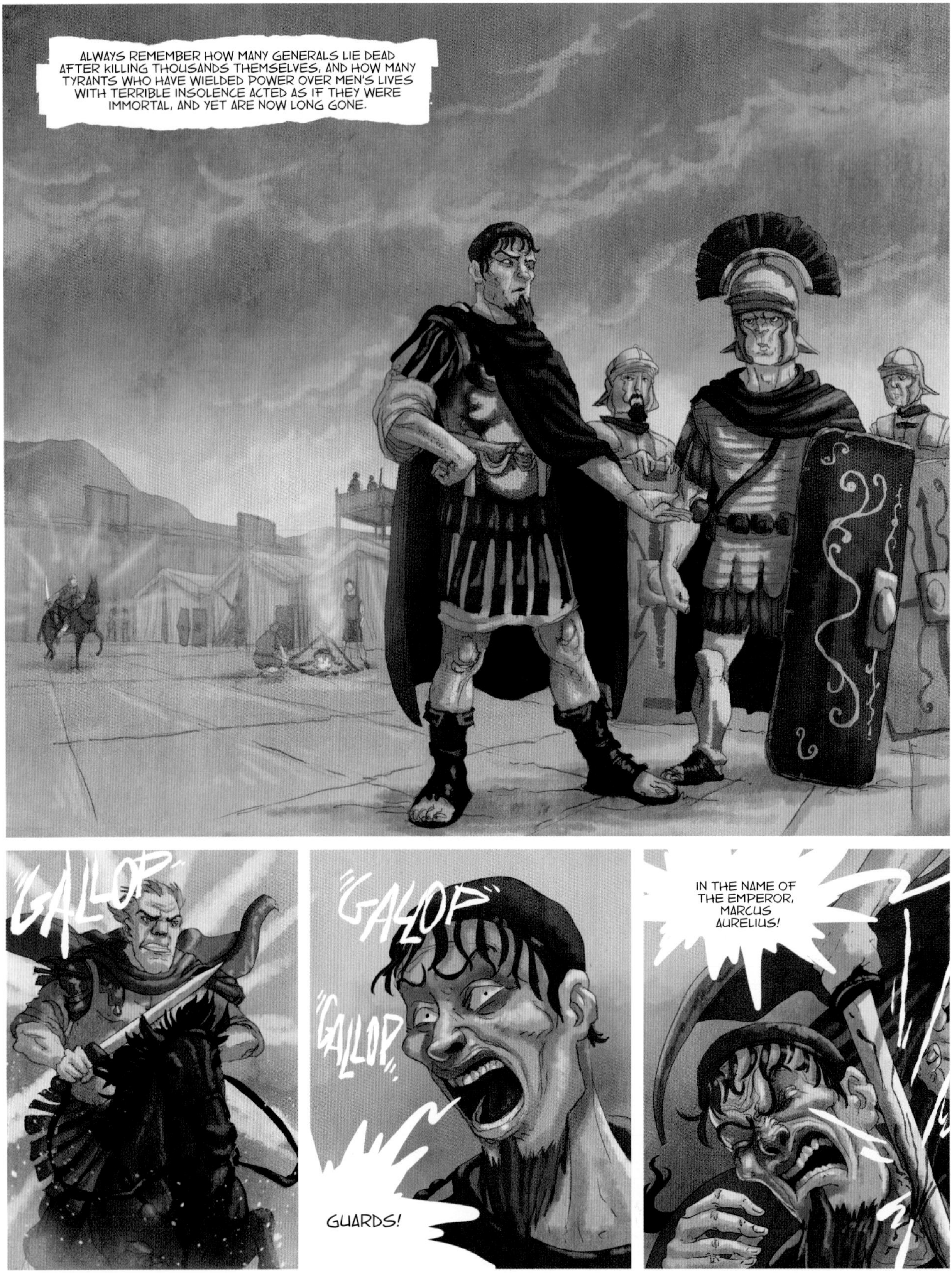
ALWAYS REMEMBER HOW MANY GENERALS LIE DEAD AFTER KILLING THOUSANDS THEMSELVES, AND HOW MANY TYRANTS WHO HAVE WIELDED POWER OVER MEN'S LIVES WITH TERRIBLE INSOLENCE ACTED AS IF THEY WERE IMMORTAL, AND YET ARE NOW LONG GONE.
GALLOP
GALLOP
GALLOP
GUARDS!
IN THE NAME OF THE EMPEROR, MARCUS AURELIUS!

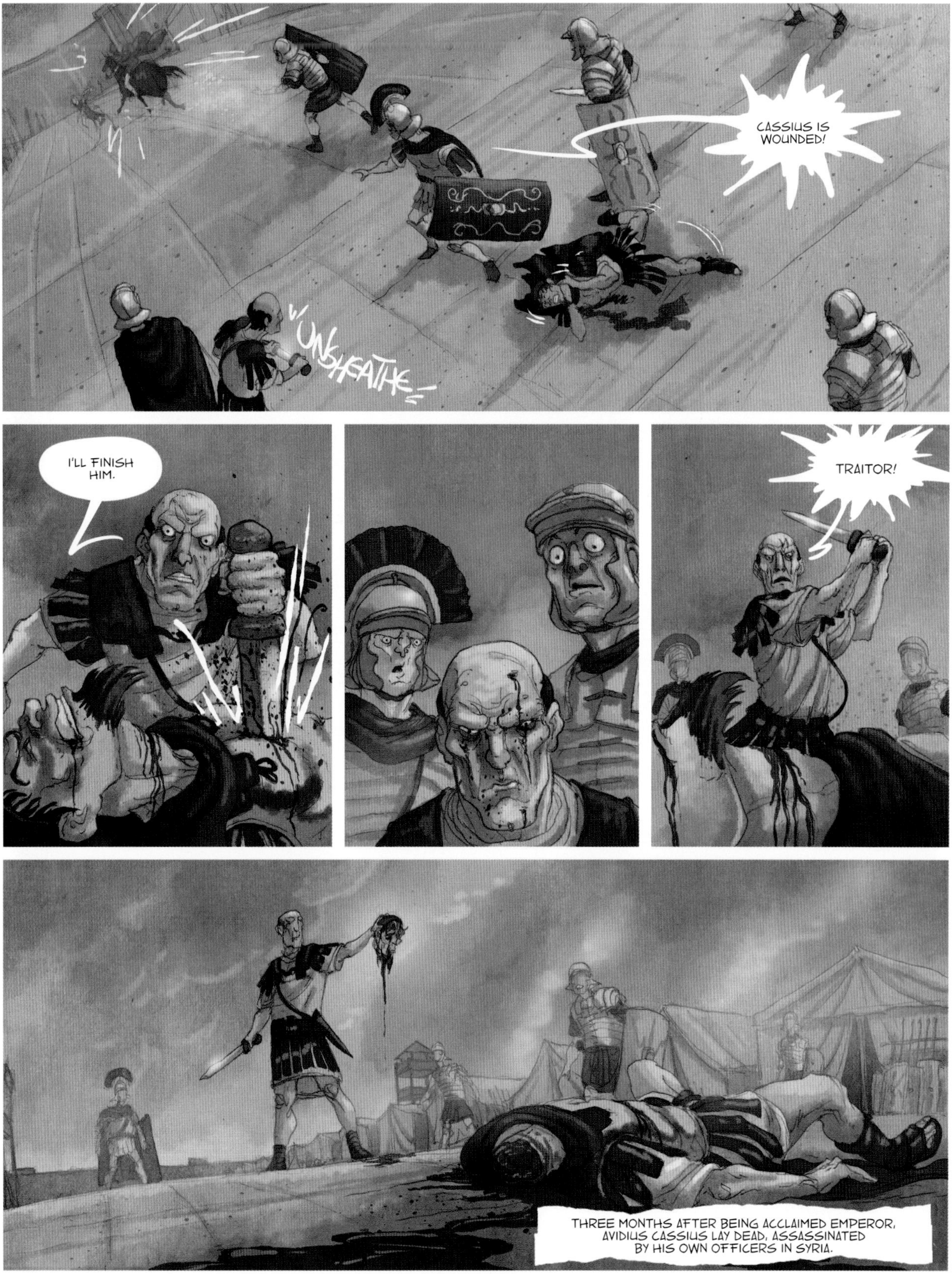
CASSIUS IS WOUNDED!
UNSHEATHE
I'LL FINISH HIM.
TRAITOR!
THREE MONTHS AFTER BEING ACCLAIMED EMPEROR, AVIDIUS CASSIUS LAY DEAD, ASSASSINATED BY HIS OWN OFFICERS IN SYRIA.

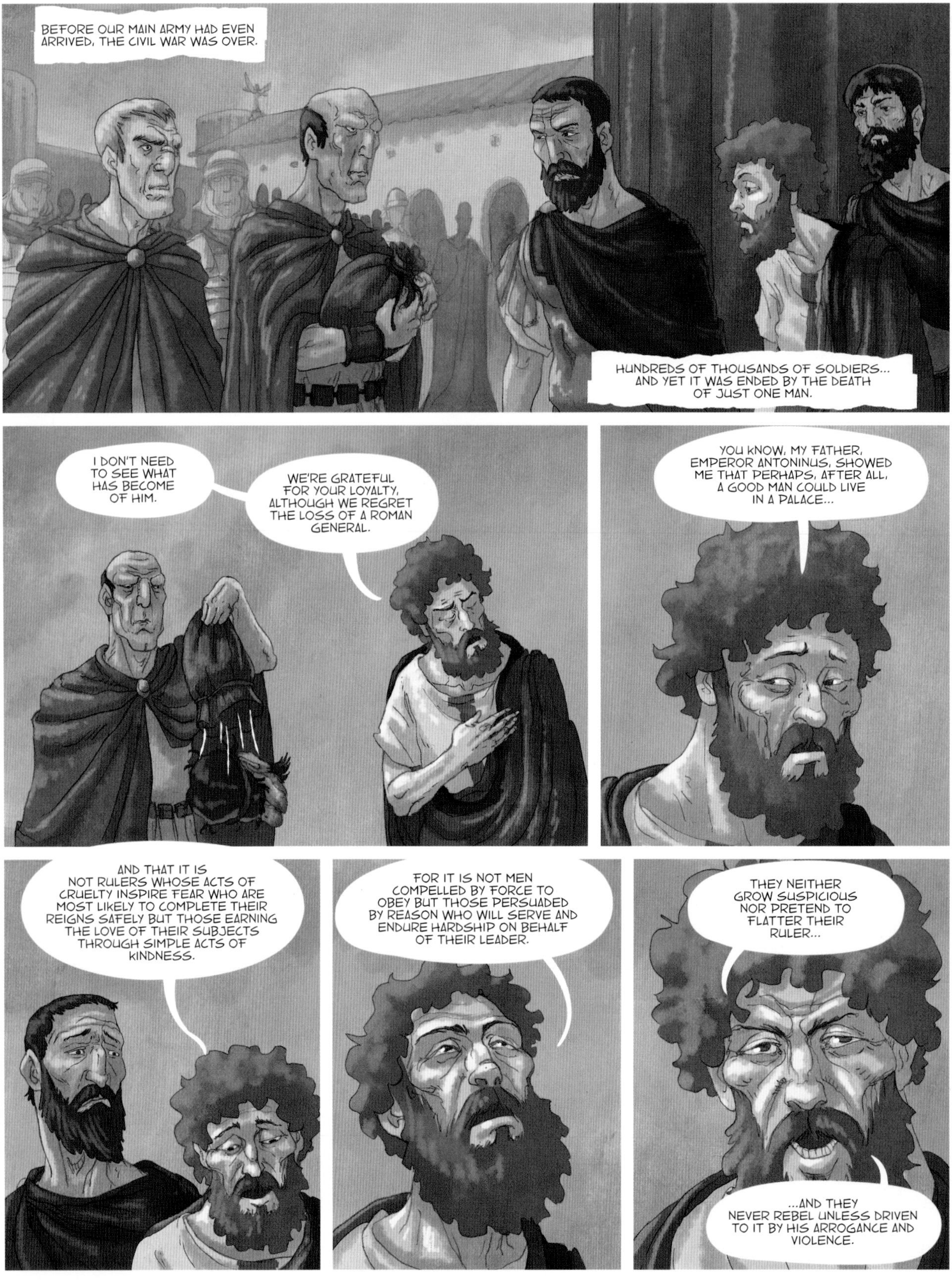
BEFORE OUR MAIN ARMY HAD EVEN ARRIVED, THE CIVIL WAR WAS OVER.
HUNDREDS OF THOUSANDS OF SOLDIERS... AND YET IT WAS ENDED BY THE DEATH OF JUST ONE MAN.
I DON'T NEED TO SEE WHAT HAS BECOME OF HIM.
WE'RE GRATEFUL FOR YOUR LOYALTY, ALTHOUGH WE REGRET THE LOSS OF A ROMAN GENERAL.
YOU KNOW, MY FATHER, EMPEROR ANTONINUS, SHOWED ME THAT PERHAPS, AFTER ALL, A GOOD MAN COULD LIVE IN A PALACE...
AND THAT IT IS NOT RULERS WHOSE ACTS OF CRUELTY INSPIRE FEAR WHO ARE MOST LIKELY TO COMPLETE THEIR REIGNS SAFELY BUT THOSE EARNING THE LOVE OF THEIR SUBJECTS THROUGH SIMPLE ACTS OF KINDNESS.
FOR IT IS NOT MEN COMPELLED BY FORCE TO OBEY BUT THOSE PERSUADED BY REASON WHO WILL SERVE AND ENDURE HARDSHIP ON BEHALF OF THEIR LEADER.
THEY NEITHER GROW SUSPICIOUS NOR PRETEND TO FLATTER THEIR RULER...
...AND THEY NEVER REBEL UNLESS DRIVEN TO IT BY HIS ARROGANCE AND VIOLENCE.

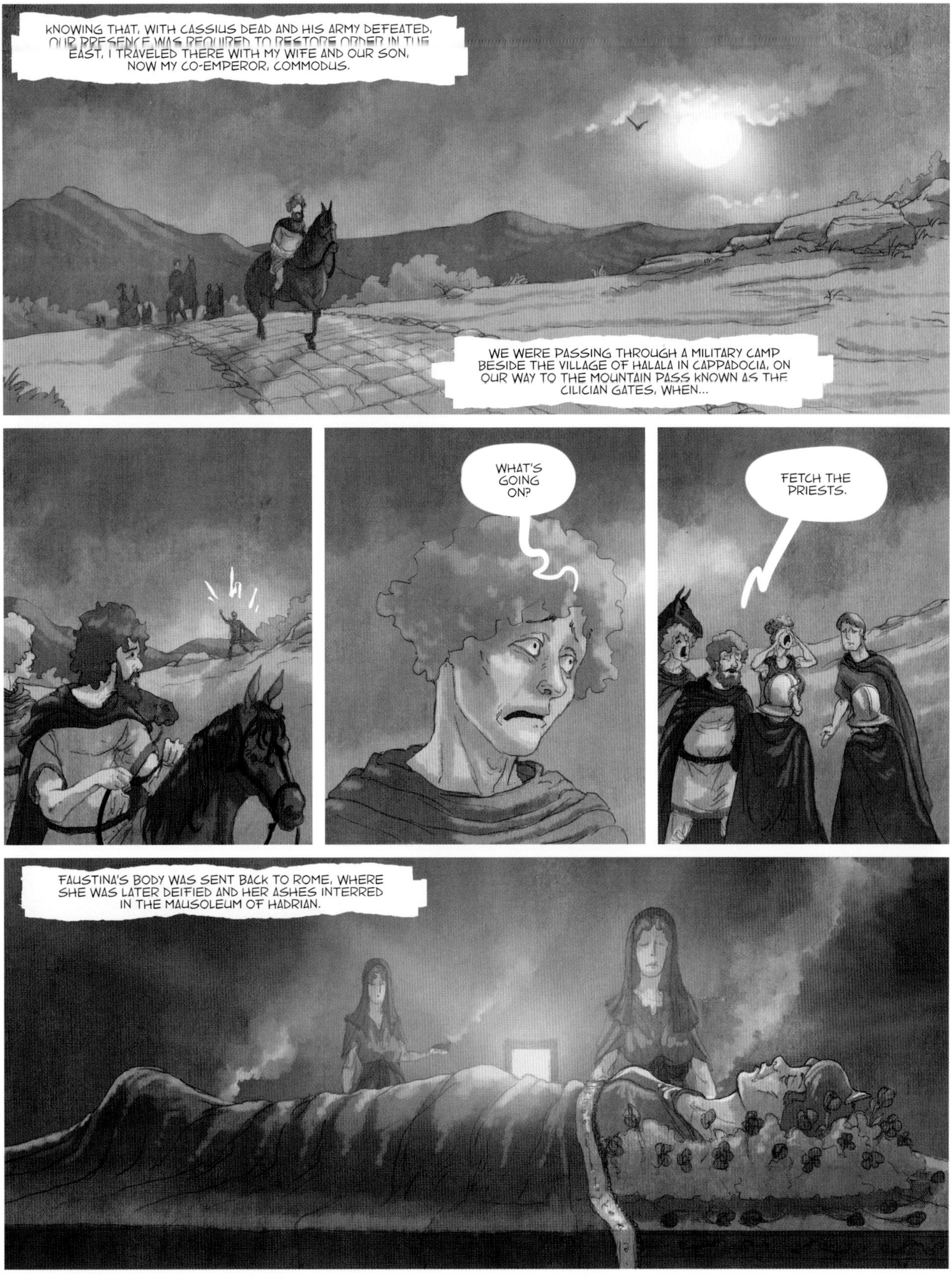

KNOWING THAT, WITH CASSIUS DEAD AND HIS ARMY DEFEATED, OUR PRESENCE WAS REQUIRED TO RESTORE ORDER IN THE EAST, I TRAVELED THERE WITH MY WIFE AND OUR SON, NOW MY CO-EMPEROR, COMMODUS.
WE WERE PASSING THROUGH A MILITARY CAMP BESIDE THE VILLAGE OF HALALA IN CAPPADOCIA, ON OUR WAY TO THE MOUNTAIN PASS KNOWN AS THE CILICIAN GATES, WHEN...
WHAT'S GOING ON?
FETCH THE PRIESTS.
FAUSTINA'S BODY WAS SENT BACK TO ROME, WHERE SHE WAS LATER DEIFIED AND HER ASHES INTERRED IN THE MAUSOLEUM OF HADRIAN.

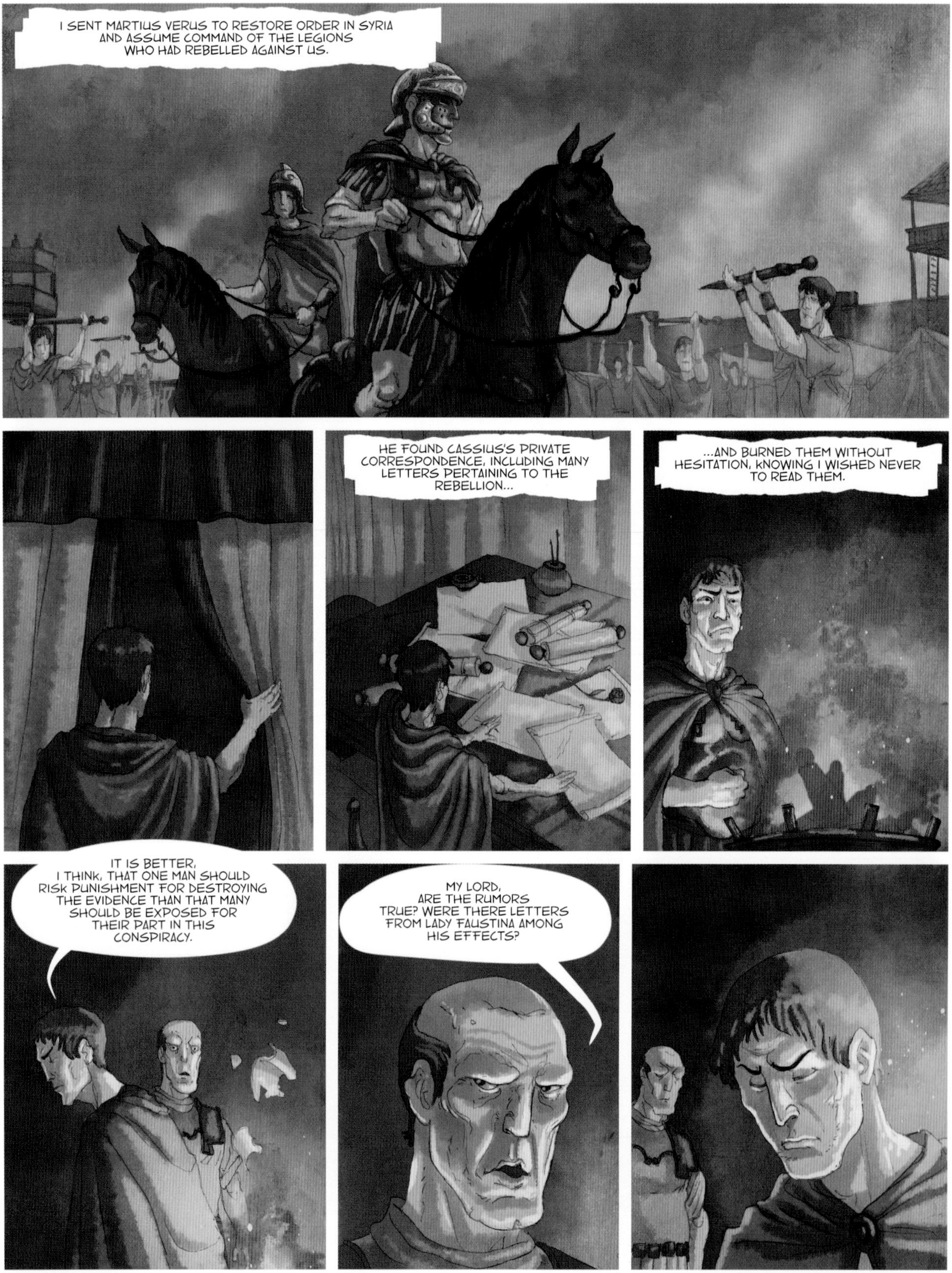
I SENT MARTIUS VERUS TO RESTORE ORDER IN SYRIA AND ASSUME COMMAND OF THE LEGIONS WHO HAD REBELLED AGAINST US.
HE FOUND CASSIUS'S PRIVATE CORRESPONDENCE, INCLUDING MANY LETTERS PERTAINING TO THE REBELLION...
...AND BURNED THEM WITHOUT HESITATION, KNOWING I WISHED NEVER TO READ THEM.
IT IS BETTER, I THINK, THAT ONE MAN SHOULD RISK PUNISHMENT FOR DESTROYING THE EVIDENCE THAN THAT MANY SHOULD BE EXPOSED FOR THEIR PART IN THIS CONSPIRACY.
MY LORD, ARE THE RUMORS TRUE? WERE THERE LETTERS FROM LADY FAUSTINA AMONG HIS EFFECTS?

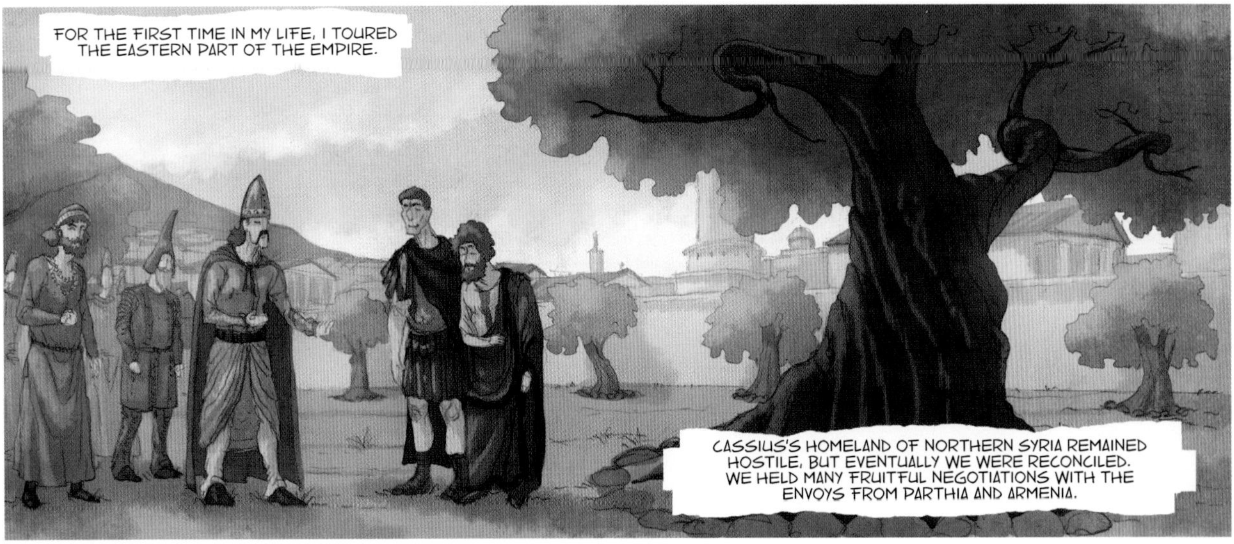
FOR THE FIRST TIME IN MY LIFE, I TOURED THE EASTERN PART OF THE EMPIRE.
CASSIUS'S HOMELAND OF NORTHERN SYRIA REMAINED HOSTILE, BUT EVENTUALLY WE WERE RECONCILED. WE HELD MANY FRUITFUL NEGOTIATIONS WITH THE ENVOYS FROM PARTHIA AND ARMENIA.

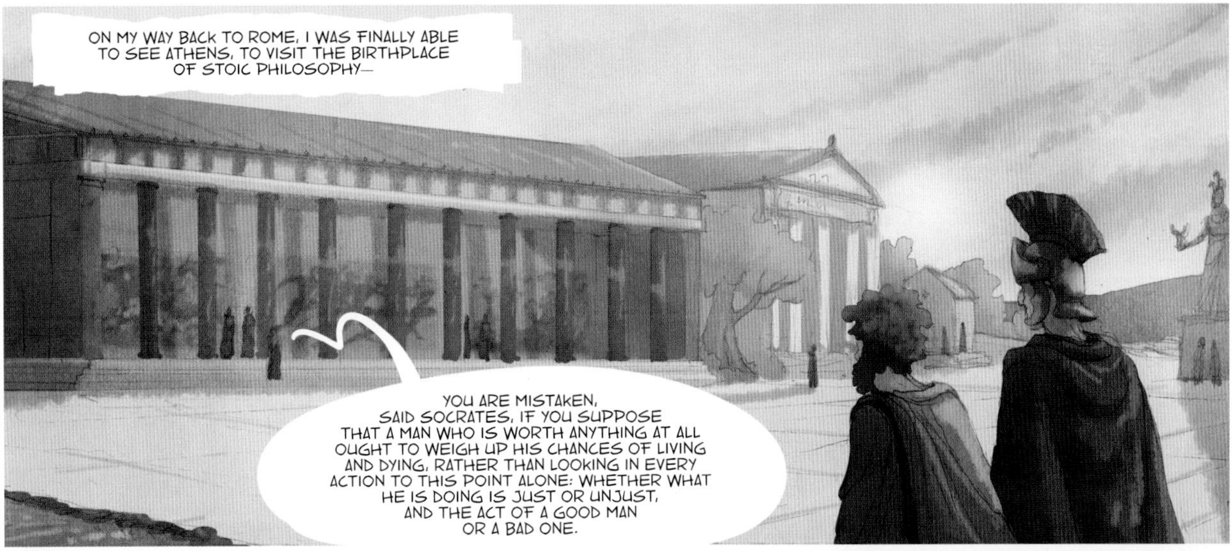
ON MY WAY BACK TO ROME, I WAS FINALLY ABLE TO SEE ATHENS, TO VISIT THE BIRTHPLACE OF STOIC PHILOSOPHY—
YOU ARE MISTAKEN, SAID SOCRATES, IF YOU SUPPOSE THAT A MAN WHO IS WORTH ANYTHING AT ALL OUGHT TO WEIGH UP HIS CHANCES OF LIVING AND DYING, RATHER THAN LOOKING IN EVERY ACTION TO THIS POINT ALONE: WHETHER WHAT HE IS DOING IS JUST OR UNJUST, AND THE ACT OF A GOOD MAN OR A BAD ONE.

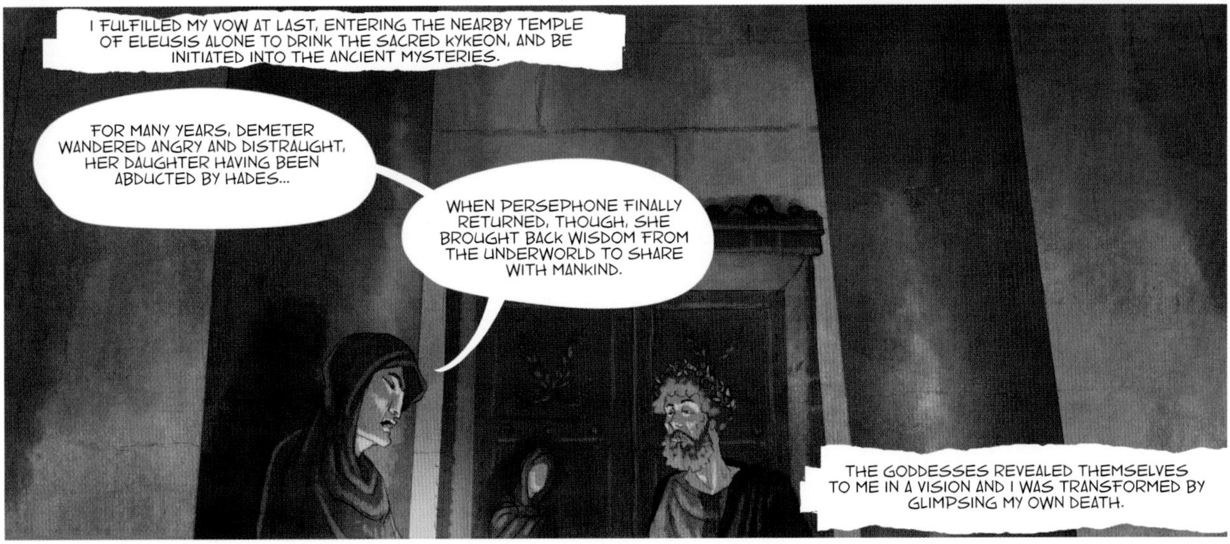
I FULFILLED MY VOW AT LAST, ENTERING THE NEARBY TEMPLE OF ELEUSIS ALONE TO DRINK THE SACRED KYKEON, AND BE INITIATED INTO THE ANCIENT MYSTERIES.
FOR MANY YEARS, DEMETER WANDERED ANGRY AND DISTRAUGHT, HER DAUGHTER HAVING BEEN ABDUCTED BY HADES...
WHEN PERSEPHONE FINALLY RETURNED, THOUGH, SHE BROUGHT BACK WISDOM FROM THE UNDERWORLD TO SHARE WITH MANKIND.
THE GODDESSES REVEALED THEMSELVES TO ME IN A VISION AND I WAS TRANSFORMED BY GLIMPSING MY OWN DEATH.

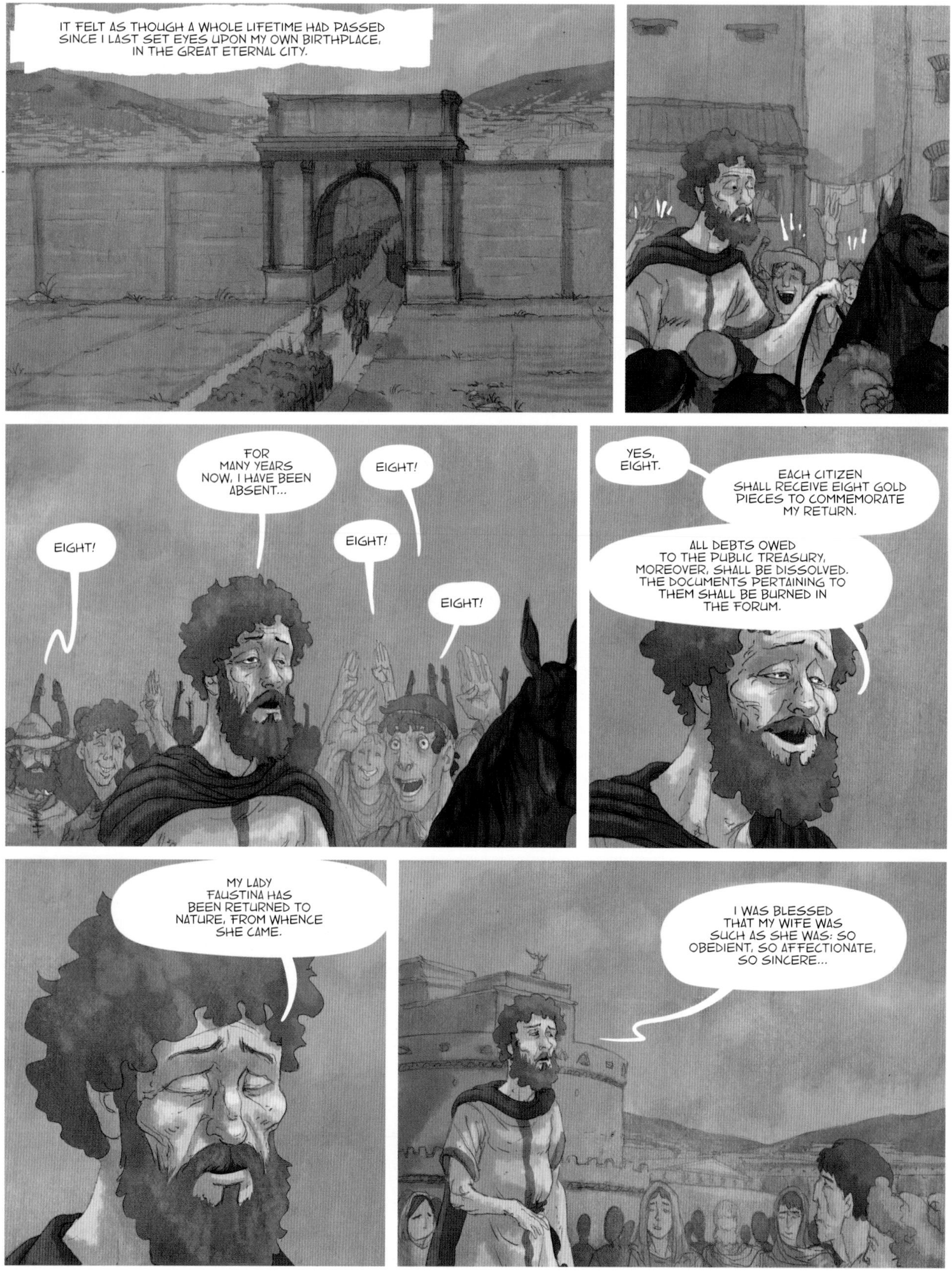
IT FELT AS THOUGH A WHOLE LIFETIME HAD PASSED SINCE I LAST SET EYES UPON MY OWN BIRTHPLACE, IN THE GREAT ETERNAL CITY.
FOR MANY YEARS NOW, I HAVE BEEN ABSENT...
EIGHT!
EIGHT!
EIGHT!
EIGHT!
YES, EIGHT.
EACH CITIZEN SHALL RECEIVE EIGHT GOLD PIECES TO COMMEMORATE MY RETURN.
ALL DEBTS OWED TO THE PUBLIC TREASURY, MOREOVER, SHALL BE DISSOLVED. THE DOCUMENTS PERTAINING TO THEM SHALL BE BURNED IN THE FORUM.
MY LADY FAUSTINA HAS BEEN RETURNED TO NATURE, FROM WHENCE SHE CAME.
I WAS BLESSED THAT MY WIFE WAS SUCH AS SHE WAS: SO OBEDIENT, SO AFFECTIONATE, SO SINCERE...

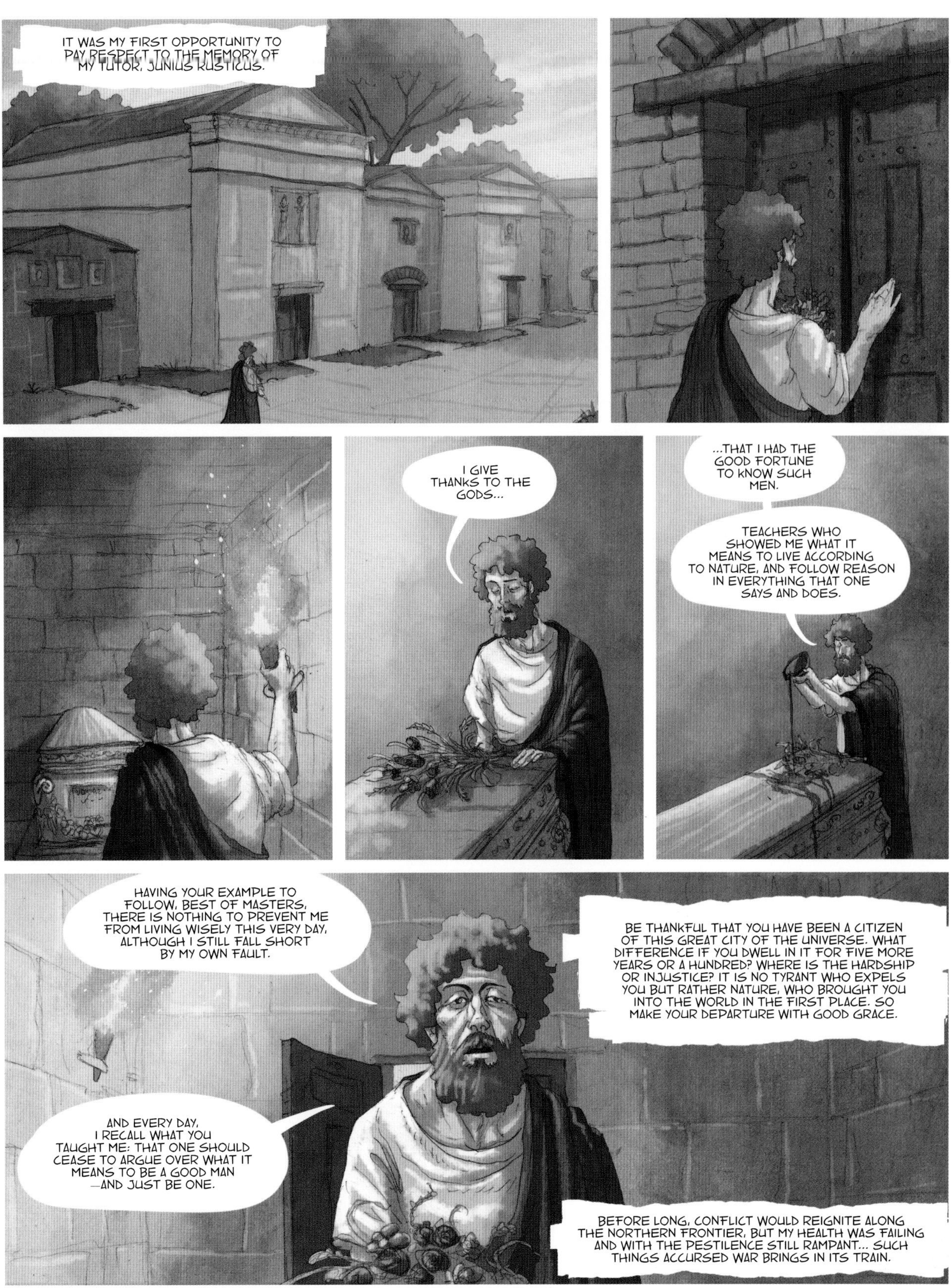
IT WAS MY FIRST OPPORTUNITY TO PAY RESPECT TO THE MEMORY OF MY TUTOR, JUNIUS RUSTICUS.
I GIVE THANKS TO THE GODS...
...THAT I HAD THE GOOD FORTUNE TO KNOW SUCH MEN.
TEACHERS WHO SHOWED ME WHAT IT MEANS TO LIVE ACCORDING TO NATURE, AND FOLLOW REASON IN EVERYTHING THAT ONE SAYS AND DOES.
HAVING YOUR EXAMPLE TO FOLLOW, BEST OF MASTERS, THERE IS NOTHING TO PREVENT ME FROM LIVING WISELY THIS VERY DAY, ALTHOUGH I STILL FALL SHORT BY MY OWN FAULT.
BE THANKFUL THAT YOU HAVE BEEN A CITIZEN OF THIS GREAT CITY OF THE UNIVERSE. WHAT DIFFERENCE IF YOU DWELL IN IT FOR FIVE MORE YEARS OR A HUNDRED? WHERE IS THE HARDSHIP OR INJUSTICE? IT IS NO TYRANT WHO EXPELS YOU BUT RATHER NATURE, WHO BROUGHT YOU INTO THE WORLD IN THE FIRST PLACE. SO MAKE YOUR DEPARTURE WITH GOOD GRACE.
AND EVERY DAY, I RECALL WHAT YOU TAUGHT ME: THAT ONE SHOULD CEASE TO ARGUE OVER WHAT IT MEANS TO BE A GOOD MAN —AND JUST BE ONE.
BEFORE LONG, CONFLICT WOULD REIGNITE ALONG THE NORTHERN FRONTIER, BUT MY HEALTH WAS FAILING AND WITH THE PESTILENCE STILL RAMPANT... SUCH THINGS ACCURSED WAR BRINGS IN ITS TRAIN.

THE

VIEW FROM
ABOVE

*Take a bird's-eye view of the world: its endless
gatherings and ceremonies, countless journeys in
both storm and calm, and the transformation of
things: coming to be, being, and then ceasing to be.*

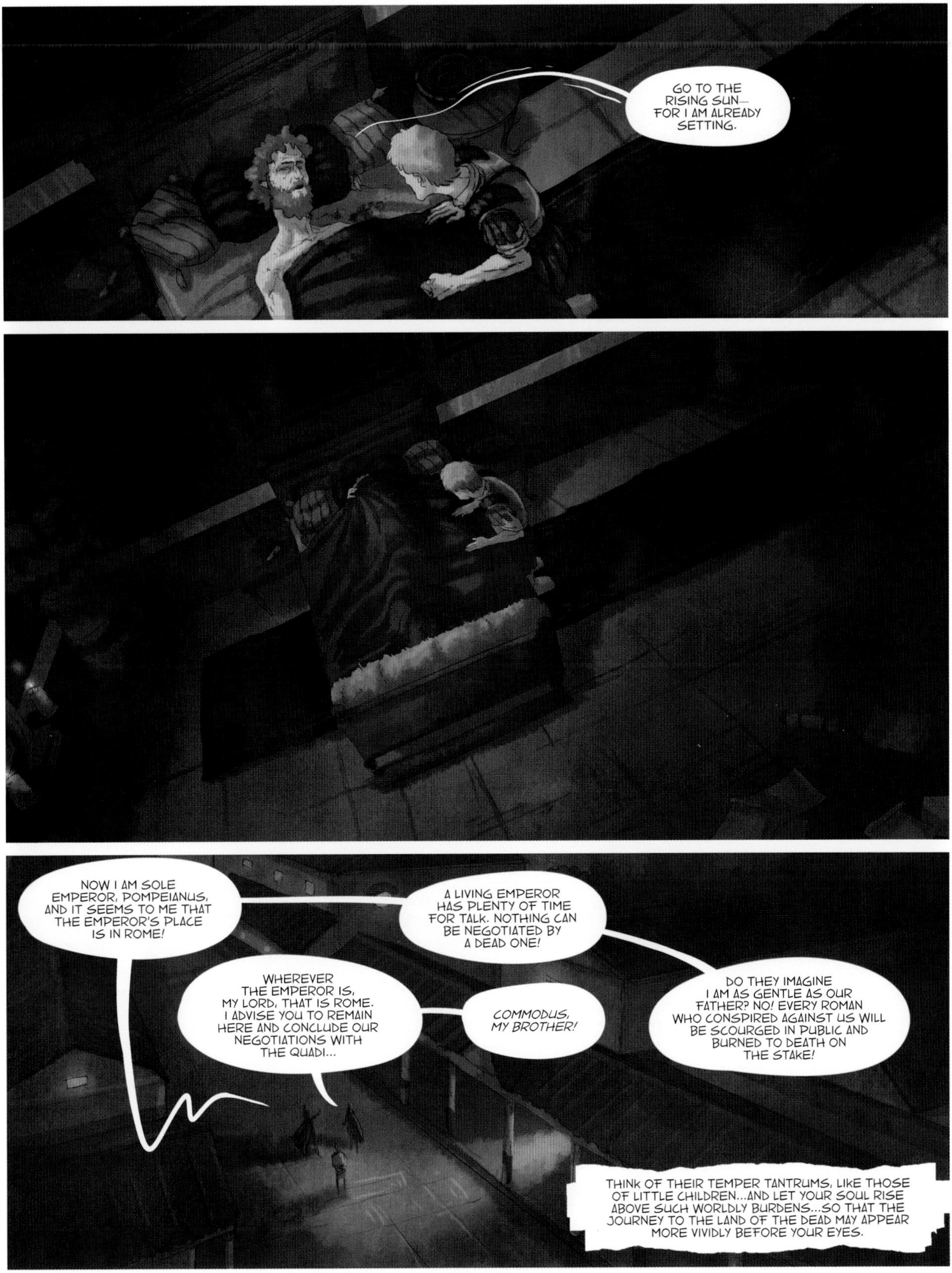
GO TO THE RISING SUN— FOR I AM ALREADY SETTING.
NOW I AM SOLE EMPEROR, POMPEIANUS, AND IT SEEMS TO ME THAT THE EMPEROR'S PLACE IS IN ROME!
WHEREVER THE EMPEROR IS, MY LORD, THAT IS ROME. I ADVISE YOU TO REMAIN HERE AND CONCLUDE OUR NEGOTIATIONS WITH THE QUADI...
COMMODUS, MY BROTHER!
A LIVING EMPEROR HAS PLENTY OF TIME FOR TALK. NOTHING CAN BE NEGOTIATED BY A DEAD ONE!
DO THEY IMAGINE I AM AS GENTLE AS OUR FATHER? NO! EVERY ROMAN WHO CONSPIRED AGAINST US WILL BE SCOURGED IN PUBLIC AND BURNED TO DEATH ON THE STAKE!
THINK OF THEIR TEMPER TANTRUMS, LIKE THOSE OF LITTLE CHILDREN...AND LET YOUR SOUL RISE ABOVE SUCH WORLDLY BURDENS...SO THAT THE JOURNEY TO THE LAND OF THE DEAD MAY APPEAR MORE VIVIDLY BEFORE YOUR EYES.

THE DURATION OF A MAN'S LIFE IS MERELY A SMALL POINT IN TIME...
...THE SUBSTANCE OF IT EVER FLOWING AWAY...
...THE SENSES OBSCURE...
...AND THE WHOLE COMPOSITION OF THE BODY TENDING TO DECAY.

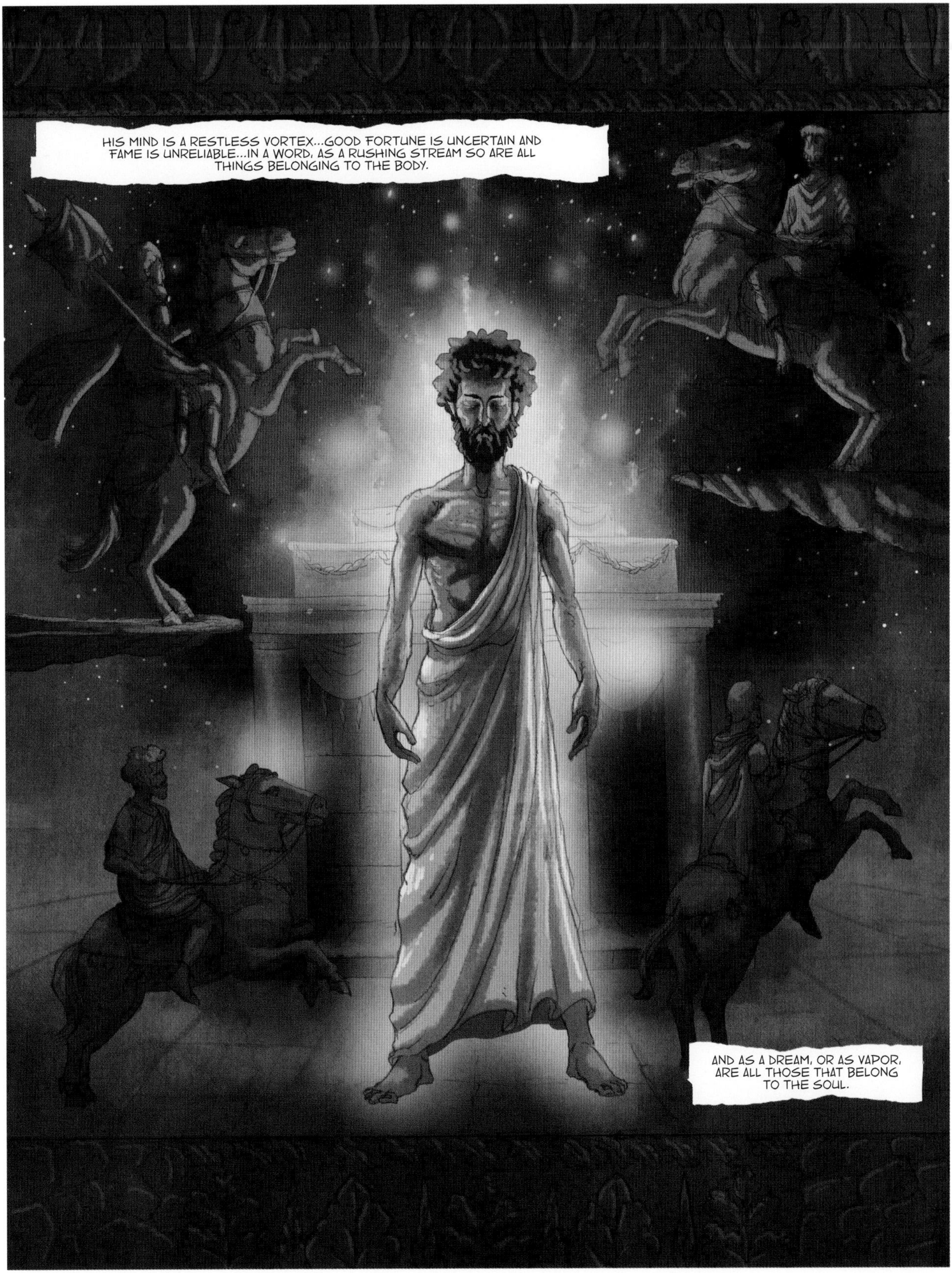
HIS MIND IS A RESTLESS VORTEX...GOOD FORTUNE IS UNCERTAIN AND FAME IS UNRELIABLE...IN A WORD, AS A RUSHING STREAM SO ARE ALL THINGS BELONGING TO THE BODY.
AND AS A DREAM, OR AS VAPOR, ARE ALL THOSE THAT BELONG TO THE SOUL.

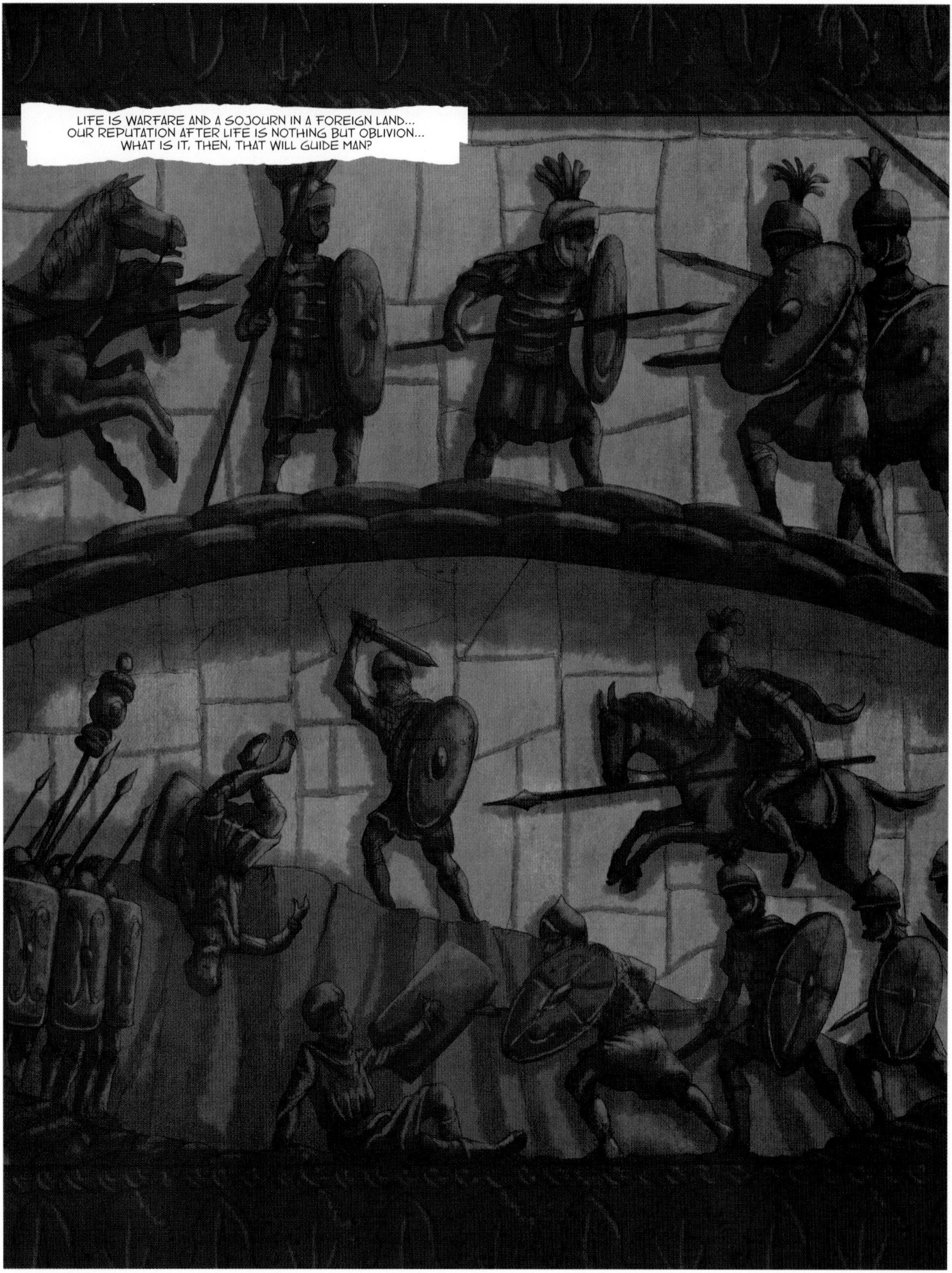
LIFE IS WARFARE AND A SOJOURN IN A FOREIGN LAND...
OUR REPUTATION AFTER LIFE IS NOTHING BUT OBLIVION...
WHAT IS IT, THEN, THAT WILL GUIDE MAN?

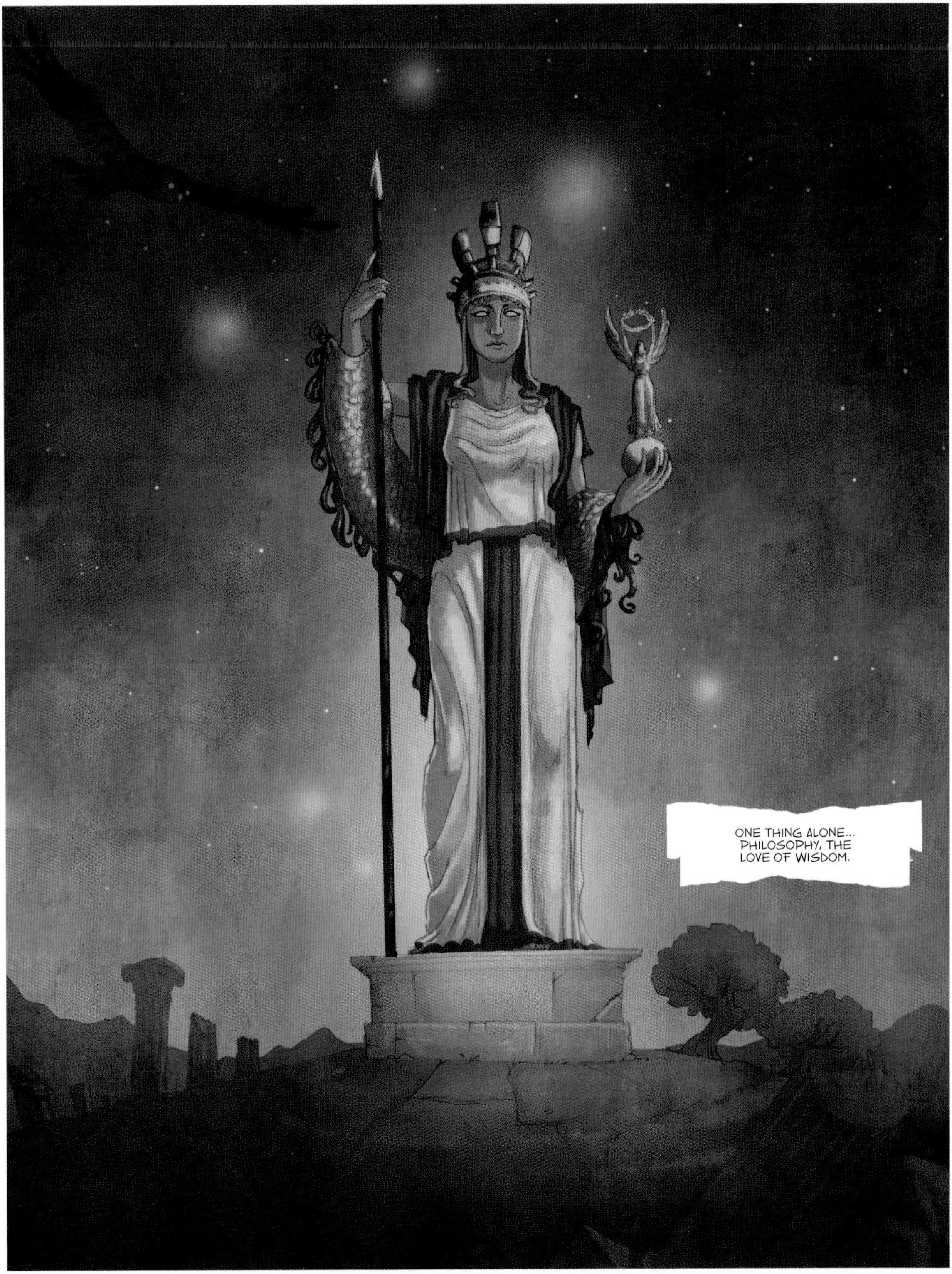
ONE THING ALONE... PHILOSOPHY, THE LOVE OF WISDOM.

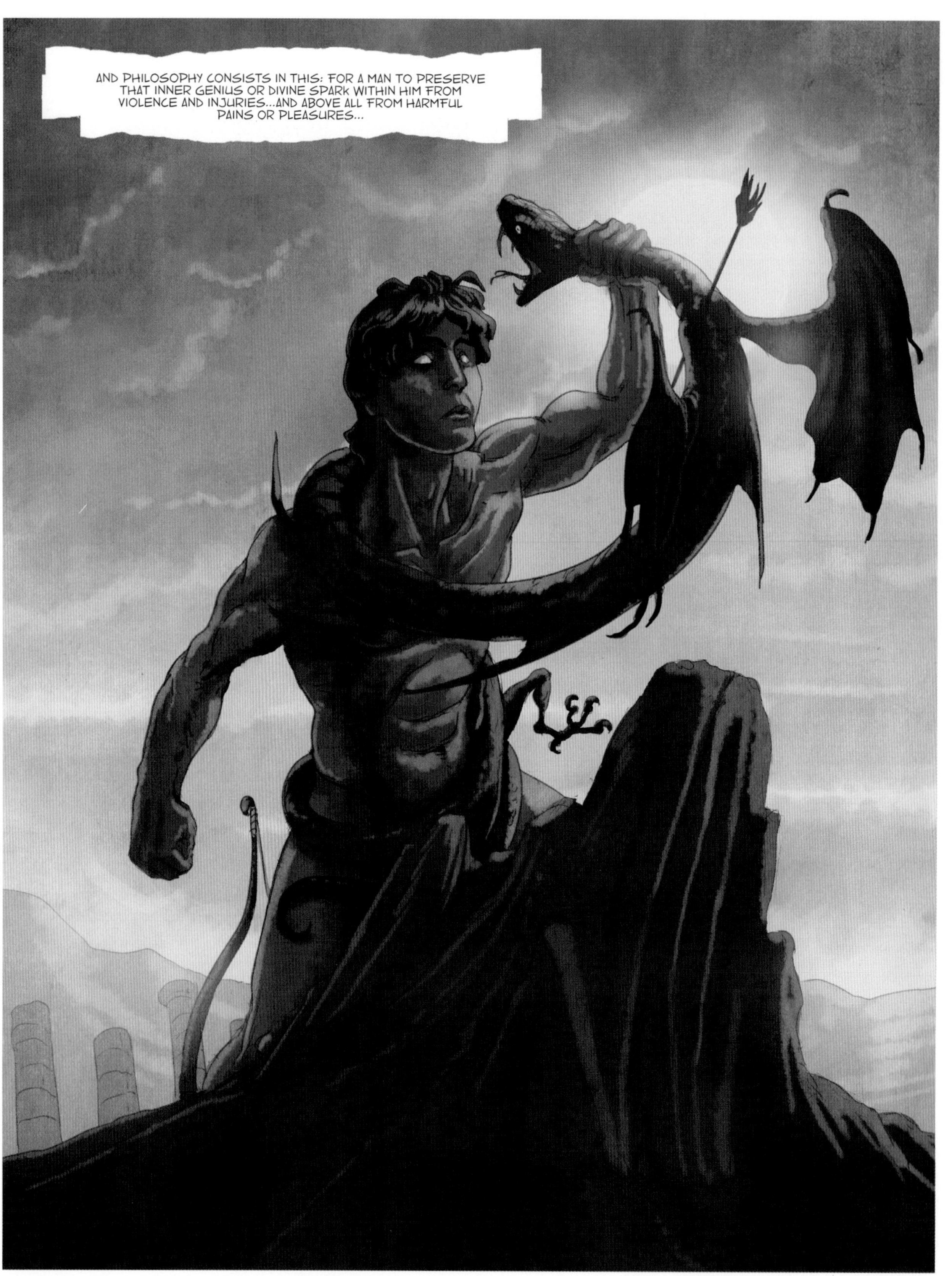
AND PHILOSOPHY CONSISTS IN THIS: FOR A MAN TO PRESERVE THAT INNER GENIUS OR DIVINE SPARK WITHIN HIM FROM VIOLENCE AND INJURIES...AND ABOVE ALL FROM HARMFUL PAINS OR PLEASURES...

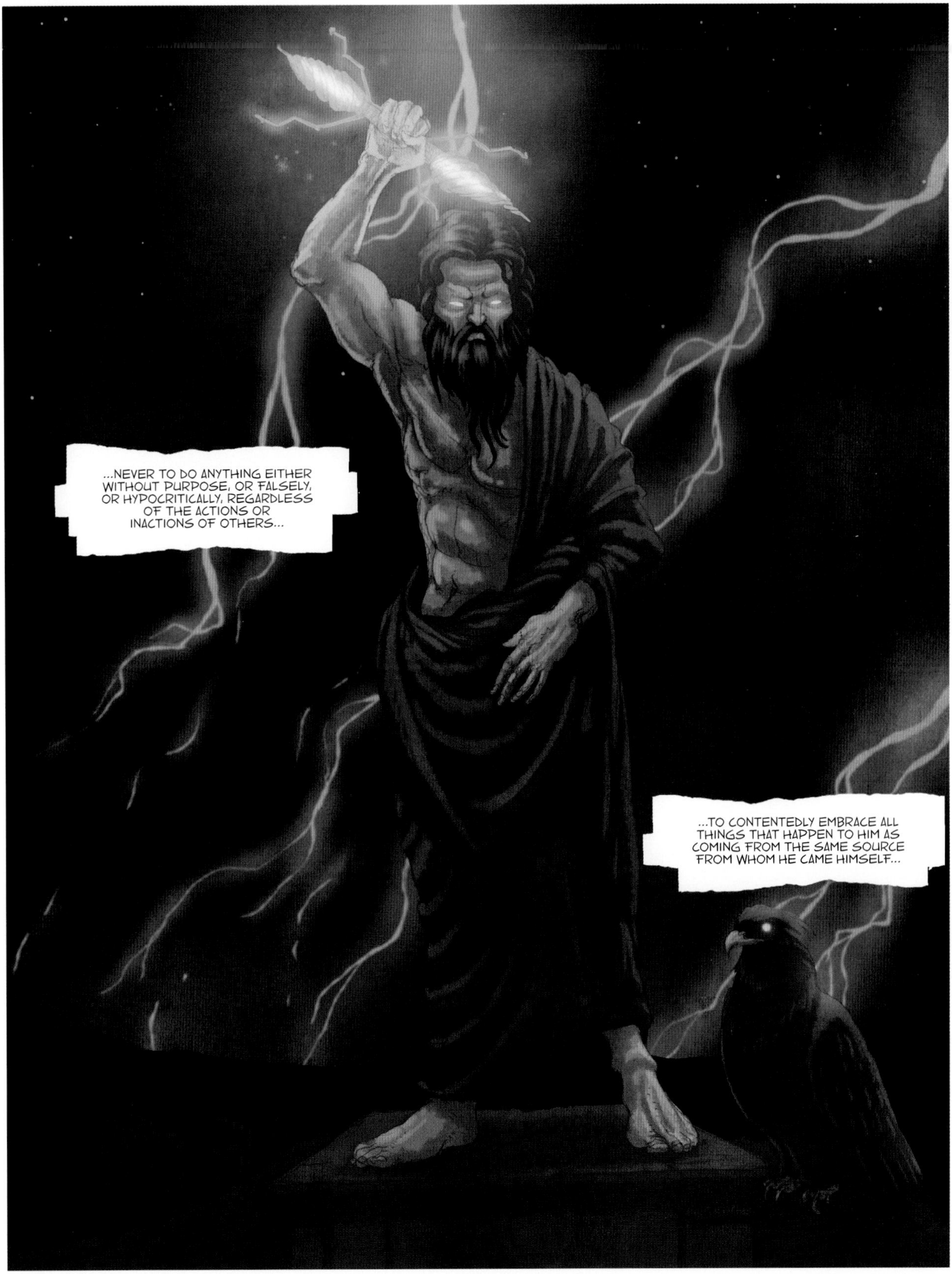
...NEVER TO DO ANYTHING EITHER WITHOUT PURPOSE, OR FALSELY, OR HYPOCRITICALLY, REGARDLESS OF THE ACTIONS OR INACTIONS OF OTHERS...
...TO CONTENTEDLY EMBRACE ALL THINGS THAT HAPPEN TO HIM AS COMING FROM THE SAME SOURCE FROM WHOM HE CAME HIMSELF...

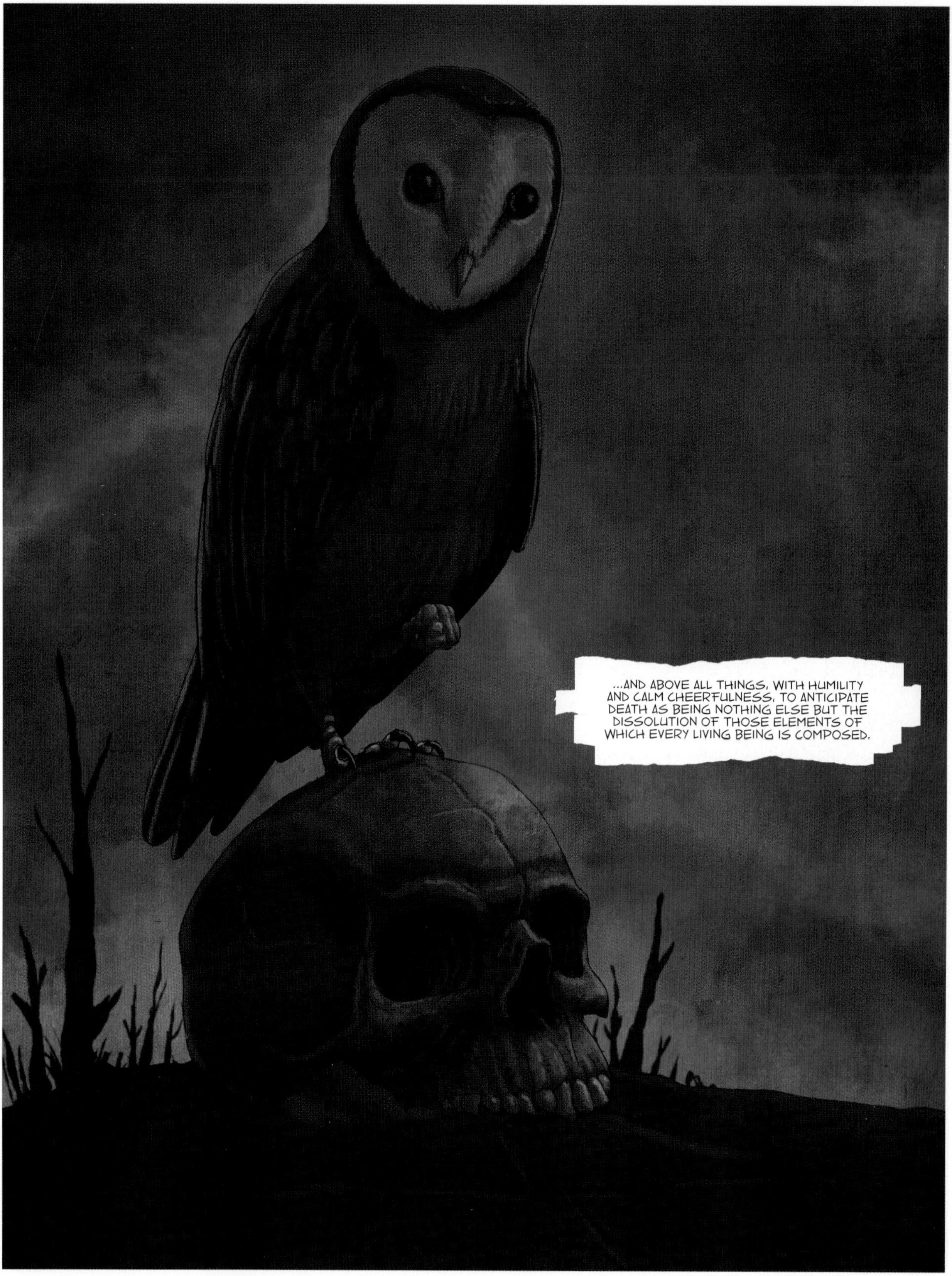
...AND ABOVE ALL THINGS, WITH HUMILITY AND CALM CHEERFULNESS, TO ANTICIPATE DEATH AS BEING NOTHING ELSE BUT THE DISSOLUTION OF THOSE ELEMENTS OF WHICH EVERY LIVING BEING IS COMPOSED.

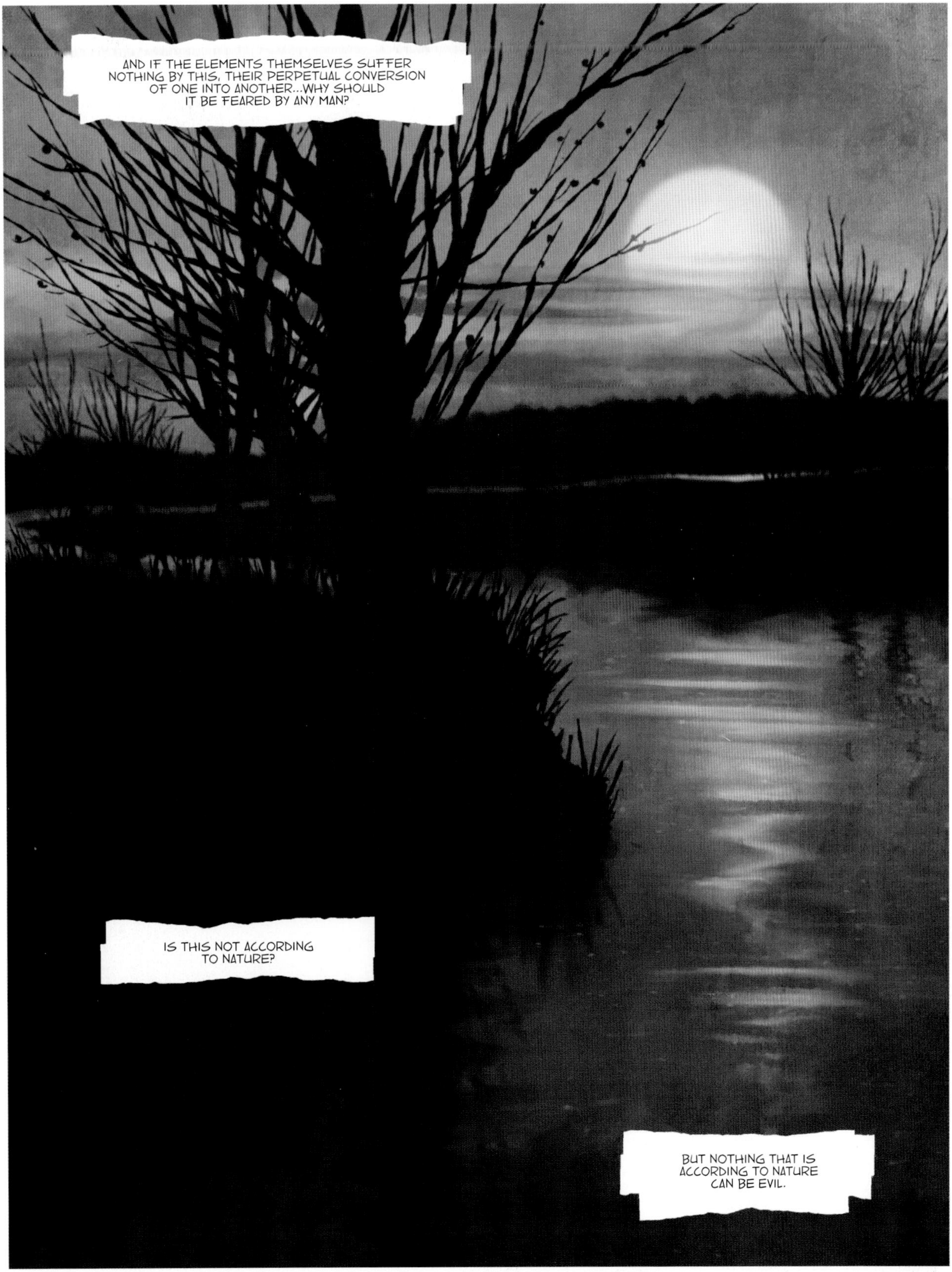
AND IF THE ELEMENTS THEMSELVES SUFFER NOTHING BY THIS, THEIR PERPETUAL CONVERSION OF ONE INTO ANOTHER...WHY SHOULD IT BE FEARED BY ANY MAN?
IS THIS NOT ACCORDING TO NATURE?
BUT NOTHING THAT IS ACCORDING TO NATURE CAN BE EVIL.

APPENDIX

At one level, *The Meditations* by Marcus Aurelius is the record of a man's personal struggle to master his own anger—his own susceptibility toward temporary bouts of madness—and replace it with reason and love.

In the very first sentence, Marcus recalls admiring his grandfather, Verus, for being conspicuously free from anger. At the end of the first book, he then thanks the gods that though often angered by Junius Rusticus, his Stoic mentor, he never himself flew into a temper and did anything to be regretted (1.17). Yet the man who most provoked him was also the one who taught Marcus how to manage his anger and how to be reconciled with his friends if an argument did come between them (1.7). Indeed, Marcus says it was Rusticus who introduced him to the *Discourses* of Epictetus and persuaded him, as a young man, that he could benefit from Stoic therapy (*therapeia*) and moral training.

Marcus returns to the problem of anger very frequently in *The Meditations*. Over and over again, he mentions using Stoic techniques for coping with feelings of irritation and rage. In one of the most remarkable passages of *The Meditations*, he provides a master list of these anger-management techniques (11.18). He calls them ten gifts from the Muses, and from Apollo, their leader, the god of the arts, and patron both of philosophy and healing.

> I. Whenever you notice yourself beginning to take offense at someone else's behavior, pause to consider your fundamental relationship with mankind as a whole. Remind yourself that humans are naturally social creatures, designed to live in communities and cooperate with one another. (Further, in your own case, insofar as you are emperor, bear in mind that you were given responsibility for them, as a ram is set over the flock or a bull over the herd.)

> II. Consider what kind of men they are at the dinner table, in bed, and so on. Realize that certain of their opinions compel them to behave as they do and that they are, therefore, enslaved by their own conceit and ignorance.

> III. If others are doing what is right, then we ought not to be displeased. However, if they do wrong, then it should be obvious that they do so through ignorance and therefore unintentionally. For as

every soul is unwillingly deprived of the truth, so also is it unwillingly deprived of the ability to do what is right. (That is why others are offended when called unjust, ungrateful, or greedy, or whenever they are accused of any wrongdoing.)

IV. Remember that you also do many things that are wrong and that you are flawed like every other human being. (Even supposing you abstain from certain faults, still you have the potential to commit them, whether through cowardice, or concern about your reputation, or some other base motive, you manage to avoid wrongdoing in your actions.)

V. Accept that you can rarely be certain whether someone is actually doing wrong or not, for often things are done for obscure motives. In most cases, we must study others very carefully before we can evaluate their actions properly.

VI. Whenever you are growing very frustrated or annoyed, remind yourself that human life lasts for only a moment, in the grand scheme of things, and that before long we will all be dead and gone.

VII. Tell yourself that it is never really the actions of others which disturb us—those are rooted in their own minds, not ours. Rather we are upset by our value judgments concerning the actions of others. Remove these opinions, stop judging their behavior to be something grievous, and your anger will be gone.

VIII. Realize that your own anger and frustration about the actions of others causes you far more suffering than the very actions about which you're upset.

IX. Remember that kindness is unstoppable if it is genuine, and you are not merely faking a smile and acting some part. For what can even the most vicious man do to harm you as long as you act consistently with wisdom and kindness toward him? (Although others may attack you externally, they cannot harm your moral character, unless you allow them to do so.)

X. Finally, Apollo himself, god both of reason and of prophecy, teaches us that to expect bad men not to do bad things is madness. This would be to demand the impossible. (Hence, each morning, we should adopt a philosophical attitude toward the future by visualizing the possibility that we may encounter foolish and vicious individuals, and imagining how we might cope with them wisely.)

You should commit these rules to memory, says Marcus, as though they were sacred gifts received from Apollo and his Muses, in order that you may "begin at last to be a man while you live."

Consider, reader, how many of these strategies may have shaped the actions of the Stoic Roman emperor depicted in this book. And how many of them could shape your own thoughts, feelings, and actions in the future, if you were to take them to heart, by bringing them into your daily meditations.

AFTERWORD

Depiction of Roman history in such detail always presents challenges, e.g., in relation to military uniforms and equipment. We've sought feedback on this from a range of experts, but our priority was to serve the story rather than slavishly maintain historical accuracy. Some additional notes on the creative decisions made . . .

Language. The language used by characters is modeled on historical sources. In particular, I tried to incorporate authentic phrases derived from sources, including a cache of private letters between Marcus Aurelius and his rhetoric tutor, Marcus Cornelius Fronto, discovered in the nineteenth century. From these we can see that Marcus liked to refer to his tutor as "best of masters," Fronto called Marcus "my Lord Caesar," and so on. Sometimes decisions were made for the sake of readability. For instance, Marcus and his brother, Lucius, are typically referred to as "Antoninus" and "Verus" respectively in formal communications. We call them by their first names (*praenomina*) throughout to avoid confusing readers.

Sources. The *Historia Augusta* is our most comprehensive ancient source for the life of Marcus, which overlaps with its accounts of the emperors Hadrian, Antoninus Pius, Lucius Verus, (the usurper emperor) Avidius Cassius, and Commodus, among others. Although the *Historia Augusta* is generally considered to be poorly reliable, the chapter on Marcus is viewed by modern scholars as one of its better ones. Nevertheless, certain anecdotes from its lives of Lucius Verus, Avidius Cassius, and Commodus, are believed to be more questionable. We have chosen to incorporate several ideas that historians have concerns about rather than adopting a more critical stance. We don't know these details are false, only that they seem uncertain. We therefore allow the reader to hear the story and decide for themselves whether, for example, Lucius Verus was as feckless or Avidius Cassius as cruel as the author of the *Historia Augusta* makes them out to be.

Creative liberties. Avidius Cassius probably wasn't made governor of Syria until around AD 166, whereas we have it happening earlier, in 163 AD, to simplify the sequence of events following the death of Marcus Annius Libo. In fact, a man called Gnaeus Julius Verus is believed to have briefly served as governor of Syria between Libo and Cassius holding that position.

Controversies. There are three particularly controversial topics people tend to mention when talking about the life of Marcus Aurelius. The first one is the idea that he was some kind of warmonger or genocidist because of the Marcomannic Wars. I hope we've shown that war was brutal for the Romans but also that the evidence suggests Marcus was perceived as too much of a "dove" by more "hawkish" factions in the military and Senate, which partly explains the rebellion of Avidius Cassius. Marcus was certainly not a warmonger by Roman standards, nor perhaps by any standard.

The second controversy derives from the claim that Marcus "persecuted Christians." This accusation is often repeated on the Internet, and even in some books. However, there's no credible evidence to suggest he was personally responsible for such persecutions. Indeed, several independent pieces of evidence suggest the contrary was true. The church father Tertullian actually calls Marcus "a protector" of Christians. A related question concerns whether Marcus turned a blind eye to the abuse of Christians by others during his rule. Our main source for a major persecution is the church historian Eusebius, who admitted to using falsehoods to spread early Christian propaganda. Moreover, the account he gives of the alleged persecution at Lyons is thrown into question due to the glaring historical inaccuracies and implausible supernatural claims it contains. (We're told that some martyrs were raised from the dead, whereas others levitated up into the sky, or survived intact inside the bowels of lions.)

Finally, there's Commodus, Marcus Aurelius's wayward son. For many people, the story of Commodus is even more fascinating than that of Marcus. Unfortunately, we simply aren't told much about their relationship, and most of what we know about Commodus relates to events after Marcus's death. So he couldn't feature very prominently in this graphic novel. People often ask how such a wise and virtuous emperor could have such a foolish and vicious son. Marcus probably had relatively little contact with Commodus in his youth, although we're told he sought out the finest tutors for his son. Nevertheless, history is full of great men who raised mediocre or bad children. It was a cliché of ancient philosophy that even good teachers can have bad students, and good parents sometimes raise bad children, through no fault of their own.

It's likewise asked why Marcus chose Commodus to succeed him. This question is more complex. I've tried to touch on historical details that relate to it at various points in the story. It seems Lucius Verus, as co-emperor, must initially have been expected, in a way, to succeed Marcus, by outliving him as co-emperor. Moreover, we're told it was Lucius who insisted that a seemingly reluctant Marcus should grant Commodus, at the tender age of five, the title of Caesar. It must have been part of an attempt by the Senate to reduce the risk of civil war, which we can see was a looming threat due to the rebellion of Avidius Cassius. The question I believe we should ask ourselves is this: May the prospect of Commodus as emperor have been viewed as a lesser evil than that of Avidius Cassius?

One unexpected outcome of working on this graphic novel has been that my views on Commodus have changed somewhat after seeing him come to life on the page, as it were. I think it's clear Commodus, perhaps for much of his youth, but certainly aged fourteen, when the civil war loomed, must have lived in fear for his life. Zé's artwork prompts us to ask ourselves: What did it feel like to be Commodus at that time? He was just a child in Rome without his father's protection. How did he sleep at night knowing that powerful individuals wanted him poisoned or beheaded? It's striking that once Marcus died, Commodus wasted no time in overturning his order to spare the lives of those involved in the rebellion. Commodus wanted his enemies dead, I suspect, because he was much more afraid of them than his father had been.

ACKNOWLEDGMENTS

Kasey Pierce, our freelance editor, for her comic wisdom and passionate Stoicism.

Calisivs Bonamansivs Aqvila for checking every page twice over to verify the historical authenticity of the artwork, including the curtains.

Maria Brine for her amusing feedback on the initial draft pages.

Mira Mortal for her creative design on the title pages.

Stephen Hanselman, Donald's agent, for getting us into this in the first place.

Tim Bartlett, our editor at St. Martin's, for his patient help and support once again.